Enrichment

For Dominique

Enrichment
A Critique of Commodities

Luc Boltanski and Arnaud Esquerre

Translated by
Catherine Porter

polity

First published in French as *Enrichissement* © Editions Gallimard, Paris, 2017
This English edition © Polity Press, 2020

This work received the French Voices Award for excellence in publication and translation.
French Voices is a program created and funded by the French Embassy in the United States
and FACE Foundation (French American Cultural Exchange)
French Voices Logo designed by Serge Bloch.

Polity Press
65 Bridge Street
Cambridge CB2 1UR, UK

Polity Press
101 Station Landing
Suite 300
Medford, MA 02155, USA

ISBN-13: 978-1-5095-2872-1

A catalogue record for this book is available from the British Library.

Library of Congress Cataloging-in-Publication Data
Names: Boltanski, Luc, author. | Esquerre, Arnaud, author.
Title: Enrichment : a critique of commodities / Luc Boltanski and Arnaud Esquerre ;
    translated by Catherine Porter.
Other titles: Enrichissement. l English
Description: Cambridge, UK ; Medford, MA : Polity Press, [2020] | "First published
    in French as Enrichissement, (c) Editions Gallimard, Paris, 2017"--Verso. | Includes
    bibliographical references and index. | Summary: "This book offers a major new account
    of modern capitalism and of the ways in which value and wealth are created today"--
    Provided by publisher.
Identifiers: LCCN 2019035403 (print) | LCCN 2019035404 (ebook) | ISBN 9781509528721
    (hardback) | ISBN 9781509528745 (epub)
Subjects: LCSH: Commercial products--Europe, Western. | Capitalism--Europe, Western. |
    Cultural property--Economic aspects--Europe, Western. | Europe, Western--Commerce. |
    Europe, Western--Economic conditions.
Classification: LCC HF1040.9.E84 B6413 2020 (print) | LCC HF1040.9.E84 (ebook) | DDC
    330.94--dc23
LC record available at https://lccn.loc.gov/2019035403
LC ebook record available at https://lccn.loc.gov/2019035404

Typeset in 10 on 11 pt Times New Roman MT by
Servis Filmsetting Limited, Stockport, Cheshire
Printed and bound in by Great Britain by TJ International Limited

For further information on Polity, visit our website: politybooks.com

Contents

Acknowledgments

In carrying out this work, we have benefited from the help of many people; it would be impossible to name them all.

We wish to thank, first, all those who participated in our seminar at EHESS between 2012 and 2016. In 2012–13, these included Michela Barbot, Christian Bessy, Sébastien Chauvin, Bruno Cousin, Emmanuel Didier, Jeanne Favret-Saada, Marion Fourcade, Marie-France Garcia-Parpet, Isabelle Graw, Catherine Grenier, Guido Guerzoni, Bérénice Hamidi-Kim, Laurent Jeanpierre, Lucien Karpic, Jeanne Lazarus, Patrice Maniglier, André Orléan, Olivier Roueff, Simon Susen, Mathieu Trachman, Emmanuel de Vienne, and Daniel Urrutiaguer; in 2013–14: Fabien Accominotti, Jacques Bournay, Delphine Corteel, Sophie Cras, Camille Herlin-Giret, Judith Ickowicz, Anne Jourdain, Michal Kozlowski, Michèle Lamont, Sylvain Laurens, Ashley Mears, Michel Melot, Alain Quemin, Thomas Piketty, Cyprien Tasset, Laurent Thévenot, Tommaso Vitale, and Loup Wolff; in 2014–15: Thierry Bonnot, Marie-Charlotte Calafat, Bernard Conein, Élice Dubuc, Stéphane Gerson, Marie Gouyon, Frédéric Keck, Anthony Kohn, Baptiste Monsaingeon, Yves Moulin, Fabian Muniesa, Frédérique Patureau, Michel Rautenberg, Bénédicte Savoy, Martine Segalen, and Olav Velthuis.

Some components of this work were published along the way, and we wish to thank in particular the editorial boards and copyeditors of *Sociologie*, *Les Temps modernes*, *Teoria Politica*, and *Valuation Studies*.

We presented our work at colloquia and in lectures at the Kunstsammlung Museum in Düsseldorf in January 2014, at the invitation of Heinz-Norbert Jocks; at the Museum of European and Mediterranean Civilisations (MuCEM) in Marseille in January 2014, at the invitation of Delphine Corteel; at the Museum of Modern Art in Warsaw in November 2014, at the invitation of the Bec Zmiana Foundation and at the initiative of Michal Kozlowski; at the Centro de Cultura Contemporánea of Barcelona in February 2015, at the initiative of Peter Wagner; at the University of Westminster in London in June 2015, at the initiative of Chantal Mouffe; on the occasion of the fiftieth anniversary of the Danish Sociological Association in Copenhagen in October 2015, at the initiative of Niels

Albertsen; at the University of Turin in March 2016, at the initiative of Massimo Cuono, where we had the pleasure of a first debate with Nancy Fraser; in May 2016 in New York, first at the New School for Social Research, at the invitation of Mark Greif, where we continued our discussion with Nancy Fraser; then at the Maison Française of New York University, where we were welcomed by Frédéric Viguier and Stéphane Gerson; and, finally, at Princeton University, in the context of the Fung Global Fellows Program.

We learned a great deal from the interventions and discussions that took place during the seminar "Valeur, prix et politique," organized by Christian Bessy at the ENS-Cachan during 2012–15, as well as during the seminar "Art/Valeur," co-organized in particular by Patrice Maniglier in 2014–16 at the Musée du Quai Branly, which gave us the opportunity to present our work at the École supérieure des beaux-arts of Montpellier in October 2015. We also presented our work and had useful exchanges at the seminar "Anthropologie à Nanterre" of the Laboratoire d'ethnologie et de sociologie comparative (LESC) in December 2013 at the Université Paris-Ouest Nanterre; during a Max Po lecture at Sciences Po in Paris, at the initiative of Olivier Godechot, in December 2014; and during a session of the seminar "Exercer la domination" at the ENS-Ulm in May 2016, at the initiative of Pierre Alayrac.

A nearly complete version of the manuscript was discussed during a day-long conference devoted to it on Monday, 4 July 2016, at the LESC at the Université Paris-Ouest Nanterre; we thank the laboratory for welcoming us, and we are particularly grateful to our readers, who are at once colleagues and friends, for their comments: Pierre Alayrac, Guillaume Couffignal, Sophie Cras, Laurent Jeanpierre, Jeanne Lazarus, Patrice Maniglier, Ismaël Moya, and Cyprien Tasset. We have also benefited greatly from observations by Bruno Cousin and Olivier Favereau and from the support of IRIS and its director Marc Bessin. Patrice Maniglier has been a constant interlocutor, accompanying and enriching our thinking, especially by making connections with philosophy, as Guillaume Couffignal has done with mathematics.

To carry out our investigation we called on numerous informants: antique dealers, craftsmen, artists, business executives, entrepreneurs, collectors, auctioneers, art critics, conservators, curators, top government officials, elected officials, and staff members of local collectivities. We thank them here for their trust and their availability.

Finally, this book would not have existed without the generosity and friendship of our editor, Éric Vigne.

This English version was built on a close and productive collaboration between the authors and the translator. We thank Catherine Porter for her careful questioning and her unfailing responsiveness as we worked together to adapt the text to a new audience.

Translator's Note

This translation (excluding the Appendix) was prepared in close collaboration with the authors, whom I thank for their endless patience in responding to my questions. The English-language text includes some updated statistics, some information added for the benefit of anglophone readers, and a small number of corrections to the original. All translations from the French not otherwise credited to a named or unnamed translator are my own.

Foreword
Charles Sabel

Sociology is at its most instructive and broadly useful when it struggles to make sense of the relation between the large structures that constrain our behavior by defining markets and institutions and the way our practical, everyday understandings of justice and fairness can both reproduce and challenge, even transform, those constraints. Sociology is at its most daring and self-sacrificing when, going further, it attempts to understand this relation with both the structures and the practical criteria of judgment in motion – when, in other words, it attempts to combine the macro- and micro-sociology of the present to bring together two terms whose poverty, especially in combination, already hints at the inevitability of partial failure. No one has pursued this audacious and invaluable program more masterfully than Luc Boltanski. Beginning with *Les Cadres* (1982), and passing through *On Justification* (2006), with Laurent Thévenot, *On Critique* (2011) and *The New Spirit of Capitalism* (2018), with Eve Chiapello, to *Enrichment* (2020), with Arnaud Esquerre, translated here, he and his co-authors have produced an extraordinary, analytically innovative chronicle of the relentless changes in contemporary capitalism. Reading the present work together with its immediate predecessor may serve to convey the promise yet also some potential limits of this approach as the continuing transformation of capitalism verges on crisis.

The New Spirit of Capitalism looked ahead to the dissolution of the bureaucratic rigidity of Fordist mass production, then well underway. The firm has been replaced as the unit of organization by the project group: a team assembled, ad hoc, under the guidance and inspiration of a manager-leader to respond to the needs of a customer. As markets shift, teams are recombined; careers are made by acquiring in each team enough expertise and experience to be recruited to the next. Together the shifting collaborations of teams and the circulation of workers yields a networked economy with open boundaries. Those who don't qualify for entrance or promotion have no function or place in this reticular capitalism. They are excluded.

But these emergent structures are deeply ambivalent judged from the vantage point of the "projective city," as Boltanski and Chiapello (adapting the general term developed in Boltanski's earlier collaboration with Thévenot) call the model of justice particular to the "neo-management" of flexibility. The variant, like all such models, links criteria for judging the fairness of individual transactions that we reflexively invoke in deciding to make an exchange and judgments about compatibility of the actions of the powerful with the foundations of our social and political order. The capitalism of projects disarms the first kind of critique, not least because it responds to familiar objections to wage labor. Thus the spontaneous creativity of the project team and the prospect of a career of ceaseless exploration offer possibilities for self-actualization excluded by the routines of Fordist hierarchies – possibilities previously best embodied in the artist's flamboyant, disdainful rejection of capitalist regimentation. Questions about the fairness of hourly compensation are moot because project team members manage their own time. If they are exploited it is through self-exploitation. For such reasons, Boltanski and Chiapello argue, parts of the labor movement and the socialist government of François Mitterrand championed the new developments instead of rallying against the precariousness they create. In celebrating talent, energy, and daring as the conditions of success, networked capitalism damps criticism most insidiously in insinuating that the excluded, by their want of endowments and initiative, if not by their vices, have all but marginalized themselves.

But the powerful in the projective city are not only obligated to respect fair terms of trade. They must also use the influence and authority derived from trading to sustain the public goods or commons on which the whole political and social community depends; to use their power selfishly, only to augment it, is a breach of the social contract that constitutes a moral order. From this perspective, the neglect of the excluded is not a regrettable oversight or a resigned acknowledgment of the incorrigible inequities of life but a breach of fundamental obligations. It is here that the critique of structure finds a handhold, but no more and just barely. Boltanski and Chiapello are rightly circumspect about the form and strategy of opposition. They remind us that the work of criticism, like the labor of Sisyphus, no sooner done, must be done again.

The picture, cheerless enough, changes abruptly and for the grimmer in *Enrichment*. The rise of new competitors, beginning with China, has blocked the renewal of industrial capitalism in its historic heartlands. Some countries, above all France, with its primitive accumulation of cultural objects from the time of the Revolution and its continuing association with good taste, respond by abandoning Fordist manufacturing. Instead they turn to production of luxury and artisanal goods, enriched (in one sense of the book's polysemous title) by narratives establishing their authenticity through connection to a past, or by pointing to some other exceptional feature that distinguishes them from standard specimens of their type. Again progressive reforms help undermine the solidarities they were intended to reinforce. In the period of the projective city, a set of laws designed to buttress traditional collective bargaining (the Lois Auroux), helped legitimate precarious employment by recognizing the (initially) exceptional cases in which it would be allowed. In the same way, the "cultural democracy" of Jack Lang, minister of culture under Mitterrand, was supposed to favor celebration of creativity outside the museums and opera houses. Now, combined, with more expressly self-interested legal changes, such as new protections in intellectual property law for forms of production variously associated with particular places, they help make the nation's own history for France today what coal once was for Great Britain: fuel for capitalism.

The analytic focus of the book shifts accordingly. In the projective city, value was created in production. The morally inflected language of exchange was therefore shared among different categories of producers – social classes broadly conceived – and embedded in a model of justice including them in a single community. In the capitalism of enrichment, value is created through narratives that link only buyers and sellers. The rich tourists who come to France to consume its cultural and culinary patrimony *in situ* and the foreign elites who buy LVMH products at home (all enriched, in another of the title's meanings, by the inequalities of financialization and globalization) share a language of evaluation with the maker of artisanal knives or the owner of a gallery offering collectable art. They can scarcely be said to constitute a community even among themselves, and still less with others in their respective home countries, from whom they are more and more distanced by their enrichment. The concept of the city has no place here; and, in its absence, critique loses even the tenuous handhold it had before. It is evoked only fleetingly. The state, having been complicit in the emergence of new forms of production, might be held to account for their consequences; the history of France belongs to all the French. Yet the authors suggest that they themselves find this insufficient. The book closes with a carefully qualified reflection on the potential for great disruptions – "when reality is confronted with major changes that put experience in direct contact with the world" – to call into question the master narratives that link our judgments of exchange and structure.

What has happened?

The first and most conspicuous explanation is simply that the facts have changed, foreclosing even the scant possibilities for critique and protest that remained until now. If Boltanski and Esquerre are silent on these subjects it is because there is nothing to say. This would bring their work into proximity with Wolfgang Streeck's recent writing on the defeat of the left by a renascent capitalism that, having freed itself of the constraints of the postwar pact with social democracy, is running the table.

But there is despair and despair. However much Streeck may be personally outraged by this outcome, it costs him nothing theoretically to acknowledge it. In his kind of social science the relation among productive groups or social class was always a strategic game, usually resulting in one equilibrium or another. If there is an unexpected, decisive victory, the scientist-observer declares the game over. Sooner or later the players come to the same realization and retire with their payoffs.

Boltanski and his co-authors are not traveling so light. Enmeshed in the structures of their day, social actors play by the prevailing rules of the game and judge whether, in the large and in the small, they are fairly applied; the observer sees the interplay of rule following and revision and the changing motives for it. But the participants can't simply turn off their faculties of judgment when judgment tells them outcomes are unacceptable. Those faculties are rooted in and expressive of our very humanity. To abandon them would be to sacrifice ourselves utterly, and for an unknown and unintelligible purpose. There is not a word in *Enrichment* to suggest that adversity will, or could, drive us to that. It is never game over with our honor, our dignity, our indignation, and our hope and imagination, even when we know we have lost.

Perhaps then it is the focus on commercial relations – the shared language of buyers and sellers – that explains the continuing commitment to the actors' moral agency and yet the absence of extended discussion of the potential resistance to the new form of capitalism. Attention to the relation between buyers and sellers might thus improve our understanding of novel sources of value and kinds of evaluation while diverting our gaze from the dissatisfaction of the broader population excluded from enriched exchange.

This observation points in turn to the risks of assuming, generally, a close relation between the immediate experience of evaluation and the generation of criticism of capitalist structures and, conversely, assuming that absent such a relation criticism is not possible. Under relatively stable conditions, such as the first postwar decades, there is good reason for these assumptions. For stability brings a shared understanding both of the public goods needed to maintain the productive and social order and of roughly who is owed what in exchange. But as capitalism, under the pressure of competition and protest, changes direction, these relations break down. Public goods are ill-defined and their provision contentious, as are the terms of exchange. It becomes difficult even to discern, as we see in the arc of Boltanski's work, who is participating in the economy and what it means to participate. The terms of exchange are too ambiguous and incomplete to suggest clues about the nature of the emerging structures, and the structures too fluid to point to reliable terms of exchange.

Under these circumstances an analytic response – the one pursued in *The New Spirit of Capitalism* and *Enrichment* – is to identify those terms and structures in each new configuration that are mutually supportive and, on the basis of this accord, to define new types of capitalism. The risk is that understandings based on emerging agreements will ignore, like the agreements themselves, the embryonic disaccord from which indignation and protest spring.

But facing the same ambiguity of terms and fluidity of structure, the actors' practical response is to look to allies outside the sphere of exchange to articulate new understandings that make sense – including moral sense – of the confusion. In a word, the actors turn to politics: the marketplace politics of politicians and parties but also to the backstage politics of institutional and legal reforms, successful and botched, and to the fumbling adjustment of established policies and programs to new conditions. It is a mistake, or, rather, an artifact of many kinds of retrospective analysis, to conclude that this jumble of initiatives and accommodations simply clears the way for and helps support new capitalisms. The same pile of discordant bric-à-brac can be the source of renewed conceptions of markets, public powers, and public goods that make exchange among individuals and groups morally intelligible and therefore legitimate again. Politics is always also a fight about which usage will prevail, and in moments of general breakdown, like the present, these stakes are sensed by all. When moral protest disappears from the sphere of exchange, or seems excluded from it, it is often on the way to such political fights.

Let me put this point generally, as my own reading of the thrust of Boltanski's reading of the last decades of capitalist development and critique of it: in times of crisis and confusion, the only way to understand structures is to see them as mutable and in motion – that is, not as structures at all; and the only way to grasp the potential of these mobile and mutable structures is to see them in the light of possible political alternatives, each associating a distinct group of allies with a bundle of institutional reforms in a constellation prefiguring new terms of exchange. This perspective, venturing further, is at once analytic and practical, or, if you like, cognitive and moral. It is the vantage point from which the observer can best understand what matters and why, and the moral agent can find and help create the rudiments of order amid tumult. In the terms Boltanski develops in *On Critique*, the turn to politics allows the actors to escape the necessarily local limits of their practical judgments without yet requiring they have access to the "overarching" or "totalizing" understanding of structures that some kinds of sociology and social criticism claim to possess.

But while a preface is perhaps a place to formulate such questions and speculations, it is certainly not the place to pretend to conclusions. Besides, you likely have this book before you because you already have these sorts of questions, and many others, in mind, along with provisional answers. You already sense how little the critiques we have speak to the problems we face, and yet how we struggle to fashion even those. So you knew too that criticism is a labor of Sisyphus. As encouragement and consolation, therefore, it may help to recall Camus' observation (from an essay published in 1942, the very darkest of times) that, in the hour of returning down the slope to push the boulder up again, Sisyphus was fully conscious of the task before him, most human in his consciousness, and, yes, happy in his humanity.

Introduction

Social actors, whether they are buying or selling, are constantly immersed in the universe of commodities. Indeed, their experience of what they conceive to be reality depends to a large extent on this universe, often more than they would care to admit. The order of commodities –things in circulation – emerges in a process through which each thing is assigned a price in monetary terms every time it changes hands. At the same time, the things in question remain diverse, so that the universe of commodities is perceived not as an opaque totality – that would make it impenetrable – but as a structured whole. Reference to the structures of this whole makes it possible to identify each of the things exchanged. In addition, because social actors have internalized a tacit competence for dealing with these structures, they are able to orient themselves in the universe of commodities: they can participate in commerce, and, most importantly, they can pass judgment on the relationship between things and their prices.

Nevertheless, these structures, along with the relations they institute between things, their prices, and the value attributed to them, draw on differences anchored in space and in history. They are modified over time in keeping with shifts in the form of capitalism. In most contemporary societies, capitalism imposes its straitjacket on commerce in things; in this regard, Walter Benjamin's analyses offer a striking framework for contrasting the structures of merchandise that subtend trade in much of twenty-first-century Europe, and perhaps in the world, with those of the nineteenth century. In "Paris, Capital of the Nineteenth Century," Benjamin nourished his meditation on history and his critique of a commodity-focused representation of civilization with a reflection on merchandise in the era of triumphant capitalism. Commodities are manifested in the immediacy of perceptible presence and indissociably – he says – as "phantasmagoria" to which strollers, *flâneurs*, yield, seeking "refuge in the crowd."[1] Benjamin stressed the forms taken by the world city, radically new forms at the time, in which were concentrated not only finance, luxury, and fashion but also the revolutionary bohemian life emblematized by Auguste Blanqui, along with industry and, above all, the proletariat. Benjamin's primary interest lay in showing how beings in this context – persons and things existing in a common space – embodied a radical break with the past. This break, marked by the creation of industrial and financial capital, was manifested concretely in the destruction brought about in Paris by Baron Haussmann's reforms and the concomitant reorganization of the urban fabric. The age of the "commodity fetish" sought to base its legitimacy on a futuristic staging of the benefits of technology; blind trust in "progress" was the instrument by means of which historians identified with victors. "And all rulers are the heirs of prior conquerors. Hence, empathizing with the victor invariably benefits the current rulers."[2]

But the figure of the *flâneur*, when transposed to twenty-first-century Paris, is immersed in an entirely different reality. This new reality is no less capitalist than the one faced by Benjamin's *flâneur*. However, "luxury" no longer boasts of being "industrial." On the contrary, it strives to make us forget that its roots lie in a specific framework of production, one all the more easily brushed aside in that it is largely delocalized, confined to the orbits of other, faraway "world cities." Capitalist accumulation is ongoing and even intensifying, but it relies on new economic arrangements and is associated with a diversification of the cosmos of commodities that depends on the modalities according to which value is assigned to them. The present study aims to describe this transformation, which is particularly apparent in the countries that have been the cradles of European industrial power, and above all in France; we shall analyze the way commodities are distributed among several different forms of valuation – that is, according to the way the price attached to a given commodity is justified or critiqued.

Our work will thus be oriented in two directions, whose relations we shall try to characterize. The first is chiefly historical. The object of this aspect of our study is an economic change that, since the last quarter of the twentieth century, has profoundly modified the way wealth is created in the countries of Western Europe. These countries have been marked both by deindustrialization and by an increased exploitation of certain resources that, without being entirely new, have taken on unprecedented importance. In our view, the scope of the change becomes apparent only when domains generally considered separate are brought together – most notably the arts, especially the plastic arts, and other cultural manifestations, trade in ancient objects, the creation of foundations and museums, the luxury industry, heritage creation, and tourism. We shall try to show that the constant interactions among these different domains make it possible to understand the way each one produces profits. Our argument will be based on their common exploitation of an underlying stratum that is purely and simply *the past*.

We shall use the term "enrichment economy" to designate this type of economy, playing on the ambiguity of the word "enrichment." On the one hand, we use the word in the sense in which one speaks of enriching a metal, enhancing a lifestyle or a cultural asset, showcasing an article of clothing, or bringing together a set of objects in a collection, to emphasize the fact that this economy is based less on the production of new things than on an effort to *enrich* things that already exist, especially by associating them with narratives. On the other hand, the term "enrichment" refers to one of the specific characteristics of this economy, namely, that it draws upon trade in things that are intended above all for the wealthy and that thus also constitute a supplementary source of enrichment for the wealthy people who deal in them. It seems to us that this enrichment economy and its effects have to be taken into account if we are to grasp the transformations of contemporary society and some of the tensions that permeate it.

Our second orientation is more analytical. It seeks to comprehend how very diverse forms of commodities can give rise to transactions that, at least in most instances, will strike the actors who participate in them – either as purveyors or as customers – as normal activities, more or less in keeping with previously constituted expectations. By the term "commodity," we designate everything to which a price is attached when its ownership changes hands. Given its phenomenal diversity, if the cosmos of commodities were not structured by modes of organization that are partly implicit, it would be hard to understand how the actors could orient themselves in it. The commercial dexterity of the various actors is quite uneven, to be sure, and depends on their experience as buyers or sellers. Nevertheless, without a minimal degree of competence, actors would simply be lost and unable to make their way in the world, given the importance that the role and the quantity of commercial transactions have taken on in modern societies. It is in this sense that we shall speak of *commodity structures*.

By relying on these underlying structures, the actors can reflect on the relation between two types of heterogeneous entities – things on the one hand, prices on the other – whose union constitutes commodities as such, instead of simply receiving this assemblage synthetically and passively submitting to its effects. But to understand the way a rational actor can seek to grasp the relation between things and their prices, we must take into account a third type of entity, which we shall designate by the term actors use – the indigenous term, as it were – namely, the polysemic term of value. It is in fact very generally the substance of a thing that is understood to constitute its "value"; in this sense, the relation between the thing and its price becomes subject to reflection, whether it is a matter of critiquing the price or justifying it. Rather than taking value as a property of things that is at once substantive and mysterious – a way of looking at things that has permeated classical economics and that continues to operate – we shall treat value as an arrangement for justifying or critiquing the price of things. The structures we shall seek to identify divide up the universe of commodities by distributing the entire set of marketable objects among various ways of justifying (or critiquing) their prices – that is, among different ways of assigning value to things. We shall see that the diverse methods for establishing value present differential relations that result from permutations of basic oppositions so that we can describe them as a transformation group in Lévi-Strauss's sense.[3] This makes it possible to reconcile the homogeneity of the cosmos of commodities (which encompasses every entity to which a price is attached when it changes hands) with the diversity of objects that comprise it, on the basis of the way that price is justified.

It is by being attentive to the dynamics of capitalism that we shall seek to connect the two approaches, historical and analytical, that have guided our work. We shall look at capitalism through the lens of commerce rather than focusing on the changes that have affected production and thus also labor – changes that, along with increased unemployment, have been the primary focus of analyses of capitalism. In this project we have benefited greatly from (re)reading Fernand Braudel, whose seminal book on capitalism puts commodities and commerce at the heart of his analyses; these entities are similarly central to studies – especially those of Giovanni Arrighi – that have sought to extend Braudel's perspective into the present day. Commodity structures have to be analyzed in historical terms precisely because they have been inserted into the dynamics of capitalism and into the link between order and disorder that is the driving force behind capitalism. On the one hand, capitalist accumulation has to be able to rely on shared expectations, and thus on commodity structures, in particular so as to limit transaction costs. On the other hand, the very logic of that accumulation means that capitalism must constantly shift its position in order to benefit from the commodification of new objects, thereby subverting its own structures.

Because it depended most notably, in an initial phase, on the development of industry, capitalism had to shift its position so as to draw the greatest possible benefit from the commodification of new objects, as opportunities to profit from the exploitation of industrial labor began to diminish. The formation of the commodity structures we see today can thus be linked to the development of an enrichment economy. The existence of a plurality of forms for making things valuable, forms that are at once isomorphic and differentiated, allows diverse things to change hands with the hope that they will be sold each time at the highest possible price so as to generate the greatest possible profit, or at least to limit losses. If there were only one way to refer to the value of things in order to justify their prices, a great number of objects that are exchanged for high prices today would find themselves depreciated. The diversification of commodity structures goes hand in hand with diversification of the gaps that commodities come to fill. In this way commodity structures tend to shape both specific things and the lack of these things, so that they are maintained in order to avoid their being neither entirely objective nor entirely subjective. It is in this respect that they contribute in a major way to shaping what is called reality, inasmuch as reality depends on what Wittgenstein called language games, linguistic maneuvers that allow actors to grasp experience through reflection.

To carry out our project, we have navigated among several different disciplines, methods, and fields of inquiry. Our displacements were not premeditated but, rather, imposed on us, as it were, by the logic of a study whose specific object became clear to us only gradually, as the findings that seemed to answer the questions we were asking brought forth new questions, drawing us toward new investigations.

With regard to disciplines, then, we followed a path that led us from sociology and anthropology toward various strands of history (the history of art, the history of technology, political and social history), political philosophy, and, especially, economics. In this last field, which is no more unified than sociology and which encompasses quite diverse tendencies (schools that disagree even about the label "economics"), our readings and borrowings led us sometimes toward works situated more or less within the neoclassical tradition and sometimes, instead, toward works associated with heterodox or critical approaches; the differences among these works appeared less clear-cut to us on the level of documentary or even theoretical contributions than on the level of institutional affiliations and conflicts between schools. It seemed to us that the most striking difference separating the "orthodox" from the "heterodox" outlooks had to do in particular with the relation that these varying styles of economics maintained with sociology: the former sought to defend the autonomy of economics – an autonomy marked most notably by the space given to translating models into one or another of the languages stemming from mathematics – while the latter did not hesitate to draw upon data produced by the other social sciences.

Our primary concern has been to disentangle ourselves from the often difficult relations maintained between sociology and anthropology on the one hand and economics on the other. Thus, at times, sociologists and anthropologists are led to neglect economics (as if relations of symbolic exchanges had an autonomous existence entirely distinct from relations of exchanges of goods); at other times, they tend to seize hastily upon models originating in economics and apply them to their own objects and thereby to justify decisions on economic policy concerning those objects; in still other instances, they are inclined to develop a critical attitude toward economics in general, as if sociology and anthropology alone had access to some truth about human relations that the science of economics, tainted by inhumanity, could not grasp. While critique is by no means absent from our work, it is aimed at contemporary capitalism and not at economics as such. Our intention has thus been to extend the efforts of scholars – undoubtedly more numerous in a not-so-remote past than they are today – who have worked toward unifying the social sciences, contesting all forms of disciplinary orthodoxy. Today, in our view, this effort must entail moving beyond the tensions between, on the one hand, approaches inherited chiefly from positivism (which are frequent in economics) and, on the other hand, approaches that stem principally from constructionism (more frequent in sociology). We have sought to move forward along this path by developing a *pragmatic structuralism*. This approach makes it possible to combine a social history with an analysis of the cognitive skills that actors use in order to act.

As far as our methods of inquiry are concerned, we have been highly eclectic in our choices, operating like gleaners, as it were. Although we have occasionally included examples from other countries to show that we are talking about a process that can be disseminated, we have focused on the case of France, which is unquestionably one of the countries in which the transformations we have sought to bring to light are most clearly manifested. Our sources were numerous and wide-ranging. We collected sets of existing statistics; we conducted formal or informal interviews, both with informants invested with institutional authority and with so-called ordinary actors, such as artists, or collectors of various things ranging from works of contemporary art to football club insignia; we went through reams of documents produced for commercial or self-promotional purposes that we found either in print form or on the Internet; we analyzed marketing manuals for luxury items, tourism, art, and culture; and we undertook to produce an ethnography of places where the formation of an enrichment economy in France could be grasped "in real time" (for example, in the Aubrac region or in Arles).

The pages that follow are thus the result of a sort of artisanal approach that was once frequently practiced in the social sciences – and in social anthropology or in history more than in sociology – but that tends to be condemned today, even though it offers great advantages in terms of freedom and especially flexibility. Since our project was free of any constraints that might have been imposed by dependence on outside financing, it could be continually redefined and reoriented in response to the results obtained. It is too often forgotten that, by limiting oneself to work based on "big data," one rediscovers an object that has already been socially constructed, and one rules out the possibility of introducing both the cognitive behavior of actors and the social changes that have not yet been subject to taxonomic identification or to technical and institutional recognition.

The process of collecting materials was all the more demanding in that what gradually turned out to be our key objects of inquiry – that is, on the one hand, the formation of an economy of enrichment and, on the other, the current state of commodity structures and of the skills that allow actors to orient themselves in this economy – have not in either case yielded, up to now, outcomes that would allow for a global, and in particular a statistical, overview. There are no data-processing or administrative centers that would collect, sift, and shape data covering the entire set of domains that must be taken into account, as we see it, if one is to grasp features in contemporary socio-economic developments that we believe to be very important. Thus we have had to criss-cross a large number of areas, from contemporary art to the luxury industry, from the national patrimony to tourism, and so on. Each of these areas calls for further study; our book as a whole can be read as an invitation to work in a new field of research. Our hope, then, is that the task will be taken up again by others who will be able to flesh out the results and further develop the hypotheses presented here.

Part I

Destruction and Creation of Wealth

1

The Age of the Enrichment Economy

The deindustrialization of Western Europe

In the last quarter of the twentieth century, in Western societies, mass production was no longer viewed as the only way – perhaps not even as the principal way – to maximize profits and accumulate wealth. For capitalism, too, the extension beyond mass production proved to be a necessity imposed by the requirement of profit as the possibilities opened up by that form of production, initially considered virtually infinite, seemed to reach their limits. While the standard form was not abandoned, the extension of capitalism entailed financialization and – in the realm of the production and/or commercialization of objects – the redrawing of geopolitical maps. Certain "emerging" countries took over responsibility for mass production as the primary path to enrichment (the accumulation of wealth), while some countries that had been among the powerhouses of world capitalism in the nineteenth and twentieth centuries concentrated on finance and on developing high-tech goods in order to retain power – from a distance – over the manufacturing of the most common goods, insofar as these were products derived from technological innovations. However, the latter countries also turned toward a much more intensive commodification of domains that had long remained more or less on the margins of capitalism.

The geographic expansion of capitalism redistributed – toward countries in which the labor force was abundant and ill-organized and in which wages were therefore low – a number of standard production sites, although the conception and sales of the objects produced remained for the most part under the control of companies headquartered in Western countries, which were still at the heart of world capitalism. Among other effects, these transfers accelerated the deindustrialization of Western Europe. Deindustrialization in the first decade of the twenty-first century is a well-studied phenomenon affecting Western economies, France's in particular.[1] Industrial employment reached a peak in 1974, with more than 5,900,000 salaried workers. In the early 2010s, this sector lost a little more than 40 percent of its personnel. During the same period, what statisticians define more broadly as the "productive sphere" decreased from 48 percent of all jobs to 35 percent.[2] This drop affected almost all areas: mining, metallurgy, machinery, ship-building, textiles, and so on, excluding only certain high-tech sectors such as aeronautics and the nuclear, pharmaceutical, and weapons industries.[3] The sectors that included intermediate goods and common consumer products were particularly affected. Their decline, which began as early as the 1960s and 1970s in the textile and leather-working areas, went on to affect manufacturing as a whole.

By "deindustrialization," however, we do not mean the shift to a "post-industrial" society that was often predicted by sociologists in the 1960s.[4] That prophecy has not been fulfilled on a global scale. On the one hand, many domains that had long remained on the margins of the industrial world – such as small businesses, education, health, and personal services – are run today (even those that do not depend on the private sector but are under state control) according to management methods that originated in the major worldwide companies and are subject to accounting norms developed in industry, a development that has been facilitated by the spread of computer technologies. But, above all, European societies make more use than ever of products of industrial origin – mobile phones, for example, or personal computers – that now count among the most common household appliances. The commodities in circulation are more numerous than ever before, but they are manufactured elsewhere. During the same period, in France, internal consumption almost doubled in global added value, as did commercial services, while the industrial sector declined by nearly two-thirds. Among economists, the explanations for this process of deindustrialization have been subject to intense debate. It is hard to determine how much importance to attribute, on the one hand, to the outsourcing of certain functions that had long been assumed by companies but were not directly productive and, on the other hand, to the increase in labor productivity. But it is quite probable that the most important factor is the importation of objects manufactured in countries with cheaper labor (depending on the sector, from 9 percent to 80 percent of the manufactured items sold in France are imported)[5] and in which the workforce is neither well organized nor well protected. This is especially the case in Far Eastern countries such as China and Vietnam, but also in post-communist Eastern European countries, for example in Slovenia, Romania, and Bulgaria.

Industrial delocalization has been inscribed in the history of Western capitalism during the last fifty years, and it undoubtedly constitutes one of the paths adopted for getting out of the crisis that capitalism underwent from the mid-1960s to the mid-1980s, roughly speaking. Often analyzed in terms of a decline in productivity and an excess in productive capacities with respect to the demand among those who can afford to buy, and the resulting steady erosion in profits from the production of manufactured goods,[6] the delocalization movement also has political roots. For the big companies, it has been a way to escape from the fiscal constraints of nation-states, and it has also constituted a response to the mobilization of the European proletariat, particularly during the decade following the upheavals of May 1968. One of the consequences of this process, but perhaps also one of its unacknowledged objectives, has been to pacify or even suppress a working class that, in the 1960s and 1970s, had proved particularly combative, especially in France and Italy. Nevertheless, the delocalization movement could not have occurred at the same pace or to the same degree without the measures of financial deregulation adopted in the 1970s and 1980s, measures that favored transfers of capital from the old industrial countries toward the so-called emerging countries, thus stimulating the creation, in countries with low wage scales, of subcontracting firms that were largely dependent on orders from companies based in the major European or North American cities.

Old and new sites of prosperity

In France, the loss of industrial jobs chiefly affected areas in which industry was the main source of wealth, thus especially the northern and northeastern regions,[7] precisely the areas in which, as numerous studies attempting to connect regional geography, economics, and political science have shown, the extreme right is achieving its best electoral results. Still, other regions where industry had played a less important role at the beginning of the period in question have become wealthy even though they have not escaped deindustrialization. This phenomenon is all the more troubling in that it is found in many rural regions that had already suffered from a weakening of the agricultural sector during the 1960s: the collapse of small farming had also led to the decline of small and medium-sized cities, leading to virtual desertification in some areas. But it is as though these regions had profited from the increased commodification of domains previously deemed marginal, as if they had reoriented themselves toward exploitation of new strata of resources: to their benefit, a number of objects, places, and even experiences that had for a long time played only a background role with respect to the primordial interests of capitalism were transformed into sources of potential wealth.

Economic geography does not allow a direct approach to this second movement because, in the absence of categories dedicated to the analysis of the process, it cannot turn to statistical data as solidly established as those for industry. Nevertheless, the field has a particularly relevant contribution to make to our research. As has been shown by Vincent Hecquet, who began with a statistical approach, and Laurent Davezies,[8] who focused on geography, the wealth of the various regions in France does not depend exclusively on the degree of development of the productive sphere – far from it; thus "the new economic geography" can separate "the territories' contribution to growth" from "the territories' social development."[9] The decline of the industrial regions in fact contrasts sharply with the growing prosperity of regions situated especially along the coasts, in the west or in the south, where population growth has been pronounced and employment and wages have increased. These regions, with greater and greater commercial activity, are developing on a basis that, if we adopt the classification used by geographers, is not "productive" but "residential."[10] These same regions include a great many retirees (49 percent of all retirees in France) who are by and large better off financially than the average,[11] large numbers of vacation homes (66 percent), intermittent or "shuttle" residents who work and live part of the time in large cities in France or elsewhere, and a number of persons who are unemployed and/or dependent on social services who find "odd jobs" in these areas, jobs roughly equivalent to work in private homes. According to Hecquet, Davezies, and others, these are "dynamic non-commercial territories" characterized by what they identify as "development without growth" based on "residential economies." In these territories, which are among the most "dynamic" and most "attractive" in France (encompassing 44 percent of the population) and which offer "residential advantages," tourism and the restaurant business are developing along with the maintenance of real-estate stock that had been in decline until recently. In the rural areas of these Atlantic and Mediterranean regions, the arrival of new residents has led to a significant increase in construction.[12] Whereas the employment base is shrinking in the industrial regions, the development of these "residential" territories is creating many new jobs in domestic service, including manual laborers, but "in local sectors oriented toward local demands (sectors that are tied by and large to specific locales)."[13]

Movements of this sort have stimulated the coalescence and deployment of forms of valorization that, although they were not unknown and not negligible, had remained in an embryonic state, since they had not been sufficiently integrated into business practices. The *enrichment economy* is one component of a social world struggling with a form of capitalism that we characterize as *integral*, in the sense that various ways of creating value are integrated within it. In this social world, buying and selling mass-produced objects, and especially artifacts that incorporate a high level of technology, have continued to have primacy, for objects of this type account for the vast majority of commercial exchanges. But there are many indications attesting to the fact that commodification has also been oriented, more intensely and more visibly than before, in new directions. Unlike what was labeled "consumer society" and subjected to critique in the 1960s and 1970s, when buyers were often represented as "passive, manipulated, and impulsive," one of the characteristics of integral capitalism is that it strongly stimulated and compensated commercial dexterity and had as its horizon the fact that *everyone is not only a consumer but also a merchant.* Following this perspective to its extreme limit, we shall deal thus with merchandise – commodities – without assuming that merchants need to be studied as a separate category.[14]

The extension of capitalism has been translated through the more pronounced and broadened role played by fashion effects, as attested, for example, by the importance attached to *brands*, and especially by what sociological literature often calls the *culture of celebrity*, whose social role has been examined in a number of studies starting in the 1960s,[15] and whose economic dimension has recently received increased attention, facilitated in particular by the development of the Internet. Similarly, the commercial importance of cultural activities has taken on unprecedented salience, as exemplified for instance by the flurry of record-breaking prices at art auctions, a phenomenon that has been compared to the processes of financializing the economy. We ourselves, however, intend to stress the development of an economy of attention, which leads a growing number of persons to seek objects that are valued less for their direct utility than for their expressive charge and for the narratives that accompany their circulation. These things reveal themselves to the observer in what is specific about them – that is, in their differences as compared to other more or less similar things; in somewhat the same way, collectors accumulate and bring together objects that have a family resemblance to one another, as if to enjoy the tension between their similarity and their diversity.

As a provisional indication of a change in the attention paid to things, we can single out the importance of the practice of collecting over the last few decades. The growing diffusion and internalization of a type of attention to things associated with the ethos of collecting cannot be evaluated solely by taking into account the number of modest collections and collectors. The schemas on which the practice of collecting rests, often described in cognitive and affective terms, also have a particular economic dimension that is especially evident if we turn to the transactions to which the exceptional items sought by a well-to-do public give rise – transactions involving, for example, art objects or antiquities, luxury goods, houses associated with artists or architects, and so on. Now, objects of this type, and the arrangements that make it possible to attach value to them, are at the heart of an enrichment economy. In this regard, we may wonder whether collecting, less as a specific practice than as a generative form involving a certain way of being with things, might not constitute a sort of operator making it possible to establish a relationship between the various realms of commercial activities on which the enrichment economy is based.

For an initial characterization of these realms, we shall focus chiefly on the case of France, which constitutes a privileged vantage point from which to observe phenomena whose presence is attested in numerous places around the world. Like the industrial economy, the enrichment economy is very unevenly distributed in spatial terms: it occupies large territories in certain countries, but it can be reduced to the scale of a quarter of a big city in other places where intensive agriculture, industry, or service activities predominate. In this sense, the spatial distribution of the enrichment economy must be conceived in terms of density rather than in terms of national boundaries, for nations are apt to evolve; as we know, such a shift occurred in the case of large-scale industrial production, which started in a few counties of rural England and ended up conquering many regions of the world. Just as we might speak of an industrial basin, we can speak of an *enrichment basin*, a space that is often established by drawing on a concentration of religious buildings (such as the Romanesque or Gothic churches in many Italian cities or, in Japan, the temples in Kyoto).

The omnipresence of enriched objects

The fields within which the enrichment economy is deployed are hard to describe synthetically, because their substantive diversity is not reduced by their inclusion in a broad category that would allow us to bring out their connections and designate them with a single term or formula. The semantic, legal, and statistical frameworks on which description of the economic and social world relies have been forged in order to give authorities a grip on an economy that is principally industrial. Thus at present there are no categorial arrangements or accounting frameworks that would allow us to determine with relative precision either the economic importance taken on by the nebulous phenomenon whose contours we are seeking to sketch here or the number of persons whose primary activity is connected with that phenomenon. This is the case in particular because the phenomenon brings together sectors (such as art and tourism), activities (as diverse as heading museums and manufacturing alligator handbags), statuses (such as short-term worker, stable wage-earner, government employee, or person of private means), and professions that are dispersed in statistical nomenclatures among sets constructed according to different logical principles, more in accordance with the old classifications of the industrial world.[16]

In addition, the existing frameworks deal with employment using two approaches whose results are difficult to put together, for some researchers look at individually declared professions, while others examine the economic sectors taken into account by national statistics; this makes it hard to analyze the indirect and induced effects of each type of activity and/or profession. As a result, we lack statistical data in support of generalizations that would allow us to highlight and follow the specific processes at the heart of this evolution. This is why, in contemporary economic literature, presentation of the economic reorientation toward the wealthy is distributed among various domains; these are apprehended according to diverse accounting forms that often rely on inconsistent definitions and categories, making an overall grasp quite difficult. The absence of an accounting framework and of categories unifying the enrichment economy is not accidental, nor does it stem from a delay in the systematic institutional registration of changes in reality; it will be understood, at the end of our analysis, as one of the conditions that make this economy profitable.

In order to indicate how the sphere of the enrichment economy is constituted so that readers will be able to follow us while relying on their ordinary sense of social reality, we must begin by turning to the objects themselves. A first indication will hold our attention: the growing visibility given to objects that are exchanged at high or very high prices in comparison with the prevailing norms. This visibility is most pronounced in major metropolitan centers, but it can also be found in a number of restored and protected sites or villages whose activity had been primarily industrial. It is prominent as well, for example, in media targeting an audience that, although fairly well-to-do, is not sufficiently wealthy, on average, to acquire many of the things that are on display not only in advertisements but also in the content presented.

In France and elsewhere, the principal organs of the daily or weekly press – whose readership is increasingly limited – offer supplements on the same themes so as to draw funds from the luxury industry that will allow at least some of these economically threatened publications to continue to exist. Among these, we find *How to Spend It*, put out in London by the *Financial Times*; *T Magazine* of the *New York Times*; and the weekly *M Le magazine* of the French newspaper of record *Le Monde*. These leisure-oriented magazines are aimed at a public with fuzzy contours but whose members, finding themselves mirrored in the magazines' pages, can see themselves appreciatively as both cultivated and wealthy. Airline magazines are another case in point: for example, *Air France Magazine*, published by Gallimard, is offered to the airline's clients free of charge. Publications like these have the advantage, for our purposes, of displaying advertisements for luxury items (watches, perfumes, clothing, real estate, upscale hotels, and the like) in close proximity to articles discussing trendy, vintage, or "design" objects, sites whose ancestral and historical values are highlighted, works of art, exhibits, and artists, and (especially in France) high-level gastronomy construed as part of the country's "non-material heritage." In these magazines, the various topics presented in ads and articles are treated without distinction, as if they were inseparable components of one and the same universe.

These media present objects chosen not so much for their usefulness or their sturdiness, as would be the case for common industrial items, as for their intrinsic preciousness, or simply for their difference, and also, inevitably, for their price. These objects are often associated with national or regional markers of identity that are supposed to guarantee their authenticity (even if their manufacture can be discreetly outsourced, as happens with ordinary objects, to countries with low wages). The fascination that these objects are meant to exercise is thought to depend on a sort of *aura* that surrounds them, conferring on them a touch of *exceptionality* that destines them to be appreciated by an elite. The objects may be antiques or items produced by luxury firms; they are often presented as handmade. They are linked to the fashion sector in many instances (watches, jewelry, handbags, and clothing), but they also may be outstanding wines or food items produced in identified and protected *terroirs* or contemporary artworks presented in galleries, at art fairs, or at auctions that attract attention through their cultural and economic dimensions alike.[17]

In these presentations, increasing importance is attributed not only to the objects themselves but also to the universes in which the objects are conceived and in which they circulate – and above all to the human beings surrounding them, whether these be "creators," such as designers, dressmakers, cooks, antique dealers, hairdressers, collectors, exhibit organizers, and so on, or "personalities," noteworthy in themselves, who associate their names and images with these exceptional items (this is the case for example with the "inspirers" of haute couture or perfumes). All of these "actors" behind "fashion, culture, and taste" are mentioned very frequently and depicted in portraits in which they rub shoulders with artists in the classic sense of the term, such as painters or sculptors. Attention is thus drawn directly toward a relatively heteroclite set of objects treated as though they occupied the same plane (a "plane of immanence," as Deleuze might say): these can be items of apparel, furniture, decorative objects, vintage items, or works of ancient or contemporary art.

The kind of profound mutation at issue here is embodied in a single building in Turin. A big Fiat factory opened in the Lingotto district there in 1922; it closed in 1982. Since then, the building has been converted into galleries featuring shops, hotels, restaurants, and a conference center. As the high point of what was one of the emblematic sites in the world of labor, the Pinacoteca Giovanni e Marella Agnelli was inaugurated in 2002, designed by the star Italian architect Renzo Piano, who already had many museums to his credit, including the Pompidou Center in Paris. In the white raised gallery of the Pinacoteca, viewers now crowd around to admire works from the collection of paintings of a former leader of Italy. How have we come from mass production of standard automobiles and the heated workers' struggles associated with the site to the silent and respectful contemplation of works of art acquired by the CEO?

The rise of luxury

The luxury industry lies at the heart of this nebulous phenomenon. In France, organized around a very dynamic professional association (the Comité Colbert), the industry experienced particularly strong growth in the early 2000s, especially in exports, with increases ranging from 6 percent to 20 percent per year depending on the product.[18] Worldwide exports of high-end consumer goods virtually doubled between 2000 and 2011; three-quarters of these originated in Western Europe, especially in France and Italy (where clothing, leather goods, and shoes account for at least one-third of high-end exports). Jewelry and fine watches came especially from Switzerland, while luxury automobiles were sold under German brand names (they won 19 percent to 29 percent of market share during the 2000s before the drop in luxury auto sales after the 2008 financial crisis). France, the leader in this sector, held 11.2 percent of the world market in luxury goods (with an annual growth rate of 9.8 percent).[19] These exports are oriented chiefly toward the developed countries (70 percent), which include the highest proportion of wealthy individuals, but the emergent countries (China in particular) are also important markets where consumption has greatly increased, from 21 percent in 2000 to 39 percent in 2011.[20] Along with the Gulf states, the emergent countries are now the chief importers.[21]

These luxury products include, among others, great wines and spirits or brand-name clothing,[22] perfumes, and cosmetics. Increasingly, some of these goods are produced in part offshore, in countries with cheap labor, but they are generally assembled and labeled in the country from which they purport to come;[23] the gap between the country of manufacture and the country of labeling and display, generally kept secret so as to avoid devaluing the exceptional object and allowing it to be categorized as just another ordinary product, is marked at most by the distinction between "made in" and "made by" or "designed in."[24] These "made in X" goods can then be sold under a brand name whose marketing emphasizes a national identity; this gives them added value and also often plays on the supposedly artisanal, "old-style" character of their manufacture, which is intended to single them out and support their claim to exceptionality. But in a period during which outsourcing and its role in increased domestic unemployment have been subject to numerous critiques, the label "made in France" can also invoke "ethical commitment and social responsibility on the part of the luxury firms,"[25] and these qualities too can boost the value added to the product.

The luxury industry also supports the contemporary art market, privileging connections between famous artists and brand-name items treated as "one of a kind" handmade objects (Hermès handbags, for instance, or Vuitton luggage). The history of the Kering group (which includes such brands as Gucci, Saint Laurent, Bottega Veneta, Balenciaga, and Alexander McQueen) offers a good example of the way one firm has flourished since the 2000s by relinquishing the industrial products to which it had been devoted earlier in favor of embracing the luxury sector.[26] Displacement effects of this sort have repercussions even in elite French graduate schools such as HEC (an international business school) or Sciences Po (a research university specializing in political science), many of whose graduates gravitate toward management or marketing and incorporate training in contemporary art into their programs. The director of one of these schools justifies its success by noting that "the students see very clearly that luxury brands are associated with contemporary art, that people such as Pinault or Arnault invest in artworks, that the major executives of the period are philanthropists. Now, those brands are their future employers."[27]

In this high-end universe, "gastronomic luxury" is doing exceptionally well: according to the geographer Vincent Marcilhac, this domain "represents several hundred thousand jobs and several tens of billions of euros in profits. It constitutes one of France's strong points on the level of commercial profits, and it plays an important role in France's image or 'brand' on the international level."[28] From the last third of the nineteenth century to roughly the middle of the twentieth, statements by producers' organizations or public authorities concerning food products were oriented mainly toward homogenizing and certifying them, while at the same time combating fraud through a series of measures addressing issues of hygiene and food safety (especially regarding milk and wine, two products about which doctors had particularly strong health and safety concerns).[29] Over the last few decades, however, the search for improvement in product quality has taken a new tack, placing more and more emphasis on "authenticity."[30] As part of this change, the meaning of the term "quality" has shifted: initially applied to products deemed stable, homogeneous, and safe – and whose improvement depended on the application of norms that implied standardization or even industrialization, thus implying lower prices as well – the term has come to designate foods deemed exceptional, unquestionably non-standard, and significantly more expensive.

This tendency is particularly evident in the case of wine, which has been studied in detail by Marie-France Garcia-Parpet. The southern and southwestern regions of France in particular have seen a shift away from massive production, in "wine factories," of inexpensive red table wine destined for domestic consumption by a broad public; instead, production began to be focused on "original" products with "character," associated with a high level of oenological culture and destined for export. This transformation has proceeded in parallel with the highlighting of *terroirs* – zones whose soil is defined not only by specific mineral properties and climatic conditions but also by reactivated or invented traditions (such as the "Confrérie de Chinon"), by the creation of labels, and by the use of historical references to famous people who purportedly lived in proximity to certain vineyards (such as Rabelais for the wines of the Loire Valley), and also by administrative measures intended to limit and regulate production.[31] One result of these maneuvers has clearly been to create effects of scarcity that can be invoked to justify price increases.

More generally, the "production of local cultural singularities" has made it possible to constitute "monopoly revenues";[32] the process of localization around *terroirs*, which we have seen in relation to wines, has been imitated for a large number of other products of more or less local origins, such as truffles, certain mushrooms (*cèpes*), beef (from Aubrac), or fowl (capons or pullets from Bresse), but also for products that are made from imported raw materials (such as chocolate) but that supposedly benefit from a form of processing associated with a local tradition. The deep roots of tradition are called upon in particular in response to economic or moral critiques, as in the case of *foie gras*, viewed as a national emblem – a phenomenon that Michaela DeSoucey has called "gastronationalism."[33] This attribution of local roots to luxury food items, dispersed over a multiplicity of *terroirs* each of which is presumed to present special characteristics unlike any other, has accompanied a growing economic concentration in the sector of luxury foods, a sector partly absorbed by the broader French luxury industry. This is attested, for example, by the fusion of the Moët Hennessy group with the Louis Vuitton group (LVMH), or by François Pinault's purchase of Château Latour in 1993 and Bernard Arnault's acquisition (for LVMH) of Château d'Yquem in 1998 and then of Château Cheval Blanc in 1999. International groups with headquarters in other countries have acquired similarly prestigious properties; Garcia-Parpet highlights "an increasing share of large groups (banks, insurance companies, management and finance companies, and so on) for which investments in French luxury foods constitute a financial investment first and foremost."[34] The development of luxury foods is thus both a factor in the expansion of world capitalism and a "tool of territorial development," because it supports local agricultural activity. It also plays a major role in showcasing two other domains that we shall now examine: tourism, increasingly focused on food, wine, and ecological concerns,[35] and heritage creation, which profits from the historical enrichment of sites, *terroirs*, and cities associated with gastronomic traditions.

A key feature of the luxury industry is its reliance on brands. Brands can be purchased by groups as non-material agents for the prestige they carry, even in cases where their products do not bring in profits and have to be offset by other products from the same group, or, in cases where the brands belong to businesses that have ceased all activity, their names can be purchased and put back into circulation in association with a narrative about the past. The prestige of a brand name is enhanced by its identification with a country such as Italy or France, political entities that are themselves treated as brands; their worth depends in a circular fashion on the exceptional items they produce and on the "art of living" they purportedly exemplify. The idea of building the image of a country as one would do for a commercial brand is relatively recent,[36] having developed in parallel with the enrichment economy. The national image may find support in any statement (or "stereotype") that is generally associated positively with the country being promoted. In the case of France, the historical and heritage dimensions associated with its monuments, landscapes, arts, foods, and perfumes can all be foregrounded (for example Versailles, Camembert, Veuve Clicquot, Chanel no. 5, Saint Laurent). But this insistence on the past has to be associated with the idea of *creation* and thus with "surprise and life," so it won't be "perceived as conservative."[37]

This introjection of the past into the present – positing a sort of equivalence between a past considered from the vantage point of the present and a present considered from the vantage point of the future (that is, already viewed as past) – is the operation that traces the outline of "eternal France."[38] The promotion of the brand "France" presupposes close collaboration between "public authorities" and commercial brands – that is, between "the *corporate* competence of the State" and the businesses or groups that have an international base. This collaboration is manifested, for example, through operations such as "Christian Lacroix providing furnishings for TGV [high-speed train] lines" or "exporting the Louvre to Abu Dhabi," in which the creation of the building was entrusted to the architect Jean Nouvel, who was charged with "updating our heritage." As for the "targets," they include above all "opinion leaders, business circles, experts in specific sectors, and journalists," not to mention the "public at large" and especially (for "not all publics are equal") "graduates of major institutions of higher education in the leading countries."[39] One of the principal aims of those who promote the "France" brand is to "influence the rankings" so as to maintain France's place in "international comparisons," in keeping with the requirements that stem from the generalization of benchmarking.[40]

Heritage creation

In addition to interest in exceptional items, a second factor in the creation of wealth is currently growing in importance. This factor is linked to various processes that can be called processes of *heritage creation*.[41] While they affect real estate in particular, they can also be extended to other types of goods. Examples can be found in apartments situated in the historical center of a large city, in residences located close to monuments or sites viewed as exceptional ("the loveliest villages in France"), or in housing near zones categorized as "parks" that have been subjected to "protective" measures after an administrative process of selection. Such measures typically require that they be maintained "as before" – often after the location in question has been subjected to an attempt to reconstitute a more or less fictional past. This process has a significant economic impact, since wherever it occurs it leads to major price increases in the associated lands and property, and it has important repercussions for tourism as well. For example, in the historic districts of major cities one now finds real-estate agencies advertising themselves as specialists in "collectable properties."

A concomitant phenomenon is what might be called *made-to-order heritage creation*. The patrimonial effect is triggered in this case when new establishments such as museums or cultural centers are created in a given locale or when local events (festivals, commemorations, and so on) are inaugurated. In addition, there are many cases in which some part of the built environment previously deemed lacking in interest and destined to be razed – often a former site of industrial production – is rehabilitated in view of housing artistic or cultural activities that are apt to give rise to "events" or "happenings." Heritage creation, whether made to order or not, can be achieved without regard to the venerability of the site or the building; indeed, these may have been entirely reconstructed, reconfigured, or even newly created, for heritage creation is based primarily on a narrative that inscribes a place within a genealogy.

One example of direct heritage creation, now classic and widely imitated, is that of Bilbao, an industrial city in decline whose luster has been restored by the addition of a Guggenheim museum designed by Frank Gehry. This operation was part of a broader project undertaken in the late 1980s at the initiative of the Guggenheim board in New York: its aim was to set up a "global museum" housed at various sites, chiefly in order to extend and diversify the existing exhibit spaces, which the acquisition of new collections had rendered inadequate. The plan included the establishment of a vast museum devoted to conceptual and minimalist art in North Adams, a small Massachusetts industrial town in decline. But that project ran up against the tension between the local authorities' insistence on highlighting local identity and honoring the workers in the former factory and the Guggenheim's wish to promote worldwide art.[42] Many similar cases can be found in France: for example, the efforts made by the authorities in Nantes to enhance the image of the city by reorienting its activities toward art and culture. Among other measures, the former site of the LU cookie factory has been transformed into a national theater, the Lieu Unique (Unique Place); an "artistic itinerary" has been set up along the Loire estuary, including a series of "installations" created by well-known artists; "events" such as exhibits or festivals have proliferated; and the establishment of luxury shops has been encouraged.[43] An example resembling that of Bilbao even more closely is the Luma Foundation in Arles, which called upon the same famous architect, Frank Gehry, to build a museum on the site of former train repair workshops (closed in 1984) for the purpose of developing increased tourism.

In more general terms, heritage creation has become a technique of "territorial development," with its experts in "local development strategies" who know how to "reveal" the "territorial agents" and to highlight their hidden "potential." The instrument of choice is "relaunching," which transforms a dormant legacy into an active heritage by stimulating the capacity of the actors to "appropriate history for themselves, even if that means transforming it." The case of chestnuts in the Cévennes, once associated with poverty, is a good example: producers have taken steps to orient their product toward gastronomy and to protect the crop legally by a Protected Designation of Origin (*Appellation d'origine contrôlée*). These "heirs of history" use history with the goal of adding value to the goods and services they provide, so as to "specify" and to "differentiate products and services with respect to their competitors." This systematic exploitation of the past via "relaunching" is what French experts call "patrimonial innovation."[44] This form of innovation often relies, as we have seen in the case of vineyards, on the reactivation of an ancestral figure whose ties with the site being highlighted may be more or less tenuous; the choice of a central figure and the way he or she is (re)invented play a major role in the success of the business, as Stéphane Gerson has shown in the case of Salon-de-Provence. This small city, a residential suburb of the industrial zone of Fos-sur-Mer, had little to attract tourists; owing to the decline of the petrochemical industry, it sought to give itself new luster, starting around 1975, by reactivating the only historical figure associated with its past: Nostradamus. The effort ultimately failed, quite probably because the local "great man"[45] has never been the glorified subject – whether hero or villain – of a work of art or fiction that could have attracted interest – unlike Count Dracula, for example, whose presumed castle in the Carpathian Mountains draws visitors thanks to Bram Stoker's novel and its numerous televised and film versions (such as Roman Polanski's *Dance of the Vampires*).

The processes of heritage creation have affected not only ancient cities and buildings deemed historical, moreover, but also rural areas, especially those in which the passage from an economy of agricultural production toward a residential economy has been most pronounced and most advanced.[46] These processes have involved villages, sites, and even entire regions. In these cases, things from the past, often falling into ruin, are – on the same basis as collectable objects – selected, rehabilitated, and associated with historical narratives designed to orient their interpretation and enhance their value. In contrast, unlike mobile objects, these entities cannot be moved; thus associating them with other entities and inserting them in a series can be achieved only at a distance, by getting them added – often with the support of a public organization – to a list modeled on UNESCO's repertory of worldwide heritage sites.[47] By means of such lists, these entities can be represented as equivalent or in a hierarchical relation to one another (for example through attribution of Michelin-type stars). The listings, which are reversible, are generally associated with commitments – especially financial – on the part of the local authorities responsible for preserving the entities in question. This type of heritage creation has given new life to regions – in France, especially mountainous ones – threatened with depopulation beginning in the 1960s and 1970s, owing to the industrialization of European agriculture that had marked the postwar decades and the resultant decline in small family farms. Such rural regions were in a position to benefit from a sort of aesthetic heritage because their "traditional" character and their geographic specificities were already anchored in the minds of a broad public, having been highlighted by writers, landscape painters, and local scholars during the nineteenth century and the first half of the twentieth.[48] It is in these regions in particular that the remaining farmers have been encouraged to take part in the "conversion of agricultural space to landscape," a process in which the regional parks were a driving force. Under way since the mid-1980s, this trend benefited from the support of European institutions; justified above all by ecological considerations, it has been coordinated in France by a government agency devoted to "nature and landscape" under the auspices of the ministry responsible for environmental issues. It has also provided a way of facing up to the problem posed by European agricultural surpluses and, especially, a way of stimulating the attractiveness of rural areas, sought for their qualities as landscapes and increasingly for their value from a residential standpoint. The Landscape Law of 1993 extended to all such spaces a "landscape-oriented attention" that had previously been concentrated on exceptional sites. Animal breeders and farmers have thus found themselves involved in agro-environmental measures and encouraged to contribute to the "common good" by supplying an "environmental service" that turns them, sometimes against their will, into landscapers.[49]

The development of tourism

A third factor in the creation of wealth is tourism, especially upscale tourism; unfortunately, the available statistical studies do not make it easy to circumscribe this sector in depth.[50] Tourism has undergone considerable development over the last several decades. In 2012, international tourism (counted in terms of the number of arrivals) reached the figure of 1,035 million (compared to 25 million in 1950, 278 million in 1980, and 528 million in 1995),[51] and it has more than doubled during the last twenty years.[52] More than half the tourist flow is concentrated in Europe, and France remains the premier destination worldwide: 25 million foreign tourists arrived in 2015,[53] and the yearly total is expected to reach 100 million between now and 2030.[54] This amounts to approximately 1.3 billion nights (a night is the unit of measure for tourism). On average, tourists in France spent 80 euros a day in 2005; thus "tourist expenditure is equivalent to the income of 8 million average French citizens." "Commercial net revenues from tourism came to some 90 billion euros in 2005 ... roughly equivalent to the net revenues in the automobile and aeronautics industries."[55] Tourism represented 7.4 percent of France's gross domestic product in 2013;[56] it employed around 1.3 million people directly and generated a million supplementary jobs indirectly.[57] The development of national and especially international tourism has been facilitated by a reduction in transportation costs, an increase in the absolute number of wealthy individuals, especially in the so-called emerging countries[58] (associated with an increase in inequalities), and financing that associates European and local support with international enterprises, especially in the hotel and transportation sectors.[59]

Tourism has stimulated the luxury industry, and specialists in tourism marketing in France emphasize the interactions between tourism and luxury, considering that "tourism creates an affinity for France, and more generally toward all of its products, everything that can be labeled 'made in France,'" along with an affinity for "luxury," "the great pillar of the image of our country in the world," a pillar that underlies one of the principal motives for visits by foreign tourists: the French *art de vivre*, the "art of living" well. Tourism is thus viewed as a "lever for exportations that occur on French territory."[60] Most luxury products are identified with the country that is presumed to be the one in which they have been conceived and manufactured. Thus they are frequently purchased at tourist destination sites (as if that made them more "authentic"), or in airports, often as gifts, or, when they are bought in their countries of origin, in "exotic" shops frequented chiefly by tourists. Thus highlighting the national culture, promoting luxury products, and exploiting the tourist business go hand in hand; this is attested, for example, by the transformation of Saint-Germain-des-Prés. Fifty years ago, this district in the heart of Paris embodied an intellectual Bohemia; now it is a high point of international luxury that exploits the history of this Bohemia and the "existentialism" with which it has been associated.

The increase in the number of tourists, both French and foreign, has played an important role in exacerbating regional inequalities in development. Indeed, outside of Paris, only the Côte d'Azur and Alps regions are widely known internationally and meet the expectations of a wealthy clientele, welcoming them in palatial lodgings that are lacking in the surrounding areas. The regions in which a "residential economy" has developed have experienced growth in the number of jobs available (often in the domestic service sector), stimulated by population increases in the territory. And this latter growth has benefited not only from increased numbers of second homes but also from increased tourism, involving both people just passing through and those whose presence is intermittent but regular. By contrast, certain other areas have more difficulty attracting tourists – areas that are saddled with former or still active industrial spaces, for instance – because they do not fit the description of regions that public authorities seek to promote.

Tourism is the point of intersection among the various domains we have mentioned. Favorable to the increase in luxury commerce, the expansion of tourism during the last twenty years has also been one of the most important factors in heritage creation in France. High-end tourism benefits from the transformation of an ever-increasing number of buildings into historical monuments and of spaces into "sites of memory." This transformation, which could be called "staging for tourism," takes place through a shift from "raw" places to places endowed with a *story*, one that is usually developed by professional historians and that offers visitors an "experience"[61] as soon as it is staged; digital technologies help to produce an "augmented reality." The effectiveness of these stories makes it possible to attract tourists to spaces that may not be intrinsically very attractive, not well endowed with either monuments or sunshine, but that are, for example, sites of former battlegrounds, especially those from the First World War.

In this spirit, many studies in the field of tourist management seek to highlight the "cultural assets" of a country such as France, where tourist facilities are expensive, so as to distinguish their own country from less expensive ones: not only those of the southern hemisphere, which are reputed, according to this marketing logic, to have "nothing to offer but sea and sun," but also those of Southern Europe, which can boast of both cultural offerings and an attractive climate.[62] To "mass tourism," which has undergone a process of standardization inspired by industrial norms, marketing agencies thus contrast "cultural tourism," associated with the definition of "world heritage," whose conception and promotion have benefited from the interest of major international organizations – for example, UNESCO, the World Tourism Organization, and the International Council on Monuments and Sites (ICOMOS) – and which has been associated with the definition of "world heritage."[63] Constructed in opposition to "mass tourism," which is denigrated on the basis of its indifference to "cultural" properties and the fact that, given a favorable climate, its touristic offerings can be realized almost anywhere provided sufficient investments are made, "cultural tourism" is supposed to add to the features generally associated with tourism – comfort, availability, and security – personal involvement and experience, a sense of adventure, surprises, unexpected encounters, and so on, characteristics that have nourished the imagery of "travel" since the Romantic era.[64] Initially organized around the "cult" of "historical monuments," seen as concentrations of culture, the notion of cultural tourism has been extended to a much broader range of places by the use of the term "culture" in a sense close to the one it has in ethnology and folklore studies. According to that logic, attested by the Cultural Tourism Charter developed by ICOMOS in 1999 (replacing the 1976 charter focused on monumentality), cultural tourism is linked to an expansive definition of patrimony, so that it now includes "all aspects considered proper to a society and an environment," with a stress on the themes of diversity (including biodiversity) and identity.[65]

The marketing of cultural tourism has closely followed this institutional turn, and it is no longer oriented exclusively toward officially recognized sites or "monuments"; while these have the advantage of making it less possible to substitute other products for those on offer and thus limiting the competition, they are relatively few in number. Tourist agencies have definitively expanded the term "culture." Thus, in a brochure published by the Malaga Chamber of Commerce designed to promote cultural tourism in the Mediterranean region, we find this definition: "Cultural tourism means traveling to places that are different from one's usual residence, motivated by the desire to know, understand, and study other cultures: a voyage rich in experiences through cultural activities."[66] In the case of international tourism, one of the goals of cultural tourism is to increase the proportion of profits that go to service providers from the destination country in relation to the proportion destined for the companies – generally based in the country of origin – that organize the trip or the visit. While a tourist staying in a vacation camp or traveling entirely under the auspices of an international tourism company contributes little to the destination country, tourists seeking "authentic" cultural experiences must move about in a more autonomous fashion, so that their expenses will be distributed throughout the territory they visit.

Seen in this context, ordinary objects can take on value and arouse interest among tourists, all the more so if their "traditional" production is on display during visits to workshops or businesses; this then becomes "craft tourism," promoted in France by the Association pour la visite d'entreprise (Association for Visits to Businesses).[67] This process of valorization is appropriated more and more often by community members who adopt for themselves the perspective initially brought to bear on them by external observers and make an effort to shape their everyday practices and objects accordingly. They may revert to making things in the ancestral manner, both to affirm a reconstructed identity[68] and to sell their products to tourists; the latter, in search of authenticity and exoticism, are looking for objects that can be brought home and added to collections.[69] Hence the trend in lesser-known or quite unexpected places toward "greeters," who offer tourists individualized visits in which the greeters' personal stories and the community's history are merged.

Responding to the demand for security is a central concern for cultural tourism, for security is also a primordial economic requirement. The task has two principal aspects. The first, a more or less conventional aspect, consists in keeping the most heavily visited places free of deviants deemed potentially dangerous, unpleasant, or even morally disturbing – such figures as pickpockets and beggars, Roma, mentally ill persons, itinerants, drug addicts, or alcoholics. But, beyond that, more generally, places celebrated for their beauty, charm, or traditional character must keep at a distance everyone who might affect their quality, which is associated with a certain "lifestyle" and a certain "know-how": poor foreigners need to be excluded, for example, and even the poor in general, at least when they are not "typical" of the locality. But security questions affect the workings of a tourist economy even more urgently when a country is threatened by terrorist acts such as those that occurred in London in 2005 and in Paris in 2015, in January and again in November.[70] Such acts, as their name indicates, aim to leave people feeling terror-stricken and shell-shocked.[71] And few groups are as susceptible to fear as tourists, on the one hand because they travel to other countries precisely in search of calm, luxury, sensuality, and even a peace that they do not always find in their home countries, and on the other hand because, without social ties in the country they are visiting, they are easily disoriented and led astray.

The expansion of cultural activities

Another indicator that an economic sphere of enrichment is taking shape is the development of a particular domain that involves numerous activities generally brought together under the term "cultural." These include the performing arts and artistic or graphic pursuits, but also publishing, ancient artifacts, museums, and organized special events, festivals, and salons. The fact that these cultural domains are in constant interaction with those we have just identified (luxury, heritage, tourism) helps make them hard to circumscribe. As we have seen, culture in the broad sense is understood as a major force for attracting tourists; at the same time, many cultural activities and sites are economically dependent on tourism. The extension of heritage creation in France is concentrated around sites and monuments that belong to the regional or national patrimony; their constitution and maintenance count as cultural activities. In addition, films and television series whose financing is partly conditioned on their localization in France promote an image of sites such as castles and landscapes associated with the most touristic regions.[72] During the last twenty years, too, we have witnessed a rapid and significant growth in the connections – especially the financial ties – that unite the vast and fuzzy domain of culture with that of the luxury economy. Companies specializing in fashion and fashion accessories – those that make watches, jewelry, perfume, and so on, but also the hotel and restaurant industries – contribute considerably to highlighting a territory in view of attracting tourists, and these same companies, especially the major producers of luxury goods, play a growing role in financing cultural and artistic activities, injecting capital that compensates for the relative decrease in state funding and other public support. In exchange, these businesses benefit from an aesthetic authority that increases the prestige of their brands and augments the advantageous profit margins generated by the sale of their products.

Despite the blurring of boundaries and the absence of focused statistical studies, since the activities and professions considered as the heart of the vast and fuzzy domain of culture are overseen in France by an ad hoc government ministry, there are accounting frameworks that allow us to follow the most stabilized aspects of this domain and, in particular, its evolution over the last twenty years. As it happens, the statistics produced by this ministry show a significant increase in the economic role of culture in the global economy and in the number of persons employed in the cultural domain. And this is the case even though these studies unquestionably fail to take into account the entire set of activities that we have tried to characterize in a provisional way; in addition, the studies do not always focus on the same types of activity.[73] Thus one study carried out at the request of the Ministry of Culture and Communication,[74] designed to measure the added value of the entire cultural sphere in 2011, estimated it to be 57.8 billion euros, or 3.2 percent of overall added value in France – as much as the agricultural sphere when agrobusiness is included (and the amount rose to 44 billion euros in 2013, according to another source from the same ministry).[75] And these figures do not take indirect economic benefits into account – for example, the benefits that accrue when cultural activities incite increased tourism. In terms of value added between 1995 and 2013, the growth in cultural activities was particularly significant in audiovisual productions, performing arts, visual arts, and heritage creation; growth in these sectors doubled or even tripled.

The domain of culture in France is divided between a commercial sector, which involves audiovisual productions in particular[76] (39.4 percent of the value added in the production of cultural commodities in 2013), and a smaller non-commercial sector, under the aegis of central or regional government agencies; the role of this sector is especially pronounced in the performing arts and heritage sites (respectively 42.6 percent and 41.3 percent of the value added in non-commodity cultural products the same year).[77] The non-commodity share in cultural activities could not have developed to such an extent without the support of the French government and, above all, of regional authorities. On the whole, this support remains at a high level, despite a certain stability or even a slight decrease in spending that reflects an effort to limit or lower public spending in general, especially since the 2008 economic crisis. In communes[78] with more than 10,000 inhabitants, cultural expenses per inhabitant more than doubled between the early 1980s and the 2000s (reaching 8 percent of the budget), with an average increase of 1.7 percent per year, devoted mainly to investment. The commitment to culture was much larger in volume (about three times higher) in cities with populations of over 100,000, where cultural expenses accounted for nearly 10 percent of their budgets. Financial support came from a complex network of subsidies from overlapping territorial authorities (regions, departments, communes, groups of communes). Spending on culture in France was directed, in decreasing order, to local cultural activities, libraries, musical expression, museums,[79] theater, and the maintenance of heritage sites. At the departmental level, spending on culture was particularly high in zones marked by the type of development geographers call "residential" along the western seaboard and in the southern region, to the detriment of the northern and northeastern industrial zones.[80]

The growth in the cultural sectors tracked by the Ministry of Culture and Communication is even more impressive if we consider it in terms of employment. According to the sources cited above, this sector employs around 700,000 people, or roughly 2.5 percent of the active workforce, and it has seen growth of more than 50 percent since the early 1990s (as contrasted with 16 percent for the workforce overall). This growth has been particularly apparent in the professions associated with theater and the other performing arts, stimulated by recent legislation governing intermittent employment (+95 percent), but it is also perceptible in the literary professions (+58 percent) and in the visual and graphic arts (+44 percent). In this last category, the increase in the number of people employed (+123 percent) has been very pronounced in the plastic arts, fashion, and the decorative arts (graphic artists, stylists, designers). But it is also noteworthy for painters (+21 percent) and photographers (+20 percent). In addition, the people employed in the various cultural sectors share basic characteristics that distinguish them clearly from the overall workforce averages. They are younger (47 percent are under forty, as compared with an overall average age of forty-four); they are more often employed in large cities, more often born in other European countries (an effect no doubt related in particular to the role of translators in the literary professions), and are generally from a much higher social class (49 percent have a father from a middle-class background). While these cultural professions employ increasing numbers of women (the proportion rose from 39 percent in the early 1990s to 43 percent in 2011), men remain dominant, especially in the fields of art and architecture, and the proportion of women is lower than in the workforce overall, where it has reached 48 percent. But it is especially in terms of educational level that the difference between people employed in cultural fields and the overall workforce, already considerable at the beginning of the period, has increased since 1991. In 2011, 44 percent of the employees in cultural fields had at least three years of post-baccalaureate education. Highest in the literary professions (66 percent), this quite elevated educational level is also often found in people working in professions to which access has long been less constrained in France by diploma requirements, for example actors (31 percent) and plastic artists (39 percent). Finally, we must point out one other defining characteristic of people working in the cultural realm, a characteristic having to do with their employment status. Nearly 30 percent have the status of independent (freelance) workers, triple the percentage of freelance workers in other fields, and even when workers in the cultural sector are salaried employees their positions are often precarious: 30 percent have short-term contracts – twice as many as the workforce average – and 26 percent work part-time, often less than half-time, and often with quite irregular work hours.[81]

In addition, the development of culture, unlike that of luxury and upscale goods, is not motivated primarily by export, because in most instances cultural commodities are not easily moved; they have to be consumed on site, as it were. This holds true of course for heritage sites, which cannot be moved, but also for a large number of activities – for example, the performing arts, art exhibits, and even literary activities – whose displacement is expensive in various respects, from transportation costs to the costs of insurance or translation. The most economical way to "export" such activities is therefore to import tourists.

The development of the various cultural domains has been driven by a significant increase in internal demand, a consequence of the considerable increase in the participants' educational level over the last four decades. Between 1991 and 2011, the proportion of the workforce with degrees representing three years of post-baccalaureate study has doubled (to 20 percent). The proportion of household expenses devoted to cultural goods and services (not including the purchase of equipment such as computers) reached 2.5 percent of total household consumption in 2007, which corresponds to an increase of 23.3 percent over cultural spending in 2000; this is especially apparent in the area of theater and the other performing arts.[82] Similarly, a study undertaken by Olivier Donnat on "French cultural practices" during the 1990s shows a slight but regular increase in attendance at shows and in visits to museums, historical monuments, and libraries, going from 4 percent for holders of a technical certificate (CAP) to 41 percent for holders of more advanced degrees. The proportion of individuals who had visited a heritage site during the past twelve months was 37 percent for people with higher education and 20 percent for those with a CAP.[83] As Donnat suggests, the growth in cultural consumption is related to the increase in amateur practices, especially in theater, where these practices grew considerably during the 1990s among young people aged fifteen to nineteen, corresponding to the rise in the level of schooling.

The figures we have just mentioned, whether they concern the added value of cultural activities, the number of persons employed, or the level of consumption in the cultural realm, may appear relatively modest. But, beyond the fact that, as we have seen, they by no means include the entire set of domains that contribute to the formation of an enrichment economy, they also fail to take into account either the indirect and induced effects of these activities or their capacity to attract participants. The tendencies that these figures reveal may be more important than their absolute value. If we compare these data with the data characterizing the industrial revolution (a comparison that we shall develop more fully later on), it is useful to recall that, in the first half of the nineteenth century, a vast proportion of the lower classes consisted of farmers, craftsmen, and servants (according to the historian Peter Laslett, at the end of the Old Regime in France, some 40 percent of adolescents in Western societies underwent the experience of domestic service);[84] workers in large-scale industries were still only a small minority. This fact shows, retrospectively, the prescience of Karl Marx, whose analyses could be judged utopian in his day, compared to those of Pierre-Joseph Proudhon, for example. The latter, as Pierre Ansart has shown, was in a sense the spokesman for the aspirations of craftsmen, who were still a driving force at the heart of the working class.[85]

The art trade

There is probably no domain in which the commercial dimensions of cultural activities have given rise to more commentary since the beginning of the 2000s than that of contemporary art; trade in artworks has undergone changes that have attracted the attention of a growing number of art historians, critics, sociologists, and journalists. In this case, as in that of stars in the music business, in fashion, or in cinema, local cultural contributions to regional economies or to a region's ability to attract residents has not seemed to interest the experts nearly as much as the global dimension of the phenomenon. This dimension entails what has been viewed as the formation of an art "market" unified from above, supported by a culture of celebrity on a worldwide scale – a market frequently described by journalists,[86] art critics, and observers from the social sciences.[87] The words used, especially in texts intended for a broad audience, evoke the vocabulary used to speak of "financial markets," such as "trend," "crisis," "collapse," "a killing" (as in the stock market), "boom" and "bust," and "scene"[88] (referring to a leading center of worldwide activity in the field). There is an emphasis on the "incredible" prices of certain works publicized by the media and, more generally, on the "colossal" sums that circulate in the upper spheres of the artistic world, as well as on the power in the hands of a small number of individuals on whom both the prices of the works and the reputation of their creators depend.

Three related phenomena, developed during the last few decades, play a pivotal role in these descriptions. First, the importance that has accrued to auctions of contemporary art conducted by the main art houses (such as Christie's, Sotheby's, Phillips, and, in France, Artcurial), and, more generally, the development of what is called the "secondary market" (to distinguish it from direct sales by galleries to collectors).[89] Second, the multiplication of rankings: starting with the *Kunstkompass*, created in Germany in 1970, hierarchical listings of the principal artists worldwide (up to a hundred) are published regularly, awarding points to each artist according to varying criteria; these rankings are presumed to exercise considerable influence on collectors' purchases (an assumption that is sometimes challenged). Other rankings have come along in the last ten years or so, claiming to classify "the most important players in the contemporary art world" on an international scale, "not in terms of fame, but in terms of influence and power"; alongside artists themselves, these lists feature critics, directors of public or private institutions and foundations, collectors, curators, journalists, and bloggers, the best known among the latter being *Power 100*, published by *ArtReview*, followed by other publications – for example *Le Monde*, with its supplement featuring "fifteen who make fashion."[90] Finally, a third phenomenon, already noted above: the relationships established between the art world and the business world, especially businesses devoted to luxury goods. Ties between the arts and business are hardly new, of course: they are attested, for example, in the numerous biographies of collectors who, from the nineteenth century on, have stood out both through their financial successes and through their roles as discoverers and patrons of artists. By contrast, what does seem new is the fact that these ties, once considered private in nature and taken as evidence of taste, ostentation, and profligate spending on the part of supremely wealthy individuals, modern embodiments of the sumptuous practices of the princes of yesteryear, have now largely become public,[91] and they serve to support the publicity with which luxury brands surround themselves in order to increase their sales. Thus these brands are likely to be associated not with the register of sumptuary expenditures, which formerly underlay their worth, but with that of commercial utility.

We must note that, while in most of the social science texts we have consulted the contribution of cultural activities to the development of regional economies and their power to attract new residents is generally presented in a more or less positive manner, almost as a social cause worthy of support, the processes associated with the emergence of an international art market are often called out, sometimes implicitly, when they play on the public's fascination with the rich and the powerful (which can easily turn into indignation), and sometimes in an openly critical way. From the 1920s to the 1980s, roughly speaking, the tendency to denounce the domination exercised by money over art and culture was associated with critiques of industrial society (we shall come back to this point); art, as an expression of the uniqueness of individuals, was viewed as the chief rampart against all-out standardization. Over the last few decades, this tendency seems to have shifted toward new schemas based on the increased proximity between art and finance.

This realignment of critical axes is particularly clear among artists themselves. Celebrity culture, highly publicized connections between famous artists and commercial brands, and the publication of rankings have established sharp lines between a handful of internationally successful artists, whose work is exhibited in museums of contemporary art and sold at the major art fairs, and everyone else. The latter continue to live – to subsist – for the most part by selling their works through galleries that have little or no access to the major fairs, by selling them directly or through local relationship networks (this is hardly a new practice), or else by taking advantage, like artists in the theater world, of efforts at cultural development undertaken at the initiative of local communities or on a regional level. The art world, like the worlds of popular music, cinema, and sports, has thus come to symbolize inequalities in earnings, contrasting a very small number of ultra-beneficiaries – the stars – with a very large number of rejects.[92] To prove this claim, one would have to be able to juxtapose an accounting of the total wealth distributed with the total number of individuals active in a given sector who are presumed to be in competition for the stakes. But the relationship itself depends on the way these totals are constructed, especially on the geographical level. This is why the contribution of famous artists – those whose activities are global in scope – to an enrichment economy is generally envisaged in a positive light only when the entity considered is the entire economy of a nation in its competition with other nations; this presupposes treating artists, and "creators" more generally, like brands whose name and "headquarters," so to speak, must retain a national character.

Arles: from railroad shops to contemporary art exhibits

As we suggested earlier, the case of the city of Arles offers an emblematic example of the transition from an industrial economy to an enrichment economy. After the decline of the dominant local industry, Arles turned toward tourism by promoting its rich ancient and medieval heritage. This transition crossed a new threshold in the early 2010s, with a shift toward culture and particularly toward contemporary art.

From the early decades of the twentieth century until around 1980, Arles was an industrial city. Its transformation from a provincial enclave began in the second half of the nineteenth century, when locomotive manufacturing facilities were set up for use on the lines linking Paris to Lyon and the Mediterranean; these shops came to play a major role in the city's economy. By 1911, they employed 1,173 people; in the larger urban area, with some 30,000 residents, more than 5,000 made their living from the railroad. Forty-five locomotives were built in the region between 1908 and 1914. By 1920 there were 1,800 employees in the shops. Along with the railroad came industrial exploitation of salt: in nearby Salin-de-Giraud, the chemical company Solvay established a facility that manufactured soda from salt, chiefly for the soap factories in Marseille; it had 500 workers in 1925. Ship-building on the Rhône and metallurgy were also important in the region; machinery manufacturing sites in Barriol (a district in Arles) employed around 200 workers in the period between the world wars. In the 1930s, the metal-working company Constructions métalliques de Provence (CMP) set up shop in Arles and became one of the most important enterprises in town. In addition to these major businesses, there was a paper mill specializing in newsprint (most notably supplying the daily papers in Marseille), a shop that made cardboard packing boxes, and agribusiness factories that produced canned fruits and vegetables.

In the 1960s, 32 percent of the active members of the workforce were employed as laborers in industry (6,000 in 1962) or as employees in industries or businesses (2,000). In the 1960s, the proportion of middle-level managers and executives also rose (from 754 and 389, respectively, in 1954, to 1,075 and 616 in 1962). Conversely, handicrafts declined: there were fewer than 500 craftsmen in the early 1960s. The population grew owing to both increased birth rates and immigration: in 1962, there were 42,000 inhabitants, of whom 84 percent were "French by birth." Immigrants from Italy, predominant in the first half of the twentieth century, came to work in industry; later, immigrants from Spain worked mainly in the rice fields in the Camargue. This workforce, chiefly laborers, was primarily male: in 1962, of 20,000 women, only 8,682 (24 percent) were employed, a proportion far below the national average.

The city's industrial decline began in the second half of the 1970s, and factory closures multiplied in the 1980s. Most crucially, the railroad shops were shut down in 1984, and the metal-working factory CMP was downsized and renamed Constructions métalliques et préfabrication d'Arles: it maintained its boiler-making shops but had only sixty salaried workers. The local economy had already lost 2,000 jobs by the early 1980s, and the losses increased in the following decades (5,000 jobs lost between 1980 and 2000). For example, Rivoire et Carret-Lustucru, a rice-processing factory created in 1952 that had had 140 employees, ceased production after the floods of 2003.

This situation led to unemployment and poverty. In 2001, the number of recipients of financial aid from the government (in the form of "minimal revenue for insertion" into the economy, RMI) rose in the commune to 2,043, or 10.5 percent of the eligible population. With an unemployment rate of around 15 percent (the highest in the Provence–Alpes–Côte d'Azur region), for the most part, according to INSEE, "pockets of high economic insecurity" were concentrated in the city. Of the residents of Greater Arles, 27 percent lived in districts covered by "municipal policy"; these included large "sensitive urban zones" in which a third of the population had an average taxable income of 5,700 euros per household. The available jobs were primarily seasonal (in agriculture, especially rice and fruit harvesting, agribusiness, and tourism); they required little skill or training and offered very low wages. Economic inequality in Arles was quite pronounced, as tax data make clear: the gross earnings of the top 10 percent were seven times higher than those of the bottom 10 percent).[93] In Arles, as in other regions, the industrial decline went hand in hand with the growth of the far right: Marine Le Pen won 25 percent of the votes in the 2012 presidential election.

In the face of this decline, the initial response was industrial, with noteworthy improvements to the port on the Rhône in the early 1990s, financed by the Compagnie nationale du Rhône: the goal was to provide harbor facilities that could accommodate 3,500-ton ships, and also to equip an industrial zone intended to support the installation of new enterprises on the site. However, only seven such businesses had been established by the early 2000s.

During the same period, the city of Arles sought to develop municipal activities in the arts, culture, and tourism. Hard hit by the departure of its principal industries, the city experienced major financial difficulties and had to find new resources. In the domains just mentioned, the city had what administrators call "assets" – masterpieces including ancient ruins (the amphitheater, the Roman theater, the Alyscamps necropolis) and religious buildings (the Saint-Trophime cloister dating in part from the twelfth century). Ninety-two sites from different periods have been included on the official list of historical monuments since 1976. But their power of attraction comes in part from the work of heritage creation that has been under way in Arles for more than a century. This work owes a great deal to the national recognition won by late nineteenth-century regionalist writers, especially Alphonse Daudet and Frédéric Mistral, who highlighted local traditions that had been revived in a spirit similar to the one that animated folkloric ethnography during the same period. These traditions were embodied most notably in the Félibrige association, which sought to preserve Provençal and establish it as a literary language. In this context, a number of folk festivals and events were brought back to life or invented. The heritage of which Arles can boast is thus constituted not only by ruins and monuments but also by the names of artists whose fame is associated with the city. Vincent Van Gogh, the most prominent among them, produced numerous paintings during his residency there in 1888 and 1889.

Bullfighting has also played an important role in the city's heritage creation, not only because of the associated festivals whose folkloric dimensions are intensified by their organizers but also in that it has attracted intellectuals and artists; this was especially true from the 1930s through the 1960s, when writers and painters saw this entertainment as a pinnacle of popular art, at once savage and ancestral. While the folkloric preoccupations of regional writers (for example, Charles Maurras, who won the Félibrige prize for an elegy dedicated to the Provençal poet Théodore Aubanel) and regionalist painters (Yves Brayer, for one) made Arles an attractive destination for people with right-wing tendencies (when he visited Arles in 1940, Marshal Pétain mingled with the *gardians*, local herdsmen who symbolized the return to the land and to traditions), the folkloric aspects of the arena, with its bulls and bullfighters evoking Spain (and the Spanish Civil War), made Arles attractive to left-leaning visitors as well. The fact that the Confédération générale du travail (CGT, a major labor union) and the Communist Party have deep roots in Arles, and the fact that the city's residents have generally voted on the left, at least until the 1980s, helped to draw artists such as Jean Lurçat and Ossip Zadkine (the Réattu Museum had exhibits of both painters in 1953), and especially Picasso, an aficionado of the feria (he was photographed in 1959 in the arena alongside Jean Cocteau and the bullfighter Luis Miguel Dominguín). Like Cocteau, Picasso stayed at the Nord-Pinus Hotel, which helped ensure the fame of that establishment. The photographer Lucien Clergue was a major factor in the "artification" of Arles: he made it a center for photography – a "middlebrow" art whose aesthetic worth has been increasingly recognized during the last several decades – first by ensuring the opening of a photography section in the Réattu Museum as early as 1965, then by setting up an international summer photography festival in the 1970s; these gatherings, now known as the Rencontres d'Arles, increased significantly in scope starting in 1982.

The city has invested in cultural facilities such as the Mediathèque in the Espace Van Gogh and the Musée de l'Arles antique, a major archeological museum; it also sponsors cultural events – among others, a festival devoted to popular music (Les Suds), another featuring harpists (Journées de la harpe), and readings in the Saint-Trophime cloister; along with the Rencontres d'Arles, these events draw around 300,000 visitors each year. With the city's support, numerous cultural associations have been created, and their widely varied activities range from the protection of Arles's heritage to the plastic arts and theater.[94] One objective of these cultural associations is obviously to attract establishments and enterprises that can stimulate the city's economic activity and create jobs. The publishing house Actes Sud set up shop in Arles in 1978, and the music publisher and distributor Harmonia Mundi did the same in 1983. A school for advanced study in photography opened in Arles in 1982 in a sumptuous private residence that the city had purchased from its owners in 1978. Similar stories can be told about PRIDES (a regional association that promotes collaborative economic development), subsidiaries of book and music publishing houses, and other industries promoting culture and heritage. The publishing and audiovisual sectors, along with the arts (including the performing arts), account for some 1,000 jobs. But these new positions, while they attract white-collar workers and managers, have not sufficed to bring unemployment down to a level equivalent to the regional average. The loss of jobs in industry has not been compensated either by second homes, a sector where there has been a significant increase compared to 1990 (+44 percent) and which represents 1.8 percent of the residences in the commune, or by tourists passing through, even though this sector has developed considerably (with a bottom line of 63 million euros in 2004). The number of employees in the tourism industry in the commune came to 812 salaried workers in 2004; jobs connected to tourist accommodation (6,414 beds, including camping facilities and bed-and-breakfast operations) represented 1.4 percent of the total in January, twice that in the summer.[95] However, these domestic and seasonal activities did not compensate for the loss of jobs in industry and agriculture.

It was in this context, problematic for the city's residents and for its budget (employment by the city rose from 635 in 1980 to 1,289 in 2000), that Maja Hoffmann chose Arles as the site for the Foundation for Contemporary Art that she created in 2004; she called it Luma, after her two children, Lucas and Marina.

Maja Hoffmann, who studied cinema at the New School for Social Research in New York, is the daughter of Luc Hoffmann, a part-time resident in Arles from the 1940s on; Luc was a founder of and major contributor to the Fondation Vincent Van Gogh, which was officially established in 2010. This foundation, housed in the Hôtel Léautaud de Donines, a refurbished fifteenth-century mansion, displays works by Impressionist painters; it has ten Van Gogh paintings on loan from the Amsterdam Museum. Luc Hoffmann, an amateur ornithologist, had previously devoted much energy and a great deal of money to the ecological protection of the Camargue region. Father and daughter are among the heirs to the Swiss Hoffmann–La Roche laboratories. Some descendants of the Hoffmann family came together in 1948 in a stockholders' pact to keep control of F. Hoffmann–La Roche SA, a pact that controls 45 percent of the company's voting rights. In 2012, the family members' fortune was estimated to be 16 to 17 billion in Swiss francs,[96] which makes it one of the top fortunes in Switzerland. Maja Hoffmann, like her father and grandmother, has a lengthy track record as a collector and philanthropist in the realm of contemporary art. She actively supports the Palais de Tokyo in Paris, the Serpentine in London, and the Venice Biennale; she is president of the Zurich Kunsthalle and vice president of the Emanuel Hoffmann in Basel, a foundation created by her grandparents to hold their collection, which was later donated to Basel's Museum of Contemporary Art. Like her father, Maja Hoffmann has for many years maintained a foothold in Arles, where she owns a home and a hotel; she also has a celebrated restaurant in the Camargue featuring organically produced ingredients.

The establishment of the Luma Foundation in Arles has been supported by the current mayor, Hervé Schiavetti, who is a member of the Communist Party. Drawn into regional administration after his studies in sociology at the University of Aix-en-Provence, he was elected mayor in 2001 and re-elected in both 2008 and 2014, despite the opposition of the Front de gauche, the anti-capitalist New Party, and Europe Écologie–Les Verts; these parties reproach him for being too close to the Socialists.

A first construction project initiated by Maja Hoffmann was rejected by the National Commission on Historical Monuments because it did not respect the perimeter of the heritage site. The current project, entrusted to the architect Frank Gehry – an aluminum tower 57 meters high – is under construction; the first stone was laid on 5 April 2015, and the museum, originally scheduled for completion in 2018, is now expected to open in 2020. The budget of 150 million euros is being financed entirely by Maja Hoffmann, in the largest private cultural investment in Europe. The tower is going up on the site of the old rail yards. Seven buildings from the complex (the former site of the Rencontres de la photographie) have been purchased by Hoffmann from the Provence–Alpes–Côte d'Azur region; they have been preserved and renovated. These old locomotive manufacturing and repair shops are located at the foot of the hill where the ancient city was established; the École supérieure Supinfocom, devoted to multimedia technologies, was opened in 2000, along with university residences, on about 27 acres of industrial wasteland partly owned by the city of Arles.

Maja Hoffmann's ambition is to make Arles "a French Bilbao" by creating a foundation intended to support a museum, artists' residences, and colloquia in synergy with other local cultural institutions; the project is designed to create "hundreds of jobs" and to give the city "international visibility," according to a logic that deploys the various facets of the enrichment economy.

An economic reorientation toward the wealthy

As the foregoing observations suggest, the formation of an economic sphere of enrichment, often described in terms of comparative advantages, has been marked by a phenomenon particularly obvious in France but apparent in Western economies more generally: a reorientation toward offering goods capable of satisfying the demands of wealthy or ultra-wealthy clients throughout the world. The number of such people has risen considerably over the last twenty years. They are based chiefly in countries such as France and the United States, where huge fortunes transmitted by inheritance were already well established and where the increase in wealth has been particularly spectacular at the top of the income scale. But the number of wealthy and ultra-wealthy persons is also growing in emerging countries, where those with fortunes have either benefited from financial operations or taken advantage of the profits generated by industrialization in countries with cheap labor. In other words, the increase in the small number of wealthy and extremely wealthy people has accompanied the increase in inequality worldwide.

> The bottom line of private financial fortunes (savings in bank accounts, financial instruments, or life insurance policies) does not represent the totality of accumulated fortunes, most notably because it does not include holdings in the form of material goods, including real estate. But since these latter goods are more difficult to identify and evaluate, the increase in the monetary total of fortunes can serve as an indicator allowing us to estimate private fortunes and the rise in inequalities on a global scale. As it happens, the total amount of money in financial fortunes increased by 14.6 percent in 2013. The wealthiest zones are the United States (50 trillion dollars) and Western Europe (38 trillion), followed by the Asian Pacific countries (37 trillion). The growth in private fortunes has kept pace with the growing number of millionaires (in American dollars), which went from 13.7 million in 2012 to 16.3 million in 2013. These millionaires, who represent 1.1 percent of households, are concentrated primarily in the United States (7.1 million households, which possess 63 percent of the private fortunes in America); their number has also gone up in China, reaching 2.4 million. The density of these millionaires in relation to the total number of households as permanent residents is highest in Qatar, Switzerland, and Singapore. In 2015, the number of millionaires continued to grow (by 6 percent), reaching a total of 18.5 million. This 1 percent holds 47 percent of the world's financial wealth. Some portion of these private fortunes is held in offshore banks, whose holdings reached 8.9 trillion in 2013, an increase of 10.4 percent over the previous year. They are estimated to correspond to between 8 and 11 percent of the financial patrimony of households, and they were expected to reach 12.4 trillion in 2018. The most important offshore banks are in Switzerland, followed by Singapore and Hong Kong. In France, tax evasion probably totaled 17 billion euros in 2013.[97]

The economic reorientation of Western countries toward the wealthy has marked a break with the type of growth that had characterized the postwar decades. We can measure the scale of the change if we recall that postwar growth was driven by national production of standardized goods whose distribution, aimed at first toward the upper middle class, was later extended to the middle classes, and even to the lower classes in the case of goods such as household appliances and cars. This seemed to confirm the idea that enrichment of the elites would inevitably benefit even the destitute in the end (the trickle-down process). Often described at the time in terms of "democratization," this economy was supposed to profit from an increase in buying power on the part of the most disadvantaged, a change to be stimulated by the redistribution of a portion of the benefits generated by increased productivity, as economists of the "regulation school" demonstrated.

One effect of this economic reorientation has been an intensification of the two-track consumption pattern, with a growing contrast between mass consumption of standardized products sold by companies with a wide distribution network to the least wealthy buyers, on the one hand, and consumption of products that are defined precisely in opposition to standardized objects and are intended to satisfy the needs of wealthier buyers, on the other hand.[98] These latter products are exemplified in the realm of food by items presented as artisanal or organic and guaranteed by a brand name or, in other realms, by personal objects (knives, for instance) presumed to have been made according to ancestral practices, with traces of the makers on display. Such products are typically guaranteed by an assertion that the items have not been produced in a series of assembly lines operated by countless anonymous workers but, rather, that they have been handcrafted by a single individual who "made them with love."

By contrast with mass production, which was legitimized in democratic terms, the enrichment economy aims to exploit the buying power of those who can afford exceptional goods. This is why the comparison between the wealthy and the rest allows us to understand the dynamics of the enrichment economy better than we would by referring specifically to social classes differentiated by their income levels and by what they can leave their heirs; the categories of rich and poor function in a relative logic of opposition rather than as categories with clear boundaries. While the enrichment economy is addressed first of all to the rich and the very rich, it has the peculiar feature of addressing the others too, as if they were rich, or, at the very least, richer than they are.

2

Toward Enrichment

The characteristics of an enrichment economy

The domains covered by an enrichment economy are not simply appended to the sectors of an industrial economy as add-ons that contribute, each in its own way, to a global bottom line. The enrichment economy is characterized by special features that have wide-reaching economic and social consequences. It is based on mechanisms that are in many respects quite different from those of an industrial economy. To prepare for the detailed analyses that follow, let us begin with an overview and several examples.

The prices of industrial products – articles intended for use – tend to *go down* sharply over time; the uses made of them are presumed to reduce their performance (used cars are exemplary in this respect). The short- or long-term fate of a standard industrial product is to become *trash*. This is so much the case that the question of trash and its disposal has become a major concern for industrial societies.

Conversely, the things at the heart of the enrichment economy may have long been treated as trash – forgotten, left behind in attics, abandoned in basements, or buried in the ground. A large percentage of the things we admire in museums or in other places where precious collections are displayed, perhaps even all such things, as the anthropologist Michael Thomson suggests in his seminal work *Rubbish Theory*,[1] have been treated as trash at one point or another. More generally, the most pertinent things in an enrichment economy may see their prices *go up over time* – the opposite of what happens to industrial products. It is precisely the work of selection between what is destined to be abandoned or destroyed and what is destined to be preserved that is at the heart of the activities, and the anxieties, of those responsible for taking inventories of a given heritage, those who, confronted with any of the objects belonging to the unlimited universe of things that are candidates for survival, have to make crucial decisions concerning their fate.[2]

In fact, the objects of the highest value in an enrichment economy are not intended to meet needs or even, in many cases, to be *used*; instead, they take on their importance with reference to a different configuration in which the logic of *collection* is central. This is true for objects from antiquity and for works of art, of course. But it is also true for many products of the luxury industry. Even if the latter may episodically satisfy a need, they are not primarily acquired to be used. Those who acquire them often already own a number of functionally similar objects (several high-end automobiles, for example, or a large number of handbags from the top designers); they are accustomed to surrounding themselves with expensive objects and putting themselves on display in front of others. Going back at least to Thorstein Veblen,[3] sociologists and economists, while denouncing the conspicuous consumption of luxury products, have sought motives behind the phenomenon. One such motive is clearly the "distinction effect," the desire to set oneself apart, to stand out. Nevertheless, it seems that expensive items are often stored away without being exposed to the eyes of others, and, when serious collectors are involved, even out of the owner's sight, since there are so many of them. It would appear, then, that such objects are accumulated mainly to be kept, sometimes to be contemplated in solitude, and placed in relations of proximity with other objects of the same kind in a logic that closely resembles the logic of collecting for its own sake.

Filling cellars with extraordinary wines offers a particularly striking illustration of this type of accumulative behavior. Aimed at acquiring complete series, the behavior is driven by a concern with *filling gaps* within sets that are being constituted. Wine collectors will seek, for example, to acquire all the vintages that were produced between two selected dates, or that meet certain standards, or that come from certain vineyards.[4] The desire to possess specific items to fill gaps defined with reference to an ideal totality constitutes one of the principal motives governing behaviors in communities of collectors. These behaviors are particularly striking when they concern beverages, because in this case they have a paradoxical character. Either the content of the bottle is used – that is, consumed – which means an indefinite delay in the formation of a complete collection, or else the collection is kept more as a collection of labels than as a collection of wines as such. Indeed, with great wines, whose nature is profoundly modified by the conditions of aging, the referential relation between the words printed on the label and the content of the bottle always has some degree of uncertainty. Similarly, to take a different example, let us consider the type of collector at whom sales of high-end leather goods are aimed (Hermès handbags, for instance). Although these goods have been manufactured relatively recently, they are sold by major auction houses that deal primarily in antiquities and works of art, in old models of watches, jewelry, clothing, "designer" furnishings, or in certain brands of automobiles that have become collectors' items. In this logic, the demand for a thing does not decrease when one approaches the satiation point, as is the case for things corresponding to needs; on the contrary, it tends – as we see especially in the case of collections – to increase as the collection grows. The most coveted item of all will be the one required for the completion of a set.

How is the value of the most sought-after objects established in an enrichment economy? Or, rather, how are the arguments that justify the price constructed? Production costs are not a primary factor: these costs are either non-existent, as in the case of ancient objects dug out of the ground, or secondary, as for example with high-end perfumes in which the content of the flask represents less than 10 percent of the selling price in shops. If we want to refer to costs, we must take into account not so much the production costs per se, in the case of ancient objects, as the costs of restoration and preservation[5] and, more generally, what can be called the *showcasing costs*.

As the foregoing remarks suggest, we can offer a schematic sketch of two ideal types of economy. An economy centered on industrial production can be contrasted with an economy based on what one might call processes of *enriching* things. Let us recall that the term "enrichment" is used not only to indicate that the things on which this economy is based are intended chiefly for the rich but also to designate the operations carried out on the things themselves in order to increase their value and their prices.

The term "enrichment economy" seems preferable to "symbolic economy," a term used more frequently in works that seek to pinpoint the specificity of a "cultural" socio-economy,[6] often with reference to the seminal works of Pierre Bourdieu.[7] The label "symbolic" strikes us as both too broad and too vague to designate the type of operation on which we want to focus. When the differentiating functions of cultural goods – the "distinction effects" – considered from the consumer's standpoint are stressed, the various lacks that these goods are intended to fill are reduced to a single dimension, which is that of prestige or social distinction, while the standpoint of the actor offering these goods, who has to stress differences among them in order to be more competitive, is underestimated or absent. But, more broadly speaking, everything that is inserted into relationships among human persons and grasped by language will have a "symbolic" dimension. Similar observations can be made about the way Jean Baudrillard used the term "sign" and his project of developing a general semiology of objects.[8] Likewise, every operation involving symbols or signs has its underpinnings and its consequences in the world of objects. By privileging the opposition between "material" and "immaterial" entities (an opposition often attributed, mistakenly, to Marx), this approach tends to ignore the fact that everything that is inserted into an economy can be envisaged in both these lights.[9] It then becomes difficult to analyze the various ways in which different types of economies combine them. Yet these *combinations*, in their specificity, characterize different ways of giving form and value to what will give rise to commerce – that is, to different economies. As for the notion of "art world," introduced by Howard Becker to designate "all the people whose activities are necessary to the production of the characteristic works which this world, and perhaps others as well, define as art,"[10] it has the disadvantage of being too restrictive and at the same time of overemphasizing human activity, while virtually ignoring the way things circulate, their prices and their value.

There is nothing that cannot be enriched, whether it comes from a more or less ancient past or is a contemporary object enriched in the process of fabrication. But a thing – any "thing" at all – can be enriched in various ways. It can be enriched physically (for example, in the case of an old house or apartment, by making the beams or joists visible) and/or culturally (for example, by relating the object to other things with which it has a certain harmony). Cultural enrichment of the latter sort always presupposes using a *narrative structure* in order to select, from within the multiplicity of potentially relatable phenomena, the differences presented by the object in question that can be considered especially pertinent and that must therefore be singled out and highlighted in the discourses that accompany the object's circulation. In this sense, enrichment economies have as their principal resource the creation and shaping of *differences* and *identities*.

Dormant resources in the enrichment economy

In the effort to understand how an enrichment economy is formed, France offers a paradigmatic example, owing to the simultaneously local and global character of its economy. The development of an enrichment economy can also be observed elsewhere, in Italy or Spain, for instance; on a more local scale, it can be studied in cities or even in districts within cities, for example, in the area around the High Line in New York.[11] It is worth noting that changes of the type we are trying to pinpoint are always rooted in an "enrichment basin" offering favorable geographical and historical conditions.

We can thus attempt to look at the formation of an enrichment economy in the way certain historians have looked at changes that have affected certain regions of Great Britain, initially on the local level, between the late eighteenth century and the first third of the nineteenth, changes that marked what has been called the first industrial revolution. As Edward Anthony Wrigley, a specialist in demographic history, has argued, this "revolution" was not simply the result of a change in the distribution of the workforce.[12] An additional and perhaps a primary cause was a change in the resources exploited for the purpose of creating wealth. Until the beginning of the nineteenth century, the principal source of wealth creation was essentially organic: agriculture, livestock, wool, wood, the use of animals for hauling, and so on. According to Wrigley, this is why the great classical economists, from Adam Smith to Malthus and Ricardo, maintained a pessimistic vision of the future, for the exploitation of additional land would not be able to compensate for population growth, as they saw it: the best lands were already being cultivated, and any new ones would produce diminishing returns. In fact, in Wrigley's view, it was the increasingly extensive exploitation of fossil deposits, and especially coal (it too was of organic origin, of course, but embedded in such a remote past), that gave the lie to the pessimistic prophecy. Coal extraction thus constituted the defining feature of industrial society. A quantitative historian, Wrigley brought to light the new role attributed to this resource in energy on which the development of mechanization depended; he analyzed the financial flows that shifted rapidly from agriculture toward mines and manufacturing, attesting to the importance quickly granted by holders of capital to this major source of wealth creation. For reasons stemming not from the nature of this wealth but from the forms of domination that influenced its distribution, industrial mechanization did not prevent inequalities from remaining as pronounced as they had been in the previous century – and indeed, for several decades, they were exacerbated. The expansion of inequality and impoverishment might have continued indefinitely had it not provoked renewed criticism from the increasingly powerful labor movement.

One can hypothesize an analogy between the phenomenon whose contours and processes we have just recalled and a phenomenon we are witnessing in contemporary France. The enrichment economy corresponds not only to growing specialization in the realm of culture and in the increasingly apparent symbiosis between the cultural realm and that of business but also to an original mode of wealth creation based on the exploitation – much more intensive than before – of *specific deposits* built up over time and for which *narrativity* constitutes a privileged mode of adding value. This is an economy that derives its substance from the *past*. Thus it relies primarily not on industrial mass production of standardized products that are sold when they are new but, rather, on the addition of value to *things already present*, such as objects from antiquity, "vintage" items from a less remote past, or monuments, buildings, or sites – in short, everything that makes up the vast domain of a country's heritage. But this also holds true for works of art that, even when they are by contemporary artists, are presumed, if their value is recognized, to be inscribed in a temporality that pulls them out of the present and considers them from a vanishing point in the future, as if they already belonged to the past, or, to put it another way, to confer on them a sort of *immortality*, since they are destined to be preserved indefinitely; this is the role assigned to museums.

Let us note, however, that exploitation of this type of wealth has so far been quite uneven from country to country, in relation to variables of which the primary one is obviously the degree to which, in the various nation-states, the holders of capital could count on a workforce that was readily exploitable even though its members had no special skills or training. While direct investments abroad were made chiefly in emerging countries with an abundant proletariat accustomed to low wages, investments in the enrichment economy were oriented primarily toward the countries of Western Europe. These countries were marked by a very substantial expansion of secondary and especially higher education in the 1960s, thus making a large, well-trained, and completely unorganized labor force available to the enrichment economy. Its members, especially when their competencies were mainly in literary or artistic areas, had trouble rising to stable salaried positions in large industrial, commercial, or financial companies, so that, facing the threat of unemployment, they tended to be willing to accept temporary, unstable, and poorly paid jobs which were often below the level they should have been able to expect based on their diplomas (that is, based on what the same diplomas had been worth in the previous job market), as long as those jobs corresponded to the cultural aspirations they had nurtured during their studies.

But a second factor also came into play: the existence, in Western European countries, of abundant strata of heritage sites. Resources constituted much earlier had been systematically exploited, preserved, and rehabilitated – in France, this process has been under way since the Revolution – because the central government saw them as internal instruments fostering national unification and as external instruments fostering national prestige; efforts to develop museums and catalog their holdings through the nineteenth and twentieth centuries exemplify this movement.[13] The resources exploited by an enrichment economy are never simply warehouses full of old things; they always require efforts to highlight the past, endeavors that rely on more or less consistent traces but that, in principle, any political entity should be able to undertake, insofar as that entity bases its legitimacy on a past that it can then exploit.

It must be noted, however, that, in France, this highlighting of what came to be called the national patrimony[14] also stemmed from what we may call – paraphrasing Marx – a *primitive accumulation* of cultural capital. The latter, on the same basis as the form of capital Marx discusses, did not have a purely commercial origin. It resulted to a significant extent from violence – that is, from the military and predatory action of the central government, which, in France, especially after the Revolution and the imperial wars, proceeded to dismantle large numbers of chateaux, abbeys, churches, and other sites and to loot the countries it had conquered and/ or colonized. As Bénédicte Savoy shows, in the early nineteenth century the first director of the Louvre Museum, Vivant Denon, orchestrated the transfer to Paris of a great number of works of art that had belonged to the German nobility, with the justification that, because "works of art" were "the fruit of the spirit of freedom," they ought naturally to "reside in the country of freedom."[15]

Changes in French cultural policy

To what extent can we see in the contemporary development of an enrichment economy a process clearly marking the shift from the twentieth century to the twenty-first? It can certainly be argued that the domains we have chosen as examples to indicate the contours of such a process (the luxury economy, works of art and antiquities, historical monuments, tourism, culture, contemporary art) are in no way really new. For each of these domains there is an abundant historiography – indeed, one that has been considerably enriched in recent decades – focusing on the way processes rather similar to the ones that interest us were deployed in earlier times, especially in Italy, Great Britain, and France. Exemplary studies have shed light on the luxury economies in Italian courts during the Renaissance,[16] the spread of luxury in eighteenth-century Paris,[17] the luxury industries in nineteenth-century France,[18] and the links between heritage creation, the development of museums, and the formation of national or regional identities in France, especially since the Revolution. Other studies have looked at the way tourism was stimulated, in the late eighteenth century and throughout the nineteenth, by the Romantic quest for the sublime and the picturesque; beginning in literary and artistic circles,[19] this tendency was extended in the first half of the twentieth century by efforts on the part of local elites to highlight the identity of a given region by celebrating both its natural beauty and its rich folklore.[20] As for the domains of art and culture, both popular and elite forms came to the fore in the preoccupations of historians, partly owing to the latter's fascination with social anthropology, especially in the second half of the twentieth century – all this to the detriment of factual political history, denounced as "event-driven."

We could invoke the increase in digital resources in the domains that interest us, of course, and stress the intensification of the economic role of these domains. But, as is always the case when one is dealing with phenomena unfolding gradually over time, the threshold effects are hard to distinguish. This is why we rely in particular on indices that point to converging changes in the way these domains have been apprehended by different types of actors operating in the political, cultural, or economic spheres, and on the way these changes have interacted. In France, as we see it, these changes began to take hold between the mid-1970s and the mid-1980s. During that period, which was marked by declining industrial employment (after 1975) and increasing unemployment, new preoccupations and new horizons started to emerge.

To simplify, we can say that this same period was marked by a decline of hope in the unlimited development of industry on the national level. During the previous decades, industrial development had been an objective shared by the Gaullist and post-Gaullist right, which had focused exclusively on the necessity of growth,[21] and the communist and socialist left, whose progressivist and reformist critique bore essentially on the uneven and unjust way the "fruits" of this growth were distributed among the various social classes.[22] The turn away from faith in industrial progress led not to the abandonment of progressivism but, rather, to a profound reorientation of that outlook, stimulated by the recent spread of ecological awareness[23] that was developing on the libertarian, anti-productivist left, in both scholarly and popular forms.[24]

Whereas the progressivism of the decades following the Second World War was centered on devaluation of the past, and most forcefully of rural areas and the agrarian way of life, the new progressivism that emerged during the subsequent period went hand in hand with *rehabilitation* of the past: emphasis on the past was viewed as one of the conditions for thinking ahead and, indeed, for the very possibility of a *future*. This development tended to modify the connotations of the reference to national heritage and, most notably, to orient that reference toward the left. One example among many: the destruction of eleven of the twelve Baltard pavilions constituting Les Halles that had been built between 1850 and 1870 to house the central food markets in Paris. These historic structures were demolished following a decision made in the late 1950s to transfer the markets to Rungis. (The sole surviving pavilion was dismantled before being purchased in 1976 by the city of Nogent-sur-Marne.) The destruction, which began in 1971, was undertaken in a spirit of modernization (the construction of a shopping complex, the Forum des Halles), despite a very powerful protest movement during which the site was occupied and used as a space for cultural events by the alternative left; a petition to save the pavilions drew 100,000 signatures. It is highly probable that, ten years later, the pavilions would not have been destroyed but, rather, "rehabilitated," not only preserved as testimonies to history but remodeled so as to be used in new ways.

It is as though the turn toward an enrichment economy had been imagined and anticipated, at least in part, after the socialist government took over in 1981, as one of the available means to compensate for a possible industrial decline. By contrast, other industrial nations tended to develop financial centers (London, for the United Kingdom) as a way of confronting the expected catastrophe, namely, the extension of unemployment beyond the categories that had been most seriously affected to that point (lower-class youth without educational credentials, workers over the age of fifty, who received special governmental support) to include young people with post-secondary education. Representing the upper class for the most part, but including more and more middle- and even lower-class youth, this cohort of educated young people had increased in number considerably[25] with the "democratization of access to higher education" that had been an important objective in the preceding period in response to critics who denounced the unequal distribution of the "fruits" of the recent economic expansion. During the 1980s, big businesses were being reorganized according to emerging management precepts: the outsourcing of numerous functions, a renewed focus on the company's original activities, just-in-time manufacturing, subcontracting, multiplication of sites identified as profit centers, networked companies, a shifting of responsibilities to operators, a flattening of hierarchies, and project-based production.[26] These reorganizations, which were clearly intended to increase productivity, weaken the labor unions, augment profits, and reinforce the power of stockholders, resulted in the firing of a very large number of workers judged "unemployable." Hiring went down, and the reshaping of the relation between educational levels and job openings led to a devaluation of post-secondary diplomas.[27]

One major difference between managing companies and managing countries, even though the latter increasingly import their management methods from business, is that the former can distribute their activities over large geographical areas, even worldwide, and above all can get rid of workers they deem superfluous in certain cases, or on certain sites, by reconfiguring themselves spatially. By contrast, it is much more difficult for nations to exclude citizens from their territory, even temporarily, in that the very existence of a nation is justified by the population for which it is responsible. Nevertheless, until relatively recently, nations have sometimes adopted policies leading to the exclusion of certain subsets of their population. The organized departure of large numbers of inhabitants of a country, whether it came about because the central government chose to offer incentives to the most fortunate members of the group or because it forcefully excluded the poorest members, was possible in the late nineteenth century; it took the form of emigration to the New World or, in the first half of the twentieth century, to the colonies with the encouragement of the mother countries. But although the number of workers, especially educated workers, who decided on their own to go abroad was still high in the 1980s, such an exodus was no longer conceivable in the form of national policy on a grand scale; departures were signs that the home country was less attractive than the destination country.[28] The question of how to employ young diploma-holders, especially those who had studied literature or the social sciences and were largely scorned by businesses, became a problem for national governments. In France, this problem came on top of other issues involving the organization of the national territory that had accompanied and followed the 1982 decentralization law and the transfer of roughly two-thirds of the public financing of culture to local governments, in view of fostering a better regional distribution of cultural activities. It is in the context we have just evoked that the problems linked to the relation between culture and the economy were significantly reconceived, and that cultural development came to be viewed, from the standpoint of the national government, no longer just as the moral necessity of maintaining the national memory, or as a requirement connected with the democratization of knowledge (which had previously been the case), but as an economic asset of prime importance.

Jack Lang, who served as minister of culture during François Mitterrand's presidency, became the principal interpreter of this transformation, displacing the conception of culture – thematized by André Malraux but also by communist intellectuals – that had predominated during the preceding period, when the state had assumed significant legal and financial responsibility for cultural activities. The progressives who had been active in the Resistance during the war considered culture in terms of a pair of oppositions that, in their eyes, justified its "democratization" – its transmission to workers. The first was the opposition between culture and the economy, mirroring the opposition between the soul and the body. Workers, who are the foundation of the economy, and especially those workers whose labor makes heavy demands on the body, must have access to culture because they (too) have souls. Culture is in some sense their due: the economy is necessary, of course, but subordinate. Culture, to play its role, must be removed from the economic sphere. The second opposition is between high or elite culture, supported by "noble" institutions (museums, universities, and so on), and low or mass culture (industrial culture, cultural commodities, or culture at the service of the commodity cosmos); the latter was viewed with loathing by elitists and reactionaries, but it was also regarded with repulsion by certain thinkers on the left inspired in particular by the Frankfurt School.[29] Seen in this spirit, cultural democratization was aimed at extracting the masses from the grip of low culture and raising them up toward high culture.

These are the oppositions that Jack Lang took it upon himself to deconstruct in a public way, beginning with a speech in Mexico City in 1982 that drew a lot of attention. On the one hand (the first opposition), he asserted that the ties between culture and the economy were not scandalous sources of corruption but normal and even indispensable. The economy does not pervert culture; culture requires the economy. Without an economy, there is no culture. Conversely, he predicted that it would be through cultural inventiveness that the economies of the world would be revitalized, and that "conquering unemployment is a cultural change that comes about through a change in cultural policy."[30] Culture is and must be at the service of the economy (above all thanks to tourism). On the other hand (the second opposition), Lang opened up the definitions of the term "culture" (following the lead of anthropology and sociology in this respect) in such a way as to break down the border between high and low culture. The concept of culture would henceforth include the so-called industrial arts, such as fashion and design, and also the popular arts, for example songs, comic books, and street art. Similarly, a nation's heritage would include, on equal footing, long-standing historical monuments recognized as such and industrial complexes showcased by the eco-museums under development at the time[31] (Lang had fought the destruction of the Baltard pavilions, which he had wanted to transform into a cultural center). Now anything could become culture, and every individual could become a creator if he or she were recognized as such. Lang proposed to replace the "democratization of culture" by "cultural democracy," which would privilege the processes – very numerous, as it turned out – known as "artification."[32] Thus the power to bestow recognition on works of art that had long belonged to agencies such as museums, academic institutions, and critics had to be transferred to public financing agencies, whether these depended on the central government or on local authorities.

This new line was not just a matter of words. Lang's argument was accompanied by concrete measures such as the creation of regional foundations for contemporary art (FRACs), which escaped the control of museum conservators,[33] or the National Association for the Development of the Arts of Fashion (in 1989). These measures provoked outrage among the defenders of culture "in the noble sense"; beginning in the 1980s, the authorities implementing the new measures were accused of "relativism," an anathema that was to resurface in force later on, when "values" became a central issue in political disputes.[34] The FRACs were different from museums in the sense that their mission was to constitute collections and to organize itinerant exhibits. These innovations disrupted the hierarchy of intermediaries in the plastic arts – a hierarchy dominated up to that point by museum officials – while giving important roles to actors who had not been certified by any official title and who enjoyed a certain degree of autonomy with respect to institutions.[35] They accompanied a proliferation of exhibit organizers ("curators"), who worked on "projects" without answering to any hierarchical body; this often went hand in hand with considerable economic insecurity and an increased dependence on major collectors and galleries.

This redefinition of culture and the measures that accompanied it were undergirded by a philosophy that has been expressed in part by Félix Guattari,[36] in a theory that associates the processes of creation and the constitution of value with the expression of differences of any order, whether the object in question is new (for example, an industrial wasteland whose beauty can suddenly be revealed) or old (for example, a Romanesque church), differences that can modify the perception of the world shared by the people to whom they are pointed out. "What can be done to ensure that music, dance, creation, all forms of sensibility, belong by rights to the entire set of social components?," Guattari asks.[37] The response lies in the conception according to which all human beings are creators whenever they realize their humanity by paying attention to differences in which they recognize themselves, and when they manifest a desire to share with others both the recognition of those differences and the recognition of their humanity inasmuch as their humanity is expressed in the attention paid to the differences. Thus everyone turns out to be oriented toward a goal, which is to *interest* other people, to arouse their *curiosity*, and this process is at the root of the formation of communities constituted around encounters among distinct beings, each of whom intends to share with the others the differences that constitute his or her singularity. From this perspective (which Philippe Urfalino judiciously characterizes as vitalist),[38] the mission of cultural agencies – above all, the agencies that distribute the funding that cultural activities need – is to put people into circulation and bring them into contact, to organize encounters in order to promote the exchange of identities and differences.

Money is the energy that allows such encounters to take place, through the financing of travel, performances, colloquia, festivals, and so on. But these encounters produce an energy that generates money in its turn, so that the economy – the libidinal economy, as it were – of exchanges of energy among actors, who are all animated by the same desire to awaken the curiosity of others by deploying their own differences while awakening themselves through contact with the differences manifested by others, rejoins the economy as understood by economists. In order to function, this generalized economy thus presupposes, on the one hand, that the participants will limit or delay the selection process, for one cannot know *a priori* what will arouse the curiosity and the creativity of others – that is, where the liberation of energy will come from – and, on the other hand, that participants will not fear excess, profusion, loss, or expenditures, for, in the absence of these, no energy can be produced. A conception to which disconsolate souls, unable to think in terms other than those of management control, object that money spent on culture – input – can easily be accounted for, and that it often leads to losses, and that the energy that culture is supposed to generate not only eludes accountability but also resists any other form of objectivization. This is the case up to the point when the importance of what geographers call the residential economy is recognized, and when mayors in urban agglomerations realize that cultural investment in the broad sense constitutes a solid asset for attracting qualified workers, tourists, foreign residents, or wealthy retirees to their cities – and also, increasingly, businesses specialized in exploiting the type of resources on which an enrichment economy is based.

A new perspective in economic analysis

Jack Lang's directives, which he implemented when the left came to power in France in 1981, accompanied and sometimes preceded a turn that was taking place among economists, especially among those who had been influenced by Marxism or by the economic outlook of the radical American left. A number of the latter thinkers had worked in French research organizations, especially INSEE. Their work accompanied the planning that took place in the 1960s and, as the 1960s gave way to the 1970s, their models sought to integrate the effects of international competition on an economy that had been conceived, after the Second World War, primarily within national frameworks.[39] In the 1980s, these economists shared a serious concern about competitiveness, but they also agreed that the economic models centered on the major industrial firms were being exhausted, although they did not give up on the project of a public framing structure for the economy. That project led them to resist the economic trend that was fast becoming dominant, the trend toward placing particular stress on demand and on the dynamics of international commerce. The work of these economists is relevant to the genealogy of the enrichment economy that we are trying to depict in broad strokes, because, even though they still concentrated on production rather than on the exchange and circulation of things, they sought to multiply the directions that competition and growth could take by tracing paths that deviated from that of the mass industrial economy. This orientation gave them common ground with economists who were attentive to sociology and, more generally, to the social and political sciences that were developing a new orientation in the second half of the 1980s: the economics of conventions.[40]

As one example of this new approach, we can look at a work by Michael Piore and Charles Sabel, *The Second Industrial Divide*, published in the United States in 1984 and in 1989 in French translation as *Les chemins de la prospérité: de la production de masse à la spécialisation souple* (The paths of prosperity: from mass production to supple specialization). The book was highly influential in Europe, especially in France and Italy, among scholars who focused on small, networked, sometimes family-run businesses, on the dynamics of proximity, and on local development policies centered in regional agencies and industrial districts.[41] In the preface to the French edition, Piore and Sabel undertook to show that the opposition on which their book was based, between "two antagonistic modes of technological progress" (assembly-line production on the one hand, an artisanal economy on the other), is particularly valid for France. While "nineteenth-century France appeared as a country with an artisanal economy par excellence," unlike "its rivals in industrial competition" Great Britain and the United States, France transformed itself after the Second World War, by a deliberate political choice on the part of its leaders, into a prototypical mass production economy rivaled only by that of the United States.[42]

The economic model that Piore and Sabel sought to promote in the mid-1980s was supposed to be valid for any type of production. But companies that had turned toward a luxury economy served as their primary models, and it was chiefly with respect to the manufacture of exceptional products that the turn advocated by the authors proved to be realistic. A case in point can be found in the textile district of Prato, in Tuscany. Faced with competition from less expensive textiles made in Japan and Eastern Europe, Prato became a paradigmatic example of local development based on networked small businesses. It succeeded owing to two factors: "a long-term shift from standard to fashionable fabrics, and a corresponding reorganization of production from large integrated mills to technologically sophisticated shops specializing in various phases of production."[43] Lyon offers a counter-example: it had stopped producing artisanal silk in the late nineteenth century in favor of industrial spinning mills, and it saw its textile industry disappear in the late 1950s. In the context of the "industrial districts" of "the third Italy," middle-sized factories benefited from the activation of familial and political solidarities in an environment shaped by dynamic regional entities; this explains the success of clothing companies such as Benetton or, later, Diesel, both of which attained the status of worldwide groups.[44]

As a second example, we can consider a book published in 1993 by Robert Salais and Michael Storper, *Les mondes de production: enquête sur l'identité économique en France*.[45] This work is particularly relevant to our effort to grasp the moment at which the orientation toward exceptional goods with a strongly cultural tenor was beginning to be considered as a way to compensate for the decline in mass production that was affecting the industrial regions in France. By relying on the notion of "possible worlds," borrowed from the economy of conventions, the authors distinguished between an industrial world in which price-based competition is driven by "economies of scale and costs" and a world in which competition relies on an "economy of variety (scope)" that includes both high-tech objects and objects of superior quality or objects that are exceptional in some other way. As it happens, one of the pitfalls of the French economy at the time was that it was too polarized toward industry, where it was not succeeding very well, to the detriment of an "economy of variety-scope,"[46] which was particularly successful in the United States, in the area of high-tech products, and in Italy, in the area of luxury goods. It follows that "the future [belonged] to products that are not strictly 'industrial'"[47] and that rely on conventions of quality. Since the publication of Salais and Storper's book, France has in fact seen growth in sales of products in areas that the authors deemed promising, such as wine, perfume, jewelry, and fashion.

A shift to different scales

In France, the orientation toward an economy centered on localities, on exceptional goods produced by artisans, on the luxury economy, and on the development of culture as an economic asset and a means of combating unemployment was first initiated by the central government through public policies whose inspiration went against the grain of those adopted at the end of the Second World War. At the outset, then, the initiative did not come from the business world, and certainly not from the large industrial firms, which were oriented instead toward delocalization, transformation into multinationals, and finance. The new public policies opened the door to active interventions at the local level. As it happened, actions of this sort, stimulated by regionalization, decentralization, and the growing autonomy allowed to local collectivities in the management of their budgets, encouraged the formation of an enrichment economy, but *from below*, as it were. The key factors were the new local cultural policies and a focus on the associative sphere, where new initiatives were encouraged and subsidized.

The public cultural policies introduced by the Ministry of Culture and Communication were characterized by "a massive use of contractual arrangements – contracts, conventions, and other protocols for agreements established by public or private organizations committed to financing and/or implementing action plans within a pre-established time period." This led to a "generalized contractualization" in 1982–8, largely under the impetus of Michel Rocard; it took the form of intercommunal development charters and neighborhood social development operations that blended urban, social, educational, cultural, and environmental concerns.[48] Thus cultural action was integrated into regional planning, which was inseparable from public action wholly based on a *regional political logic*; in other words, "cultural action" was approached not "as a sector for action" but in its global dimension, inscribed in a politics of regional development. Key factors in the program's success were "strong involvement by elected officials," "a dialogue with associations and communes," and "intense coordination among the services: culture, regional planning, tourism."[49] In short, the implementation of this policy was based on processes of "concertation," "dialogue," "joint elaboration," and "shared responsibilities," during which cultural actors – actors in theater and film, dancers, painters, sculptors, writers, librarians, and so on – found themselves led, and in some cases compelled, to keep on working, making contacts with mayors, local officials, managers, and so on. These processes could be seen as exemplifying the "encounters" on which Jack Lang counted for an intensification of creativity at all levels.

The increase in the number of people employed in the performing arts is often attributed in part, or even wholly, to the adoption of special legislation providing a degree of financial security for intermittent workers. However, this explanation does not apply to other workers in the cultural sector, and it underestimates the role played in this augmentation by regional planning since the 1980s. The policy introduced by Lang, based on contracts involving both public authorities and private interests, encouraged the development of associations, especially in the performing arts, and it also supported development in the non-profit sector. (With the exception of "social work," the arts, theater, and other cultural activities were the only domain in which salaried employees working for organizations belonging to the non-profit sector – around 100,000 – were nearly equivalent in number to those employed outside of that sector.) The combined budgets of non-profit associations in the economy of culture, which amounted to 8.3 billion euros in 2011, add up to roughly 10 percent of the combined budgets of all non-profit associations in France.[50] But the Lang policy has led to income precarity for a significant number of workers in the cultural domain. The salaried workers employed by cultural associations in 2011, estimated at around 170,000, were working more frequently on short-term contracts even though their educational levels were higher than those of workers in other sectors.[51] Contractualization thus had features in common with the "project" culture that characterized the change in management methods implemented in businesses from the mid-1980s on and that may have served as a model.

As for festivals, they are especially plentiful in France. They are typically devoted to literature, comic books, theater, and above all music (1,972 musical events were produced in France in 2013). The creation and development of festivals during the second half of the 1970s and in the 1980s was first envisaged by actors on the ground, most often public figures serving as instruments of local development in interactions with government agencies; their projects benefited from the government's decentralization measures. The budgetary equilibrium of such festivals, which depends – in proportions that vary on a case-by-case basis – on public subsidies, ticket sales, and private funds, is nevertheless fragile: when a festival is cancelled – sometimes owing to movements connected with the renegotiation of the status of intermittent workers – or even disappears altogether – most often owing to a reduction in public financing – the repercussions affect not only the culture workers involved but the entire set of local services and businesses.

Onto this development of the enrichment economy *from below*, which has benefited from governmental initiatives and subsidies that are often justified as measures intended to curtail unemployment, an expansion *from above* has gradually been grafted, as the prospect of profit has led to growth in investments in luxury goods, heritage sites, tourism, art, culture, and so on; the profitability of private capital has seemed all the less risky in these domains in that they have been supported or encouraged by public authorities. Investments oriented toward an enrichment economy are even more difficult to quantify and summarize than jobs, given the absence of transparency and the lack of an adequate accounting framework. But various indices, such as the development of luxury firms, suggest that these investments are significant and that they increase regularly, as do the profits generated.

Intensification of relationships between public cultural action and private enterprise was deemed necessary early on, in order to give substance to the idea that culture could make a significant contribution to economic growth. This intensification has taken the form of symbolic and material support on the part of public authorities for what can be designated as "culture industries," thus making it clear that such industries are fully entitled to state support, with a primary emphasis on sectors judged prestigious on the international level – for example, haute couture, cinema, and of course the national heritage. The tourism sector, placed under the authority of the Ministry of Foreign Affairs in 2010, is another exemplary case, since public efforts in favor of tourism, a real national "cause," cannot be effective without support from private interests in the areas of transportation, the hotel and restaurant industries, and upscale commerce, all of which are highly concentrated around a few major companies. As evidence, we can consider the demand, approved by law in 2015 after lengthy debates, that stores in designated tourist zones in Paris be allowed to stay open on Sundays and in the evenings. But the concern for stimulating investor interest is also taken into account on a more local level, with the promotion of heritage sites and regional attractions. The tourism secretariat thus includes among its "poles of excellence" a "wine tourism pole" that aims to "bring together the various actors in viticulture and tourism," most notably by organizing "winery visits." An "ecotourism pole" focuses on tourism by boat, on foot, by bicycle, or on horseback; this form of tourism is expected to benefit the development of rural regions by increasing the commodity value of the landscapes and increasing familiarity with local gastronomic products.[52] This is why, among the personalities that make up the Tourism Promotion Council, alongside diplomats, local elected officials, and journalists, we find a representative of the National Group of Independents, a CEO of a high-quality food processing company, and the president of the Federation of Wines and Spirits.

The emphasis on tourism and, more generally, the highlighting of regions and areas offering important heritage sites that attract well-to-do residents (for example, chateaux, abbeys, exceptionally well-preserved villages, outstanding wine-growing regions, and "traditional arts and crafts") are profitable above all for those who own property in the area, whether or not they themselves actually live there. These developments have thus helped increase the revenues drawn from heritage sites as compared with those drawn from work; this shift has been among the defining traits of the changes that have affected the bourgeoisie in France over the past thirty years.[53]

Let us look, for example, at the Forum d'Avignon, created in 2007 with the support of the Ministry of Culture and Communication; it is presented on its website as "a laboratory of ideas and a space for international encounters at the service of culture and its dialogue with the economic and digital worlds."[54] Its mission is "to recall that culture is an investment – and not a cost – that is at once individual, collective, and financial, and that its triple nature – artistic, economic, and social – shares actively in the development of the economy and of the territories." It brings together "artists," "creators," "entrepreneurs," and officials from public agencies, as represented by the twenty or so personalities on its board of directors; the board addresses problems such as tax issues affecting creators, intellectual property rights and authorial rights, "cultural entrepreneurship," or the contribution of culture to the development of regional "powers of attraction." The Forum is increasingly interested in the impact of digital developments on the financing of the cultural sector. The existence of such an organization is emblematic of an enrichment economy, for it seeks to make three dimensions of the enrichment economy compatible: first, promotion of the nation itself as a brand in international competition (the brand "France"); second, development of the various regions, so as to maintain activity in them and, if possible, increase their powers of attraction; and, third, exploitation of those resources.

From ornamental patrimony to heritage creation

The case of chateaux belonging to the aristocracy is particularly relevant to our attempt to show how measures to highlight regions undertaken by the public sector have converged with the interests of the patrimonial elites. In her work devoted to the sociology of nobility, Monique de Saint Martin's discussion of chateaux helps us to sketch a sort of phenomenology of the way the enrichment economy was gradually established and the way measures initiated by the central government – especially concerning taxation – met the expectations and economic interests of the old elites.[55]

Let us recall that, in France, private parties own nearly half (49.57 percent in 2014) of the protected heritage sites, some 22,000 monuments.[56] In addition to funds for maintenance and restoration that come directly from the state, these property owners benefit from a favorable tax status. One criterion for attribution of this tax break – guaranteed public access to the building – was called into question in the 2010s, according to a Senate report, for it did not correspond any longer "to contemporary touristic practices." In fact, "a well-managed cottage or a bed and breakfast arranged in a way respectful of the building's history can attract a broader public and generate more public revenue than opening the site a few weeks a year." The notion of "economic and regional valorization of the building" as a substitute for opening it to the public is justified in this report by invoking Viollet-le-Duc, for whom "the best way to preserve a structure was to find a use for it."[57]

A heritage site par excellence, a chateau more than any other object embodies the sense of belonging to the nobility, because it anchors the relation between a name, a title, and a history. A nobleman is constructed as such inasmuch as he remembers that he has a history, that he is History, and that, if this historical memory is to be maintained and transmitted, it needs, like all memories, to be inscribed not only in bodies but also in things and in situations designed to promote contact with those things. In the case of the French nobility, chateaux are concrete emblems of the difference or gap without which the sentiment of nobility cannot be maintained, inasmuch as their transmission is inscribed in the succession of generations that make up family lines. In Monique de Saint Martin's analysis, the relation between owners and chateaux, at least as it had been maintained more or less until the 1970s, was separate from the building's properly economic components, and even from its aesthetic aspect. On the one hand, a person who inherits a chateau may boast of being merely its "custodian." On the other hand, a family chateau may be sought doggedly after it has been lost, even though a person who has inherited the name, has succeeded in buying the chateau back, and has restored it to the family line may actually find it "very ugly."[58] Chateaux that "quite often are no longer of great economic value and make no money, or very little, are often said by their owners to be a source of expenditures and 'charges' or 'debts.'"[59]

The same remarks apply as well to the chateau's furnishings:

What owners appreciate are not so much the aesthetic properties, the style of the objects, furniture, or paintings, as their history, their origin: it is not so much a Louis XV chest of drawers or a Louis-Philippe armchair that is admired in a small drawing room as the commode that belonged to great-grandmother C or the armchair on which the Duchess of R from the chateau of X used to sit. The commercial value of such objects may even be unknown; the familiar objects simply sit there, their owners pretending not to notice them. Most often it is not a masterpiece by some more or less famous painter that occupies the place of honor but a portrait of the Marshal of X or the Duke of R, preferably an ancestor with whose historic exploits all family members, young and old alike, are expected to be familiar; the story of the adventures and vicissitudes of the painting itself is often better known than the artistic qualities of the painting or the history of the painter.[60]

One of the interesting aspects of Saint Martin's work is that she depicts the nobility and its relation to objects at a time when its members' efforts to maintain their status require new strategies that intersect with the formation of an enrichment economy. At this point in time, the past – history, and thus the narratives that accompany the objects in question and mark their value – is no longer valued exclusively with reference to a family lineage – that is, to a private subset of interested parties, closed off in its difference; the past has taken on an additional dimension that is at once economic and public. Seen from this perspective, the enrichment economy, and the processes of heritage creation in particular, can be viewed as extensions of the relation of the aristocracy to the world of objects, at the price of a radical transformation that shifts the referential orientation of these objects from the private toward the public, from the family toward the territory (regional or national), and at the same time connects them with the evolution of capitalism. Families whose fortunes rested on economic capital of the industrial variety and/or with the development of conversion strategies, on jobs requiring advanced university studies and benefiting from high salaries, could consider their "ancestral" homes as costs, "burdens," or, at best, an enjoyable legacy favoring the maintenance of familial and social relations. With the transformations of capitalism, the patrimony associated with the quest for distinction has gradually been transformed into capital capable of generating a profit through commercial exchange, and also through tourism.

The practice of opening chateaux to visitors developed in France starting in the 1970s and 1980s, and it was given favorable treatment by tax legislation adopted on 23 December 1964 and 5 January 1988. The first law "allows owners to deduct from their taxable revenue the entirety of expenses incurred in restoration and maintenance if the 'private historical monument,' officially registered as such, is open to the public at least forty to fifty days a year." The second allows "private historical monuments open to the public at least 80 to 100 days a year, according to the circumstances, to be transmitted from one generation to the next tax-free." The theme of "chateaux for everyone" or "chateaux open to all" developed rapidly among owners as a manifestation of their good will "as citizens" "in the service of the public good." "One of the new duties of descendants of the nobility [is] to preserve in their families the chateau or home they have inherited and, to this end, to be able to allow visitors access within carefully defined limits, and perhaps to serve as guides, commenting with telling anecdotes and historical information." More and more often, spaces in chateaux can be rented for receptions and weddings, and bedrooms are transformed into "(paying) guest rooms."[61] Certain grand chateaux (such as that of the Marquis de Breteuil) have been converted into veritable businesses, embracing "visitors' activities, seminars, professional colloquia, parties organized by company boards, concerts, weddings, restaurants, and so on."[62]

The transmutation of private homes into heritage objects, essential elements for enrichment basins, has come about in France in conjunction with the development of a politics of patrimony, showcased for example with Jack Lang's 1984 creation of "Journées portes ouvertes dans les monuments historiques" (open house days for historical monuments). Coordinated at the national level by an office in charge of heritage sites, these events were initially centered on visits to buildings usually closed to the public, especially places from which government authorities exercised power; it was later extended to properties managed by regional entities, and also to a number of private properties, especially "historic" homes whose owners have thus been recognized as "partners" in the politics of heritage creation.[63] The insertion of private owners into this apparatus increased both the reputation of the goods they possessed and the value of those goods as capital. Such public–private partnerships rely on owners' associations set up to "protect the patrimony." The oldest of these associations, "La Demeure historique" (Historic Homes), includes almost nothing but chateaux of the aristocracy (2,000 in 1989) and "Vieilles Maisons françaises," whose much more numerous members (18,000) do not always hold titles.[64]

The process of turning homes of aristocratic origin into heritage sites thus had a double and more or less contradictory character. On the one hand, the process allowed a memorial relation to objects to be extended to social classes that, although foreign to the nobility per se, had discovered their own "roots." Their members, generally urbanized, often with university education and occupying upper managerial positions in modern companies, envisaged the objects and homes of their families of origin – often from the peasantry – as treasures worthy of being admired and preserved owing to the mere fact that they came from the past and could be invested with memorial power. The owners associated these objects – which, a few decades earlier, would have been scorned, or even abandoned – with narratives that invested them with value, initially for themselves and their children, as testimony to the family's past. This democratization of the "chateau" effect, which can lead to showcasing the slightest little farm or even just a barn, enhanced with a narrative referring to the family's history, is paralleled by the transformation of other goods endowed with powerful personal memories into heritage objects capable of taking on a capitalistic tenor. The process of transforming patrimony into capital is stimulated by an increased demand for residences and goods anchored in the past. This demand is spurred in turn by the spread of what could be called a *patrimonial ethos,* an ethos shared by large numbers of people who, although they themselves have not inherited real estate, invest their earnings from work in homes and objects apt to give them a sense of historicity. The practice of collecting is a somewhat comparable development, as is its "twin," the search for genealogical origins ("collecting" persons rather than objects). A trend initiated chiefly by the descendants of "great" families, genealogical research has become a widespread passion in recent years.[65]

Local mutations in global capitalism

The concomitant and interrelated processes of deindustrialization and the development of an enrichment economy attest to a profound shift in the strategies employed by Western capitalism to retain its central position. These paired phenomena constitute two responses to the crisis that began affecting capitalism toward the end of the 1960s and during the 1970s. This crisis, whose epicenter was in the United States, was marked by a significant drop in returns on capital (more than 40 percent between 1965 and 1973). Robert Brenner attributes the crisis to surplus production capacity on the part of businesses with the highest fixed capital.[66] The situation did not allow these companies to maintain either their previous levels of profit or their competitiveness in the face of the systemic struggle for predominance that was under way at the time. Starting in the late 1960s, that struggle pitted established companies against new entrants whose costs were lower.

Still, we can follow Giovanni Arrighi when, in his responses to Brenner's analyses, he stresses the intensification of conflicts between labor and capital from the late 1960s to the mid-1970s.[67] These conflicts were particularly pronounced in Europe, especially in France and Italy, where they marked the exhaustion of "Fordian" arrangements. In a framework subjected to a Fordian (or Keynesian) mode of regulation, the production of industrial goods was achieved locally at the cost of increased standardization of products and labor. Redistribution of the profits derived from increased productivity was supposed to lead to increased revenues for salaried workers, which would enable them to acquire the goods produced for themselves. But workers' demands (most often transmitted via labor unions) concerning salaries, working conditions, and job security intensified simultaneously with stagnation in the expected earnings from increased productivity. During the 1960s and 1970s, these combined developments triggered a major crisis in the capitalist mode of regulation: salaried workers received the larger share of increases in earnings, and stockholders, who saw their profits decrease as a result, responded in part by reducing their investments in production.

Taking back the initiative, the institutions of "central capitalism" (in Jonathan Nitzan and Shimshon Bichler's sense),[68] acting in concert with economic and political agencies of central governments, began by re-engineering the production lines and management structures of the big companies in the hope of increasing their productivity, especially by shrinking the scales on which productivity was measured (a process facilitated by the development of computer technologies), sometimes down to the level of workshops and departments or even individuals, so as to eliminate workers deemed unproductive or useless. This skimming resulted in a situation of structural unemployment whose effects were initially attenuated by government aid and especially by monetary inflation, so that consumption could be maintained in the face of mediocre economic growth.[69] However, as this new policy proved inadequate, central capitalism adopted the strategy of using legal arrangements for financial deregulation that favored the rapid circulation of capital and direct investment abroad, in countries where wages were low (those later labeled "emergent") and where there was a plentiful supply of workers lacking job security.

That strategy led to delocalizing an increasing segment of local industries and to underutilization of the productive capacities of Western European countries, where many potential workers found themselves without jobs. The rise in unemployment was a factor in disrupting what had been called up to that point the working class, whose members, more and more dependent on protective measures and support from central governments, came to constitute a sort of "plebeian" class. Associated with intense movements toward the concentration of capital, the strategy had the effect of restoring "central" capitalism's hold over "peripheral enterprises" – that is, local and dependent businesses – and empowering it to influence price fixing so as to generate higher than average profits, reinforce stock values, and thereby extend its scope in the struggle for differential accumulation.

The displacement of production, encouraged by a significant decrease in the costs of transporting merchandise (owing in part to the increased use of shipping containers in the 1980s), had the effect of maintaining a relatively high level of consumption and an abundance that the so-called consumer society needed to maintain itself, since everyday products (clothing, household appliances, and so on) manufactured in low-wage countries were less expensive than products made locally. But this shift in production sites also raised the question of how the people remaining behind would find work, and in particular the young people coming out of a rapidly expanding university system, a majority of whom came from the upper or middle bourgeoisie.

This is the context in which the shaping of an enrichment economy has to be interpreted. The process consisted in putting previously marginal forms of wealth creation at the heart of economic activity, which had long been dominated by manufacturing. Economies based on tourism or luxury goods already existed, but they had far less importance than they were to acquire later on, chiefly because their principal customers were less numerous and more locally rooted. But the wealthy and ultra-wealthy individuals who had benefited from the financial, industrial, and digital economies, as well as from the lowered costs of travel, were increasing considerably in number and becoming much more mobile. The development of an enrichment economy stimulated exports, which included more and more high-end goods. But it also enabled the highlighting and exploitation of resources that either could not be moved (such as landscapes and monuments) or were difficult to transport. These factors led to a doubling of the objects offered for consumption (this was particularly clear, as we have seen, in the case of food products): things manufactured in low-wage countries, intended for low-income households, were sold at relatively low prices, while things intended for the wealthy, identified with reference to their local and historical origins (which protected them from competition by conferring on them a specificity with monopolistic effects), could be offered for sale at high prices.

The intensification of trade in these exceptional goods also benefited from a change that constituted one possible exit, and perhaps the main one (though Giovanni Arrighi deems it temporary), from the crisis capitalism was undergoing, which has been labeled the "financialization of the economy."[70] This phenomenon, triggered by a repatriation of capital toward its most liquid forms in response to the lowered profitability of productive investments, including on the part of non-financial enterprises, was amplified when the system of fixed exchange rates was ended in 1973, a move that stimulated speculation on currencies and the creation of new financial products intended to play the role of insurance in order to diminish the uncertainty of derivative contracts, which had themselves rapidly become speculative instruments. The growing role given to financial activities almost certainly benefited the development of an enrichment economy, in two different ways. First, by increasing inequality. Financial gains are concentrated at the top, in private fortunes. Much more than is the case with industrial profits, these gains favor the wealthiest to the detriment of the middle classes, not to mention the mass of workers excluded from the profits drawn from this type of trade.[71] Indeed, ultra-rich individuals constitute the most sought-after clients in an enrichment economy, the most interesting in pecuniary terms, especially in the real-estate sector. Second, by increasing the level of uncertainty of returns on speculative investments. The sometimes gigantic sums that have fallen into the hands of the lucky agents of successful financial operators have presumably[72] been used, at least in part, for the acquisition of goods of high patrimonial value, such as exceptional homes, antiques, or works of ancient or contemporary art, rather than being reinvested on the financial markets in new operations whose outcome would be more or less uncertain. Rather than being investments destined to bring in profits, these acquisitions thus have played the role of permanent placements that shelter capital by investing it in goods that are very likely to maintain their prices over time at a high level, even while remaining relatively liquid, in the sense that the investor could plausibly hope to sell them eventually, even in the worst of cases, without loss.

Partisans of things[73]

In the effort to understand the formation of an enrichment economy, we must go beyond a sociology or ethnology of the rich,[74] of their way of life, their patterns of consumption,[75] their tastes, their preference for luxury goods, and more generally everything in their behavior and approach to life that is rooted in a quest for distinction so as to maintain the gap that separates them from the other social classes.[76] As useful as it may be, such an approach often tends to take an atemporal turn, if only insofar as one can bring to light traits that characterize the dominant classes, whatever the period or even the culture considered. What is required for our purposes is a dynamic analysis of the relation between different ways of generating wealth. This detour constitutes a necessary preliminary to an understanding of the changes over the last few decades that have affected not only the dominant classes – for which the term "bourgeoisie," inherited from the nineteenth century,[77] hardly suffices to evoke the most contemporary features – but also the overall divisions of society.

For, as has been demonstrated by an overabundant historiography focused on the decline of agrarian feudalism and the formation of industrial societies, while the defining features of social divisions clearly depend in part on their anchoring in specific political configurations, these divisions are fundamentally based on the way wealth is generated. This is why we have begun not with the study of people, and particularly the wealthiest (the top 10 percent), for whom the objects we have mentioned as examples seemed to be chiefly intended – the analysis of their tastes, their conspicuous consumption, or the role played in the exercise of their domination by the symbolic markers that surround them – but with the objects themselves and the way they have been invested with their particular value – that is, with the processes through which they acquire the status of wealth. We shall thus focus primarily on the processes through which things possessed, things that count as heritage objects, are transformed into *capital*, in the sense that they are integrated, through exchange, into a process of circulation that aims at accumulation and profit.[78]

Considered in terms of the formation of a specific sphere of wealth creation, the development of an enrichment economy is manifested as much by the intensification of the relations woven among these sectors as by the growth in each of the sectors we have mentioned, taken separately. Thus, for example, the development of trade in luxury goods maintains close ties, on the one hand, with an increase in public attention to cultural and artistic activities, considered in their conjoined aesthetic and commercial dimensions, and, on the other, with the growth of tourism and heritage creation, two processes that mutually stimulate each other. The multiplication of such links seems to us to be the most striking phenomenon, for it attests to the orientation of contemporary capitalism toward a systematic exploitation of wealth relying on the exploitation of "tradition" and, more generally, of the past.

This change tends not only to affect the structure of society in certain ways that may be deemed local or sectorial but also to modify the cognitive operators on which actors rely to form a representation of social space and to orient themselves within it. Some three decades ago, given the gradual disappearance of the French peasantry, these cognitive operators were still centered largely around positions of managers and engineers, workers and employees, which constituted its poles of attraction, or, one might say, its *attractors* – that is, they were centered around activities connected to varying degrees with productive work, dependent either on private firms or on organizations linked to a central government. Lately, these operators seem to have reorganized themselves around business, as attested for example by the proliferation of business schools.[79] But, if we go deeper into the details, we can see that this change in orientation has tended also to modify the nature of the activities that played the role of attractor, at least on a symbolic level, partly because the role of these activities was increasingly important but also doubtless because they were subjected to an intense work of representation. Thus we find in the position of attractor, on one side, the fuzzy notion of *creator* and, on the other, a category of increasing importance in ordinary social taxonomies whose label is essentially pejorative: in French, the category *bobo*, which can be associated with the English "hipster."[80] The success of these terms is probably connected to the fact that this category emphasized a new social configuration, bringing together within the same persons traits that had been viewed as socially antagonistic, some having to do with commerce and others with intellectual and cultural life. This is why the extension of *bobo* is extremely variable and its definition extremely fuzzy, allowing it to encompass all cultural actors down to the most subaltern, for this category serves as a channel connecting the world of the "rich" to that of the "creators." In addition, it serves increasingly as a basis for critiques of the "system": this term, used in the 1930s to designate the despised "elites," is coming back into use today.

Given the importance, in an enrichment economy, of the circulation of objects that are promoted through reference to the past, whether these objects already exist or whether they have allegedly been manufactured through "traditional" procedures, we shall approach this economy by returning to the *things themselves* – that is, by stressing the modalities of their valorization and the forms that support their circulation and make them estimable in terms of wealth. We shall contemplate these things especially in the particular moments of their "social life" (to borrow Arjun

Appadurai's expression),[81] in which they circulate, *change hands*, and are objects of *commerce* (taken in its broad sense, which can include conversational exchange) – that is, when they are exchanged for money or for other objects or advantages, or when they are transmitted through inheritance or through donations, particularly to institutions. These are the moments par excellence in which things are subjected to a *test*[82] during which the question of their value arises, a question made manifest either in the form of a price, in the case of direct sales, or in the form of an estimate made by relying on the commercial exchange of things deemed similar.

Part II

Prices and Forms of Valuation

3
Commerce in Things

In the preceding chapters, we introduced the first part of our project, the goal of which is to identify an economic change that is taking place today, especially in Western Europe. This change is characterized by what we are calling an economy of enrichment, centered on the exploitation of a source of wealth creation that had not been used before – at least not to the same degree and not as systematically – to produce profits and nourish capitalist accumulation. We have sought to show that this new resource is, paradoxically, *the past*. The enrichment economy relies principally not on promoting new objects but, rather, on enhancing the value of existing ones, objects often drawn from deposits of outdated things that may have been forgotten or reduced to a state of trash. These "found" objects are supplemented by newly created ones whose value is indexed to the past – for example, to the value of a *brand* whose prestige comes from its anchorage in the past, as is apparent with the leading brands of the luxury industry.

The commodity condition

Our next step is to examine the ways in which the type of things valued in the enrichment economy can be inserted into the commercial universe. The objects on which the enrichment economy relies circulate among a multitude of other things whose valuation derives from differing forms of logic. Still, all these things have a common feature: they *change hands* – that is, they *circulate* among large numbers of persons who are all qualified to become their owners. These persons can possess and resell them, as long as prices can be established in each case. In a free-market society, the character of property is not defined by statute. No material goods are out of bounds except for certain objects owned by public authorities, most notably art objects or antiquities preserved in government-owned museums.

This type of society has been called, especially since the 1960s and 1970s, a *consumer society*, a designation that usually has pejorative connotations.

The label stresses the fact that people confronted with a multitude of diverse objects can buy them if their monetary resources are adequate. But we contend that such a society is also, increasingly, a *commercial society*, in the sense that the actors are expected to be able to negotiate and are encouraged to become sellers themselves.

From this standpoint, we shall not emphasize differences between goods whose prices depend solely on supply and demand according to a classic market logic and goods that escape market logic, goods whose prices depend on a "value" or an "evaluation" established in an extra-economic manner (in the case of works of art,[1] for example, by means of the artist's reputation, confirmed by gallery owners),[2] or goods whose prices depend on a hierarchy of qualities (as established for instance by rankings or awards).[3] As for "the market" itself, a notion that is not the central focus of our project, it contributes very little information about "procedures for determining prices," as Michel Callon and Fabian Muniesa have pointed out.[4] In fact, markets bring sellers and buyers together around goods that already exist and are available; their principal function is to coordinate supply and demand. The process presupposes a principle of similarity according to which the goods involved can be substituted for one another, so that the results of an indefinite number of exchanges can be aggregated.[5] The principles of substitutability and aggregation raise questions that we shall address here, first by noting that the value of any and all goods has to be determined in a specific way, and then by treating each exchange both as a *test* and as an *event*. This is why we stress the notion of *commerce* rather than that of *market*; in this respect we follow Karl Polanyi when he seeks to tease apart and analyze the various "institutions" on which exchanges are based.[6]

Thus we shall call into question ordinary *commercial competencies*; the way these are acquired deserves to be the focus of empirical research.[7] These *competencies* are unevenly distributed among people, as a function of their divergent experiences; however, all individuals authorized to engage in commerce must have a minimum of competence so they can get their bearings in this composite universe populated by diverse objects that can all be bought and sold. (The need for such minimal competencies is apparent *a contrario* in the fact that persons deemed to lack them are placed under the authority of a competent person, as in the case of children or of adults who cannot function autonomously and are assigned custodians.) These competencies have to do with *things* themselves, on the one hand, and with *prices*, on the other; in other words, they have to do with *things* inasmuch as things are associated with *prices*. At a minimum, these competencies must allow actors to become familiar with the *relative prices* of things.

Whether they occupy the position of buyer or seller, individuals have to be able to find reasons to act when they are confronted with what might be called *commercial tests* – that is, they must be capable of relying on *commodity structures*. Like all structures, these may be more or less explicit.

Let us recall that we are using the term *commodity* to characterize every *thing* that *changes hands* in association with a *price*. Although commodity structures undoubtedly differ at least in part from person to person and from group to group, and although their degree of explicitness varies greatly, these structures must nevertheless have a more or less *common* character so that transactions can occur.

In our effort to sketch out a model of these structures, rather than starting with a detailed description, we shall present three of their components. First, they entail a *qualification of objects* – supported by institutional entities to varying degrees – on which all parties can agree, thereby *determining* the things that give rise to commercial circulation. Second, they entail the *prices* that are associated with these same objects when the objects *change hands*. These prices are supported by a common *metric* expressed in monetary form. Like all metrics, this one is available to translate highly diverse measurements into a single system. However, unlike the size or weight of physical objects, price is not an intrinsic property of the thing being priced: after all, a thing understood to be the same thing at time t and at time $t+1$ can be priced differently at those two moments, and two things viewed as identical can nevertheless be bought and sold at different prices according to the situation. Considered as signs, prices have a relation to things that is thus at most on the order of an *index*, to borrow a term proposed by C. S. Peirce.

A *thing*, anything at all, is transformed into a *commodity* when, in a situation of exchange, a price *is assigned* to it. This is far from being the case for everything on every occasion. As we know, there are things to which no one has ever dreamed of assigning a price, for example because they are too common (this was the case for air, before pollution inspired an appreciation of places in terms of air quality), and there are things that are explicitly removed from the cosmos of commodities, either by virtue of social norms that often evoke their dignity (in contemporary societies, human beings are the example par excellence) or because they are viewed as things that cannot be owned by private parties, even if they can be rented, as is the case with certain common goods (an individual cannot buy a work of art belonging to the public domain, the *Mona Lisa*, for example, but individuals can purchase access to museum space in order to contemplate the painting).

A third component of commodity structures is a reference to the *value* of things. Instead of seeing value as coming *before* price and locating it in things themselves, as the classical economists did, and instead of confusing value with a theoretical equilibrium price (under the organizing surveillance of an auctioneer), as the neoclassicists did, we locate value *after* price. Indeed, in our view, reference to *value*, which lacks any metric of its own, is relevant only insofar as it permits the prices of things to be *criticized* or *justified*. Our conception of commodities thus dispenses with convoluted debates over the relation between use value and exchange value; by the same token, we can avoid debates over the fetish character Marx attributed to merchandise, a fetishization whose supposed unveiling has provided fodder for theories of reification in Marx's wake.

By relying on these components, we shall be able to look a little more deeply into commodity structures, analyzing what we call *forms of valuation*. These forms help to partition and therefore to structure the universe of commodities because they are associated with modalities – that is, both arrangements and arguments – that make it possible to formulate propositions concerning the value of different things and also to set up tests on which to base arguments. The various forms of valuation generate arguments that serve to mediate, in a sense, between objects and prices. On the one hand, the arguments are based on specific properties of a given object that are deemed relevant. On the other, they serve to criticize or justify the object's price.

On the circulation of things

We propose to study the circulation of things only when the thing in question is associated with a price.

It is true that the circulation of things has been studied, most notably in anthropology, in terms of the relation between gifts and counter-gifts or, more precisely, in terms of putting a thing into circulation and thereby triggering the circulation of another thing in exchange. The gift has been represented, especially in Marcel Mauss's celebrated study,[8] as associated with an act of return in the form of a counter-gift; this association led Pierre Bourdieu to speak of "the twofold truth of the gift," at once interested and disinterested, a selfish calculation and a generous act, a contradiction resolved or "masked" by the interval of time separating the two acts of giving.[9]

The notion of the counter-gift has been criticized on the grounds that a gift does not systematically lead to something in exchange.[10] On these grounds, Philippe Descola proposes to distinguish among the concepts of gift, exchange, and predation. With a gift, something is given and no counterpart is expected; with an exchange, something is given and something else is given in return; with predation, something is taken and no counterpart is offered.[11] Another way of looking at the circulation of things has been in terms of transmission via filiation, in which something is yielded with no counterpart. While certain "gifts" may trigger counterparts less systematically than "exchanges" do, as Descola acknowledges, what is at issue here is not the definition of "gift" but, rather, the fact that, in anthropology, the circulation of things is most often envisaged only in relation to the presence or absence of counterparts that take the form of other things, or perhaps of actions. In other words, what has become the most common, the most banal mode of circulation of things in most societies (indeed, no doubt in virtually all early twenty-first-century societies) – that is, the circulation of things associated with prices, or what we are calling commercial exchange, in which things are viewed as commodities – seems to have gone largely unexamined.

Prices themselves have attracted little specific attention from sociologists and anthropologists. When they are afforded marginal mention, it is most often in the context of a separate subject, one that has become a theme in its own right, especially since Georg Simmel:[12] that of money. It is significant, moreover, that in a study titled "Gifted Money,"[13] where Viviana Zelizer brings together the themes of gifts and money, the question of price never comes up.

Prices have not been completely ignored, of course, especially in relation to art objects, when prices are in some sense exceptional, or appear "arbitrary," or seem to result purely from a power play and thus draw media attention, although still without necessarily being well understood. But they are most often treated as marginal, peripheral, as we can see in the work Pierre Bourdieu devoted to trade in private homes;[14] or, where prices have been a central focus, it has been in the context of a form of commerce considered "exotic" from the European and North American perspective, as illustrated in Clifford Geertz's work on the suk in Sefrou.[15] In other words, the commercial circulation of things endowed with prices seems to be taken for granted in most so-called capitalist societies to such an extent that it is not questioned; it remains in the shadows for philosophers, anthropologists, and sociologists, who leave them without compunction to people in the field of marketing, from whom they intentionally keep their distance.[16]

Studying commerce in things requires us to define – in broad strokes, for the time being – what is meant by the term "things," so as to ward off misunderstandings as far as possible. By "things," we mean material and movable forms. We are thus setting aside commerce in what is said to be immaterial. Real property, while immovable, will be treated according to the model for appraising movable things. As for what are commonly called "services," these encompass quite diverse activities that are presumed to be unified only through opposition to "goods." Nevertheless, the circulation of things cannot take place without "services," especially in the enrichment economy, where valuation of things often occurs via "personal services." While we shall not deal with "services" as such, then, we shall not fail to take into account the activities included under this term. On the contrary, they play a necessary role in the establishment and justification of the prices of things.

The death knell of commerce in material things has often been sounded to celebrate the arrival of a presumed "immaterial" era. The importance taken on by the information economy and worldwide web is undeniable. At the same time, however, we have to reckon with a paradox: while the reign of the immaterial is said to have arrived, there are more material goods than ever before, and their future has become a problem in itself, one of the greatest ecological problems of our time.

Commerce in things generally has a legal basis.[17] Things change hands according to contracts, and changing hands implies a change of owner. To make a thing an object of commerce is to modify the way in which the territories of ownership are populated. Commercialization in this sense is the opposite of renting. One could imagine a world in which a minority of owners would not sell things but would instead rent them to people who wanted to use them. Such a world would be so inegalitarian that it would probably not last very long. We could hypothesize that the increasing importance of commerce in things has introduced a certain stability into the world, by giving most people the impression that ownership of a small number of material things produces some sort of equality, or at least blurs the sense of inequality. But this is an illusion that is becoming more and more fragile. For the development of what is called the immaterial economy has come about precisely because payment for access – that is, payment according to the logic of renting rather than that of changing ownership – has been privileged. In addition, the most critical property rights are very seldom granted, and only at prices that put them out of reach for ordinary mortals, namely, intellectual property rights: these make it possible, above all, to reserve for oneself the exclusive right to reproduce the thing in question or to charge for simple access to it.

This approach, in which we examine commerce in things and take their prices into account, leads us to deviate from two major sociological traditions. The first consists in treating things with an emphasis on the work involved and, more broadly, on the professional practices behind the production and even the commercialization of these things; this approach generally leads to giving special importance to the distinction between goods and services. The second consists in treating things as social signs of intergroup relations. Nevertheless, even when prices are taken into account, it is still possible to focus, as Viviana Zelizer has done, on the way the price is paid and to proceed as though the form of the expense were socially marked; this would make it possible to differentiate among different sorts of currencies that are perceived as defining social bonds.[18] Although the issue of how the price of a thing is paid – in cash, by credit card, by electronic transfer, and so on – is not unimportant, it is not a primary focus of our own work.

Changing hands

Commerce in things takes place during transactions that are at once *events* and *tests* – that is, transactions that blend the world – what is happening – and reality, inasmuch as reality is constructed and as it qualifies what it selects from the world.[19] A transaction is an event to the extent that, when a change of hands takes place in the world, it always has a circumstantial character: I bought a certain pen at a certain place and at a certain time, whereas I may not have planned to do so, or I bought two when I had planned to buy one, or I bought this one when I had thought I would buy the one next to it, and so on. But, at the same time, the sale was contractual: the thing had been assigned a price, and a change of ownership occurred. Thus a transaction is also a test that takes place in a certain format, internalizing the circumstances within a constructed reality.

A thing is not a sign but, rather, a material object that can be seen; it can be heard if one taps on it or if it emits a sound, like a clock ticking; it can be smelled, as one breathes in the odor of glue in a new book upon opening it for the first time; and it can be touched.[20] Nevertheless, as is the case with signs, whose meaning is established on the one hand with respect to other signs and on the other with respect to an external reality to which they refer, a thing, considered from the standpoint of its value, is also defined with reference to something external to it, namely, the lack experienced by the person who is seeking the thing.

Let us add that not all the qualities of a thing are disclosed by the test of looking or by the tests imposed by the other senses. For a thing to reveal its qualities, it has to be experienced, and not just in the moment but over a more or less lengthy period of time. In the commercial moment, it is especially by relying on the description offered by the seller that the buyer can hope to eliminate any ambiguity. But the seller may not be sincere, may lie, or may hide certain information that is not available to the senses. The buyer needs to be able to trust the seller, and, for this to happen, the buyer must make sure the seller is telling the truth about the thing in question (although it is of course possible for a seller to be sincere but mistaken).

Commerce in things is thus confronted with *uncertainty*. This uncertainty may bear on the persons who are interacting or on the thing that is the object of commerce. But the level of uncertainty can be unequal, depending on the viewpoint of the parties involved. From the viewpoint of the person offering an object for exchange, the uncertainty has to do especially with the intentions of the person who may take it. Has that person decided to take it, and under what conditions? Does that person really have the means to produce what is required in exchange for the thing? From the viewpoint of the person who might take the thing, the uncertainty has to do with the thing itself. Does it meet that person's expectations? Or, in other words, is it capable of compensating for a lack, filling in a gap that is driving the person's search? This uncertainty bears inextricably on the person who is making the offer. Has that person not dressed up the thing so it will appear more appealing than it really is? Can one trust what that person says about it in describing the thing? Finally, does that person really own the thing on offer?

These uncertainties may take on different characteristics, however, depending on whether the transaction takes place remotely or locally, according to the distinction analyzed by Fernand Braudel.[21] What Braudel calls internal commerce is a situation in which the persons interacting have a certain prior familiarity with one another, through direct experience, by reputation, or as a function of their status. These are also situations in which the object of commerce is usually fairly well known to both parties, or, we might say, typified. The ideal type for such a case is the marketplace in traditional rural societies. In such a situation, face-to-face contact allows the person who covets a thing to put the person offering it to a *test* in various ways. Internal commerce thus tends to be governed according to the mode of interaction that is described as stemming from practice.[22] Commerce carried out in this mode makes it possible to diminish uncertainty not only about persons but also about the things involved – that is, about whether the thing on offer actually has a referential relationship to the lack that has motivated the search. In this mode, the specific properties of things (often called their "singularity") are not obstacles to commerce. Things that are presented as similar, in a certain light, may turn out to be dissimilar, in the sense that the interaction can make it clear that they do not correspond to the same lack. Conversely, things that appear different may turn out to correspond to the same lack. The success of these adjustments depends on the competence that the interacting persons bring to bear on the situation in order to reach agreement.

By contrast, in the case of external commerce, senders and receivers are unknown to one another and, in principle, may be anyone at all. Precisely because the thing in question comes from elsewhere, the receiver may have trouble identifying it accurately. For agreement to be reached in this second kind of situation, of which worldwide trade in things difficult to evaluate constitutes the ideal type, the relation has to be supported by forms interposed between those who are proposing something and those who are seeking something, forms recognized as well founded by both sides. These forms often emerge from practical relations that seek trust (this is why they may rely on familial or community relations),[23] but they have no chance of being imposed in an effective and lasting way unless they are sustained by institutions. From a linguistic standpoint, onto the pragmatic adjustments that are always made when a commercial situation is initiated, the action of institutions grafts a *semantics* that the actors in a transaction can use so as to facilitate its progress and reduce the costs that must be accepted if agreement is to be reached (the transaction costs); this semantics is designed to stabilize the qualification of specific things in terms that will have legal validity.[24] Institutions also have the role of determining at least some qualities associated with the persons involved; in particular, they establish the property rights that those persons have over the things in question. In other words, institutions give legal expression to the attachment between things and persons.

In the process, institutions reduce the uncertainty that is always inherent in commercial situations. Freed from the viewpoint adopted toward things by individual persons, who are necessarily situated in particular contexts, institutions can claim to be qualifying things in themselves and appreciating them as they would be revealed to the gaze of an unembodied being.[25] This type of claim is accompanied by the presentation of guarantees bearing upon both persons and things. The person who offers a thing is indeed its owner (she has a title to the property); she indeed possesses the identity she claims as her own (she has identifying documents); as for the thing on offer, it can be described in terms that correspond accurately to its characteristics, or at least to some of them, and the description can in principle be known to all. The action of institutions does not completely eliminate the uncertainty of the situation and the concern it arouses, but it tends to shift these feelings away from the persons between whom the transaction is occurring and from the things that are the object of the transaction onto the institutions that guarantee both persons and things.

In the case of transactions involving words, the principal role of a semantics of commerce is to stabilize the relative value of the terms and their references in the case of a transaction requiring words, and thus to stabilize the meaning of the state of affairs. And, in the case of transactions involving things, the role of a semantics of commerce is to stabilize the relation among the various things proposed and to orient the referential relation between certain lacks and certain things – that is, to propose a more or less stable point around which the price of those things can oscillate. By deploying such a semantics, institutions make possible a virtually unlimited extension of circulation zones by removing the obstacle of distance.

Nevertheless, the significant modifications introduced by the Internet into the means of production and transportation and, simultaneously, into the means of selling and buying have considerably reorganized the relation between remote and local commerce for a great many things, especially those we call standard, although the distinction still applies for certain objects, such as works of art. Why can someone buy a vacuum cleaner or a computer on an e-commerce site at a fixed price or a nineteenth-century gold watch offered on an auction site, while no collector will buy a painting by Picasso on such a site (at least given the way sales sites are currently organized) but will instead go to examine the painting in person, or delegate someone else to look at it and report back, before proceeding to make a purchase? To be able to answer this question, we need to hypothesize that the value of things is established in a variety of ways, and that these differing valuations have consequences for the ways things are offered for sale, whether locally or remotely.

The process of determination

For a thing to be commercializable, a necessary condition is that it be determinable and determinate: in other words, its qualification, or the characterization of its properties, must be such that it can be shared with seller and buyer alike.

Classification of the entities that make up one's environment is a universal phenomenon. As Lévi-Strauss notes, systematic classification "clearly cannot relate just to practical purposes"; rather, "it meets intellectual requirements rather than or instead of satisfying needs." It aims to introduce "some initial order … into the universe" by marking what "can be seen, from a certain standpoint, "as 'going together,'" for "classifying, as opposed to not classifying," has a value of its own, whatever form the classification may take."[26] The various ways of classifying and distributing things among categories, which are most often designated by name but which may also remain implicit, are generally common within the context of a collectivity, although the various subsets of which the collectivity is composed, in their practical relations to things, can bring into play partially divergent classifications.[27]

Nevertheless, our focus here is narrower than Lévi-Strauss's. In the vast universe of classifications, the type of classification that interests us concerns things only inasmuch as they are *commodities*. This method of classification is distinctive in that it encompasses things in two very different respects. On the one hand, it takes into account certain of their properties – usually qualities perceptible to the senses and/or functional properties associated with use; this occurs constantly in our ordinary relation to objects. On the other hand, it is concerned with the way in which a *price* – which is not a quality of things, since it depends on circumstances and on the format of the transaction test – can be attributed to a thing in the course of an exchange. Considered in this light, two things with identical functions – for example a plastic footstool and a Louis XV footstool, both of which can serve as seats – will not be determined as belonging to the same class, not only because, during a sale, they will be priced very differently but especially because the way the prices are set and the argument used to justify (or criticize) those prices will be very different in nature. We shall thus say that objects considered as commodities are distributed among classes that take into account not only their perceptible and/or functional properties but also the form of valuation that is used to establish their prices. Two plastic stools of industrial origin can be determined as belonging more or less to the same class. We could say the same thing about a Louis XV armchair and a wing chair from the same period. In ordinary circumstances, nothing keeps either of these from being treated as more or less substitutable for the other. But it requires extraordinary circumstances for a plastic chair and a Louis XV chair to be determined as belonging to the same class – for example, circumstances in which sitting down is a question of life or death, and in which the number of postulants would be much higher than the number of seats available for sale. And, under the effect of panic, the various seats, whether ordinary or precious, would lose their status as commodities, in the sense that the establishment of their prices would no longer depend on anything but the urgency that prevailed in such a situation. It would not be an exaggeration to say that they would become priceless.

More generally, for a price to be attributed to a thing (whether it is predetermined by the supplier or revealed at the conclusion of the transaction), the thing must be *determinate*. An indeterminate thing cannot be appreciated for a simple reason: since prices have no meaning except in relation to one another, the price of any one thing can be established only in relation to the prices of other things. If the thing in question is not determinate, there is no way to grant it a place in the cosmos of commodities, no way to compare it with other things and thereby to assign it a price in relation to other prices. The price of an indeterminate thing can be anything at all, which amounts to saying that the thing is priceless. Thus, for example, a pebble, as such, is not appreciable. I pick it up on the shore and offer it to you. You may reject it, accept it without giving me anything in exchange, or give me a few cents as an act of charity if I look really poor or mentally ill. This indeterminate naked pebble is not a commodity and has, in itself, no price. But, by contrast, it can be appreciated inasmuch as it belongs to a pile of pebbles destined to be crushed to make construction material (the pile can be weighed and priced) or inasmuch as it has been chosen by an artist who spotted it, selected it, and used it in such a way as to make it a work of art. To say that the thing is determinate thus necessarily signifies that it has been attributed to a class of commercial objects and also, usually, that it has been given a name that allows it to be easily determined by being attributed to that class.

Raw materials, especially when they are extracted from under ground (as opposed to raw materials from living sources), have properties that are more readily determinable than are those of elaborately worked artifacts. This is no doubt why precious metals, which have not only the property of being rare but also that of purporting to be uniform, are in some sense predestined to play the role of general equivalent that has been conferred on them. Owing to their plasticity, they have some independence with respect to the form that is given them at certain points in time, since they can always be melted down and brought back in a different form. Where precious metals are involved, the principal information, often difficult to establish, bears on the degree to which the final product also incorporates other metals. This is why, even in this latter case, and perhaps above all in this case, institutions based on political authority have been set up to establish and guarantee the value of things that incorporate these metals, in relation to the percentage of precious metal included in alloys.

As the example of precious metals predisposed by their plasticity to serve as general equivalents suggests, commerce in things, during which their prices are set, is confronted with a central question regarding their singularity. All things are singular in the sense that they are all supports for differences that may be recognized or not, depending on the scale adopted for their consideration. One can grasp this by taking metaphysical recourse to fractal objects – for example, a coastline, whose segmentation is a function of the scale used.[28] A given contour, appearing smooth on one scale, reveals the irregularities that mark it when it is represented on a smaller scale. But the metaphor of fractals is not limited to spatial representations. It is also valid for all the operations of establishing equivalencies on which categorization rests, whether these bear on human beings brought together in groups or on things distributed under nomenclatures of types or species, at the price of smoothing over certain of the differences that distinguish them in order to highlight the specific relation in terms of which they have been juxtaposed.

The question of the singularity of things and of persons – of their properties, in the first case, and of their lacks, in the second – is at the heart of commercial relations. In fact, in a possible world in which every thing and every lack would be irremediably singular, their adjustment would be highly implausible and afflicted with radical uncertainty. Moreover, it is in order to leave room for this implausibility that the logic of love (a relation that needs no justification) is invoked, whether the term is taken in the sense of an elective relationship among persons or in a theological sense. In both cases, the intent is to mark the gap that separates relations that do not depend on systems of equivalence from relations that are established by the ordinary forms of commerce.

Nevertheless, we shall also exclude raw materials from our study. In fact, we shall limit ourselves to the realm of things that are not only material and movable but also reproducible. If one can extract raw materials, such as oil, from a deposit, or if one can renew the production of a raw material, as with rice, the mode of production involved is not that of reproduction in the strict sense, even though one could theoretically imagine a mode of production by reproduction – for example, a situation in which synthesized raw materials are produced in the same way that an imaginary world of human and animal clones might be produced. However, given the way reality is socially organized, in these early years of the twenty-first century the question of digital reproduction – a central concern, from both the legal and the economic standpoints, especially where the accumulation of profit is involved – distributes things very clearly on one side or the other, as reproducible or not. The only major rupture at the moment has to do with the mode of digital reproduction, for example of music, films, or books, which are nevertheless no longer material, mobile things, even though they are supported by such things (computers, tablets, smartphones); access to these immaterial and immovable things is commercialized, but not ownership as such, for ownership would make it possible to reproduce them at will.

In addition, the fact that things have to be determined does not prevent new determinations from appearing, while others disappear or, more precisely, no longer appear except as recorded in archives, or even perhaps in material form in specimens preserved, typically, in a collection. Any classification of things is thus destined to evolve, and new classifications can be formed when hitherto unheard-of things are invented. Among the most characteristic items introduced in the 2010s, we might cite the smartphones and tablets we have just mentioned, multifunctional objects that combine the functions of telephones, cameras, and computers but that cannot be reduced to any one of these qualifications, and thus have inaugurated new classes of objects.

Price and metaprice

Considered in isolation and in itself, as it were, a price is meaningless. It is a sign written in the language of arithmetic, referring both to a thing and to a currency; in other words, it is simultaneously inscribed as a measurement within a monetary system and assigned to a thing.

In a commercial transaction, the price is never anything but a sign associated with a thing. From this perspective, the price is not interpreted as a sign of the relative social positions of persons; it is not the symbol of a social distinction. "That watch has been sold for $100" informs us that, under specific circumstances, someone paid $100 in exchange for a particular watch, in cash, with a check, by credit card, or through an online transfer. An indication of this sort tells us nothing about the watch except its price and the fact that the price is expressed in a certain currency.

Although each thing is singular and so is each exchange, a change of hands is achieved by using a general equivalent – money – so that this metric, valid in a sovereign political community, can always be invoked even in situations of circulation that do not refer to money directly (as in barter or inheritance). As the monetary metric can be involved in any transaction whatsoever, and as the quantity of money at a given operator's disposal is limited (even if it is very high), it is always possible to establish a parallel between the sum of money expended to obtain a specific thing and the sum that would have been expended to obtain a different thing. Consequently, it is always possible to consider that the sum in question would have been, or would be, better used elsewhere (or should have been set aside for use in a future exchange). This way of looking at involvement in a transaction, which is the chief consideration of agents who invest in view of future profits, is always more or less present, or at least latent, in ordinary commercial relationships. Why deprive oneself of a $25 restaurant meal in order to buy a coveted new $250 watch when, with patience, one might well find a used version of the same model on an auction site at a much lower price?

During an exchange, the diversity of things is reduced by the fact that all things are translated into an identical metric that establishes, or seems to establish, a form of equivalence among them. "My kingdom for a horse" is an utterance – a cry! – whose strangeness reveals the speaker's despair. However, if "the kingdom" and "the horse" are associated with a metric capable of establishing an equivalence between them, in a given situation nothing prevents the marginal usefulness of a kingdom from being equivalent to the marginal usefulness of a horse.[29] We shall thus assume, as neoclassical economics does, that a single semantics, that of prices, makes it possible to carry out the translation between these two entities, despite their extreme heterogeneity: a kingdom and a horse. This assumption does not hold, however, in most transactions that actually occur, and that is why King Richard's utterance, impelled by despair, seems to us to border on the absurd. For the modes according to which a kingdom (something that is usually transmitted or conquered) is evaluated and acquired have little in common with the usual modes according to which a horse is evaluated and acquired (a horse being usually evaluated in terms of the services it can render, and usually exchanged for money). And the reasons for wanting to acquire a kingdom are very different from the reasons for wanting to acquire a horse.

The always possible detour by way of money is what permits us to relate things among which there would be no common measure – since they differ in most respects – if their prices were not taken into account. The consideration of prices alone allows us to situate them in the same space for calculation. Nevertheless, this operation confers a relative character on the things considered in terms of their prices, at least to the extent that the price of a given thing is always viewed in comparison to the prices of other things expressed in the same currency or converted into other currencies. There is no such thing as the "price of a priceless thing" in the sense that such a thing would be ideally, and in a sense essentially, incapable of valuation, even though in practical terms it may turn out to be encumbered with a price.

The price of a thing is not its description. This is why, on the one hand, quite different things may have the same price, while, on the other hand, identical things may have very different prices, depending on the circumstances and on the format of the test. Given that every price depends on the state of affairs in which it is revealed, there is no reason for prices to be stable in space or time. For them to be stable, at a minimum, the thing in question would first have to have been *determined*, in the sense we have given this term: that is, the definition of the thing or things to which the price refers would have to have been stabilized. Next, the circumstances of the exchange would have to have been stabilized, in particular by making the exchange independent of the personalities of the partners involved, so that the price would not vary if the seller were replaced by a different seller and/or if the buyer were replaced by a different buyer.

Each price thus has meaning only insofar as it is inserted into a field of relationships in which we have identified, for the time being, three components. First, the relation between the price and the thing submitted for exchange. The price is thereby, on the same basis as a linguistic sign for Saussure,[30] a twofold entity in the sense that it exists only in relation to a thing with which it is nevertheless not confused. Second, the relation between the price of a thing and the monetary circumstances on which the actors in the exchange – buyers and sellers – can count, a relation whose intensity brings to bear a constraint on the actors' inclination to commit themselves to a given transaction. But these two relations, invested in each singular exchange (which always has a circumstantial character), become meaningful themselves only in the presence of a third component, namely, the relation between each particular price and the prices of the various things whose interconnections constitute what is customarily considered to be reality. Each price is thereby associated with a value, not in the economic sense, here, but rather in the linguistic sense (for Saussure, the term "value" derives from its use in aesthetics to mark variations in tone),[31] since its salience appears only through reference to other prices, revealed by other exchanges (whether these prices are related to things considered, rightly or wrongly, as similar), or to things treated as radically different.

In more or less stable situations, where there are no surprises in the relation between prices and things, the conventional price, which we can call the *standard* or *regular price*, is generally viewed as the "fair price." By referring to this "fair price," one can formulate a reproach aimed not so much at the order of prices considered as a consistent entity as, on the moral level, at the persons deliberately imposing prices viewed as excessive and allowing those persons to realize a big profit, either because the sellers are making personal determinations and are charging different prices according to the characteristics of the buyer or because they are exploiting shortages in a period of scarcity – as Raymond de Roover has shown with respect to the economic thinking of the scholastics.[32] The metric of prices thus seems sufficient in such cases to allow judgment to be passed on the fairness of the exchange. But the same cannot be said of situations in which the structure of relative prices appears highly disorganized: this is something social actors grasp owing to their own experience, but also owing to information spread by the media through reports of "unbelievable" prices established in one place or another (for example, the current pricing of works of art when they are sold at "exorbitant" auctions) or through complacent displays of luxury at its most excessive. In these historical situations, the prices of things no longer seem to be in harmony with the importance that social actors, for the most part, have been accustomed to attributing to them.

Beyond the three relational components previously mentioned, we now need to identify three principal properties of a price.

The first is that prices are *real* to the extent that they effectively sanction the result of the *test* constituted by every commercial exchange. In language echoing that of the early Wittgenstein, we can say that prices are *facts* in the sense in which, *by taking place*, they belong to a certain *state of affairs*.

The second is that prices have the advantage of relying on a metric that allows for collectively shared measurements. These two properties confer on them the type of robustness that is generally attributed to entities said to be *objective*.

But prices have a third property: they have a *circumstantial* character (and it is in this respect that one can say that the prices that emerge at the conclusion of every exchange have to be understood as *events*). The price of a thing is not attached to it as though it were a relatively stable property such as, for example, its dimensions or its substance. On the one hand, the price of a thing can vary according to the circumstances of the exchange and especially according to the power relations that are instituted between the participants – this is the case, for example, when the vendor has an urgent need to sell, or when the client lacks ready access to other situations of exchange, either because they do not exist or are not close at hand (monopoly situations) or because the client is attached to the vendor by other types of social bonds. On the other hand, the price depends most often on the way in which the thing is inscribed in temporality. And temporality comes into play in different modalities in relation to the economic sphere with which the thing is associated, especially depending on whether this sphere belongs to what we are calling the *standard* form or instead to the *collection* form. In the first case, the price of a thing will go down over time, while in the second case it is very likely to go up. Thus, for example, the price of a certain old watch will diminish over time if it is sold on the used goods market; conversely, its price will rise if it is perceived as an antique watch destined for collectors.

The circumstantial nature of prices makes problematic a question that occupies a central position in economics, that of their *aggregation*, particularly when actual transactions depart from the idealized model of pure and perfect competition; this is the case for a large number of commodities, perhaps even for most. It should be noted in passing that this question is very similar to the one that sociology encounters when it has to come up with conceptual means and methods for understanding the formation of *collectivities* on the basis of the interactions among persons who, being at once singular and endowed with multiple properties, are disposed to connect with one another via a plurality of different relationships under different historical circumstances and thus to be *aggregated* within different "categories" or "groups."

Similar problems arise if we consider not prices or persons but things themselves. Even in the case of industrial products, the shift on the part of clients from one particular product to a substitute raises the thorny problem of the modes through which different objects are determined to be equivalent. For, if prices are indeed set with reference to a collective measurement, the same thing does not hold true for the things themselves: their similarities can always be found wanting when their *differences* are taken into account, and this can lead to endless confusion and debate about whether a specific less costly item is indeed similar to a specific more costly item. In many cases, it is the *latest difference* (in Bourdieu's sense)[33] that will distinguish a costly but *fashionable* item from a functionally similar but outdated or otherwise unfashionable item.

If, as we have indicated, a price taken in isolation is meaningless in itself, we must then consider that, rather than a single price, there are always at least two, one belonging both to the event and to the test constituted by the change in ownership of a thing, and at least one other, with which the first is compared but which is not, generally speaking, the price paid. This "second" price is what we shall call a *metaprice*, in the sense in which it does not apply to the thing involved in an exchange; instead, it refers to the operations during which prices are set.

Certain economists and marketing professionals have identified a large number of prices with different characteristics. "Pricing" – price-setting techniques derived from marketing practices – differs from price-setting based on costs (direct and indirect manufacturing costs plus a sort of marginal cost conceived as compensation for the risk taken by the entrepreneur); pricing techniques are designed to take into account in particular the consumer's "consent to pay," so as to institute a range of "acceptable prices" that are set at different levels for different "segments" of the potential public. Price-setting thus becomes a central element in the "strategic management" deployed by vendors, so that the same item can be sold at quite variable prices according to the place and the circumstances of the transaction.[34] As examples, we can cite the following: the establishment of "thresholds of acceptability" to which variable or marginal "multiplier coefficients" correspond; situations, especially those involving high-end or luxury products, in which the inverted relation between lower prices and increased demand is taken into account; the determination, for a given product, of a price spread in relation to a categorization of potential buyers perceived as belonging to groups whose expectations and means are presumed to be different; methods of price-setting that rely on a practice of "price-tracking" that makes it possible to establish a price with reference to the competing prices proposed by other vendors for objects deemed "similar" (this procedure is illegal in the European Union but widely practiced nevertheless); temporary "promotions" of certain products or "loss leader" prices intended to attract attention to a product, a practice that may imply a loss accepted for a predefined period in the hope of making up for it by an increase in the volume of demand by loyal customers able to tolerate higher prices at a later date; and, last but not least, yield management, which – in the case of transportation, for example – determines prices as a function of the relation between supply and demand at a given moment, as users of the French high-speed train system (TGV) know first-hand: the price for a given destination can increase by a factor of 10 depending on the date on which the purchase is made and the date of travel.[35]

The various *pricing* techniques, developed under the stimulus of supply-side economic theories, tend to make prices "flexible" – that is, they tend to distort the relation between things and their prices. These techniques are meant, of course, to counter *price controls*, those established by government authorities or by some other regulatory body. Rather in the way that, in their "proper usage," grammarians are accused of rigidifying language instead of leaving it to popular inventiveness and the inspiration of innovative writers, these administrative entities are accused of pinning down arrangements of equivalence in order to fix in place an economic activity that supply-side economists conceive along vitalist lines, as changeable and in essence free. Don't price controls, in this view, inevitably spur transgressions, "black markets" in the case in point? Nevertheless, the impetus toward flexibility, especially when it occurs in a period marked by profound change in the sources of wealth creation and profit formation, tends to disorient a number of actors whose cognitive maps and interpretive abilities prove inadequate, and who are thus encouraged to seek to acquire means that will allow them to pass a *judgment* considered "reasonable" and also more or less "stable" concerning the price of things – that is, both on the nature of the things in question and on the level of their prices.

A *metaprice* can take the form of the kind of prices developed most notably by marketing professionals. The metaprice is distinguished from the "real" price in that, without being either the price resulting from an event or the price resulting from a test, it can nevertheless appear simultaneously in the circumstances of the event and in the format of the test. We can say that, in the statement "this watch is worth $100," "$100" can designate a "real" price if the watch in question has actually been sold and bought for $100; it can designate a metaprice if "$100" corresponds to an assessment of the watch, in which case $100 could be a reserve price for an auction featuring watches, a quote for watches of the same type, or a price fixed for insurance purposes if the watch belongs, for example, to a museum collection.

Metaprices proliferate, and it would be worthwhile to study them systematically, following the model of pragmatically oriented analyses of social reality. They come into play in particular in the composition of insurance prices, estimates of remedial costs (for instance, following incidents of pollution),[36] estimates of future goods, or interest rates; they can take the form of quotes (for objects in collections, such as stamps, for example), or they can function as "reserve prices" in the case of auctions, and so on. Similarly, in bargaining situations, the highest price, stated first by the vendor, and the lowest price, stated first by the customer, can be viewed as metaprices inasmuch as neither is very likely to be achieved at the conclusion of the transaction.

Metaprices are not facts; they do not belong to events, but they appear in the situations that precede and follow events. They are *meta-* in that they are a structure for reflection on prices (discussion, comparison, criticism, justification, and so on). They are attributed to things under the heading of *estimates*, which can be based on very diverse and unequally realistic foundations; in other words, metaprices can be viewed as *potentialities* treated as capable of realization but only if they are projected into different circumstantial contexts – other places or other times – whose contours are simply sketched out, or even just *imagined*, without leading to any effort to realize them.

Metaprices are fictional entities, in the sense that they have little chance of being realized in the situation of exchange under consideration, and even in the sense that nothing guarantees that another situation exists somewhere in which they would actually be applied. Nevertheless, they have real effects on the interactions between the partners in the exchange. In the best of cases, they can facilitate coordination by serving as reference points. Conversely, they can make coordination more difficult by establishing chimerical expectations, sources of frustration that can readily be transmuted into criticism.

However, a metaprice can sometimes converge with a real price: for instance, in a case where the quote for a certain type of watch is $100 and where a watch of that type is sold and bought for $100, the exact amount of the quote. This type of situation is extremely rare, and, to take an example in which the quote plays a very important role, that of a stamp in a collection, not only is the real price of a collector's stamp historically, from the very beginning of stamp collecting, always lower than the quote, but the gap between the quote and the real price has increased with commercialization via Internet sites.[37] It is true that, in the case of controlled prices of standardized objects, as is the case for books in France, the metaprice is often the same as the real price. Nevertheless, it is important to recall that the market for new books coexists with a market for used books, and that, on this secondary market, books presented as new, provided by press services, for example, or books in like-new condition can be sold at lower real prices, in which case the price of the new books becomes a metaprice.

Critiquing the price

The price at which a thing is offered or yielded can often be contested, because the conditions under which a transaction takes place are often contestable. Such situations, which for neoclassical economics are signs of an "imperfection in the market," are perhaps in reality the most common ones, if only inasmuch as actual commercial relations rarely conform to the economic model of the perfect market.

Contesting a price, as Albert Hirschman has shown, can take two different forms.[38] The first is silent; it is manifested by the abandonment of one supplier for another (the "exit" modality) – in other words, by competition. The second is expressed verbally (the "voice" modality), and it is called for especially when the commercial environment is insufficiently competitive.

Challenging a price always entails bringing into play a difference in *power* between seller(s) and buyer(s). The power differential can be interpreted through the model of pure and perfect competition, as is the case, for example, when it is clear that sellers can fix the price of a thing to their own advantage because they have a monopoly on the supply of something desired by a large number of buyers. It can be the case if a single seller holds the desired item, or if several sellers agree to join forces (in a tacit or covert agreement that is often described as a sort of conspiracy aiming to undermine the competition) in the face of a multiplicity of buyers, each of whom acts independently and enters into the exchange with no power beyond his or her own. The defense of the buyers' interest thus presupposes two operations. The first consists in uncovering the secret bond that unites the sellers – for instance, exposing a "yogurt cartel" in which major groups in the agro-food industry have secretly agreed to fix the price of yogurt. This operation can take the form of an investigation followed by a penalty imposed, for example, by an independent authority (such as, in the United States, the Federal Trade Commission or the Antitrust Division in the Department of Justice) if the existence of a secret agreement is brought to light. The second operation consists in seeking to promote unity among buyers, by setting up associations such as consumer organizations or by creating unions in a workplace.

Another operation (which may be associated with the first) consists in showing that the information possessed by the parties involved is *asymmetrical*, in situations where the challenge to a price may be based on the fact that there is a significant imbalance between the information available to the actor who holds the thing in question (the seller) and the one who wishes to acquire it (the buyer). In situations like these, certain operators may conclude that the price has not been set in relation to the thing itself but depends on the relation instituted, in the circumstances of the exchange, between the seller and the buyer, a relation that can be expressed in terms of power. This is the case if the seller has an urgent need to sell something (for instance, she has to flee her country for political reasons) and has no possibility of putting several buyers in competition, or, conversely, if the buyer has a pressing need for a thing that he cannot find elsewhere at a lower price.

In a situation of pure and perfect competition, contesting a price would always be expressed tacitly by exiting from the transaction and giving preference to a different seller. However, as has often been demonstrated, it is very hard to show in a convincing way that a given commercial situation actually entails pure and perfect competition. Such competition in fact relies on conditions so demanding that they rarely occur together in the concrete situations of exchange that interest sociologists. These conditions include the following, among others: perfect and total homogeneity among the objects in competition (they are of the same "quality"); equal geographic accessibility and thus equal costs of access (this condition is met only in a face-to-face marketplace); and complete independence of each exchange in relation to other exchanges and with respect to other types of interaction, in particular a complete absence of relations of dependence among sellers (monopolies), among buyers (boycott), and between sellers and buyers (clientelism). All these conditions are constitutive of the neoclassical models.

Finally, to validate the argument that pure and perfect competition exists, it must be possible to bring together a vast set of presumably independent exchanges. Yet aggregating these multiple exchanges is problematic. Each exchange takes place in a particular situation. To aggregate them, one must be able to show that they are perfectly independent of one another while being similar in all respects. First of all, the objects offered must be identical (which is plausible only when specimens of a single prototype are involved), or at least more or less similar (but in this case their similarity can easily be contested). Next, the circumstances of the exchange must also be identical.[39] This is rarely the case, if only owing to differences in geographical distance or ease of access. A buyer living in the heart of a city, for example, will agree to pay more for an item near her home than it would cost in a discount store in the suburbs.

More generally, the price of a thing is always more or less circumstantial, since it is the result of a test during which the thing changes hands, a test that is on the order of an event and thus cannot be dissociated from the circumstances in which it occurs. Prices can be, and often are, more or less regulated or controlled (under pressure from a governmental authority) – that is, they can be standardized, at least in a specific geographic area. In other words, laws or regulations may require that things of a certain type be offered at the same prices wherever they are sold, as is the case for books in France; here the intent may be to conflate prices with metaprices or to control the situations in which prices are lowered, for example the period when sales are allowed (which does not preclude dumping). But, for large numbers of things in circulation, prices depend principally on each situation of exchange. This is particularly true for used or second-hand goods, whose similarity with other objects that have certain (but not all) properties in common can be contested, and which are offered for sale in widely varying commercial circumstances.

During each exchange, taken separately, a thing finds its expression in a monetary amount, a metaprice, that can be fixed by the seller before the exchange or can be determined following a negotiation, as is the case where bargaining occurs. But since each exchange is a singular event – the encounter between a seller and a buyer in a specific context – the price has a circumstantial character. The "same" thing may have changed hands, or may change hands in the future, at different prices, and "similar" things may be offered at different prices in different situations of exchange (the latter case being the basis for competition). A world in which knowledge about things was limited to their prices would be subject to arbitrariness and contingency. In the absence of information about the sellers and the buyers, and especially about the things exchanged, and thus in the absence of metaprices, knowledge of prices would not suffice to submit the exchanges to an ordering principle, and competition would be haphazard. If this contingency is to be reduced, a price must be associated with specifications bearing on the things (and the persons) involved, if only so that one can say about a thing that it is "the same" at different points in time and about two things that they are "similar" – that is, that these things can be inscribed in a test format.

It follows that the prices of things are always open to contestation, in particular through reference to metaprices, so that arguments and, where possible, concrete arrangements for testing must be available in order to justify them. Thus even in situations that purport to involve competition (situations from which the buyers are presumed to be able to exit), the sellers are inclined to justify the things they are offering, and this is one of the functions of advertising. This requirement of justification is also imposed on the buyers, whether they must justify to third parties the price they have agreed to pay for a certain item or whether they intend to criticize the price proposed. The requirement of justification is suspended only in situations where the power relation between the partners in the exchange reaches such a high degree of asymmetry that the sellers can dispense with justifications ("take it or leave it"). For example, a company or a government may have a monopoly on the sale of an absolutely necessary thing (a supply of electric power or a train ticket), while a buyer with an imperative need for that thing has no hope of obtaining it elsewhere at a lower price and thus cannot exit. Or buyers may agree to boycott certain things at the price being proposed, which supposes recourse to strategies of *voicing* (the seller cannot hope to find another customer who will pay the price that he is asking for the thing). We must now clarify the way in which the price and its justification are connected through recourse to the notion of value.

Value as justification for a price

We shall define *value*[40] as an arrangement for *justifying a price*. The price of a thing does not always need to be justified, and in practice the prices of the ordinary things that we acquire on an everyday basis are rarely subjected to justification. When the justification of a price does occur, it may be a response to a challenge to the proposed price (the classic case where a justification responds to a critique), or it may be presented prior to the purchase, to reassure the potential buyer, as it were, that there are good reasons for the act he or she is about to perform. From this standpoint, the question of value can be clarified if we detach it from its ontological and moral significations.[41]

Connecting value to the price of a thing may allow us to solve what can be called the mystery of value that has been facing sociology since Émile Durkheim addressed the issue. Indeed, Durkheim himself expressed astonishment at the "value" of luxury items, "which cost most ... not only because they are often the most rare; it is because they are also the most esteemed": similarly, he was struck by the fact that a postage stamp, "a thin square of paper, ... may be worth a fortune." While Durkheim understood that value did not lie in things themselves, he attributed the fixation on things to "collective ideals," so that "a value judgment expresses the relation of a thing to an ideal." This is why, in his view, a (good) soldier would die to save his flag, even though "a flag is only a bit of cloth."[42] However, Durkheim simply posits the link between the value of a thing and the collective ideal without explaining it (it is indeed inexplicable), and he conflates two senses of the word "value." On the one hand, in his effort to establish the relation between value and such things as luxury goods or precious pieces of paper, he fails to refer to the prices of the things – yet astonishment about the value of a thing is meaningful only in connection with astonishment about its price. On the other hand, the value of a flag depends on the fact that it symbolically represents the nation of which the soldier is a subject: by saving the flag, the soldier is defending his country. This confusion has frequently been carried over, especially when Dewey is also a source of inspiration,[43] into the most recent economic sociology. It leads to a moralization of economics and its critique, linking "value" to "values," and considering that "all the really interesting questions about economic value are always, inextricably, tied to questions about moral economy," as David Stark argues.[44] Stark relates prices, in the sense of economic analysis, to the ordinary expression "paying a price," taking as an example a painter who has won fame "without paying a price" for it – that is, without being creative. The term "price," for Stark, refers to the relation between "differing orders of *worth*."[45]

If a price cannot be understood in itself but can be understood only in relation to other prices, referring to the value of a thing from the standpoint of an exchange presupposes that there are several forms of valuation applicable to that thing, hence the establishment of metaprices. Indeed, if things were always exchanged in the same way, and thus for the same prices, there would be no need to refer to value, and there would be no metaprices.

The value of a thing, when it comes into play in an exchange (which is generally the case), is not stabilized once and for all; rather, it is the result of a *process of valuation* that belongs to the order of events rather than to the order of facts. This is the case in most of the exchanges that punctuate daily life, but it is also the case when actors use pre-established methods for determining value, resorting to mathematical calculations. Thus, for example, the determination of the value of a business can be very different depending on whether it is based on an estimate of the actual prices of its various components (compared to the prices of things deemed similar that have been exchanged during the same time period) – this can be called its legacy value – or whether, instead, the firm's potential for growth and return on investments are emphasized – that is, whether the estimate has been made according to the logic of capitalization. The value of a thing, insofar as it is an interpretation, thus depends on the way in which that thing is evaluated.

If one wishes to challenge the framework of a transaction viewed as a test, one must be able to criticize the test as being affected by circumstances (for example, power relations) – that is, one must refer to the value of a thing in order to negotiate its price while proposing one or more metaprices. This requires the existence of a semantics that includes several forms of valuation.

A buyer who wants to obtain a reliable watch so she will be on time for her professional appointments may find that the price proposed by a merchant selling used watches is excessive for a watch that is several decades old. But this buyer has not understood that the watch in question is a Brand X watch, highly sought after by collectors. As a second-hand watch intended for use, the watch is clearly of limited value and cannot be negotiated at a high price. But as a watch intended for collectors, its value is high and its price continues to rise. One and the same referent can thus be the object of two or more forms of valuation, each of which emphasizes different relevant properties, so that the two statements "the old watch in Paul's chest of drawers" and "Paul's splendid Brand X watch" designate the same thing.

In fact, value presents properties that are almost the inverse of those presented by prices. For people with ordinary economic competence, but also for professional economists, those of the classical school as well as modern practitioners (for example, when they are seeking to determine the "fundamental value" of a financial product in order to distinguish it from its "speculative value"), value is supposed to refer to a property of a thing that is more constant than its price, the latter being always subject to fluctuation; in other words, value would refer to a property that is in some sense incorporated into or *inherent in* the thing. Value is thus treated as though it were more *real* than the price, so that the distinction between value and price can be described as a tension between two ways of positing what is *real* rather than artificial. The problem is that – as has been demonstrated by the failure of classical economists to constitute a specific metric for value based on work – value does not possess a metric of its own that would allow it to be objectified independently of the price. Thus a circumstantial *reality* – that of prices – is opposed to an ideal or fictional *reality* – that of value.

As opposed to prices that are real in the sense that they are the result of the specific test constituted by an exchange, value always has a fictional character. Even when it is translated into the metric of prices (as is the case with insurance, for example, or with official price controls), value never has a sufficiently imperative character to constrain exchanges and impose on them a rigid translation in numerical terms. It is to solve this problem that we have distinguished between *real prices* and *metaprices* – that is, all assessments of value that are expressed in numerical terms without resulting from an exchange, whether they are dictated by institutions, generated by actors who rely on familiar examples or on imaginary, dreamed-up assessments, or even determined by custom. It is always through reference to these metaprices that social actors judge prices, criticize them (when they find a given price too high), seek to justify them, or even claim to be lowering a price by offering a "discount." And it is with respect to the question of *value* in its relation to *price* that the analysis of metaprices is necessary, inasmuch as the value of a thing is very generally expressed in the form of a metaprice to distinguish it from its real price. Saying that "this watch is worth $100" can mean different things, depending on whether the assertion is a statement of fact – "I bought it for $100" – or, as is often the case, whether the assertion is aimed at setting the stated price of the watch against what is deemed to be its "true" value, as in statements such as: "I got this watch for $50, but it's worth at least $100," or "You're offering me $50 for this watch when it's worth twice that much."

What does it mean when someone refers to a thing as being of such value that it is "priceless"? A claim of this sort signifies that the thing in question is exempt from exchange but that value can be attributed to it nonetheless. This is the case for the human body, its components and its products, which may in legal terms be placed outside the realm of commerce and cannot be the object of patrimonial rights (as spelled out in France today under Article 16 of the Civil Code). But this is also the case for things that are viewed as symbolic expressions of a collectivity and that are usually the public property of a national government in today's societies (thus, in France, such things are inalienable: they cannot be sold). Still, suspending the commercial circulation of an object is a complex operation, supported by institutions, and the act can always be contested, threatened, and eventually reversed. Where art objects in inalienable public collections are concerned, the value attributed to them actually remains related to a pricing metric via their declared insurance value.

The reference to value plays a central economic role inasmuch as it allows potential buyers to *criticize* prices. But it is also present every time a supplier seeks to ward off the always possible criticism of the proposed price of the object of a transaction by *justifying* that price, either during the exchange or prior to it. This justification can take quite different forms according to the sphere to which the goods in circulation belong. It can be based on manufacturing costs, as it often is for standard industrial goods; it can be based on certain qualities of the objects that contribute to their value, such as durability or technological sophistication; especially in the case of objects at the heart of the enrichment economy, it can be based on the inscription of these objects within a tradition or, more generally, on the *memorial power* attributed to them. It could thus be shown that the maneuver consisting in justifying the proposed price ahead of time constitutes one of the main tasks of advertising; this is particularly obvious with goods construed as part of a legacy and with luxury items, which rely on brand names and whose profit margins are high.

These operations of criticism and justification are based on an artifice that supports naturalizing the reference to value. It consists in situating an object's value *prior to* its price, as if it belongs to the thing itself before any evaluation has occurred, instead of recognizing its presence when and where it is manifested – that is, *in the wake* of its price, in the sense that the reference to value is not expressed overtly unless specific actors reach the point of passing judgment on the price. When that happens, the tension between price and value can of course be stimulated by the avidity of the partners to the exchange who, as potential sellers and/or buyers, have an interest in over- or underestimating the price of the thing, by praising or denigrating its "real" value so as to draw maximal monetary profit from the transaction (standard economics interprets this situation in the idiom of rationality and opportunism). But, as we see clearly when the judgment comes from actors who are external to the transaction and may even know about it only by hearsay, or when the judgment bears less on the price involved than on the very fact that a particular thing has been offered for a price, criticism deployed in the field of exchanges is also based on moral norms, explicit or implicit, thus obliging efforts at justification to shift onto the same ground.

Price as an element in the construction of reality

Because an economy involves the exchange of things that have prices, the *manifestation* of economic relations is essentially a matter of bookkeeping. Thus an economy may even be considered a by-product of *accounting*. It involves making explicit what happens when relations subject to accounting are established. Just as, in linguistics, a speaking subject possesses knowledge of a language that linguists seek to bring to light or to theorize, an accountant possesses the economic knowledge that economists seek to bring to light and to theorize. Without some form of accountability, there is no economy. This being the case, we can distinguish between economies in which the actors' actions, the motivations for their exchanges, are or can be wholly defined in accounting terms and economies that function only provided that there is a separation, in the way the motives for an exchange are conceived, between the aspects and motives subject to accounting and those that stand out as exempt from accounting, so that the accounting dimension can be concealed or even criticized.

For its part, sociology has forged a conception of reality as constructed, and consequently a conception of critique as an enterprise of *deconstruction*. These related conceptions owe a great deal to the diffusion of philosophies of language; with both analytic philosophy and phenomenology as starting points, these philosophies of language have led to a paradigm shift known as *the linguistic turn*. So-called mainstream economics has not deigned to pay attention to this change, seeing in signs, whether linguistic or monetary, "*only a veil* placed over an independent objective reality."[46] This attitude has helped deepen the gap between economics, which has remained faithful to the old forms of positivism, and the other social sciences. Still, by focusing on language as the principal constituent of social formats, sociology may have been led to equip itself with a mutilated representation of reality. In particular, it has tacitly excluded *prices* – those performative entities impressively anchored in reality – from its descriptive grids, while leaving their analysis to economics. Yet, in complex societies, prices constitute an essential element of social reality as instruments for establishing equivalences based on a common metric, equivalences thanks to which things can give rise to transactions and change hands without those transactions being inscribed in relations of reciprocity that involve persons in multiple dimensions.

But, as we have emphasized, since a price cannot be dealt with in isolation, the social construction of reality depends on the *structure of relative prices* – that is, on the relation between the prices of the various things that, in a certain area at a certain point in time, are submitted for exchange (a relation that is thus paralleled by a *structure of relative metaprices*). Social actors, bringing into play the social construction of reality as a whole, can engage in an action only if they succeed in capitalizing the data, on the basis of their own experience or of information transmitted by others, so as to constitute cognitive maps of a sort that allows them to orient themselves in the social world. These cognitive arrangements are put to work every time it is necessary to reduce the level of *uncertainty* which, to varying degrees, hovers over most exchanges and threatens to prevent them from reaching closure if the expectations of the partners involved fail to converge.[47] As it happens, in order to coordinate with one another, actors have to exercise not only a strategic rationality but also an interpretive rationality, on the one hand, in order to try to detect the *properties* of the thing submitted for exchange (which economics often designates with the overly amalgamating and thereby overly vague term "qualities") by juxtaposing it to other things[48] and, on the other hand, in order to *judge the price* of the thing by immersing it in a universe made up of a plurality of metaprices capable of playing the role of salient points or markers.

We see this clearly, for example, in situations in which a foreigner, perhaps simply a tourist, is suddenly plunged into a situation in which it is impossible to compare the price of a specific item with the universe of metaprices with respect to which this singular price is relevant. By contrast, a reality can be envisaged in which those who find themselves involved in a situation they take to be "normal" or "self-evident" – a qualification in widespread use, since the work of Alfred Schutz,[49] especially in ethnomethodology – or even as "natural," when the things exchanged are more or less known in advance and when the structure of relative prices seems more or less stable and predictable. Such a situation has the particular effect of allowing coordination among the expectations of all the actors who, in various capacities, participate in the exchanges. This state of affairs characterizes the economy of bazaars par excellence, as in the case of the suk in Sefrou analyzed in minute detail by Clifford Geertz.[50] Thus Geertz can write that "the bazaar is the nearest thing to be found in reality to the purely competitive market of neoclassical economics."[51] We must note, however, on the one hand, that the bazaar is at once and inextricably the place of an exchange of objects and of a generalized exchange of words that guide "the search for information"[52] and, on the other hand, that the transactions in a bazaar, which are mostly "person-to-person," also depend – especially where the handling of disputes is concerned – on ties that the actors may have woven outside of the marketplace and on their relations of authority.[53]

The situation described by Geertz contrasts with the one that prevails in complex societies whose dominant feature is capitalism, in which commercial relations are established at a distance and in which relations between seller and buyer are separated by chains of mediation of varying length, so that the decisions made by the agents and companies that control the supply are not directly confronted with the expectations of widely dispersed consumers, each one of whom behaves as if he or she has been turned over to the solitude of the supermarket. In these societies, the structure of relative prices, as an essential component of reality, oscillates between periods of relative stability and moments marked by distortions which, beyond a certain threshold, tend to increase in sometimes catastrophic ways the uncertainty that always threatens the exchanges and, with them, reality as a whole.

One of the effects of the constant modification of prices is to destabilize the relation between things and their prices, and especially to destabilize the perception of that relation or the confidence that people may have in it. This is especially true when the number of price variations crosses a certain threshold, especially if the variations are closely spaced in time, so that the social actors are sensitive to them because they have learned the earlier prices by heart. This effect may be echoed, and thus reinforced, by the media that inform the public and express astonishment at the increase in the prices of certain things and the decrease in certain other prices (for example, when the prices of specific paintings offered for auction are stressed). In such instances, the relation between the thing and its price tends to be perceived as arbitrary.

The idea that prices are arbitrary is, moreover, almost the only way in which critical sociology analyzes prices. This theory, in harmony with the general orientation of critical sociology, aims to show that reality is arbitrary so as to "make reality unacceptable." To show that reality is arbitrary is to show that it is "only" the result of power relations (thus of domination) for the purpose of providing arguments for changing reality by changing the power relation in question. But this leads to aporia. For one cannot make such a demonstration without relying, implicitly, on a reality that would not be merely a semblance. Thus Bernard Lahire, studying a matter connected with the identification and sale of paintings by Poussin, seeks to show that a crude "daub" can reach a very high price if the power relation tilts in favor of those who have an interest in raising the price (art critics and experts with ties to art merchants).[54] But speaking about "daubs" presupposes that one is implicitly passing judgment on the "real" value of the painting in question and on what it deserves – that is, on the price at which it should be sold if only the power relations were different. This shows that criticism of a price, as Lahire conceives it, cannot fail to rely, at least implicitly, on an estimation of what is, or rather should be, the "real" price of the thing had the reality of that reality not been called into question.

As it happens, this attitude is not the exclusive property of critical sociologists; it is shared quite broadly with social actors. In fact, the latter seek to profit from price variations when these are in their favor. But, from another standpoint, they cannot live in a world in which prices, and especially relative prices, are modified endlessly, because in such a world it becomes impossible to pass judgment on objects, to the extent that prices play a central role in ensuring the reality of reality. For no one can live in a world in which reality is perpetually shifting ground, constantly prey to the "flux of life" which must be stabilized.

How do social actors manage to put up with the variability of prices, or profit from them, on the one hand, and maintain the reality of reality, insofar as possible, on the other? To answer that question, we can now go back to the set of notions presented earlier that connect determination, price, metaprice, and value. Social actors proceed by falling back on the artificial distinction between price and value. The prices, however, are those actually paid; each price is caught up at once in an event and a test and is inscribed in a monetary system. And each price paid is confronted with something presumed to be an attribute of the thing acquired: its value. This attribute is thought to be inherent in the thing, essential, and thus more stable, more fundamental, than the price. Yet to describe and measure this attribute, we have no language other than that of prices, since there is no metric specific to value. The reference to value is crucial for maintaining the reality of reality: that is, here, the relative prices of various things and their metaprices.

Firmly maintaining the thematics of value and the possibility of a difference between price and value, which presupposes a metaprice, is all the more important in that reference to value is the only argument available to actors who seek to criticize a price and present it as arbitrary – that is, as the result of a power relation and not as grounded in reality. In fact, without the possibility of referring to value and mobilizing it as an argument to justify prices, the actors would be totally at the mercy both of the arbitrariness of prices and of the changes in the relative prices of things that result from shifting tendencies in capitalism. In other words, they would be totally at the mercy of capitalism.

For the logic of capitalism is a logic of displacement that leads to shifting capital and activities away from the areas where they bring in the smallest returns (that is, where they are the least profitable) toward areas in which they bring in the most profit. Innovation is one of the components of this logic of displacement. And this logic typically leads to endless modifications of the relations among the relative prices of things.

This modification of the structure of relative prices and metaprices is one of the expressions, perhaps even the primary expression, of the relation between capitalism and central governments. On the one hand, to make reality predictable, governments must attempt to maintain the relative prices of things so as to reduce the gap between metaprices and prices. On the other hand, driven by the quest for maximum profits, capitalism leads to constant modifications in the relations among relative prices, and thus to increased gaps between metaprices and prices. Here we are at the opposite pole from a conception of the economic theory of "natural," "fair," or "real" prices. Such prices, as Foucault points out, "inasmuch as they are determined in accordance with the natural mechanisms of the market they constitute a standard of truth which enables us to discern which governmental practices are correct and which are erroneous."[55] In such a conception, free competition leads to a "dual profit,"[56] benefiting seller and buyer alike.

We maintain that the logic of capitalism leads to endless modification of the relative prices of things, a dynamic that central governments seek to diminish or to moderate but are never in a position to eliminate entirely. This dynamic is more or less perceptible and powerful at different moments in history. Why do these modifications matter? Because they change the structure of reality. And they do so not only because they make certain things affordable and others not, but especially because of the relations they create between things and their prices. The logic of capitalism appears all the more clearly when the relations between currencies via exchange rates – that is, the relations between central governments – come into play. The notion of relative prices presupposes the establishment of a relation between the prices of various things expressed in a specific currency. But, as we see in the ordinary experience of tourists, for example, there are many ordinary situations in which, for a given item, the actors have to deal with metaprices expressed in different currencies. In such situations, the criticism of a price that appears too high can be based just as well on a metaprice for the desired item relative to other items as on the relative value of the currency in which the price of the item is expressed compared to its expression in another currency. Following the same logic, purchasing an item might be viewed as a bargain if its price is deemed low relative to its metaprice in a different currency.

During a transaction, each participant seeks to have the thing he or she covets at the lowest possible price, but at the same time each would like things to have the prices they warrant, and the actor may be uneasy if the price appears arbitrary. At the heart of every actor in a commercial society, there is thus a tension between a logic that can be called capitalist, a logic in quest of profit that seeks to benefit from changes in price and from shifts in the relation between things and prices, and a different logic that is troubled by these shifts because they make reality itself suspect by modifying the relation between things and their prices and between the relative prices of things. Such tension thus creates, in addition, a loss of confidence in the governing authority, inasmuch as that authority is supposed to guarantee the stability of reality, which entails, at least in part, the stability of the relation between things and their prices. This is all the more developed in free-market democratic societies, whose motto, Foucault suggests, could be "'Live dangerously,' that is to say, individuals in these societies are constantly exposed to danger, or rather, they are conditioned to experience their situation, their life, their present, and their future, as containing danger."[57] This culture of danger is embodied most notably in the appearance of detective stories and spy novels.[58]

The distortion of the price structure becomes manifest to the actors when the outcome of certain exchanges – processes that, being on the order of *events*, always have a singular character – discloses prices that appear enigmatic, because on the phenomenal level they seem to be wholly disproportionate to the thing exchanged. Such an impression can be formed, in fact, only by implicitly comparing the relation of one particular price for one particular thing to the relations between other prices and other things that make up the framework of reality.

These processes have rarely been taken into account by economic sociology, except in situations of hyperinflation, for example in Latin America, where the very possibility of a "prediction" tends to disappear because the "relation between individuals and goods" is profoundly disturbed by the "incoherence of systems of equivalence."[59] In the case of hyperinflation, all prices grow brutally and unpredictably. But the distortions of price structures can also take less spectacular, less rapid, and more disparate forms, manifested in some cases by a rise and in others a fall. Changes like these are frequent and particularly intense during periods marked by the appearance of new sources of wealth creation that result in valorizing things previously judged of secondary importance or even completely ignored, thereby increasing the prices of those things relative to the prices of other things. This was the case during the first industrial revolution, with the gradual shift in an economy that had had an organic basis for the most part (agriculture, wood, wool, the use of animal power, and so on) toward an economy in which the exploitation of mineral wealth played a growing role. The second industrial revolution then brought an intensification of industrial mass production of standardized objects that competed with artisanal production. But the same can be said of our own day, under the influence of three interrelated phenomena that we have already mentioned. First, the deindustrialization that has accompanied the outsourcing of the production of everyday objects toward countries where wages are low; second, the expansion of profits drawn from financial activities; and, third, the development of a new sphere of wealth creation, the one we have identified and characterized as the *enrichment economy*.

4

Forms of Valuation

Structure and transformation group of forms of valuation

Let us consider things that circulate in association with prices that are justified by values. Our hypothesis is that the ways in which these things circulate can be distributed according to a structure that organizes forms of valuation in a transformation group.[1]

We have emphasized that things, in order to circulate, have to be determinate: in other words, they have to have been shown by linguistic means to possess a stable set of qualities that allows them to be considered together. But, at the same time, it has to be possible to differentiate them from one another. Let us take two things that are different but that are *determined* in the same way: that is, they belong to the same category. If their prices are the same, why buy one rather than the other? And, if their prices differ, why buy the more expensive one rather than the cheaper one? The structure that we are proposing should make it possible to answer these puzzling questions.

Any such structure must allow us to establish how things that are determined to belong to the same category can be compared through the introduction of differences, but it must do this while inscribing the things in question in a temporal context. This is why the structure must take into account two axes in terms of which things are distributed. The first axis makes it possible to expose the differences that the things in question present; the second organizes the way in which these things can be assessed, even though the assessment itself cannot be *presented*, properly speaking: in other words, along this second axis, the commercial potential of things is inscribed in its relation to time, or, more precisely, in temporal uncertainty.

Before going into detailed discussions of these two axes as they apply to forms of valuation, we must say something about what we mean by "form." A form is a structure that makes it possible to connect things with the perspectives from which they must be envisaged if they are to be correctly appreciated. Considered from the outside – that is, from a disengaged overall vantage point – forms can be identified with the conventions with which the constructivist economics of conventions is concerned. Nevertheless, for these forms to be capable of operating concretely in the practice of transactions, they have to be situated at a point of indistinction between the things themselves and the perspectives from which those things are determined; in other words, they have to blur the gap between realism and idealism, a gap whose emergence always signals the initiation of a critical approach. When forms of valuation come into play – that is, when they cause their conventional dimension to be taken for granted – they have several functions. On the one hand, they specify the various perspectives that can be adopted toward the things that circulate through exchange and limit the number of those perspectives. On the other hand, they distribute the applications of the various perspectives in such a way that the applications can be justified by properties identified in the things themselves. In other words, a thing must in some sense prove on its own that the perspective from which it is being considered is appropriate, so that the perspective applied will not appear purely subjective or arbitrary.

However, we do not propose to adopt an all-seeing vantage point and explore every perspective that can be applied to anything, as if we could produce an exhaustive list. Moreover, such a project would be very unconvincing and probably unrealizable, for the possible perspectives are as diverse and changing as are the societal and historical contexts in which they are anchored and thus as diverse and changing as the kinds of things whose exchange they facilitate. And if the exchange of commodities indeed has a universal character, it is by no means always and everywhere commercial, at least not in the same way or to the same degree.

Our decision to give priority to forms that are situated along the axis of difference on the one hand and along a temporal axis on the other invites a reconsideration of what Lucien Karpik has called "the economics of singularities."[2] By contrast with Karpik, we support the idea that the circulation of things is organized more by their valuation in conventional forms than by the opposition between things belonging to the order of the singular and things belonging to the order of the serial. Moreover, each form constitutes a collective resource to which agents can refer when they have to orient themselves in the world of objects – that is, when they need to make distinctions or bring things together so as to rank them, sell them, or buy them.

Let us now look at these forms in their broad outlines. When a thing is presented for exchange (the act of presentation will constitute the vertical axis of the forms in the graphic representations that we shall introduce shortly; see figure 4.1),[3] it can be described in two types of language: on the one hand, in the language of *analysis* (focusing on distinct properties that can in principle be measured and codified); on the other hand, in the language of *narrative* (featuring events and/or persons). An analytic presentation of a thing produces a double hierarchy: a hierarchy among things offered at different prices and a hierarchy among things presented as different from one another in analytic terms (for example,

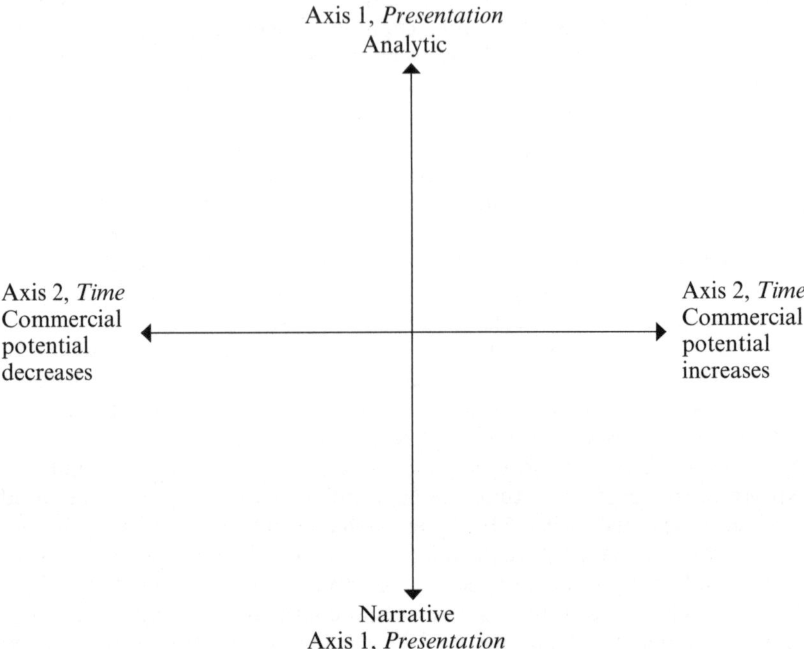

Figure 4.1 Structural dimensions of the forms of valuation

through indications of weight, dimensions, age, rankings attributed by a consumers' association, and so on). With a narrative presentation, tension is created between incommensurable relations: a given narrative is not hierarchically situated with respect to other narratives, whereas the different prices of things organize the things in question hierarchically.

In a "naturalist" ontology, one difference between things and humans is that we humans have a tendency to behave as though we know what things are made of and therefore what they are capable of doing, while we behave as though humans are endowed with unlimited potential. This is why the presentation of a human being in an analytic manner is criticized as "reification."[4] In any case, as we shall see, the theory of reification does not account very well for the ways in which value is attributed to things, in particular because numerous things can be associated with narratives that attribute human qualities to them, and because these narratives, too, contain an element of uncertainty. A contrasting tendency, which we also reject, consists in treating things as human beings, most notably by endowing them with agency.[5] We shall maintain the division between people and things as a necessary condition. If things were like people, there would no longer be any reason to assign prices to them. Our ontology presupposes that there are beings that undertake exchanges – human beings – and beings that are exchanged – things – and that, even though things may deteriorate over time, if they are to be exchangeable they must remain unchanged in terms of their determinations.

But this requirement – the constraint of determination, a necessary condition for the circulation of things – means that presenting things in terms of their differences, whether in an analytic or a narrative manner, introduces tension among the things presented. This tension shares some properties with the contradiction that inhabits the fabrication of new human beings potentially capable of taking their places in an already constituted collectivity.[6] But, in the latter case, it takes a more drastic form. In fact a postulant for admission to the human collectivity, in the case in point a foetus, must – this is the first constraint – be identified as belonging to the human species (and not, for example, as the offspring of a supernatural spirit or as a monster) and must be attributed to categories of belonging (sex, kinship, and so on); these requirements seem to parallel those introduced by the constraint of determination in the case of objects of commerce. But, where human beings are concerned, the second constraint, the constraint of differentiation, is immediately positioned at the limit – that is, as a constraint of *singularization*. Every human being is inherently a unique, singular being, as manifested by the fact that each is endowed with a proper name.[7] This singularity is necessarily related to the principle that human beings cannot be endowed with prices and made objects of commercial exchange in view of profits. The institution of slavery, defying this principle, thus tends to call into question the very membership in humanity of the persons enslaved.[8]

In each form, one of the two axes of presentation is privileged, either the analytic or the narrative; the two function as a pair of opposites. The hierarchy among things that are presented analytically is based on the greater or lesser number of differences ascribed to things in the analytic process. It may be argued that a certain number of things, those we call standard, and which are copies, receive identical analytic presentations. How is the analytic presentation organized in such cases? Here we need to introduce a distinction between prototype and specimen (we shall explore this new distinction more fully later on). Things that can be presented in identical analytic terms are specimens produced on the basis of an original analytic presentation, that of the prototype. With standard objects, then, their differences are supported by analytic presentations of the prototypes.

If a thing is grasped in terms of its relation to time (this relation constitutes the horizontal axis in figure 4.1), its description contains an irreducible uncertainty. On the one hand, one may hope that the perceived value of the thing in question will increase over time, thus justifying the argument that its current price is lower than it will be later on. On the other hand, one may suppose that its perceived value will diminish over time, thus justifying the argument that its current price is higher than it will be when the thing goes back into circulation. These temporal orientations thus guide the appraisal of what we shall call the *commercial potential* of things, a potential that can be manifested over time by a decrease or an increase in value. This potential, while it concerns the uncertainty about the future of a thing, is nevertheless always understood in relation to the thing's past. In fact, things that have no past tend to see their commercial potential diminish over time, whereas things endowed with a past may well see their commercial potential increase.

Paying attention to the two modes of *differential presentation* of things (analysis vs. narrative) and to the two temporal orientations that direct the estimation of their *commercial potential* (loss of value vs. gain in value) makes it possible to sketch out a combinatorics of the principal perspectives from which one can identify and differentiate commercial objects in a commercial society. These perspectives are associated with forms of valuation of things, each form obeying its own logic. These same perspectives also designate market spaces which, while they may partly overlap, are nevertheless relatively distinct, so that they help structure the cosmos of commodities. On the one hand, these structures organize competition according to rules of commensurability and incommensurability among certain objects (it is reasonable to compare the prices of two new utilitarian automobiles of similar size, but it is aberrant to compare the price of a utilitarian vehicle to that of a collector's model; to do justice to these two objects, one must consider them from different perspectives). On the other hand, these structures make it possible to open up as widely as possible the field of things that are capable of being transformed into commodities by multiplying the relations in terms of which a thing can be envisaged on its own, or with respect for its dignity, as it were, even as it is endowed with a price. This process would be limitless were it not subordinated to law, which is itself a process supported by moral and/or social norms. This latter process, which prevails at certain points in time and in certain areas of exchange, regulates an always disputed and more or less shifting borderline: the line separating things whose commercialization is accepted from things that are (or ought to be) excluded from the cosmos of commodities, such as, for example, things belonging to the realm of intimacy.[9]

This structuring of the cosmos of commodities and of the arrangements that make it possible to attribute value to objects is favorable to commerce for at least two reasons. On the one hand, it permits a seller to realize the greatest possible profit from the sale of each thing. This would not be the case if everything were considered from the same perspective, which would obviously have the effect of devaluing a large number of things. Considered from the same perspective as a new utilitarian vehicle, a collector's model would find itself relegated to the category of low-level used cars, ready for the junk heap. Conversely, a new utilitarian automobile would be of little interest and could not be offered at a high price if it were being assessed from the standpoint of a collector.

On the other hand, this mode of organization also structures the competencies of the actors. It provides them with schemas of perception and evaluation and with descriptive languages that, although very unevenly distributed, can make use of common sense in a commercial context, rendering it possible to limit misunderstandings or at least to supply actors engaged in legal disputes – which arise very frequently in the world of commerce, a world based on competition for profit – with arguments toward which the parties can converge in an effort to bring their disagreements to an end. If things were put on sale without any way for the actors to get their bearings thanks to a limited number of forms of valuation, the actors could not coordinate with one another, and, since the price of things would be constantly called into question and negotiable, the circulation of things would be limited or even impossible. But a single form of valuation would not leave room for any hope of maximizing the profit from each thing. The fact that commercial potential may be negative or positive makes it possible, in addition, to classify things according to whether they are slated to disappear or to be preserved. If there were only a single mode of commercial potential, either everything would be destined to disappear or everything would have to be preserved.

By crossing two modalities of presentation of a thing – analytic or narrative – with two modalities of estimating the thing's commercial potential – destined to decline or capable of increasing – we shall sketch four perspectives from which things can be envisaged and evaluated.

Objects considered from the same perspective are viewed as having a *family resemblance*. But they are also seen as having differences on which the set of metaprices attributable to them is based. The forms thus generate arguments that are associated with a particular thing to justify its metaprice in relation to the metaprices of other things that are relevant in the same context. These forms make it possible to justify prices: they privilege the setting of prices that are likely to be deemed reasonable, and they can also provide a basis for criticism of prices.

However, these forms also play a contrary role. Owing to their plurality, they create spaces of incommensurability that structure the cosmos of commodities. Seen from a certain perspective, the value of a particular thing is incommensurable with that of relevant things seen from other perspectives. The dispersal of value has repercussions on the distribution of prices. The prices of relevant things seen from different perspectives can be expressed in the same monetary metric without being confronted with one another and without giving rise to comparisons. And, at the same time, the competition between objects that could be determined as belonging to the same kind – in relation to their function, for example – but that are assessed with reference to different forms of valuation, is very

FORMS OF VALUATION

	Analytic presentation	*Narrative presentation*
Negative commercial potential	Standard form	Trend form
Positive commercial potential	Asset form	Collection form

limited or even non-existent, so that things that seem to be substitutable for one another become non-substitutable (a second-hand Ford Fiesta cannot be substituted for a collector's Model T; a standard cup purchased at Target is not in competition with a designer cup from Tiffany's; and so on). Similarly, it goes without saying that, if the parties to an exchange coordinate with each other with reference to the standard form, a car fresh from the factory can be offered at a price higher than that of a used car that would serve the same purposes, just because the first one is *new*. Or, if the parties' coordination is based on the collection form, it is clear that an original work of art can be presented at a price higher than that of a copy, even if the copy is perfect, simply because the first one is the *original*. The fact of being new or original thus constitutes, prior to any more detailed examination, a basic difference with which things may be endowed. In other words, the process of valuation aims to limit the effects of *substitution* and thus to limit competition. Or it aims to specify the small number of objects with which the object submitted for exchange can be placed in competition by excluding a large number of other potential competitors. The constitution of monopolies or quasi-monopolies is the horizon of this process and is probably the dream of all the operators who intervene in the space of a transaction. It is in fact in these situations that the supplier's power over the determination of the price is greatest and, consequently, that an object's commercial added value is likely to be highest.

We must emphasize that the differentiation of things, whether it is expressed through a narrative or an analytic presentation, is motivated by competition. The requirement of differentiation responds to the expectations of each seller who means to realize a profit by negotiating the thing being offered at the maximum price. The seller must thus try to counter the buyer's propensity to turn toward other things that are determined in more or less the same terms and, consequently, deemed more or less similar, especially if they are offered at lower prices. As it happens, in contemporary Western societies (it was probably not the case earlier, at least not to the same degree, not even during the three prosperous decades in France following the Second World War), potential buyers already possess a large number of things, especially standard objects with a technological dimension. They can therefore be content with what they already have without embarking on new transactions. When a new object is presented to them, that object has a better chance of arousing their interest if the difference between this object and already existing objects is emphasized in such a way that the latter can be judged obsolete. Even though built-in obsolescence may be legally prohibited, we know that obsolescence can be provoked. This happens frequently today with standard artifacts that have significant technological components: they may be manufactured in such a way that they will work only for a relatively short period of time, or their compatibility with other objects in the same technological sphere may become problematic after a certain period of time, as we see for example in the case of digital networks and devices.

The principal way in which sellers can try to protect themselves against the risk of competition and make a profit when they exchange their holdings consists in highlighting the *difference(s)* between the thing they possess and are offering for sale and other things offered by other sellers or already possessed by a large number of buyers – things that, considered all together and from a distance, may be judged more or less similar.

Increasing the differential value of an object amounts to privileging certain comparisons to the detriment of others that might seem reasonable; in other words, it amounts to *partitioning* the class with which a thing is associated in such a way as to create subclasses. The thing in question is indeed a Chinese statuette or an automobile, but not just any Chinese statuette or automobile. The Chinese statuette is an antique dating back centuries; the automobile can achieve exceptional speeds. This process is inherently limitless. One can always try to introduce a new difference or modify the system of differences. The process of differentiation can thus be pursued until the class to which the thing is attributed contains just one item, which is the very thing being offered up for exchange: for example, an unparalleled masterpiece.[10]

Constraints of determination and constraints of differentiation enter into tension. The first presupposes linking the thing in question to classes that are sufficiently large and recognized (such as styles) for its determination to be unproblematic. But the second presupposes partitioning those classes so as to render the thing incomparable in order to justify its higher price with respect to other less expensive things that a buyer might be tempted to substitute for it.

One of the effects of the structure of forms is that it favors an extension of the cosmos of commodities, enabling that cosmos to incorporate more or less anything. But the structure of forms can also do justice to each thing, since an object that is devalued from one perspective can be appreciated from another: in other words, this structure can make it possible to draw the maximum profit from the exchange of anything at all. The displacement of things from one form to another is not only a possibility but a condition of the forms' existence. If things could not circulate among the forms, the forms could not exist as such, independently of one another.

The way in which objects are offered for assessment, the way they are arranged in a certain environment, their mode of presentation, the arguments intended to bring out their particular features, and so on, prove to be profoundly different in each of the four forms we have identified. Nevertheless, the overall arrangement is coherent and robust enough to function as if it went without saying and to allow the actors to shift easily between transactions belonging to different forms, because well-formed expressions according to one form of valuation are logically connected with well-formed expressions according to a different form. These connections are possible because the syntax internal to each of the four forms of valuation is isomorphic to the external syntax on the basis of which the forms are generated and thereby also in a relation of isomorphism to the internal syntax of each of the others. One characteristic of this syntax is that it transcends the distinctions that play a major role in accounting categories, such as those between movable and immovable goods. It can thus be shown that, depending on the way in which an immovable good is determined, such a good can be appraised as a standard immovable good (the individual house analyzed by Pierre Bourdieu),[11] as a collectable immovable good (one of the exceptional residence described by Marc Augé),[12] as a trendy immovable good (as in the case of gentrification),[13] or as an asset (an apartment on Park Avenue in Manhattan).

Each of these internal syntaxes is, like the external one, structured by the intersection between the axis that ensures a *differential presentation* and the axis along which the *estimation of commercial potential* is situated. But while in the case of the external syntax each axis can take two different modalities (analytic or narrative, increasing or decreasing value over time), each internal syntax can adopt only a single modality on each of its axes. It is on this condition that the forms can be both differentiated (two syntactic systems that operate for the same modality on the two axes would be indistinguishable) and motivated with reference to each other. The various internal syntaxes thereby maintain inseparable relations that are at once external and internal. They make each other mutually comprehensible in the sense that the specificity of each one is immediately graspable with reference to, and by contrast with, the others. Each of these syntaxes generates categories making it possible to qualify objects according to specific modalities. But the categories belonging to each internal syntax can be interpreted by means of implicit transformational rules as functions of categories occupying a similar position in each of the other syntaxes. It follows that the entire arrangement on which the valuation of objects is based can be envisaged as a transformation group, in the sense given this notion by Claude Lévi-Strauss.[14]

A semantics encompassing the categories generated by these syntactic systems, "always half-way between percepts and concepts," as Lévi-Strauss says about "mythic reflection,"[15] can be applied to a matter composed of distinct or even unique things, both by differentiating that matter and by homogenizing it, since what the semantics applies to is grasped on the one hand in terms of its substantive diversity – that is, in a discontinuous fashion – and on the other hand in terms of its belonging to the cosmos of commodities envisaged in its continuity. "Making use of the means at hand," as Lévi-Strauss says, this semantics composes itself, diversifies, and recomposes itself by taking advantage of "all the opportunities" available in order to "renew or enrich the stock, or to maintain it with the residue of earlier constructions and destructions."[16] It thereby supplies operators that allow it to traverse a vast field that has no *a priori* limits, so that it can extend to objects that it had not previously recognized, whether they are actually new or pre-existing but not previously considered in terms of their commercial circulation. This is rather like the way a metaphoric logic puts schemas in circulation between diverse domains of objectivity so as to bring out an element that could be common to them, or, to borrow another comparison from Lévi-Strauss, like the "commercial codes that, condensing the past experience of the profession, allow it to face, economically, any new situation (provided, however, that it belongs to the same class as the old ones)."[17] This is why each of the forms we have identified can give rise to two different approaches; we shall characterize the first of these as *limited* and the second as *extended*.

In its limited aspect, each form can be considered on the basis of exemplary cases that are at its heart – that is, on the basis of objects that, owing to their properties and their uses, lend themselves to operations of valuation that lead to the deployment of the principal characteristics of the form under consideration. These exemplary objects, with respect to which the components of each form find themselves strongly correlated, concentrate the relevant information on each of the forms of valuation.[18] Thus an analysis of the standard form in what is most specific about it can focus on the valuation of industrial objects that incorporate a significant technological component; an analysis of the trend form can take fashionable clothing as a case in point; an auction of art objects will constitute a good example of the asset form; and the properties of the collection form will become particularly self-evident in a comparison of practices of accumulation – of watches, stamps, or paintings, for instance – that share the property of being systematic and are oriented by interest in the past.

But to the precise extent that they have to face a "heterogeneous repertoire,"[19] one that must be inflected when the contours of the commodities are modified, the forms of valuation can always – again, rather like "mythical thought" – be extended and "work by way of analogies and comparisons," as in the case of *bricolage*, a sort of tinkering in which "creations, like those of the *bricoleur* [tinkerer], always really consist in a new arrangement of elements, the nature of which is unaffected by whether they figure in the instrumental set or in the final arrangement."[20] This is why, in the practice of exchanges, and driven, as it were, by the need to give a value to things in order to justify or criticize their prices, each form can be extended to domains whose properties differ from those of the exemplary objects that may seem the most apt to illustrate the form in its specificity.[21] And, in the process, a given form will encounter no limits except those that are imposed on it by the concomitant movements of the other forms.

Thus, for example, in an industrial society in which the Fordian mode of production has become predominant, it has been possible for standardization to be extended not only to new domains, such as the slaughtering of animals or sales techniques, but virtually to the use of human beings as well, a situation that has been one of the chief targets of critiques of that social form. The standard form has thus come to embody an economic cosmos in what might be its most specific aspects and, with that cosmos, the society itself in which that form had become dominant. The collection form, for its part, can also be extended, especially in Western European countries, where it tends to develop by bringing together and ordering an ever-growing number of objects, domains, and even experiences that are nevertheless distant from its prototypical core; real estate in the central and oldest sections of big cities and touristic and cultural arrangements more generally are good examples. This is the case to such an extent that, just as it has been possible to see in the standard form the paradigm of a certain type of industrial society, even if many things remain unstandardized, similarly one can plausibly see the collection form as the paradigm for another type of society that is emerging, even if collections, in the literal sense, do not play a central economic role in these societies and even if the subjects in these societies are by no means all avid collectors.

Capitalism can be fully realized only if there is a structure of the sort we are identifying, one that makes it possible to bring together and order a multiplicity of things by extension. But this dynamic has the effect of constantly putting the structure to the test, or even, potentially, of modifying or undoing it. Our goal is to expose the structure as it functions currently; thus we shall offer a kind of snapshot of commercial society.

Analytic and narrative presentations of things

For a thing to be put up for sale, it has to be determinate, and, for a value to be attributed to it, the thing has to be presented. In fact, a thing does not say, on its own, what it is, and the way in which it has come into existence is most often unknown to the parties potentially involved in an exchange. Its valuation relies, moreover, on the fact that human beings are in general stimulated and affected by things they have not yet experienced, things with which they are acquainted only through the intermediary of reported information that is difficult or impossible for them to test or verify.

The presentation of a thing is made, first of all, by the principal artisan of the valuation, namely, the seller. Such a presentation may be made "upstream" – that is, it may be developed by the producer of the thing, if the producer is not also the seller – but the presentation is then most often directly taken over by the seller, all the more so if the producer has deployed the presentation publicly on a wide scale, through advertising campaigns that associate an image and/or a slogan with the thing. But a buyer can also propose a presentation of the thing, especially if buyers come together in consumers' associations that aim to test and assess products by comparing them to the presentations made by the sellers, or by expressing their opinions and observations in a series of Internet-based exchanges.

An analytic presentation consists in breaking down the properties attributed to the object until they are fixed in a minimal form that is easily storable, reproducible, and transmissible, one that facilitates comparisons. This type of presentation is particularly well adapted to external commerce in situations where a number of things can be described in similar analytic terms.

Having recourse to the transcription of properties that can be translated into numerical terms, as we see par excellence in the case of technological objects (but the approach can also be couched in the words of ordinary language, often in the form of slogans), this procedure for presenting an object can often be summed up as a process of codification. Generally speaking, an analytic presentation breaks the thing in question down into its relevant properties; each of these properties is represented by a sign, and the juxtaposition of properties provides information that purports to be exhaustive and objective, making it possible to recognize the thing from a distance without recourse to direct experience. Such a presentation is virtually atemporal, in the sense that references to time are scarce, except for the date of manufacture, the lifespan projected for the object, or the period during which it will be covered by a guarantee; there is never a reference to a chain of events.

The second descriptive modality that we are envisaging consists in attributing value to a thing by means of a narrative. While an analytic presentation is limited to the thing itself and is designed to represent the thing in its pure "thingness," as always identical to itself without regard to the context in which it is situated, narration makes it possible to associate the description of the thing with an evocation of situations in which the thing is or has been immersed and/or with an evocation of persons who have or have had a relationship with it, for example, the persons who made it or those who currently possess it. Unlike an analytic presentation, with its almost atemporal character, a narrative presentation incorporates a chronological orientation that makes this mode of representation particularly suited for taking the past into account – not only the past of the thing itself but also the situations, events, and persons with whom the thing may have been associated previously. The person who acquires a thing endowed with such a presentation is inscribed in turn in the accompanying narrative: by entering into possession of an object, that person can introduce his or her own life story into the story of that object.[22]

For at least two reasons, narrative presentation makes it possible to activate the memorial functions to which analytic presentation does not give access. In the first place, for human beings, narratives are much easier to commit to memory than analyses – a fact that, according to cognitivist studies, is one of the traits that distinguish persons from the architecture of computers.[23] In the second place, the structure of narrative allows the past to be represented and embedded within a single story of the evocation of the past that also incorporates reference to a present in which the past is remembered. Nevertheless, we must note that, for the same reasons, narratives are less stable than analyses. An analytic presentation, once established, may remain unchanged, especially if it has benefited – as is often the case – from an institutional guarantee. By contrast, a narrative presentation, although it may give rise to a written transcription intended to fix it in place, is inherently mobile and mutable. Its primary vocation is to be transmitted from person to person, and this mobility opens up the possibility of a plurality of interpretations that may generate multiple and sometimes contradictory variants, some of which may nourish the intention of challenging the original narrative on which the valuation of the thing whose history it is retracing rests.

A narrative presentation, to the extent that it stresses events, however brief they may be, aims to attach the names of singular or collective persons to things. These persons may be famous, perhaps heroic; they are most often dead, although living persons may also be invoked. Such persons are said to be real when various forms of attestation pertaining to them exist, making them historical characters. They are said to be fictional when they exist only in an oral tradition or in a story or a series of stories, if there is no other form of attestation. No one questions the historical existence of Napoleon. But there is reason to question the physical, historical existence of Oedipus. And certain characters – Harry Potter, for instance – who exist exclusively in literature are fully fictional. Still, on the one hand, in certain novels, the characters bear close resemblance to real persons, often the author (as is the case for instance in Patrick Modiano's stories); on the other hand, certain fictional characters are endowed by readers with a quasi-autonomy that allows them to escape from the exclusive control of their author (Sherlock Holmes is a good example).[24] Narratives bring into play famous, historical, mythical, or fictional persons such as these by associating them with events, with places, and often with objects, all the more so if the stories have been presented in films.

Nevertheless, for such a narrative to be considered as participating in the valuation of a place or an object, it must be associated with two different references that are connected through a *trace*. First, the famous persons (such as protagonists in historical events) or the collective persons (for example, nineteenth-century French peasants) to whom reference is made must be kept at a distance, whether they are dead or inaccessible. Then, references to things or to places must be at once *material* and *current* in character. In addition, it has to be possible to attest – and this is the role of the narrative – to the existence of a physical relation (such as touch) between the vanished or remote heroes and the current material objects that are supposed to have retained their traces. Narrative presentations of this type play a major role in the collection form, both in its limited dimension and in the dimension that extends to include the economy of enrichment. The relation between the names of vanished heroes and things or places, widely used in advertising, favors both identification with a hero (which is always the case with heroic literature that presents models to be imitated) and the possibility of realizing such identification via things that can be appropriated and exchanged or via places that can be visited.

The problem of valuation by means of images

In the distinction we have just proposed between analytic and narrative presentations of an object intended for exchange, we have at least implicitly stressed language, especially in the form of texts. A text used for narration can also serve analytic presentations, although in such cases it is frequently associated with numerical data. But what role is played by the images that very often accompany the presentation of the object?

The predominant role given to images, especially still photographic images, in advertising, which blossomed following the development of glossy magazines after the Second World War, might suggest that photographic images are the principal medium used to showcase things. Isn't it chiefly by means of images that advertisements seek to make the objects being marketed look attractive? We shall nevertheless distance ourselves from that position, for from our standpoint it confuses two different semiotic operations that surround the market test and that are based on different conceptions of potential buyers, and even on different anthropologies. In the first case, the operations fail to take into account the ability of actors to reflect on their own actions (relying, rather, on conceptions that appeal to something on the order of an unconscious); in the second case, they endow the actors with intentionality and with the capacity to orient their intentions in a reflective way that motivates their actions.

Advertising, especially since advertisers began making use of depth psychology (a process that has been under way since the 1950s), relies on an anthropology focused on "desire." In this view, the task of advertising is to stimulate the "impulses" that inhabit actors so as to "create desires" to which actors will succumb without much reflection.

Photography appears to be a good medium for exercising this seductive function, because it allows advertisers to present any object whatsoever in an environment that has given rise to a work of representation and valuation of that object. The photographic image of the object refers to an "encyclopedia" in the semiotic sense, composed of "model images" with which potential buyers can be assumed to be already generally familiar. In an associationist logic, the desires aroused by a model image are supposed to shift onto the image of the thing offered for sale. This is the case, for example, with bottles of brand-name sparkling water from a spring located in Italy: their photographic image is associated with a stereotypical photograph of an Italian village, so as to orient desire toward the water sold under this brand name rather than some other.

We could argue – as advertisers themselves do, moreover – about the commercial effectiveness of such associations, but it is important to note that these associations do not include a connection between the thing and its price; in most advertising photos the price is not mentioned. It seems likely, moreover, that such photos are specifically intended to attract the potential buyer's full attention to the image of the object so as to minimize reflection not only on its qualities but also and especially on its price, and thus to deflect a possible critical movement that would consist precisely in creating a tension between the thing advertised and its price, on the one hand, and competing *things and their prices*, on the other.

It is in this sense that such strategies of seduction deviate from the logic of valuation. They propose no arguments that could intervene in sequences of critique and justification. We may suppose, moreover, that, on the contrary, when they are not accompanied by texts, photographs and still images more generally – whose strong evocative power can be called on to trigger associations – have only weak argumentative force owing to their character as snapshots, their impoverished syntactic articulations, and perhaps above all their weak access to metalanguage, which is a specific property of the natural languages that makes it possible to use the same code to refer to an object in the world and the symbolic means that represent it. This is, furthermore, why the developing magazine industry had to invent a specific rhetoric that included both images and texts, exemplified in the captions that accompany magazine photographs. Journalists deem these texts indispensable in order to "give meaning," as they say, to the pictures – that is, to orient their interpretation. The principal function of a caption is in fact to make manifest a meaning, a single meaning, which is something that the mute image cannot do on its own. For one cannot comment on an image by means of another image without having recourse to a text; thus a caption is just another way of using an image.

These remarks are not meant to suggest that the recourse to images, most often surrounded by texts, does not play an important role in the valuation of things; that would be counterfactual. But, in each of the forms of valuation we have identified, the use made of images is subordinated to the type of justification that is made of the relation between things and their prices. In other words, superficially similar images will be associated with different meanings according to the presentations, analytic or narrative, in which they are embedded. It is this differential use of images that we propose to examine more closely here.

In the standard form (analytic presentation), the relation between image and text (or data) is aligned with the distinction between *outside* and *inside*, especially when the objects in question have a significant technological component (a camera or a personal computer, for example). The image reflects the *design* of the thing but says nothing about its *potential* – that is, about what the thing is capable of doing – as compared with other things that, seen from the outside, may look similar or superior. Images are thus particularly important when the differentiation between things stresses appearance. But since standard objects are intended for use, their allure, which photographs emphasize, is usually not enough to defend a particular price relative to the prices of other objects whose performances, announced by textual or numerical data, appear superior. Similar observations can be made about objects envisaged from the perspective of the asset form, which also depends on an analytic presentation. In this case, the image of the thing matters even less, to the extent that the object's price can be justified by taking into account its degree of liquidity and the added value that one can expect to realize when it is sold. Photography can of course be used for the purpose of assessment by experts. But it must itself then be the object of expertise in order to guarantee its "objectivity."

The relation between images and texts poses different problems when the presentation is narrative. Images, even stationary ones, can play an important role in the establishment of a narrative if they are accompanied by texts. Here we have to distinguish between figures in which the valuation of objects is handled via the collection form and those to which the trend form applies.

In the case of the collection form, as the objects undergoing valuation are not destined for use, the relevance of the distinction between outside and inside is relatively secondary (even though it can still come into play when the objects collected have technological dimensions and have been relevant, in a more or less remote past, with respect to standard objects – for example, watches, pens, or old cars, whose price will depend in part on how well they work). Most often, the valuation of objects in this form will rely on the manifestation of their *authenticity*. It will be important to defend their *memorial power* by bringing in elements that will make it possible to differentiate between the authentic object, in the sense that it has been in physical proximity with a person or an event situated in the past, and a reproduction, a copy, or a fake. An image of the object, and especially a photograph, can help. But a photograph on its own is of little use in distinguishing the original from an exact copy without the help of a *narrative* that presents the *history* of the object. Photography cannot readily accomplish this task because it does not incorporate temporality. Conversely, a narrative can base its arguments on *encyclopedias* that are historical in nature. Without recourse to such encyclopedias, photography cannot facilitate differentiation between an old but impeccably restored monument and a monument reconstituted on the basis of old images (as was done for the historic districts of Warsaw that were systematically destroyed by the Nazis between 1939 and 1945 and reconstructed in the 1950s as replicas inspired in part by Canaletto's paintings).

The situation is somewhat different with objects whose valuation depends on the trend form, because in this case the value attributed to objects, which justifies their prices, depends on a staging of the proximity between these objects, or objects of the same style, not with personalities or events belonging to the past but with famous persons – movie stars or other media celebrities, for instance – who are presumed to be present in the same spatial and temporal contexts as the potential buyers, even if the latter are unlikely to cross paths with the former. These objects may also be associated with current or recent events (for example, the dress worn by a particular actress during the Oscar awards ceremony). The narrative effect can then rely more strongly on photography by presenting these objects (or objects of the same style) in proximity with the bodies of the celebrities who were their first owners. In this case, the "encyclopedia" is supplied by the media and can be treated as information that is already known, if not by everyone then at least by those persons whom the suppliers may deem potentially interested in those objects.

Nevertheless, even in this case, recourse to texts is necessary to consolidate the relation between objects and persons by documenting the way in which a given person came into the possession of a certain object: for example, a text can indicate that the person received the object directly from the hands of its "creator," who conceived it on the occasion of a festival organized by a brand for the launching of a product. A text can also provide information about the way a given item can be used (on what occasions, in what places, in combination with what other things, and so on). In the trend form, the narrative organization of valuation undoubtedly owes a great deal today to the rhetoric of glossy magazines, which, along with comic books, constituted the chief innovations of the twentieth century in the relation between texts and still images: these innovations have sought to transpose onto the space of a page the narrative arrangements by means of which films have managed to construct an original language that integrates sequences of spoken words and moving images into a single temporal sequence.

On the reproduction of things

In each form of valuation, the question of the reproduction of things is central, but it comes up in different terms and calls upon a series of opposing pairs.

First, we must envisage the possibility that a thing can be reproduced and then presented, especially in the analytic mode, as "without differences" from another such thing. This possibility is embodied by two contrasting pairs, "prototype vs. specimen" and "original vs. copy." We need to distinguish between the two pairs because, when we are dealing with a "unique item," we consider it possible for a thing to be at once a prototype and a specimen, while we cannot say that a thing is at once an original and a copy. The original and the copy refer to the thing by attributing it to a singular or collective person, as well as to the precise period and place of its production. The "prototype vs. specimen" pair, even if it can be associated with a person as far as the prototype is concerned, may as a general rule be detached from persons insofar as persons are named or namable in the production process. These pairs can of course intersect: a painting by Picasso can be at once an original, a prototype, and a specimen, in the sense of a prototype of which only a single specimen exists.

A thing can also be reproduced with variations. This type of reproduction corresponds to a "model vs. imitation" pair. Certain salient features are presented as being reproduced, while other characteristics reveal pronounced differences between the model and the imitation. What unites them is a certain style. As it happens, the style may be associated not only with things but also with persons to whom the creation of a thing is attributed. Thus we can speak, for example, of the Caravaggio style or the Chanel style. This is the possibility to which the pair "real vs. fake" refers. A thing is said to be "real" when its presentation is considered as linking it to a person who created, touched, or produced it, while a "fake" thing corresponds to an incorrect attribution. Someone passes off a painting as a "real" Vermeer, as if Vermeer had painted it, whereas it is actually a "fake," painted by a counterfeiter living in the twentieth century. This does not mean that it is a copy, for the counterfeiter has reproduced only Vermeer's style – that is, a set of features common to other paintings attributed to Vermeer that are "real." The "real vs. fake" opposition is equivalent to the "authentic vs. inauthentic" opposition.

The "original vs. copy" and "real vs. fake" oppositions are often confused, especially with reference to art, but it is a mistake to treat them as if they were equivalent. This is easy to understand if we think in terms of two cases that, moreover, do not enter into the forms we are establishing: movies and relics. One does not say about a film that it is "fake," even though there may be countless copies of it, legal or illegal. Conversely, "real" and "fake" relics are deemed to exist, but the problem of "copies" of a relic never arises. The possibility of creating and passing off a "fake" film for a real one is quite remote: one would have to invent a fake production team, which would multiply the risk of discovery, owing to the number of biographies implied at a period when a great many traces of persons are retained. When a work of art is restored, it is possible that its attribution to a given artist will be changed. The struggle against counterfeit works and copies consequently has to be the object of a distinction between, on the one hand, battling against the circulation of illicit copies, which requires not the competence of historians or critics, and the like, but of persons and technologies capable of overseeing and controlling the flow of things, and, on the other hand, struggling against the circulation of fakes, which, in this case, requires the competence of historians, critics, experts, and so on. The problem, for the work of art, is that it may be at once a copy and a fake. The idea that a given work may be both is often a starting point, but it is a mistake to confuse the two.

For a thing to be "real," it has to be regularly, frequently, even continually subject to some form of surveillance, or at least to reliable attestation of its presence, so that it can have a "narrative identity."[25] If one cannot tell what has become of a thing during a certain period of time, the possibility arises that it may be a copy or a fake. The problem posed by a fake is that of inconsistency with other elements that, for their part, form a consistent whole. The problem posed by a copy lies in the appearance of a difference in resemblance (and without any question of mimicry). From one perspective, the differences are imperceptible: the things look "the same." From another perspective, a difference appears: a certain thing has been "copied" – that is, it has appeared after an earlier thing and has been created in relation to the first. In the accusation that something is a copy, the copy is presumed to have come after the original. In the accusation that something is a fake, the fake object is presumed to be situated with respect to a "real" one, but this may take place before, during, or after the production of the real thing. If one "discovers" an early work of a painter known up to that point only through mature works, one may wonder whether the work discovered is real or fake, with reference to the later works that are already treated as real.

The status of these contrasting pairs differs according to the form of valuation applied for at least two reasons. First, in each form, each pair participates in a more or less significant way in the valuation of things. The "prototype vs. specimen" opposition is at the root of the standard form; the "original vs. copy" opposition creates great differences in prices and metaprices within the collection form; the "real vs. fake" opposition does the same within the asset form; the "model vs. imitation" opposition is the basis for the organization of things in the trend form. Then, within each of these forms, the same question arises: if they are susceptible to activation, who has the power to activate these oppositions?

In the standard form, the "prototype vs. specimen" opposition cannot be understood without information about who has the exclusive right to reproduce specimens on the basis of a prototype. Specimens of a single prototype constitute series that include elements that are *a priori* unlimited in number. It follows that, depending on the case, the differential function can be applied either to the prototype or to each specimen. In the case of standard objects produced in series and sold when they are new, the differential function applies to the prototype. The prototypes are differentiated, and each thing produced is differentiated from another thing with reference to the prototype of which it is the specimen.

But the distinction between prototype and specimen can also be expressed, for example, in the collection form. As we shall see, in the domains where this form is used for the valuation of things, a distinction is posited between, on the one hand, things that, even if they are no longer produced, were manufactured in the past in a greater or smaller number of specimens and, on the other hand, things of which few specimens exist or things that can even be considered as unique specimens of their kind, thus concentrating prototype and specimen in a single object, as it were. Moreover, the collection form is characterized by a prohibition on reproducing things. This form must in fact maintain a price differential between the original and the copy. It is very hard to maintain such a differential if the original and the copy appear identical. This is why reproduction of the original is avoided. But the original can be reproduced when its price remains high owing to its memorial force, whereas its copy will have a much lower price that is likely to decrease rather than to rise or to remain stable over time.

In the case of objects that belong particularly to the standard form and are thus specimens of relatively undifferentiated prototypes – that is, of prototypes whose specimens enter readily into competition with specimens of other prototypes – the work of valuation is able to raise the price at which each specimen can be negotiated only slightly. In cases of this type, profits will depend chiefly on the number of specimens sold, each specimen being able to offer only a weak profit margin. Competition among suppliers (producers and/or sellers) will take place mainly through prices and through distribution. Nevertheless, distribution circuits targeting clients whose willingness to pay a given price differs may make it possible to increase profits if the product is slightly differentiated, in particular by its packaging. All sellers will seek to lower the prices of their products with respect to competing products and to distribute their own products as widely as possible so that a buyer who is relatively unconcerned with the differences among prototypes can always find an available specimen. The easiest way to increase profits will thus consist, in this case, in increasing the number of specimens sold (economies of scale), while at the same time lowering the manufacturing costs, in particular by putting pressure on variable costs and especially on salaries (for example, by outsourcing the manufacturing process to a low-wage country). From the perspective of profit, the value added by labor will contribute significantly to the added commercial value.

Conversely, when the emphasis is on differentiation between prototypes and also, as is very often the case with luxury products, on their anchoring in the past, the quest for profit tends to rely less on value added by labor and more on added commercial value. In these differing cases, the height of the price of a thing is limited only by the thresholds of acceptability tolerated by the various strata of potential buyers. And it is with reference to these thresholds that more or less elevated profit margins can be realized.

Lacks, totalities, and scarcity

A *lack* introduces a force capable of inciting a buyer to acquire a new thing, even though he or she already has other things that, seen on a broader scale – one on which certain differences are no longer perceptible – can appear similar and can be described in identical terms. However, what we are calling a *lack* is not conceived in psychological terms and does not refer to a subject's inner life. On the contrary, the force that stems from a lack is objective, in the sense that it is generated by the things themselves. The lack is produced by a system in which things take on meaning. A "lack" is thus, on the one hand, a substitute for a "desire" (and everything that ensues from desire: impulse, longing, envy, and so on) and, on the other hand, a substitute for utility. A given thing is lacking not because it would be useful; it is lacking, rather, with respect to a systemic dimension of objects among themselves: the object is missing with respect to a totality. With lack, the force that arouses the compelling need to acquire something shifts from the libido of a subject to the system of things in itself.

However, there are two different ways to conceive of a totality: as a *complete set* or as a *complete thing*. A complete set and a complete thing are, in general, ideal totalities destined never to be realized, or realized only very exceptionally. These totalities are distributed differently in relation to analytic and narrative presentations, and thus in relation to the four forms of valuation we are examining. *Complete sets* organize lacks in the collection and trend forms, which rely on narrative presentations, while *complete things* organize lacks in the standard and asset forms, which call for analytic presentations. To clarify these distinctions, we propose to explore the collection and standard forms in some detail.

In the collection form, anything at all can be given value through reference to a narrative of the past. It is generally supposed that the memorial power of things (their relation to persons or events) on its own ensures their degree of scarcity. But in fact it is the arrangement of the collection itself that generates relative scarcity, in connection with the complete set of relevant differences. When certain differences are absent from an accumulation that is meant to constitute a complete collection, the collector needs to add what is lacking. Such lacks exist for everyone who embraces the same system of differences – that is, everyone who makes or adheres to the same type of collection. These differences may be present among a large number of objects (as in a stamp collection) or among a small number (as in a collection of Fabergé eggs). But all collectors have a compelling reason for wanting all the pertinent differences to be represented; this creates, on the one hand, a competition among collectors and, on the other hand, a scarcity of the things that bear the differences that are present in a small number of them. This scarcity increases as the number of collectors in competition grows larger.

Such an arrangement, associated with the collection form, generates objective lacks within a totality and, as a result, produces relative scarcity. It thus also has an effect on the prices and metaprices of the objects collected. It is distinct from the analytic presentation of the thing itself. The fact that a certain pair of glasses has a very high price can be justified by the fact that they were worn by Sigmund Freud; this is different from justifying their price by arguing that they are rare – in other words, that a large number of collectors need them owing to a lack (in their collections of glasses worn by psychoanalysts, for example).

We are thus seeing two types of arrangement: one allows the price of an object to be justified in terms of its own value (Freud's glasses), while the other generates relative scarcity by virtue of the systematic character of the collection, inasmuch as the collection is based on a system of pertinent differences, a scarcity that also acts on the price in an external manner – that is, without justifying the price by referring to the object's intrinsic value. The collector has a compelling reason for acquiring a certain thing that he or she does not yet possess because that thing is lacking and is thus needed to complete the collection.

Let us now consider the possibility of a lack that does not occur within a set but is supported by a thing, or, more precisely, several things, that can be described in identical terms. In the standard form, each thing is inscribed in the same determination of things, characterized by a broad functionality: a camera is used to take pictures. In the (relatively infrequent) case that someone invents a new functionality – an apparatus that can both take pictures and be used as a telephone – a new determination of a thing is created. In the standard form, each thing is described and subjected to valuation in an analytic manner with respect to other things. The magazine of a consumers' association can thus present notations serving to classify ten digital cameras that are being offered for sale concurrently.

In the standard form, a lack is not produced by a thing in relation to several other determinate things of the same type at the same time, for that would amount to making a collection – of digital cameras, for example. Rather, lack is inscribed in temporality: it is produced by the evolution of prototypes in the direction of progress. This evolutionist ideal is particularly clear in the case of technological objects. It is derived from the habitual conception of science and technology according to which they are oriented toward constant progress.

There is thus also, in the standard form, a system of differences that, being new, appear as improvements, advances. When these differences appear concretely, they create a lack with respect to existing things – that is, they generate compelling reasons for acquiring the new thing. What is at stake, once a new determination of the thing in question has been developed, is the creation of a new lack according to this evolutionist logic. The iPhone is a famous case: a new and improved version is marketed every year by Apple, the new improvement being presented as filling a lack found in the previous version, which by the same token becomes obsolete. From this perspective, the complete thing is the one that incorporates all possible evolutions, or, in other words, the one that would be the end point of evolution. Just as collectors have no reason to buy new things if their collections are complete, except to have duplicates, someone who buys a complete thing would have no reason to buy a new one, except to have one in reserve.

The differences introduced by the evolution of a thing stem primarily from an analytic presentation, and thus they generally offer either an improvement in an already named quality (lighter, faster, more durable, and so on) or the addition of a new quality. A distinctive feature of the standard form is that it offers things that incorporate the possibility of their own surpassing by new and improved things, going in the direction of progress. Sometimes these improvements are included or anticipated but incorporated only gradually in order to "program obsolescence." In such cases, the thing is surpassed not in the sense that it would no longer be in fashion, as is the case in the trend form, but in the sense that it is outdone by a better version of itself. This orients buyers toward a certain number of things to the detriment of other such things, and it creates a relative scarcity that generates competition.

In the other two forms, lacks are organized in still other ways. In the trend form, fashion offers a system of differences that creates lacks in a temporal context, as is the case for the standard form, but in the trend form these lacks operate in cyclical rather than evolutionist terms. This form does not feature constant progress; rather, it features eternal returns, each endowed with a variation. From this perspective, the totality is a set that encompasses the entire cycle. If a person were to possess all possible varieties of jackets, those currently in fashion but also those that are outdated, to the extent that fashion is cyclical that person could always be in fashion, pulling whatever is currently à la mode out of the closet. As in the standard form, the totality is tied to a suspension of time.

In the asset form, lack is supported by the thing itself and not by a set of things. But a lack is produced by the fact that several persons want the same thing, and thus each person, in a kind of mimesis, lacks a thing that is sought by others. The complete thing would thus be the thing sought by each actor inasmuch as all the actors concerned are seeking it in order to sell it at a profit.

The arrangements for creating lacks and thus for creating scarcity are essential to making profits and to creating added commercial value.

Institutions and forms of valuation

The forms of valuation that we are in the process of describing are supported by institutions. From our perspective, institutions differ from "ordinary persons" through the fact that, unlike persons, they have no bodies.[26] It is precisely this property that authorizes them to adopt an all-encompassing viewpoint and posit definitions that are valid for all. Ordinary persons, because they have bodies, are always situated in particular contexts, and thus their vantage points on the world are always partial and/or self-interested. This is why, as John Searle has shown,[27] they delegate to institutions the semantic task that consists in shaping the formats on which social order relies – or, to put it in different terms, the task that consists in undertaking what sociology has been calling for some forty years the construction of reality: these formats declare "the whatness of what is." But, conversely, precisely because institutions have no bodies, they can express themselves only through the intermediary of spokespersons who are always susceptible to speaking, not, as they claim, in the name of the institution, but in their own names and in their own interests.

This architecture accounts for a reduction in uncertainty that leads to a stabilization of reality. As it happens, the work of constructing reality always presupposes choosing among different interpretations of what has happened or is happening in the world. The suspicion that is manifested toward spokespersons is supported by the actors' own experience of the world (understood as "everything that happens"), on the basis of which they can critique the depictions of reality that are offered by institutions. In fact, since the world is intrinsically contradictory, the way an institution makes it coherent can always be rejected as being only one interpretation among others. This is precisely what is accomplished by the operations that characterize critique.

Three components are particularly essential in the construction of reality: language, things, and prices. As reality is most often oriented toward permanence, for institutions the task is to produce, first of all, qualifications, norms, and narratives, whether they do so via statistics, law, education, or scholarly research. But the construction of reality is also carried out by institutions through a certain number of things that are selected for preservation, as in the collection form.[28]

As for prices, they are, as everyone knows from everyday experience, a central constitutive element of reality. Prices are not directly regulated by institutions, except in the case of price controls. However, it is precisely because they do not have an institutional character and because they are perceived as resulting from blind mechanisms – those described by "economics" – that prices are "innocent." They can be deemed "innocent" because they are generated by no one in particular, since "free" competition is presumed to be responsible on its own for setting prices "freely." If prices are "innocent," they can be held responsible for establishing a border between things for the wealthy and things for those who lack wealth, a border that central governments cannot themselves institutionalize, not even in statistical terms, since the official vocation of central governments is the common good.

One of the contradictions of the science of economics may stem precisely from the tension between things and their prices. Things in fact undergo numerous processes of qualification that in some cases have a legal basis and that often rely, through more or less complex networks, on institutions, even governmental institutions. These qualifications are structured like a semantics. But prices are left free so that they have, as it were, a strictly pragmatic character, since they depend on the circumstances of particular transactions. This is the case even if they are expressed in a framework – that of currency – which for its part is indeed subject to institutional monitoring and support. But this framework provides only a general metric; it intervenes only rarely, if ever, in the structure of relative prices, except in situations of crisis. Only in extreme cases – hyperinflation, the simultaneous presence of several competing currencies – does it become necessary to stabilize the metric once again and presumably to be concerned with relative prices. If price structures become too distorted, central governments (or other types of political entity, such as the European Union) can intervene, typically via their monetary policies (where inflation is concerned) or via a particular category of prices, for example through taxation; in the case of real estate, they can intervene to limit the rise in rental prices in districts where buildings are increasingly oriented toward either touristic activity (hotels, restaurants) or sales of luxury products, or are bought and sold as assets, but are in any case no longer, or less and less, intended for durable housing benefiting city residents (for examples, it suffices to look at London, New York, or to a lesser extent, depending on the district, even Paris).

Each form of valuation – standard, collection, asset, and trend – relies on institutions.

So that the standard form can function properly, institutions guarantee the standardization of norms and the legal protection of prototypes along with the major brand names: this allows owners of the rights to a prototype to retain the exclusive right to reproduce it in the form of specimens and to put those specimens up for sale, provided that norms ensuring their compatibility with other objects are respected (and thereby excluding other types of things that are not in conformity with the norms governing their functions, safety, and so on).

To be inserted into the collection form, a thing has to be assigned a value in relation to a narrative of the past that gives it memorial force. Institutions, primarily museums and universities, guarantee this memorial force through narrative presentation and by endowing certain things with a kind of immortality – that is, by selecting them to be preserved in collections that cannot be sold. While museums may seem to offer "spaces for resisting the effects of the growing commercialization of art," as Chantal Mouffe argues,[29] it is precisely when they present works of art in a context that distinguishes them from "commercial products" that museums help solidify the presence of these works in the economy of enrichment.

From the perspective of the asset form, things viewed as assets are bought (exchanged for a sum of money) solely so that they can be sold again – that is, transformed back into money. In this case, where institutions guarantee the stability of the currency, one can buy certain things with the prospect of reselling them at a higher price in a context in which other prices remain relatively stable.

When a thing is assigned a value from the standpoint of the trend form, even if it is utilized, it is considered not primarily with reference to its intended use but, rather, as a sign marking the position occupied by the parties to the exchange in the web of social relations, in a constantly renewed movement of resemblance and difference. As this form has a cyclical character, it needs to draw from the past to maintain the cycle and to be out of phase with what is recognized by institutions. What is institutionalized is already out of fashion.

Structuralism and capitalism

The phenomena on which our analyses focus can give rise to two approaches, both of which bring into play reference to structures, although the latter are envisaged very differently in the two cases.

A first approach deals with structures in the sense that it takes as its object configurations of constraints whose interactions produce a force field. Considered from a dynamic viewpoint, the relations between these constraints are linked in a causal chain and take the form of more or less irreversible processes. This approach can be called systematic.

The second approach also deals with structures, but even though these latter structures have a collective or shared character, as it were, they reveal their agency only when they are incorporated into the competencies that the actors deploy when they have to act. In this sense, these structures can be characterized as cognitive – but only on condition that the action is not envisioned in a behaviorist (stimulus–response) optic; it must be envisaged, rather, as depending not only on interactions among actors but also on the relation that all the actors maintain with themselves and with their own actions – that is, envisaged as bringing feedback loops into play. This second approach is often characterized as microsociological, since it deals with actors at close range; it is also called "pragmatic," since it takes into account the conditions of the action and the reflective processes that accompany it. As both of these approaches have guided us in our work, we shall attempt to clarify their articulation.

Competition from a systemic viewpoint

In the case that concerns us, that of commodities, defined by the encounter, in an exchange, between a thing and a price, these two approaches both stress the quest for advantage and competition in the effort to generate and secure a profit, although the manifestations and effects of competition are envisaged in two different lights: on the one hand, inasmuch as they stem from systemic mechanisms and, on the other, inasmuch as they bring the actors' capacity to reflect into play.

Among the various features generally associated with capitalism, the one that plays the principal role in the picture we are drawing is competition for profit. Indeed, the displacements of capitalism (what Braudel calls its dynamic) rely on the play of this competition. We have thus drawn on causal analyses that aim to explain this dynamic through the lowering of rates of profit in a certain sphere of operations and the search for new spheres that promise higher rates. These analyses, which are often said to be made from a Marxist (or, sometimes, Weberian) perspective, can also be compared with Niklas Luhmann's conception to the extent that Luhmann defines a structure as "a limitation of the relations allowed within a system," a structure that can take on an "internal guidance system" permitting "autoproduction."[30] These analyses have a systemic character in the sense that they conceive of capitalism as a self-maintaining global process oriented toward the unlimited accumulation of capital, whose movement depends on the causal relation between forces that either work together or oppose one another in such a constraining way that capitalism can be described without descending to the level of the actors, and especially without bringing their reflective capacities into play. Hence the stress on the necessity that governs the system and is imposed on all parties.

No one escapes the force fields described – accurately – as asymmetrical, not even the holders of capital who profit from them. For the latter, who sometimes adopt an objectivist posture toward themselves, especially when they describe past actions, often claim that they too have acted under the constraint of necessity, so as to ensure the survival of their business, their portfolio, their family assets, or even their country, and so on; that is, they declare that they have acted so as to perpetuate these holdings for their own sake and that they have only carried out the "will," as it were, of capitalism, whose more or less content but always faithful servants they have been. A systemic description of this type is valid under certain conditions. It sheds light on a reality considered from a position of overview and over the long haul, inasmuch as this reality is shaped and transformed through the effects of processes whose stages are causally linked. Useful on the macrohistorical level, such a description proves inadequate if we change the scale and, moving closer to the actors, have to account for the way in which they help drive these processes through their activities and, more precisely, through their exchanges. It thus becomes hard to avoid reckoning with the actors' reflective capabilities and the way these intervene during every exchange.

Capitalism and markets

The distinction just evoked is at once epistemological and ontological. The two approaches do not disclose the same reality. It is thus reasonable to wonder about the relations between the two realities that these two different approaches bring to light. One way of doing this is to project each approach onto the other in a thought experiment. Shifted to a macro-analytic scale, the approach that incorporates reflective individuals amounts roughly to positing a universe governed by the decisions of a small number of actors invested with exceptional power – something that is not very credible, at least in most historical contexts.

Conversely, placed on a micro-analytic scale, the perspective that inspires broad overviews bearing on long time periods and stressing the necessity generated by a play of constraints in a context of competition remains effective only when it is applied to situations, fairly rare ones, in which either a single supplier or a small number of suppliers (who have agreed to act in a coordinated way, whether explicitly or through collusion) hold a monopoly on access to goods sought by a large number of clients, who desire them in order to satisfy compelling needs and where, as a result, power relations are both manifest and irrefutable.

This thought experiment leads us to emphasize the relation between two ways of conceiving of the sphere of exchanges. The first invokes capitalism; the second, liberalism, with an emphasis on the workings of markets.

These two regimes can be identified with each other, as is often done by the critical vulgate of neoliberalism; conversely, they can be distinguished from each other, as Fernand Braudel has done. Braudel, noting the generality and banality of the market, saw one of the major features of capitalism in the exploitation of differentials making it possible to institute a relation of force and thereby to put pressure on the workings of a market. From this perspective, we can see – still following Braudel – in the "transparency" of markets a sort of moral ideal weighing on capitalism, in the manner, so to speak, of a liberal superego. We have sought to combine these two positions by showing that, if the analysis of contemporary capitalism has to take into account systemic constraints and power relations, it nevertheless cannot ignore certain of the central characteristics of exchange in a liberal context.

These can be summarized as follows. First, sellers, but also, in their own way, buyers, are, to varying degrees according to the situations, in competition with one another from the standpoint of advantage and gain. None of them is obliged to limit his or her hopes for profit in connection with attachments of another order, even if, envisaged from a moral viewpoint, that "possessive individualism" can be criticized, in the name of fidelity to various spheres of belonging (nation, family, social class, or even humanity). Secondly, sellers are always free to sell or not to sell the goods they hold and, similarly, buyers are always free to acquire or not to acquire the goods offered for sale. This is the case even if an asymmetry of financial means and power confer on that freedom a more or less "formal" character (the "free fox in the free henhouse").

This is the situation that makes price the principal tool for coordination in an exchange. The sellers, wishing to sell only at a certain price, will want to acquire an advantage over the competition by stressing the differences that characterize the things they are offering for sale. In this process, they will seek – as Edward Hastings Chamberlin was the first to emphasize[31] – to escape from competition by occupying a quasi-monopolistic position, even if only temporarily. As for the buyers, endowed with unequal means of payment and wishing to buy only at a certain price, they have the possibility of turning away from the commodity proposed. They may refrain from buying by telling themselves that they already have what they need. Or they may challenge the relevance of the differences highlighted by the various sellers, each of whom seeks to win out in the competition that opposes him or her to the others (for instance, buyers may purchase something used instead of a new item, judging that the "pre-owned" one will be just as useful as the other).

In the practical course of exchanges, these decisions rarely bear on things judged for themselves but generally concern things inasmuch as they are associated with prices. From the standpoint of commodities, things cannot be dissociated from their prices. It is (almost) always the combination *things + prices* that circulates through the intermediary of exchange. We note, however, that such situations of exchange do not necessarily have an imperative character, since the seller may choose not to offer (below a certain price), and the buyer may choose not to acquire (above a certain price). Even though these situations are generally asymmetrical, if one considers the inequalities of means and power, they do not provoke an absolute obligation except in cases in which the seller has a monopoly on goods of prime necessity.

The role of the capacity to reflect

Here is where reflection comes in. For the seller has to convince the buyer that what he or she is offering is worth a certain price so as to remove the hesitations of the buyer, who is free to criticize the price at which the thing is being offered. The deployment of this reflective capacity relies on the comparison between different *things* + *prices*. Since buyers and sellers alike are reflective and most often "reasonable" persons, and not simply agents of a system who would act blindly or under constraint, they must equip themselves with arguments that make it possible to justify or criticize the relation between a thing and a price, something that they can do only by associating with that thing a discourse capable of expressing the respect in which it is valuable (at a certain price) in comparison with other things (associated with other prices). As it happens, if these arguments and the discourses that incorporate them are to have a certain degree of effectiveness, they must be intelligible both to a buyer confronted with a seller's requirements and to a seller facing a buyer's reticence.

What we are calling the forms of valuation have an effect on the organization of commodities only inasmuch as they intervene in the composition of discourses about things considered as commodities – that is, things associated with prices. But it is precisely because they operate not on things themselves but on the discourse produced about things that these forms are structured. And this is how they help guide, in return, the structuring of commodities. A universe of choices considered independently of all discourse can perfectly well be described – in a logic that we shall characterize, to simplify, as positivist – as a set that would be governed only by constants, functions, or stochastic interactions, or even envisaged as an amorphous and chaotic set (on the same basis moreover as the elements of the world itself, as long as they have not been incorporated into the framework of a reality constructed by the intervention of a controlled use of language, of which law constitutes a paradigmatic example). By contrast, on the same basis as any other expression, a discourse about things must bend to the modes of arrangement that, in a certain cognitive framework, alone make it possible to generate an effect of signification. And this, through a play of repetitions and differences, comparisons and oppositions, makes it possible to grasp a thing the way one grasps a term or a name – that is, by showing oneself "sensitive to the set of semantic oppositions that define its content negatively and fixes the field of its possible uses differentially."[32] On the same basis as words, considered as signs whose value – in the Saussurian sense – is defined by the place they occupy in language, things are always identified differentially, with respect to other things, and thus they can become commodities by being associated with prices whose appropriateness will be justified or criticized through reference to the prices of other commodities.

The structure of the forms of valuation

This is also why the discourse of valuation is itself presented as differentiated and turns out to be distributed among a plurality of structurally similar forms that present rule-governed differences with respect to one another; this allows sellers and buyers to converge or diverge, by activating their imaginations, on the question of what particular qualities the thing submitted for exchange may have that would justify its price. To function, the field of discourse of valuation has to be both pluralized and unified, and it has to be based on categories whose structure is maintained even though it is the object of rule-governed transformations. If there were only a single discourse of valuation used for everything – for example, an exclamation of the type "that's super" or "that's better" (and such a discourse is implied, moreover, by the way the term "quality" is often used in economics) – the comparison between things would not have enough reference points to allow criticism or justification of the price of each thing. Everything would be comparable with everything else, and this would tend to pull the cosmos of commodities toward an amorphous and chaotic state.

But, from another standpoint, if the different forms of valuation consisted in categories unrelated to one another, the cosmos of commodities would tend to dissociate and split apart in a multiplicity of isolated units between which no comparisons would be possible, and this would call into question the unity of the measuring instrument used to compare things as commodities – that is, pricing arrangements. Each of these isolated units would then have to be endowed with a specific measuring instrument, a possibility somewhat similar to that of the dispersion of language among an unlimited series of private languages evoked by Wittgenstein. This is why the distribution of discourse about things at the heart of a transformation group constitutes, in the case that concerns us, an optimal figure.

We must be careful, nonetheless, to avoid considering these different ways of attributing value to things as purely formal models similar to the ones the econometricians have imagined. As is always the case for discourses that grasp elements of the world and that, owing to the very fact that they have grasped them, engage these elements in reality (as totalizations that are selective but are also by that very token organized and predictable, apt to be substituted for the world, which is ungraspable in its totality and thus unpredictable), the forms of valuation we are considering work for concrete entities. They operate on the basis of disparate elements that may be attached to outdated ways of envisaging things whose memorial potency has nevertheless not completely faded away, but they operate above all by taking into account the way things are affected by the use made of them.

The various ways of using things may be those of commerce, invented locally and on a case-by-case basis by clever salespersons, or those of so-called ordinary people. For if the fact of changing ownership modifies only the legal status of a thing, the fact of falling into new hands, when these hands grasp the thing in order to develop practices, can go so far as to modify the thing's character – what Michel de Certeau, in *L'invention du quotidien,* called the "arts of doing," which he associated, using the analogy developed by Claude Lévi-Strauss in *The Savage Mind,* with "tinkering."[33] The forms of valuation we have identified are nourished by these disparate elements, but they adapt the elements to structural constraints that select the respect in which the things must be considered in order to be compared with other things so they can be correctly appraised. The respect that is privileged, which emerges in relation to the context in which the thing is immersed (as in Wittgenstein's famous image of a duck/rabbit), modifies not just the way in which the thing presents itself to be seen and appraised but also the way in which those who enter into contact with it are expected to react to its presence. This means that discourses about things must be envisaged also as discourses addressed to persons, a fact that both orients those persons toward the forms of life that are appropriate to the things in question, given the way value is attributed to them, and coordinates the expectations that the persons may have about them.[34] The forms of valuation can thus be envisaged both from a structural viewpoint, when one is interested in the way their differences have to be articulated in order to be intelligible, and from the viewpoint of a pragmatics, and even more specifically of a "normative pragmatics,"[35] when one stresses the way in which these differences insert themselves into situations in which the challenge is to reduce the uncertainty about a price by making an explicit reference to value.

Part III

Commodity Structures

5

The Standard Form

The model for the standard form

The invention of the *standard* form is one of the principal innovations on which the development of industrial society has depended since the nineteenth century. The defining characteristic of this form of valuation is that it applies to objects closely tied to a particular mode of manufacturing, whereas the other forms can be applied to objects of diverse origins, only some of which are produced in the standard manner. The standard mode of manufacturing entails reproducing a *prototype* by producing a potentially unlimited number of *specimens*. Standardization of this sort supports production while favoring economies of scale and gains in productivity, but that is not all: it also establishes the relevant properties of the prototype via an *analytic presentation* that is usually registered in a patent granting the holder a monopoly over reproductions of the prototype. The standard form also allows for public descriptions of the relevant differences between a given product and others whose appearance and/or functional capacities are similar but not identical. Thus the standard form makes it possible for sellers to justify the asking price; by supplying instruments for comparative measurement,[1] it also makes it possible for others to critique the asking price. In economies that rely on the use of standards, consumers are supposed to be able to access all the information they need to make thoughtful choices and, in particular, to relate the price of the product to its qualities.

This way of reducing the consumer's uncertainty is fully effective, however, only if the comparison deals with *new* products: the properties of these products may be deemed *defects* if there are discrepancies between the actual objects produced and those in the canonical description. Things whose valuation relies on the standard form are always intended for *use*. Yet because use subjects things to random transformations that may go unnoticed even in a fairly thorough examination, in a transaction involving a used object the seller and the potential buyer do not have access to the same amount of information. This *asymmetry* increases the buyer's *uncertainty*, as demonstrated in an often cited article from the early 1970s about the used-car market.[2] An increase in the level of uncertainty thus accompanies the *trajectory* of the standard product.[3] Describable and guaranteed when it leaves the factory, it is always destined, sooner or later, to become *trash* – that is, something that no one wants or can use any longer, something that its owner will try to get rid of by abandoning it, destroying it, or recycling its elements so as to reinsert them in a productive cycle. This is why the standard form can be said to exploit the present.

The arrangements for assigning value associated with the standard form can be schematized by distributing the objects involved along two axes (see figure 5.1). The vertical axis, which can be called *the differential axis of analytic presentation*, has at its base objects designed to satisfy generic needs, often intended for everyday use; their prototypes are minimally differentiated, so that competition between products will depend primarily on the distribution network and on prices. The objects involved are often based on relatively old technologies. As an example, let us take ballpoint pens: with objects in this category, the brand name and the model are ultimately of little importance to the user, who grabs one to satisfy an urgent need such as jotting down an address or a telephone number. At the summit of the axis of analytic presentation, on the contrary, we find highly differentiated objects, often based on more recent technologies; with such objects, an innovative character is an important argument in the competition for buyers. Here, computers and cell phones are good examples.

The horizontal axis, which distributes objects according to their relation to time, indicates *commercial potential*. It concerns the period of time during which the product is expected to give satisfaction to its owner before it becomes trash. In this context, one often speaks of the product's *quality*. However, the *obsolescence* of a product can be programmed so that the user will be forced to replace it before it *fails*; this is often the case with information technology. On the far left of this axis, we find products intended for short-term use, as is the case par excellence with products said to be "throw-aways" – for example, razors; on the far right, by contrast, we find expensive watches that users are supposed to be able to wear for a lifetime and even pass along as heirlooms.

To say of a standard object that it will last a short time signifies that it has weak commercial potential; to have strong commercial potential, a product must be durable. As we have seen, the distinguishing feature of the price of a standard object is that the price is highest when the item is "new," and it begins to decline at once, even if the used object appears to be no different, materially and functionally, from its new counterpart, except for the fact that it is presented as used. Let us consider a "reconditioned" object, one whose owner, having perhaps merely unwrapped it, returns it to the seller, who wants to offer it for sale again – for example, a white refrigerator, immaculate except for a small, visible scratch. A scratched refrigerator, even if it is perfectly operational in technical terms, can be sold only at a discount, at a lower price than a new one. If a product is "durable," it can presumably circulate for a long time and change hands more than once; thus its commercial potential unfolds in the form

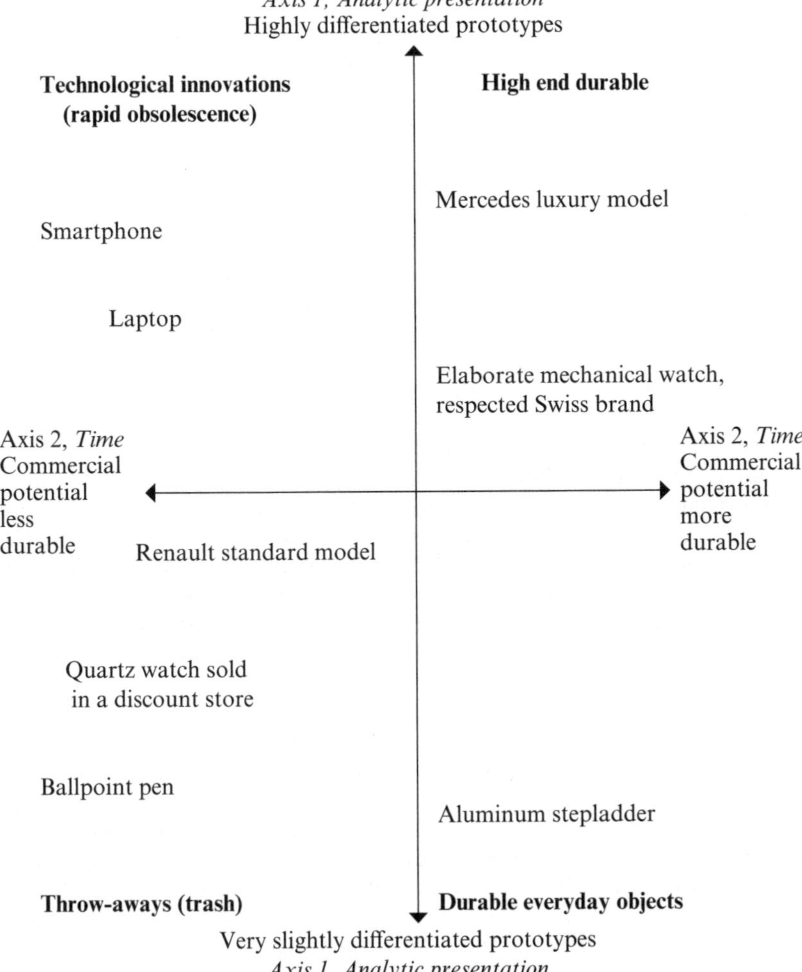

Figure 5.1 Structural schema of the standard form[4]

of a broad circuit of exchanges. By contrast, objects endowed with weak commercial potential generally change hands just once, when they are sold as new products, and they quickly end up as trash.

By taking the two axes into account, we can also draw a diagonal line that ranks objects, as marketing often does. Thus *low-end* objects – that is, objects that are minimally differentiated and not very long-lasting (for example, a toothbrush) – are contrasted with *high-end* objects – those that are at once highly differentiated and very long-lasting (for example, a Mercedes).

The standard form and industrial production

The world in which the standard form is used is centered on utility. Only objects (generally artifacts with a certain technological dimension) that are explicitly intended to carry out a predefined function at the time they are conceived and fabricated, and perhaps most clearly at the time they are offered for sale and purchased, can be assigned value through recourse to arguments on which the standard form confers relevance and coherence. This has no doubt been the case for a long time for objects destined for armies and commissioned by central governments, especially weapons and uniforms; it has also been the case for tools and machinery used by industry in production lines. Here, however, we are interested chiefly in objects intended for everyday use by private persons in the ordinary course of life.

These objects are predefined with reference to the functions they are meant to perform, and thus they rely on a nomenclature of functions, even though the functions may range from highly specific to quite open-ended (as is the case with tools used in information technology), and even though different individuals may use a given object in very different ways. This predetermination by function supplies a descriptive language and evaluative criteria that facilitate communication between the seller and the potential buyer. But predetermination by function does not suffice when it comes to exploring in detail the capabilities of each object offered for sale – that is, estimating prior to purchase how well the object will actually perform when it has to carry out the tasks required of it and the length of time during which its use will prove to be satisfactory.

This instrumental relation to objects has often been considered a feature specific to industrial societies, and on this basis it has been among the pivots of the numerous critiques that, since the nineteenth century, have called disenchanted modernity into question by contrasting it with the enchanted world of tradition. One has to go beyond the instrumental approach, however, to characterize the most original aspect of the standard form. For one thing, the criterion of utility obviously did not wait for the appearance of standardized objects to serve as a basis for making judgments about things. For another, the causal links that tie the development of the standard form to the industrial revolution are far from mechanical and linear.

We have no intention of trying to draw a broad synthetic picture of the various industrial revolutions and their stages; this history is now so thoroughly documented, so diverse, and sometimes so contradictory that it discourages any effort to synthesize.[5] But we note that, at least until roughly the last third of the nineteenth century, what is known as the first industrial revolution affected in particular the sectors involving energy, transportation, the means of production, and the manufacture of certain semi-finished products such as cotton cloth, timber, and flour, without profoundly modifying the universe of things that were exchanged in the ordinary course of human relations. Thus, as Patrick Verley has written, it would be "totally anachronistic to evoke standardization in connection with the industrial production of the first half of the nineteenth century."[6] Especially in rural communities where cash was scarce, the things used for everyday tasks were still often manufactured at home or in very small proto-industrialized workshops. To be sure, with urbanization, the formation of a proletariat, and the development of the middle classes in the first half of the nineteenth century, the proportion of things purchased rather than made at home tended to increase. This development was stimulated, at the bottom of the social ladder, by the work of women in business enterprises and by the length of the workday, which left women less time for household tasks. It was also influenced, toward the top of the ladder, by the spread of a new type of relation to material culture, an "industrious"[7] relation that paralleled the growing role of women in the domestic economy.[8]

But the everyday objects made outside the home were for the most part fashioned according to procedures and forms of organization that stemmed from those used by previous generations. This was the case even when the makers profited from the development of machinery, whether indirectly, in the sense that the process included transforming semi-finished industrial products, or directly, when part of the energy used was not of human or animal origin but, rather, supplied by machines installed near workshops. Still, we must note that manufacturing establishments of the latter type were relatively rare during the first industrial revolution; their development was based on the use of steam-operated machines that were costly and cumbersome, while the energy supplied was centralized and relatively inflexible, since its transmission to the various tools used by workers required complex systems of axles and pulleys. And, even in workshops that used steam, the proportion of tasks accomplished by hand, especially in the finishing stages, remained high.

It was only with the second industrial revolution, at the end of the nineteenth century and in the first third of the twentieth, that the growing use of electric motors favored the diffusion of machinery on smaller scales and the development of tools that worked autonomously.[9] This was also the period during which new manufacturing methods allowed for interchangeability among the various components making up a standard object and thus made repairs easier: a part that turned out to be defective could be replaced by a new one. This possibility, which posed complex technical, organizational, and commercial problems and was introduced into production facilities only gradually during the last third of the nineteenth century (the earliest examples were in the United States, with sewing machines and bicycles), is often viewed as one of the major features contributing to the development of the standard form.[10]

One can thus conclude that, for a long time, the objects that entered into commercial circulation – which increased in number especially starting in the second half of the eighteenth century and continuing throughout the nineteenth, in tandem with the rise of itinerant peddling in rural areas[11] – retained a character that could be described succinctly as traditional, the concurrent development of industry notwithstanding. These products did not differ in any essential way from the objects supplied by artisans or made in small local workshops. This was true not only of clothing made by tailors or dressmakers working at home on made-to-order items, for example, but also of all sorts of tools and instruments intended for household use, not to mention food products that were still mostly made at home. One of the features of the non-industrial mode of production that accompanied the development of commercial exchanges during the industrial revolution was that it did not harden the opposition between new objects purchased first-hand and used objects purchased second-hand: that opposition became central only when the standard form began to take off: "A great number of shops do not sell newly-manufactured products but rather second-hand items."[12] Inspired by the writings of Louis-Sébastien Mercier, Laurence Fontaine shows the diversity of this trade in used goods, especially on the part of women, in eighteenth-century Paris.[13] In 1725, for instance, alongside 3,500 tailors and dressmakers (who made new clothes or altered old ones) in the city, there were 700 merchants selling used clothing and as many selling used women's lingerie; in addition, some 6,000 to 7,000 people were engaged in selling second-hand goods.[14] Thus the importance of traders in second-hand clothing persisted, at least among the urban lower classes: for a long time these merchants remained the main source for acquiring clothes that had been used, transformed and exchanged again and again until they were so worn they became unusable. The proliferation of second-hand shops, whose success was based on the fact that they sold on credit, was thus associated with an economy of recuperation rather than an economy of consumption.[15] This reuse of objects, whose downward trajectory passed through the various strata of the social hierarchy, contrasted sharply with the fate that objects were to encounter with the development of mass production based largely on the standard form, one of whose features is that it confers on objects, often rather quickly, the status of trash. The accumulation of trash has thus become one of the most critical and most criticized aspects of mass production.

Prototypes and specimens

Thus the industrial revolution and mechanization cannot be credited with a radical transformation that brutally replaced artisanal objects, admired for their fanciful aspects and their diversity, with manufactured objects, denounced for their unattractive uniformity. The theme of radical transformation fed into the artistic critique of capitalism, a critique often confused with that of industrial society in general. The artistic critique dramatizes the opposition between things made in a so-called traditional way, so that no two things are alike and each one can be characterized (like the individuals who make them by hand) as "authentic," and things made in the era of mechanization and exchanged in shops for money; in the latter case, the products allegedly have the effect of alienating not only the workers who make them and the shopkeepers who trade in them but also those who covet, buy, and use them. However, one can just as well acknowledge that objects labeled artisanal – wooden clogs, to take just one example – can be very similar to one another, at least in a certain region, as the ethnologists who collect them reverently are well aware, and that objects labeled industrial can be sought for their diversity, as the collectors who collect and compare them precisely to stress their differences are well aware.

It is often forgotten, moreover, that a certain uniformization of things was produced early on by the institution of Christianity. The funerary sculpture of the Roman era was inspired, as Erwin Panofsky showed, by "an almost boundless variety of beliefs and experiences – the official religion, the literary and representational tradition of mythology, strange mystery cults and even stranger philosophies."[16] Tomb sculptures came in unlimited forms, and the burial of bodies coexisted with cremation. But, according to Panofsky, "the Christian faith gave unity of direction to man's confused desire for immortality," or at least to discourse on the subject, and, in a ricochet effect, to grave markers, which were "to be reduced to relative simplicity and absolute consistency by the unifying force of Christianity."[17] The same movement toward uniformity occurred in Germany in the fifteenth and sixteenth centuries, with an effort to stabilize the identification of religious imagery, especially that of Christ. Starting in the fifteenth century, as David Freedberg points out, images intended for meditation, which had become inexpensive and easy to obtain, were available to a large part of the population. At the same time, "they became standardized in undreamt-of ways."[18] Everyone meditated[19] with the help of identical reproductions of images, in which Christ, in response to criteria that had become uniform, was recognizable. As Freedberg puts it, "The old difficulties of recognition, the old urgent need for it now ease; you and I meditate on images of whose identity we may be sure."[20]

The retrospective illusion that things were made uniform owing to the industrial revolution – an illusion conflating hatred of factories, machines, and money as opposed to the craftsman's workshop, manual dexterity, and the nobility of gifts – conceals a disjunction in the order of things that was to become predominant especially in the first third of the twentieth century, when products identified as *standard* began to invade the sphere of everyday exchanges.[21]

The development of the standard form did indeed introduce an unprecedented innovation into the universe of objects, but one that can by no means be attributed entirely either to machinery – even though it emerged in the wake of mechanization – or to money – even though its formation was stimulated by the quest for profit. Anchored not only in technological changes but also in organizational and legal developments that accompanied a transformation in class relations, the standard form was distinguished not as much by uniformization and serialization as by a redistribution of things in relation to a difference that, without being absolutely new, had never before been so decisive. This difference was articulated around a nodal point that concerned the relation between *things* and *persons*, a relation that, on this basis, can be called ontological. Until the standard form appeared, the ontology of beings was essentially grounded in a separation – inherited from Aristotle's metaphysics and taken up again in its broad outlines by the scholastics – between so-called natural beings, "whose coming to being is from a nature," and "productions" – that is, beings whose coming to being is "from craft," in which some matter, which is not generated but rather pre-existent, is brought together with a form that "is in the [artist's] soul." Thus the object produced is not "said to be what it is from" (a bronze sphere is not called bronze but "brazen," *of* bronze).[22] But the form itself pre-exists as essence, so that what is engendered is a composite of matter and form that receives its name from the form and owes its existence to the artist's activity. By relying on the distinction between matter and form, each of the beings whose arrival in the world resulted from human activity – artifacts – could consequently be envisaged as an arrangement whose quiddity ("what it is said to be intrinsically")[23] was generated by that action on pre-existing matter carried out by bodies imbued with the intention to confer form on them. It followed that, in every artisanal object, one could see at least implicitly the result of a sort of fusion between things and persons, in the sense that every artifact was thought to preserve in its very substance not only a trace of the intentions of the person or persons who had made it but also a trace of the intentions of the person or persons who had wanted to possess it and had placed an order for it.[24]

The standard form does not abolish this way of conceiving the relation between artisanal objects and persons, which has transited from the myth of the *chôra* (reformulated in Plato's *Timaeus*) to ordinary metaphysics via a Christian reinterpretation of Greek philosophemes that was spread widely through classical education in schools,[25] but the distribution of the concept has been modified. The innovation introduced by the standard form – a way of engendering things and also of attributing value to them – in fact depends on the distinction between, on the one hand, the creation of a *prototype*, which may exist as a fully realized object or only in virtual form and, on the other hand, the production of objects that reproduce the prototype in a theoretically limitless number of *specimens*. Only the latter are sold and inserted into the cosmos of commodities. In this new arrangement, within the prototype are concentrated the traces of all the human intentions that presided over the conception of the object, whose description is stabilized in the form of a patent that fixes its relevant properties according to modalities that evoke codification: a legal act guarantees that the patent holder has a monopoly over the production of specimens that reproduce the prototype and thus has a monopoly on the profits that selling them can procure. But the specimens – which are the sole objects of appropriation by clients, each of whom may consider the object that he or she has acquired and will use as if it were a singular object, since it is now his or her possession – no longer bear, as individual items, the traces of human intentions that remain concentrated in the only entity to which the specimens refer: the prototype. It is through this arrangement involving a prototype and specimens that we can understand the rupture introduced by the standard form with respect to the uniformization of things that could be produced in the absence of a prototype by an institution such as the Church – tombstones, for instance, or images of Christ.

Thus the standard form can be said to introduce, among things, beings that have unprecedented properties, in the sense that, even though they are products of human activity, they have the particular feature of being *objects in themselves* – simply things and nothing else – since their share of humanity is concentrated entirely in the prototype. Only at the moment of appropriation do these things have a chance to recover a human aspect, so to speak, by becoming a thing belonging to someone who invests them with a desire and inflects them solely by making use of them – in other words, by submitting them to a treatment that, caught up in the various circumstances of life, always has something specific about it. By contrast, if such things, even in perfect condition, fail to find buyers and begin to clutter stockrooms, they will count among the rejects negotiated at low prices and destined to be sold off at a discount. In the regime of the standard form, objects are linked with human beings only through the intermediary of ownership, which alone can give any particular specimen its own identity.

This is no doubt why stores in which specimens are presented for sale generally avoid showing different specimens of the same object side by side and in large numbers, especially if the things in question are costly and invested with affect (as are high-end or luxury products, par excellence), and it is probably also why the factories where such things are made and where they can be seen in their serial multiplicity (for example, on the assembly line) are not generally open to potential buyers, or are modestly veiled from public view, as if to erase them from the collective consciousness of potential consumers. But, from a different standpoint, it is also because of the perfect conformity of specimens, and because they do not exist as individual objects, that potential consumers can place their confidence in them by shifting onto them the confidence they may have in the prototype and in the company where the prototype was conceived. This is why the valuation of things in the framework of the standard form introduces a maximal gap between new and used objects. Only a new object can in fact claim to be in perfect conformity with the prototype to which it refers and can thereby deploy its "thingness" in a pure state, since it is only through the intermediary of appropriation and use that human intentionality can be invested in the object once again.

The proliferation of things without persons

The transformation of the relation between things and persons brought about by the development of the standard form, a transformation that shifts the identity of things onto the prototype alone, can be understood as a sort of projection onto things themselves of the radical asymmetry between intellectual work and manual labor in which Marx recognized one of the principal defining features of capitalism. Whereas the traces of the intellectual work that was necessary to produce the prototype are revealed and celebrated in its very body, so much so that it sometimes becomes a respectfully preserved object of veneration (a phenomenon structurally analogous to the cult of origins, thus enabling passage from the standard form toward the collection form), a specimen is appreciated only inasmuch as it is presumed to be nothing but a perfect reproduction of the prototype: in other words, it is appreciated not for itself but only inasmuch as it represents – in the sense that an agent or proxy can represent – the prototypical properties that characterize its model. This is the case to such an extent that discovering the slightest difference between the prototype and one of its specimens – a task assigned to quality control – is tantamount to discovering a defect in the specimen, whose lack of perfect conformity alters it and strips it of all commercial value.

Mechanization is indeed responsible for the possibility that one object (the specimen) may *repeat* another (the prototype) – that is, the possibility of an act of generation and multiplication without differentiation; this constitutes a tour de force that had never been realized, either in the realm of nature or in that of culture, before the advent of the standard form. But this act was possible only to the extent that it went hand in hand with a radical change in the organization of labor and of the legal framework surrounding it. This change from handwork to factory production transformed a process based on a combination of dispersed workers – among whom it would have been theoretically possible to distribute the attribution of the various components of the finished product (Marx called this a "subjective" division of labor) – into a mode of production (which Marx called "objective") in which the manufacture of specimens that come out of the factory is attributed solely to the production arrangements themselves.[26]

This mode of reproduction is attributed to strictly mechanical action that is presumed to transpose none of the particular properties of the agents who set the machinery in motion onto the body of the thing produced, whether the work is actually done – it hardly matters – by a machine or by a human person, since agents of either sort will have accomplished the task expected of them only if they have followed the instructions and prescribed protocols to the letter. Whereas the work that allowed the construction of the prototype is presented as belonging to the mode of *creation*, the work of reproduction is envisaged according to modalities on the order of having things done, modalities that thus, to varying degrees, evoke servitude. This way of conceiving of the division of labor, which doubtless originated in military structures, from the discipline of combat to the organization of arsenals, reached its culmination and became the ordinary way to fabricate the most common objects, when the standard form was in full development, with the invention and gradual implementation of the Taylor method, one of whose chief objectives was to free capitalist enterprises from the power that workers were capable of exercising over production.[27] Organization according to the Taylor method is characterized principally not by the importance it grants to machines but by the fact that it entrusts the inevitable human interventions to persons who are easily and rapidly replaceable, since each of them has to accomplish only one partial and relatively unspecific task requiring only generic competencies.

Moreover, it is precisely because it was accused of treating workers as if they were machines and of mechanizing human beings that the standard form, when it reached its fullest extension (embodied par excellence in Henry Ford's automobile business), was the object of intense critiques in the 1920s and 1930s. There were early echoes of this in literature, for example in Aldous Huxley's *Brave New World* (1932), a science fiction novel set in the year 632 of an era called "Our Ford," in *The Flivver King* (1937), a novel by the socialist utopian writer Upton Sinclair satirizing the Ford factories, and also in films, for example in René Clair's *À nous la liberté* (1931), which represents a Fordist organization as a prison regime, or Charlie Chaplin's *Modern Times* (1936).[28] In the same period, Walter Benjamin wrote "The Work of Art in the Age of its Technological Reproducibility" (1936),[29] both stressing the singularity of the original work and the threat that reproduction introduced into its aura and extending the fear of a possible extension of the standard form that would end up controlling even what, for the philosophers of the Frankfurt School – Adorno in particular – constituted civilization's last rampart against mechanistic barbarianism: the world of art and culture.[30]

This form of organized production was not only capitalist in the sense that it stimulated profits by allowing increased exploitation of the workforce and the extraction of added value; it was also capitalist to the extent that it constituted the analytic presentation of an object as property, and thereby infinitely increased the gap between owners and non-owners. Based on codification, standardization created a radical asymmetry between those who owned the code of analytic presentation and those who merely reproduced or applied it. The generalization of patents and the spread of intellectual property rights arose first in the universe of communications (and especially in the economics of book publication). Extended to the totality of things – material and immaterial – likely to circulate in a commercial form, this phenomenon exercised an effect of dispossession that has often been aptly compared to that of the enclosure of the commons in which we have been able to see, after Marx, a forerunner of capitalist accumulation on a much larger scale. With the extension of industrial property associated with the development of standardization, the owners of the means of production no longer necessarily possessed the instruments and equipment required for producing standard objects; ownership fell in particular to those who held the intellectual property rights to the code embodied in the prototype and/or in a schematic representation of the prototype on which the improvements and codifications of the industrial design, based on a standardization of the symbols used, conferred legal authority. It was first and foremost possession of the patent making those property rights official that gave its holder the possibility of becoming an entrepreneur, if he or she could convince investors and banks that it would be profitable to extend credit by providing the means of producing and commercializing an *a priori* limitless series of the objects whose properties had been established in the patent and thus could no longer legally be manufactured by others.

The asymmetry that the deployment of the standard form introduced into the relation to artifacts was manifested not exclusively in the field of production but also in that of consumption and use. With the spread of standard objects, buyers lost the power to define in advance the properties of the object that they were thinking about acquiring. That power on the part of buyers was explicitly contested, moreover, when the standard form reached its peak, inasmuch as it proved too often to be exercised in an irrational, even absurd manner, subject to the "whims of fashion," as Henry Ford argued in his memoirs.[31] Ford was seeking to justify the decision to center a business around the production of a single model, the most rationally conceived, in relation to a selling price deemed optimal. (This critique, which can be called "Veblenian" in orientation, is in Ford's case directed explicitly against women accused of being diabolical forces behind what we are calling the trend form.) All this so as to be in a position to resist the irrational desires of individual persons and to give oneself the means – as Marx put it – to produce consumption and consumers.[32] In the framework of this new arrangement, prototypes could certainly retain some traces of the intentions of the potential buyers. But these intentions, collected through the intermediary of market research – this being one of the principal tasks of marketing – were no longer connected to the choices and desires of a particular individual; they were reconstituted on the basis of statistical aggregations that attributed them to a category or to a niche group of potential buyers.[33]

The internal tensions of the standard form

The standard form is what made "mass production" possible. The term, forged in the 1920s, caught on quickly. However, if we follow David Hounshell's analyses, the designation is best suited for describing the project emblematized by Henry Ford as it took shape and gradually evolved between 1923 and 1925, roughly speaking. What Peter Drucker has characterized as the "economic revolution" carried out by Ford cannot be reduced to the invention of the assembly line. It lies above all in Ford's demonstration that a company could bring in the greatest possible profits by maximizing production while reducing production costs – that is, by sidestepping the monopoly theory.[34] Nevertheless, the types of management and marketing that underlay the success of the Model T Ford came up against pitfalls as early as the second half of the 1920s, when Ford's rivals developed more sophisticated cars and, more importantly, put into place production techniques that allowed for rapid renewal of the models and an almost continuous creation of new differences. The standard form in effect ran into a contradiction that can be characterized schematically as follows. Reduced production costs and lower selling prices require large investments in production equipment. But, to amortize these investments, the production and sales of specimens corresponding to a single prototype have to be maintained over long periods of time. To be sure, in the standard form, the number of specimens produced is in principle unlimited. But if the objects proposed for sale remain identical to the prototype that generated the series, demand for those objects tends to fade, especially if the objects are robust, as the Model T was, and if they do not present enough technical defects to require their renewal. This state of affairs tends to discourage new investments.

This is why Ford reluctantly gave up producing the Model T – even though he deemed the model perfectly rational and adapted to the needs of the masses – and plunged into serial production of specimens of a different prototype, the Model A. This renunciation, accepted for financial reasons, put an end to the hopes that had been placed in the unlimited development of the standard form as an extreme manifestation of technological rationality. It implicitly supported the critique developed by Thorstein Veblen, who, from the turn of the century on, never stopped denouncing the preeminence of commercial motives over production requirements and the power exercised by financiers over inventors and engineers.[35]

It must be said that the rapid exhaustion of the standard form, which was maintained in its absolute form only in communist countries (and may well have contributed to their ruin),[36] was accelerated by a transformation in consumers made possible by the standard form itself. The development of the standard form initially accompanied and stimulated a change in the role of objects in the expression of social differences. The multiplication of standard objects – "pure" objects – accompanied the lifting or attenuation of the status barriers that maintained a link between social position and goods purchased in the context of the development of liberalism, which legitimated the acquisition of goods by any person with the financial means to buy them. This production regime thus adapted to the way liberal society arranged class relations and inequalities by attributing them for the most part to inequalities in monetary resources. Manifestations of social position thus shifted above all onto the ownership of artifacts acquired in their new state, and this shift tended to diminish the weight of other status symbols. But it also tended to trigger competition among persons to acquire objects treated as so many distinctive signs, and this in turn stimulated competition among things, each of which had to manifest the differences that identified it. Since social differences manifest themselves especially through the possession of things that others do not possess, producers and merchants were prompted to propose ever more differentiated objects, thus triggering obsolescence of the objects already in place and encouraging their renewal before they were no longer usable. It is, moreover, by taking this limitation of the standard form into account that one can understand the importance in contemporary capitalism of what we have called the trend form. This phenomenon was already noticeable in the period between the wars, when producers undertook to standardize the construction of individual houses and furnishings. But these attempts ended in failure because they had to do with things that people saw as constitutive of their private lives.[37] Unaware that tastes are socially constituted (something sociologists soon undertook to teach them, but in vain), potential buyers had a tendency to turn away, when they had the means, from these standardized products, even though their relative prices were quite advantageous, in favor of more expensive products that were more likely, in their eyes and in the eyes of others, to manifest what they perceived to be their own individuality – that is, their tastes.

The response of businesses to this situation was to set aside the hopes that had been placed in absolute standardization in favor of what has been called flexible mass production, by putting in place arrangements authorizing variability in the prototypes. Standardization was not abandoned, but it was modulated so as to allow for the production of specimens incorporating differences obvious enough to satisfy the expectations of ostentatious distinction; in this way there was no need to modify manufacturing tools and assembly lines in their entirety. On the level of commercialization, by profiting from the teachings of psychologists and sociologists, businesses developed marketing techniques that allowed them to grasp and orient consumer tastes which had previously been assumed to be spontaneous and unpredictable.

But the problems that were supposed to be solved by processes aiming to reconcile standardization and differentiation quickly proved to be inexhaustible, as evidenced by their return in full force in the 1980s, when capitalism had to confront a situation marked on the one hand by excess production capacity and on the other by the exhaustion of solvent demand. As had been the case fifty years before, some of the solutions proposed consisted in promoting a radical new version of flexible mass production, called "supple specialization," and the revalorization of manufacturing modes calling for diversified competencies within shops that mobilized locally rooted skills and traditions.[38] One can see in this option, which relied on case studies from Italy and France in particular, a prefiguration of the economic turn marked by the passage to an economy of enrichment.

The unease created by the standard form

As the foregoing analyses suggest, the weight taken on, in a given society, by a certain form of valuation of things may be such that the influence of that form stretches far enough to penetrate practices that do not involve commerce directly and may even inflect the ways in which the overall social formation is represented, whether describing it, celebrating its benefits, or critiquing it – that is, the form's influence may extend even to the most widespread ideologies, those that can be called dominant.

We see this clearly in the case of the standard form, which, because it chiefly concerns objects that come from factories, has been associated with a particular form of society known as industrial, whether in celebration or reproach. In fact, industrial society has sometimes been glorified as the bearer of progress conceived both as improvements in the material conditions of everyday life and as the bearer of freedom when it is associated with the development of democracy.[39] Conversely, it has sometimes been condemned as a differentiating factor, contributing to a perceived increase in inequality of conditions, and at the same time, perhaps paradoxically, as a factor in the uniformization of ways of being, contributing to exploitation and alienation.[40] The term "alienation" – a notion derived from Hegel, reinterpreted by Marx, and taken up again by numerous authors, sometimes implicitly, with differing inflections, especially in Germany between the wars – has come to designate the distinguishing feature of the condition of modern humans: that is, the loss of the possibility "of possession or mastery of oneself, or of a personal identity ... owing to external constraints."[41] One can get a sense of the extension taken on by this critical philosopheme, which has really become a commonplace likely to undergo multiple migrations (in both directions) between serious philosophical discourse and political sloganeering, by recalling its expression in quite similar terms both by thinkers belonging to the far left (often connected to the Frankfurt School) and by conservative thinkers, for example Spengler or Heidegger.

The thematics of alienation, which profoundly influenced social philosophy and sociology during the period when the potential of the standard form was asserting itself (that is, more or less between the last third of the twentieth century and the 1970s), extended to human beings – especially to those who belonged to the popular classes or the lower bourgeoisie – the repellent effect that the proliferation of industrial objects had on the elites (who were nevertheless their primary beneficiaries). Daily life was invaded by standard objects whose similarity, as specimens of a single prototype, or as prototypes conceived to be distinctive yet almost identical, aroused stupefaction and disgust in the elites. As Christian Borch has shown,[42] these sentiments could be shifted from objects to persons. Evidence for this can be found in the uses of the theme of crowds, introduced by Gustave Le Bon and Gabriel Tarde, who stressed the loss of all individuality and even of all singularity on the part of human persons when they found themselves in proximity with others amid huge gatherings, and they emphasized the centrality of processes of imitation, each person becoming a copy of the others, just as things were reproductions of a single prototype.[43]

This theme was relayed a little later by that of the masses, as disembodied and dispersed crowds manipulated from a distance by political propaganda and by the media.[44] The new theme took hold most fully during the interwar period, when totalitarian authorities claimed to embody the power of an entire people in a single person, a leader or guide, and put this divestiture on display by staging grandiose parades in which a multitude of human beings dressed in the same uniforms and making the same gestures at the same moment became analogs of the standard objects that were also being produced *en masse* by the industrial potential developed under the aegis of central governments. We need to recall that this vision of a massified society, as a typical expression of modernity, was shared both by those who advocated it and made it the source of the exorbitant power they had seized and by those whose intention was to oppose it in the name of human rights and individual creativity. Yet the latter, for the most part, directed their condemnation not only toward the massification of human beings but also toward the massification of things; to the proliferation of standard objects that were all alike, they opposed the diversity and even the singularity of things produced by the hands of artisans or, better still, of artists. And this was the case whether their conservative ideological orientations inclined them to nostalgia for the old rural world or whether, influenced by Marxism, they interpreted massification in terms of alienation. Everything that seemed to escape standardization could then serve to support the conception of a world not only freed from capitalism but, more broadly, no longer dominated by economic constraints.

These critical thinkers, as if blinded by the predominance of the standard form, were not sufficiently attentive to the economic processes that accompanied the circulation of things, especially in the realms of art and culture, processes that might have seemed to them to be incidental in relation to the heart of capitalism. Envisioning the progression of capitalism only in the form of a generalized standardization, they did not anticipate the transformations of capitalism that would allow exploitation of domains of objectivity and experience from which one could envisage a reconquest of both society and subjectivity. As it happens, one aspect of those transformations was the extension given to forms of valuation from which standardization was absent or in which it occupied only a peripheral place; the strengthening of these alternate forms went hand in hand with the development of commercialization in new directions.

Nevertheless, these condemnations of technological modernity have helped inflect the general representations of the social world and the modalities of its critique. In the development of critiques of consumer society, advertising, fashion, and the media that unfolded in the 1960s and culminated in the questioning of "the society of the spectacle"[45] – the supreme stage of alienation as "degradation of being into having" where "having is degraded into appearing" – and of the "simulacrum,"[46] one can see elements of a critical description of a social world in which the trend form, without being radically new and without taking precedence over other sources of profit, had at least begun to play a much more important role than it had in the past. We could doubtless make remarks of the same sort regarding the numerous critical descriptions that, especially from the late 1990s on, analyzed the passage from a consumer society to a commercial society, focusing especially on the domination of money and the market in a world presumed to be entirely in the grip of neoliberalism and finance. This critique was able to draw on the deployment of what we have called the asset form, especially in the case of sales of works of art. The publicity given in the media to the transformations that have affected the circulation of ancient and (especially) contemporary artworks and antiquities, with the development of awards and auctions on the international level, supplied many concrete examples that have been invoked to support the idea that contemporary society is almost totally dominated by the power of money and the quest for profits.

6

Standardization and Differentiation

The historical dimension of the forms of valuation

As social forms, the various ways of attributing value to commercial objects unquestionably have a historical dimension. Nevertheless, it is difficult, if not impossible, to establish their genealogy. Each of them appears as a relatively coherent structured whole, even though each consists of more or less disparate elements, residues of earlier constructions that have their own histories and are comparable in this respect (like language, in Wittgenstein's well-known metaphor) to an ancient city, with its roads and houses from different periods and in different styles. It could be argued, then, that large quantities of more or less similar things, especially objects intended for armies, were being produced well before the implementation of the standard form, or that the advent of printed books ushered in that form. Still, as Roger Chartier has pointed out, standardization cannot be attributed entirely to printing, for at least up to the eighteenth century the printed text was "open to mobility,"[1] in the sense that reissues of a given work introduced many differences: corrections were made during print runs, for instance. Moreover, in France, authors' manuscripts were extremely rare before 1750, for, once copied, the original was considered worthless and therefore destroyed; the practice of buying and selling autograph manuscripts, along with the collection of autograph signatures, did not develop until the late eighteenth century.

We may thus raise questions as we follow the many current debates both about when collections appeared and about the similarities and differences between the old "curio cabinets" and modern collections.[2] We may also wonder, with regard to the trend form, whether interest in objects as indices of belonging and as signs of distinction is a universal trait, or whether it can be traced back to the fifteenth-century Italian principalities, to seventeenth-century French court society, or to the appearance in eighteenth-century England of a new relationship to consumption, luxury, and what historians call populuxe; these questions have become widespread themes of debate and discussion in essays ranging from enthusiastic to critical. The same kinds of remarks could be made regarding the asset form. We could no doubt find, in more or less remote eras, examples of "precious" objects circulating rapidly for speculative purposes, as in the famous case of tulip bulbs in seventeenth-century Holland,[3] or, conversely, objects being removed from exchange and held in reserve as treasures.[4]

One position, characterized by an obsessive quest for antecedents, pushes the point of origin ever further back; getting lost in the details, it often ends up with the relativist – thus historically cynical – observation that there is never anything new under the sun. In contrast, we can characterize our own position succinctly as structural. This approach seeks to identify the times and places in which pre-existing things and practices have found their meaning profoundly modified because they were entering into new configurations under the influence of changes that might at first affect only a small part of their environment and might appear marginal.

In the case that concerns us here, modifications that may seem to have come about very slowly and almost continuously, if we focus on things as such, take on a much more pronounced character historically if we consider things as commodities. Or, in other words, everything was already there, capable of circulating and changing hands, by being bought, used, kept, transmitted, or abandoned, but the things exchanged were not yet commodities in the sense we have given the term, because the cosmos of commodities had not yet been fully constituted. Commodities, considered as such, require structures that allow very different objects to be treated as equivalent when they are exchanged, by being associated with prices. For things to be able to be identified as commodities during such exchanges, one must be able to refer them to a more general mode of being. Now, one of the key characteristics of this mode of being is that it reorganizes the relation between homogeneity and heterogeneity – that is, between the fact that everything can be reduced to a price and the fact that diversity among things is maintained through forms of valuation. In other words, this mode allows us to envisage the whole gamut of diverse things, on the one hand by identifying them precisely through what is different about each one, specific to each one, and on the other hand by viewing them as if they were all amenable to the same treatment. As things, they are distributed among categories that take their diversity into account and organize their plurality. But, as commodities, they are objects of arrangements that treat them as though they were all of the same order.[5]

One indicator of the need to diversify products that are at risk of losing their differences when they are plunged into the cosmos of commodities is the heightened importance taken on by brands, starting in the late nineteenth century, a phenomenon reinforced by the growth of marketing.[6] Brand names became a driving force, especially in the interwar period. Advertising began to focus on brand names; it dramatized their images and conferred on them a broad reach that aspired to universality. Brand names, familiar and known to all, thus became an important element of social reality. This arrangement was not aimed exclusively at stimulating sales; it also played a central role in the transformation of power relations between manufacturers and retailers, and it was thus central to the changes in capitalism that accompanied the rise in power of the standard form. "During the entire modern period," Patrick Verley writes, "merchants have drawn more profit from selling products than makers have made from their work. The former have tended to control the latter."[7] This power relation held steady and even grew stronger in the last third of the nineteenth century, when standard products for everyday use (such as food and toiletries) appeared, arriving in retail shops after transiting through wholesale businesses, so that it was almost impossible to know their provenance. Buyers' confidence in these products depended essentially on the trust they had in the shopkeeper, the only human person with whom such products could be associated and who could vouch for them. The system of brand names was designed to allow "makers to be emancipated from shopkeepers" by ensuring a way of identifying objects that would be relatively independent of the seller's identity. It aimed to shift the client's trust to the manufacturer, who had previously remained in the shadows, so as to ensure the client's loyalty no matter where the product was sold, and to exercise monopoly effects by discouraging substitutions that might be proposed by rivals wishing to direct buyers toward other seemingly similar products that they had in stock and wanted to unload.[8]

Brands and the advertising that familiarized the public with them had both to deploy and to counter the properties of the standard form. On the one hand, they had to reassure the public that the products existed, by stressing their impersonal dimension. Advertisers had to assure prospective customers that the products they might covet would always be available, always present, and always in conformity with their prototype – that is, with the analytic presentation that defined the prototype, provided that those products were purchased new. Emphasis on the fact of being "brand new" was intended to reduce consumers' uncertainty and to discourage them from acquiring used objects of the same type at lower prices. It also served to reassure consumers with a guarantee or a written warranty that could extend beyond the moment of purchase, as well as the assurance of follow-up service if the object purchased failed to perform properly. But, on the other hand, the brand also had to respond to relatively contradictory requirements. Especially if the object was expensive, it had to create the impression that, while it would always be available, even on a purchaser's whim, from one day to the next, it also remained relatively rare: this was achieved by highlighting the object's exceptional qualities as compared to those of other seemingly similar but ordinary things. Above all, the brand had to rehumanize the object, by orienting the potential buyer's attention in three different directions. First, toward the maker (or the founder of the factory), who often gave his or her name to the brand (Gillette, Ford, Chanel, and so on). This was often done, especially in the period when the standard form was being deployed but was still fragile, by associating each specimen of the product with an image that was supposed to be that of the head of the factory from which the product was supposed to have come, and sometimes with a signature, the graphic trace of a human being. Second, toward the potential consumer, by associating the product with a stereotypical image of the type of persons for whom it was intended – a child, a homemaker, an executive, a young person, and so on. (This procedure is taken to an extreme in the trend form, where photographs of real people who are celebrities are substituted for pictures of generic individuals.) Third, toward the product itself – especially when, in view of worldwide diffusion, that item can no longer be identified through reference to a localized person – by associating it with a symbolic system modeled on heraldry and charged with both representing the product and supplying stable reference points, as was the case, among the oldest examples, with the Bibendum of Michelin tires (1898) or with Citroën's chevron (1922); Citroën was one of the first automobile companies to work systematically at building a brand image.

These means are primarily intended to reduce the uncertainties of distant consumers by encouraging them to have confidence in information supplied in the analytic presentation of the product so as to justify its price. This information, largely controlled by the producer, is supposed to be public; advertising can supply it only to a limited extent through images and/or texts. In order to form an opinion about the product proposed and to compare it to other products that are supposed to be suitable for similar uses, the potential buyer has to trust the producer and/or has to know someone who has had prior experience with the object. This has led to the creation of consumers' associations: originating in the late nineteenth and early twentieth century,[9] such associations developed alongside consumers' institutes starting in the 1970s, stimulated most notably by the critical work of the American attorney Ralph Nader.[10] These consumer institutions select objects with ostensibly similar functions that are sold under competing brand names and subject them to tests whose results are made public. Such evaluations, designed to supply consumers with information from a source that is less self-interested than that disseminated under the brand names, are formalistic in their own way: they are based on a classification system that uses a grid deemed applicable to different prototypes so that the specifications tested can be broken down into a set of relevant properties.

From trade in things to the circulation of commodities

There is perhaps no more eloquent example of things coming to be envisaged as commodities than the commercial arrangements known as department stores, whose appearance in the second half of the nineteenth century was prefigured in Paris by a proliferation of arcades, or covered "passages," as described in Walter Benjamin's analyses.[11] In department stores, as in international fairs and exhibitions, things are distributed among different departments, each of which presents a plurality of objects offered at different prices; the fact that these objects are brought together in a single place makes it possible to highlight both their similarities and their differences, thus triggering effects of substitutability. But whatever their substance, their form, their function, or the reasons invoked to make them attractive may be, these diverse things, distributed among different areas, each directed by a specialized salesperson (the "department manager") who can orient prospective buyers and answer their questions, are all subject to similar commercial treatment: prior to sales, this takes place at the level of relations with suppliers, insurance agents, and stock managers, and afterward at the level of service centers, guarantees, and especially the accounting office, since incoming and outgoing commodities are recorded in largely unified accounting forms.

Regarding these procedures, let us note another, primordial fact concerning the relations of objects to time, to space, and to persons. In the department store configuration, all the items exhibited appear in the same present moment and also in the same space, regardless of their origins, geographical in particular. But, even more significantly, they are detached from the persons who made them and sent them on, so that buyers can confer a personal identity on them only by associating them with the person of the seller and, conceivably, with the personality that the department store has managed to acquire, as a legal and collective entity, chiefly through the medium of advertising. And this is the case even though the gradual development of brands, especially in the first half of the twentieth century, has tended to restore to objects a kind of substantive identity that supposedly remains constant wherever these commodities are sold.

This homogenization of the commercial relation to heterogeneous objects constitutes a historical process of primary importance: it breaks with the economies that, to varying degrees and on different bases, can be characterized as pre-capitalist. To be persuaded of this, it suffices to read descriptions of the most frequently used forms of exchange in French society in the eighteenth century – that is, less than a hundred years before a radical transformation emerged with the revolution in commerce that brought to light their way of being as commodities. By referring to the analyses of Jean-Yves Grenier, along with the important commentary Alain Guerreau devoted to Grenier's work,[12] we can attempt to summarize the state of affairs that prevailed around the middle of the eighteenth century.

The number of objects in circulation was relatively small, since much of the economy was based on home production and on rents that were often paid in kind. The production and sale of objects constituted a secondary mode of enrichment whose benefits were converted into ground rents, so that "income from the control of land had a strictly dominant position."[13] Currency was far from unified, a situation that led Alain Guerreau to state that "there was no general equivalent under the Old Regime," where there were "as many monetary relations, thus of set valuations of currency, as there were forms of exchange,"[14] owing in particular to the fact that multiple metals were involved. The objects in circulation were "determined entirely by a specific structure of identification and personalization, which tended to induce a very weak substitutability," so that "adjustments were partial, localized, and uncertain"[15] and that "goods produced for exchange" were highly individualized.[16]

Barter predominated over monetary exchange.[17] For goods such as luxury items or works of art, gifts made in exchange for status and prestige, grants made in exchange for privileges, and even occasional extortion or theft remained significant means of circulation.[18] Since objects were defined through reference to persons and in relation to a place, they circulated readily on the local level, but with more and more difficulty and at higher transaction costs as distances increased. Under these circumstances, "spatial variables" played a primary role (as attested by the attention paid to these variables by the earliest eighteenth-century economists, who associated differences in price with spatial differences; that attention disappeared from nineteenth-century economic thought). The space of commercial circulation was not a Cartesian space but "a set of points equipped with differential properties and connected by distances,"[19] where "every center of production enjoyed relative autonomy with respect to the overall situation."[20] Transportation difficulties, including the poor state of the roads and the number and diversity of tolls, made it difficult to navigate the distances between these salient points. Given that profits were tied to the exploitation of spatial differences, "interest in homogenization" and in the "fluidification" of exchanges was weak.[21]

As Jean-Yves Grenier has shown, the determination of profits depended in large part on "power relations" that were tied to "control of the exchange [of goods] and not of the production process."[22] (Fernand Braudel called this "commercial added value," to distinguish it from the surplus value drawn from the exploitation of labor.) Either these power relations were expressed in the form of regulations legitimized by the monarchy,[23] or they were dependent on advances that preceded and enabled the circulation of commodities. But credit retains a personal character even when it relies on institutions, so that "economic domination is not realizable without a broader social power." This leads Grenier to say that, in a situation of this type where "the objectivization of social relations is incomplete," one can observe the importance of "capital" without being able to speak of "capitalism," because "the relation is invested in a much larger framework that creates, as a sub-order, the conditions for an economic relationship" in such a way that "henceforward nothing makes it possible to unify the forms of economic domination that thus fall outside the concept of the social relation of production."[24]

According to these analyses, there were indeed, in the economies of the Old Regime, great numbers of objects (although far fewer than there would be a hundred years later) that passed from hand to hand. But the things that circulated (and people circulated as well – historical demographers have traced their frequent displacements, countering the retrospective illusion of villagers who never left home)[25] could not all be called commodities, because they were not all subject to the same sort of control, and this restricted the possibility of a global grasp relying on a single mode of totalization. As the determination of things was largely subordinated to that of persons, it followed the "fundamental [divisions] of the concrete social organization"[26] – that is, it preceded any relations of power or personal dependency.

The emergence of the various forms of valuation can thus be understood by contrast with the way things circulated under the Old Regime. First of all, given the fact that currency was not unified and thus could not serve as a common metric for prices, on the one hand, and given the importance of barter, on the other, we can hypothesize that price occupied a less central place than the one it has acquired with the standard form (which is based on the prices of "new" objects); indeed, for one historian who sought to classify them, Old Regime prices constituted "a literally indescribable jumble."[27] Consequently, the act that consisted in turning away from one thing in favor of another as a response to their respective prices – a gesture that allowed a form of price-based critique – was almost irrelevant, if not inoperative. Moreover, the things in question could be produced as approximate copies of one another; questions of maintaining exclusivity or prohibiting reproduction did not arise. Indeed, it was only starting with the introduction of the patent system, and more generally of intellectual property rights, that monopolies on reproduction of manufactured objects could go into effect.

Things do not present themselves as predetermined by the prices that the supplier wants to obtain for them or as predefined by the highlighting of a value that, even though it is intended to justify the price of the thing, ultimately has only one expression, which is monetary. With the development of the commodity form, the distribution of things among typical situations and among uses adjusted to practical constraints – that is, to the circumstances of action – was not abolished. But it no longer governed the circulation of things – things that, as commodities, are determined instead through reference to profit expressed in monetary and accounting terms – so that circulation itself became, explicitly or implicitly, the *telos* of exchange.

Still, this homogenization cannot extend all the way to uniformization – as certain analysts of the standard form at the time of its full development came to think – insofar as the logic of capitalism, which has the goal of drawing the greatest possible profit from trade in every instance, requires, to this end, that the *means* used to posit the value of each thing be diversified. Although commodities are endowed with prices expressed in a common metric and unified inasmuch as they are polarized in terms of money and profit, they are nevertheless distributed – but under the auspices of a different relation, that of the value attributed to them. Prices in themselves are signifiers with no signifieds, so that, even ranked hierarchically, they never suffice to give meaning to the circulation of goods.

Yet precisely because they fluctuate (and a given price can qualify the most varied commodities), these signifiers face a critique demanding that the things to which they refer be made clear, and that the prices attributed to them be thereby justified. The arrangements for bringing together things treated as similar from the standpoint of the way a price is assigned to them are what we have called the forms of valuation.

The effect of standardization on the constitution of forms of valuation

Histories of Enlightenment economic thinking, in a period when economics had not yet reached the point of denying its political dimension and redefining itself along the lines of the hard sciences, have chiefly emphasized the ideological changes that, following Mandeville,[28] legitimized individual interest[29] and the changes in the juridical order that, with the French Revolution, drew on free-market liberal themes[30] to abolish constraints on the circulation of persons and goods in order both to detach things from persons and to foster free exchanges. But this reorientation of the point of view brought to bear on things would not have sufficed to modify the structures of commerce profoundly, or to favor the deployment of commodities, without a transformation of the things themselves. This transformation was linked to the invention and diffusion of the standard form, which did not really come into its own until the last third of the nineteenth century. By permitting the production of a theoretically unlimited number of specimens reproducing a single prototype, the standard form considerably multiplied the number of objects proposed for exchange while lowering their prices. That was not its only effect, however. It also tended to detach things from persons, and, by loosening up spatial constraints, it made access anywhere to anything possible for anyone, provided the price could be met. The anonymity of things was matched by the anonymity of buyers, who henceforth intervened in the space of commerce only as consumers.

It is precisely this generalized anonymization, often more desired and invoked than real, that constitutes the principal feature of a market society. Anonymity has been, as we know, one of the central points around which revolve, on the one hand, the critique of commercial relations and, on the other, the prophetic character attributed to the market. On the side of critique, the anonymity of commercial relations associated with a critique of standardization – although those themes were never clearly distinguished, given the degree to which the development of capitalism was identified with that of the standard form at the time – was at the heart of the anticapitalist arguments developed, especially in Germany during the interwar period, by philosophers more or less associated with the Frankfurt School, who denounced an extension of standardization that was shifting from things toward human beings themselves, resulting in a *reification* of social relations and of persons.[31]

Looking in a different direction, one can identify political philosophies that emphasize the liberating role of the market and associate it with democracy.[32] And of these, of course, there is above all economics, which had acceded to the status of a science and proceeded to redeploy itself primarily, with the neoclassicists of the second half of the nineteenth century, around the production and circulation of objects that belonged to the standard form. In this shift, economics no longer took into account either spatial considerations or the personal relations that connected things to those who made them and to those who acquired them. But the principal effect of a recentering of economics on the standard form was the recentering of that form around the relation between two entities. On one side, there are human persons equipped with desires; on the other, things equipped with prices. Still, this relation can function, in the manner of an impersonal and self-maintaining mechanism, only if desires are defined as relatively malleable, apt to be modified and adjusted to circumstances; and if things are defined as substitutable for one another, preference for a particular thing at a particular price can shift to a different thing, similar to the first but offered at a lower price. *Substitutability*, which plays a central role in this model, presupposes that a unified cosmos of commodities has been constructed, that it can rely on a general classification of goods so as to allow them to be compared, and, finally, that things are guaranteed to be in conformity with their model, provided that they are offered for sale only in their new state. These are all properties that only the standard form can ensure.

We can thus hypothesize that the development of this form had the effect not only of fostering the creation of an autonomous cosmos of commodities but also of conferring a specific mode of structuring on that cosmos. Still, the latter has been growing increasingly complex as the development of capitalism, in search of new sources of profit, has given rise to an extension of the notion of commodity that has allowed it to encompass entities – things, but also experiences, and even persons – that had remained on the margins of the standard form. In the period during which the standard form was increasing in power, commodities were structured principally around the distinction between standard and non-standard objects. Reference to the fuzzy plurality of non-standard things served as support for the critique of standardization, and, since standardization was associated with capitalism, the same reference served as support for a certain critique of capitalism (a type of critique that has been characterized as artistic criticism in the wake of César Graña's work,[33] to distinguish it from social criticism).

The plurality of non-standard things thus came to constitute a sort of *outside* of capitalism, but, since the principal property of these things was defined in negative terms (they were what they are only owing to the fact that they were not standard), this outside could remain relatively vague and weakly structured. It included, first and foremost, objects in the domains of art or culture, but also everything connected with personal experience in its most individual aspects – in other words, those that are non-commodifiable – as for example the experience of travel, or that of luxury. More generally it included the experience of the mind,[34] related to the experience of the dandy, who is precisely defined by the fact that he withdraws, at his own risk, from the attraction of standard things that has taken hold of the masses and from the standardization of his experiences under the influence of capital, which seeks to take over everything. In this spirit, the rejection of standardization finds its high point – particularly in the work of Georges Bataille[35] – in the sacralization of excess that is expressed, indissociably, by gratuitousness and by expenditure, but expenditure as pure loss, as in the potlatch, a form of expenditure whose matrix is sexuality. The possibility that capital will take control over everything – especially art and culture – has been staged in a particularly dramatic way by the principal actors of the Frankfurt School. But such control could be conceived, during the interwar period, only in the form of an unlimited extension of standardization.

Following this logic, it is possible to associate the shaping of the three other forms whose contours we have traced (the trend, collection, and asset forms) with a gradual extension of capitalism toward what, during the period when it was being nourished in particular by profits obtained through the production and commercialization of standard objects, constituted its outside. The defining feature of this extension was its subjection to a double constraint. On the one hand, it had to integrate standard objects into the cosmos of commodities, the very notion of which was developed through contact with the standard form, while maintaining the form's homogeneity. And, on the other hand, it had to take into account the heterogeneous character of the new things that were suited for full immersion in this cosmos – that is, things that were likely to become sources of monetary profits that would satisfy the requirements of existing forms of accounting. This way of articulating homogeneity and heterogeneity is what gives consistency to commodity structures as they are deployed today. They are based in fact on primary oppositions that are multiplied within a limited plurality of forms, at the price of transformations that allow them to be adapted to the diversity of the objects encountered, so long as these objects can be distributed among the four forms generated by this transformation group.

Material economies, immaterial economies

The four forms we have identified certainly do not encompass all the means that could potentially be put to use for the valuation of things. But, given the structures of commodities in their current state, it appears difficult to attribute value to anything without calling on one or another of these forms; this is true even if the thing in question is relatively distant from the paradigmatic objects that are at the heart of each form and serve as convenient exemplars. Nevertheless, we may suppose that the expansion of commodification, conjugated with the important technological changes that are currently affecting the universe of commodities and reshaping its contours, especially by blurring the boundaries between material and immaterial components, will make it harder and harder to attribute value to all things by subsuming them under one or another of these forms.

Over the last few decades, modalities of wealth creation that seem to fall outside the forms of valuation on which our analyses bear have taken on unprecedented scope. Beyond the economy of finance, which has contributed greatly to making cash available to nourish the economy of enrichment, we can invoke the profits generated by goods that are often characterized as immaterial, not only in the sense in which they have a "symbolic" dimension – this is the case for anything when it becomes an object of exchange – but in the sense that these goods are considered independently of their physical placement; they devolve more precisely from the joint development of the Internet and digitization,[36] innovations that have been associated with "immaterial capitalism" or "cognitive capitalism."[37] These latter approaches generally tend to underestimate the constantly increasing importance of the circulation of material things, even though commerce in such things now takes place chiefly through Internet sites that are heirs to print catalogs for mail-order sales or that serve to organize sales between private individuals.

To illustrate the economic importance of these goods, the profits earned by those who own property rights to intellectual content – independently of the supports on which the content depends – are often taken as examples. The advent and vertiginous growth of the Internet have undoubtedly been considerably enhanced by such profits. Still, let us recall that the legal and economic questions they raise are by no means entirely new. They have been raised, most notably starting in the eighteenth century in the case of books, ever since property rights applying to intellectual content (an author's text) began to be distinguished from property rights applying to the material support (a printed book) that allows the content to be inscribed, preserved, and disseminated. The question of "piracy" – that is, the illegal exploitation of a content protected by laws governing intellectual property rights – arose well before the development of the Internet and digitization, and, as Robert Darnton notes with respect to books, "piracy was so pervasive in early modern Europe that bestsellers could not be blockbusters as they are today."[38]

Even so, the development of the Internet and of digital media has profoundly complicated these problems, especially because the people and companies that have property rights over software and websites, to which access may be free or not, can profit from these arrangements in order to inspect and record the addresses and behaviors of potentially vast numbers of persons who visit their sites; this gives them the possibility of selling address lists, information about web surfers' behavior, or advertising space that can have a narrowly targeted and at the same time very broad impact. Where advertising is concerned, however, we must note that similar roles have long been played by print media, which were to a large extent financially supported by advertising until they began to be challenged by competition from the Internet. Still, in this case, the term "selling" does not quite fit; it would be better to refer to "renting," since the advertising spaces yielded to a client for a contractually limited period of time remain the property of those who hold the property rights to the supporting medium, whether this medium is materialized by paper or, on a screen, by computer algorithms.

These remarks are not intended to minimize the role played by the digital economy and the web in the economic changes that have marked the last few decades on a worldwide level; rather, they are meant to suggest that a study of that role would presuppose raising once again, the question of the forms of valuation that we are developing in this book based on commerce in things. It would not be a matter of seeking to insert digital content, as an economic good, into the four forms that we have identified or of creating a fifth form that would be exclusively devoted to such content – doing the latter would disrupt the structural approach to commodities. It would be appropriate to undertake a specific study, parallel to the one we have pursued concerning commerce in things, that would take into account the evolution of intellectual property rights and the economic consequences of their growing importance.

Let us add that it is difficult to estimate the effects that the growth of an economy based on commerce in "immaterial" goods, as opposed to one based on commerce in things, might have on the way value is attributed to things, and perhaps more generally on the forms of wealth themselves, if the economic logic of access were to become predominant in relation to so-called full and complete possession. Several possibilities could then be envisaged. One might be the redistribution of goods among different universes, each of which would be defined by a particular type of control, as we see already with the increase in the role played by rented or paid access without changes in ownership. Another could be the emergence of new structural constants, which would lead to the extinction of the transformation group that we have analyzed and its hypothetical replacement by other formations. For, as Claude Lévi-Strauss pointed out, "each anterior state of a structure is itself a structure."[39] The forms of valuation that provide the foundation for commerce, most notably by favoring the emergence of metaprices capable of playing the role of focal points toward which the critiques and justifications on the part of sellers and buyers can converge, are – as our entire work seeks to illustrate – historical formations. On that basis, they have no claim to immutability.

$$7$$

The Collection Form

The modernity of the collection form

What we have said about the historical dimension of the forms of valuation applies above all to the collection form. The history of collections is a well-documented field today, thanks to the work of many historians, specialists in art history, anthropologists, researchers from other disciplines in the social sciences, and even from philosophy and psychoanalysis.[1] We are thus in a position to reflect on the relations between the treasure troves accumulated by medieval princes or religious orders (in which relics occupied an important place), the curio cabinets that proliferated in the sixteenth and seventeenth centuries (which brought together disparate objects chosen for their strangeness), and, finally, what can be called *systematic collections*, which began to appear in the first third of the nineteenth century. These relations have been studied either in order to try to establish continuity among these different modalities of collection or, on the contrary, in order to mark their discontinuity; the latter efforts have often been inspired by Michel Foucault's analyses and by the disjunction that Foucault established between an episteme founded on a theory of signatures and one founded on a theory of representation.[2]

To put it succinctly, a systematic collection has a *serial* dimension. It brings together things *that have a certain relationship to one another* and that are distributed according to *differences* recognized as *pertinent*, which are organized in a *system*: for example, items of pottery made in a certain place during a certain period but differentiated in terms of size, color, shape, the figures that decorate them, and so on. With systematic collections, the principle of selection is generally a specific property, often functional in origin, that subsumes an organized cluster of secondary properties. The systematic collection form seems to have emerged initially in the domain of the natural sciences, as a way to classify and present minerals and animal or vegetable material;[3] it was later applied to other types of sets composed of artifacts produced by human hands, whether these artifacts were works of art or utilitarian, folkloric, or ethnological objects.[4]

Nevertheless, the history of collections interests us especially in its relation to the process of forming commodities and to the evolution of commercial societies. A first indication comes in the nineteenth century, with the new interest shown in forming systematic collections; this development left many traces, particularly in literature.[5] One of the first works devoted to collections and collectors – and undoubtedly the most famous and most penetrating of them all – was Honoré de Balzac's novel *Le Cousin Pons*, published serially in 1847.[6] But other examples from French literature attesting to the same interest can be cited, especially Anatole France's first novel, *Le crime de Sylvestre Bonnard*.[7]

As a way of understanding the new interest in collecting in the second half of the nineteenth century, we offer the following hypothesis. It hinges on the *ambiguous relation* that the development of a practice of collecting and the nature of the objects collected maintained with the formation of a cosmos of commodities, and thus with the development of capitalism. On the one hand, the practice of collecting was perceived as a sort of metaphor for capitalism. On the other, it was considered as being in some sense the obverse of capitalism. These opposing perceptions call for analysis.

Let us begin by looking at what brings collecting and capitalism together. In the first place, seen from the outside, the *systematic* character of collecting seems to be oriented toward accumulation for its own sake – since the objects accumulated are not destined for use – and pursued without limits in a quasi-obsessional way. In the second place, the character of the objects accumulated and the way they circulate are what seem to drive accumulation. The things sought by collectors were, first of all, precious objects possessed under the Old Regime by persons of quality (generally belonging to the upper tiers of society), often made to order for them by renowned artists or craftsmen. Given the personalized character of their manufacture and their destination, these objects could not be confused with the more ordinary products intended for a bourgeois or even petit-bourgeois clientele, products that recent historians often characterize by the term "populuxe." In the wake of the great political and social upheavals that accompanied the French Revolution and the Napoleonic Wars, a number of such things that had previously been confined to protected spaces (such as chateaux or religious edifices) found themselves tossed out onto the street, so to speak, and "without a master," as the law put it: these were goods that belonged to everyone and to no one. Some of them, acquired by looting, lost their identity and became virtual trash. Those that resurfaced in the hands of dealers in art or second-hand goods became available for exchange: they could circulate and be acquired by any person capable of perceiving their "value" and meeting their prices.

The episode of the fan, in Balzac's *Cousin Pons*, the first major narrative marking the entry of the theme of collecting and the figure of the collector into French literature, is particularly significant in this regard. Pons discovers, in a shop on the rue de Lappe, a fan that he decides to offer his cousin, the *présidente* of Marville; the shop owner had found the object in Dreux, where a chateau, Aulnay, had been "pulled down" during the French Revolution. As it happened, Madame de Pompadour had stayed in that chateau. Pons thinks that the fan had belonged to her, and he believes he can attribute the image on it to the painter Watteau. In an earlier passage, Balzac mentions the "Auvergnats" and the "Black Band," alluding to the speculators accused during the Revolution of purchasing goods belonging to the nation, picking them over and selling them off ("Auvergnats, those satellites of the Black Band who sacked châteaux and carried off the marvels of Pompadour France in their tumbril carts").[8] It was during the period that followed the Revolution and the Napoleonic Wars that interest in second-hand goods – bric-à-brac – developed (and the term "bric-à-brac" itself was forged); during the same time, the major art collections, private and public, were enriched, most notably after the looting of German treasures, a phenomenon studied by Bénédicte Savoy,[9] or the looting of Italian treasures that continued to feed the collections of wealthy French and English buyers, as Francis Haskell has shown.[10] The same thing happened after the Russian Revolution in 1917. Gorki had been instructed by Lenin to create a commission of experts to sort through "the objects of great artistic and material value" that had been abandoned in the houses and apartments of emigrés and had been "looted" by domestic servants.[11] Things that had been kept out of sight were "brought out" (*sorties*),[12] to use a term favored by flea market traders; it had the advantage of obscuring the differences among things that were sold, found, or stolen. And it would doubtless be possible to show that the development of collections quite regularly followed periods of political change, often periods of revolution or war that had resulted in throwing into the street – thus reducing to the status of trash – thousands of objects that had until then been preserved as precious treasures in closed spaces such as ancestral homes, chateaux, convents, or churches.

But the astonishment aroused by the new relation to objects that accompanied the development of the practice of collecting increased still further when objects that had been systematically sought after, sometimes with considerable obstinacy, turned out to be quite ordinary, their value being determined solely through reference to the systemic and totalizing character of the accumulation in which they came to fill lacks. This is particularly clear in Anatole France's *The Crime of Sylvestre Bonnard*, published in 1881,[13] a little more than three decades after *Cousin Pons*. Sylvestre Bonnard is a learned man, a member of "the Institute," short on funds. A manuscript collector, he heads for Sicily in search of a rare manuscript copy of *The Golden Legend*. In Sicily, he meets a young French woman married to Prince Dimitri Trépof, a Russian who is immensely wealthy, seductive, and a major collector. The young woman explains to Bonnard why she and her husband are wandering off the beaten track:

> We are going just where you are going – to Girgenti. I must tell you all about it. You know that my husband is making a collection of

match-boxes ... Dimitri has been a collector of all sorts of things; but the only kind of collection which can interest him now is a collection of match-boxes. He has already got five thousand two hundred and fourteen different kinds. Some of them gave us frightful trouble to find.

Later, Trépof's wife shows Bonnard her loot.

"Oh!" declared Madame Trépof, "it is ugly, but it is rare! These boxes are not exported at all; you can buy them only where they are made. Dimitri has six others just like this in his pocket. We got them so as to exchange with other collectors. You understand? At nine o'clock this morning we were at the factory. You see we did not waste our time." ...
   I felt – must I confess it [says Sylvestre Bonnard, the narrator] – a thorough sympathy with these intrepid collectors. No doubt I would rather have found Monsieur and Madame Trépof engaged in collecting antique marbles or painted vases in Sicily. I should have liked to have found them interested in the ruins of Syracuse, or the poetical traditions of the Eryx. But at all events, they were making some sort of a collection – they belonged to the great confraternity – and I could not possibly make fun of them without making fun of myself.[14]

Collecting is not only a metaphor for capitalism, it is a capitalist practice in itself, and therein lies its ambiguity: to the extent that, as a practice of accumulation that mimics capitalism, it does not have the goal of monetary enrichment, it can be viewed as the obverse of capitalism. Cousin Pons is poor, and monetary issues are foreign to him. The same is true of Sylvestre Bonnard, who is completely disinterested. As for the immensely wealthy Prince Trépof, he spends his fortune to the sole end of accumulating things that lack not only commercial value but aesthetic value as well; he is entirely possessed by a totalizing project that he never succeeds in completing. Just as Cousin Pons deprives himself of everything so he can withdraw the objects he admires from their status as commodities, Prince Trépof has the power to transform a wholly trivial commercial object – a match-box – into a sought-after thing that warrants any sacrifice. Still, it is precisely to the extent that their enterprises aim only at totalization (as opposed to commercial gain) that they have the power to confer value on anything at all, whether the object in question was formerly precious but later forgotten and turned into quasi-trash or the humblest of commodities – like match-boxes – just as capitalism creates wealth by taking advantage of a multitude of disparate resources.
One of the most typical examples of systematic collection, inaugurated in the second half of the nineteenth century, is stamp collecting, which spread very quickly on a large scale. This type of collection had the advantage of offering, within an immutable form, a great diversity of

sought-after objects, including some at very high prices and others – the most numerous – at little cost. Another advantage of stamp collecting is that it was very quickly oriented toward children and adolescents, for parents and teachers saw it as an educational tool, especially in the areas of history and geography. As Steven Gelber has shown,[15] the practice of stamp collecting expanded when it became apparent that a collector's stamp was an object that could be bought and sold. This practice could thus become an instrument for education in commerce, allowing young people with bourgeois and even petit-bourgeois backgrounds to become familiar with certain aspects of the capitalist cosmos, all the better because the practice appeared playful and disinterested. The decline of the practice among young people probably has to do with the fact that its educational role has turned out to be less and less necessary, since, by virtue of the extension of capitalism, familiarity with it has become coextensive with preparation for life in commercial society (not to mention the fact that electronic messaging has largely replaced postal mail since the early 2000s).

But if the role of stamp collections has declined, the practices of collecting have taken on unprecedented importance in recent decades. First, in quantitative terms: according to studies (chiefly from the English-speaking world) devoted to the sociology of collecting and collectors, in contemporary Western societies roughly one person out of four would admit to being or having been a collector.[16] Their collections are obviously very uneven in size, and they involve very diverse objects whose commercial value can range from a few dollars – as for example with collections of postcards, sports team pennants, or beer cans – to several million – as with certain collections of ancient or contemporary art. In addition, the communities that have formed around the exchange of specific objects defined by their type or kind have unquestionably seen their numbers grow and their level of activity increase; there is evidence of this in the development of specialized press organs, clubs, and especially, since the early 2000s, Internet sites that facilitate exchanges, mainly through auctions, as with eBay. To take just one example, there is a French-language site devoted entirely to exchanges and discussion among collectors of watches made in the USSR between 1940 and 1960.

The unprecedented character of the collection form, as it is characterized here, appears all the more clearly if we relate it to the way in which value has been attributed to relics in Catholic and Orthodox churches. The idea of a continuity between "collecting" relics and collecting works of art[17] has often been defended, with the claim that both sets are things whose value comes from exceptional beings, although commerce in the first category is "illicit" while commerce in the second is legitimate.[18] This association, which gives the impression that valuation via the collection form has been in place for several centuries, is nevertheless erroneous in the sense that it ignores the specificity of relics. To be sure, relics are endowed with a memorial force associated with a singular person. But they have value only within an institution, and their value is measured by the veneration of which they are objects. The Catholic code of canon law (canon 1190), which forbids commerce in relics, says this quite clearly: among all objects, relics, most particularly those "honored by a great popular veneration," cannot be alienated or transferred without permission from the Holy See. When relics are offered for sale on Internet auction sites (and this happens quite often), their prices tend to be low.

But we can better understand the difference between relics and works of art if we take into account the fact that relics are divisible by religious institutions, and that each piece is of equal value. This is why the body of a given saint can be disseminated in many different places. The body of St Vincent de Paul, for example, is said to be distributed among ninety-seven relics spread among fifty churches in Paris.[19] But no museum, public or private, would take the initiative of dividing up the relics it has in its collections, for in the museum director's eyes such a division would rob the relics of their value. It would be like dividing a painting by Leonardo da Vinci into ninety-seven pieces: each piece would be worth little, and in no case would it be worth as much as the complete painting. This difference between relics and artworks in collections is clarified if we take into account the fact that human remains, destined to be exposed temporarily or permanently in places of worship, came from an "original" person, and, to be preserved and exhibited, such remains have to be transformed by one or several persons. Immersed in a religious institution (Catholic or Orthodox), human remains are associated with the proper name of the original person, but the person or (more often) persons who carried out the transformation may remain anonymous. Knowing the name of the person who opened the corpse of the saint or dug up or gathered the bones hardly matters, even though in some cases the names can be known and are registered during investigations conducted within the religious institution to "authenticate" the relics. What is essential is the name of the saint associated with the relics who is the object of veneration. The artistic regime is the exact opposite of the religious regime in the way it works: the artistic regime grants great importance to the name of the person who carries out a transformation and little importance to the original person when a work is composed of elements drawn from the human body, such as hair, blood, urine, and so on, as in practices that were quite common in the art of the 1970s. It can be argued that in some cases there is no difference between the two. But it is the proper name of the transforming person, the name/signature of the artist, which makes possible the presence of these bodily elements drawn from the original person, *even* when the artist and the original person are one and the same.[20]

Systematic collection as an arrangement for valuation

We shall explore later on the idea that collecting, and particularly systematic collection as an arrangement based on accumulation, may have served as a matrix for the gradual development of a specific form for attributing value to things that plays a central role in the economy of enrichment. This form, as it was being established, helped shift the modalities of wealth creation when, as the production of standard objects was increasingly outsourced to low-wage countries, the dynamics of capitalism turned much more strongly toward exploitation of the past. As it happens, the extension of commercialization toward things that, since they are already present, do not have to be produced presupposed the establishment of arguments and tests very different from those on which standard production was based. But, before analyzing the extension of the *collection form*, a process that is at work today in a growing and diverse number of commercial situations, we must say something about collection as an arrangement for valuation. This arrangement is the basis for arguments and tests that determine the specificity of the collection form; these arguments and tests can maintain sometimes virtually literal, sometimes more distant and even metaphorical, relations with empirical collections and with the way they are arranged. Thus we shall propose a schematic account of the principal distinguishing features of the collection arrangement.

A collection is an accumulation of entities that, in order to be collectable, must possess *bodies*. Thus, for example, books – material things containing utterances and ideas – can be collected by bibliophiles as things, but not on the basis of the ideas they contain. A library used as an intellectual resource (for example, the library of a researcher or a writer – all the more obviously if it is made up of digitized books contained in a computer-based medium) is not a collection. In addition, the objects in a collection must (ideally) be movable, so that they can be juxtaposed in a common location in a way that brings out their differences.

A collection, in our sense, must contain things, and the things must be arranged. The fact of being endowed with materiality and being involved in the world of bodies confers properties on things that are indispensable for appearing in this type of arrangement. Unlike ideas, which are transmitted by written or spoken language, and unlike other works, such as those included in the performing arts, which belong to the register of events (happenings), things possess a durable material unity that readily permits their appropriation by an individual or collective person, their determination as separate units, their matching, storage, transport, and exchange. When old things are in question, things that are no longer produced and no longer protected by patents, they can easily be appreciated for themselves without taking the potential rights of their inventors into account.

Things that are inserted, at a specific point in time, into a collection fall under the legal heading of property, whether private (belonging to an individual or to a collective such as a foundation or a business) or public (belonging to the central government or to some other governmental agency). There is no such thing as a collection without an owner. But things in a collection do not require support from legal fictions different from those on which property in general is based; unlike intellectual property, for example, they do not need a more complex description. This is true even if certain things – for example, works of art[21] – may fall under different regimes of property: ordinary, patrimonial, or intellectual.

Objects in a collection can be exchanged and circulated. Their circulation fosters the formation of collectors' communities, groups in which exchanges may take place. A collector is rarely the only one who accumulates a certain type of object, and collectors virtually never practice the activity of collecting in isolation, except for certain pathological cases or cases in which an artist puts together a collection precisely in order to produce a representation of that type of activity – and in the latter case the product can be characterized as a metacollection rather than a collection properly speaking.

To be sure, some actors accumulate objects and arrange them in relation to one another in a solitary fashion. But in most cases such actors fall into the category of mentally disturbed or deviant persons. With the development of interest in *art brut* ("raw art," a forerunner of "outsider art"), a number of such accumulations have been retrieved and exhibited,[22] and some have achieved considerable fame – in France, for example, the celebrated Palais idéal du Facteur Cheval.[23] This interest in *art brut* doubtless led several artists, especially in the 1970s, to focus on the theme of collection as a solipsistic activity.[24] In France, an important moment in the movement that led numerous artists to take an interest in collection arrangements was marked by an exhibit organized in Paris in 1974 at the Musée des arts décoratifs titled "Ils collectionnent ..." ("They collect ...").[25] The exhibit included collections of tops, gas masks, whistles, glasses, cigarette lighters, stones, sand, pens, pipes, tools, bottle tops, votive offerings, light switches and plugs, and so on. The catalog lists seventy-nine different types of collection: the exhibit can truly be called a collection of collections.

Because they can be exchanged, things in collections are economic goods to which a price is attached when they change hands. When an object in a collection is the property of a central government, it can be inalienable (as is the case in France). It nevertheless receives a *metaprice*, which is the amount for which it is insured (this price is estimated when the object enters into a collection or when it is loaned for an exhibit). There is no such thing as a "priceless" object in a collection. But things in collections can also be transmitted through inheritance, as gifts, or as donations to a government agency in exchange for a tax exemption at the time of transmission. Public collections, composed of things acquired through purchase, as gifts or as donations (and sometimes by extortion or confiscation), have continued to be enriched either by items from personal collections or by collections already constituted in their entirety. But once they are in public custody, the things acquired, if they cannot be resold, may nevertheless be relegated to storage, set aside, or even forgotten, like trash left behind in a warehouse, whether or not they appear in inventories (which are often incomplete).

Excluded from exchange, these public collections still play an economic role, with implications for the entire field of collectables. To grasp the economic dimension of the collection schema, we thus have to surmount the distinction between private and public. We have to consider at one and the same time individual enterprises of accumulation (often described, or written off, as whims, hobbies, or manias) and large-scale state-level institutions devoted to constituting and preserving a heritage characterized as national or even global.

In terms of costs, unlike the form that prevails in an industrial economy, the collection form does not give priority to the hours of labor or to the other production costs involved when it comes to justifying the price of objects. But the form must nonetheless take into account other costs, which are by no means negligible: namely, *preservation costs* – not only the costs of storing and maintaining the objects collected but also the costs of insuring and in some cases restoring those objects.

Anything can be added to a collection as long as it can be referred to a principle of totalization. Thus nothing that has a form (whether this form is attributed to "nature" or results from human intervention) and that presents variables in relation to other forms likely to be considered in terms of a series is *a priori* uncollectable. Still, the vast realm of collectables, taken as a whole, comprises *fields* that include things deemed of very unequal value, as is evidenced by the incommensurable prices at which they are negotiated. We may find among collections, on the one hand, a series of relatively recent objects, fairly easily obtained and relatively inexpensive, even if they have been collected over a certain period of time and by a large number of people, and, on the other hand, a series of things that are hard to obtain and very costly. Fans of collections, even though they readily acknowledge that all these collections have something in common and that all collectors are cut from the same cloth, whatever their objects of preference, agree on distinctions between "beautiful" or "exceptional" things and "ordinary" or "banal," even "trivial" things. Thus they have a tendency to justify the very unequal prices that things obtain in exchanges by referring to qualities that are viewed as intrinsic to the things themselves and that consequently do not depend on the activity of collectors (rather like actors operating in the financial markets when they evoke the "fundamental value" of stocks, treating that value as inherent, in contrast to the prices that these same stocks can attain during phases of speculation).

Collectors' items

Things that have been overlooked or forgotten, even *trash* – that is, things whose principal characteristic is precisely that they have low prices or are deemed worthless[26] – can become collectors' items alongside "valuable objects," "beautiful things," or "noteworthy works" acquired at high prices. The former may have been acquired at low prices, or "found" – that is, extracted from the environment for free, or even stolen. Nevertheless, if we acknowledge that things to which value has already been attributed, things that have been the object of a monetary exchange, often owe this status to the very fact that they had been included in earlier collections (this is made evident when their itinerary has left material or memorial traces), then we can postulate that there are very few collected or collectable objects that, at some stage of their existence, have not existed as trash before being noticed, gathered up, classified, and taken in hand. This is eminently clear in the case of archaeological, prehistorical, or paleontological collections, all of which comprise things that have been extracted from the soil in which they lay. Still, this property can doubtless be extended to most if not all objects in collections, so that it would not be an exaggeration to say that collections are the result of *digs*.

Things that are collectors' items *already exist*. Thus they come from the *past*, although the past in question may be remote or (as in the case of contemporary art) recent. By and large, these things were not produced for the purpose of collecting; thus the economy in which they are inserted is one in which production does not play a determining role in valuation, unlike the economy associated with the standard form. It is rare for a collector to acquire such objects by placing an order with a supplier, although certain things (for example, high-end luxury cars) can be produced in limited series intended specifically for collectors.

Collected items are not subject to use. This is equally true for things taken from so-called natural environments (for example, pebbles) and for articles that result from human activity (for example, pots or buttons). None of these things is acquired in order to perform practical functions corresponding to needs (unlike stones acquired in order to build a house or shoes purchased for walking). They are not acquired even for the purpose of display, in a logic of social distinction (for example, boots of a certain brand and at a certain price). In other words, interest in the items collected is not dictated by considerations that rely on externalities, whether these considerations are material (sturdy shoes for walking in the rain) or social (eye-catching shoes that make a statement). To be sure, if we wanted to remain within a neoclassical framework, we could say that these things do have a certain utility. But this utility is related exclusively to the place they can occupy in a given collection.

While objects brought together in a collection do not give rise to use, they arouse two types of interest that are generally closely connected. The first sort of interest is stimulated by what the item, considered in terms of what is singular about it, is capable of evoking. The second sort of interest is focused on the tension, made evident when the items collected are juxtaposed, between *repetition* and *difference* – that is, between what a certain number of things have in common and what distinguishes them from one another. The "beauty" of things, often evoked by collectors to justify what they call their "passion" (a property that does not belong to things as such but, rather, refers to the sentiments they arouse), takes shape at the intersection between these two types of interest.

Let us start by examining the first type, which may apply, moreover, to objects brought together in "curio cabinets" as well as to objects situated in what we are calling *systematic collections*. Stemming from the past, the objects gathered up and collected bring up memories of persons, events, or states of affairs with which they are thought to have been formerly associated. In this way they are comparable to what are called "souvenirs," a term designating things capable of arousing mental states on the order of evocation or recollection. This is the case, for example, of a dip pen that once belonged to Marcel Proust, a paving stone ripped out of the rue Soufflot during the "night of the barricades" in May 1968, or "the watch my grandfather wore" that was taken from him on his deathbed. Such things are charged with a *memorial force* whose gradient is a function of the importance granted by collectivities of any size to the person, thing, event, or state of affairs whose memory the things evoke.[27]

The second type of interest, which is particularly evident in systematic collections, is what distinguishes a collection from a *heap*. A collection is generally presented in the form of an accumulation of things whose juxtaposition is justified through reference to a property that is said to belong to each of the things brought together. What these things have in common is most often a visible property. This property may be self-evident to a non-expert viewer, who will perceive something like a *family resemblance* (for example, among pots, watches, or keys), taking into account the functions these things fulfilled when they were still in use; alternatively, the property may be perceptible only to the viewer who knows something about the history of the objects assembled (as in the case of things originating in the same place, from the same period, and so on). A systematic collection is thus based on a premeditated *repetition*. The property that is presumed to be shared by the things brought together makes it possible to say what the collection is collecting: its *state of things*. In the absence of that "something" that the objects are presumed to have in common, the accumulation would break down into a *heap* – that is, a group of objects in a proximity that nothing justifies, that results from contingency, chance, or the deleterious action of time. *Being in a heap* is the mode of being of trash. It is only when things are removed, by human hands, from the contingent proximity of other things with which they had appeared together in a heap, and then placed in contiguity to things with which the object in question has something in common, that an object gains access to the field of the collectable.

But the figure of repetition does not suffice to characterize the collection arrangement. Things made in factories, according to certain standards, intended to be as similar as possible to a prototype (for example, bolts made from the same mold) and brought together in a single place, do not constitute a collection. Here again we are in the presence of a heap, but a heap of bolts of the same kind. There are, then, two types of heap. In one case, heaps bring together heterogeneous things among which differences are perceptible and innumerable; in the other, heaps bring together things presumed to be similar (even if close examination – through a microscope, for example – might reveal differences). Collections fall between these two opposing types of heap: the one in which everything is different (a jumble) and the one in which everything is the same (a stockpile of specimens from a single prototype).

The distinction between accumulation and collection can be spelled out in yet another way. Accumulations are in principle open or unlimited. To things already accumulated, one can endlessly add other things that bear some degree of resemblance. But adding on the basis of similarity may lead to an accumulation of more and more divergent things, because resemblance can be spread from one thing to another – for instance, in relation to the order in which interest is paid to one feature and then another (as for example in children's word games based on associations of sounds: "fire truck" – "truck stop" – "stoplight" – "lighthouse," and so on). In this type of accumulation, the connection between each new thing chosen and the previous ones may be made on the basis of properties that can vary. But the more slippage there is from one property to another, the more the accumulation as a whole will resemble a heap (as in displays of second-hand goods where there is a jumble of everything, including a kitchen sink).

The objects that figure in a given collection have to present not only resemblances but also systematic *differences* in relation to one another. Thus each of the things brought together on the basis of a certain similarity must also present features that differentiate them from the others, although these differences must not be so vast as to outweigh the family resemblances. The proper form toward which a collection tends is thus that of an accumulation of small differences among things that, considered from a greater distance, as it were, can be envisaged in their similarities. This form is unstable. If the differences among things are too significant, the collection regresses toward the heap form of the first type (a jumble). But if the differences are too hard to discern, the collection tends to approach the heap form of the second type (a stockpile). An analogy from cartography may help to clarify this: depending on the scale adopted, a map may represent the contours of an island in the form of a continuous line or a broken line.

The differences among the things that figure in a single collection have to be susceptible to organization in the form of a system of pertinent differences. The collection form thus sketches out a certain ontological framework within which a plurality of entities, *a priori* indefinite in number, is ordered by the relation of these entities to a *governing principle* that, as it is realized in their juxtaposition, blurs their relation to other things in the world, things that are generally kept at a distance from the environment in which the things collected are placed. The collected objects are thus detached from a *remainder* and placed in the perspective of their relations to one another. By the same token, the differences that nevertheless separate them must be explicitly described. Still, the descriptions can never account for all the differences among the things assembled, for these differences are always heterogeneous and excessive. The work of interpretation thus consists in distinguishing among several types of difference. Some of these are not noted. Others are attributed to contingency and treated as accidental defects that have an individual character. Still others, finally, are deemed *pertinent* and evaluated according to a certain gradient of solidity and stability. They can be indicated by a term in such a way that the presence of the specified difference can be reidentified on an *a priori* indefinite number of things likely to bear such a difference.

The relation between what we have called the *governing principle* (which specifies what type of thing is accumulated in the collection) and the *differences* deemed pertinent under a given governing principle can prove variable. What we call the governing principle is never more than one difference among others, placed for a time in a position that makes it possible to close the list of collectables. Thus, to take a very simple example, air mail can be the governing principle of a certain stamp collection in which the differences between countries will be treated as the pertinent differences. But if the governing principle selected is a particular country, then the difference between regular mail and air mail will become pertinent. Finally, the various types of difference we have just indicated are not necessarily stable. A previously unnoticed feature may become a pertinent difference, while differences once deemed pertinent may stop being taken into account or may come to be viewed as defects, and so on. In other words, the *conventions* according to which a certain field of collectables is organized, and the length of time these conventions last, depend first and foremost on the actions of operators, the length of time the field has been in existence, the power relations manifested in the field, the presence or absence of specific institutions, and especially, no doubt, the number of exchanges and their level in terms of price. Conventions and exchanges are in a circular relationship. The principal role of conventions is to facilitate agreements concerning the appreciation of the things in question under the circumstances of an exchange. But, at the same time, the conventions are shaped and solidified in the course of officially completed exchanges.

When *patterns* organizing a certain field of collectables are put into place (which is not always the case, especially if the field in question is relatively new), the accumulation of objects undertaken by operators is governed by a more or less shared representation of the totality to be constituted by the collection once it is complete. We need to distinguish, then, between *objective totalizations*, those on which the various accumulators embark, and *ideal totalizations*, which, even if they are never completely achieved by anyone, constitute the vanishing points toward which the various accumulations are oriented. The interactions within a community, whether it is a well-established and durable community or one that is still being formed, make it possible to establish a system of principles of juxtaposition and of pertinent differences that, through reference to shared conventions, can regulate geographically scattered enterprises, each of which is rightly experienced as personal and even as singular. In fact, the constitution of a field of collectable things within which a plurality of systematic collections is developed presupposes that individual accumulations – which owe a great deal, of course, to chance encounters, the diversity of tastes, and even fantasies on the part of an individual collector – are nevertheless governed by reference to an *ideal collection*. Such a collection includes the complete series of objects subject to a single governing principle and distinguished from one another by the fact that each bears differences judged pertinent according to modalities that are themselves conventional.

In a format of this type, an accumulation that gives rise to a collection governed by reference to an ideal totality does not simply contain things as such (if it did, it would be hard to distinguish from a heap). A collection properly so called includes three sorts of entity. First of all, necessarily, there are *things*. But, secondly, there must be *differences*, and we can even go so far as to say that a collection is above all a *collection of differences*, even if those differences become pertinent only insofar as they are deposited in things. Considered in this light, the things in question matter less for themselves than in relation to the *differences* of which they are the material *supports*. In the logic of collecting, then, two things characterized by the fact that they are supports for the same pertinent differences constitute *duplicates*, so that one of the two is deemed excessive; it can be removed from the collection and be exchanged – a common outcome – for a thing that is lacking, a thing that supports differences not yet present in the collection understood as an objective totalization. Let us add that, while different things bearing pertinent differences may turn out to be valued differently and exchanged for very unequal prices, the differences that constitute a certain field of collectables all have equal weight.

A collection, as an objective totalization, includes a third sort of entity that can be designated by the term *lack*. It is a question of pertinent differences in the system of the ideal collection, differences that are supported by things that do not figure, or do not yet figure, in a given collection seen as an objective totalization.[28] Each collector operating within a certain field of collectables, oriented toward a single ideal totality, will seek to fill in what is lacking – that is, will try to acquire new things which bear certain pertinent differences that are not present in the things he or she already possesses. To say that every collection is composed at once of things that bear differences and of *lacks* means that things that are missing are always present, at the heart of the collections, but precisely in the form of lacks. It follows that the activity of collectors is above all guided by a concern for supplying what is lacking. It is because they are imbued with this concern that collectors engage in exchange.

For the collector, these lacks may be quite precise, in the sense that the things on which they figure are already identified, even if it is difficult to gain access to them and to incorporate them into the ongoing collection. But they may also have a relatively uncertain representational presence.

Their existence may, sometimes, be only postulated (as when one speaks, in paleontology, of a "missing link"). In such cases they are sufficiently hypothetical for the things on which they might figure to be the object of research, often lengthy and uncertain, but at the same time they may be anticipated with enough assurance to orient the research in certain directions rather than others. In either case, it is the dynamics of the collection itself, guided by the contours of the ideal totality taking shape (which each objective totalization helps to specify), that orients the research.

Thus all collectors, in order to pursue their accumulations, must meld two very different states of mind. On the one hand, they must set out in search of new things with an unbiased outlook: they must be "open-minded" enough to welcome and acquire (when they encounter by happenstance) an object whose pertinence might have escaped them, as it had escaped others, because it had not up to that point been registered with reference to the ideal totality. On the other hand, they must orient their choices in a way that gives primacy to things that are capable of filling gaps, supplying what is lacking, with reference to the contours of an ideal totality that they, as collectors, are helping to draw. When they speak of what motivates them, collectors generally conflate these two orientations by grasping them in a single idiom, that of "desire," understood as a sort of impulse that grips and guides them in an almost involuntary way toward objects that they have to acquire "at any price." Yet this sort of subjectivization of the impulse that inspires them leaves aside the fact that they are especially attracted by lacks – that is, by entities that, even though they are absent, nevertheless have an *objective* mode of being, since the objects to which they correspond figure in the *pattern* of the ideal collection. Thus their "desires" are not internal, not rooted in their subjectivity; they arise, rather, from the arrangement of the *state of things* with which collectors are confronted.

The fields of the collectable may be mutable, especially if they are recent and bear upon objects that are readily accessible and not very expensive, or, on the contrary, they may be stabilized and equipped with instruments, supported by catalogs, experts, associations, and so on. But they are rarely institutionalized in the narrow sense in which their contours and their functioning would be the object of legal stipulations or would be placed under governmental control. Institutions may have to rule on the authenticity of things – that is, on their attribution – so as to distinguish originals from copies or counterfeits. But it is not their place to rule on what is, or what ought to be, the way a given collection is organized. Or, in other words, a given field of collectables and the system of governing principles and differences on which this field is based are not *codified*: that is, neither the field nor the system is backed up by written instructions and definitions claiming legal authority. Their acceptability – as in the case of dialects, by contrast with national languages that have been stabilized under the authority of grammarians – thus depends above all on the tacit recognition granted them by those who participate in exchanges and on the capacity of those participants to maintain grounds of understanding, despite the slight displacements (especially spatial, in the case of dialects, and temporal, in the case of collections) that continue to modify the participants' interactions.

Price and value of collectors' items

Let us now consider, just as schematically, the mechanisms of exchange and their effects on the formation of prices and on the determination of collections as wealth.

In a certain field of collectables, characterized by the existence of more or less shared conventions that support ideal totalizations, the various operators rapidly enter into *competition*. Their preferences converge around certain things rather than others, and this convergence tends to limit the range of things being sought. To reach their goals – that is, to fill in lacks that become objective only when the totalization in progress is confronted (if only in an imaginary fashion) with an ideal totalization – collectors will tend to focus on things that bear pertinent differences. If they cannot manage to procure such things, they can obviously opt for things farther removed from the heart of their collections, but then they risk seeing their collections regress toward simple accumulation. It must be noted that this reorientation of the interests of most collectors toward certain things rather than others is not necessarily the result of a change in tastes or in individual "passions," or even of a "fashion" effect. It is triggered by the very logic of collecting, which pushes collectors to fill in certain gaps.

The formation of a field of collectables may lead to a rapid and sometimes considerable rise in the *prices* at which the things that support pertinent differences in the field are negotiated. Such increases in the prices of collectables depend, first of all, on the narrative presentation of the thing (its memorial force), secondly, on the originality of the thing (whether the item is a reproduction or not), and, thirdly, on the differences each thing bears within an ideal totality.

Things that are no longer produced and no longer used, having attained the status of quasi-trash, can once again enter into exchanges if potential buyers identify in them the presence of differences that can fill in some of their lacks. Thus an obsolete ballpoint pen, of a type that has not been produced for a long time, one that does not work as well as a more recent model and has been forgotten at the back of a drawer, may be the object of renewed interest if collections of ballpoint pens are being developed. Someone may then discover that this obsolete pen contains pertinent differences within the conventional framework that governs such collections. Let us note that a change in price is in no way connected to the substantive properties of the object. It is still the same thing. The passage from the state of trash to the state of an appreciated thing thus depends solely on the possibility offered by collections to *bring together* different things under a single governing principle that serves as the background against which their differences can stand out. In this sense, the collection arrangement can be said to accomplish, on its own, a creation of value that owes nothing to the things themselves but that operates *ex nihilo*, as it were. This transmutation is by no means a mysterious miracle, nor does it depend on the outdated charm attributed to old things. Thus it must be credited neither to some sort of "magic" nor to a search for "distinction." It results from the lacks that the collection arrangement brings to the fore.

Still, within a single field of collectables, this rise in prices is differential. For if a collection has to bring all the pertinent differences together under a certain governing principle, and if these differences all have the same import, the objects that bear these differences are not equally accessible. It follows that certain lacks (in differences) may be much more difficult to fill than others because the objects that bear them are not readily accessible or have already been appropriated. These are the objects whose prices are most likely to rise.

Moreover, the price of each thing is relational: the price of any collectable, when it is made public, is a metaprice that serves as a benchmark for all the things in a given totality. This is why, when a work by a certain artist, or an object whose value has been heightened by historians or anthropologists, enters into a public collection maintained by a major institution, the prices of all works by that artist or all objects in the same category will rise, pulled upward by the immortal character of the piece that has entered the museum. In the same way, collectors or gallery owners, in order to maintain or increase the prices of works they already possess, have an interest in ensuring a high price for a work belonging to one of the totalities that are particularly well represented in their stock, for example by buying such a work at a high price on the secondary market. But this is also why many works, most notably when they are handled by an intermediary such as a broker, are sold at prices known only to the broker and the buyer and are not made public, so as to avoid depreciating the other works in the same totality.

The increase in the prices of things sought after but not readily accessible stems from the fact that, in the logic of collecting, the least onerous solution, which would consist in filling lacks by fabricating, or commissioning a craftsman to fabricate, *copies* of things bearing pertinent differences, is not acceptable. In addition, if a copy of a collectable item is made, as happens sometimes in museums where a copy is exhibited in order to preserve the original from deterioration, the price of the copy remains far below that of the original, since the latter is established in relation to other originals from the same totality.

As historians who have studied artists' workshops and the art trade have shown, the rejection of copies is a relatively recent phenomenon;[29] this is attested, for example, in Gérard Labrot's study of the Neapolitan art market in the seventeenth and eighteenth centuries.[30] Similar remarks could be made about the importance attributed to signatures on paintings. "An irregular, even rare practice for the modern period," according to Charlotte Guichard, signatures became a major index of authenticity only in the first half of the nineteenth century. Guichard points out that this change "coincided with the development of the art market, which benefited from the dispersal of aristocratic collections tied to confiscations during the Revolution."[31] The rejection of copies, which developed in the nineteenth century, paralleled the establishment of the distinction between an art destined to fill various social functions (religious edification, manifestation of authority, decoration of public spaces or private dwellings, and so on) and "pure" art, "art for art's sake," in which things are destined above all to occupy places in specific collections, whether these collections belong to princes or to museums under the authority of a government agency (the concept of the latter appeared during the same period).

The reorientation of art toward collections that can be called systematic (to distinguish them both from ordinary practices and from curio cabinets) had the effect of banning copies and establishing a decisive separation between the original and any duplicates, a separation that had earlier been seriously blurred owing to the existence of a great number of works of intermediate status (as is evident in the case of Leonardo da Vinci's *The Virgin of the Rocks*). From the late nineteenth century on, the creation of fakes – that is, reproductions or adaptations that are passed off as authentic and original, and sold as such – and the penalization of counterfeiters would come to constitute particularly pertinent indicators of artistic success. In certain cases ("design" furniture, for instance), things figuring in collections have indeed been produced again. But such reproductions, characterized as "reissues," concern a limited number of things whose quantity is controlled (as opposed to serial production, which continues as long as there is a demand), and the new specimens put into circulation are not intended to be confused with the original works, still less with the prototype on the basis of which the reproductions are created.

The depreciation of copies goes hand in hand with the valorization of *authenticity*, which, although largely overdetermined, relies heavily on *attribution*, envisaged in a logic of causality.[32] An object is authentic when one can know its origin and determine its causes from the moment when it was thrust into reality, either because it was made by an agent (usually an individual to whom a name is attributed), or because it was discovered (as with the objects with which archaeology and paleontology are concerned). Authenticity also implies that we can follow or retrace the steps in its path to the present day. But the cult of the authentic and the original, which arose in Europe toward the end of the eighteenth century and spread very broadly, interests us here only in the context of the determining role it played in shaping the prices of collectors' items.

With the exception of things made in such a way that their prices were already very high at the time of fabrication, have remained high over time, and have consistently been treated as treasures (objects incorporating precious metals or stones, for example), the very fact that the collection arrangement has taken over certain things, most notably with reference to their memorial power, is essentially responsible for their increased prices. Thus it is appropriate to relativize or at least to nuance the distinction between "fine things" and "ordinary things," a distinction that plays an important role in the discourse of collectors and – especially – in the discourse of the merchants from whom they buy things. What characterizes the "fine things" that draw high prices is largely the fact that they have been hoarded and then collected over long periods of time and have been endowed with great memorial power, whereas this has happened with "ordinary things" only recently. It is thus in the course of their history, marked by successive passages among various treasure troves, curio cabinets, and collections, the memory of which is in some sense deposited in the objects themselves, that the most sought-after things are credited with the value that makes it possible to justify their prices.

The collection form allows for the reference to the "intrinsic value" of a thing – a value often presented in terms of what makes the object unique and thus incommensurable with any other – to be closely tied to its "market value" (that is, its metaprice), a value made concrete by a price set in the test of an exchange. The tension between these two ways of judging – evaluation and appreciation – turns out to be neutralized, as it were. To be sure, the price of an object can be treated as if it were more or less tied to the circumstances of the exchange (a judgment of the pragmatic order), while the value of an object can be bound up with what is deemed essential about it (a judgment, in a sense, of the semantic order). This is why the value of a thing can always be evoked in order to challenge its price. Nevertheless, a given domain of collectables appears more or less stabilized when the prevailing arrangement maintains an acceptable relation between the price of a thing (revealed in an exchange) and its value (likely to be judged "purely subjective"); this situation tends to limit the number of transactions that give rise to critiques. The most important among these arrangements are those that ensure the validity and autonomy of the agencies on which the definition of value depends by separating them decisively from the agencies that weigh in on the shaping of prices.

Transactions among art collectors provide a good illustration. The value acknowledged in works of art relies on a number of arrangements for evaluation that have an institutional basis; these arrangements themselves often depend more or less directly on the public domain or, especially in Europe, on central governments. Participants include conservators, historians, and critics who, on various grounds, are associated with museums or universities.[33] The judgments made by these actors are not supposed to take prices into account. This indifference to "economic" considerations is (or was for a long time) thought to be a condition of the validity of the judgments made. But, from another standpoint, the autonomy of the agencies of valorization is (or was for a long time) taken to be one of the conditions ensuring the justification of the prices of artworks during transactions among artists, merchants, and collectors. For the price of a work to be justified, it needs to appear miraculously adjusted to the value that it has been acknowledged to have in arenas where judgment is supposed to have been passed by placing prices under a veil of ignorance. But, for this fiction to be credible, the actors and the arrangements that ensure artistic valorization have to be different from those who take part in the transactions.[34] Indeed, if these groups of actors are too closely connected or merged, the valuation of a work of art runs the risk of being denounced as a *maneuver* intended to support or increase the work's price.

It is perhaps a situation of this type that is targeted today in protests by artists, and especially art critics, who call into question the growing role played by collectors, not only in the appreciation of works but also in their evaluation,[35] to the detriment of institutional agencies and critics.[36] The protesters associate this development with a set of changes marked most notably by the weakening of arrangements for public financing, but also by the growing importance of awards in the evaluation of works and artists. The creation of the *Kunstkompass*, at the beginning of the 1920s, was initially met with indignation (certain artists mentioned went so far as to demand that their names be removed from the list), before the awards multiplied[37] and diversified, to the point of becoming – as is the case now – unavoidable instruments of evaluation and appreciation of works and artists. Without contesting the power that is attributed to collectors today, we must nevertheless note that, if that power is undeniable on the financial level, institutions and in particular public museums still retain an important role of consecration. Attesting to this are the fact that, at least in France, aspirations on the part of private collectors to create major museums quickly become virtual affairs of state, and also the fact that a significant portion of the estate taxes owed by collectors is covered through donations of consecrated works from the collections to the central government.

The fields of collectables

The passage from the state of trash to that of a sought-after object owes a great deal to the action of primary collectors who also hold artistic authority, whether they are recognized artists, patrons of the arts, or organizers of exhibits or other artistic displays. This authority, acquired during earlier tests in the various art worlds, confers enough power on the actors to elevate rapidly the status of the things that they have singled out; part of the worth attached to their names is transferred to the things in question. Collecting and preserving what they like (or, in the case of artists, what they say are sources of inspiration), these actors gradually generate – starting from random encounters with certain objects and their exchanges (exchanges of things or exchanges of statements about things) – the conventions that will allow tastes and desires, considered initially as the expression of individual originality, to be shared by others. This is the case even if, in the absence of previously established conventions, these primary collectors are at the outset more like accumulators who pick up things that suit them and put them side by side without any sort of systematic organization. The reference to their very person is what tends to transform such accumulations into collections. Indeed, when artists whose creative activity has gradually made them famous are involved, their identity and the features that turn out to be attached to that identity become the constitutive principle (the governing principle) of a collection that is designated by their names (as when we speak of the "Breton collection") and whose deployment of objects is thought to reveal the depths of the artist's personality.

Examples abound. They often depend on external, intellectual, aesthetic, and/or political developments. Among the best known, we can mention the constitution of *art nègre* in Paris between 1910 and 1920, roughly speaking; that of *art brut*, especially in France and Switzerland, in the 1950s; or, more recently, works of art constituted from traces left by street graffiti artists, a movement that began in New York during the 1970s. In each of these cases, the activity of the initial collectors, individual innovators, and artists very quickly aroused the interest of collectors properly speaking, and consequently of gallery owners, followed later by museums or other public institutions. These secondary collectors, initially without specific competencies, tend to appreciate things by taking into account above all the personalities of the artists who were the first to spot these objects. Thus it is said that the first systematic collectors of "primitive art" appreciated the things they were acquiring through reference to the noteworthy artists who had been the first to possess them, and who had valorized them by projecting onto them part of the value attached to their own work ("this one comes from the Vlaminck collection").

We must note, nevertheless, that processes of this type are not limited to the famous examples that we have just recalled. They always accompany the formation of any new field of collectables. The case of Stevengraphs, analyzed by Michael Thompson, is a classic example.[38] These are figures woven with silk threads of different colors whose mechanized production, based on Jacquard looms, was invented by Thomas Steven, a manufacturer in Coventry; they were first presented to the public at an exhibition in the city of York in 1879. Produced serially, relatively inexpensive to purchase, tableaus of this sort with very diverse motifs (ships, religious images, representations of a nude Lady Godiva on her white horse, and so on) constituted typical examples of industrial art destined to enrich the homes of the English middle and lower classes between the end of the nineteenth century and the first third of the twentieth. Eventually, as the interest of buyers waned, production ceased, and the models, preserved in Coventry, were destroyed when the factory was bombed in 1940. Stevengraphs gradually passed from the status of inexpensive popular items appreciated by a broad public to a state of quasi-trash, forgotten in attics or displayed in a disorderly manner among a multitude of other things on the shelves of the most modest second-hand dealers. They were invisible, worth practically nothing, until the 1960s, when they began to become appreciated and sought-after collectors' items. Their prices rose rapidly in just a few years, until they reached levels well above their starting point as industrially produced commercial objects.

Michael Thompson has sought to reconstitute the way this "return to life" worked and to identify the actors behind it. The revival of interest was linked first to the publication of articles in *Collectors' Magazine*, then to better documented and more systematic works written by academics and art historians. It seems that the formation of a group of connoisseurs and collectors interested in Stevengraphs was initially the doing of separate individuals – "eccentrics," as Thompson calls them – who, each in his or her own way, and for different reasons, came to see these isolated and depreciated objects in a new light. These individuals eventually came into contact with one another, chiefly through specialized magazines, so they were able to exchange specimens and trade information about them. Stevengraphs thus became collectors' items sought by a large number of people. The reconstitution, by the earliest connoisseurs, of what must have been complete series from the Coventry factory and the identification of the traces that appeared on the back of certain specimens – examples that were thus considered particularly rare – served as the basis for shaping conventions that could guide collectors. The latter could henceforth form the project, impossible to realize, of achieving an exhaustive collection, coming up with an idea of the prices of the various items brought together under the newly developed governing principle, identifying what they lacked, and passing judgment on the prices of things that were proposed to them.

The fields of collectables are thus rarely stabilized once and for all. And this is so in particular because the various fields interact, and each of them is therefore subject not only to the constraint of its own governing principle but also to constraints imposed by the operations of constitution, reinforcement, and weakening that affect other more or less adjacent fields. These interactions are achieved by collectors' efforts to initiate or pursue the development of their own object collections.

Each of these fields of collectables thus finds itself constantly distorted – although to varying degrees according to their level of rigidity – under the effect of a *dynamics* that has to do above all with competition among collectors. To sketch out a model of this dynamics, we have to take into account the fact that different collectors do not all have the same means (financial means in particular); in addition, they start collecting at different times. Those who have been operating for some time (perhaps as innovators, who may have played a role in the formation of a new field of collectables) may keep on adding to their collection, which they do not consider complete. But others are newcomers, starting from scratch. The situation of the two groups is profoundly asymmetrical.

The operators who are among the earliest to occupy a certain field of collectables have an advantage for at least two reasons. On the one hand, they contribute, during their activity (which may extend over a lifetime), to the establishment of a new system of governing principles and of differences that tend to rigidify over time. These operators are thus able to influence the *determination of the differences* that will become conventionally accepted in the future, and by the same token they are able to influence the shape of the ideal collection, the one that new collectors will take as their model.[39] On the other hand, having been the first to exploit the buried layers of things dispersed among various sites, mismatched and often viewed up to that point as trash, these same operators are able to acquire relevant items at low prices and profit from the valorization that accompanied the juxtaposition of these things, now matched with others in systematic collections. The initial accessibility of things that bear pertinent differences allows experienced collectors to fill a great number of lacks and, as a result, to move quickly to develop collections (which are, let us recall, collections of differences and not only of things). During the process of accumulation, these collectors presumably acquire a number of *duplicates*, which they can exchange for things bearing the differences that are so necessary in the logic of collection that they have undertaken but not yet objectivized in the things already present (or they can exchange duplicates for a monetary equivalent that will allow them to acquire items they lack). Still, the existence of lacks that are hard to fill does not stop nagging at them; it is an obstacle to their hope of one day seeing the objective totalization of their collection and the ideal totality in relation to which they are orienting their efforts – a totality whose representation, moreover, they often continued to shape.

New entrants into a stabilized field of collectables are in a very different situation. The external layers have been in part exhausted by the early arrivals, and they are much more difficult and costly to exploit, most notably because the intermediaries (second-hand goods dealers or brokers) have acquired some information, however rudimentary, about the prices of the things they hold. Still, the existence of numerous duplicates, put back into circulation by seasoned collectors, makes it possible for newcomers to fill gaps that concern differences presented by a relatively large number of things. But these newcomers rather quickly find their undertaking hindered by the difficulty of finding and acquiring things that present pertinent differences. In fact, such things, of which there are few duplicates, are almost always already held by experienced collectors who have no interest in putting them back into circulation, knowing that it would be extremely hard to locate other things presenting similar differential values. Such a situation leads fairly quickly to blockage in a given field of collectables that is governed by an established system of principles and of differences. For newcomers, who have little chance of reaching a level of totalization that could compete with that of the major established collectors, there are several possible strategies they can adopt if they want to continue collecting.

A first (weak) possibility consists in *shifting* from one field of collectables to another. When their efforts to accumulate in one field are hampered by the difficulty of acquiring the things they lack, which have become too costly, collectors can abandon the collection under way and initiate a new collection in a different field (we know of one experienced collector who started twenty-five different collections during his lifetime, all of which remained incomplete).

A second possibility, usually costly and thus reserved for wealthy collectors, is to try to buy treasure troves that have already been established, or "dead" collections. Opportunities of this sort come up mainly when an inheritance is being transmitted. The transmission or dispersal of a collection when the collector has died is often one of the most critical moments confronting things in the course of their "social lives." When objects are detached from the projects and attention of particular persons who had been careful to act in the best interest of those objects (an interest to which those individuals had linked their own interests and sometimes their identities), the only protection remaining to the objects is the law, which lends itself to diverse interpretations. Their possession may be disputed among various heirs, or among private persons and public authorities; in either case, they are vulnerable to disruption, and they offer new collectors opportunities for interesting transactions.

A third possibility calls for particular attention. It consists in attempting to make a slight shift in the system of governing principles and of differences within a certain domain so as to reopen opportunities for access to collectable things. Neither the pertinence of existing things nor, consequently, the validity of the major existing collections is called into question. In the cases we shall examine here, which can be called ordinary because they are internal to the fields of collectables and they belong to the everyday activities of collectors, the scope of a governing principle and the differences taken into account are gradually modified. This is often an almost imperceptible process, carried out by a combination of individual acts whose successes, at the moment of sale or purchase, constitute the chief tests of validity.

We must note, nonetheless, that such shifts, made in response to internal forces at work in the fields of collectables, also draw on external forces of the aesthetic and/or political order. It is thus impossible to understand the valorization of "primitive art" without taking into account both colonialism and the efforts made, in particular by ethnologists, to valorize the cultures that colonialism was in the process of destroying.[40] Similarly, the birth of *art brut* cannot be separated from the changes that were occurring during the same period both in the domain of art (with the spread of surrealism) and in that of psychiatry.[41] Even the popularity of "rustic" art that overtook bourgeois households in the 1960s and 1970s has to be seen in the context of the decline in rural life and the way dealers in second-hand goods or antiques took advantage of it. In this case too, new groups and new classes, comparable to Balzac's "nouveau-riche bourgeoisie," grabbed things that had been populating the universe of trash. Thus it is always the destruction of a certain world that produces the flood of flotsam and jetsam on the basis of which new collections are constituted, collections in which some of this trash will be valorized.

One might think that the prices at which such things are negotiated, things that had been forgotten or buried and then brought back to life because they had come to interest new collectors, would depend chiefly on their *scarcity*. Now left to themselves and without protection, these things have been subject to the assaults of time and destroyed, buried, looted, or lost, so that, abundant at the time when they were appreciated for the use that could be made of them, they ought to be very few in number. The survivors – if we can use that term to speak of inanimate beings – would thus attest to a sort of natural selection. It seems, however, that this is by no means always the case, as we have already seen with the Stevengraphs studied by Michael Thompson.[42] When a new order of collectables is constituted, it often turns out that the things collected are, on the contrary, numerous and widely accessible. Only gradually, as collectors competing for the same things (because they have to fill the same lacks) begin to proliferate, does the scarcity of these things – whose reproduction is in principle excluded – become one of the main elements determining their prices. Up to that point, the things were indeed in existence, often overabundantly, but confined to spaces of relegation and mixed together in total disorder – that is, in *heaps*. They were not necessarily *hidden* in the sense of being absent from the field of perception; nevertheless, even though they may have been *visible*, they were not *noticed*, as if those who saw them were incapable of identifying them and thus incapable of recognizing what might be special about them and worthy of interest. We maintain that things are not collected because they are rare; rather, their scarcity arises from the very fact that they are collected. The economic interest of collecting, as an arrangement, would thus be to *produce scarcity* by taking as raw materials things that are the most abundant – that is, trash.

Thus the collection arrangement can be viewed as a *selection* arrangement. It is precisely this work of choosing between what is destined for destruction and what is destined for preservation that is at the heart of the activity of collecting, and of the anxiety experienced by those who take on the task of establishing the inventory of a patrimony and who, confronted by objects belonging to the unlimited universe of things that aspire to survive, must make the crucial decision determining the fate of each one.[43] In the case of collections, selection is based on the conventions that stabilize the systems of governing principles and of pertinent differences. But these conventions – which constitute, as we have seen, stakes in struggles between collectors and, in particular, between established collectors and newcomers to the field – are relatively flexible, because they rarely involve legal considerations, so that it may not be impossible to shift them, if only ever so slightly, in such a way as to reopen to competition a field of collectables that has appeared closed.

The structure of the collection form

The space of the collection form can be envisaged in terms of the intersection of two axes, that of the presentation of a thing and that of its commercial potential (see figure 7.1).

Let us look first, as we have done for the standard form, at the *axis of presentation* and examine the way it allows us to organize and rank things that are pertinent to the collection form. It is oriented by the relation between two possible states of things, viewed either as *prototypes* or as *specimens* produced with reference to a certain prototype that is already established. At the base of this axis, we can situate collections that bring together things viewed as specimens of determinate prototypes. This is the case par excellence of the numerous collections that bring together artisanal or industrially produced objects that initially fell under the mode of valuation proper to the standard form but have been reappropriated through the logic of the collection form, often after having undergone a more or less lengthy period of degradation. For example, we can consider the accumulations of trivial objects that comprise the majority of ordinary collections whose existence we have already noted: objects such as match-boxes, pipes, empty bottles of beer or whisky, or Thompson's Stevengraphs. Having been sold at relatively low prices at the outset, then having lost all commercial value, artifacts in this category that have become collectors' items and are still available see their prices go up rapidly and sometimes dramatically.

As we move up along the axis of presentation, we continue to find collections that bring together specimens that correspond to prototypes, but prototypes that have been produced in much smaller numbers. This is the case for objects placed in circulation by the luxury industry: high-end watches, for instance, or exceptional antique cars. As an example, let us look at the watch collection that the plastic artist Arman offered for sale in 1992 (a multicollector, Arman named one exhibit of his works an "accumulation of collections").

> It included pieces as rare as a Patek Philippe with calendars and phases of the moon, in gold, from 1955, and rare models of the earliest electric watches by brand names including Hamilton, Elgin, and Illinois. Among some three hundred items he also had Rolex watches from the 1930s and 1940s, and – the stars of the entire exhibit – two watches that had belonged to Andy Warhol: a Kingsley in rose platinum with a diamond-studded index and a Vacheron Constantin in gold from the 1950s.[44]

This makes it clear that the items in the collection could be valorized principally in some cases in relation to their differential value within the series and in other cases, rather in terms of their memorial power.

Finally, as we move toward the summit of this differential axis, we find collections composed of objects for which the gap between prototype

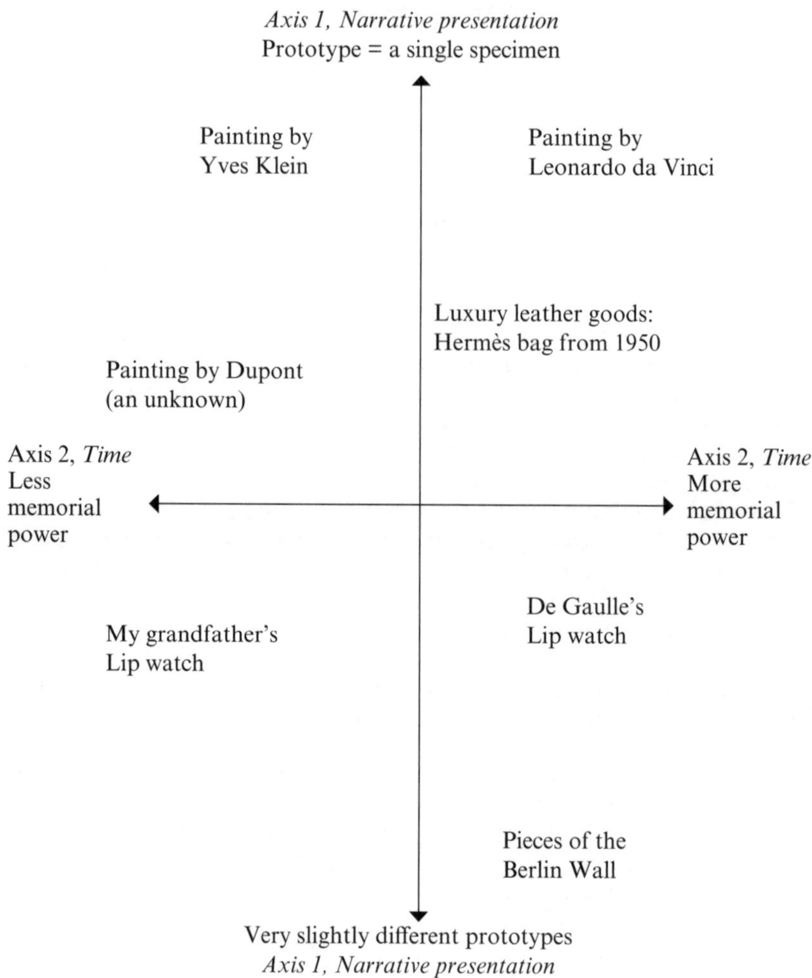

Figure 7.1 Structural schema of the collection form

and specimen tends to be attenuated or even abolished. This is par excellence the case of highly celebrated artworks, whether these are very old (Leonardo da Vinci's *Virgin of the Rocks*, for example) or modern or contemporary works (such as Balthus's *La chambre turque* or Yves Klein's *Monochrome bleu*). With regard to works such as these, we can borrow the analysis developed by Claude Lévi-Strauss in *The Savage Mind* when, in the chapter titled "The Individual as a Species," he seeks to reduce the distance separating the logic of proper names from that of categorial entities.[45] He then envisages the possibility of species that would have just a single specimen (as is the case, for instance, for the phoenix). And, similarly, one can treat objects often called "unique" or "singular" as prototypes, but prototypes of which just one specimen exists.

Let us now examine the second axis, the one that incorporates the dimensions of *commercial potential*. We have seen that, in the context of the standard form, this axis indexed the duration of use that can be expected of things destined to be used, with single-use objects at one pole and objects of higher quality, supposed to be usable throughout a lifetime, and even transmitted to heirs, at the other pole. Obviously, this cannot be the case for the collection form, since the latter valorizes things one of whose properties is precisely that they escape the test of use or, in other words, of being past their useful life. We have just seen, moreover, with the example of works of art, objects that occupy a central position in the order of the collectable, that, once these things are selected, they are endowed with a fictitious immortality and thus find themselves exempt, as it were, from the grip of time. The question of time resurfaces nevertheless, but in a different way.

Alongside the differential power of collectables, handled by the first axis, a second property plays an important role in the valorization of things that belong to the collection form: the degree to which these things are likely to produce memory effects, or what we are calling their *memorial power*. This power, conferred on things that may be relatively unimportant, taken at face value, has to do with the fact that at some point in their career they were in physical contact with persons or events that matter. This property – *physical proximity* – accounts for two previously noted pertinent features of collectors' items. The first is the fact that their valorization depends to a large extent on the *narrative* that accompanies them. Whereas industrial objects can be described through a combination of standards – that is, by a form of codification – collectors' items can be described through stories that recall, in particular, the conditions in which they appeared and the persons who created them or to whom they once belonged. *Narrativity* is part of their way of being in the world.[46]

Linked to the question of memory, there is a second feature of major importance in the economy of things belonging to the collection form: the requirement of *authenticity*. In other words, each collectors' item must bear a guarantee, generally incorporated into the accompanying narrative, that the very thing before one's eyes, considered in its pure materiality, has indeed been in physical contact with places, persons, or events now buried in the past but still present in human memory. This is why no *reproduction* – not even a perfectly executed *copy* – can replace the original item within a collection; nor, quite obviously, can it reach an equivalent price when it is subjected to the test of exchange. The processes of attribution, rather than the intrinsic properties of the thing, thus play a fundamental role in establishing the prices of the objects that interest us here.[47]

But the memorial power conferred on things depends on the more or less individual or collective character of the persons, places, or events that these things evoke. Thus "memorial power" must be understood not as an immanent property but as a quality socially attributed to an object and discernible by means of indices that make it possible to measure the object's degree of fame, which can vary over time depending on the way history is written.[48] We can thus identify, at one pole of the temporal axis, things whose memorial power is weak, for what they evoke is important only to a limited number of people, or even to a single person. This limited memorial power is the one invoked when the quality of "souvenir" is attributed to an object that has a more or less "personal" character. Such an attribution indicates that the object is indeed of great "value" to the person who has it, or perhaps for the members of a family group for whom it evokes a deceased relative, but there is no claim that the object is of any value to others (for example, the Lip watch that belonged to one of our grandfathers). Conversely, at the opposite pole of the same axis we find objects endowed with great memorial power, because they are credited with having been in physical proximity to persons, places, or events that have remained present in the memory of a very large number of people, even of entire peoples (for example, the model T18 Lip watch that General de Gaulle is said to have offered Winston Churchill).[49] This is the case par excellence of collections bringing together things whose principle of accumulation is related not to a function or a period but to a memorable person.[50]

The same remarks apply as well, of course, to objects that aspire, without great success, to the status of works of art and to objects whose status as works of art no one would dream of contesting, whether or not they are appreciated on the "aesthetic" level. Thus a given painting, unfamiliar to most people or viewed as a "reject," may be of great value to the mother of the person who created it one day in the vain hope of becoming recognized as an artist. And, conversely, another painting attributed to a famous artist whose works are well represented in museums, a painting supposed to have been produced by that artist's own hand, will be endowed with considerable memorial power on the basis of that attribution alone. But if disgruntled experts claim that the work is not by the master but by an apprentice working in the master's studio – or worse, attribute it to a copyist – and manage to make themselves heard, then the work's memorial power will decrease, leading to a dizzying plunge in the price at which the painting can be negotiated. And yet the object remains exactly the same, at least considered solely in terms of its material qualities, absent its narrative dimensions.[51]

8

Collection and Enrichment

The usefulness of useless things

It would clearly be quite a stretch to suppose that the development of an enrichment economy depended on the increase in the number, activity, and wealth of collectors, in the proper sense of the term. And this is why the relation we have posited between the *formal arrangement of collecting*, on the one hand, and what we have called the *collection form* as a modality of valorization, on the other, shifts according to the particular case along an axis that goes from literal application to synecdoche. Still, the shift of capitalism toward new domains of activity, as the opportunities for profit offered by mass production were tending toward exhaustion (at least in Western Europe – that is, in the countries where capitalism was born), would have been difficult without the recourse to new forms of valorization, forms with dual roles.

These forms had to supply a structural base favoring large-scale commercialization of things characterized by their "singularity" and by their "scarcity," two qualifications that stemmed from the fact that they had been identified through opposition to standard objects. Things said to be "exceptional," whose "scarcity" was considered "natural" and "absolute" (by David Ricardo,[1] for example) because they were not reproducible, were once viewed not only as being relatively marginal but especially as constituting exceptions to the "economic laws" that had been established through reference to industrial production. These things, as they were transformed into layers whose exploitation could create wealth, had to find a language in which they could be appreciated: that is, they had to be associated with arrangements that could establish their prices and, especially, make those prices justifiable on the basis of arguments that would reveal their value.

But at the same time these specific forms of valuation were also charged with making the prices of objects that were being extracted from such buried layers *intelligible* in relation to the prices of things stemming from other forms: standard objects first of all, but also fashionable objects – those appreciated in the *trend* form – and objects appreciated as *assets*.

Thus while, as we have seen, an enrichment economy is by no means addressed solely to "collectors," the collection form is a cognitive operator that makes it possible to appreciate the value of things judged "exceptional" by envisaging them from a point of view comparable to the one from which a "collector" would consider them, a collector being a fervent accumulator of things that are no longer useful but are appreciated both because they have been bequeathed by the past and because they lend themselves to being organized in a serial mode that articulates their similarities and differences.

The practice of collection has generally been considered a pastime or *hobby* and, consequently, as a marginal or even parasitic activity grafted onto other modalities of access to wealth, whether these modalities come from inheritance, from work, or from financial operations. It is moreover precisely because the activities involved in collecting are presented as *hobbies* – that is, as superfluous – that they have been able to maintain the unique position they have always occupied in the economic order. The practice of collecting, no matter how much or how little time and money may be devoted to it, is in fact inscribed in a cognitive structure that has accompanied the development of capitalism and that rests on a series of homologous oppositions. These include the relation between work and leisure (or non-work); between what is necessary and what is superfluous; and between action oriented toward business and action oriented toward disinterestedness – that is, in this case, toward leisure, passion, spending, all of which, in this context, have an orientation that is at once aesthetic and sexual (ever since the first half of the nineteenth century, the "mania" of systematic collectors has been considered a substitute for sexual activity).[2]

These oppositions have been grafted onto a distinction that played a central role among the bourgeoisie in France and elsewhere throughout the nineteenth century and the first half of the twentieth, the distinction that contrasts practices and ways of being as functions of gender. On the masculine side, we find business, money, work, science, sports, and outdoor activities; on the feminine side, we find taste, fiction, indoor activities, and religion. Activities stemming from the vast domain of "culture" or "the arts" can be associated with one pole or the other according to the modalities of the practice (professional, institutional, and lucrative on the masculine side, gratuitous or associated with pure expenditure or taste on the feminine side).[3] Steven Gelber has shown how stamp collecting, when it first began in the 1850s and 1860s, was viewed as a feminine practice, in which the decorative aspect of the vignettes was emphasized; this lasted until the formation of an organized market gave stamp collecting a new character that it would retain until the mid-twentieth century, that of an educational practice intended in particular to stimulate, in boys, a tendency to accumulate possessions and engage in commerce.[4]

One feature in particular conferred a certain salience on the systematic collection form as it developed during the nineteenth century and, indeed, was largely responsible for the attractiveness of the form in the bourgeois universe: it served as a support structure for practices that escaped the distinctions we have just evoked. In this zone of marginal importance, the tension between what was associated with beauty and gratuitousness, on the one hand, and with usefulness and interest, on the other, could be suspended (often by invoking the ancient notion of *otium*, leisure time).[5] Stories featuring collectors appeared with some frequency in the literature of the second half of the nineteenth century, well before major collectors became objects of biographies or published their own autobiographies. These fictional accounts incorporated anecdotes that blended the register of passion inseparably with that of commerce. They staged narratives that were at once stories about love for things, impelled by a desire that had nothing to do with calculation, and stories about money, often presented (especially by Balzac) in a way that highlighted their most sordid aspects and invoked attitudes and behaviors associated with critical representations of finance, such as harshness, greed, and especially deceit. Thus Balzac's Cousin Pons – to go back to one of the earliest and best-known illustrations of the personal *character* of a collector – is truly satisfied only when he has managed to acquire the "beautiful" things that he covets at a price below what he thinks of as their "real" price – that is, either below the price that others less shrewd than he would be inclined to pay or below the price at which the object might be negotiated in the future. This satisfaction can be described by Balzac as both aesthetic and commercial, because it is based, in both regimes, on the buyer's capacity to recognize the value of *small differences* that escape the eyes of others, and particularly, during the transaction, the eyes of the seller – a situation of what we have called *asymmetrical information*. Asymmetries of this sort stimulate a desire whose fulfillment depends on differential gaps. The satisfaction of having bought a thing for less than its asking price boosts and objectivizes the pride of a connoisseur who knows how to identify small differences and also the social distinction of the person who is proving himself or herself superior to neophytes. For connoisseurs like Pons, it is thus as though the items were no longer *purchased* – unlike the case of any standard object acquired from a catalog – but instead were in some sense *giving themselves* to the connoisseur and to no one else.

The articulation between the collection arrangement and the development of modes of consumption dependent on an enrichment economy is pertinent from yet another standpoint, that of the relation to what is *useless*. As Russell Belk has remarked, the development of collections becomes a salient phenomenon only in societies characterized by an excess of wealth.[6] As it happens, the increase in wealth has been one of the obstacles confronting the expansion of capitalism, whose justification has relied on the thematics of *need* and has aligned itself simultaneously with necessity, utility, and the scarcity of things required for the pursuit of life, and also (especially in Marxist terms) by the maintenance of a workforce. But that form of capitalism, characteristic of the decades following the Second World War in Europe in countries where the war had produced penury, was rapidly limited by the unequal distribution of the monetary resources needed to acquire mass-produced consumer goods; in other words, it was limited by the difficulty of expanding solvent demand, a difficulty that gave rise to ever-increasing recourse to credit.[7]

A large proportion of potential consumers had difficulty acquiring the goods offered for sale, while those who had the means to purchase factory-made goods had already done so. This situation, which tended to perpetuate itself and to become even more acute in the process, led to an overcapacity to produce. Why buy a second car – a more recent model, when the one already at hand sufficed to meet transportation needs – a new refrigerator, or a new television? Or a new watch, a particularly interesting example if we recall that the invention of quartz watches in the 1970s made that instrument very reliable and very inexpensive, even before electronic developments put watches inside mobile phones; the rapid and widespread diffusion of these instruments thus made wearing a watch less useful. As it happened, after an intense but brief crisis that affected Switzerland in particular (for Switzerland held a quasi-monopoly on watchmaking), it was precisely owing to a resurgence of the watchmaking industry that a particularly active and profitable luxury economy was re-established in that country.

Compared to the thorny problems posed by the exhaustion of the form of capitalism that was justified by recourse to the problematics of need and consequently of necessity and utility, the generalization of the collection arrangement offered a resource capable of relaunching consumerist accumulation by basing it on a different thematics, one that, far from referring to usefulness, emphasized on the contrary the value of accumulating useless things – in other words, accumulation for its own sake.

Here we can evoke the intuitions of Georges Bataille when, in *The Accursed Share*, he reversed the problematics of scarcity, which had been at the heart of economic thought at least since Malthus.[8] Bataille saw *excess* as one of the principal challenges societies have to confront.[9] If the formulations that associate excess with transgression could be left behind, it might be possible to revisit the problematics of scarcity in order to identify one of the paths followed by the agents of capitalism to get out of the crisis of the 1960s and 1970s and stimulate the generation of profit. That endeavor consisted primarily in relaunching the process of accumulation by displacing it toward spheres of economic activity that were largely exempt from a requirement of justification based on utility, as is characteristic of the enrichment economy. We must nonetheless note – following Bataille – that each social formation develops a specific way of stimulating and consuming excess, for example by war, competitive destruction, or *ostentatious magnificence*, as was the case in fifteenth-century Italy. In this last instance, as Malcolm Bull has shown, artistic representations, featuring reinterpretations of mythological themes and magnified human bodies that were at once denuded to reveal their splendor and surrounded by sumptuous adornments, had become symbolic expressions of a worldly power that was inextricably political, military, and pecuniary – and difficult to depict through the bleak iconography of Christian inspiration.[10]

But in post-Cold War Europe – democratic, meritocratic, fond of ethnic considerations – none of these forms of consumption was legitimately available to counter the threat of insufficient consumerism. In this context, the collection form was of interest because it supplied a model of accumulation for its own sake that could reconcile the extravagance of completely gratuitous expenditures with the principal features associated with the capitalist ethos as thematized by Max Weber:[11] meticulousness, a sort of restraint bordering on the most sordid avarice, an aptitude for calculation, and the deployment of frenetic activity that was at once disinterested and inclined to tilt toward a quest for profit. This was particularly the case when the things accumulated were detached from the collection arrangement and transferred to the *asset form*. The collection arrangement makes it possible, in fact, on the same basis as financial operations when they are removed from investment in the strict sense, to generate scarcity from the starting point of everything or nothing (and these come down to the same thing), including trash, since, by relying on the construction of serial forms of totalization, the practice of collecting creates lacks that demand imperiously to be filled. Viewed in this light, the collection form thus possesses a specific property that represents an undeniable advantage with respect to the capitalist universe, which is simply its capacity to generate wealth without massive recourse to human work and, consequently, without having to worry either about handling masses of potentially rebellious workers or about managing technological arrangements subject to frequent breakdowns and costly maintenance – and without even having to rely on justifications involving the thematics of need.

Thus the collection form, without jostling egalitarian sensibilities too forcefully, has been able to frame sumptuary expenses attributed to a pastime sublimated by the attraction of beauty, or even seen as a sort of beneficent activity undertaken to the advantage of all – as though the very possibility of accumulation for its own sake were completely unrelated to the destitution of the multitude of those who are excluded from it and in which globalized capitalism could nevertheless simultaneously discover the most reliable source of future profits based on the "democratization of commerce" – that is, on its extension down to "the bottom of the pyramid" in countries and classes that had been largely kept out of the consumerist sphere.[12] Or as if scarcity itself could be "produced," just as industrial capitalism produces the experience of necessity in which Sartre thought he recognized the "original structure" underlying the human adventure.[13]

Collecting in thrall to marketing

The collection arrangement does not apply directly to all the objects whose exchange and circulation create wealth in the context of an enrichment economy. This arrangement, which becomes particularly apparent if we look, for example, at commerce in artworks and antiquities, may appear less appropriate, at first glance, for domains such as luxury and tourism, the processes of heritage creation that involve rooted, non-transportable things, or even the broad and vague cluster that is called "culture," a domain that, partly deposited in things endowed with bodies, also manifests itself in the form of texts, words, schemas, and "ideas." It is nevertheless permissible to think that, in the regions or countries where capitalism has shifted in part from a production economy toward an enrichment economy, the collection arrangement has supplied a *repertory* of schemas available to be reworked so as to trace the contours of an extended form of valorization of things.

How are these apparently unconnected activities – the pursuit of luxury, tourism, heritage creation, and culture – related to one another, and why is the collection form central? The starting point must be tourists, especially the wealthiest tourists, whose increasing importance in the economies of Western countries (and especially in France) we have already noted. Heritage creation is one way to get affluent tourists to move about and to attract them to one particular locale rather than another; the attention of prospective tourists can be secured by recourse to culture, and especially to narratives. But, once they have been drawn in, once they have been told a story, tourists must still be enticed to buy things. Yet these things cannot be standard objects that they could just as well have bought at home. The objects thus have to rely on the collection form and enter into the category of luxury items, or at least tend in that direction. Since the collection form is not oriented toward use, it can be a way of justifying the accumulation of things that, in terms of their utilization, would be seen as more or less similar and thus substitutable. This form, when it is *extended*, thus constitutes a powerful engine for buying and consequently for generating profit. Those who draw the greatest benefit from this linkage, those who are already the wealthiest, can also be tourists in countries other than their own.

We shall thus try to sort out, in an *extended* approach, what the collection form owes to the features that characterize the collection arrangement, but we shall also try to show how, as its repertory was gradually developing, these features were selected and redeployed: some of them occupied central positions, while others were marginalized and associated with properties borrowed from other formations so as to cover a much broader set of situations. We shall start with the hypothesis that this form plays a role of the first order in the valorization of exceptional items destined for a wealthy public. According to this hypothesis, the collection form would take on ever-greater salience and would now be extending its sphere of influence to the detriment of the standard form.

> ## Marketing as know-how for valorizing commodities
>
> Just as reading books about management is one of the most illuminating ways to grasp the changes brought about in the control and exploitation of human work, books about marketing are a source of precious information about the way in which capitalism methodically takes advantage of the different modes of commodity valorization. These two bodies of knowledge, concerning management and marketing respectively, are complementary with regard to the extraction of profit, the first because it is centered on value added in the sphere of work, and the second because it is centered on value added in the sphere of commodities.
>
> The elements that characterize the collection form in an enrichment economy are found in particular in marketing manuals devoted to art, luxury, and tourism published in France between 2005 and 2015, as will be attested by a series of citations from the following manuals:
>
> M1: Eugénie Briot and Christel de Lassus, eds, *Marketing de luxe: stratégies innovantes et nouvelles pratiques* (Cormelles-le-Royal: EMS, 2014).
>
> M2: Michel Chevalier and Gérald Mazzalovo, *Management et marketing du luxe* (2nd edn, Paris: Dunod, 2011).
>
> M3: Isabelle Frochot and Patrick Legohérel, *Marketing du tourisme* (3rd edn, Paris: Dunod, 2014).
>
> M4: Henri Mahé de Boislandelle, *Marché de l'art et gestion de patrimoine* (Paris: Economica, 2005).
>
> M5: Benoît Meyronin, *Le marketing territorial* (Paris: Vuibert, 2009).
>
> M6: Karen Neilsen, *Le mécénat mode d'emploi* (Paris: Economica, 2007).
>
> M7: Christine Petr et al., *Marketing de l'art et de la culture* (Paris: Dunod, 2009).

The juxtaposition of processes associated with an enrichment economy and the collection arrangement seems fairly coherent in the case of antiquities and works of art from the workshops of old masters, even watches or automobiles from prestigious brands whose production has been interrupted. But, in the case of other sectors that play important roles in an enrichment economy, the features borrowed from the collection arrangement have to be inflected or adjusted to allow their valorization.

Places, insofar as they are objects of commerce, can generally be valorized in the same way as things, but with the constraint that they cannot be moved. The exemplary case of a place valorized according to the standard form is that of the serially manufactured individual house. In the collection form, places such as monuments, neighborhoods, cities, villages, or rural sites, even entire regions, are most notably valorized by processes of heritage creation. In this case, things that come from the past and may be undergoing a process of degradation are selected, on the same basis as collectors' items, then rehabilitated and associated with a *presentation narrative* – that is, a historical narrative intended to orient their interpretation and to augment their value. One consequence is that long-distance association has to be substituted for the physical juxtaposition that characterizes collections of objects.

The narrative presentation

The story of the brand or product is often based on a real story about one or the other, but nothing stands in the way of suggesting a fictitious story about the brand, as was the case with Bell & Ross, founded in 1991. The story had minimal effect on the firm's up-front costs, but it was largely responsible for the future success of its products. (M1, p. 131)

Storytelling is a method of communication based on narrative; its purpose is to unify the various elements of the experiential sphere ... The objective is to work up stories that will have a strongly evocative power and will arouse strong emotions in consumers ... When someone tells the story, the author is going to stir up feelings that will make the consumer more receptive to the message. The story will focus the consumer's attention with its discourse .... The narrator will use anecdotes, funny and entertaining stories, and unexpected details, and will integrate historical elements (including legends that are highly prized by tourists). The emotional intensity elicited will make it possible to enhance the memorability of the experience. (M3, p. 113)

The concept behind phantom visits is to propose a unique experience through a guided visit to a city center that breaks sharply with traditional guided tours. These phantom visits generally take place at night or at the end of the day to benefit from the dusk, which creates a very special atmosphere. The object is to offer a city from a very different angle by using storytelling, which will focus on legends about the sites, local mysteries, and ghost stories. The visit also includes more "classic" information, historically valid facts, about the city's history and culture. (M3, p. 115)

Working on the sense of a place means integrating identitary, relational, and historical components. What is at stake here is the construction or reconstruction of stories that confer a meaning on a given territory. (M5, p. 16)

Considered from the standpoint that interests us here, the notion of culture can be interpreted within a logic that opens pathways to the collection form. This is the case when buildings or ruins are declared "historical monuments," attractions "created by humans," which are more powerful factors in determining tourists' choices than those based on "natural resources (beaches, nature preserves, etc.)."[14] But the term "culture" can also be understood in a sense derived from the one attributed to it by ethnology and folklore studies. According to this logic, ordinary objects – cloth, soap, or knives, for instance – can be collected, valorized, and preserved in museums, like the plastic bags exhibited in 2013 in Lausanne's museum of contemporary design and applied arts.[15]

The subject of luxury poses different problems. Let us first recall that the existence of luxury is by no means really new. Luxury and the manufacture of luxury items intended for the wealthiest consumers have been striking facts in various historical formations, both as economic phenomena and as objects of moral debates in which the desire to illustrate the benefits of luxury (as was Voltaire's case) is sometimes opposed by simple indignation, often Christian in inspiration, especially in periods and in places marked by practices tending toward the formation of capitalism: as examples, we can point to the city-states of northern Italy during the Renaissance[16] or to Western European metropolises such as Paris and London in the nineteenth century.[17]

The term "luxury" has not always been claimed by the enterprises that are nonetheless associated with it in the early twenty-first century. We can bring this variation to light by looking at the *Lettre mensuelle du Comité Colbert*.[18] In 1976, firms presented themselves as stemming from the "fields of art, fashion, and creation." In the following decade, "luxury" appeared as a "new idea."[19] In fact, it was viewed as "obsolete" in the 1970s, as we see from a comment regarding a survey published in the same *Lettre*:

During the last few months, have you bought any luxury products?
  Yes: 42.
During the last few months, have you bought any perfume, jewelry, etc.?
  Yes: 87 percent.
Commentary:
The French do not see the word "luxury" (for which no one has found a satisfactory substitute) as pertaining to themselves; it is probably charged with obsolete and even negative connotations. We know, moreover, that it is no longer used in the language of communication. There used to be "luxury trains"; who would refer to the Concorde as a "luxury plane"? The items that the word covers are, in contrast, quite accepted: 87 percent.

But a generational change that also corresponds, as Thomas Piketty has shown, to an incipient modification of the relation between work and patrimony is transforming the meaning attached to the word "luxury": now "luxury is a young phenomenon, totally integrated in the way things are for the new generations."[20]

As the same survey explains:

> As all the answers to the questions have been spelled out according to age groups, let us note in a general way that, the younger the interviewees are, the better they analyze and "live luxury." The following example is very revealing:
>
> In buying a luxury product, you thought "I've done something crazy": under 24, 14 percent; over 65, 31 percent. "I did something to please myself": under 24, 53 percent; over 65, 18 percent.
>
> The oldest interviewees still feel a certain guilt; the youngest apparently have no complexes around luxury that falls within the framework of impulse purchases.

With the formation of an enrichment economy, justifications of luxury and of the prices of luxury items have taken a new turn that owes a great deal to the way in which they have benefited from social arguments and relationships associated with the collection arrangement. The thematics of collection have penetrated luxury on the one hand through the new personal, organizational, and financial links (identified in the previous chapter) that have been woven, especially during the last couple of decades, between luxury firms and the world of contemporary art. Luxury firms also endow themselves with "arty" images, for example by buying works and organizing exhibits; or, more directly, by asking known artists to associate their names with models that they are supposed to have inspired or conceived; or by asking artists to decorate the sites where these models will be presented for sale. The firms can then blur the banalization of objects reproduced in numerous copies – even if the number is limited – by attaching the signature of an artist, considered not as if he or she had personally made the work of art but as if the artist had set forth a certain number of rules for the production of the work that made its determination possible.[21]

The new representation of their activities that luxury firms have thus sought to establish, and that owes a great deal to the valorization of their links to art, has benefited from the extension given to the term "creator." This has consisted largely in treating the objects that the firms put into circulation as though they were things worthy of figuring in collections and destined for buyers who had the ethos of collectors. This orientation may seem all the more paradoxical in that, during the same period, the universe of luxury relied more and more on industrial arrangements. Whereas the creation "by hand" of objects intended for a single client, or produced in very limited series, once occupied the center of this universe, fabrication by hand today is reserved for extremely expensive objects.[22] The artisanal workshops that are still operating are mostly devoted to the creation of prototypes and/or serve as showcases for the major companies in the "luxury industry," whose product lines are discreetly manufactured and managed industrially (and often outsourced, as we have seen)[23] in order to respond to a growing demand, especially for export.

Nevertheless, these firms strive to maintain or construct an identity associated with a proper name (the "brand") that is intended to mark them as lasting and designed to support their claim to exceptionality. Whereas in the fairly recent past the exceptional character of luxury items was most often justified by their innovative character, it is now more and more often justified by reference to tradition or, to be more precise, by the construction of subtle compromises between tradition and innovation – that is, between features drawn from the past and features projected into the future. This alchemy owes a great deal to insistence on the timeless fame of certain brands, on the connection that their histories are said to maintain with those of historical personalities, countries, regions, and, especially families, whose members have devoted themselves generation after generation both to maintaining certain traditional skills and to supporting innovation, that term being understood in its aesthetic dimension. This explains, for example, why the big globalized luxury firms are competing to purchase very old brands, ones that are declining or even failing, but whose past and pedigree make them worth the price and justify investments intended to bring them back.

The constraints of the collection form for luxury objects

A luxury brand has national roots. (M1, p. 82)

Most of the time, luxury businesses have only one or two factories producing prototypes and a few product lines. The rest is carefully controlled but produced by subcontractors. (M2, p. 44)

In the world of luxury, it is almost impossible to visit factories ... It is very hard to visit automated factories, when they exist, for that is not what the brands want their clients to retain. (M2, p. 6)

One of the procedures that has allowed elements from the collection arrangement to be integrated into the luxury industry has been the production in *limited series* of certain items put into circulation. This practice breaks with the canons of the standard form, in which series are in principle unlimited and their production continues as long as there is demand (except in cases of planned obsolescence, as we have seen). In many instances, customer orders for certain things produced in a limited series face a waiting period of a year or more. In other instances, when the initial series has reached its limits, the production of objects in conformity with the original prototype is presented as a *reproduction* or a "reissue (the latter term is used frequently for example with furniture in the *design* category). But while the objects in the original series may become collectors' items and see their prices increase over time, "reissued" objects, even if they are in every respect similar to the originals, will generally lose part of their value as they age, on the same basis as any standard product.

In addition, firms specializing in luxury goods have made abundant use of the marketing technique known as *storytelling*[24] in support of commercial strategies that aim to singularize their products, models, and brands by associating them with historical figures, with famous persons (such as actors), and/or with well-known contemporary plastic artists. The story that is told may also be the story of the brand owner's family, whose historical roots are supposed to guarantee the venerability of the things produced and offered for sale (for example, the story of the Italian boot-making Ferragamo family), or the story of the "creator" who imprints his style on the brand (for example, Yves Saint Laurent, who became an icon of taste celebrated in literature, film, and televised fiction). This way of valorizing things – embellishing them with their own history and associating that history with stories of individuals who either created or possessed them and in any case *physically touched them*, since in a way they lived with them – plays a central role in the collection arrangement.

One of the major defining features of the collection form is scorn for reproductions. The enrichment economy thus borrows from the collection arrangement this preference for the *authentic*, even in the case of the luxury industry, which, however, is not loath to produce a portion (and sometimes the largest portion) of its production industrially and in series: hence the importance of attaching to a standard object the name of a particular person who is said to have deposited his or her traces on the object, even though there may not be a firm basis for such a claim.

> The luxury client is neither a concept nor a category, it is a human being who dreams and purchases luxury for an incalculable number of more or less acknowledged and wholly intertwined reasons: status, reward, seduction, pleasure, happiness, amusement, freedom, relations with others, access to creation, access to good taste, surprise, comfort, the desire to be unique and to purchase accordingly, and aspiration to supreme well-being. (M2, p. vii)
>
> Even if the products are made in industrial quantities, as in the case of a perfume, they [the clients] want to believe that the object has come directly from the creator's workshop. (M2, p. 6)
>
> Luxury items have always been subjected to a deep and refined process of aesthetic research .... It is almost always a question of a work of art. (M2, p. 5)

If we turn now to buyers of exceptional goods, we have to acknowledge that, by approaching them as if they were real or potential "collectors," luxury firms place the emphasis on a prestigious lifestyle in which buyers are prepared to take pride, if only to the extent that it justifies the accumulation of things that are costly and useless. In fact, luxury objects, even though they can be presented as intended for use, are not acquired primarily in order to meet and satisfy a need. Their purchasers already possess, by and large, a number of functionally similar objects (several high-end automobiles, many leather bags from top brands, and so on). The fact of appearing before others, of being seen in public surrounded by costly objects, can obviously be a source of pleasure. And these distinguishing effects, which have been invoked since Thorstein Veblen[25] by sociologists and economists in an effort to account for – and to denounce – expenditures on conspicuous consumption of luxury goods, certainly play an important economic role. Nevertheless, in many instances these costly things seem to be collected in such numbers that they are stored away without being exposed to the eyes of others or even, in the case of major collectors, to their owners' eyes. They are thus accumulated chiefly in order to be preserved and placed in relations of proximity to other objects of the same type, in a logic close to that of the collection form.

On the use of the collection form by luxury firms

The study of two major groups manifesting strong growth, LVMH and Kering, whose owners and principal directors are based in France (or in Belgium, in LVMH's case, for tax purposes) and whose revenues are very high (46.8 billion euros for LVMH and 13.6 billion for Kering in 2018, as compared to 29 billion and 9.7 billion respectively in 2013), allows us to document the way in which the collection form functions at the center of a reorientation of capitalism.[26] This reorientation can be read very clearly over time if we follow the changes in the Kering group's activities from the 1960s on. LVMH and Kering share the distinguishing feature of targeting the fortunes of the wealthiest consumers, both in the richest regions of the world (Europe, the United States, Japan) and in those where the conjunction of strong growth and significant inequalities in income and patrimony guarantees the presence of great wealth (in particular China, India, Mexico, and Brazil). In order to capture this wealth, the two companies rely on commerce in luxury goods with high profit margins, goods endowed with brand names "rooted" in the past of a country whose very lifestyle is depicted as a patrimony (Italy, France, and Switzerland in particular, but also China). These goods, which are on display in a large number of magazines, are either standard products endowed with a "collector effect" (fashionable clothing and accessories) or else products likely to be collected (wine, jewelry, watches); certain standard products (for example, leather goods) can even become collectors' items, and any of them can be hybridized or associated with contemporary art.

From lumber to luxury goods: the transformation of the Pinault group into Kering

The LVMH and Kering groups both bring together brands associated with luxury products. However, the groupings have different historical origins. The LVMH group resulted from merging the luggage company Louis Vuitton with the champagne firm Moët Hennessy, the latter being itself the result of the 1971 merger between two champagne producers, Moët et Chandon and Hennessy.

The history of the Kering group brings to light the displacements of capital, and thus of capitalism since the second half of the twentieth century in France, and beyond in the world's wealthiest regions.

In 1963, François Pinault created an eponymous group specializing in the lumber business, eventually including its distribution and its transformation. The group was thus devoted to commercializing a raw material destined to produce standard objects. Beginning in the 1990s, the group extended its distribution activity to electronics (with the acquisition of Cfao in 1990), mass-market furniture (a controlling interest in Conforama, 1991), standard products in general (a controlling interest in Au Printemps, including 54 percent interest in the mail-order company La Redoute), and cultural products (a controlling interest in FNAC, 1994). In 1994 the group changed its name to Pinault-Printemps-Redoute (PPR), to acknowledge its transformation into a firm dedicated to distributing standard items, thus a firm present in virtually all aspects of daily life among the middle classes, from furniture to clothing, including electronic and digital technology along with books, records, and other cultural goods. The group completed its ambit, in effect, by adding an enterprise that distributed office supplies and furnishings (a controlling interest in Guilbert, 1998) and another that distributed micro-computing equipment (the acquisition of Surcouf, 2000).

Nonetheless, in the 2000s, the PPR group had to reckon with several mutations. On the one hand, digitization was dematerializing most cultural goods, first and foremost those involving music and video productions, as far as the group's activity in that sector was concerned (via FNAC); on the other hand, the development of the Internet considerably increased competition in online sales of standard products. Moreover, inequalities in revenues and personal holdings were increasing, and it was becoming particularly advantageous to focus more specifically on the wealthiest among potential customers.

In 1999, the PPR group entered the sector of luxury goods by acquiring 42 percent of the Italian brand Gucci and then the Yves Saint Laurent and Sergio Rossi brands. The luxury apparel firm Gucci itself acquired the jewelry firm Boucheron the following year and the Bottega Veneta and

Balenciaga firms in 2001. Gradually increasing its share in Gucci's capital, PPR finally acquired 99.4 percent in 2004, following a takeover bid.

At the same time, starting in 2002 and continuing until 2013, the group gradually backed out of all the enterprises distributing standard products that it had acquired during the previous decades, shedding them one after another: Guilbert (2002–3), Pinault Bois et Matériaux – the original core enterprise from the 1960s (2003), France Printemps (2006–7), Conforama (2008–11), Surcouf (2009), FNAC (in stages, starting in 2010), Cfao (2009–12), and La Redoute (2014).

During the same ten-year period, the group pursued the acquisition of luxury brands and also firms focused on sports (such as Puma). During 2013 alone, PPR acquired majority stakes in two jewelry brands, one Chinese (Qeelin) the other Italian (Pornellato), a deluxe designer brand (Christopher Kane), and a leather goods firm (Croco). To make its new transformation visible, the group changed its name once again: abandoning PPR (which had been reduced in 2005 to Pinault-Printemps-Redoute), it became Kering, almost entirely specialized in luxury goods and, to a limited extent, in sports-related products.

Capturing the wealth of the wealthiest

Why, at the beginning of the twenty-first century, did a group wholly transform itself in the space of a decade, completely changing its activities and even its name, abandoning the distribution of standard products to focus on producing and trading in luxury goods? The reason is straightforward: the group was managed by holders of capital who made the same observation that economists in the academic world were making, namely, that inequalities in revenue and in individual wealth were increasing in a large number of countries. But whereas certain economists proposed to reduce these inequalities, the holders of capital proposed for their part to profit from them – that is, to offer products and services that would allow them to capture the money of the wealthiest without at the same time allowing these wealthy consumers direct control over company decisions. The problem in the displacement of capital is that it can in fact make it possible for investors to hold rights over those who are proposing ways to attract it. This is most obviously the case for stockholders in a company. But in the case of luxury products, and of objects belonging to the collection form in general, the new owner holds the luxury object or the collectors' item without being able to exert personal influence over the fate of those who have produced it and offered it for sale, and without being able, either, to make free use of the brand name of the object acquired, since brand names are protected by intellectual property laws.

As a market analysis of luxury brands worldwide carried out by Xerfi Global for the period 2013–18 explains, the quest for wealthy consumers requires luxury groups to reason in terms of income inequality and personal wealth:

The emerging countries hide a significant and rising class of wealthy consumers.

Per-person income and income inequality can be used to measure the market potential of consumers of luxury products. Income per person is higher and more equally distributed in the developed countries, making them important markets for personal luxury goods.

However, developing countries such as Mexico, Brazil, Russia, Indonesia, and China are characterized by lower per-person income but also have significant inequalities. If we consider the size of the populations of these countries, great inequalities consequently imply a significant number of wealthy consumers. The growing revenues of these countries illustrate why they have become the target of luxury industries.[27]

The Kering group's annual report also emphasizes, among the growth factors in the luxury market, "the number of HNWIs" [high-net-worth individuals], not only in "developed countries," where most of them live, but also in "high-growth countries," has increased rapidly in recent years.[28] The number of wealthy clients in the world is evaluated at 12 million in 2012, representing 46,200 billion dollars overall, and it was expected to increase by 6.5 percent per year, reaching 55,800 billion in 2018.[29]

Thus most luxury product sales occur where these extremely wealthy people live. Europe is the number one region in terms of revenues in the luxury sector, evaluated at 74 billion euros or 34 percent of worldwide revenues in 2013 (the four countries with the greatest revenues were Italy, with 16 billion euros, France with 15 billion, the United Kingdom

INCOME DISTRIBUTION

	Norway, Sweden, Denmark, Germany	Netherlands, France	United States	
Very high	Norway, Sweden, Denmark, Germany	Netherlands, France	United States	
High	Japan	Canada, United Kingdom, Italy, Spain		
Medium	Czech Republic	Poland	Russia, Turkey	Mexico, Brazil
Low		India	China, Indonesia	
	Egalitarian	*Almost egalitarian*	*Almost inegalitarian*	*Inegalitarian*

Per-person income

From Xerfi Global's market analysis (p. 34)

with 12 billion, and Germany with 10 billion). The United States alone accounts for 62.5 billion euros in revenues. Japan (17 billion), China (15 billion), South Korea (8 billion), and Hong Kong (7 billion) are the Asian regions with the highest revenues in luxury goods.[30]

For Kering, the revenues of the luxury branch in 2013, which rose to 6.4 billion euros, were thus logically derived as follows: Western Europe, 33 percent, the Asia-Pacific region, 41 percent (with 10 percent from Japan alone), and North America, 19 percent. For LVMH, revenues from the "watches and jewelry branch" (TAG Heuer, Hublot, Zenith, Bulgari, Dior Watches, De Beers, and Fred), which rose to 2.7 billion euros in 2013, were divided among Europe (34 percent), Asia (40 percent, including 13 percent from Japan alone), and the United States (12 percent).

Values and prices of luxury product brands

Luxury goods can capture part of the wealth of the wealthiest in a more significant way than standard products, because the profit margin set at the time of the exchange can be especially high. For LVMH, in 2013, the operational margin rate for apparel and leather goods rose to 32 percent (operational results of 3.1 billion euros for sales amounting to 9.8 billion); the rate for wines and spirits was 33 percent (operational results of 1.3 billion euros for sales amounting to 4.2 billion). This rate is much lower, however, for watches and jewelry, reaching "only" 13 percent (operational results of 375 million euros for sales amounting to 2.7 billion euros). The same year, in the Kering group, Gucci realized 1.1 billion euros in operational results from overall revenues of 3.5 billion.

The central notion of "brand" lies at the heart of the model for this type of enterprise, hence the importance of protecting it via intellectual property laws and the struggle against counterfeit merchandise.

But what is the price of a brand? Taking into account high margin rates, a brand is clearly not reducible to production costs, nor can it be apprehended by the work of its employees alone. Kering and LVMH use different calculation methods to evaluate the brands among their assets. For Kering, the value of Gucci, the most important brand in the group, is calculated on the basis of future income from license fees received on the assumption that the brand will be exploited in the form of lease contracts by third parties;[31] this so-called royalty method is also used by LVMH. The latter group also uses a method based on "comparable transactions (i.e. using the revenue and net profit coefficients employed for recent transactions involving similar brands) or of stock market multiples observed for related businesses." However, LVMH also uses two other methods: "the margin differential method, applicable when a measurable difference can be identified between the amount of revenue generated by a branded product in comparison with a similar unbranded product," and that of the cost of reconstituting an equivalent brand, in particular in terms of the costs of advertising and promotion.[32]

These different calculation methods applied to brands[33] allow us first of all to demonstrate the full extent to which values justify prices. In addition, they help reveal what ultimately characterizes a brand: it is at once a thing endowed with a price comparable to that of similar things that are sold and bought, a name that has a reputation and for which significant expenses (for advertising) are tolerated in order to maintain or even increase that reputation, a name protected by intellectual property laws that can thus be exploited by bringing in royalties, and, finally, a name that allows an enterprise or a group to generate a profit margin in relation to production costs and to other names. In comparison, the vineyards owned by LVMH are evaluated on the basis of their market value alone – that is, with reference to recent transactions in the same region.

One major difference between standard products and luxury brands is that standard products are typically developed within a large company, in a research and development department, for example, while a luxury brand is generally launched by a person in his or her own name and is then purchased and developed by a large company. In order to grow, luxury firms are thus led to acquire new brands, ones that already exist but are not yet in the fold. Once acquired, these brands are at once preserved in their "artistic" positioning and reoriented in economic terms. Kering thus applies a management model, which it calls "freedom within a [financial] framework,"[34] for brands, as their annual report explains, "that offer genuine and significant potential to improve financial performance, which [Kering] can identify and exploit in the long term."[35]

A luxury brand usually involves a proper name (often that of the founder, such as Yves Saint Laurent with Kering or Marc Jacobs with LVMH) that is associated with a territory – whether a very localized region as with wines (Ruinart, Hennessy, Moët et Chandon, Krug, Dom Pérignon in Champagne, or Château d'Yquem with LVMH) or a larger region, even a country (France, Switzerland, Italy) – and also with a date of creation. Proper name, territory, history: these three intertwined qualities are at the heart of the economy of enrichment, and they can be inscribed in, or are compatible with, a patrimonial politics directed by public authorities, either on a local or a national scale.

Apart from the Château d'Yquem, most of the oldest brands go back to the seventeenth and eighteenth centuries for watchmaking (in the case of Kering, Jeanrichard dates from 1681, Girard-Perregaux from 1791 in Switzerland), to the nineteenth century for jewelry (Kering: Boucheron, 1858, in France), and leather goods (LVMH: Louis Vuitton, 1854), and to the twentieth century for fashion (Kering: Balenciaga, 1919; Yves Saint Laurent, 1961), or even the twenty-first (Kering: Stella McCartney, 2001). The narratives associated with these brands anchor them in a territory or even in a localized craftsmanship. Thus the Bottega Veneta brand (Kering), founded in 1966, is presented as having originated in the Veneto region of Italy and as having been "originally specialized in the leather goods made famous by the celebrated technique of *intrecciato*," a method invented by craftsmen to reinforce soft leather. As Kering explains in its annual report, the company seeks "brands that have a truly distinctive identity: well-rooted values and a sought-after legacy."[36]

But anchoring in the past is not enough: the process has to be brought up to date. The products of the enrichment economy succeed only if they entail an alliance between the "contemporary" and the "traditional" – that is, only if there is a narrative that anchors the present in the past or, for more recent brands, a narrative that presents products as if they were unquestionably going to be anchored in the past. If they were associated only with the present, the objects would be tainted by the idea of disposability – that is, they could become unfashionable; if they were associated only with the past, they would already be unfashionable, outdated, trash. The alliance by way of a narrative connecting past and present is what allows objects to attain "immortality." Thus Gucci is presented as "the combination of tradition and modernity, craftsmanship and innovation."[37] Another example is found in the "Pom Pom" collection of the Milanese jeweler Pomellato, for which "every ring is created around stones that are unique in their rarity, large size, or irregular shape. This results in sophisticated, excessive, contemporary jewels whose value combines culture with an unconventional flair."[38]

Standard products with a "collector effect" and collectors' items

The various luxury products of the LVMH and Kering groups are put on display and brought together in articles as well as in advertisements in many journals and magazines: wines and spirits, clothing and leather goods, perfumes and cosmetics, watches and jewelry.

Nonetheless, these products can be sorted into two different sets. On the one hand, many of them are still products made in the standard way, and like standard products they are characterized by depreciation once they have been offered for sale. This is the case for fashionable clothing, in particular, and to a lesser extent for leather goods. These products are distinguished from those in the ordinary standard form, however, in that they are endowed with what we call a "collector effect." In other words, while fashionable items of clothing are unquestionably destined to go rapidly out of fashion, thus inscribing themselves in a cycle proper to the trend form, their presentation nevertheless takes place in the collection form: the term "collection" is used explicitly to designate "fashion weeks" during which a given designer's fall–winter collection is presented, followed a few months later by a spring–summer collection.

On the other hand, wines, jewelry, and watches function directly as collectors' items. Their value may in fact increase over time after their initial sale; they are sought by collectors and resold as collectors' items on the secondary market. The jewelry brand Boucheron presented its 2014 collections during the Biennale des Antiquaires in Paris: it showed novelties alongside older objects, thus preparing the future of the former as collectables.[39]

It is significant that these objects can be associated or even hybridized with contemporary art. Thus in 2013 the champagne brand Dom Pérignon called on the artist Jeff Koons to create a sculpture, "Balloon Venus for Dom Pérignon," for the launching of Dom Pérignon Rosé 2013. A champagne brand in the LVMH group, Ruinart, was proud to be associated with international contemporary art fairs; it called on the artist Piet Hein Eek to create a work in homage to the house's legacy and imagined two collections in limited editions. Finally, let us recall that the two founders of these groups (who remain owners, as of this writing), Bernard Arnault of LVMH and François Pinault of Kering, are the two greatest collectors of contemporary art in France.

One of the most successful instances of the use of the collection form by the luxury industry is that of the LVMH group's showcase brand: Louis Vuitton. The company was originally a rather ordinary luggage manufacturer; it distinguished itself by the adoption of a monogram, invented in 1896, thus after the founder's death. The operation by means of which these ordinary objects, produced in series, became luxury objects and collectables was particularly well presented in an exhibit at the Grand Palais in Paris in 2015–16. In fact, this exhibit presented trunks as collectors' items, associating them with a narrative that evoked "the work of Louis Vuitton": the luggage-maker became a "creator" ("he renews fabrics and motifs, as much to protect himself from counterfeiters as to stand out") and was linked with stars of the contemporary art scene (Damien Hirst, Richard Price, Takashi Murakami), with writers ("the Louis Vuitton House has accompanied the travels of well-known writers and anonymous amateurs for whom writing is a necessity"), with musicians ("Whether for a violin, a guitar, or a conductor's batons, the protective cases are conceived by the luggage-maker as jewel-cases made of velvet and benevolence"), and with movie stars (a "Deauville bag in monogram fabric that belonged to Elizabeth Taylor" or a "wardrobe trunk in monogram fabric that is believed to have belonged to Katharine Hepburn").[40] The principle of collection as a way of valorizing things that would otherwise have been quite ordinary and worth very little was first deployed by Gaston-Louis Vuitton ("Apart from the old trunks, I also collect everything that has to do with the luggage-maker's trade, in particular old tools such as hammers, pliers, planes, ... old papers, that is, bills, letterheads, address cards"); it was also spelled out in the presentation of "hotel labels from the personal collection of Gaston-Louis Vuitton."[41] The intersection with another dimension of the enrichment economy, tourism, was all the more easy to achieve in that tourists move about with luggage, but the term itself had given way to the nobler one of "voyage" or "travel," by "automobile," train, ship, or plane.

The collection form and contemporary art

The role played by the collection form in the insertion of contemporary art into an enrichment economy also needs to be clarified. The link between contemporary art and collecting may seem to go without saying, especially given that trade in contemporary artworks plays a very important role today in the commercial activities spurred by collectors' practices. This is all the more the case when, as frequently happens, collectors acquire works less for the purpose of decorating their homes than for the purpose of accumulation: relying on the collection arrangement, they seek to fill lacks in a serial totality. This intent to acquire may seem secondary to the extent that these collectors, especially the wealthiest ones, spend time with artists, to the point of sometimes considering themselves as co-producers of their works.[42] Thus the great collector François Pinault is described as being on familiar terms with artists and their galleries, from New York to Paris by way of Basel, and as taking pride in devoting a considerable part of his life to them: "To love artists, one needs time."[43] But the proximity between collectors and artists must not be allowed to obscure the fact that the former would not qualify as collectors if they did not become owners of works.

Besides, what is at issue is not so much the motivations declared by collectors and made public by the media and in works that celebrate these persons as the changes in state that affect the objects signed by artists when the productions of these artists have been recognized by collectors and have thereby been constituted as works of art. This process makes it possible to resolve a seeming contradiction between contemporary art and the collection form. We have seen that the collection form is oriented toward the appreciation of things extracted from the past. Now, nothing seems more contemporary than contemporary art, not only because it is shaped in the present, but also to the extent that it boasts of being turned toward the future. This seeming contradiction can nevertheless be overcome if we take into account the forms and stages of what can be called *turning into art*: that is, the process through which things attain the rank of *work of art*, either because the persons that have shaped them claim the status of artist, or because that status is granted them by others, from the outside, as it were, and sometimes without the artists themselves having asked for such a status; this latter case is exemplified by such phenomena as the so-called *art nègre* or *art brut* and, more generally, by the itineraries that have recently been studied under the term "artification."[44] One can confer on any artifact whatsoever the label of "artwork" only once it has succeeded in penetrating into the sphere of circulation where goods of this sort are exchanged; thus the clearest indicator that a thing has been transmuted into a work of art is its integration into a collection. This remark applies especially to modern or contemporary art, which, unlike art forms of earlier eras, has found itself more and more often deprived of external functions and has essentially become art for collectors.

Yet it must be noted that the process through which any objects whatsoever attain the status of artworks is highly selective. This is a way of saying, in passing, that few activities produce as much *trash* as artistic activities. It suffices to think of the vast numbers of canvases that have never found buyers and that are no longer anything more than *stuff* deteriorating in basements. Or we might consider public monuments that are not classified as historical: the authorities responsible for the national patrimony, for example, are reluctant to assume maintenance costs for the thousands of monuments to the dead of the First World War. We could make similar remarks about museums – which are by and large official agencies of authorization and preservation – within which the proportion of works that lie in storage and have never been exhibited, and may never even have been catalogued, is considerably larger than the proportion available for public viewing. And this is so even though the fact that they have been cared for so as to avoid their destruction still offers these works a modest chance of rehabilitation.

If we take into account this process of radical selection, we might consider that one of the principal signs attesting that an artifact has achieved the status of an artwork concerns its mode of temporal existence. In fact, selecting an artifact from among a mass of similar objects destined to become trash (which, as we have seen, is the ordinary fate of things in the standard form) and conferring on it the status of a work of art signifies that current viewers are asked to look at the work the way viewers are expected to look at it in the future. In other words, viewers are asked to carry out a retroactive movement by situating themselves, with regard to the work, in the present but from a vantage point to come, as if the work already belonged to the past or, rather, as if it were, in its essence, so to speak, exempt from the corruption of time. This movement, which consists in envisaging things from the standpoint of their possibility of access to a sort of *immortality*,[45] constitutes one of the distinguishing features of the collection form.

The interactions between collectors' strategies for selection and artists' efforts to escape obliteration, which would be their normal fate from the vantage point of the present, produce effects of competition, on one side among artists, who seek to maintain their existence over time by capturing the attention of collectors, and on the other side among collectors, who seek either to fill in gaps or to shift the contours of the collectable by creating ties with and promoting artists not yet highly esteemed whose works are therefore affordable. These processes have occupied – and still occupy – an important place in the collective shifts that affect judgments of taste and whose effects are exercised simultaneously on the orientation of markets and on processes of aesthetic innovation.[46] Aesthetic innovation has often been associated with the role played by a "norm of originality" characteristic of modern art or "art for art's sake," a norm whose rise in potency, especially from the second half of the nineteenth century on, is thought to have accompanied the avant-garde rebellions against the conformist effects of arrangements of academic control.[47] In the wake of Pierre Bourdieu's work,[48] and also that of Raymonde Moulin,[49] it has been possible to see in the emergence of this "norm of originality" the result of the formation of specific and "relatively autonomous" fields within which artists and "creators" compete for recognition. Without challenging this type of structural interpretation, which stresses the strategies for achieving distinction on the part of the *creators*, we may nevertheless wonder whether it does not lead to underestimating the role of the *selectors* – that is, where artists are concerned, the role of collectors in interacting with merchants and critics. What has been called "art for art's sake" is above all an *art for collectors*. Far from being devoid of all external (or "social") functionality, as some have claimed, "art for art's sake," it can be argued, has its own functional (and social) orientation, imprinted on it by the constraints that collectors have to face in order to complete or extend their collections.

For collectors, as we have seen, and especially those newly arrived in the field, may well encounter difficulties as they try to get their hands on items that have become rare and expensive but that they need to supply what is lacking in their collections. They can then try to modify the contours of the collectable and to shift the criteria of pertinence, a process that leads them to turn toward new artists whose works are abundant, inexpensive, and thus easily accessible (whether these artists are lesser old masters heretofore forgotten or disdained[50] or young artists who are still unknown). This project entails work carried out in association with art critics and curators for the purpose of valorizing such newcomers. Their specific differences will be incorporated into narrations and associated with certain names, often by associating different "creators" in such a way as to produce the effects of "schools." When these operations succeed, the interests of a growing number of collectors will then tend to be oriented toward works that have been "recognized" by the persons or agencies, private or public, that play a role of mediation between the worlds of art and the worlds of collecting.

In other words, the multiple differences between works of different artists (even though these artists may tend to imitate one another at certain moments) depend on the simple fact that the artists are different individuals who find themselves selected by the agencies of mediation, in somewhat the same way – if we may be allowed the metaphor – that in a Darwinian perspective individual differences are selected by the environment from which the entities among which these differences are presented draw their subsistence. We can see this process at work currently in the so-called emerging countries – China, India, or Brazil, for example – where new collectors, motivated in part by nationalism, valorize works created earlier by artists from their countries of origin who had remained up to that point relatively unknown or underappreciated, notwithstanding the fact that some of the artists in question had settled in Europe or in the United States. The introduction of such works in new collections tends not only to raise the rankings of the works but also to modify the contours of the vast imaginary collection we know as the history of art by imbuing it with a global dimension.[51] These processes have the effect of increasing the prices at which highly reputed art objects are exchanged, because prices are influenced by the constant growth in the number of collectors and also in the number of museums that must solicit "creations" to keep themselves supplied: in other words, they must select new differences from within the environment when the works bearing already canonized differences have become too expensive or unavailable owing to their incorporation into public collections.

The strategies for shifting the contours of the collectable can prove to be lengthy and difficult to carry through to fruition. If they are to have a chance of being crowned with success in the short or the long term, those who deploy them have to be able to claim a certain influence on the entire set of operators acting within a given domain, and this supposes a pre-existing accumulation of specific competencies and also of a certain renown. As it happens, the latter often depends on holding a position of authority such as, in the domain of the arts, that of influential critic, conservator of an important museum, commissioner of a widely recognized exhibit, or major collector highly reputed for reliable good taste and sound business sense. In the case of collectors, their capacity to link their personal activity to that of private institutions such as foundations, and especially to public institutions, museums above all,[52] plays a very important role in the accumulation of power that allows them to shift the contours of the collectable.

The contradiction of the enrichment economy

The case of France is exemplary: the enrichment economy is more highly developed here than anywhere else, although it is not recognized as such. France is the number one destination in the world for tourism; it has a strong cultural sector with a system for compensating intermittent workers and many artists; it also has the two worldwide giants of the luxury industry in LVMH and Kering, whose principal stockholders are also two of the greatest art collectors in the world. One may wonder why the enrichment economy, relying on the collection form, although this economy is an object well implanted in the weft of reality, is nevertheless not construed as such, and in particular why it is not taken into account by the institutions of central government.

It is as though what we call the collection form, extended to the enrichment economy, has not yet given rise to the same enterprise of generalization as the standard form extended to the industrial economy, either on a descriptive level or in a critical mode. Thus the development of tourism in France has been relatively little studied in relation to its importance, and critical approaches to the subject always concentrate on mass tourism, conceived as a sort of standardized and therefore degraded form of travel, whereas the quest for profits from tourism concentrates more and more on exceptional forms of travel that propose to exploit authentic experiences available to cultured amateurs upon contact with heritage sites valorized for their unique historical features. More generally, the relation between commercial exploitation of the past and the development of ideologies emphasizing culture (the term being taken both in its elite sense and in the sense it has for social anthropologists), tradition, and local color have not yet given rise to broad overviews. Thus the world of art and culture can always be treated as though it were somehow external to capitalism, a fenced-off preserve, besieged to be sure but resistant – all this without taking into account either the significant profits generated by that world or the new forms of exploitation confronting the increasing numbers of people who work in it. As far as economic literature is concerned, luxury, tourism, culture, and heritage creation are grasped according to various modalities. Yet, as we have seen, these diverse activities are by no means independent of one another.

The connections among them have nevertheless not been officially recognized, either by economic institutions or by the official French institutions for statistical analysis, making it all the harder to bring the connections to light and study them in statistical terms. The enrichment economy, in this sense, finds itself in a position rather like that of the industrial economy before the statistical innovations of the 1930s up to the reform of the national accounting system and its statistical apparatus. At the same time, it lacks the visibility of the digital economy that is often presented as a radical turning point, and this presentation, conversely, tends to make people forget that the digital economy bears in part on objects; in this context, the emphasis on discontinuities obscures the continuities that have been crucial to the development of the enrichment economy.

One might think that we are dealing here simply with a delay on the part of institutions with respect to a change that is affecting social reality, and that this delay will be overcome in the near future. We may wonder, nonetheless, if this charitable hypothesis is the right one, and if the blindness of political, economic, and statistical institutions may not have a deeper cause.

For, if we examine the problem more closely, it appears that the relevant institutions in France are playing it both ways: on the one hand, they do not recognize the enrichment economy as a coherent totality, and they maintain in a separate sphere the relations they themselves sustain with the various activities on which this economy rests. On the other hand, as we have seen, through the intermediary of the language used, through price controls, and through the way they consider things in themselves, these institutions in fact govern the organization of such activities, inasmuch as they all have a commercial dimension. But the commerce associated with the various activities involved relies on forms of valorization that are not only different but even appear to be opposed to one another.

Thus it is not enough to explain the absence of recognition of the enrichment economy by a lag in the semantic, legal, and statistical frameworks on which the description of the economic and social world rests, as though, having been forged on the basis of the industrial economy, these frameworks had not yet been adapted to the changes in the economy, changes that are presumed to have escaped the attention of state administrators and, in particular, that of the national accounting system.

While novelists have been able to dramatize the changes of this type,[53] there are nevertheless, as we have seen, no categorial arrangements or accounting frameworks that make it possible to determine with relative precision either the economic importance that is taken on by the nebulous phenomenon whose contours we are attempting to trace or the number of persons whose principal activity is connected to that phenomenon. This is the case in particular because the phenomenon brings together sectors (for example, art and tourism), activities (for example, museum direction and the production of crocodile bags), statuses (for example, that of people living in precarious economic circumstances, secure wage-earners, government employees, and people living on income from their assets), and professions that, in the official nomenclatures, are dispersed among sets constructed according to various logics of assembly that are more in harmony with the old classifications of the industrial world.

As a consequence, we lack statistical series capable of supporting the totalizations that would make it possible to highlight the specific processes at the heart of this evolution toward an enrichment economy and to track these processes as they evolve. This is why, in contemporary economic literature, presentation of the economic reorientation toward the wealthy is distributed among different domains, which are apprehended according to diverse accounting forms that often rely on heterogeneous definitions and categories.

But, given the amplitude taken on by the various cultural activities and the significance of the French government's role (while the government did not initiate their transformations, it has consistently supported individual cultural endeavors since the 1980s), we can attribute to an *institutional effect* the fact that these closely related activities nevertheless remain unconnected. Not only is there no centralized effort at qualifying them that would seek to establish their interrelationships and to unify them, but, quite to the contrary, governmental institutions are actively working to keep them separate, or at least to represent them as independent phenomena.

Why? First of all, it is because there is a borderline that the institutions cannot fail to recognize. This is the borderline between cultural goods, whose purpose is to elevate the spirits of all (in the sense of culture as defined by Malraux, an object of democratization), and commercial goods, especially if they are intended for the wealthy. To associate explicitly, in an institutional logic, on the one hand art, often idealized and treated as if it were really achieved only when it is oriented toward "art for art's sake," and on the other hand the sale of perfumes or the proliferation of boutique hotels has something socially intolerable about it: it would be to accept the "commercialization" of everything and thus to expose oneself to becoming the target of moral critiques of commercialization.

But this is not the only reason. Such a juxtaposition, if it were to take an official form, would endanger the entire economy of enrichment. In fact, the links between tourism, culture, and luxury have to remain unofficial in order for each of these sectors to retain its own dynamics. And this is so despite the fact that none of them would experience such powerful dynamics without the benefits conferred on it by the relations it maintains with the other two.

The absence of recognition of the enrichment economy thus benefits the forms of capitalism that are engaged in it. On the one hand, they produce only for the wealthy, but they can claim to be producing for all, on the sole condition, obviously, that all become rich, but only in the long run. As for the difference between high culture, which is supposed to be exempt from commercialization, and ordinary things, which are commercialized, the former plays an essential role in this arrangement because things stemming from high culture can be sold at high prices only by being valorized with reference to their non-commercial dimension. This latter is attested, as it were, by connecting such high-culture goods with works that are kept in museums; this confers on them a promise of eternity, a promise likely to be extended, in a quasi-metaphorical way, to all the goods that have managed to be qualified through reference to the arts. Finally, the persons in charge of state institutions, for example the directors of the budget who are responsible for supporting and stimulating the activities arising from the enrichment economy, emphasize the difficulty of separating, among the entire set of "consumer goods," those that belong to the domain of luxury from ordinary goods. As it happens, the fact that such a division is not institutionalized allows the luxury firms, brought together in France in the Colbert Committee, to decide for themselves what does or does not belong to the category of luxury goods.

There is thus a contradiction at the heart of the enrichment economy. Important features of this economy aim not to resolve the contradiction but to render it, if not acceptable, then at least customary, as if it went without saying, so that people can learn to live with it. This contradiction is particularly well illustrated in the use of the "France" brand we evoked earlier. The way it is put in place and managed attests to its participation in the enrichment economy, conjugating political interests – the will to maintain a discourse about the "values" of a community – and economic interests: those of the large luxury groups that, seen from abroad, embody the very image of France. As a highly placed official in the Ministry of the Economy and Finance has explained, "the image of France is Vuitton, Chanel, and so on. There is polarization around the major brands, for they convey the image of France. They have created the concept of the art of living, French style, as much as they benefit from it."[54] But what this "art of living" shows, as anyone who leafs through Air France magazines or the supplements of the major French newspapers can see, is first of all a culture: this is why one finds, under separate rubrics, advertisements for expensive watches, articles describing the lives of contemporary artists, and advice for making the most of one's stay in Paris.

The contradiction at the heart of the enrichment economy is not a contradiction between a homogenization that would be inherent in the capitalist logic and a heterogeneity of cultural objects – that is, between a valorization of uniqueness, authenticity, particularity, and specialty on the one hand and "the bland homogeneity that goes with pure commodification" on the other, as David Harvey maintains in a study on wine and the city of Barcelona.[55] The problem is not, in fact, that capitalism is confronted with "two dilemmas – veering so close to pure commercialization as to lose the marks of distinction that underlie monopoly rents or constructing marks of distinction that are so special as to be very hard to trade upon."[56] David Harvey conceives of capitalism only in its standard form; what is missing in his analysis is precisely the collection form. Now, as soon as we take into account the existence of several forms of valorization, one of which takes advantage of the exploitation of differences in the past of things, the contradictions posited by Harvey disappear.

9

The Trend Form

Trend, sign, and distinction

The *trend* and *asset* forms complete the transformation group that has enabled us to characterize commodity structures as both unified and diverse. The trend form, like the collection form, involves things that rely on narratives for their valorization, but that are destined to depreciate very rapidly: their mode of temporal existence is thus the symmetrical inverse of that of the collection form. As for the asset form, like the standard form it relies on the analytic type of valorization, but the objects it envisages are not destined to depreciate over time; on the contrary, this form counts on the possibility of an increase in their market potential.

The different forms of valorization necessarily overlap in part; thus they open up paths enabling objects to pass from one form to another. On the one hand, the trend form may tend toward the standard form, since most objects in the trend form, if they succeed in pleasing consumers, are destined to be taken over quickly by mass production, which leads to their depreciation. On the other hand, it can tend toward the collection form, to the extent that its objects derive their differential value from differences whose appearance is attributed to the intervention of "creators": this aspect of objects in the trend form predisposes them to become collectors' items over time. As we shall see, this twofold aspect is linked to the dual character of the trend form, which has to gamble both on the quest for distinction and on processes of imitation.

The trend form is based on the commercial exploitation of social hierarchies first and foremost: hierarchies of wealth and/or class, but also hierarchies that rely on other differentiating factors such as celebrity, age, physical beauty, or even gender or ethnic origin. While the trend form is associated particularly with fashions in clothing, it can actually valorize anything at all, especially through the intermediary of design.

Attention to trends tends to appear in every social formation where three conditions are present simultaneously. First, things in circulation must be numerous, diversified, and subject to frequent and rapid changes: certain items appear on market shelves while others disappear. Second, these things must be very unequally distributed among the actors, groups, or classes occupying different hierarchical positions in one respect or another. But there must also be a certain degree of fluidity in the social formations involved: those who are the least privileged in one respect must have the opportunity to acquire things that evoke objects possessed by those who are more privileged in this same respect. This process is possible only when the attribution of things, such as items of clothing, is not statutory in the sense that it is not based on legal codes or their equivalent (unlike, for example, the attribution of uniforms or military decorations, which has a statutory basis). Third, there must be a relation between the rhythm of renewal of the things in question and the hierarchical position of the actors. This relation is established in back-and-forth exchanges among things and persons: either persons who are privileged in some respect prove to be the first to acquire things that have recently appeared, or else these things appear because persons privileged in the same respect are seeking them.

In an arrangement of this type, *lacks* are generated by social hierarchies. The "old" lack the quality of being "young"; the "homely" lack being "handsome" or "beautiful"; "nobodies" lack being "famous"; the "poor" lack being "rich"; the "ordinary" lack being "chic"; and so on; they experience lacks because others have these qualities. It follows that relations to specific things are spread via the relation of those things to persons. In fact, the acquisition of new things is a way of filling lacks that are neither justified by need (as in the standard form) nor driven by a demand for totalization (as in the collection form); they are actually revealed only to persons confronting hierarchically structured collectivities. The things themselves, when we consider them in this light, are appreciated first and foremost not for their usefulness, even if they do give rise to some use, but as *signs* – that is, as markers of a person's position in the social fabric. The totality within which lacks appear is thus itself of the semiotic order. It is constituted by the entire set of signals that are apt to be grasped as indices of social status, or, rather, it is made up of the relations between these "indirect" indices and brands or symbols referring to legally guaranteed qualifications. While legally protected brands are difficult or impossible to modify, these systems of indexation, open to all, as it were, are constantly reworked in a cyclical manner by a twofold movement of imitation and distinction.

The trend form does not simply mirror pre-existing social hierarchies, arrangements established once and for all and based on institutional (or even legal) footings that are objectified by titles or canons (as we might speak of canons of beauty), or even based on unquestionable hierarchies of wealth. It recognizes only the signs through which these hierarchies are expressed. As it happens, these signs are subject to variations in relation to the contexts in which they are manifested; thus the trend form identifies them only in contexts favorable to the expression of the trend. In other words, a trend imposes the signs that, at a given moment in time, are truly fashionable because they are associated with actors whose presence is revealed on stages dedicated to manifestations of the trend.

The traits that can be attributed to the trend form, or to its premises, have been of particular interest to sociologists and historians,[1] for, by paying attention to them, these scholars can translate them into the more familiar idiom of groups and hierarchies and, in so doing, can situate things in places different from the ones usually assigned them when the things in question are considered from the standpoint of economics or history. Thus, in an article that Pierre Bourdieu and Yvette Delsaut devoted to haute couture, we find an enlightening analysis of the fashion effects that play a determining role in the trend mode.[2] By the late 1970s, a number of researchers had begun to call on structuralism as a resource allowing them to describe social phenomena by applying methods that had originated in linguistics. This led them to conceive of the circulation of things through homology with the circulation of signs,[3] as we see most notably in the work of Roland Barthes[4] and Jean Baudrillard.[5] The trend form rests less on a semantics than on an empirical and practical semiology, and that is why it has been so fascinating to semiologists. It has an allure like that of a Moebius strip. An actor is fashionable if he or she conveys signs of a trend; at the same time, the signs conveyed by such actors, or by the actors on whom the trend depends, are fashionable.[6] From the perspective of a Saussurian semiotics,[7] these actors could be seen as coveting things and appropriating them for themselves solely or chiefly for their differential meanings – that is, in relation to what could express the differences between these things and other things. This type of approach proved compatible with a critical perspective that, setting its sights on consumer societies and/or class-based societies, tended to interpret the relation to difference according to the logic of an incessant quest for distinction aroused by effects of domination.

By emphasizing the "symbolic" dimension of goods (the term "symbolic" often being set in implicit opposition to "material"), this critique, anchored in Marxism, could easily be reinterpreted in the terms of very different morally inflected critiques. Some of these critiques drew on a progressive or even socialist celebration of the industrial order, as Thorstein Veblen did; some invoked a form of anti-chrematism, Catholic in inspiration, that opposed "useful" things, which are necessary for the "needy," to "useless" things, which are marked with the sign of dissipation and waste. Others, purporting somewhat vaguely to have been inspired by Adorno or perhaps by Heidegger, stressed an "authenticity" anchored in the autonomy of the subject, as opposed to the inauthenticity of "mimetic desire" which, driven by the "desire for the desire of the other," would plunge alienated persons into the anonymity of the impersonal "one" or "they."

Considered in this way – that is, in the most general and almost transhistorical terms – the trend form could be folded into the vast domain of the fashion effects that lead actors in a given society to conform to contemporary tastes, or to "good taste," and to seek what is "in fashion," "up-to-date," or "the last word"; in such a situation, actors who aspire to "social recognition" imitate those who are presumed to have achieved it already. These effects have been perceived and condemned or ridiculed, especially in places and periods in which the social order has appeared to be sufficiently mobile for actors to try to inflect its contours by modifying their own ways of being, living, and displaying themselves to others – in other words, especially when a shift in the flow of money seems to call social categories into question. This is the case when a previously subaltern group seeks to rise to the level of the dominant group, a situation attested, for example, by a literature particularly abundant in the eighteenth and nineteenth centuries that targeted either the efforts of members of the bourgeoisie to imitate the nobility, or the simultaneously imitative and distinction-seeking frenzy that developed in the micro-societies surrounding royalty, among persons confined to various ranks who were all attempting to modify their positions by winning favor with the prince.

Nevertheless, the trend form cannot be associated exclusively with the mimetic and distinction-seeking processes that develop within elite groups. As we see it, the trend form properly speaking is involved only when the tendency to follow a trend, a tendency that has a virtually anthropological character, is articulated with capitalism – that is, when actors equip themselves with specific instruments to channel the trend in view of making a profit. These instruments make it possible, in particular, for actors to displace the power accumulated by persons owing to their celebrity onto commodities so as to induce potential buyers to pay higher prices for them. This is one of the tasks of marketing, an activity whose vocation, according to Peter Drucker, is to "create the client."[8]

This movement, which has accompanied the rise of capitalism, got its start in the second half of the eighteenth century, as two transformations were under way: on the one hand, that of the dynamics of social differentiation and, on the other, that of the production and circulation of commodities whose semiotic dimension was explicitly taken into account with increasing frequency by sellers and buyers alike. The constitution of the trend form, in the late eighteenth century and throughout the nineteenth, a form that was eventually systematized and amplified by the development of marketing, has thus been associated with a double movement of diversification and unification of the arrangements for production and commercialization. In the direction of diversification, we can observe the shaping of a "luxury" economy that must not be confused with the creation of very costly products intended for a small elite; rather, it entailed a proliferation of things for which prices were disproportionate in relation to their utility in the strict sense. The growth in consumption, especially in urban contexts, was accompanied by a diversification in manufacturing techniques and in chains of value that tended to separate exceptional goods more and more sharply from more or less similar goods that were accessible to certain upwardly mobile urban strata.[9] These latter goods, produced in greater numbers, were often imitations of the former. While objects initially destined for an elite were often imported (as with porcelain from China, for example) or derived from imported raw materials, the goods intended for the wider public, inspired by the imports, interpreted the latter in a way that allowed them to be produced in the country where they were to be sold, often using locally available materials.[10] But this diversification of the arrangements for producing objects went hand in hand with unifying processes of a semiotic nature, manifested by the migration of differential values associated with things from the luxury economy toward that of more common goods. Especially if they were produced industrially and if their commercialization depended on fairly extensive sales networks (which was more and more often the case), luxury goods were in a sense swept up into what Cissie Fairchilds calls populuxe goods, intended for the lower and middle classes in urban areas in the eighteenth century (tableware, dry goods, and so on);[11] produced in large numbers by artisans who copied one another, these goods were relatively uniform even though the production processes involved did not yet entail any techniques for standardization properly speaking.

More precisely, the formation of commodity cycles that hinge on the relation to trends tends to reveal the transitory character of the differences that are initially introduced by way of luxury commerce and that can be criticized as "artificial" and "arbitrary." The fact of emphasizing the cycle as a whole tends in particular to render certain luxury products overfamiliar; these then risk being reduced to the same level as more ordinary products that bear the same differences, inasmuch as both types simply constitute moments in a single cycle.

The most pertinent dimension of the trend form is thus, in this respect, the fact of anticipating and controlling the life cycle not only of products as material entities but also and especially of the differences supported by those products. In fact, considered through the lens of the trend form, production concerns more than making things. It concerns, also and especially, the creation and management of differences that can be deposited in various objects and that can shift, according to a variable rhythm, from things produced in small quantities and sold to wealthy persons at high prices to things produced serially and sold at lower and lower prices. At point $t1$ in time, the objects in which new differences are introduced are expensive precisely because they alone bear these differences, even if their cost is also justified by the higher quality of the supporting object (which points toward the standard form). At points $t2$, $t3$, to tn, the differences introduced at $t1$ are shifted onto less expensive objects offered to a broad public; this marks the formation of a new cycle. These temporal processes provoke a rapid rotation of commodities whose obsolescence results not from material wear and tear but, rather, from semiotic erosion.

The structure of the trend form

As we did for the standard and collection forms, we have sought to situate the trend form in a space drawn at the intersection of two axes (see figure 9.1). The first is an axis of narrative presentation, which expresses the modality according to which things are valorized so as to be differentiated from seemingly similar things in order to make it harder to substitute the latter for the former. The second is an axis of market potential, which has to do with the way the price of a thing, justified by the value recognized in it, is likely to evolve over time. We shall begin by examining this second axis, which plays a central role in the trend form.

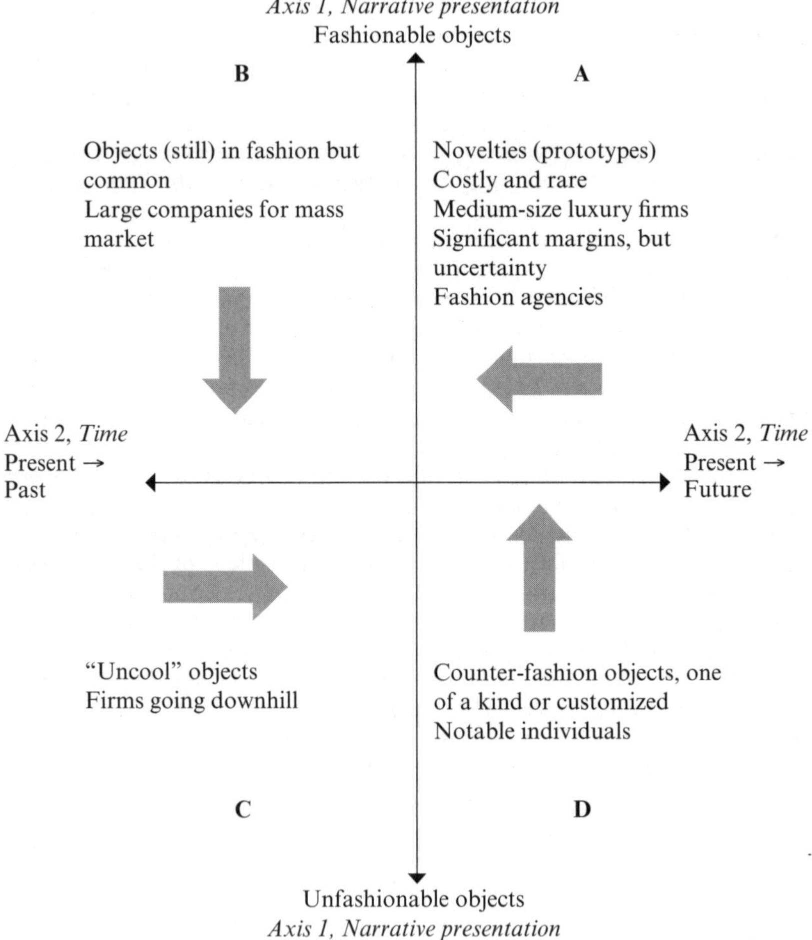

Figure 9.1 Structural schema of the trend form

In this form, the present is the fundamental temporal dimension. An object may be characterized as fashionable or "trendy" when it is inscribed in the reality of the moment. But the present is caught up in a continuous temporal flow oriented from the past toward the future, so that past time and future time are similarly inscribed, implicitly, in the present, in the form of persistence or traces in the case of the past, and in the form of anticipation in the case of the future. One can then contrast the objects at the left on the horizontal axis, which exist in the present but are in a way pulled toward the past and already outmoded, to the objects present at the right on the axis, which are in the grip of a future whose advent they announce. The latter are par excellence the ones that can be qualified as fashionable.

The narrative presentation takes charge of differentiation. Since things in the trend form are valorized through reference to persons, the emphasis is placed on one or more specific differences conveyed by the things in question that put them in proximity to other things currently possessed or coveted by attractive persons – that is, by "influencers" whom those to whom the things are proposed would like to resemble. It is through our familiarity with the persons who appreciate these things that we come to know the things themselves. The people whose proximity enriches the items are living individuals. We might pass them on the street or even be personally acquainted with them if they did not inhabit a different world – that of movie stars, for example.[12] This is the main reason why references to persons whose social power carries over to things are conveyed not only by narratives but also by photographs or films: by making celebrities visible, capturing them occasionally in their "everyday lives," these media in effect increase the reality of their (hidden) presence among us. The differences between things are associated with persons belonging to groups whose strength they manifest and concentrate [e.g., film stars], but these persons are also singular individuals with distinct personalities, tastes, and so on [e.g., Angelina Jolie]; thus the differences between things can be multiplied indefinitely and can at the same time be singularized, as it were. In the case of the trend form, then, it is always the most recent difference that makes all the difference (for example, wearing the same watch – that is, a watch of the same brand and model – as the one worn by a particular American movie star on the plane taking her to the Cannes festival). "Being in fashion means being in the latest fashion," as Pierre Bourdieu once noted.[13] It is likely, then, that the new turn taken by the advertising industry around the mid-1980s was related to the growing importance of advertisements heavily dependent on photographs or films featuring things whose valorization called upon the trend form. Whereas ads oriented toward the valorization of standard objects claimed to "inform consumers by presenting them with the qualities of the product," the new style in advertising, which turned to well-known photographers or film-makers, sought to substitute "the spectacular" for "the informative" by awakening "the imaginary" in a "logic of seduction," by featuring "celebrities," creating "atmospheres," and playing on "second-degree" relationships.[14]

The reinforcement of the differences that account for the specificity of the thing celebrated is thus displaced from the object itself toward the persons and contexts that are presumed to have an affinity with the commodity whose sale is being promoted by the advertisement. Differences that might seem secondary or infinitesimal thus take on considerable relief.

But these small differences, which suffice to prevent a given object from being substitutable for another, are also the "latest" differences, because they have a temporal dimension, if only to the extent that select individuals are presumed to be surrounded with – and the earliest beneficiaries of – *model* objects that have arisen from the imagination of "creators" or designers. The intersection between the way the trend form valorizes objects, through narratives and images that bring (famous) human beings into the picture, and the temporal dimension of the trend form is what accounts for one of the form's specificities, namely, that it relies simultaneously on *mimicry* – being similar to a certain famous person and at the same time similar to all the ordinary people, so to speak, who, since they also want to resemble that person, are really "up to date" – and on *distinction* – being separated from the great mass of people who, unable to follow the trend, seem definitively cast aside. The tension between mimicry and distinction is governed, in the trend form, by the importance taken on in this form by the notion of *style*. In fact, the reference to style authorizes a vast set of interpretations and variations that can extend to *customization*, which constitutes, in the trend form, the way of responding to the demand for authenticity attributed to buyers. By customizing the things with which they surround themselves, consumers are presumed to be able both to be "in fashion," or even to anticipate a trend by combining the fashionable objects they acquire in such a way as to make what is specific about them obvious, and, at the same time, to project a "self-image" that manifests their own singularity and thus their authenticity – a phenomenon that is particularly clear in the case of fashionable apparel. This is why marketers of fashionable objects stress the plasticity of the commodities offered for sale: the objects can be presented as "prosumer platforms" so as to suggest that the buyers themselves are "creators" and not just passive consumers of "finished products."[15]

The narrative presentation in the trend form contrasts objects in relation to the degree to which the properties of a given object are determined through reference to trends – that is, in relation to the degree to which the most recent difference can be valorized at a particular moment in time. This makes it possible to justify the object's price by distinguishing it from objects that are similar in other respects but lack this latest difference. At the top of the axis, we thus find objects whose qualification emphasizes the fact that they are indeed fashionable; at the bottom, we find objects that are exempt from fashion, either through ignorance or through a decision to set them apart.

The intersection of these two axes allows us to distinguish four spaces. In A (the upper right quadrant of figure 9.1), we find fashionable objects qualified as *models* that look toward the future. They generally exist in a limited number of specimens, or even only in the form of prototypes, and they are offered for sale at high prices. Their conception and manufacture is handled by firms employing designers, conceptualizers, fashion specialists, and so on, who often act on the advice of fashion agencies or "style bureaus." These agencies regularly supply their clients, who come primarily from the domains of fashionable apparel, textiles, and cosmetics, with "trend notes" that are "guides for creative anticipation" for the forthcoming months or years,[16] and that are presented in salons, which play a driving role in the spread of fashion in these domains.[17] These agencies, which employ stylists, colorists, photographers, and also semiologists, work to ensure coordination between the productions of different firms. Their interventions help define the contours of what can be considered characteristic of the trend that is being formed, or of its "spirit," and this will nourish in turn the descriptions, both linguistic and photographic, offered to a broad public by journalists who specialize in taste, fashion, design, and lifestyle.

Unlike the generally costly and rare objects that appear in zone A, those in zone B, while they are also determined through reference to trends, are more broadly distributed. Their valorization emphasizes the differences introduced earlier whose pertinence is presumed to be already widely known to a more or less considerable number of persons potentially able to acquire them. Let us take the woven leather bags offered by the leather goods firm Bottega Veneta as an example. These bags symbolize the renaissance of the firm (which belongs to the Kering group). But the style of the bags, which owe their prestige first and foremost to good management of the visibility conferred on them by numerous clients belonging to the jet set, is rapidly imitated by less select rivals, which diminishes their exclusive character and consequently their value.[18] The objects in zone B are generally offered for sale at prices lower than those for objects in zone A, of which the zone B objects could be taken to be poor imitations, often deemed imperfect. They do present the differences that constitute – or have constituted – a fashion trend, but, on the one hand, they give these differences a stability that is overly obvious and almost ostentatious and, on the other hand, the differences are incorporated into things that, seen from other angles, do not have the qualities of the objects on which the most recent differences have been made manifest. For example, the form may be similar but the material different. This is the case, for example, with the type of leather jacket known as perfecto, which was adapted by a highly reputed brand and made of leather from lambs (rather than the leather from cattle used for the old biker jackets) and was then reproduced in a plastic material. Such objects can be devalued by being characterized as imitations (*simili*, a term used in French by Pierre Bourdieu, has become a concept)[19] and can be judged *common* owing to their widespread availability at low prices.

In zones C and D, we find objects that are exempt from the demands of fashion, but in very different ways. In zone C, there are things that, considered from the standpoint of trends, can be judged seriously outdated or "uncool." The valorization of these things can rely on numerous arguments (for example on sturdiness or comfort, in the case of corduroy pants), while ignoring the question whether they are fashionable or not, a question that is not pertinent in this context of exchange. In zone D (oriented toward the future), we find things that, without being fashionable, are nevertheless determined – unlike the things observed in zone C, oriented toward the past – through reference to fashion, but this time so that they can ignore, challenge, or surpass it. These objects can be characterized as counter-fashion. This is the zone in which we can situate things of which there is only a single specimen, valorized inasmuch as they are considered absolutely original, unlike any other, things whose existence attests to the spontaneous creativity of those who have conceived, created, or chosen them while obeying only their own fantasies, whether these are artists, creators, or dandies. The latter often get their ideas, moreover, by drawing on obsolete or outmoded things (things from zone C), whether they adopt, modify, or customize them with personal touches, or whether they take their inspiration from them as they create new objects that both "resemble" and slyly wink at things from an earlier time that have become obsolete. Objects of this type, over time, often end up in collections.

But these objects, whose visibility is ensured by their presence in proximity to the persons who have made them their own – a presence that, when those persons are well known to the public, is often relayed by media attentive to tastes and lifestyles – can in turn serve as models for designers, creators, journalists, and especially experts from the fashion agencies who take inspiration from them to orient and coordinate the activity of firms specializing in the fabrication and commercialization of fashionable objects (zone A). The "watchful" activity of the fashion agencies profits from the "drift" of trend-spotters, who linger in streets, museums, and cafés – in short, more or less everywhere – to "stalk" the latest trends,[20] but it also benefits from conversations with "fashion creators," figures in "contemporary art" and "avant-garde milieus."[21] During this transfer, singular and counter-fashionable objects are reinterpreted by specialists in fashion, design, and marketing whose work consists in creating prototypes capable of preserving the component of authenticity that derives from the relation between the original object and a singular person, even as the objects are adapted to the constraints of a more or less industrialized (and often outsourced) production process ranging from limited series to extensive reproduction.[22] A similar movement leads to feeding the search for new trends by drawing on the stock of vintage objects – that is, by turning toward the past, thereby forging a compromise with the collection form. The fashionable object, because it is new, is thus endowed with a history. We must point out that the attraction exercised by vintage objects over the trend form is doubled owing to the tropism of this form toward youth. The reference to vintage objects anchors them at once in the past and in the future, because, for reasons that are not merely economic, fashion-conscious urban young people surround themselves with objects found in yard sales and second-hand clothing stores; this is the current form of the interest André Breton and the Surrealists manifested for flea markets, an interest that prolongs the fashion for the Romantics' "bric-à-brac" (to which Nerval referred at the end of his novel *Sylvie*).[23]

This sketchy analysis suggests that the general movement animating the trend form can be expressed not by a diagonal going from relatively undifferentiated, throwaway objects to highly differentiated durable objects – as in the case of the standard form – but, rather, by a circle symbolizing the way the temporal dimension, central in the trend form, structures the flow of differentiated things and the transfers of trends that traverse the various zones of the schema. If we start from zone A (objects that are new and fashionable), we see the transfers operating toward zone B (objects that are still fashionable but common, targeting mass markets); then, with time, they plunge down into the hell of zone C (uncool objects), from which artists, creators, or dandies can draw out elements to nourish their inspiration and can choose objects that they will customize or imitate by inventing similar things that suit them better (zone D); many of these singular objects will be able in turn to be invested by the fashion specialists of zone A and serve as models, with the introduction of at least one new difference so as to create prototypes likely both to embody the fashion spirit of the moment, in its distinctive aspects, and to be manufactured and commercialized in series.

The economic constraints of the trend form

In the trend form, the production costs of an object (more or less recaptured in the price) are essentially the production costs of its metaprice – that is, the costs incurred at various points along the chain of value that make it possible to forge arguments justifying the highest possible prices. These costs include marketing, research, and identification of the most significant current trends, along with the costs of determining and stimulating emerging trends that have not yet been picked up by rivals. They also include the costs of advertising and those of public relations more generally – the costs of organizing events, salons, festivals, and perhaps especially of orienting or even controlling the media, most notably through the purchase of advertising space; this is often the case for the press devoted to fashion and interior decoration, in which the authors of the content pages take care not to offend the providers of the advertising pages. But it is also a matter of the costs of efforts to anticipate and shape "the trends of tomorrow." Investments in these efforts may serve to pay "creators" and artists, as well as the fashion agencies that are thought to be able to predict future trends because they invent them.

It happens quite often, then, that, in the metaprice proposed for a fashionable product, the costs of the material production of the object are quite low compared to the costs of marketing, advertising, public relations, and the set-up and maintenance of distribution networks. For example, the makers of fashionable objects stemming from the "culture of appearance" (clothing, jewelry, but also watches and even cars) frequently offer them, at the beginning of a cycle, to "stars," so the latter will be seen and, most importantly, photographed in physical proximity with these objects.

We must note in addition that, in the context of the trend form, the price gap that separates a fashionable object from other things that are more or less equivalent in terms of their functionality and use is itself one of the differences attached to the object that come into play in its valuation. Price becomes an argument for justifying the price, and this tends to cancel out the distinction between value and price. In this form, the price is thus not the result, *ex post facto*, of an appreciation of the product that takes into account its production costs plus the hoped-for margin of profit; rather, it constitutes in itself one of the qualities intrinsic to the product. The capacity of a thing to adjust to lacks (and to give rise to them) increases as a function of the price of the thing, which is a consequence of mimicry; this phenomenon can also be observed – as André Orléan has shown – in the case of financial products, when their circulation takes a strictly speculative turn.[24] In cases such as these, demand does not tend to decrease when the price goes up and to increase when the price goes down. It tends, on the contrary, to increase when the price does, because the price of the thing is one of the qualities that stimulate demand.

But this process is eminently temporary. The distinction between what is new – which pays due regard to the fact that it has never been used – and what is second-hand – a central distinction in the standard form – has an equivalent in the trend form: the distinction between what is new – in the sense that it has just appeared – and what is "on sale," offered at a discount. The price of an item on sale is often accompanied by another price, the price of that same item at an earlier moment when such items were at the height of fashion; this second price, which is present only to mark the difference between the original and the sale price, becomes from that point on a metaprice.

When there are sales, the semi-luxury clothing shop ceases for a few weeks to be presented as "a universe of personalized service with a precious décor" and is transformed into "a warehouse universe with self-service," while at the same time the "social level" of a large part of the clientele is modified.[25] The multiplication of sales, including sales of objects presented as stemming from the cosmos of "luxury" (clothing, cosmetics, fashion accessories, tableware, household linens), goes hand in hand with the discounting techniques, systematized by marketing, that appeared in these specialty niches in the United States toward the mid-1970s. The major brands multiplied their outlet stores, making these more numerous than their regular stores (Ralph Lauren, for example, had 105 regular stores and 146 outlets in 2007). This distribution channel, representing as much as 30 percent of sales in the luxury industry, is rapidly expanding in the United States, in Europe, and also in Taiwan and in Japan. Nevertheless, if brands that benefit from the trend form, especially when they are attached to luxury industries, seek to extend their distribution areas in order to benefit both from significant profit margins on every unit sold and from an increase in the number of units, they risk finding themselves back in the field of standard production and of seeing the profits they derive from their differences decline. This was the case, for example, in the 1970s, when luxury clothing brands associated with haute couture (such as Dior and Pierre Cardin in France and Valentino in Italy) used the device of "licensing" to plunge into the distribution of "derivative products" bearing their logos, products sometimes close to the heart of their trade (such as stockings or perfume), sometimes quite remote from it (such as eyeglasses or cigarette lighters); this process had the effect of eroding the companies' claims that their products were "exceptional."[26]

A fashionable object rarely has the identity and the stability, with legal underpinnings, that characterize the prototype in the standard form, and the differences that make it unique (the most recent differences) have to be open to reappropriation and/or reinterpretation, even when they are protected by a patent or a registered model, by makers who introduce these differences in cheaper objects produced in large numbers. Trendiness is on the order of style, which, as is also clear in the domains of artistic or literary creation, can be adopted by anyone who is in a position to perceive its interest and novelty and to use it for inspiration in creating variants, *a priori* unlimited in number, without being accused of "plagiarism." Thus, for example, in the case of fashion, a "goth style" will be characterized by "a bundle of diverse influences," including "an assemblage of materials (velvet, lace), color (black), motifs (Scots plaid), and cultural references to other movements such as punk or *new wave*."[27] It is moreover because styles can be easily imitated that these trends are short-lived, for they must constantly be modified by trendsetters in order to stave off their competitors' efforts to take hold of them by adapting them to the means of production at their disposal, and especially by adapting the prices at which the objects will be offered for sale in relation to the threshold of acceptability of the targeted clientele. Thus each of the styles that comes into fashion must become more or less outmoded even before it is reappropriated by brands whose profits depend on the number of specimens sold and which for that reason mean to make the style accessible to the mass of potential buyers.

The major brands that wager on fashion trends always profit, at least at the beginning of the process, from revenues based on difference. But this advantage tends to fade as production increases (zone B of figure 9.1) and as the style behind the fashion is taken over by small businesses whose flexibility allows for rapid adaptations. This happened in Paris in the Sentier district in the 1980s, following a pattern taken up again today in an industrial form by big companies such as Zara, H&M, and Benetton, companies all born in the innovative districts of the "third Italy."[28] But the brands are also simultaneously confronted with the appearance of new pertinent differences deposited in things that exist in the form of models or are created in very small numbers by trendsetters (zone A).

Owing to the rapidity of distribution cycles, the trend form generates enormous quantities of *trash*, even more than the standard form does. The trend form might even be described as trash-driven, since part of its logic impels it to make things outdated ("unwearable," in the case of clothing), things that in terms of functionality and use value could perfectly well give their users satisfaction for a long time. This is why the trend form has become a symbol of the *wastefulness* of which "consumer society" is accused; indeed, critics of the trend form focus principally on this feature.

In the context of an economy in which the trend form plays an important role, the work incorporated in an object can be broken into two quite different parts. First, there is the work involved in manufacture, which can to a great extent be outsourced to low-wage countries; here, the procedures follow those of the industrial manufacture of standard objects in countries where factory workers operate under conditions resembling slavery (as for example in Bangladesh)[29] and recalling the proto-industrialization of Western societies.[30] Second, there is the work involved in determining the differences that will create the trend and the work of exploiting these differences – that is, the production of lacks that these things will come to fill. This is why, in the countries where the leading firms in the trend economy are based, so-called immaterial work can play a predominant role, maintaining the largely illusory belief that these companies have become "post-industrial."

Fashion workers need to have specific traits that predispose them to succeed in the type of tasks for which they are hired. In most cases, university-level training both in the area of business and management and in the area of literature, taste, or the arts is a requirement. But workers in the fashion industry must also have assets of a different sort, corporeal or incorporated assets that can hardly be called "immaterial," for human bodies are no less dependent on the order of matter than are things: these include youth, good looks,[31] and good manners. This is one of the reasons why these workers often come from the old entrepreneurial bourgeoisie, from the liberal professions, or, in Europe, even from the nobility. Above all, they have to live in places and milieus in which new trends are likely to emerge. This, for example, is the reason why the highly qualified persons employed by the major companies live mainly in well-appointed buildings near business districts when they specialize in management, finance, or information technologies, while those whose professional work is focused on questions of taste, fashion, design, or communication tend to live in neighborhoods undergoing gentrification (in Paris, the northern and eastern districts).[32] These "trendsetters" must in effect evolve in an environment in which they can "feel" an emerging trend so as to grasp it and put it into a form that is compatible with the organizational and financial possibilities of the firms that employ them. This is also why these firms regularly seek new collaborators among the youngest candidates, who are presumed to be bearers of tomorrow's trends.

Turning now to the profit side, we observe cycles that accompany the often very rapid migrations of the differences that produce fashion trends. In zone A, the profit margin can be very large. But it is also dependent on unpredictable factors that can themselves be very broad in scope. First of all, there may be radical uncertainty (as is also the case in the worlds of publishing[33] and film-making) about the potential success of the new differences introduced: these may not be adopted, or may not start a trend. Managing this uncertainty depends in part on the quality of the assessment made of the trend cycle. A new difference may not bring about a windfall because it is introduced too soon, while the productivity of the previous differences is not yet exhausted, or because it is introduced too late, when other differences proposed by competitors have already gotten the upper hand.

But it may also be a matter of an incorrect estimation of the disposable income of the world's wealthiest individuals and a misreading of the uses to which they are prepared to put their money. This is how the anticorruption campaign carried out by Chinese authorities in 2013–14 could bring the sales of perfumes and alcoholic beverages sold in China under the "France" label down by 30 percent. In the case of luxury industries that sell products whose valuation rests in large part on the trend form, the need to face up to this uncertainty is one of the reasons both for the growing concentration and financialization of these sectors and for their rootedness in families. On the one hand, the brands have to be backed up by groups that have financial resources powerful enough to let them bear the costs of the strategies of planned obsolescence, so they can absorb the failures that the introduction of new products may incur and so they can try to control the distribution networks despite possible losses.[34] On the other hand, the requirement of flexibility, driven by the need to make rapid strategic decisions, fosters a form of familial integration that guarantees the cohesiveness and consistency of an authority that presents itself as collegial.[35] These family structures are also among the reasons why the luxury industry is particularly well developed in Europe, where family members may have a kind of solidarity that allows them to bear several losses in a row before they realize significant benefits, unlike shareholders, who require immediate and ongoing profits.

More generally, an economy that depends principally on the trend form has a parasitic relation to straightforwardly industrial economies that are based on exploitation of the workforce. Its prosperity depends on a multiplicity of global factors that it cannot easily control or even assess. The relation to uncertainty entails, in this type of economy, both uncertainty at the outset about profits, which can be considerable when a trend-based opportunity has been seized before a competitor steps in, and uncertainty about significant losses, when the possibility of quickly exploiting a new trend has been misjudged.

Finally, the need to produce a constant flow of differentiated merchandise, and to keep introducing successful new differences while intervening in a very taut field of competition with other companies that are also trying to be the first to declare and commercialize the latest appreciable difference, creates a situation of permanent tension for firms whose prosperity or even whose very survival depends on the trend form. They are condemned to being as *flexible* as possible so that they can cope with the uncertainties on which their profits depend. This tension is not limited to investors alone. It has large-scale repercussions on those who ensure the work of creation or exploitation of trends in the countries where fashion-dependent firms are located. These indispensable collaborators are largely condemned to short-term and precarious employment, for the body of salaried workers in this type of economy constitutes the chief adjustable variable that allows firms to handle the risks on which their successes and their failures depend.

From the trend form to the collection form

The economic properties of the trend form that have just been evoked, properties particularly apparent in the luxury economy, help clarify the reasons for the increased importance of the collection form. In sum, recourse to the collection form has made it possible to attenuate some of the contradictions that weigh on the trend form. On the one hand, this recourse can help stabilize an economy that is based on valorization of the latest differences and is thereby constantly threatened by the cyclical character of the benefits that this economy makes it possible to reap; on the other hand, it can help increase the standing or worth of activities that are often condemned both for their futility and, with the rise of a sensitivity respectful of environmental integrity, for the vast amounts of trash they generate. As we have seen with respect to the important ties between the collection form and the luxury economy, the most unstable and transitory objects, like the trinkets that come in and out of fashion, can find themselves associated with objects valorized for their ancestral character and their patrimonial worth. The former, set on the same level as the latter, in a sense, have found themselves thus ballasted by a form of immortality whose scope has dignified the firms that produced them; these firms can then boast of a sort of ancestrality in the shifting universe of brands, on which the increasingly rapid displacements of capital has nevertheless conferred an eminently chaotic character. As for the trash, the fact that certain "worthless" items, even if they constitute only an infinitesimal proportion of the commodities sent to the trash bin, can be rehabilitated and collected, even exhibited in museums, tends to credit the idea that luxury firms are working for eternity and that they play a role in increasing the "national patrimony."

What is called luxury in its modern expression – that is, since the development of industrial production has forced luxury to be redefined with reference, and in opposition, to the standard form (somewhat the way the emergence of photography gave rise to a redefinition of painting) – is in fact caught in a contradiction. On the one hand, it has to remain anchored in tradition – that is, in what could be designated by the oxymoron "an atemporal past" – so as to be distinguished from the prevailing industrial production. On the other hand, it cannot escape the logic of the trend form, which is characterized, on the contrary, by a temporality marked by shorter and shorter cycles as the strength of the industry and the scope of its distribution networks permit a growing rotation of production and products.

Luxury and the constraints of the trend form from the standpoint of marketing[36]

[Each] brand will have to define its own "luxury" – that is, its way of being competitive as a luxury brand – by spelling out both the norm from which it means to distance itself and the differentials on which this distancing will rely. (M2, p. 29)

One of the conditions for the existence of a brand is differentiation of its identity. This implies that the brand in question exists in relation to other brands from which it differentiates itself. (M2, p. 233)

In the luxury industry, one must ... always remain in sync with the artistic and aesthetic trends of society. (M2, p. 59)

A luxury brand will come out better if it creates fashion rather than following it. (M1, p. 85)

The difficulty is that products for mass consumption gradually improve the quality of their packaging. Luxury products have to keep ahead and improve constantly. (M2, p. 58)

On the one hand, luxury operates, among other things, as a social distinction: it is the sign of a practice reserved to the "happy few" – meaning those who distinguish themselves from the masses. At the same time, contemporary luxury is carried by brands, and these remain tied to the logic of production volume and product distribution. How, then, can distinction be produced serially? Such is the dilemma facing luxury brands. (M2, p. 10)

It is very easy ... to pass from a situation of profitability to heavy losses, as soon as sales decrease and products are no longer adapted to consumers or, for whatever reason, no longer in fashion. (M2, p. 49)

The luxury economy thus finds itself caught between two contradictory requirements, one tugging it toward the standard form and the other toward the trend form, whereas it seeks to be anchored in the collection form. In other words, it is subject, on the one hand, to a requirement of quality, with the term understood in the sense of product robustness and longevity, as is the case in the standard form, where "quality" defines the "high end." And, on the other hand, it is subject to a requirement that the differences manifested by these products be constantly renewed, so that by continually stressing the latest difference it can drive the commodity cycle that will necessarily lead to making unfashionable, at time *t2*, the differences that were introduced at time *t1*. Yet the problems raised by the management of this contradiction have continually increased as the extension of the demand for luxury products has been stimulated by the unification of markets, a phenomenon that has been driven in turn by the increase in the number of wealthy individuals on a worldwide level. To face up to this, the luxury economy has had to turn more and more clearly toward *populuxe*, which has led it to resort in turn to industrial production that is outsourced for its part too, except for the prototypes, toward low-wage countries, thus coming perilously close to mass production.

In response to this contradiction and to try to attenuate it, the luxury industry has leaned heavily on the collection form and, first of all, on activities connected to the plastic arts. Reference to the latter, because they are at the heart of the collection form and are its most striking expression, or perhaps its sign, has allowed in turn, as if by contagion, for reinterpretation of a multiplicity of other activities from which the luxury industry benefits (for example design, or the interior decoration of shops), as if it were there, too, a matter of artistic and thus *creative* activities, not only likely to produce the new differences needed to feed the commodity cycle but also likely to inscribe the commodities involved within the field of things worthy of being collected – that is, destined to remain eternal and ultimately to be "museified." The impetus given to the collection form by the luxury industry has been a major factor in stimulating the spread of that form and, with it, the extension of the fields of the collectable.

But this operation could not have been carried out so quickly and on such a large scale had it not profited from the economic crisis that affected the media. By using some of the exceptional profits it was bringing in, the luxury industry undertook to support the media parasitically by taking maneuvers tried out initially in publications addressed to women or "professionals" and extending them to the most venerable and "serious" media outlets. These maneuvers not only resulted in making advertising for luxury goods indispensable to the survival of businesses specializing in print media; they also resulted in drawing the contents toward a point of indistinction where the properly editorial domain and the space devoted to advertising merged, as we have already seen in the newspaper supplements devoted to "the art of living"; without this development the principal media could not survive. Such shifts, which conferred a sort of public authority on the domain of luxury, so often denounced in the name of a morality condemning ostentatious wealth, would not have been possible if new arrangements had not proliferated between the luxury industry and other actors (primarily the media but also other institutions – museums, for instance – and, more generally, national or local services that support creation). These arrangements involved private parties such as foundations and agencies, public institutions such as art centers, and numerous associations with both private and public sources of funding. Thus a "milieu" was formed that brought together people of differing professions, statuses, and roles but whose interactions helped to establish ties between brands and culture – that is, to support culture with money from luxury brands and to reinforce the power of those brands by allowing them to benefit from the prestige of culture.

10

The Asset Form

Characteristics of the asset form

When they are viewed as assets, things are purchased (exchanged for a sum of money), but only for the purpose of being resold (that is, transformed once again into money). The resale is often presented as speculative when it is made soon after the purchase. But, even if it takes place after a longer period of time, the item is still treated as an asset, inasmuch as it is regarded primarily with reference to its metaprice and inasmuch as its preservation is intended to protect or maintain inheritable wealth. This is particularly clear in situations in which estate planning advisors put the long-term"interests of the family" ahead of their clients' whims, taking on the role of "protecting the rich against themselves."[1]

The asset form places things at the outer limits of the commodity cosmos, since commodities are produced from encounters between commercial and non-commercial goods. The process takes a particularly spectacular turn when the assets subjected to massive trading are certificates of ownership that exist only in written form, but it can also involve things considered in their materiality.

"The direct form of the circulation of commodities is C–M–C, the transformation of a commodity into money and the reconversion of money into commodities," Marx wrote.[2] Now, in the asset form, the relation to money is inverted, closely resembling the transformation that, for Marx, was typical of capitalism: M–C–M, or, ideally, from a capitalist viewpoint, M–C–M′. We can say that there is M–C–M when we are speaking of a *placement* – that is, when there is a requirement of resale in the short or long term, but when the requirement of profit does not have priority. In this case, the anticipated metaprice is equal to the sale price. By contrast, the requirement of profit becomes the primary factor in the form M–C–M′: one expects that the resale (in the short or long term) will bring in more money than the initial cost of the commodity; in this case, we speak of an *investment*. But whether the transaction is a placement or an investment, in the asset form a thing is a commodity transformed into money, treated as quasi-money, or treated as a substitute form of money, and it serves to build up wealth that may be intimately connected to its owner; indeed, the owner may even take physical possession of it. Thus, although it has often been emphasized that placements in art are of relatively little interest to banks,[3] we must keep in mind that a commodity may be used in place of money, as when wealthy heirs choose to pay their estate tax to the central government by donating artworks to public collections.

As an asset, a commodity has value only in the relation between a price and a metaprice, insofar as the latter is a possible future price: its value is its anticipated metaprice. To valorize a commodity is to assign it a metaprice that, at minimum, will be maintained. The more the anticipated metaprice goes up, the more the price will go up. No one says, about an object considered as an asset, that its purchase price was too high or not high enough on the basis of its value. Such claims can be made only by someone relying on knowledge of its metaprice on other occasions – for example, a metaprice attributed to the object in the past or the metaprice of a similar and comparable object. Its purchase price can be said to be above or below its metaprice.

We must stress here that an object, as an asset, does not produce revenues. Its income-generating capacity can be analyzed only at the time of resale, taking into account the capital gains or losses realized (that is, realized in the difference between the sale price and the metaprice). There is a significant difference, here, between investment assets and placement assets; the profitability of the latter is measured at regular intervals, most often annually. Since William J. Baumol's celebrated 1986 study arguing, on the basis of an analysis of 640 transactions involving paintings between 1652 and 1961, that works of art were not very profitable, and notably less so than financial placements,[4] many other researchers have studied the profitability of collectors' items as assets (aside from French Impressionist paintings, which have attracted exceptional attention). These studies, ranging from contemporary Italian art[5] to bottles of wine[6] to Australian aboriginal art,[7] have generally focused on auction sales, especially those conducted by the major houses such as Christie's and Sotheby's,[8] where prices are made public and readily accessible, unlike those negotiated in secret or discreetly with gallery owners or brokers.

The development of the asset form is nevertheless closely tied to the rise in sales at auction and to the transformation of these sales in relation to sales in the standard form, inasmuch as the latter relies on the distinction between new and used commodities. Thus, in France, a law that came into effect on 25 June 1841 provided that, in sales of furnishings, only used goods could be sold to the public at auction; this was intended to protect retail merchants by giving them the exclusive right to sell new merchandise. Beyond the fact that, especially from the second half of the twentieth century on, auctions have made it possible to establish ever more spectacular record-breaking prices for works of art,[9] they have undergone a considerable extension with the creation of Internet auction sites. Yet this extension has maintained the distinction between new and used goods, since, for furnishings to be sold at auction on the Internet, they "must be used – that is, they must have entered into the possession of a person for his or her own use, either as gifts or as purchases, at some stage of production or distribution" and, if they are new, they "must come directly from the production of the seller if the latter is neither an artisan nor a merchant."[10] Still, it is not just because an object is sold that it belongs to the asset form.

Art objects as assets[11]

Considered as an asset, an art object in fact supplies its owner with a profit (a financial product if there is liquidation) that can be measured by value added in a given time period. (M4, p. 151)

Buying power: Generally speaking, it is recognized that purchasing works of art and antiques constitutes a way of preserving buying power. The resale of these objects, made easy today, serves as a guarantee. (M4, p. 81)

Capital gain: The possession of artworks or antiques does not generate regular income the way financial investments do; it leads only to a capital gain or loss at the time of resale. (M4, p. 143)

Price: The price of an artwork depends on its physical properties: size, materials used, date of creation, pedigree, and, of course, the name of its creator ... However, the same work will have different prices depending on the date and the place of sale. (M4, p. 90)

The big question is how the price is determined. In the realm of art and antiques, the price often results from a negotiation and rarely from the application of a stable pricing system. (M4, p. 246)

Profitability: The profitability of art objects, especially paintings or prints by known artists, is established, to be sure, but rarely in a spectacular fashion .... Investing in art objects thus proves profitable if it involves recognized and clearly identifiable objects or artists, this condition being the common denominator of the studies under discussion. (M4, p. 143)

Time: Certain categories of objects ... escape the process of devalorization related to aging. For example, certain products such as wines and spirits can improve over time and gain as much in use value as in exchange value, thus in price. Finally, objects known as antiquities resist devalorization best of all. (M4, p. 65)

Trend (reversal of): Fashions and tastes are actually very fluid; no artist is protected against the reversal of a trend, not even the greatest. (M4, p. 152)

The commodity form in which funds are stockpiled has to be a more robust way of maintaining buying power than if the funds were left in an exclusively monetary form. The metamorphosis of money thus has to bear on objects that have a greater chance of keeping their buying power when they are resold at the end of a given time period than money does when it is left dormant.

In the asset form there are two types of totality, depending on whether one adopts the logic of placement or that of investment. In the logic of placement, the totality is constituted by the entire set of goods – that is, by all the entities that, if they were purchased, could store up money. In the logic of investment, the totality is constituted by the entire set of goods that, if purchased, could be resold for more money than the amount needed to acquire them. Metaphorically, goods of the second type constitute a *portfolio*; thus lacks are created within an ideal portfolio. Goods of both types have to be readily resellable; consequently, they have to be able to restore, in monetary form, the funds that were necessary to acquire them.

The asset form can be envisaged from the starting point of three questions. First, is the durability of the object that serves to store money well established (is it better established than that of money itself)? This first question has two facets: one concerns the durability of the thing in which money is invested and the cost of maintenance; the other has to do with whether the thing can be resold at the time and place of the owner's choosing. In other words, what is its *liquidity*? A subordinate question is whether the thing is transportable, either in the form of a title of ownership or in a material form. Finally, will the object, if it is resold, bring in more (or less) money than had to be provided in order to acquire it (profit or loss): that is, will the future metaprice of the object be higher than its price?

Subjected to the filter of these three questions, things that can serve as complements in a basket of goods or in a portfolio and can fill lacks are thus fairly limited in number. They have to be guaranteed by an institution; they have to be liquid (available for exchange at any time and at any place); they have to be known, but not so visible that their displacement would be hindered; they have to be mobile and displaceable via the sale of the title of ownership or, preferably, via the sale of the thing itself; they have to be durable, meaning that their maintenance costs will not be too high; and their price must be able to rise over time.

Many things, even most things, cannot be handled by the asset form, or, to be more precise, the asset form enters into tension with the other forms we have envisaged. A thing immersed in the standard form or in the trend form cannot shift directly into the asset form. In the case of the standard form, the price of a commodity is highest when the thing is new, and it decreases steadily thereafter, whenever the thing is sold as a used item. The trend form could be articulated with the asset form in that it is cyclical and thus leaves room for hope of a higher price. But it introduces such uncertainty, owing to this same cyclical character, that the future metaprice of an item is just as likely to be lower if the trend shifts. This is why the asset form is articulated in a privileged way with the collection form, in which the prices of objects may rise over time and depend in any case on institutions that guarantee them; however, these processes follow the logic proper to collecting, which creates a certain tension with the asset form. Such articulation between the asset and trend forms is often denied, and, as Raymonde Moulin has remarked, "economic calculation does not figure in collectors' descriptions of what they are about." When questioned about whether their purchases are also assets, collectors oscillate between "outrage" and "cynicism."[12] Their denials are echoed by critics who stress the weak liquidity of collectors' items, the opacity of information, the high transaction costs, and the limited opportunities for arbitration in the case of conflicts – all these factors explain why funds for investment in art have not been developed.[13]

To be assets, things have to last, which excludes a number of fragile works composed of materials of uncertain life expectancy or even deliberately chosen by an artist for their ephemeral character. In addition, as assets, things have to be preserved under particular conditions: high-quality wine has special storage requirements, for example. And the durability of things as assets has to last beyond the context of the sale, inasmuch as the things purchased are expected to circulate further. In the case of auctions, the auction house is a determining factor in the price of a thing:[14] the sale of objects in a prestigious house such as Christie's or Sotheby's increases their prices and may even make it possible for things to be sold that might otherwise remain unsold, or sold at much lower prices, in a different transactional context, such as an online auction. The impact of auction houses on prices is especially salient when the collection form, the importance of which is well understood by the directors of these houses, is mobilized to allow the things on offer to appreciate with respect to one another if they are sold together, as though the ideal totality were presented in a staging that advances a narrative valorizing that totality. This phenomenon is illustrated, for example, when the furnishings, decorative elements, and tableware of a famous ocean liner (the *France*), a luxury hotel (the Crillon, the Plaza Athénée), or a prestigious restaurant (the Tour d'Argent) are dispersed at auction, attracting buyers who associate each of the things sold with the history of these locations, as if each item bore some trace of the celebrities who frequented the sites. Thus Artcurial's sale at auction of 3,500 items from the Crillon brought in roughly 6 million euros in 2013, whereas the estimates had anticipated only 2 million. But the curtains of a famous luxury hotel, whatever stars they may have protected from the light, remain curtains, and they can bring a high price only if they are presented as filling a gap in a totality that includes the plates, chairs, tables, and so on, of the same hotel; stripped of the memorial power of the totality in which they had been inserted, they will not interest the same auction house and can be sold only at the price of other used curtains in a different transactional context.

On the liquidity of things as assets

Let us now consider the objects belonging to the asset form in terms of their analytic presentation. When things are envisaged as assets, their differences are pertinent neither in relation to their uses nor in terms of their position in serial sets; thus a large number of their properties, whether these are substantive or narrative, are neutralized. The differences that remain pertinent are those related to the degree to which the objects can easily be converted into money – those differences, one might say, on which their *liquidity* depends. The term "liquidity" refers here to the possibility that the person who holds the objects will be able to draw the anticipated revenue from them no matter where or when the transaction takes place. The liquidity of an object may itself be a function of various factors that the holder of the thing in question must be in a position to appreciate.

Let us look at five such factors. A first dimension is the *transportability* of the object – if not the object itself in its materiality, then its title or deed. A second is the degree to which transactions concerning assets can be discreet – most notably in order to avoid taxes – as opposed to being hard to shield from national or international controls. Things in the collection form may also be considered "national treasures" and thus be legally prevented from leaving the country, or even subject to a right of pre-emption on the part of a central government if it seeks to insert them into public collections, thus withdrawing them "forever" from the possibility of resale. A third factor concerns the existence of valid instruments over a geographic area of some size that makes it possible to determine the characteristics of things and associate them with a reference price; when such tools exist and are reliable, a thing so determined can be negotiated at a similar price in other places.[15] From this perspective, the implantation of the same auction houses and galleries in major cities throughout the world increases price stability.

A fourth factor: things have to be able to find a buyer easily and be sold rapidly. As it happens, sales of collectors' items, when they are assets – that is, when their prices are high – generally remain seasonal, and time is required to organize auctions and find specialized merchants who can guarantee the nature of the items; in addition, the transaction costs are apt to be high. Thus for Australian aboriginal art, following the seasons of the southern hemisphere, prices are higher at auctions held from May to July and lower from December to February.[16] The liquidity of collectors' items as assets has increased only in a relative way through Internet transactions, in that more of the items exchanged in that context are produced according to the standard form (postage stamps, for example) and are sold at lower prices, whereas high-priced collectors' items produced in limited editions or even in a single exemplar (a Hans Bellmer drawing, for example) are not offered on the Internet. This difference can be attributed, on the one hand, to the question of guaranteeing the authenticity of the things offered for sale and, on the other hand, to the fact that, while standardization offers the buyer guarantees of the properties of a mass-produced object that has become a collectors' item (a piece of furniture or a watch, for example) and of which the buyer may have seen exemplars, a potential buyer of a work that is unique may have a greater desire to assess it by being in the presence of the thing itself. Finally, the group of potential buyers of collectors' items as assets is growing because the patrimonial class is expanding and becoming wealthier. If inequality were to diminish, the liquidity of this type of object would decrease correspondingly.

Let us take postage stamps as examples of collectors' items that are readily convertible into assets with great liquidity. As we have seen, stamps have been privileged objects of collection, but they have also been easy to use as assets. Stamps are small in size, easy to transport and to hide, and they can also be presented in *catalogs* that offer both a description of each object and its price. The latter takes into account the price received for goods deemed similar during various earlier transactions, and this fictive price plays a regulatory role during new transactions. It is established and set by "experts," holders of an institutional authority delegated to them by the numerous philatelic associations spread throughout the world and grouped in federations. The same type of stamp, for example a Penny Black (the first stamp in history), whose price is generally high, is thus likely to be negotiated at comparable prices in different markets, with variations that depend on the circumstances of the transaction and the condition of the stamp.[17] This, for example, is why, during the period between the two world wars, the political authorities of the Soviet Union tried to limit philately, for fear that stamps would be used, especially in external commercial relations, as quasi-currencies capable of rivaling the ruble.[18]

We can contrast the case of stamps with that of certain second-hand goods just as sought after by collectors; here, prices can vary considerably depending on the situation in which they are evaluated. A dealer, questioning the role of "experts" in his area, thus wrote the following in his memoirs:

> To know, one first has to see. But that is not enough to propose a price: even if I hold a Daum vase, an ivory statuette, or a violin, its price, in my eyes, depends on several criteria. Is this the price for which I would buy it in a second-hand shop? Or in an auction house? Or is this the price for which I would sell it? And, in this case, where? On the sidewalk at the Vanves fleamarket, at the Biron market at Saint-Ouen, at the Village Suisse, at the Louvre des Antiquaires, or in the Carré Rive Gauche?[19]

These remarks apply more generally to all objects when they are treated as assets. In the absence of formal inscriptions, these resources cannot readily generate goods likely to see their prices stabilize no matter what the transactional context may be. Their exchange owes a great deal in each case to the personal relations that surround a given transaction and to the information that each participant has, not only about the things being negotiated but also about the other participants, as has been demonstrated in studies of the "bazaar economy."[20]

We could make similar remarks about paintings on canvas, as well as old books and manuscripts. These objects have the advantage that they can be transported fairly easily and discreetly, thus allowing their possessors to escape taxation;[21] this is more difficult in the case of a real-estate asset, for example an apartment in the heart of Manhattan or Paris, which cannot be moved and which is usually subject to taxation.

The negotiation of things as assets may bear only on the title of ownership, however – that is, on a written document whose exchange is registered by government agencies. For such a transaction to remain discreet, complex financial arrangements may be required, such as recourse to offshore companies, while the goods themselves may remain stationary, stored in warehouses located in free ports.

The possibilities for negotiating a painting at similar prices in different circumstances are very uneven, depending on the level of "recognition" that has been achieved by the artist. While the price of a canvas by an artist who is little known, or appreciated only by a limited number of admirers, will be uncertain, the price of a work attributed to a famous artist and included in reputable catalogs will be relatively stabilized. One of the roles played by the major auction houses, where prices (but not the buyer's identity) are made public, is precisely that they set the prices of paintings and confer on them the status of liquid assets, thus allowing works of art to serve as virtual equivalents of money.

The commercial potential of assets

When things are treated as assets, their *capitalization* is defined in relation to the axis of commercial potential. Capitalization – that is, the realized value of the future flow of profits that can be expected from an asset – aims to estimate the current price of an item – that is, the sum that an actor would be prepared to pay at once to ensure ownership of the item in the hope of a future profit, rather than investing that sum in a different operation involving its relation to other goods. The process of capitalization leads actors to compare the purchase price of a thing to its metaprice – that is, the estimate of what it may bring in, or cost, in the future. Capitalization presupposes constructing a specific relation between the present and the future. The asset is appraised in terms of the future revenues that it may generate, which presupposes setting the point in time at which these revenues will be received. But such an appraisal allows the actor to set the top price for the item, as current capital, only if it is balanced by a rate of realization that takes into account both the cost in time – generally indexed on the prevailing interest rate – and the cost in risk, as an estimate of the likelihood that the revenues will actually be available at the end of a given time period. The latter cost is itself dependent on an appraisal of the relation of the benefits that can be expected from a risky operation and the anticipated cost of the efforts that would be required to reduce the risk. The axis of commercial potential, in the asset form, is thus oriented neither toward a horizon on which things are destined to become trash – as in the standard form – nor toward their preservation in order to make them immortal – as in the collection form – but, rather, toward a *present* whose content, defined in terms of capital, is determined with reference to more or less distant future moments.[22]

On the axis of commercial potential, then, at one end we find assets promising future profits whose realization will take into account prices subject to moderate risk, provided that the negotiation takes place in the short run, for example because the circulation of the assets will benefit from mimetic effects encouraging speculation – as can be the case for financial assets[23] but also for works of art. In this situation, the preference for immediate gains – that is, for the *present* – wins out over confidence in the future. At the other end, we find assets offering the hope of future profits in the long run – that is, revenues at a level that will make up for the increased costs in time and especially in risk.

In the first case, the rhythm at which assets change hands will be rapid; actors will seek to submit each asset to the test of exchange in the hope of an immediate profit as long as there is an upward trend – that is, as long as one can expect that numerous actors will be ready to acquire them with the same motives – and also ready to get rid of them as fast as possible when the trend reverses and other actors can also be expected to try to liquidate them quickly, as we know all too well from financial crises in which the effects of mimetic speculation are blatant.[24] But one could undoubtedly find many more processes of the same type that have developed in situations of mimetic enthusiasm for various things sought after by collectors, as when, in the late 1980s and early 1990s, Japanese investors paid increasingly high prices for French Impressionist paintings, which they held in particular esteem.[25]

In the second case, the rhythm at which assets change hands will be slower, although the tendency to hold onto them may be attributed to diverse motives. The object of a given transaction may be either an investment – when the decision to hold onto it is based on the hope of a profit that will increase over time – or a placement intended to hold a significant sum of money *in reserve* in order to shield it from wealth-destroying circumstances. This second option may be based on a comparison of the unequal risks attached to different kinds of assets. This is the case, for example, when sums earned through commerce in very volatile assets are set aside in reserve – warehoused, as it were – by being placed in assets from which only moderate revenues can be expected, but whose capacity to resist the test of time seems particularly great provided that their level of liquidity seems adequate. This possibility – which follows the prevailing tendency, in banks, to suspend the distinction between savings and holdings[26] – is no doubt widely exploited by collectors of expensive artworks. Relying on the solidity of the works that they collect, works whose value is supported, as we have seen, by the institutional authorities in charge of rendering things "immortal," these collectors can both cherish the works for their precious qualities and treat them as particularly robust goods likely, on this basis, to play the role of a virtual reserve currency when considered in terms of the asset form.

From this perspective, things appreciate insofar as buyers estimate that there will always be future buyers who will appreciate them just as much. This is why the name of the creator of an artwork is the most important factor in its price, not only for European and North American art but also, for example, for Australian aboriginal art,[27] for artists' names are warranties for the future, once the narratives of the creators' existence have been taken up by those who write history and then by institutions that possess other works by these same artists. Although several scholars have maintained that artworks are less profitable than financial placements, these works appear no less durable in the logic of constituting a legacy intended to be held by the same family and, in the long run, by the same *patrimonial* class. After all, the history of capitalism is also a history of huge, highly capitalized companies that were omnipresent on a worldwide scale at some point in time and later disappeared, their existence forgotten or reduced to a mere memory after just a few years.

In contrast, collectors' items can be held for several centuries; this explains why the asset form has been able to develop so robustly. But the consistency of prices, in the case of the most expensive works, cannot be attributed, contrary to what certain economists suggest, to a "quality" presumed to be incorporated in the work itself and presumed to have imposed itself over the years. If this were so, it would make prices the best indicator of the worth of artworks and would justify the role attributed to awards and prizes in aesthetic judgment and in the use of works as assets. Rather, the consistency of prices is based on the fact that, if the prices of certain works are maintained, it is first of all because they are assets, and because those who own, buy, and sell or transmit them have an interest in maintaining them at such high levels.

In this light, we can understand better why the selection of the most famous artists in history, those whose fame has persisted over time,[28] corresponds fully to the valuation of the asset form, while in the meantime the status of works by these artists has been modified, passing from the status of treasure to that of quasi-currency. When we draw up the list of paintings sold at auction for record prices between 1701 and 2014,[29] it becomes clear that the most expensive works in the eighteenth century, sold in those years in Amsterdam, Rotterdam, or London, are those of artists whose works brought in very high prices two centuries later (for instance Gérard Dou or Anthony Van Dyck). The most remarkable case is that of Rembrandt, whose works have regularly been purchased at record prices for three centuries (in 1798 in London by the English banker Sir Francis Baring, in 1811 in London by Prince George IV, in 1913 in Paris by the American businessman Benjamin Altman, and in 1961 in New York by the Metropolitan Museum). New fortunes help maintain or establish collectors' items at high prices as assets, whether the works in question are ancient or more recent ones that are being included in turn in a narrow circle: works purchased by Americans in the early twentieth century (Henry C. Frick bought a Frans Hals at a record price in 1910, Benjamin Altman a Rembrandt and a Mantegna in 1912–13); by Japanese in the 1980s and 1990s (Yasuo Goto bought a Van Gogh for a record price in 1987, Tomonori Tsurumaki a Picasso in 1989, Ryoei Saito a Van Gogh in 1990); and also by Brazilians in the 2010s (Lily Safra bought a Giacometti for a record price in 2010).

For a long time many analysts have considered that works of art and venerable objects treated as assets were used as means for saving, intended to preserve capital rather than to increase it,[30] while investments in contemporary art were riskier and had a more speculative character, forming a bubble ready to burst the moment an economic crisis came along. Still, we may wonder whether the transformations of the art market linked to what is called globalization, a phenomenon marked by unification and rapid transmission of information, have not modified this distribution, with the most expensive contemporary artworks now being treated as reserves of capital. This transformation might make it possible to understand the growing resistance of the art market to economic crises. Whereas the 1929 stock market crash had a considerable effect for almost a decade on the contemporary Parisian art market, obliging most art galleries to close,[31] the consequences of the 2008 crisis were short-lived, especially where artists whose works command the highest prices were concerned. As early as 2010, the index of contemporary art prices began to rise again, setting new auction records starting in 2014 (driven above all by sales of works by Jean-Michel Basquiat, Jeff Koons, Christopher Wool, Zeng Fanzhi, Martin Kippenberger, and Peter Doig).[32]

The fact that several exceptional pieces reaching very high prices are regularly negotiated among a small number of major collectors helps support the capitalization of these assets by lowering the level of uncertainty as to their real – that is, current – value, as objectivized in a price.[33] The high cost, which may sometimes appear exorbitant, that certain actors agree to pay, and that it would be tempting to interpret within the sacrificial logic of the potlatch,[34] actually plays a more prosaic economic role, in the sense that it helps support the value of the entire set of assets of the same type, considered as capital. It thus makes it possible to minimize the possibility of a collective destruction of collective wealth, an eventuality that always threatens accumulations of things, even the most noble and immortal. It is as though, on the occasion of these sales at auction, each of the participants were acting in two different ways simultaneously: on the one hand, as individuals endowed with their own interests in competition

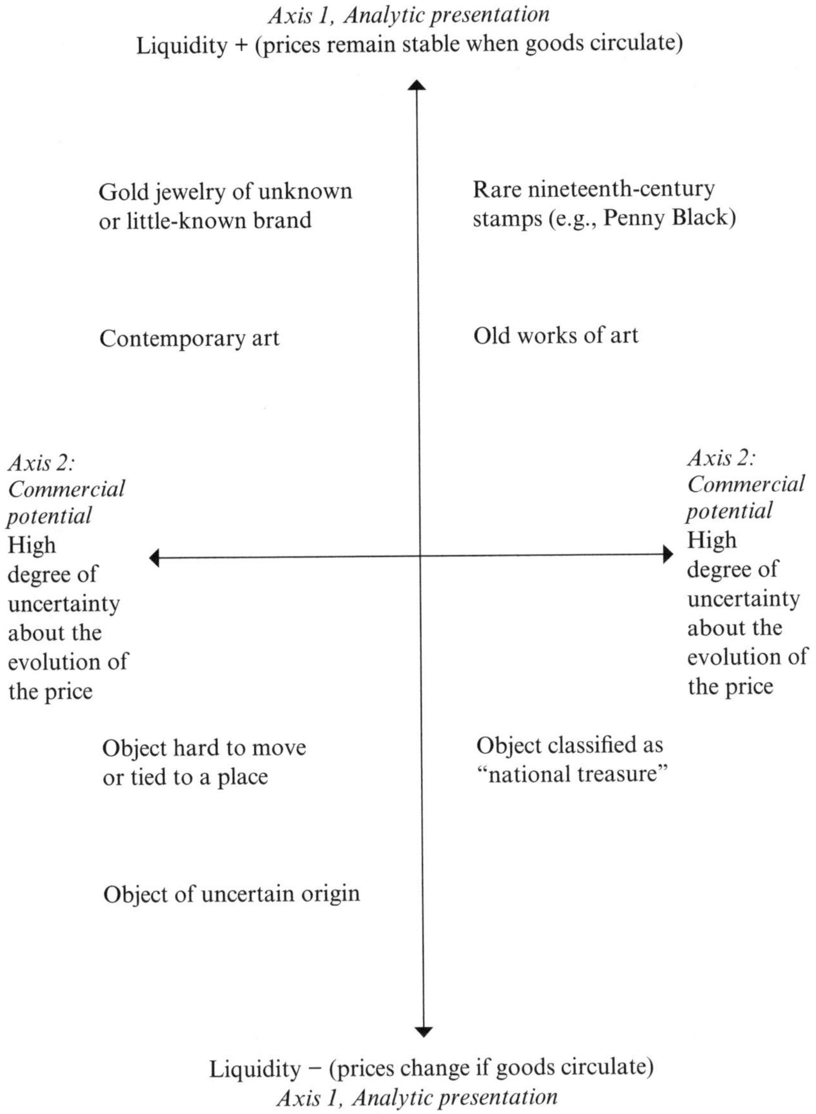

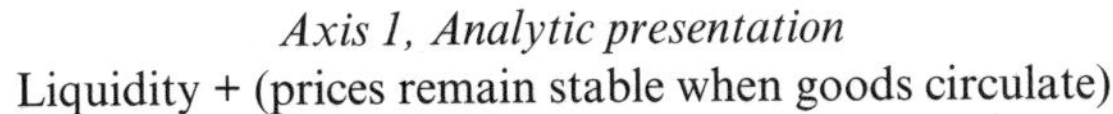

Figure 10.1 Structural schema of the asset form

with other individuals who desire the same object and, on the other hand, as participants in a small but worldwide collective whose members know one another for the most part and often maintain personal relationships. This group is formed by the set of extremely wealthy major collectors who also have an interest in seeing that the value of the collectors' items they own is maintained and attested by the prices at which they exchange things among themselves; this encourages them to develop specific forms of cooperation, one manifestation of which is competition to drive up auction prices.[35]

Part IV

Who Profits from the Past

11

Profit in a Commercial Society

Competition and differentiation

Value and profit are linked. If it is the case, as we have suggested, that reference to value comes up primarily in relation to exchange and when it is a matter of criticizing the price of an object or justifying it in the face of a critique, it is clear that critique and justification are focused primarily on determination of the margin – that is, on the relation between a given price and other possible prices (metaprices); the margin may be favorable to the buyer, if it is small, or to the seller, if it is large. A defining feature of capitalism lies in the fact that it sets different profit centers in competition with one another. Each center seeks to sell at the optimal price, so as to draw the maximum profit from the sale of goods that are in its possession and that it has obtained at a certain cost, whether it has created those goods or purchased them. Thus it is easy to see that the arrangements likely to defend the value of the goods on offer occupy an important place in this framework.

Following the same logic, we can connect the various forms of valuation with the dynamics of capitalism. The constitution of different forms that can be arranged in a transformation group accompanies the dynamics of capitalism, whose logic entails pursuing an unlimited accumulation of capital by shifting from one terrain to another. These shifts have the effect of extending and homogenizing the cosmos of commodities while nevertheless respecting, insofar as possible, the substantive diversity of the commodified objects, so as to adjust to the different sorts of lack that could justify their acquisition, or even to create such lacks. Commodities are thus distributed among the different spheres to which the different forms of valuation correspond. While the same requirement of profit guides these transformations, the fact remains that, in the quest for profit – and profit always has to be as high as possible in the face of competition – there is more than one path to follow, depending on the distinguishing features of each kind of commodity and of the forms that allow a given commodity to be valorized.

As we have seen, the limits reached by the profits that can be drawn from mass production are almost certainly, at least in the Western European countries, the driving force behind the shift of capitalism toward new domains or, rather, toward domains that had remained marginal as long as standardization continued to look like the royal road to profit. To sketch out an analysis of these assorted ways to generate profit, we need to start with the standard form. From the standpoint of profit, what distinguishes standardization is that it places its bets on serial production. The objects are produced by the profit centers that offer them for sale. The production process is very costly. It presupposes heavy investments in fixed capital and the mobilization of a large number of workers who must be paid. This is why the growth of a capitalism based on standardization has gone hand in hand with a considerable expansion in the number of salaried workers. Specimens are manufactured in view of producing the greatest possible number on the basis of a prototype that is very costly to create.

But, for sales to multiply, the price at which each specimen is sold has to be conceived so as to be able to satisfy the largest possible solvent demand. This system encourages producers to reduce as far as possible the per-unit margin to be realized by the sale of each specimen so as to capture all the solvent demand; the producers wager on the profit to be generated by the sale of the highest possible number of specimens (and on economies of scale at the level of production), unless they have managed to create a difference in the prototype that institutes a situation of monopoly or quasi-monopoly. According to the same logic, the competitive relation among profit centers can easily take the form of a price war, each center seeking to lower its prices so as to attract the potential demand. The salaries paid to the large number of workers required for production pose a key problem. Maintaining them at a low level minimizes production costs. But this also tends to hinder the extension of the solvent demand that has to be sought in order to sell the largest possible number of specimens. The search for an equilibrium between these two requirements has been one of the orientations of the Fordist mode of production, as analyzed by the French Regulation School (for example, in the works of Michel Aglietta and André Orléan). Finally, the way the workforce is organized and the way workers' behavior is managed play a central role in this arrangement. Workers who become "undisciplined" or "rebellious" owing to salaries that are too low increase production costs and even introduce a threat to product quality. But workers whose inadequate salaries limit demand threaten the system with a risk of excess production.

The risk of saturating the solvent demand is provoked not only by the weak buying power of the potential consumers but also by the numerous specimens already in circulation that can be acquired second-hand, not to mention the objects already owned. This accounts both for the importance granted, in the standard form, to the fact that the objects are new and for the considerable price differential between new and used objects. Potential buyers have to be persuaded to prefer new objects, despite the price differences. To capture the solvent demand, the competing profit centers have to highlight the robustness of the products they are offering. But robust products do not have to be replaced often. It follows that the expansion of profit drawn from the production and sale of standard objects requires not only the creation of new models, in order to win out over the competition, but also the constant conception of new prototypes, so as to render the specimens already in circulation obsolete – that is, to disqualify them and thereby depreciate them. This constraint had not been particularly noticeable at the beginning of the age of standardization, when standard products proposed to take over functions that had been handled until then by traditional means, but it quickly became significant when the world began to be inundated with a countless number of standard specimens already in place. This process stimulated a search for new "markets," but these ran into the limits of solvent demand in the countries where they might have been introduced. In other words, as Joseph Schumpeter maintained, in this system of production and sales, the creation of new objects is always destructive.[1] In the early stages, when the use of standard objects comes in to supplant the old ways of doing things, the system has to count on the destruction of ways of life – the disqualification of customary practices as archaic – in the name of an imperative of technological progress. Then, when standardization has become the principal means of production of everyday objects, the system has to bet on the destruction – the transformation into trash – of the specimens already in place in the name of continuous refinement – that is, the valorization of differences always purporting to be new.

To interpret the displacements of capitalism, we have to take the limits imposed on profit in the case of standardization into account: on the one hand, the sites where standard objects are produced shift toward low-wage countries, so as to reduce production costs and support the profit margins of sales, and, on the other hand, commercialization extends to domains that have previously remained outside the primary area of capitalist profit. The extension of the cosmos of commodities is what nourishes the development of an enrichment economy. This economy manifests three distinguishing features that can be articulated differently, depending on whether the thing from which profit is expected is valorized by betting on one or another of the three alternative forms of valuation that we have identified. First, one can place less importance on production and more on commercialization for the generation of profit. Second, one can wager on the growth in the margin produced by the sale of each unit rather than on the sale of a great number of units, each of which would bring in a weak margin. Or, third, one can place less emphasis on attracting money from the poor – a strategy that was a stimulant to standardization – and focus on the money of the rich, in expenditures that can always be transformed into an increase in wealth.

To describe these paths to profit as they have been followed by the standard form or as they rely instead on other forms, let us start with the distinction between two ways of producing added value that are associated with two critical analyses of capitalism: that of Marx, who stresses the extortion of added value from labor, and that of Braudel, who stresses the appropriation of added value from commodities.

Surplus work value and profit

Since the nineteenth century, some analyses have defended the idea of a historical break marked by the development of what they have called "capitalism" characterized by the *unlimited* accumulation of capital, referring to accumulation acquired neither through war nor through looting but through "formally peaceful means," as Max Weber put it.[2] Capital accrued in this way, as it circulates, becomes concentrated in the hands of a *limited* number of persons, either individual or collective; the latter may include, for example, societies of stockholders. These analyses have sought first and foremost to account for the possibility of profit, having dismissed as inadequate all explanations based on the division of labor, the rationalization of production and commerce, or the need to remunerate capital in a competition-based economy where autonomous agents participate in interactions in which each tries to further his or her own interests maximally by entering into exchanges. These processes, according to the analyses we are considering, do not allow us to understand how capital could accumulate at the heart of *profit centers* and in the hands of the persons who own and direct these centers. In fact, the multiplicity of exchanges, each of which is governed by the encounter between an offer and a demand, and all of which have a complementary character owing to the fact of the division of labor, ought to result in the eventual neutralization, in a given area, of the advantages temporarily acquired by each partner in an interaction.[3] These analyses thus all have a *critical* dimension in that they stress the asymmetries, juridical in nature, that are attributable to the *ownership* of capital and its transmission through *lineages*, whether such transmission has a familial basis and rests on inheritance or whether it takes an organizational, political, or networked form and orients capital toward profit centers where it accumulates without being redistributed.

Many interpretations have been proposed to account for profit, with diverse factors being singled out for emphasis – for instance, innovation and the qualities of the entrepreneur (Schumpeter);[4] a monopoly effect aiming to limit competition (Chamberlin);[5] actions taken in situations of uncertainty entailing non-problematizable factors (Knight);[6] or access to positions of power from which competition can be paralyzed (Veblen).[7] But, among the variety of available interpretations, we shall focus on two analyses in particular, one that places the emphasis on *value* and the other on *profit*. Both seek to explain how the exchange of a commodity can generate profit, inscribed in *accounting* terms on the *balance sheet* of a *profit center*: in other words, profit is objectified by the *margin*, which may be positive, negative, or neutral, separating the monetary equivalent of the commodity in question between two balance sheets.

To schematize the first explanation, we shall rely on Marx's *Wages, Price, and Profit*, a summary written in simple, lapidary terms for a broad public.[8] The text stands out by its focus on the human labor that has to be expended to give a commodity a form in which it can be exchangeable, and it stresses the possibility of added value generated by the exploitation of unpaid (surplus) work – that is, it focuses on *surplus labor value*. It emphasizes the difference between the price paid for a commodity and the price at which that commodity is sold. But if this difference is not to be neutralized in a series of exchanges among interdependent agencies, we must suppose that the place and time of the first exchange – during which the commodity is purchased – is not in direct interaction with the second exchange – during which the commodity is sold – in other words, we must suppose that the commodity undergoes a *displacement*. For Fernand Braudel, this displacement is essentially geographic (external commerce);[9] however, we shall try to show that the term can be extended by envisaging other forms of displacement that have the same effect of increasing the price of the commodity displaced.

In the speeches Marx gave in 1865 during the two sessions of the First International Working Men's Association, published as *Wages, Price, and Profit*, he sought to refute the economic theories according to which "the value of labour or any other commodity whatever is ultimately fixed by supply and demand," which, according to him, "regulate nothing but the temporary *fluctuations* of market prices. They will explain to you," he adds, "why the market price of a commodity rises above or sinks below its *value*, but they can never account for value itself." Reversing an argument of classic economic theory, Marx considers that, "at the moment when supply and demand equilibrate each other, and therefore cease to act, the *market price* of a commodity coincides with its *real value*, with the standard price around which its market prices oscillate .... This holds true of wages and of the prices of all other commodities."[10] We know how Marx proposed to elucidate the mystery of "real value." His answer was based on the determination of the "expression common to all" commodities, which is a "certain amount of labour" considered as "social labour ... crystallized" in all commodities;[11] this allowed him to declare that "*price*, taken by itself, is nothing but *the monetary expression of value.*"[12]

Marx was the first to grasp and even anticipate the formation of commodities as the specific ontological modality of things when they are not merely exchanged through the intermediary of a monetary equivalent but, rather, take their reason for being from their capacity to transform, through exchange, a certain quantity of money into a greater quantity – that is, when they are no longer envisaged as ends in themselves but only as intermediaries in the process of accumulating capital. This change is schematized by Marx through the opposition between two forms of circulation. Let us recall that, in simple circulation, the seller hands over a commodity in order to obtain an equivalent in monetary form so as to purchase a commodity of equivalent value (C–M–C).[13] In a capitalist economy, the capitalist gives money in order to obtain commodities for the sole purpose of reselling them to transform them back into money (M–C–M), so as to obtain, at the end of the operation, more money than he or she had put into circulation (M–C–M′).

But, by starting directly from the analysis of human labor before considering things in themselves, Marx does not free himself from dependence on a substantive representation of value, which he derives from the differential between use value and exchange value and which culminates in a critique of fetishism. Marx describes with precision how, in pre-capitalist societies, heterogeneous things find themselves dispersed among different modes of being. But he immediately relates this dispersion to the heterogeneous character of human labors as they are distributed among persons, most notably in the framework of the domestic unit, so that the objects produced by these labors are socialized even before they actually appear and begin to circulate through exchange.

This approach via labor has two effects. First, it sustains a critique that, in certain formulations, can be interpreted as if it targeted the very fact of establishing equivalences among things (and, in the case of labor, among persons) through their monetary expression, an interpretation whose effect would be to abolish the identity and the singularity of these things or persons. The genealogy of this critique goes back quite a long way; it appears, for example, in a number of New Testament parables that call monetary equivalence into question (as in the case of "workers of the eleventh hour") and even any form of equivalence (as in the case of "the prodigal son").

The second effect of this approach lies in the fact that it seeks a substantive basis for the equivalence, which leads to making labor, in the form of abstract social labor, the origin of the value of each commodity, but in a transfigured and alienating fashion, in the process of exchange. As a result, communitarian bonds are replaced by an illusory community that is realized only through the mediation of money. But such a critique, which places the reference to value upstream from commodities and exchange, instead of situating it downstream where it plays the role of justifying prices, misses one of the fundamental contradictions of the capitalist regime: on the one hand, capitalism is based on a heterogeneous plurality of transactions that are circumstantial and therefore not totalizable; on the other hand, the capitalist regime cannot do without reference to value, however value may be defined, as a way of giving meaning to the multitude of transactions on which the formation of profit is based.[14]

The way Marx analyzed profit, which has inspired many studies oriented toward the search for an equivalent for labor that could be manifested through the intermediary of a specific metric, has run up against numerous difficulties, as we know.[15] Moreover, Marx himself had anticipated these difficulties in part, for instance by positing that "the quantity of labour necessary for the production of a commodity changes continuously with the changes in the productive powers of the labour employed."[16] On this basis, the existence of surplus labor value had the ambiguous status of a hypothesis that was both profitable and enlightening (without relying on it, for example, one could not understand the importance of outsourcing production to low-wage countries) and hard to illustrate in numerical and accounting formats.[17] Nevertheless, we can attribute the limits that have hindered analysis of the changes in capitalism during the 1960s and 1970s to polarization around a narrow conception of surplus labor value.[18]

Surplus market value and profit

We are borrowing the concept of surplus market value, or "trading profit," from Fernand Braudel.[19] For him, the possibility of generating a trading profit characterized capitalism even more than the extraction of surplus labor value in Marx's sense; Braudel saw the latter as a feature of the "industrial 'mode of production'" (which he did not consider "the be-all and end-all of capitalism").[20] This does not mean that he associated the development of capitalism with that of the "market economy." He meant, on the contrary, to point out the difference between the market economy, which, in his view, had been present in virtually all societies throughout history, and capitalism, which operates in what he called "the zone of the anti-market," where improvisation and "the law of the jungle"[21] prevail, and in which the realization of "super-profits" is achieved primarily through luxury commerce. In the wake of Werner Sombart, Braudel attributed crucial importance to luxury commerce in the formation of capitalism, because luxury goods are goods whose prices can be easily changed "so as to make a profit upon arrival."[22] In the case of "long-distance" or "external" trade, which he often took as exemplary, what he called "super-profits" consistently play "on the price differences between two markets very far apart, with supply and demand in complete ignorance of each other and brought into contact only by the activities of a middleman."[23] But the connection Braudel often made between (geographic) "distance" and "information" suggests that the effects of displacement are far from being exclusively geographic. Those who have "the inestimable advantage of a good communications network … were thus able regularly, quite naturally and without any qualms, to bend the rules of the market economy," most notably by eliminating competition in such a way as to benefit from quasi-monopolies that make it possible to manipulate prices.[24]

The analyses we have just summarized in broad strokes, published by Braudel in the late 1970s, have been more or less swept under the carpet, if not by historians who have pursued the analysis of market networks envisaged in a Braudelian perspective,[25] then at least by a large number of studies focused on the workings of capitalism, studies that emphasize the virtually absolute primacy granted the notion of market as the term is used in neoclassical economics. This is sometimes the case even retroactively, as Guido Guerzoni illustrates with perspicacity when he examines the many studies that purport to describe the workings of an "art market" in Italy in the fifteenth and sixteenth centuries. There, a closer examination of the circumstances allows Guerzoni to bring to light complex and very diverse modes of circulation – gifting, theft, inheritance, cronyism, lending, and so on – of works that pass from hand to hand in an economic context dominated by princely courts and by luxury, a context that is far from wholly market-based.[26] For our part, we consider Braudel's theses highly relevant to a critical analysis of capitalism.

When a commercial object is moved, at each step along the way it is considered from a different "point of view" in relation to the place it occupies in the set of ordinary things, a place on which its differential value depends (the term "value" is used here in the sense in which Saussure applied it to the relation among signs).[27] Thus the "meaning" given to the item in question is posited in relation to that of other things, and the item's price, when it is the object of a transaction, can likewise be called relative, since it is judged with reference to the prices of the other things that give rise to local exchanges. This type of commerce presupposes a confrontation of profoundly asymmetrical viewpoints. The first is local, or indigenous; the second is global, or allogeneic. Whereas, considered from an indigenous point of view, the thing in question is determined with reference to the set in which it is embedded and where it finds its price, so that two positions distant from one another never include exactly the "same" things, the distinctive feature of the allogeneic (or global) point of view is that it has the possibility of following the trajectory of a thing between different positions in which its price will be determined in different ways, while the thing in question is considered to remain "the same thing." In other words, the allogeneic point of view allows for an overview of an entire commercial itinerary.

The most effective trader, in this respect, is one who controls a plurality of viewpoints, and who may thus be characterized as polyvalent. The capacity to play on the differential between viewpoints is what accounts for the power of external commerce and perhaps, more generally, for displacement as a component of capitalism. It is fair to suppose that capitalism has had, and still has, the property of relying on actors who take advantage of their knowledge of different forms of valuation of commodities. At each stage in its trajectory, a given commodity is in fact exchanged at its local price, so that there would be no point in condemning the merchant for dishonesty. But the profound asymmetry that is established between actors whose point of view is indigenous (or local) and those whose point of view is allogeneic (or global) generates a differential that tends to accumulate the bulk of the profits in the hands of those whose point of view – or whose overview – is broadest.

Still, to speak of an "overview" is an inadequate approximation if one does not raise the question of the arrangements and tools on which it depends. In the modern era, these arrangements and tools have been the ones that favor external commercial expeditions. They have been developed, as we know, to a large extent at the initiative of centers of political power – that is, nation-states or city-states. These have been the only entities in a position to place very diverse means – especially military means, in connection with navigation technologies, but also intellectual means, on the order of geography, cartography, and perhaps especially history, and the interest in linguistic and ethnographic knowledge of indigenous peoples throughout the world – at the service of the risky enterprises on which the success of external commerce depends. But the possibility of an overview has depended above all on the development of instruments of communication, especially commercial correspondence,[28] and on the development of financial networks, bills of exchange in particular.

Finance is characterized not only by the fact that it allows for *detachment* in relation to the substantial properties of merchandise, by substituting sums inscribed in account books for commodities themselves, but also by the fact that it permits the accumulation of gains that can be realized eventually through a series of operations. This is the case even if these operations are based on the disparity between local relative prices of commodities whose qualities and market value, determined differently at each stage in their trajectories, can be compared and accumulated only if financial instruments are available. Such instruments make it possible to connect actors who, although they are situated in different spaces (geographically or otherwise), can have an overview of the entire merchandising process because they recognize the validity of accounting instruments underwritten by profit centers that are in a dominant position. One of the most troubling and best studied examples of this type of commercial circulation in the modern era is the three-way business operation initiated in France, where specially designed ships were loaded with utensils intended for West African kingdoms that captured human beings for the slave trade. The captives (about 25 percent of whom died during the crossing) were resold to American plantation owners, and the ships returned loaded with luxury goods such as coffee and cacao to be sold at high prices in Europe. This trade provided only about 6 percent in profits, because it required heavy investments, especially for the construction and outfitting of ships,[29] and it faced significant risks.

In cases like these, the possibility of exchanging heterogeneous things (as indeed all things are) depends on the dissymmetry between the indigenous points of view, based on local instruments, and allogeneic points of view, based on global instruments, financial instruments above all. Far from distributing wealth more or less equally by coming full circle, as do gift exchanges in the so-called traditional societies, such exchanges tended, on the contrary, to benefit profit centers where the advantages drawn from the circulation of commodities were accumulated.

One may also wonder whether the effects of these shifts, hard to contest in cases where surplus market value is obtained, may not also intervene in cases where gains are obtained by the exploitation of human labor (surplus labor value). Let us consider the example of outsourcing to low-wage countries. Such delocalizations, designed to mitigate the decline in industrial profits in Europe and in the United States, shift production to countries where the relative price of human labor is as low as possible. It is true that, in certain circumstances (as with the manufacture of clothing in Bangladesh or the assembly of electronic equipment in Guadalajara, Mexico),[30] these displacements amount to substituting a work regime of virtual slavery for a wage-based workforce; however, this is not necessarily the case. The workers used locally by Western firms may consider themselves properly paid in comparison to the relative price of labor in their own country. It is the differential between the price of local labor in Europe and the price of local labor in low-wage countries that is the source of profit, since the commodities produced are intended to be brought back for sale in Europe. Yet these operations could not be carried out, or would not produce the same profits, in the absence of deregulated financial instruments that allow a circulation of capital available for rapid displacement and re-engagement in places where investments are most profitable.

Displacing commodities or displacing buyers

According to Braudel, the maximization of surplus market value has been made to depend on a displacement of commodities. Let us look first at examples of geographic displacements. They are evident in cases where luxury products associated with a label or brand known for its national or regional roots are exported to more or less distant countries where consumers acquire them owing to the prestige of the country of origin. In the case of luxury products, profits can be all the higher in that industries combine surplus labor value and surplus market value. Like every industry, the luxury industry, whether it deals in perfume or cosmetics, apparel or watches, produces and offers for sale objects manufactured according to procedures and norms resembling those of standard industries, and it does so more and more often by outsourcing part of the production to low-wage countries. The objects, which represent prototypes, are produced in ever-greater numbers in order to satisfy a growing worldwide demand. But as each individual item benefits from operations that intervene at the top of the value chain – that is, design, marketing, advertising, and distribution, which are not outsourced[31] – and profits above all from a process of valuation that stresses the traditional character of these items and their origin in countries such as France and Italy, countries highly appreciated for their "art of living" and for their authority in matters of "taste," each item can be sold with a much higher commercial profit margin than that of a standard product, even though the manufacture and commercialization of the latter are not in fact radically different; however, the growing standardization of luxury products is blurred or even concealed.

Second-hand trading, which plays an important role in supplying collectors of antique or vintage objects, is also an example of negotiations in which the prices of objects sold depend in large part on their displacement. On this point, we can follow a text in which a merchant dealing in second-hand goods, Hubert Duez, sets out to reveal some trade secrets.[32] A first remark: being in the position of middlemen who skim off surplus market value by displacing existing objects, dealers do not differentiate between the constraints imposed on them when they are buying and those imposed when they are selling. In each case, the objects have to be displaced in such a way as to be bought where they are cheapest and sold where they are most expensive. One must never buy an object at its point of origin, for example: "It's not in Marseille that you should buy a 'Veuve Perrin' tureen [a type of earthenware made in Marseille in the eighteenth century], but in Brest ... In a word, it's at its place of origin that an object is most expensive .... The farther away you get from the place of origin of your favorite objects, the more you'll multiply your chances of getting a break."[33] This is the reason why things do not have prices that are inherent to them and independent of the place where they are negotiated.

The merchant's goal is to "get a break" – that is, to come across a second-hand object that can be sold for a much higher amount than the purchase price. To succeed, dealers have to avoid shops and salons where "the merchandise has already been picked over"; rather, they need to "be present at the moment of unpacking where the unsorted contents of cleared-out houses, apartments, basements, or attics arrive directly." For "the 'break' is something *forgotten* (an object made of silver in a silver-plate case) or *mistaken* (a piece of eighteenth-century earthenware at a nineteenth-century price)."[34] To "get a break," the buyer has to be capable of *identifying* objects when the seller does not know what they are: this happened one day when an "old merchant" showed Hubert Duez a "bizarre object, a 'schmilblick,' a kind of upside-down U, 30 × 30 cm in size, fastened to a pedestal." The author, who recognized the item as "a seventeenth-century goldsmith's press," asked the price, but the merchant was unable to respond. To "get a break" is to be able to recognize, in "a chest full of random stuff," an object that bears pertinent *differences* that are immediately transformable into price differences: "it is by rummaging through drawings that one has the best chance of coming up with a good deal, a 'hit' that we call 'a difference.' They are riding high but their rating is still very reasonable."[35] And this presupposes "paying the greatest attention to the small details."[36]

Considered not as a buyer but as someone offering a product to a potential buyer, the second-hand dealer has to develop a pricing policy, and our author takes up the matter. Bargain, yes, but especially to "please the client": consequently, "we post higher prices. Thus everyone is happy: the buyer has had a discount and the seller has sold at his price." But the discount must not be too large (no higher than 30 percent), for an excessive discount would indicate "that the first price posted was not serious," and that is the mark of an "improvising merchant."[37] One should refrain from making an "aesthetic judgment" on the thing offered for sale and just concentrate on its price: "No one makes an aesthetic judgment on anything at all, for everything sells. An object despised by some will enchant others."[38] Let the buyer take the initiative and propose a price: "If someone asks you the price, answer 'make me an offer,'" to show that you are "ready to make a serious effort." Make decisions about selling (and buying) very quickly; it is "out of the question to say 'I'm going to think about it.'"[39] If you have a "good thing" that you haven't managed to sell, "raise the price," and then "amazingly, it goes."[40]

The central activity in the enrichment economy, tourism, also profits from geographical displacement. But in this case the cost of things, or, rather, the cost of access to things, depends on their being rooted in a specific site. Thus movement into a tourist-welcoming site is what generates a profit, by leading buyers to spend money on the spot for food and lodging, leisure activities, and/or luxuries at a level equivalent to or higher than what they would have spent in their place of origin. Considered in terms of merchandise, tourism poses particular problems, because access to commodities is achieved by way of their distribution in a country, a region, or a site where hotels or monuments are located but where people also live. The quality of the merchandise offered for sale consequently depends on the activity and even the way of life of the locals, and above all on their greater or lesser degree of willingness to welcome visitors who come to spend their money on the residents' home ground.

This is presumably why the development of tourism is never simply an undertaking on the part of capitalist enterprises but always involves the intervention of a central government, especially in the case of cultural tourism as opposed to mass tourism (the latter can be channeled toward restricted areas, such as vacation clubs). For it is up to governmental authorities not only to assess potential dangers[41] and to guarantee the security of tourists but also to manage the quality of the greeting that tourists receive from the locals: for example, their honesty in delivering a certain number of services (restaurants, hotels, taxis, shops, and so on), their availability, and their courtesy. For these reasons, no enterprise is more naturally collective than tourism, whose success depends on the tacit coordination of a large number of participants, all of whom must have internalized the importance of the quality of welcome not only on the part of each individual with something to sell but also on the part of the collectivity as a whole. The reputation of a tourist destination depends in fact on this overall quality; once back home, those who have already visited the site are all potential influencers inclined to send new visitors that way.

Outsourcing that shifts the workplace, long-distance sales of luxury products requiring the transport of commodities, and tourism promotion that attracts customers from afar can be aligned in a series as three different processes permitting sellers to escape from the saturation of solvent demand through recourse to spatial displacements. If "enriched" products are purchased on site by tourists, it is because their enrichment is based on the overall environment in which the products are immersed and with which they are associated, through narratives, to the history of that environment. This effect is reinforced by the fact that buying things at exceptionally high prices is part of the exceptional experience of tourism. This is why luxury firms in Europe realize a very high proportion of their profits from non-European buyers. Nevertheless, these firms must also sell their wares in other countries while controlling their distribution networks as much as possible, for if the flow of tourists into a given country or region should diminish owing to security concerns, the firms need to be able to capture the same buyers elsewhere.

It is easier to understand the critique that is addressed to tourists from a moral standpoint, condemning them inasmuch as they are seen as the opposite of "travelers." Whereas travelers are presumed to seek out the unknown, whether this entails places or persons, in a logic marked by the ethics of selflessness and risk, reflecting an ideal embodied in the figure of the ethnologist on the ground, tourists are accused of going to see things with which they are already familiar, of taking no risks, and of intending to buy on site things whose authenticity is presumed to be maintained by their belonging to a "land" and a "culture." But this contrasting picture omits a third actor, the trader from afar who also shifts position, but solely to realize profit by putting commodities into circulation between two collectivities that have different ways of evaluating the things whose circulation the trader intends to monopolize. It is through opposition to such self-interested traders that the image of the traveler praised for selflessness came into being in the nineteenth century. The figure of the tourist cancels out the opposition between the remote trader and the traveler, because one of the defining features of the tourist condition is that it occupies an unstable position between selflessness and self-interest, the tourist constantly shifting from one to the other.

Shifts among forms of valuation

Still, geographical displacements are far from the only factors at issue. In many instances, in fact, by taking different forms of valuation into account, one can interpret the way objects circulate during their "economic life" as a matter of shifting from one form to another. This is the case, for example, when an object first produced and exchanged as a standard commodity is revalorized through reference to the collection form after a period during which it has had the status of trash; it can also happen when an object initially appraised according to the logic of the trend form is brought back toward the standard form in the course of successive transactions or, on the contrary, reappraised in the collection form. As for objects initially evaluated in terms of the asset form, they may have been initially relevant to one or more of the other three forms, as for example when a certain automobile, a standard product par excellence, is acquired by a celebrity, allowing it to be appraised with reference to the trend form before becoming a collectors' item likely at that point to be acquired as a placement or with the intent of reselling it quickly at a profit.

In relation to profit, the forms of valuation function in such a way as to permit displacements of things from one form to another, thus making it possible to sell at high margins, according to the logic of one form, things that, identified with reference to a different form, would have been impossible to sell except perhaps by liquidation at very low prices. This is the case when a standard object nearing the trash stage and disdained even by buyers of second-hand goods comes to be transferred into another area of sales where it can be valorized with reference to the collection form: this is evident with certain inexpensive articles of furniture, several decades old, whose prices rise considerably when they turn up in "vintage" shops, or with certain old cars that become collectors' items. The possibility that objects fitting the definition of "standard" – meaning that their prices ought inevitably to decline as they age – might migrate toward other forms of valuation, especially the collection or asset forms, permits hope that they will generate renewed profits once their use value is exhausted. A similar process accompanies the valuation according to the trend form of clothing or other objects produced industrially in low-wage countries and in a quasi-standard fashion; once these objects are transported to wealthy countries, their sales prices are incommensurable with their production costs, and consequently their sale realizes a very high profit margin.

Similar observations can be made about other forms of displacement. For example, the shift of a collectors' item to the asset form, where its substantive properties and its pertinent differences are largely lost from sight (a painting or a piece of furniture signed by its creator and treated as an asset is as likely to be found in a bank vault as in an apartment) but where its price becomes instead a defining attribute, since the possibility of reselling it at a high margin depends on potential buyers who, acquiring it with the intent of reselling it in turn at a profit, are attracted by expensive objects whose prices they think may keep on rising. Similarly, fashionable objects, having become outmoded and "uncool," can see their prices rise if they pass into the collection form, or even the asset form, if they have been in the hands of celebrities. These shifts among forms of valuation, when they are successful, allow an object to escape its otherwise inevitable transmutation into trash, whether this means becoming obsolete in the standard form, downgraded in the collection form, unfashionable in the trend form, or depreciated in the asset form.

Among the various forms of valuation, virtually all displacements are possible, but on one condition, which concerns the return toward the standard form of objects initially evaluated according to one of the other three forms. This condition holds that any object whatsoever that is pertinent in a different form can be displaced toward the standard form only if it occupies the position of prototype in that form. The possibility of such a displacement is rare for objects that find themselves in the collection form. Generally speaking, the prohibition on reproduction in effect prevents a collectors' item from becoming a standard object, although that possibility does exist; for example, a museum may offer for sale, as "derivative" products, standard reproductions said to be "identical" to masterpieces on display. By contrast, the trend form, owing to its cyclical character, can more readily bring outmoded objects to which a designer adds a slight difference back into the standard form, thus allowing the objects to serve as prototypes for a new generation of specimens.

In addition, from the commercialization of a single product one can derive a profit generated both by important per-unit margins (as in the collection form) and by the sales of a large number of specimens (as in the standard form) by playing on the diversity of marketing sites. This is the case, for example, with high-end perfumes. Let us consider a well-known Parisian perfume manufacturer. In the flagship store of the parent company, each of the flasks corresponding to a particular perfume with its own specific name is arranged as if it were a unique piece, exhibited in an elegant environment decorated in a nineteenth-century style so as to evoke aristocratic distinction, or else complemented by contemporary works of art so as to appeal to a younger, more modern clientele. The stocks are kept in the storerooms, out of sight, and the salesperson will go there to retrieve a sample once a transaction has been completed. The extensive sales staff will take the time to guide buyers, inviting them to sniff different essences sprayed onto small triangles of blotting paper that they can put under their noses, and so on. And of course regular buyers will be known in advance by the staff.

The buyer of the same perfume in a duty-free shop at an airport will have a very different experience. At a shop in one of these sites, which are presented like shopping malls, a small number of salespersons face buyers who come from all over the world and are in a hurry; some of them will shop at this site only once in a lifetime. All this gives their transactions a hasty and anonymous character. Whereas in an upscale store the act of purchasing is in a sense valorized in and of itself, an act marketers call *experiential* (it is supposed to leave a pleasant memory), in a duty-free shop the act is motivated by the hope of acquiring at lower cost something that would be more expensive elsewhere. By the same token, the standard character of the product purchased, dissimulated in the upscale store, in particular through a kind of "mythic packaging" that evokes a "limited series,"[42] is transparent in the airport shop.

Profiting from the wealthy in the capitalist cosmos

The goal of making a profit not by mass sales of specimens each unit of which delivers only a weak margin, as is the case with standard objects, but on the contrary by a maximization of the margin obtained from each unit sold, even if these are few in number, tends to direct the objects that give rise to valuation in the trend form, the collection form, and above all the asset form primarily toward wealthy consumers. In fact, only the wealthy can afford costly goods that offer a high profit margin. The development of an enrichment economy thus allows capitalism, on the one hand, to be less dependent on a mass of workers who are readily inclined to protest (an attitude viewed as "insubordination") and, on the other hand, to take advantage of the money of the wealthy (as opposed to that of the poor) and/or – and there is a difference – to take advantage of the money that circulates in wealthy countries (as opposed to poor countries); the expenditures may also be made by central governments or public collectivities rather than by private persons.

Still, compared with the expenditures made by wealthy consumers in previous centuries, those made in an enrichment economy signify something new. They no longer aim to mark the prodigality of the very rich toward those who depend on them, so as to avoid the "defaming" accusation of avarice and to make their magnificence manifest, the way Italian princes sought to do in the sixteenth century.[43] Nor are they even aimed at acquiring the sort of objects that used to allow the bourgeoisie to express their taste and distinction and to mark their distance from the lower classes. These contemporary expenditures are undoubtedly motivated by the quest for exceptional objects and by the enjoyment procured by access to exclusive and comfortable places. But they can also be financially profitable, and in this respect they are inscribed in a new way within the capitalist universe. In fact, the objects that give rise to such expenditures and that are accessible only to the wealthy – hotels or luxury products, exceptional apartments, art objects and antiques, and so on – are also, with increasing intensity, objects of investment for profit centers that expect to reap returns.

Such returns on an investment do not directly reach all the actors who have made luxury expenditures on their own account. But it enriches as a whole the class of those who have interests in the profit centers that are at the heart of an enrichment economy, which is itself integrated into economic and financial circuits on a broad scale. The individual expenditures of the wealthy thus collectively enrich the dominant classes. The extension of capitalism to new objects destined for wealthy consumers allows these consumers to participate individually, through their expenditures, in the prosperity of capital – that is, in their own enrichment insofar as it is collective; despite the competition between them when they are doing business, this level of participation helps create solidarity among them. All have an interest in ensuring the maintenance of the commercial value of the goods from which they profit, both as users and as owners. It is thus no exaggeration to say that, if exploitation of the poor, which has long been the mark of capitalism, impoverishes the poor, this newer sort of "exploitation" or profiteering tends to enrich the rich. Wealthy individuals of course always draw part of their income from exploitation of the poor, in particular in an indirect way through the intermediary of the profits realized in the financial economy, in the digital economy, and in direct investments abroad that continue to underwrite standard production. But this type of economy still tends, at least in Western Europe, to deprive the poor of the minimal social utility that the possibility of being exploited brought them – that is, the possibility of figuring among the potential sources of the enrichment of the rich. This is no doubt the basis for the affirmation, at once true and false, and often repeated over the past few decades, that exploitation has disappeared, to be replaced by "exclusion."

It can thus be said that the development of an economy of enrichment in the former industrial countries where the wealthy are always most numerous – a phenomenon that accompanies the displacement of mass industries toward peripheral countries where the majority of the population is poor – exploits to the outer limits the possibilities offered by trade in commodities to generate the profits on which capitalism feeds. This is achieved by various means: valorizing things cast aside or "remaindered" through the intermediary of the collection form, which allows for the recuperation of trash; intensifying the rhythm of the processes of obsolescence by way of the extension given to the trend form, which, conversely, leads to the relegation of scarcely used things to the trash bin; or attenuating the difference between material things and their monetary equivalent by making a profit from the circulation of things treated virtually as though they were financial products, something that is permitted by the asset form. To mark the specificity of the type of capitalism that benefits from the four forms of valuation we have identified, we shall use the term *integral capitalism*.

Integral capitalism does not escape the characterization of capitalism that stresses a requirement of unlimited accumulation, but it pursues accumulation by extending the cosmos of commodities, by exploiting new strata of wealth, and by articulating different ways of valorizing things and putting them in circulation with a view to maximizing profits. As we see it, this regime of capitalism, in association with the development of the financial economy and the digital economy, favors the growth of an enrichment economy. The latter is articulated with another process that has been noteworthy since the 1990s on a worldwide scale, namely, the expansion of mass production and of the type of capitalism associated in Europe with the industrial revolution into regions of the world that had previously remained largely rural. It is conceivable that the development of the enrichment economy can be attributed by and large to that expansion and the profits it generates, including in countries undergoing deindustrialization, primarily by way of financial circuits. In addition, in countries where the enrichment economy is becoming increasingly important, the sale of standard objects entirely or partially produced in the countries to which mass production has been shifted continues to play an important and even a predominant economic role.

But a defining feature of the enrichment economy is that it feeds on profits drawn from trade in things that, even when they are manufactured industrially, give rise to a valorization based above all on the other three forms we have identified. The enrichment economy is thus associated with particular ways of exploiting a highly qualified local workforce on which responsibility for the tasks of valorization falls. In this sense, the profits generated by this economy depend in part on the extraction of surplus labor value. Nevertheless, a defining feature of the enrichment economy is that it wagers on arrangements that allow an extraction of a surplus market value that is undoubtedly much greater than is currently the case for standard objects, which face a high level of competition. Let us also recall that, whereas a mass economy is oriented toward exploitation of the poor, either as workers or as consumers, the enrichment economy is oriented toward profiting from the wealthy. Now, as Braudel's analyses show, it is above all on trade in "rare" or luxury goods intended for the wealthy that the possibility of particularly high surplus market value relies.

As these remarks suggest, integral capitalism is not an avatar of capitalism that could be characterized as "post-modern" in the sense that it would no longer rely on profits drawn from surplus labor value, or even on the manufacture and circulation of material things. Rather, it is a form of capitalism whose flexibility allows it to profit from a much larger gamut of things than in the past, things whose diversity is not only maintained but valorized in such a way as to exploit the *differences* that are instituted among several states of commodities. This is the case even as these states are integrated into a single force field within which financial flows (which are strictly a matter of accounting, and are therefore indifferent to the material specificities of the objects and arrangements that sustain them) create a form of interdependence or even a sort of solidarity among the holders of capital.

Nevertheless, on this basis of tacit solidarity, struggles take place for the appropriation of benefits that depend on the way the differences among things in the various forms that we have identified are exploited. These struggles have to be considered in relation to the question of who controls the determination and the valorization of the differences – that is, in relation to the question of the *power* that, in the context of capitalism, is manifested especially through the ability of an actor to highlight certain differences under that actor's control, and thereby to devalue the differences from which competitors count on profiting. In industrial economies based on the standard form, the principal agent of production, whether this is the owner of the means of production or an agent reporting to stockholders, has control over the description of the pertinent features of a product, expressed in the form of standard properties, which concern both the prototype and the specimens that reproduce it; the agent seeks to maintain and protect these properties through recourse to the legal system, intellectual property law in particular. In the case of the asset form, those who hold power over the pertinent differences among commodities are those who, whether they are owners or not, can base differences of appreciation on assessments bearing on the future, especially on future profits; when they also have access to enough capital, this capacity can help make such assessments become reality. If we consider, finally, the appreciation of objects that fall under the collection form, we note that control generally belongs to the agent holding the power to define the pertinent differences among the objects in question, differences on which the assessment of their value will depend.

One of the significant differences between industrial and enrichment economies has to do, however, with the fact that, in an enrichment economy, the agents – persons or institutions – that compose the narratives incorporating the descriptions of differences on which the value of things depends, narratives ensuring the validity of the commodities in question, have to be viewed as relatively independent from the agents that can profit financially from the appreciation and circulation of those commodities – independent, most notably, from the agents that hold the property, unless the goods under consideration belong to the public. Despite this provision of independence, which stipulates "disinterestedness," owners retain significant power over the valorization of objects. But this power is manifested indirectly in relation to the degree to which the owners have control over those responsible for composing the narratives presenting differences, and thus they retain the ability to twist to their own benefit a discourse purporting to be truthful that is reinforced by institutions and generally, in France at least, by agencies dependent on the state. This indirect power plays a crucial role when the items held are capitalized. It is quite conceivable that the arrangements associated with the collection form confer a much greater stability on the determination of the value of objects than is the case for industrial objects and especially for financial assets. The construction of a narrative of the past is based on very large institutions and often has national underpinnings, so that, once established, it proves more robust than a narrative dealing with the future or even one wagering on the present.

12

The Enrichment Economy in Practice

Thus far, in describing the enrichment economy and the collection form, we have focused on their broad historical and structural dimensions. However, the development of this economy and the extension of the collection form of valuation have been incorporated into changes at the local level in quite variable ways. These changes have affected both urban and rural enrichment basins. The former have received greater attention: Bilbao and Barcelona are exemplary, because the transformations in cities have been embodied by emblematic buildings such as the Guggenheim Museum or made visible through exceptional events such as the Olympic Games.

We seek to show how such mutations can also occur in rural enrichment basins and in small cities, where, although they may take less well-known forms, they are at least as spectacular, radically upsetting social relations, economic activity, and uses of space. A case study will allow us to show the practice of enrichment as it unfolds by bringing to light the way actors take hold of local resources and produce narratives. We base our observations primarily on a field study carried out in the Aubrac region in France, more particularly in the village of Laguiole.[1] In this instance, a dynamic that was initiated in the 1980s calls upon the various pertinent features of the enrichment economy that we have identified: the declining importance of the old form of wealth creation centered on livestock; a rise in tourism; the phenomenon of heritage creation at various sites; high-end gastronomy; the development of narratives about the past (for the most part invented); and the institution of a process for manufacturing – producing knives, in this case – that is represented as ancestral and local, a process whose valuation rests principally on the collection form and to a lesser degree on the trend form. In the twenty-first century, the "artisanal" manufacturing of objects that have been produced industrially in the city of Thiers since the nineteenth century is encountering competition from objects bearing the same name – standard products now outsourced to low-wage countries (China and Pakistan).

An enriched village: Laguiole in Aubrac

The village of Laguiole was profoundly transformed between the 1960s and the 2010s. As we see from a large-scale study undertaken in the early 1960s as a cooperative research project (RCP) under the auspices of the French National Center for Scientific Research (CNRS) by a team of social scientists led by Georges-Henri Rivière,[2] the village was then the principal center and the most populated area of the Aubrac Aveyronnais. Whereas the other communes of this region had fewer than 800 inhabitants in 1962, and the dominant professional activity by a wide margin was raising livestock, Laguiole had around 1,200 inhabitants, and only 46 percent of the active workforce was engaged in agriculture; of the rest, about 20 percent worked in business, banking, insurance, or the hotel industry, around 15 percent in private and public services, and 10 percent in the construction industry.[3] Laguiole was typical of the region in that its principal industry was livestock breeding, along with cheesemaking. The highly detailed information provided by the CNRS study includes no mention of knives. The researchers intended to add items from this region to a collection (they took a *buron*, a traditional shepherd's cottage, back with them) destined for a museum of folk arts and traditions, in conjunction with an empirical scientific study.[4]

The basic issue in the "economic anthropology" part of the study was set forth by Jean Cuisenier, a participant in the RCP who later succeeded Georges-Henri Rivière as director of the Museum of Folk Arts and Traditions in Paris:

> Research project on the economic and social implications of the changes in livestock breeding and animal products in the Aubrac and on the future prospects for the placement of their products.
>
> A cooperative research project has been undertaken focusing on the Aubrac region ... From the standpoint of economic anthropology, the Aubrac region is in fact of special interest. A large portion of the resources of the population comes from livestock raising according to ancestral techniques and methods. Thus there is a whole network of quite particular economic flows that need to be grasped: flows between villages in the zone of summer grazing and neighboring villages, between owners and the herders in the "*burons*," between agricultural exploitations and farm families ...
>
> But the livestock economy in the Aubrac region is condemned to disappear in its traditional form. Its products – animals for butchery and cheeses from Laguiole – have to adapt to new forms of commercialization and to the constraints created by the opening of the national frontiers to a vast Common Market ... How can the shift from a traditional livestock economy to a highly industrial economy be accomplished?[5]

Fifty years later, the activity of the village, now counting 1,300 inhabitants, is chiefly oriented toward the visitors who come through all year round and overwhelm it in the summer. Tourism has developed gradually in the region, in part because people from the Aveyron area who have moved to Paris tend to come back during their summer vacations, something that had already been noted in the 1960s by one of the researchers who participated in the RCP Aubrac: "While in 1910 the returning émigrés still quickly resumed their old ways of doing things, those who come back to Aubrac now are for the most part Parisians on vacation who come to rest and have a good time during the period when everyone in the village is working."[6] Nevertheless, until the 1980s, as the local tourist guidebook explains (written in its first edition by a priest, Father Calmels, then updated by Abbot Ginisty), the attractive elements highlighted were mainly the forest ("one of the great tourist attractions"), the church, a museum "owing to the initiative of Canon Gaidou," which "makes it possible to preserve and show to visitors some of the most characteristic objects of life in earlier times," cheese, and festivals (held August 8 and September 25).[7]

From that point on, tourism became an economic activity that has generated at least 3,000 salaried positions in the department of Aveyron. Revenues from touristic activity rose from 163 million euros in 1993 to 360 million in 2011. Still, with its 11 million hotel nights in 2011, Aveyron came in far behind a department such as Hérault, with more than 40 million nights that same year. The tourists who came to Aveyron during that period included families (41 percent), couples (39 percent), and single individuals (only 5 percent). These visitors were primarily from the middle classes: 26 percent retirees, 23 percent salaried workers, 14 percent from intermediary professions, and 6 percent blue-collar workers, as opposed to 20 percent from upper management and the higher intellectual professions. The estimated average daily expenditure per person of these tourists, who were almost all French (nine out of ten), came to about 32 euros.[8]

Still, one restaurant with an international reputation for its chefs, Michel Bras and his son Sébastien, attracted a wealthy clientele. Three interconnected attractions oriented the crowds of visitors in the 2000s: the knives, the natural setting, and the food, along with the occasional festivals. During our site visit to Laguiole in August 2013, an owner of vacation rental properties told us that "there's no unemployment here; everyone has a job"; "government ministers often come here," because "it's pretty much exemplary." He explained this by listing an assortment of things: the "high-quality" Aubrac cheese and wine, the knives, and the Aubrac plateau ("it's a special landscape").[9]

As it happens, all these activities take the form of heritage creation: that is, they exist as if they have been there forever and had to be preserved over the long run in order to maintain an "identity" that would draw its power from its rootedness in the terrain. Heritage creation can be defined as the shaping and presentation of a material or materializable element, as if it were inseparable from the land (the *terroir*) in which it had been present from its "origin," thus as if it possessed a memorial power making its survival imperative. To create a heritage site as part of the patrimony, at least three types of operation are required: one must show the origin of the element, bring it up to date as much as possible in order to project it into the future, and determine a minimal number of factors justifying the claim that "the same element" has been present from the beginning. The greatest continuity is ensured by narratives and place names: these ensure heritage creation by associating a site, a time period, and some specific element. This is why place names (Aubrac and Laguiole, in the case in point) are central stakes in the process. But the problem with words is that they circulate and can come to designate quite different things, thereby threatening the "identity" of the elements. This leads to interventions by institutions that are endowed – especially by the legal system – with the power to regulate and even prevent the circulation of words by reserving them for certain persons or certain uses: for example, by creating an *appellation d'origine contrôlée* (AOC) that restricts the use of a given label to products with a specified provenance and manner of production.

The transformation of habitats through heritage creation

Heritage creation transforms human habitats in two ways. First, their appearance has to be modified so as to create a look that mixes the "ancestral" past with the present. What must be rejected and effaced insofar as possible are marks of the recent past. Thus plaster is removed from walls to reveal the underlying stones, creating the appearance of "yesteryear" – that is, making the walls look as they are presumed to have looked in the nineteenth century. Inside buildings, other evidence of an earlier era is exposed: for example, a black-and-white photo of the local school taken in the early twentieth century decorates the principal guest house in Laguiole. This house, a former Catholic school run by nuns, has been set up primarily for hikers, along with a bookstore. Farms on the outskirts of the village have turned into bed-and-breakfast establishments. But, like the school, these farms – the Moulhacs', for example – have integrated contemporary elements in their décor as well. The B&B and the farm are owned by village residents whose families have been there for several generations and had previously made their living from other activities (in selling hardware and other items in the first case, in agriculture and livestock breeding in the second).

Nevertheless, visitors to Laguiole generally do not stay very long. The B&B takes in hikers who rarely stay more than one or two nights.[10] The Moulhac farm attracts a more affluent clientele, people who come to enjoy the cuisine at the Bras' restaurant and stay two or three nights.[11] However, the wealthiest tourists can stay on the restaurant site: the Bras' establishment includes a hotel complex, contemporary in design, on a promontory that overlooks the village.

New "traditional festivals" in the village

The transformation of the built environment in Laguiole, both in appearance and in function (a school and a farm converted into tourist lodgings), has been accompanied by a mutation in community activities. Fairs used to take place there several times a year – hence the name "Place du foirail" for the main town square – but these have disappeared. Twelve fairs were held in 1965, which accounts for the long-standing availability of large numbers of hotel rooms.[12]

However, several new festivals featuring "ancestral traditions" have been instituted. Perhaps the most noteworthy is the festival of the fatted steers, celebrated at Easter on the square called "la place du nouveau foirail" ("the square of the new fair"), which dates back only to 2000. But it highlights a race of cattle that is also "ancestral": the Aubrac line. Around 200 steers of related lineage – Aubrac, Fleur d'Aubrac (a hybrid between Aubrac and Charolais), and other organically raised animals of Aubrac lineage are exhibited and entered in a competition at the end of which winners are designated, breeders and butchers do business, and meals featuring beef are organized.

Heritage creation around food

Food and gastronomy are thus also pivotal elements in heritage creation. In addition to Aubrac beef, other food products are highlighted in Laguiole as locally produced: an orange-blossom brioche called a *fouace*, honey, jam, dried *cèpes* (boletus mushrooms), and especially cheese. The eponymous Laguiole cheese has been protected by an *appellation d'origine* since 1961. It is used to cook *aligot*, a dish made of mashed potatoes and melted cheese.

While the cuisine of the restaurants at the heart of the village is centered mainly on dishes based on beef, aligot, and cheese, it takes a more sophisticated – and more costly – form in the Bras family restaurant, whose reputation is based on the high marks awarded by the major gastronomic guides and where reservations are made several weeks or even months in advance. However, even on the Bras menu one finds a mix of contemporary and traditional dishes, blending local products and methods that can be called avant-garde in the field of haute cuisine. This alliance is also found in the restaurant opened by Bras in the museum of contemporary art in Rodez, featuring paintings by Pierre Soulages; this museum, opened in May 2014, received 250,000 visitors during its first year.

The menu listing the offerings of the Bras brasserie at the Soulages museum consists in descriptions of dishes that exploit local history:

> The *fouace* is a traditional cake typical of the Aveyronnais region. Its recipe respects tradition to the letter, producing a dense but tender dough, perfumed with orange blossoms.

Tripes used to be served before mass, or after a hunting party ... Each region in the Aveyron has its own particular recipe.

Cold cuts preserved in salt, dried, smoked, or served fresh are characteristic of the Aveyron.

The *bourriol*, a galette made from rye flour, wheat flour, and potatoes dampened with whey was once a replacement for bread.

The wine list is divided into two categories: "From here" (Estaing, Côtes de Millau, Marcillac, etc.) and "From nearby" (Gaillac, Jurançon, Languedoc, Corbières, etc.).

A landscape to contemplate

The Bras family stresses not only the products used in cooking but also the Aubrac landscape itself as an anchoring point. As the restaurant's presentation brochure explains: "Here on the Aubrac plateau we live according to the rhythm of nature. For if we can keep on preparing local dishes, it's because nature is at the heart of every moment of every day." The building, designed by architects Éric Raffy and Philippe Villeroux, was built in 1992; it has large bay windows offering panoramic views.

This landscape "to be contemplated" is also an attraction for hikers, for Laguiole is located on one of the paths leading to Santiago de Compostela. The effort to carve out new hiking paths in order to expand "green tourism" further has run into obstacles, however: most of the surrounding lands are private, so the permission of the owners must be obtained before paths crossing the land can be created.

The logic of heritage creation focused on the land itself may lead to its designation as a regional nature preserve; an association dedicated to the project has been working on it since 2002.

The association's website justifies the project of a regional natural park by bringing together terms such as "patrimony" and "territory," "vulnerability" and "preservation," and also "valorization:"

A semi-mountainous rural region, the Aubrac has a *patrimony* that is still well preserved. Its rural economy, its landscapes, its skills and knowledge, its environment, and its *cultural heritage*, all widely recognized assets, are nevertheless *vulnerable and threatened.*

To *preserve* and *valorize* the treasures of this exceptional *territory*, local communities, the state, and relevant professional groups have undertaken to create a regional natural park.[13]

The development of such a park, like the "protection" of the *appellations*, makes it clear that heritage creation in France takes place owing to a mix of local private and public actions implicating the national government. It is not constituted on the model of a public "problem" in the sense that it would be subject to criticism, indignation, or scandal. Dissent focuses, rather, on the way the costs and benefits are distributed. Each project of heritage creation is based on a local collective "identity" attached to a "territory" – here, the residents of Laguiole and beyond, those of the surrounding Aubrac area, with their local way of speaking, which was once scorned but has become a point of pride (for example, Laguiole residents insist on pronouncing the village name in the old way, as "layol" rather than as "laguiol" with a hard "g"). The self-awareness of this community is established through a sense of belonging based in particular on family names and the presence of forebears ("he comes from here").

In the 1960s, according to the RCP, "the revenues from craftsmanship in Aubrac were less than 10 percent of the revenues from agriculture," and, in Laguiole itself, "crafts were virtually non-existent" except in vestigial forms; the only continuing activities were those "tied to building construction and maintenance" (the extraction of raw materials, structural work, electricity, roofing).[14] During a work session in Paris in 1965, one researcher estimated that, "in Aubrac, there are few artisans," while another observed that in Born there were "no artisans; everybody works along 'do-it-yourself' lines."[15] In Laguiole, the local dignitaries at the time were the notary and the priest, and on the day of the Fête-Dieu the whole village knelt in the streets and prayed aloud.[16] In the 2010s, there was no longer a priest in the village, but the enrichment economy had brought a new social hierarchy to the surface, with private entrepreneurs at the top. These business owners exploited the past both for personal enrichment and for the benefit of the community; some became involved in public life as well. The "Aubrac house" (where a *buron* is on display) and the now defunct Museum of Folk Arts and Traditions (with the offices of the regional natural park project nearby) were financed in the 2010s by four local businesses: the cheese cooperative of Laguiole, the Bras gastronomic enterprise, the cutlery makers of La Forge, and a distillery.

Cutlery valorized by the collection form

At the heart of the heritage creation on which the village of Laguiole embarked lay a treasure: the eponymous knife.

In the early twentieth century, the name "Laguiole" was routinely applied, in France and elsewhere, to a knife of a certain form: foldable, with a handle made of plastic, wood, or horn and finished with metal ends, one of which held the blade and was decorated with a bee motif.

Yet the knives known as "Laguiole" that could be found most often for sale in France and in the world were not those produced in Laguiole. Only a small number of knives were produced in the village; these were presented and sold as artisanal products, at relatively high prices. A large number of inexpensive Laguiole knives were manufactured according to standardized processes in factories located in China and in Pakistan.

Why were Laguiole knives produced in a standardized way far from their namesake village? Why did village residents keep on producing limited numbers of knives, often with slight differences from one another, in the "artisanal" way, when there was a market, in France and beyond, where far more knives that all looked alike could be sold more cheaply?

To answer these questions, we cannot fall back on an explanation according to which the village "missed the boat" on the way to industrialization and did not know how to convert its businesses by scaling them up for a worldwide market so as to export knives produced in a standardized way, nor can it be argued that local enterprises outsourced their production to China and Pakistan because the labor costs were too high in France. These claims are unacceptable because between the 1920s and the 1980s hardly any knives at all were produced in Laguiole. While knives were indeed made there in the nineteenth century, their production gradually came to a halt after the First World War. A few businesses continued to sell this type of knife, but they got their stock from Thiers, the major industrial center of cutlery in France.

As it happened, during the 1980s, while the last cutlery factories in Thiers were closing, giving way to workshops of fewer than a dozen people, members of the municipal council in Laguiole wanted to launch the local artisanal production of knives. Four young people received training. As one of them explains: "We didn't know where we were going, we didn't know what we were going to do, we were just told that 'we want to give you a little boost but afterward you'll have to create a business.' And we did."[17] A few years later, the enterprise "La Forge de Laguiole" was created in the village. During the 2010s, Laguiole was invaded every summer by mobs of tourists who came to buy knives from one of some twenty outlets, all of them selling knives produced locally.

The "artisanal" manufacture of a knife in Laguiole

A knife made in Laguiole is composed of a blade, a handle, and bolsters. Three sorts of blades are used: carbon steel, stainless steel, and Damascus steel. The carbon blade, which was widely used in the nineteenth century and a little less often in the early twenty-first century, has the "disadvantage" of oxidizing and blackening in contact with an acid substance (as found in certain fruits or vegetables, such as tomatoes). Stainless steel blades are the ones in most common use today. A Damascus blade is a laminate composed of several layers of steel bent and hammered together like the layers in puff pastry; it is known for its hardness and slicing ability. The materials most commonly used for the handle are horn and wood, but other materials such as plastic or ivory are occasionally found. The two bolsters, made of brass or galvanized steel, encircle the handle and protect the knife from damage when it is folded.

Several steps are required to make a knife: preparation of the parts, assembly, fine-tuning, and polishing. Cutlers say they can make a "standard" knife ("the simplest model," for example a 12 centimeter-long two-piece knife with a horn handle) in forty-five minutes to an hour. However, to make a more sophisticated knife, a "collectors' item," can take several hours.

In the larger enterprises, the production process may look more like "standardization." Whereas the Honoré Durand company, which employs sixteen cutlers, is said to produce around 20,000 units a year, La Forge de Laguiole declares that it makes around 120,000 per year. Quality control, which is characteristic of standard manufacturing procedures and which makes it possible to minimize the differences between objects, plays a decisive role, but it is in constant tension with what is presented as an artisanal activity:

In one of the major cutlery-producing facilities in Laguiole, once the knives are polished they undergo quality control, the last step before they are released for sale. "We do visual quality control," a guide explains to visitors. "We look for the slightest little flaw; we'll find it. Our rate of return to the shop is between 20 and 25 percent; that's a lot. But remember that these are knives created by men and women, with natural materials, so there's a double possibility of error or defect – both from the human side and from the material – which is natural. So we inevitably have more flaws with wood or horn than with synthetic materials. When the knives are inspected, when we find defects, we send them back to the shops they came from. If it's just a matter of polishing, we send them to the polishers. Or if the problem is in the handle, because a piece of horn is split, we send it back to the work-shop: the cutler will break the knife down, unscrew the two blades, change the two sides and put it back together; then it will be sent to the polisher and, normally, back for a second quality control."[18]

"Cutlery" is one of the crafts recognized by a governmental decree since 2003. The decree is worded in terms of opposition to industrial manufacture, as attested by an editorial devoted to knives from the trade journal *Excalibur*:

In France, but also elsewhere in Europe, the advent of the industrial era dealt a heavy blow to the arts and crafts. For many of these trades the blow was fatal. Fortunately, handicrafts today, which carry forward skills and traditions that are often centuries old, are rising up from the ashes and becoming once again a major economic component of our society, employing nearly five million people. Artisanal cutlery, too, has come a long way, because it had almost disappeared completely ... Since then, interest in cutlery, especially high-end knives, has never flagged.[19]

Artisanal production is characterized by individual responsibility for production, and this is what distinguishes it, at bottom, from standardization. Each cutler makes a knife from beginning to end: "'There is no assembly line, everyone makes his own knife from A to Z, everyone is responsible for his own work,' a guide in a cutlery workshop explains. 'Everyone works for himself, not for others. We always talk about knife-making from A to Z. Every cutler starts his own knife and finishes it.'"[20]

Standardization is presented as a practice that uses workers who make the same components, assembly-line fashion, aided by robots, while artisans are said to produce single objects personally, with their own hands, from their individual workbenches. "In our shop, the assembly is not going to be done by machines or robots. It's going to be done by hand," a guide in a different cutlery workshop declares.

If several cutlers are employed by a given company and are not working on a freelance basis, each one of them is still encouraged to be a "businessman in his own right" – that is, to valorize his own "know-how." In fact, the work is organized so as to establish a link between the object produced and the specific person who produced it. In this sense, the link is modeled on the one between a work of art and the artist who made it with his own hands, invoking a conception of art pre-dating the one that had been developing in embryonic form since the 1960s and more forcefully since the 1990s, according to which a work of art is conceived, moreover, as an object that can be executed by someone other than the artist but according to rules set down by the artist and with the artist's signature.[21] This latter conception has been generalized in the contemporary art market but it is challenged by defenders of tradition who are conservative where art is concerned and who continue to refer to the earlier conception. The artisanal enterprise is thus organized according to the logic of "the author's hand," which makes it possible to present certain pieces explicitly as works of art, collectors' items, and in the process to draw all the other pieces presented in the same direction.

A collectable knife

To understand the social change in which the knives made in Laguiole are immersed, we need to recall the way knives were used in the "original past" – that is, in the nineteenth century. They were first used by farmers who made their living from livestock breeding and agriculture. As quite a few Laguiole residents had moved to Paris, like a large number of others from the Aveyron region (known as "bougnats"), to work in restaurants and cafes, the Laguiole knife was enhanced with a corkscrew so it could take on the new function of opening wine bottles.

What became valorized later, in the knives made in the early twenty-first century, was their durability: in the cutlers' words, they were "guaranteed for life." Generally speaking, the local cutlers promised to repair any knife made in Laguiole. Still, since the processes of production have evolved over the last couple of decades, La Forge de Laguiole acknowledges that replacement parts for the knives made during the first few years of the company's existence are no longer available.

Laguiole knives are durable because they are made of "quality" materials and because they are made by hand. The most prized specimens are not the ones that have the greatest use value but, rather, those that are destined to be collected. These latter are often made by cutlers who have been designated *meilleur ouvrier de France* (best worker in France) or are in the running for that title. Thus La Forge de Laguiole has two *meilleurs ouvriers* in its employ: they work across from one another on separate workbenches near the entry to the shop, making one-off items. Another cutler, "Benoît l'artisan," makes it known that he, too, was a finalist in the 2011 competition for the title. Another *meilleur ouvrier de France*, Jean-Michel Cayron, works for the Honoré Durand company, as the guide leading a visit to that shop explains: "And now to show you the quality of the work we do here, this is a piece made by Jean-Michel Cayron. You're seeing 250 hours of work. The handle is ivory. The knife is appraised at €13,000. Our cutler made this blade when he was twenty-three years old. And it's thanks to this kind of work that he has twice been named *meilleur ouvrier de France*, the first time in 2007 and again in 2011."

What is valued now in a worker's performance is no longer a reduction in production time, as was the case for workers immersed in the universe of industrial production, but on the contrary an extraordinary lengthening of production time – from 45 minutes to 250 hours for a single object, crafted by a single creator.

Still, the logic of the second definition of a work of art, according to which a work is executed according to rules set by an artist and is then signed by that artist even though he or she did not produce it personally by hand, can be found again as soon as a company hires a designer, relying here on the trend form. Thus La Forge de Laguiole has called on several highly regarded designers, such as Philippe Starck, Matali Crasset, Christian Ghion, Andrée Putnam, and Ora-ïto. These designers "interpret" the Laguiole knife, sometimes very freely, so that the form of the resulting product bears little resemblance to the most common form of a "Laguiole," as is the case for example with a cake knife designed by Matali Crasset for the pastry chef Pierre Hermé.

The "simplest" knives benefit from this proximity to the most "sophisticated" and most costly products. So that they will have a unique character, they are often personalized: the cutlery companies, including the largest, La Forge de Laguiole, offer to engrave the name or the initials of the recipient on the blade, conferring on it an exclusive, visible difference.

Laguiole knives are inscribed in a larger movement of collecting knives and bladed weapons. Some knives even have no use value at all: "For some, the knife is the preferred medium for artistic work. The American Fred Carter, like his compatriot Gary Blanchard, makes knives that he sculpts and engraves. The object looks exactly like a knife, but the blade is neither tempered nor sharpened: it is an art object intended for display."[22]

In the 2010s, knife collecting is probably less dynamic and less prestigious than collecting luxury products such as leather goods by Hermès or Rolex watches. This is why, as an article in the journal *Excalibur* explains, knives "are not really the best niche if one is thinking about safe placements" – that is, about assets – but "one should, rather, consider the law of supply and demand to the extent that an enthusiast always agrees to pay more to obtain the item he or she has been coveting for a long time."[23] Still, this is the same logic of collecting that is shared with other types of collectors: "To be a collector is necessarily to have a good nose, to be able to sniff out a good opportunity when a model is put on the market. If [the knife] has been made in very small numbers and if it has met with great success, its price, 'under the table,' may climb toward the highest peaks."[24]

The peaks in question are of course far from those reached by contemporary art. Nevertheless, at prices that can rise above 20,000 euros, as is the case for knives made by Jean-Michel Cayron, or for those of the best American cutlers, whose prices can range between 10,000 and 20,000 dollars,[25] these artisanal knives far outstrip standard industrially produced knives that are sold for a few euros and destined to be thrown away.

Museification as a means of commercialization

For a work to qualify as a work of art, some arrangement for eligibility – often a consortium plus the walls of a gallery or a museum – is required. Similarly, objects such as the knives made in Laguiole, in order to be offered for sale as collectables rather than standard items, have to be presented in an equivalent arrangement.

This staging is less likely to take place in contemporary art galleries – which generally display works alone, without their creators, except in the case of performances where the artist appears on stage – than in museums, particularly museums of ethnology and folklore. The private cutlery firms in Laguiole, from the smallest to the largest, are presented to visitors as living museums in which what is on display is not only the object for sale but the activity of the person who made it; these firms are thus expressly participating in "craft tourism." Here, the artisan's body is no longer that of a worker disciplined by the bourgeoisie so his labor power can be exploited within a barracks-like factory; it is, rather, the embodiment, to be admired, of a presumed "ancestral" skill, wholly integrated into a museum-like space.

Certain businesses, such as La Forge de Laguiole, Honoré Durand, and Benoît l'artisan, offer guided tours of their workshops at specified times, the way one might offer tours of a chateau, and they attract large numbers. In 2012, Honoré Durand received an estimated 175,000 visitors and La Forge de Laguiole about 85,000[26] (in comparison, the cooperative Jeune Montagne, which offers tours of its cheese production facility, received 134,500 visitors). At Benoît l'artisan, the tour takes place in three stages: an employee begins with a history of the Laguiole knife and a presentation of the company; then, in the workshop, a cutler explains how a knife is made; finally, the first employee takes the visitors into the shop where knives are sold. At La Forge de Laguiole, in addition to guided tours, wall panels explain the various activities of the employees at work, while in the entry hall the knives for sale are arranged like art objects in glass cases, with discreet tags indicating their prices; if a designer was involved, there is a larger label naming the "artist" who designed the knife. The Honoré Durand company has taken the enterprise of museification the furthest by setting up, next to the sales area and the demonstration space, a "museum" announced as such, where tools and knives from Laguiole dating mainly from the nineteenth and early twentieth centuries are on display. Guided tours provide opportunities to attach stories to these objects.

In the late nineteenth century, a study by Camille Pagé in six volumes presented an exhaustive view of cutlery "from its origins" up to the time of writing, with a principal focus on the then current situation. The bulk of the work is devoted to the cutlery industry in Châtellerault, where the work was printed, and to that of Thiers; only a few lines deal with cutlery in Laguiole. Mention is made of the workshops of Pagès, Calmel, Mas, and Glaize, which employed about thirty workers and produced knives that were "solid" but that left "something to be desired where finish is concerned." In comparison, the number of cutlery workers in the administrative districts of Thiers and Saint-Rémy was estimated at between 15,000 and 18,000,[27] employed by 600 to 700 manufacturers. According to the mayor of Laguiole, cited by Pagé: "A knife very much in vogue in this region is called a *capujadou*: the blade is very thick, and it does not close; it is a kind of dagger that looks a little like a Corsican horn. Like the old sheath knives, it needs a case so it can be put in a pocket."[28]

Indeed, the Laguiole knife featured in the illustration is a straight knife, without a corkscrew or a trocar (a sharp-pointed surgical instrument): in short, it looks nothing like the "Laguiole" in its most common twenty-first-century form.

If the RCP Aubrac study essentially devotes no attention to knife-making in Laguiole in the 1960s but instead stresses the importance of trout farming and cheese production (described as "well known" but assessed as having "not much of a future" because they are not "modern"),[29] it is not because the researchers failed to see an activity that was right there under their noses – only one cutler is mentioned in the report – but because, as was the case with other artisanal trades such as "sawyers, joiners, clog makers, and millers," among which cutlers figure without distinction, the activity of knife-making, if it had not disappeared altogether, no longer existed except as a "relic." In the 1970s, the knives sold at the few available outlets in Laguiole had been purchased from manufacturers in Thiers, as a retired merchant explains:

> In the 1970s, only C. sold knives. Most of the knives he sold were made in Thiers. He gave himself a certain air of mystery by leading

his customers to believe that he made practically all his knives and that he was more or less the one who ensured Laguiole's knife-making skills. I knew the P. women, both widows. From my early childhood on, I don't remember having seen any knives made in their store. At the start, the G. cutlery was a bistro where he sold knives in the back. At the rear of the store there was a cutlery workshop. He also sold fishing and hunting equipment in the bistro. G. bought his knives from an artisan in Thiers who had a business with two or three workers. G. even had business cards made where you saw a cutlery workshop in the rear. He said he had taken over the P. work-shop, and he posted the year of foundation, but it was all smoke and mirrors.[30]

The narratives offered by cutlery workshops in the early twenty-first century begin with the origin of the knife, situated in the early nineteenth century. One guide in a shop claimed that the form of the Laguiole knife resulted from a crossing of a Spanish knife with an older local knife:

The Laguiole knife is about two hundred years old, but it was originally Spanish. Why? Because in those days, in Auvergne, there wasn't much work in the region, and young men left for Spain to find jobs. It was a young guy from the region who wanted to buy a typically Spanish knife, a *navaja*. The navaja is a knife like this [he showed a knife]. He bought it, brought it back to Laguiole, showed it to more or less everybody. People told him that he had a good knife, but that it wasn't very practical, because the handle was all twisted and hard to hold. So the people in Laguiole, what they did was, they took that knife and took it apart, they modified it to make it more like a knife that was already typical of the region, the old Laguiole, and put the two together – that's how the [new] Laguiole knife got its shape.[31]

The story sometimes features an idealized image of a nineteenth-century shepherd in this Catholic region, associating another product of the "*terroir*," cheese, when it comes to interpreting the sign of the cross found on certain knives: "'On one side of the knife,' a guide explains, 'you drew a sign of the cross. And that cross is called the shepherd's cross, because the shepherd, when he was working in the fields, would take out his Laguiole and stick it into a piece of bread or a piece of cheese, and he said his prayers before he started.'"[32]

But these stories can vary from one cutler to another. Thus when it comes to interpreting the origin of the bee design on the knives, one will bring in Napoleon, another will refer to the natural setting (the landscape):

One guide in a workshop explains: "A Laguiole knife, it has several symbols, and the most famous one of course is the bee. According to a legend, it was Emperor Napoleon the First in person who authorized the people living in Laguiole to put that bee on their knives, it was to thank them for fighting bravely in his armies."

But a salesman in another shop, questioned by a visitor about where the custom of inscribing a bee on the knives had come from, responded that the bee was the symbol "of the cycle of life" through pollination; it was a reference to the "flora of the Aubrac." Later, one of the visitors went to find the salesman and told him that he had heard that the bee was connected to honey and to the use of the knife for honey.[33]

The problem of the origin of materials

Since knife-making skills had disappeared from Laguiole before the 1980s, their transmission relies on a fiction designed to suggest that those skills had come from the territory itself; a narrative was required to ensure continuity with the past. However, the knife-makers faced an additional discontinuity, one that involved the origins of the materials used. Origin is generally a determining criterion for establishing distinctions in terms of intellectual property. In 1973, the problem had already arisen for "Limoges porcelain": because the raw material was no longer of local origin, the Council of State ruled that porcelain made in Limoges could no longer benefit from the *appellation d'origine*.[34] This is the dilemma expressed in the "Theseus paradox":[35] how can Theseus' ship still be identified as the same ship if all of its constituent parts have been replaced? How can a Laguiole knife remain the same if the materials used in the present version are no longer the same as those used in the original version from the past?

The fact is that in Laguiole few – indeed, virtually none – of the raw materials used in knife-making are of local origin. A number of knives, simple in form, are made with a handle (called a "side") of juniper wood, a variety that does not grow in the Aubrac district but has to be imported, mainly from the Hérault region. Moreover, this wood was not used for knife handles in the nineteenth century; Camille Pagé mentions only *cormier* (a now rare fruit tree), walnut, boxwood, pear wood, ebony, and "wood from the islands."

The problem of origins arises in a particularly acute way for two emblematic materials: horn and steel.

Horn is the material most commonly used for Laguiole knife handles. Like bone, this material has been used from the nineteenth century on. In the nineteenth century, though, as Camille Pagé wrote, "there is no substance that can compare to ivory for whiteness, solidity, and the ease with which it lends itself to the most delicate works."[36] Horn was used mostly in Thiers and in Nogent for producing "knives that close."[37]

A horn consists of two parts: an upper part, solid, which is called "the point" (*la pointe*), a small portion of the whole, and a lower part, hollow, called "the bottom" (*le bas*), by far the larger portion. Higher-quality knives are made from the point, in which direct cuts can be made. The bottom of the horn is much too thin to be used as is for making handles. It can be treated by being cut, heated, and pressed, but it is of lower quality than the point. In contact with water, the point of a horn tarnishes and flakes, and the bottom may be deformed as well, which is why it is said that a knife "guaranteed for life" can be wiped off but must not be washed. La Forge de Laguiole has stopped making knives from bottom pieces of horn because working on the raw material produced defects that led quality control to send the knives back repeatedly for reworking, so that the use of bottoms became more costly than the use of points.

It turns out that the horn used in Laguiole at the beginning of the twenty-first century came mainly from zebu horns imported from Africa. But this importation, which might be supposed to have resulted from recent globalization, is in fact an old practice. In fact, according to Pagé, in the nineteenth century "the East Indies and South America supplied France with the horns [from cattle] needed for its industries."[38] Horn from cattle was thus the principal form used, ahead of horn from buffalo (which came from Asia – Calcutta, Siam, Singapore, Coromandel), goats, and deer.

According to the stories told in the cutlery workshops, horns from Aubrac cattle were used in the past to make knives, but these horns are no longer large enough to make big handles, for cattle-breeding itself has changed, as one guide explains:

Everyone had stopped working with horn from Aubrac cattle. Because before, they didn't use cows, they used the thicker horns from steers, often fairly old ones, which had thick and very hard horns. Today, we have cows that are sold when they are three or four years old. When you have some land, it's a shame to go looking for horn in Africa when you have them right under your nose and can't use them. In fact, they're really only good for making fertilizer for flowers. The horn remnants are ground up and you come across them later in fertilizer for geraniums.[39]

In a move characteristic of the trend form, La Forge de Laguiole, which was trying to solve this problem, announced as "news" in the fall of 2013 the fact that they were making knives with horn from Aubrac cattle "in the old way" and that they were the only company able to do so. ("It's a great innovation, so much so that we're going to present it as the big news at the home and housewares show in Paris this fall.") The new knife made with horn from local cattle is presented by La Forge de Laguiole in the following terms:

The cows from Laguiole, from Aubrac, also have their knife. Conceived at the heart of the famous Aubrac plateau, and faithful to a tradition going back centuries, for the first time this knife has a handle made from the horn of the Aubrac breed of cattle. Celebrating the return to its origins, the blade "straight from the forge" underlines the importance of the territorial know-how and recalls the roots of the Laguiole knife. A stylized bee, magnified by a smooth spring, speaks out in praise of tradition and modernity. A leather string made from Aubrac cowskin, delicately rolled around the traditional suspension ring, is one more nod to this cow with her "gentle and joyous gaze." This knife is much more than an object, it is a hymn to the village of Laguiole and to its territory, the Aubrac.

The problem of the provenance of the steel is twofold. First there is the question of the origin of the material itself, then the question of where it was forged. The steel used was often of Swedish origin, from the Sandvik company (12C27 or 14C28N). To relax the tension introduced between this foreign element and the local claims, those who used it justified doing so by insisting that it was "the best steel in the world," because "it was also used in Thiers, in France, in the world." Spokespersons for La Forge de Laguiole, in contrast, view 12C27 steel from Sandvik as "commonly used in cutlery" because it is "not very expensive" and "it is produced in great quantity in Sweden." They explain that La Forge de Laguiole chose a different steel, the T12, supplied by a French manufacturer in Grenoble, "which corresponded well to the philosophy of the business." In other words, "we go further and further astray when we fail to find a solution nearby."

But the problem becomes more complicated in the sense that, besides the fact that it does not originate in Laguiole, the steel used is not forged there either (with the notable exception of La Forge de Laguiole). The blades of all the other companies continue to be forged in Thiers. Thus most of the knives made in Laguiole can be attributed to hands other than those of the village cutlers – and those other hands have created the essential element in a knife, namely, its blade.

Distinguishing Laguiole's knives from those made elsewhere

Among the various activities involved in the production of knives, one of the most important consists in informing visitors, thus potential buyers, about the differences between the knives made in Laguiole and those made elsewhere. What is at stake for the Laguiole cutlers is to distinguish their products, on the one hand, from the knives made elsewhere in the region and in Thiers, their direct competitors in the collection form, and, on the other hand, from those made in China and Pakistan, competitors in the standard form.

Several businesses in the nearby municipalities sell Laguiole knives. Just a few kilometers away, in Espalion, the Lacaze store, where sales are divided more or less between knives and fishing gear, offers knives in the

Laguiole format made in Thiers but engraved with the notation "Lacaze" or "Lacaze. Espalion." A little further away, in Rodez, a small easily removed transparent label specifies "Made in P. R. C." (People's Republic of China).

The question of distinguishing between a "real" Laguiole – that is, between one made by hand in Laguiole itself – and a "fake" (the standard version made in China or in Pakistan is viewed as the "fakest" of all) is highlighted by many knife-makers in Laguiole, and thus it is a subject of conversation for visitors who want to be sure of what they are buying. After a report on a widely watched television channel showed a shop owner who sold as local products knives that were actually manufactured in China, the owner in question posted a large sign saying: "Our store does not sell any Laguiole knives made in China or in Pakistan." In La Forge de Laguiole, a video prepared for visitors to the factory is devoted entirely to the problem of "fake" knives manufactured abroad.

The knives made in the standard way are represented as objects that will not last long, throwaways destined to end up shortly as trash (as one salesman said in a cutlery shop: "Those knives are of poor quality, you just use them once a year"); they are not designed to be kept "for life," still less to be passed on to heirs. The difference can be embodied in the sale price: a standard knife may cost around 10 euros, while the price of the "simplest" knife at La Forge de Laguiole is around 100 euros, ten times as much. Even so, certain knives made abroad may be sold for higher prices, 40 to 60 euros or even more, thus canceling out the distinction in terms of price.

The criteria that make it possible to distinguish a standard knife from an artisanal and collectable model are thus established on the basis of the quality of the materials and of the production. Among other differences, the standard handle is not made of wood or horn but of plastic; the blade is not steel but iron, and the bolsters are flimsy, as one guide in a workshop explained:

> So, these supposedly magnificent Laguioles, I have a few here. They have a bee, they're marked Laguiole, and in this model the handle is plastic [he strikes the handle against a table], the blade is tin plate, it's a poor quality blade. The bolsters, I told you earlier that they're massive, that they serve to protect the knife; here they're just small brass leaves that are glued on. So, as soon as you drop it, you'll find the knife in one place, the bolsters in another. These knives are of really poor quality.[40]

Still, certain models are made in Pakistan or China with materials that are also used in Laguiole, and the distinctions are more subtle (the steel of the blade is of "poor quality," the "spring" is "going to stretch," and so on). This is why, as with works of art, the knife-makers of Laguiole rely on "certificates of guarantee" for their products, delivered at the time of sale. Nevertheless, sellers of knives made far from Laguiole establish their

own "certificates of guarantee," which means that new differences have to
be found, this time based on the local parlance:

> "So what can you do to avoid buying fake Laguioles, knowing that
> these are sold everywhere in France and even in Laguiole?" one guide
> asks. "Every time you buy a Laguiole knife, you have to ask for a
> certificate of guarantee. Here, all our knives come with a certificate,
> there's our address, our telephone number, and this will serve as your
> guarantee. But after you get a copy of a Laguiole knife, then you get
> a copy of a certificate. For the certificate to be valid, it has to be dated
> with the day of purchase, and it has to have an accurate description
> of the knife you bought: its size, the material used for the handle, and
> the type of steel. It mustn't be a generic certificate. Now I'm going
> to show you a real fake certificate: you see right away that there are
> little blue, white, and red flags more or less everywhere. This is surely
> to make you believe that the product was made in France, and I can
> certify that this one is very far removed from French manufacture.
> 'We attest that you have just bought an authentic bougna Laguiole.'
> But there you have the wrong territory and the wrong term, because,
> earlier, people from here who moved up to Paris were known as
> *bougnats*, spelled with a 't.' If you buy the famous 'Laguiole bougna,'
> you're nowhere near Laguiole; you're actually in Pakistan. And one
> indication that could have proved that this was a scam is the address
> given: it's a post office box."[41]

This competition between the standard and the collection forms of the
same item arises from the fact that the Laguiole cutlers have not legally
protected the name of their village or their knife as a model. So, as the
guide in La Forge de Laguiole says, "there's no such thing as a fake … you
find real Laguioles from Laguiole, and Laguioles from elsewhere, but all
Laguioles are Laguioles." Still, there is some ambivalence in the relation to
standard manufacture. It is possible, in fact, that the standard form produced on assembly lines that allowed the form of the knife and the name of
the village to spread may have also created its international celebrity. But
now that they have achieved fame and the value of the village name and
the knife's form are widely appreciated, the village residents want to claim
exclusivity for themselves.

"A name, a brand, a village"

One of the key constituents in movements of heritage creation, and of
the crossing of collective identity with capitalism, something that Jean
and John Comaroff call "Ethnicity, Inc.,"[42] is intellectual property. The
latter applies in particular to the names and forms that are at the heart of
heritage creation. In the case we are examining, neither the name Laguiole

nor the form of the knife were protected before the 1990s. The situation changed during that decade, but the village residents were neither the instigators nor the beneficiaries of the change.

How the residents lost the ability to dispose freely of the name of their village

An entrepreneur specializing in ceramics, located in Saint-Maur-des-Fossés, sought to manufacture a variety of objects in high-tech ceramics, most notably artificial hips, pens, and knives with ceramic blades.[43] He had received a "Laguiole" knife from an uncle in the early 1990s, and he discovered that the name Laguiole was not a protected trademark. He then decided in August 1993 to patent the name with the National Institute for Intellectual Property (INPI) for more than thirty categories of products. He had standard products manufactured, mostly in China: pens, glasses, garden tools, casseroles, and so on. The reference to "Laguiole" knives, which were also among his products, is quite explicit, for the logo of the brand is a stylized bee. He presented his strategy with the slogan "A name, a brand, a village." But, for him, producing objects intended for more or less everyone could only be accomplished abroad ("industry in France is over and done with"), and artisanal production was destined to remain "a niche market."

In reaction, the commune of Laguiole brought an initial suit, which it lost in 1999. Still, the judge decided that the name "Laguiole" applied to knives was a generic term, since many were manufactured outside of Laguiole, in particular in Thiers, and so the village name could not belong to the entrepreneur from Saint-Maur-des-Fossés either. But, despite this ruling, the entrepreneur remained the owner of the name as a trademark for his other Laguiole products (Laguiole Licences).

In 2010, the commune brought a new suit against the entrepreneur from Saint-Maur-des-Fossés, focusing on the fact that the brand's reference to a French village leads the consumer to a mistaken belief as to the provenance of the products, which were in fact manufactured abroad. However, in September 2012 the judges of the Tribunal de Grande Instance, a high court in Paris, ruled that the fame of the village had not been sufficiently established among the French population as a whole; a survey ordered by the commune itself had shown that a majority could not identify it accurately. The commune was thus condemned to pay damages with interest to the entrepreneur from the Val-de-Marne. A few days after the court ruling, Laguiole's municipal council announced the removal of the road sign identifying the town at the entrance, a gesture that won a lot of media attention.

In the village, the legal proceedings brought by the municipality divided more than they unified. Some residents felt that the amount paid for the trial could have been invested in public activities (creating associations, building a town swimming pool) or in maintenance or heritage creation

("I'd like to see the mayor resurface the streets, because there are pot-holes everywhere"). For their part, the cutlery workshops that supported the mayor's action deplored having to pay royalties to the entrepreneur of Saint-Maur-des-Fossés, emphasizing the fact that his products were simply standardized items made on assembly lines in China, in reaction to which they had developed all their "artisanal" activity ("he [the entrepreneur of Saint-Maur-des-Fossés] makes a profit by having things made in China – barbecues, pens, watches, napkins, towels, sneakers, and so on. We have nothing against the Chinese, but we think Chinese Laguiole isn't really us," one salesman in a shop complained).

The cutlers of Laguiole have also had recourse to the protection offered them by intellectual property laws, however, by registering brands, logos, and models for their own products. One of the cutlery shops on the main square has taken the bull as its emblem, modeled on the sculpture that dominates the square, and has a little bull engraved on the blade of its knives. "Honoré Durand" and "La Forge de Laguiole" are registered as trademarks. Benoît l'artisan owns two logos, "La Maison du Laguiole" and "Benoît l'artisan." In 2007 he also created a line of knives called the Tribal, "a Laguiole but with a more modern shape"; "unlike the familiar Laguiole, it is a registered model, an exclusive item that you can only find in our shop," a salesman explains.

The defense of an interest presented as a common good – the name Laguiole – with a trial that was for the primary benefit of private entrepreneurs – the cutlers' associations – but was very costly to the community created tension in the village. Since registering other brands and models did not suffice, and since legal avenues had failed, the residents of Laguiole decided to appeal to the political authorities – that is, to the possibility of modifying the laws. In this struggle, an additional front then opened up in another area, the commune of Thiers.

A geographic indication to "highlight the treasures of the territories"

The residents of Laguiole turned toward a legal solution to try to defend what they considered a collective public interest – something that was also, in fact, a merging of private interests directly aimed at insuring for themselves a monopoly on the accumulation of capital resulting from the exploitation of the name Laguiole. Their defense was expressed by the desire to create an arrangement that would provide a formal geographic indication for non-agricultural industrial and artisanal products – that is, products that did not come from "farming, the lumber business, the agro-food business, or the sea." One cutler explained, even before the law was passed, that there was going to be a law, but "there ought to have been one a long time ago."[44] "What the people of Laguiole are worried about today is protecting the Laguiolais territory," another testifies. "They've been trying for five years to work out a protected geographic indication for the manufactured projects using the names of places or territories."[45]

Attentive to this particular local problem, the government decided to resolve it in a general way through a proposed law pertaining to consumption that was presented in 2013 and adopted in 2014 (articles 23 and 24). According to the impact report published on that occasion, the administration considered that "the absence of protection for the names of these products contributes to the increase in similar products mostly manufactured abroad, and this creates unfair competition for the businesses involved when they are trying to maintain their production and thus jobs in the historical zone of production and to guarantee the traditional skills in the manufacture of these products." In addition to the Laguiole knives, the French government estimated that there were around a hundred industrial and non-food products that included a geographical origin in their name, for example Calais lace, Aubusson tapestry, Limoges and Berry porcelain, Moustiers earthenware, Breton granite, Cholet handkerchiefs, and Vallabrègues baskets.

As the impact report points out, geographic indications are recognized on an international scale as a type of intellectual property on the same basis as commercial trademarks. According to Article 22 of the international agreement on aspects of intellectual property rights that apply to businesses, the term "geographical indications" refers to "indications that serve to identify a product as originating in a territory of a Member [of the European Union], or in a region or locality within that territory, in cases where a quality, reputation, or some other determinate characteristic of the product can be attributed essentially to that geographic origin." Still, there are two distinct types of protection at the European level that are already applicable to food products: one that implies a strong relation to a place, the *Appellations d'origine* (AO; for example, "Bordeaux" wine), the other implying a weaker relation, the geographic indications (IG; for example, "Marennes Oléron oysters"); these protections refer moreover to a set of specifications that spells out a certain number of requisite qualities. To the extent that, as with the knives made in Laguiole, the materials used for the non-food industrial and artisanal products often do not come from the region where they are assembled, the AOP does not suffice to protect them, while the geographical indication can.

The law on consumption[46] thus modifies the code of intellectual property by creating within it a geographical indication clause written as follows (emphasis added):

Art. L. 721-2. — A geographic indication consists in the *determination of a geographic zone or of a specified place* serving to designate a *product*, other than agricultural, forest-related, food-related, or from the sea, that *originates* in it and that possesses a *determinate quality, a reputation, or other characteristics that can be attributed essentially to that geographical network*. The conditions of production or transformation of that product, such as cutting, extraction, or fabrication, respect a list of specifications that have been accredited by a decision made in the context of the application of article L.411-4.

Art. L. 721-3. — The demand for homologation or modification of the specifications was registered with the National Institute for Intellectual Property by an agency of defense and management, defined in article L. 721-4, representing the operators concerned.

A geographic indication connects a "product" and the name of a space ("geographic zone" or "place") through a relationship of "origin" (*originaire de*, "originating in" or "native to"); the relationship must be supported by an "attributable characteristic," which may be the product's "reputation." Here we can see the key role played by "memorial power": a "reputation" is in fact nothing but one aspect of the memorial power that can be attributed to a thing or a type of thing. Still, in order for it to be able to be protected in its collection form, the thing in question also has to correspond to certain criteria, and this requirement introduces a constraint proper to standard products, which must correspond to a set of specifications registered with the institution charged with controlling intellectual property in France, the INPI.

The problem is that the word *originaire* does not indicate how the relationship of origin with regard to a space is established, and it has led to concerns on the part of the cutlers in Thiers, relayed through their elected representatives in the French Parliament. Despite the geographic distance between the two communes, can the "origin" of the Laguiole knife be extended to Thiers, where large numbers of knives in the Laguiole form are manufactured, some of which are sold in Laguiole itself? André Chassaigne, a representative in the National Assembly from Thiers, expresses this concern as follows:

> The meaning of the adjective *originaire* is ambiguous. Does it refer to the first original manufacture – but how to prove that that really occurred in a given place? Does it refer to the first registration with the INPI? To the extent that the end of the sentence brings sufficient clarification, I propose to eliminate the use of this term …. Calais lace, "originating in" Calais, is also produced in the Caudry basin: even though they are not adjacent, these two production zones came together to register a single label of geographic origin. Similarly, Basque linens and fabrics "originate in" the Basque country, but they are also produced in the Béarn region: by Lartigue in Oloron in particular, also by Ona Tiss in Saint-Palais and Tissage Moutet in Orthez.[47]

In this discussion where the meaning of "origins" is at stake, writing the historical narrative – in other words, controlling memorial power – is the determining factor. Senator Alain Néri, another elected official speaking in a public discussion in the Senate on behalf of the cutlery industry in Thiers, defended the idea that "the production zone constituting the territory of the geographic indication must be defined by taking the history and the historical expertise of certain artisans into account," for "history demonstrates that the first Laguiole knives were quite obviously produced thanks to the expertise in Thiers."[48] And, highlighting the extent to which memorial power constitutes a factor of valorization in itself, he went on to specify that "the definition of the geographic indication thus has to take these legacies, this past, these traditions, into account: for *without a past and without traditions, there is no value added to these productions*, which are among the treasures of France!" (emphasis added).

These demands for precision were rejected by the government, however, on the grounds that the matter would be settled by the set of specifications. On the Laguiole side, of course, the desired outcome is to deprive Thiers of the possibility of benefiting from the geographic indication, as a salesman in a cutlery shop explains:

> The people in the Thiers cutlery industry who've been making Laguiole knives for a long time say: "don't forget us, we're here, we'd really like to be part of the geographic indication for Laguiole." We tell them: "Laguiole is Laguiole, Thiers is Thiers." It's true that we've done it on our own, without the Thiernois. We have absolutely nothing against the population of Thiers – they're neighbors with whom we've been cohabiting for a long time – it's just that these are two different territories. What's at stake is pinning down a label guaranteeing to people that the product actually comes from the place people are thinking of. If the Laguiole geographic indication were extended to Thiers tomorrow, people wouldn't understand why. If people want a Laguiole geographic indication, it's to be sure that their Laguiole really comes from Laguiole. If only because of that, the label shouldn't be shared. The Thiernois are free to work out a label with a Thiers geographical indication.[49]

But, alongside the cutlery debates, people defending the local agro-food industry are concerned about the weakening of their own links with the territory created by the geographic indication, and they seek a narrower criterion, as Deputy Brigitte Alain proposes:

> The geographic indication has to be able to certify that the raw materials that are the principal components of the product benefiting from this protection do in fact come from the geographic zone in question … This amendment reflects the concerns that have arisen about the geographic indications protecting food products, whose quality may well suffer from an insufficiently strict definition.[50]

The government and the rapporteur – the deputy in charge of drafting the final report – also referred to the set of specifications, considering that, with such a constraint, "there would no longer be very many candidates for geographic indications, and the arrangement would lose much of its interest."[51]

In a June 2015 brochure designed to promote geographic indications for manufactured products and natural resources, the secretary of state for business, arts and crafts, consumption, and the social welfare economy thus lauds the new arrangement in which the enrichment economy is valorized, using a number of terms that sketch out its discursive architecture (emphasis added):

> And what if we were to look at our territories as jewel cases overflowing with *treasures*? And what if we were to bring to light these resources, which contribute to forging *the soul of our country*? We have to *highlight the wealth of our territories* and give them the visibility they deserve.
>
> The Consumption Law of 17 March 2014 anticipates the possibility of creating, gaining recognition for, and protecting, through the National Institute of Intellectual Property (INPI), geographic indications (IG) for manufactured products and national resources,
>
> France is a precursor among European countries: manufactured products and natural resources benefit up to now only from limited protections.
>
> Geographical indications will recognize, while *valorizing* them, products, territories, expertise, and professionals. The resulting attractiveness plays a role in economic, territorial, cultural, touristic, and social development of territories ....

The French art of living is not an empty shell or a fine theoretical ideal. This art of living is a reality experienced on a daily basis. This art of living is the sum of all those resources, all that expertise, and it forges *our identity*. Born of our requirements, of those of *our ancestors*, who forged *its histories and its geographies*, this art of living will have a future if we are determined to recognize it, protect it, transmit it, share it, and embody it constantly through our choices, our actions, our policies.

The enrichment economy is built in enrichment basins, which are best positioned to highlight a heritage and resources that are always unevenly distributed in space. By relying on legal protections guaranteeing intellectual property, the nation (like the European Community, along with international institutions insofar as they consolidate national policies in this area) supports capitalism in these enrichment basins via regulations governing proper names and forms. To this end, it relies on memorial power, inasmuch as that power is made up of written history and reputation blended together.

To be sure, a nation can be conceived, and is often conceived, as a brand (the brand "France," hence the label "made in France"). But such brands have to be based on small-scale basins. Applauding the creation of geographic indications for manufactured products during a public discussion,

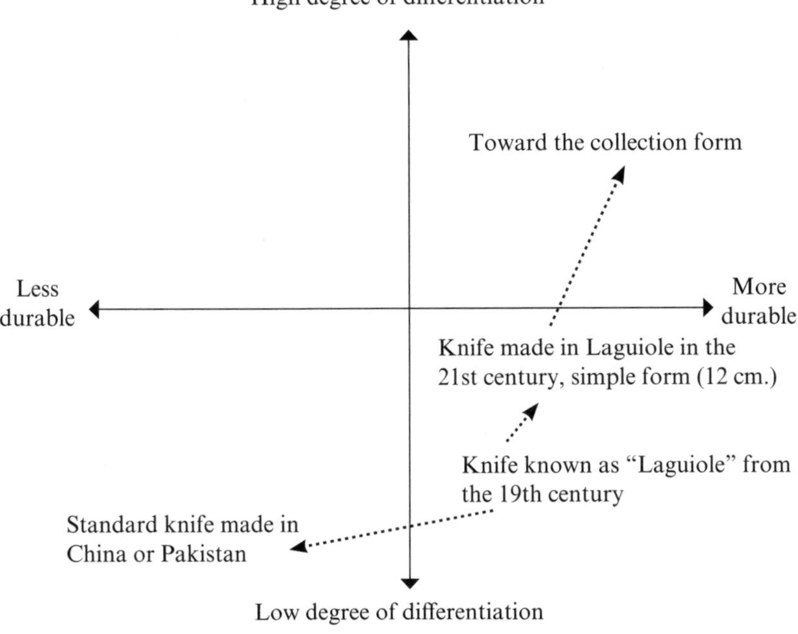

Figure 12.1 Standard form

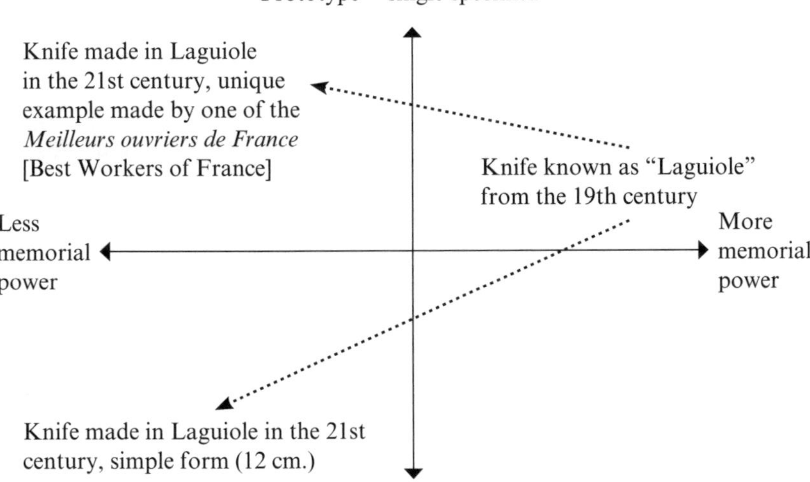

Figure 12.2 Collection form

Senator Stéphane Mazars exclaimed, addressing the government: "Your arrangement, Madame Minister, is more than *made in France*, it is *made in 'territories of France.'*"[52]

Whereas, in the industrial economy, by granting monopolies on the national level, the nation was able to privilege the emergence of national enterprises (for example railroads, energy, water, and telecommunications), in the enrichment economy France favors the development of small-scale capitalist enterprises, local capitalism, through equally protectionist measures and the establishment of monopolies – thus for example precluding the possibility of using the name "Laguiole" for commercial purposes outside the local context.

13

The Shape of the Enrichment Society

The organization of things and persons

The emergence of new sources of wealth creation is one of the main factors commonly invoked to interpret changes in the way a society is shaped. On the one hand, if the different types of resource on which the accumulation of capital rests are to be valorized, they must be exploited by different types of *persons*. On the other hand, because a society is composed of both persons and things, as layers of wealth and modalities of enrichment shift, the orientation of revenues and the distribution of *property* – which is a major dimension of society – are modified.

As it happens, property is the principal arrangement that governs the composition of societies, because it fixes the distribution of things among persons and also, conversely, as Marx noted, the distribution of persons among things. For persons are dependent on the things they possess as much as things depend on the persons to whom they belong. To be sure, people have expectations (which are by no means solely instrumental, moreover) with respect to things. But in return, if only to see these expectations satisfied, people must devote themselves to the cause of the things they own, for things inevitably deteriorate if they are deprived of care and left, as it were, to their own devices. Whatever their content, and whether they are material or immaterial, the goods on which a person's fortune rests, if they are not assisted – that is, if they do not also give rise to *expenditures* (of attention, time, money, and so on) – imperceptibly turn into burdens or trash. The forms of valuation we are examining are articulated with these processes on the horizon of profit: either the deterioration of things is accelerated so as to require their renewal, as in the standard form or the trend form, or their preservation is emphasized, as in the collection form or the asset form.

Whether it is displaced or stabilized, wealth must always be maintained, which is to say, kept ready for exchange. A possession that does no "work" (as Schumpeter would have put it)[1] may well be endowed, on paper, with a metaprice. But, as capital, this patrimony remains imaginary as long as it is not submitted to the test of circulation, which alone has the power to make it real by associating it with a price.

This is also why kinship structures play a central role in the organization of social life, in contemporary free-market societies as well as in the old status-based societies. It is indeed on the basis of kinship that things, or most things, are transmitted from generation to generation. A thing whose owner is dead cannot remain for long "without a master" – as French law puts it – without being destroyed.[2] The existence of things requires humans to choose whether or not to abandon them; and the possibility of this choice probably constitutes one of the obligations on which the primacy of kinship relations rests, a primacy that no political system, not even communism, has managed to abolish. But this possibility takes different forms depending on the relation between the lifespan of things and the lifespan of persons.

One of the most radical changes introduced by mass production of standard objects has entailed populating the world with things conceived in such a way that they will have a much shorter lifespan than people do; this is the case for most technological artifacts. And, during the same period, the life expectancy of humans has gotten longer, so that, in the case of standard products, the question of their transmission from one generation to the next has become secondary. Conversely, things of the type that occupy the heart of an enrichment economy have a lifespan with no predictable end and can thus, in principle, circulate endlessly, provided that they find human beings to take care of them – that is, to protect them against the ravages of time to which they are subject on the same basis as are all beings, animate and inanimate alike, and whether or not these are artifacts or "natural" entities. These latter goods serve the interests of their owners only if the owners take responsibility for maintaining them, for keeping them in good condition, and, as it were, for ensuring their quality of life (this was recognized in older legal structures which referred to the behavior of "a good father of the family," a term taken from Roman law and only recently eliminated from French law). It is in fact only on this condition that a thing can retain the possibility of circulation and of being appreciated (in other words, it can retain its *metaprice*) and can remain a patrimonial good capable of providing income, of serving as a monetary reserve, or of being exchanged for a sum of money that can be reinvested in another business deal: that is, it can be turned into capital. In the enrichment economy, at any given moment in time, the field of possible outcomes available to persons is ballasted with the weight of the properties that they have in one way or another inherited, and that they can, or cannot, put back to work; in this sense, then, the present is always governed by the past.

Who can profit from an enrichment economy?

When it comes to analyzing the way the development of an enrichment economy has been able to modify the composition of society, it is essential, first, to identify the goods whose possession allows one to invest in this economy and, second, to analyze the distribution of these goods. Knowing that an enrichment economy is based above all on exploitation of the past, we shall say that the goods that can prove to be profitable are goods that, in one way or another, not only come from the past – which is the case for property in general – but also *signal* that fact. They denote or connote the past more or less explicitly, either by incorporating it in a semantic mode (an antique is understood as such only through reference to the past) or by being charged with memorial power in certain discursive contexts (for example, that of an industrially produced perfume whose name and brand evoke a legendary past).

How are these goods distributed? The answer that comes immediately to mind is that they are in the hands of those to whom *old* objects belong, objects from which these owners can profit by reselling them (surplus value) or – if the goods take the form of real estate – by renting them (income): in other words, these goods belong to possessors of a *patrimony*. But this answer is insufficient, because the age of a thing is not, or not only, a physical quality; it also obeys a narrative mode of determination. An old object is not only aged, it is also associated with a story (a history), and it is in large part with reference to this story that its price is justified. Now, such stories have to be composed and maintained if their memory is to be preserved. Story-makers thus play a considerable role in the valuation of goods whose prices are justified by their memorial dimensions; these actors may be historians, critics or historians of art or of literature, anthropologists (when so-called ethnological objects are involved), or even novelists whose narratives help adorn certain places with a prestigious halo and increase tourist activity in these places to a significant degree. It is thus conceivable that actors who "produce" the past benefit, or might benefit, from the opportunities offered by the development of an enrichment economy, even if they do not themselves own goods anchored in the past and do not trade in such goods. The same holds true for all those who are responsible for restoring, preserving, or displaying objects from the past, such as museum conservators or the various experts involved in restoring prestigious objects or buildings. Plastic artists may also contribute to the fashioning of the past, or aspire to do so, to the extent that their works – if the artists succeed in gaining recognition for them – will be positioned among things that, presumed to be immortal, are already, in the present moment considered from an imaginary standpoint, projected into the future and thereby adorned with the aura of a past.

Of what order are the goods held by actors of the sort we have just enumerated – goods that, being anchored in the past, ought to place those actors at the heart of an enrichment economy – when the actors are not themselves owners of memorial objects but, rather, are among the *personnel* charged with inventing and maintaining the memory of things? The mere fact of participating in the preservation of a heritage is an insufficient criterion, for this is also the case of staff members, significant in number, who ensure the material maintenance of exceptional objects and places; in an enrichment economy, people in this category play a role more or less comparable to that of *servants* in pre-industrial economies, since they are assigned to the service of things without being given the power to transform them by endowing them with a history. The goods in question clearly equate with *culture*, which is determined entirely through reference to history, since it is composed of proper names, verbal statements, schemas of thought, and objects that, following a series of selections, have found themselves embodied in works deemed worthy of being preserved in libraries, monuments, or museums. This heritage, transmitted by families and schools, can be reinvested with each new generation in new cultural operations and can generate profits. It is thus quite fitting to speak, following Pierre Bourdieu, of *cultural capital*. This form of capital clearly has a mode of existence that is at once individual – since each of the individuals in which it is deposited may profit from it personally – and collective – to the extent that its maintenance, transmission, and deployment depend on the participation of a large number of actors and on the way their actions are coordinated. But this is no more and no less true than for the other forms of capital, and especially industrial capital, whose private appropriations, to be profitable, must be immersed in a productive fabric consisting mainly of infrastructures that are not privately owned but typically belong to governmental entities.

It is thus reasonable to think that an enrichment economy benefits different types of actors who can profit from the past on various grounds, and that it is beneficial above all to those in possession of a heritage that can give rise to a commercial exchange which will turn it into capital. Patrimony of this sort may be incorporated into objects or embodied in persons. In relation to these two possibilities, actors can be ranked more or less hierarchically in terms of the importance of their holdings measured in the first instance by an estimate of the metaprice of their possessions – an estimate produced for tax reasons, for example, or during the transmission of an estate – and in the second instance most notably by the actors' educational level, their professions, or their earnings. The two possibilities are of course not mutually exclusive. Still, while it is presumably rare for collectors and traders in art, antiques, or even expensive real estate to be totally lacking in embodied cultural capital, it is conversely quite common for holders of this latter sort of capital, even at the highest levels, to be totally lacking in costly patrimonial objects. From this situation we can deduce that patrimony incorporated in things takes precedence over patrimony incorporated in persons, since those who benefit from the second sort and who seek to valorize it – that is, to transform it into capital – have to place themselves at the service of those who hold patrimony embodied in things or, at the very least, of those who control access to such patrimony.

"Losers" and "servants"

How can we characterize the individuals or groups least likely to profit from the development of an enrichment economy except as "losers" or "servants," people who have been left behind or left out? These are not simply actors who possess little or no patrimony – whether incorporated in things or in persons – in their own right; the category includes, more radically, all those who belong to groups whose anchoring in the past has not been the object of a collective work of valorization, or even of shaping, so that memorializing that past, which is at best strictly a family or community affair, not only brings no external benefits but can even stigmatize the group.

Among these "losers," one finds persons and groups who made their living until recently as blue-collar workers in industrial centers that are now in decline, and who lived in nearby urban areas. These centers and the associated housing clusters have generally been either abandoned or "rehabilitated." But for the most part their former occupants have not profited from the recent reclassifications of production sites and relocation zones that have accompanied the (re)valorization of the industrial patrimony. In fact, rehabilitation efforts have been focused exclusively on buildings and material infrastructure whose arrangements and destinations have been profoundly modified; their former populations, excluded, no longer had any place in the landscape. These processes of *gentrification* – which have been the object of much recent study[3] – have been characterized chiefly by the way they combined respect for *things* whose anchoring in the past had been valorized with disdain for *persons* whose anchoring in the present condemned them to degradation. But the things in question still had to be old enough to attract attention once again, and this was by no means always the case. Workers who had lost their jobs when factories closed and residents in inferior or dilapidated housing thus met the same fate as the so-called soulless sites where they had ended up: abandonment.

The possibility of reinterpreting local memories within the patrimonial frameworks established in France especially from the 1980s on, and thus the possibility that workers could profit from the past, played out very differently depending both on how much commercial potential the external actors responsible for policy implementation saw in the workers involved and on the workers' ability to exploit that potential. Thus farmers who stayed "on the land" (a small fraction of the old peasantry) could profit from heritage-creation arrangements that allowed them both to give a traditional allure to their products – local cheeses, for example, as in Laguiole – and also to initiate a shift toward environmental ("green") tourism.[4] This was particularly feasible in moderately mountainous regions, where agricultural industrialization was less extensive than on the plains; folklorists and, later, ethnologists had been taking an interest in those regions for decades. Through contact with ethnologists, the members of the populations in question had acquired the ability to see and present themselves as they were seen by others, from the outside. Thus they could offer proof, as it were, of their ancestral authenticity by surrounding themselves with objects bearing the marks of a tradition (often reinvented, moreover) while blending into their environment. Those who work the land are expected to be one with the landscape.

By contrast, other subaltern actors, even though they too came primarily from traditional cultures, had not had the same opportunities because, having been transplanted, they did not enjoy the same ancestral traditions as the objects present in their environment. Lacking memorial power in the broader context, their memories were conflated with their personal and familial histories, so that, even conveyed to a third party (such as an ethnologist or a sociologist) in the form of stories, they had little chance of coinciding with any "site of memory" and thus little chance of contributing to the success of an effort at heritage creation. This is the case par excellence of the immigrant populations from the other side of the Mediterranean, who are stigmatized by being treated as though they lacked a past, no matter how long they have been on French territory and in spite of efforts on the part of novelists "from an immigrant background" to inscribe them in a history. This is true, for example, of "former North African miners" from a mining operation in Loos-en-Gohelle in the Pas-de-Calais discussed by Michel Rautenberg: objects of a "cultural action undertaken at the initiative of a 'National Theatre,'" these actors have never risen to the status of subjects in the enterprise of "patrimonialization through culture and art."[5] The study by Stéphane Gerson cited earlier offers another example: Gerson focused on the unsuccessful attempts on the part of various actors in Salon-de-Provence to create a patrimony for that community, which had been affected by industrial decline, by turning to the ancestral figure of Nostradamus.[6] Among the numerous initiatives, generally focused on celebrations of "Provençal culture," that accompanied the collective effort at heritage creation, an association of students of Algerian origin ("Nejma") had the idea of highlighting Nostradamus as a "cosmopolitan figure," "open to other cultures," so as to valorize "a 'biculture' blending the North African origins of its members with the local patrimony." In 1984, they set up "an Arab *suk* [street market] and a seventeenth-century slave market in the Village Renaissance." But this creative effort led nowhere.

Since at least the nineteenth century, struggles over the past have played an important role in class struggles. Testifying to this, for example, are the efforts undertaken by unions and competing parties claiming to represent the people – first of all the French Communist Party, especially from the 1930s to the 1970s – to endow themselves with a tradition that would have its own pilgrimage sites, its monuments, its heroes, and its folklore. Reference to these "traditions" supported the "repertory" (to borrow an expression from Charles Tilly)[7] of actions carried out by workers during strikes and social conflicts. Reference to the past plays at least as important a role – although a different one – when the claims emanating from subaltern groups are translated not in the idiom of social class but in the language of ethnicity. They then take the form not only of demands bearing on working conditions and standard of living but also, and perhaps especially, of demands for recognition.[8]

These demands for recognition are often supported today by activities that, in different ways, are related to the world of art, as is the case when so-called traditional objects, often connected with the sphere of religion, valorized for their decorative aspects and introduced into circuits of exchange, undergo a process of ratification; the same process can occur with practices that claim both to express the subaltern condition in its specificity and to be aesthetically innovative, as was the case with hip-hop starting in the 1980s.[9] These displacements of social demands toward identitary expressions are an indication, among many others, of the way the development of an enrichment economy tends to modify manifestations of belonging and of social conflict, going so far as to affect even those who are *a priori* the most excluded from such manifestations.

Let us add that some of these outsiders – who are deprived of a past susceptible to valorization – can nevertheless earn salaries in an enrichment economy, either because the economy has been implanted in a former industrial zone (such as the Louvre satellite museum opened in Lens in northeastern France in 2012) or because the outsiders in question have moved toward zones where such an economy is developing; however, they are relegated to the least stable and most subaltern positions. Often temporary or seasonal, these jobs are stimulated by the expansion of tourism but also of cultural activities, including activities that depend on the central government or on regional entities. At the bottom of the ladder, outsiders may find work as custodians ("surface operators") or as "maintenance agents" and, at a somewhat higher level, as security guards (those in museums have the highest status); they may even win positions in administration, hospitality, or event organizing, although the latter positions are often reserved for students. The enrichment economy is associated in this way with the formation of something like a "proletariat," but one whose contours have little in common with those of the industrial proletariat. Scattered and transitory, the new proletariat is virtually devoid of organization. Its members, judged in part in terms of personal qualities (flexibility, congeniality, likeability, honesty, and so on) that evoke the qualifications for domestic employment of yesteryear, but also in terms of youth and physical beauty, have no access to the "repertory of actions" set up by decades of workers' struggles.[10] Mobilizing them constitutes a difficult task, a daunting challenge for the new union organizations that are trying to establish themselves by invoking above all the fight against job insecurity; the organizers are struggling to find specific forms of action that would give them leverage to defend personnel who have very little legal protection, and whose employers have a vast "reserve army" at their disposal.[11]

The return of "*rentiers*"

The term *possédant* (owner), which has been part of the vocabulary of social critique in France for two centuries, whether that critique is from a socialist perspective or linked to the revolutionary right[12] (as was the case with the writer Georges Bernanos, for example), has long been used to designate a vast aggregation stretching from the upper industrial bourgeoisie to a lower bourgeoisie of *rentiers*, people whose income came exclusively from their ownership of property. The term was often used in critical contexts where *heritage*, and consequently *family*, were stressed alongside an *ethos* marked by money, calculations, rapaciousness, and avarice, long embodied in literature by the figures of the local factory owner or (although with lower status) the shopkeeper. By the 1970s and 1980s, the term was tending to disappear from ordinary taxonomies, or else it was retained specifically because of its somewhat old-fashioned flavor; this was the case in the Communist Party in its waning years. The term gave way to other modes of classification that had initially been proposed by academic sociology. These modes placed emphasis less on the possession of material things that were "transmitted from father to son" – that is, inscribed in a patrimonial order – than on the transmission of immaterial and embodied values such as language, culture, relationships, and (especially) competencies sanctioned by academic degrees, any of which could give access to privileged social positions.

Thus to the old bourgeoisie consisting of "owners" we can contrast *cadres*, members of the managerial class, a group whose extensive media representation throughout the same period has been extended by novelists, film-makers, and social scientists. During that time, the old lower middle class typified by shopkeepers, a group once denounced for stinginess and narrow-mindedness, was replaced by the "new middle classes," which made a thundering entrance into the sociology of the 1970s and early 1980s. These new classes were characterized no longer by an ethos of restraint and thriftiness but, on the contrary, by the amount of their consumption, most notably of cultural tools (such as hi-fi equipment or cameras) and also by their cultural practices, which often took associative forms.[13]

This change was linked to the fact that the members of the upper bourgeoisie and the middle classes were earning salaries in increasing numbers. This trend began in the period between the two wars during the currency devaluation and then the crisis of the 1930s; it became massive in the postwar years.[14] Most analysts of that period associate it with *modernization* – that is, with the supremacy of industrial society, in which access to affluence or even to wealth, and thus to consumption, validated the competencies deployed in salaried work within large companies that produced goods.[15] Production of the standard objects that came out of these enterprises depended on personnel made up not only of laborers and employees but also of supervisors, engineers, and managers. In that context, there was emphasis less on the possession of a patrimony – in the form, for example, of a large house in a provincial or rural environment that had been received as an inheritance – than on the income that people earned as a function of their diploma-attested competencies or, to use an expression that was just starting to emerge at the time, on "human capital" invested on the market of salaried work.[16]

The question of social inequalities and their causes tended to shift onto the same terrain, whether inequalities had been considered as "just" recognition of unequal gifts or competencies, or whether critics had attributed them to the transmission of "cultural capital" via families and schooling. During the last few decades in particular, the study of social inequalities has ceased to focus exclusively on salary differentials (or on the risks of unemployment) but has also taken into account income differences tied to the possession of a patrimony. Struck in particular by the increased costs of housing in large cities, scholars have stressed the differences in income, especially among young people, between those who rent their homes or make monthly mortgage payments and those who have a house or an apartment thanks to an inheritance. This is the case for the synthesis presented by INSEE on earned and unearned income in 2014;[17] the factors on which its estimations are based include ownership of the housing in which "households" (in INSEE's sense) reside and the rising costs of real estate during the 2000s.[18] Taking into account what can be estimated as the rental value of the residential units people own meant a "change in standard of living" attributed to 37 percent of the persons involved: a shift to a lower level for tenants and to a higher level for property owners, the latter being much more numerous when we look at the upper levels of income distribution, especially from age fifty on. Ownership of a residence, especially when it is received as an inheritance and not purchased on credit, constitutes an important asset that makes it possible to rise in the world of enrichment, where working conditions often differ from those in the wage-earners' world in its stable forms; those conditions are characterized by interplay among a plurality of forms of activity ranging from independence and solo entrepreneurship to participation in associations or involvement in short-term projects.

But the gap in standard of living that has to do with housing conditions, and whether one owns or rents, is just one indicator among others of the role, undoubtedly once again a very important role, assigned by the development of an enrichment economy to patrimony in the formation of income. In fact, in large cities and in zones and regions where the economy is chiefly residential and, even more clearly, in proximity to patrimonial and touristic sites that attract large numbers of visitors, real estate and building lots, which may long have been viewed by their owners as an agreeable inheritance whose maintenance costs had to be met from salaried income, turn out to be important sources of income, either in the form of rent payments or in the form of added value when they are offered for sale. This process of enrichment, which benefits from the considerable expansion of tourism, has been stimulated by the creation of Internet sites and legal arrangements that make it possible to rent secondary or even primary residences for short periods to visitors passing through. As one ad for a site set up for person-to-person rentals (Airbnb) noted: "My guest room pays for my vintage motorcycle! Extend your income by renting your home in Paris."

These new opportunities favored the formation of a large stratum of lower- and mid-level households relying on income from property ownership. Although they do not constitute an explicit category in France (that is, the category is not recognized as such by the government, so it doesn't figure in administrative nomenclatures), these people nevertheless manifest *de facto* solidarity in the defense of their specific interests, which leads them to privilege territory, conceived not as a space of production but as a place for living and vacationing that can be valorized through reliance on processes of enrichment. Examples of this phenomenon include buildings in historic city centers that have been classified as historical landmarks, "authentic" cottages belonging to fishermen or winemakers in "the loveliest villages in France," ancient *terroirs*, with their high-quality foods and great wines, or ancestral manors where investments with guaranteed returns have allowed them to be turned into "Relais & châteaux" offering prestigious tourist accommodation.[19]

The members of this stratum of independent wealth profit, to varying degrees according to the size and nature of their patrimony, from new economic opportunities that have arisen chiefly from real estate, buildings and building sites, and land transmuted into "places of memory." These latter attract affluent visitors seeking cozy, nostalgic places of refuge, in which the *past*, which owes its calming power to the fact that nothing more can happen there, finds itself *reinscribed*, as it were, in a present that, as a simple staging of a past, is disconnected, positioned at a safe distance from danger and above all from conflict. But these environments retain their value only if they are protected, not only from natural risks, not to mention war, but also from the sort of permanent risk that the presence of poverty has always constituted. The patrimonial class, whose re-emergence has been fostered by the development of an enrichment economy, is inclined to ensure such protections in order to maintain the conservatism, regionalism, and nationalism that are the political attitudes most in harmony with the interests of the things whose survival they are responsible for ensuring and from which they profit.

The development of an enrichment economy has contributed to a degree that is undeniably difficult to measure with precision to the reconstitution of the "patrimonial class" based on independent means that Thomas Piketty's studies have brought to light. Analyzing the evolution of the capital-to-income ratio during the twentieth century, Piketty has shown how this ratio, which was very high up to 1914 (the value of the national capital was equivalent to six or seven years of the national income), sank in the wake of the First World War until it was reduced by two-thirds, before it began to climb back up. It has continued to rise over the last several decades, especially since 1990, so that, "by 2010, the capital/income ratio had returned to its pre-World War I level."[20] The relation between the enrichment economy and the re-emerging patrimonial class is even more apparent if we take into account the nature of the goods that comprise this capital. Its principal component today is no longer agricultural land, whose value has plunged since the early twentieth century, but real estate: in other words, private capital, which, in France, constitutes more than 95 percent of the national patrimony.

What Piketty calls "capitalism without capitalists," which characterized France in the 1950s, when "public power in France held between 25 percent and 30 percent of the national patrimony," and when the French economy was driven by growth, has thus been replaced by "a quasi-stagnant society" in which "wealth accumulated in the past will inevitably acquire disproportionate importance."[21] We have been witnessing "a strong comeback of private capital in the rich countries since 1970, or, to put it another way, the emergence of a new patrimonial capitalism" accompanied by an increase in inequality.[22] In addition to real estate, which is in first place, this private capital includes financial assets and also "valuables" such as jewelry or works of art, held above all as "reservoirs of value" (estimated to amount to between 5 percent and 10 percent of the national income).[23] Alongside a patrimonial class made up of the extremely wealthy (the top 1 percent – in France, some 500,000 people), a significant "patrimonial middle class" is developing; according to Piketty, its emergence is "an important, if fragile, historical innovation" in recent decades.[24] It contributes to the formation of an "inheritance society ... characterized by both a very high concentration of wealth and a significant persistence of large fortunes from generation to generation."[25] Evidence for this can be found in the rise, since the 1980s, "in the annual flow of inheritances over the long run, that is, the total value of bequests (and gifts between living individuals) during the course of a year, expressed as a percentage of national income," which had fallen to its lowest point around 1950.[26] Inheritance "has thus nearly regained the importance it had for nineteenth-century cohorts."[27]

Piketty's conclusions are confirmed by the trends of recent years.[28] The surveys used by INSEE[29] show that inequalities have continued to increase since 2010 owing to the rise in poverty among the unemployed and among wage-earners who were already poor, and above all owing to the "dynamism of those with very high incomes,"[30] "nearly two-thirds" of which is driven by the "growth in property income."[31] Revenues from property represent 30 percent of their total income, as compared to 22 percent seven years earlier. Now, "the patrimony of households is very concentrated within the population: at the end of 2009, more than 20 percent of the net patrimony was held by the wealthiest households – 1 percent of the total population."[32] While almost all of those with "very high incomes" benefit from transferable securities (between 95 and 99 percent), income from real estate is also very high, since 70 percent of the households in this category also declare real-estate income, as compared to less than 15 percent of "the great majority" of people.[33] The proportion of patrimonial income in overall household incomes goes from 3 percent for lower-income households to 30 percent for those at the top of the scale. Finally, the analysis of the relation between the level of patrimonial wealth and savings shows that, if the rate of savings generally rises in correlation with the patrimonial level, the holders of expensive inherited real estate have a tendency to save less because the patrimony they hold itself constitutes savings.[34]

Let us note, nonetheless, that the available indicators do not allow us to establish with precision the difference between *patrimony* and *capital* – that is, to distinguish actors for whom the possession of inherited assets plays the role of a back-up savings account and/or of a resource that can be rented, temporarily or permanently, in order to draw income (a possibility in most cases only when the inheritance consists in real estate) from actors who give themselves the means *to put their patrimonial holdings to work* by multiplying transactions in order to gain added value – that is, in order to transform their holdings into *capital*. This last possibility opens up opportunities that also concern patrimony in the form of transferable securities, because operations of this sort can be carried out by buying and selling objects of value.

14

Creators in the Enrichment Society

The economic condition of culture workers

People who possess cultural capital play central roles in an enrichment economy; the increase in their numbers in Europe since the 1960s, and especially in the last two decades of the twentieth century, was unquestionably one of the factors that contributed to the growth of this type of economy. This was especially true for people who had earned degrees in literature or the arts; shut out from employment in business, many were able to find jobs in the new economic context and devoted themselves to enhancing the value of exceptional things. These actors were thus *a priori* beneficiaries of the enrichment economy.

Still, the way profits can be made from the possession of literary or artistic cultural capital, which may be associated with commercial competencies when this capital is engaged in an enrichment economy, deviates, to varying degrees according to individual situations, from the modalities of salaried work that have long prevailed in businesses oriented toward the production or sale of standard objects, even when these processes have been re-engineered to meet the demands of project management. The development of the enrichment economy has thus come to be an important element in what has been described as "the crisis in salary-based societies."[1]

A first glimpse of this situation is offered by Cyprien Tasset's composite picture of the positions obtained by people who have earned academic degrees in a variety of fields.[2] Tasset based his study on a "generational" survey carried out in France in 2007 by the Center for Studies and Research on Qualifications, a survey that set forth the professional situations of persons who earned graduate degrees in 2004.[3] For a certain number of fields of study, Tasset's synthesis provides data on the status of graduates in 2007: by percentage, how many were unemployed, how many worked part-time, or had jobs with open-ended contracts, or had managerial status; how many worked in "intermediate professions";[4] and the median salaries for each subcategory. Other information pertained to the status of the graduates' fathers (whether or not they belonged to the managerial class as defined by the French National Institute of Statistics and Economic Studies, INSEE). The resulting picture allows comparisons between young people who had earned engineering degrees or doctorates – graduates whom one might expect to find employed in businesses oriented toward industrial production or finance, but also toward the public sector – and graduates of art schools (who had earned a baccalaureate degree followed by four years of higher education) or others who had pursued literature (at the "Masters 2 [M2] research" level); one might expect this latter group to have gravitated in larger numbers toward the enrichment economy.

Three years after they completed their studies, 87 percent of those with engineering degrees and 92 percent of those with doctorates were employed at the managerial level; they had the highest median monthly incomes (€2,150 and €2,170 respectively); very few were unemployed (4 percent, 6 percent), and the vast majority benefited from an open-ended contract. The situation of the second group, graduates of art schools or holders of M2 degrees in literature, art, or other fields in the humanities, was different. Of the art school graduates, 17 percent were unemployed; of those with M2 degrees, 13 percent. Only 60 percent of the two subgroups combined had open-ended contracts; far fewer of them had managerial status compared to those with engineering degrees or doctorates; and roughly half of them were classified as employed in the intermediate professions. The median salary for the art school graduates was €1,400; for those with M2 degrees, €1,450. Many members of each of the sets we have just described had fathers in the managerial class, but this was more frequently the case for the first set (50 percent) than for the second (37 percent). These data suggest that, alongside the classic tracks for access to higher positions in business or in the public sphere, there are other academic and social itineraries that are riskier but more open to social mobility, giving access to activities that are more often related to the enrichment economy.

These indications have been confirmed in studies carried out by the Ministry of Culture and Communication, studies designed to present "the incomes and standards of living of professionals in culture" on the basis of the INSEE Tax and Social Income Survey for 2005–12.[5] In the absence of other statistical sources, the data collected by the Ministry of Culture and Communication constitute the only unified framework allowing us an overview of the standards of living of people who work for the enrichment economy. In fact, this ministry, whose usefulness, and thus whose very existence, is sometimes called into question, is undoubtedly the agency that has the greatest interest in giving consistency to the disparate actors whose activity touches domains more or less under its oversight, and for that reason the ministry is interested in considering them as if they constituted an identifiable social group. This mode of totalization by no means covers the entire set of actors who work for an enrichment economy; it concentrates attention on the best established among them, to the detriment of those whose activity is episodic, unstable, or precarious or those who exercise a primary activity, such as teaching, that leads them to be classified under other administrative and statistical rubrics. The "culture professionals" (in the ministry's sense) are brought together in the following categories: practitioners of the visual arts and other artistic trades, performing artists, journalists, publishers, literary writers and translators, architects, archivists, documentalists, and art teachers (working outside of the national education system). Although the scope of the INSEE survey is restricted and leaves aside those persons – doubtless the most numerous – whose activity depends on the enrichment economy without being easily identifiable on the basis of a nomenclature of trades recognized by the central government (the existing nomenclature is already outdated, moreover),[6] this study allows a first glimpse of the features that characterize the forms of employment in the area that interests us. These features can be summed up as follows.

Compared to other categories of employees, culture professionals are characterized by a high level of education (at least three years past the baccalaureate), by high social origins (more than half have had fathers in the managerial class [*cadres*]), and by residence in the Île-de-France (in proportions ranging from a third to more than half, depending on the profession). Two-thirds live as part of a couple with a partner who is a *cadre* contributing his or her income to the household, and more than half own their own homes. For this reason, their "household income" is higher, to varying degrees depending on the situation, than individual earnings from work, as a function of the "household composition" and the presence or absence of inherited wealth. This latter, which most often involves home ownership, may also be the source of financial surpluses and income received from rent. Income generated from inherited wealth is found among culture professionals at a decidedly higher level than in the overall set of working households.

The average annual salaries of these professionals are "generally equivalent to those of the working population as a whole,"[7] but their income from work is 26 percent lower than that of salaried workers with identical qualifications. This gap is partially filled, for a quarter of culture workers, by substitute income such as unemployment payments or even retirement income. Substitute income is especially important for professionals in the performing arts (it constitutes from 30 to 60 percent of their annual income), owing to the legal provisions established for intermittent workers, but it is also important (accounting for about 10 percent of annual income) for journalists, publishers, and professors of art. It follows that, in this milieu, "revenues from professional activity constitute only part, a more or less considerable part, of the means available to an individual for subsistence; household composition, inherited wealth, and income from government programs, financial investments, or real-estate holdings may constitute other sources of revenue that complement the wages earned."[8] These complementary sources are on average 13 percent higher than those of the entire active population. Despite the multiple supplements, the "standard of living" of culture workers remains 12 percent lower than that of workers exercising a profession "at a comparable level" outside the domain of culture. In addition to this gap, the income of culture workers is characterized by the diversity of its sources. This is true not only of substitute income but also of the wages earned: the latter often comes both from a primary source of employment and from complementary jobs that may be outside the domain of culture.

The same diversity is found in the status of the positions occupied: 80 percent of the members of cultural professions are salaried, but the proportion of freelance workers is also considerable, especially in the visual and plastic arts and among writers and translators. As for salaries, they are distributed between two poles. At one extreme, there are workers who hold stable positions in cultural enterprises: this is the case, for example, with editors in the publishing world, and with people working in programming or production in the performing arts, including sound engineers. Their average salaries are the highest among culture workers, and their situation is close to that of managerial-level workers in other sectors. At the other extreme, there are workers who combine salaries from different sources, often in the form of payment per unit of work performed as a function of the plurality of their complementary forms of employment. Finally, freelance income and salaries can be combined; this is the case for more than 10 percent of visual arts professionals and authors of literary works. Culture workers are thus distributed between relatively stable jobs organized around businesses in the classic sense of the term or around public agencies, at one pole, and dispersed among jobs that are often organized in the context of associations, at the other. Cultural associations, which are qualified to receive subsidies, on the one hand, and which pay partial and temporary salaries for work concentrated on specific projects, on the other hand, can play the role of relay between financing agencies (especially regional entities) and a multiplicity of persons – actors or artists, for example – whose activity is dispersed according to contracts, "programs," or temporary "residencies."[9]

At the outer limit, one finds people in very precarious situations, largely dependent on substitute income and even on minimal social subsidies (these play a central role for 7 percent of culture professionals). The most fragile of these are undoubtedly missed by the ministerial survey, especially because individuals in such situations, while they may well be involved with "culture," are not technically speaking "professionals." Cyprien Tasset's thesis includes many interviews that make it possible to sketch a profile of such workers.[10] Shut out of urban centers by the high costs of daily life (housing in particular), and having neither inherited wealth nor family support, they are cut off from the networks of relationships that are indispensable in this milieu for keeping up with what is going on and getting involved in projects. Benefiting from minimal social subsidies without which they could not subsist, they most often find themselves dispersed among various temporary activities without being able to claim any specific trade. Nevertheless, they keep on doing things – painting, writing, performing, and so forth – in order to nourish the project, typically formed in adolescence, of living a life oriented toward culture; they keep trying to remain close to a romantic image of the artist that bears little resemblance to the experience of artists who have had to learn, in order to survive, to organize their activity in a way that allows them to tap into the funds that circulate among private enterprises, government-sponsored agencies (such as museums, cultural centers, or outlets for certain subsidized goods), regional entities, and foundations.

This asymmetrical distribution of employment situations goes hand in hand with a particularly broad gap in income levels (from more than €47,000 in annual revenues to less than €3,000), and especially in "standards of living," if profits from inherited wealth are taken into account for the most well-to-do, along with income brought in by a spouse or partner for those who do not have resources of their own. These supplementary sources of income play a particularly important role when the "culture professional" does not come from a family with high social status and has no inherited wealth. The gap between the income contributed by a spouse or partner and the income earned by an individual personally "is especially large in the household of visual artists, literary writers and translators, and art professors, where the revenue of the spouse or partner is quite likely to be a support, sometimes an indispensable support, for the pursuit of the artistic activity."[11]

One of the interesting features of the data collected by the Ministry of Culture and Communication is that it breaks with the at once bleak and sublime depiction of the artistic life passed down from the nineteenth century, by showing that persons who engage in cultural activities are indeed, for the most part, "professionals," as it were, on a par with other professionals. Their standard of living is a little below the one they would have were they in a profession classified as "at the [upper or middle] managerial level," in public service, or in a business, and, for those who are of middle- or upper-class origins, having inherited wealth and/or a managerial-level spouse or partner brings resources that can make up for the relative weakness of income from cultural activity.

Two other frequently defended theses must also be nuanced. The first, which focuses on the wide range of income levels, and especially on the rare culture professionals who bring in very high incomes as a result of their exceptional success, consists in the claim that all those who commit themselves to this path are ready to accept great sacrifices and to take great risks in the hope of belonging, one day, to the small number of the elite.[12] But this emphasis leaves out the fact that, while exceptional successes are indeed exceptional, those who do not reach that level and who are, by composition, in a sense, the vast majority, manage nevertheless to attain a standard of living that is not very different from the one they would have had if they had opted for classic careers.

The second thesis associates the rise of the *precariat* with the rise in poverty. Financially precarious situations, in the sense in which the actors are always immersed in uncertainty about the future of their professional activities, further the poverty of those who are already poor to begin with because of their social origins and their schooling. Still, members of this group are in the minority, at least according to surveys of cultural activities. A diversification of employment situations and a tendency to hold multiple jobs have certainly accompanied the development of cultural activities and perhaps, more generally, during the last few decades, that of an enrichment economy. It has profoundly modified the way in which those who participate in these sectors earn their living and thus the way in which those individuals spend what they earn and how they occupy their time – indeed, their entire lifestyle.

Members of the latter group have to acquire competencies that combine knowledge of government bureaucracy (to obtain funding) and business (to manage their finances) if they are to attain a standard of living they find acceptable in relation to that of their family of origin and that of their friends. These competencies are thus inseparably both relational and commercial, and they involve activities that take up a significant amount of time – time that is thus not devoted to creative activities as such. These activities are indispensable for remaining informed about new trends and new projects, negotiating contracts, mastering the intricacies of funding arrangements, making oneself known (in particular via social networks), and *making oneself stand out*, in a highly competitive situation, in dealings with very diverse agencies and persons. The latter may include other artists participating in commissions charged with selecting projects, business managers, administrative managers of regional agencies, elected officials or others with political responsibilities, directors of foundations or cultural centers, and so on – all of these being entities on which commitments and proceeds depend. The acquisition of the requisite competencies, which takes place partly in schools and partly through the trials and errors of daily life, is one of the conditions of access to the informal status of *creator*, someone who, in an enrichment economy, tends to occupy a place comparable to the one occupied in earlier years, when the industrial economy predominated, by someone with the formal status of *executive* or *manager*. Let us now look closely at the modalities of this process of self-valorization.

Self-promotion by creators

We have already seen how, from the 1930s on, critiques of mass production of standard objects shifted their focus from things to persons. These critiques were permeated by a twofold fear: that the uniformization of things in the standard form and the primacy granted to functional objects would lead to the destruction of the "aura" around beautiful objects, whose "value" – in the aesthetic sense – would no longer be recognized; and that the uniformization of persons in the service of standardization would lead to a decline in "values" in the moral sense. Some might see this thematics as merely an avatar of antimodern thinking, apt to take a tone that was sometimes emancipatory and sometimes elitist; for us, though, the thematics brings with it an intuition that is certainly not groundless. It has to do with the mirror relation established between the way wealth is generated and the way persons who create or profit from this wealth are appreciated; and there is a similar relation between the arrangements that serve to justify price differences among things and the "values" that are invoked to justify inequalities among people. It is as though, within a single regime of wealth creation, things and persons alike could be objects of modes of appreciation that are by no means foreign to one another.

It is undeniable that, in the era of mass production, the standardization of things has gone hand in hand with an organization of labor and, especially in the framework of the welfare state, with administrative arrangements for social dealings that have tended to standardize persons or, put another way, have tended to apprehend persons only insofar as they could be codified. In the organization of labor within businesses, the standardization of persons has been stimulated by hierarchical arrangements, such as those separating research divisions from assembly lines, and by unequal treatment of persons depending, primarily, on the degree to which they offer useful differences within a given organizational framework and, secondarily, on an estimation of their capacity to maintain their performance levels over time. While people doing assembly-line work, conceived precisely to make them easily replaceable, earn low salaries, other persons, who are expected to be reliable over time – engineers, for example – earn higher salaries in positions characterized by a certain degree of autonomy. In what Randall Collins has called a "credential society,"[13] indications of competence and reliability have increasingly been tied to the possession of diplomas delivered by institutions judged trustworthy, often because they were underwritten by the national government.

As for administrative arrangements for societal support, their implementation has also relied on a strict codification of persons. In the systems adopted by welfare states, salary grade systems – integrated, in France, into collective conventions – have allowed unions to control the adjustments, within businesses, between work assignments (coded in terms of the level of competence required), diplomas (treated as coded indicators of incorporated competencies), and status (for example, executive or managerial). Other modes of codification have framed the programs responsible for people unable to work, whether they are unemployed, ill, or disabled. The implementation of this mode of dealing with persons rests on a large number of organizational, administrative, and statistical arrangements, all centralized and interconnected; in other words, it relies on a vast bureaucracy.[14]

If we limit ourselves to the case of "culture professionals" (assimilated in administrative nomenclatures to the category of "managers") and, more generally, to the case of workers in the enrichment economy, it is not hard to see that the environment in which these workers carry out their activities is very different from the one in which, forty or fifty years ago, a manager in a business was immersed. Let us single out a few indicators. "Culture professionals" and their ilk often work at home, which also means that they play dual roles: they are at once workers and supervisors of the intensity and regularity of their own work. Their hours are not limited to fixed time periods, and they can adjust their schedules as they like, so that work time can blend in with personal time. On the one hand, this superimposition of work time on personal time makes obsolete the distinction between payment by hours worked and the purchase of the person of the worker, a distinction on which the salary system had been based since the nineteenth century. On the other hand, this blurring of lines can sometimes create the illusion of a "refusal to work,"[15] because work is not performed at dedicated sites or within limited time periods; rather, it is extended to all places and all moments of a worker's existence.

A great number of workers in the enrichment economy do not belong to a particular company but depend on two or more employers, or are simultaneously salaried and independent. Their careers are not linear; rather, they are indexed on the worker's seniority, and such workers must continually adjust their personal positioning to the developments that affect the professional environments in which they work. They are often evaluated in terms of their reputation, which, while it may grow, can always be called into question. Engaged in several different activities, they may devote more time to one than to another at any given moment, working in alternation between two or more jobs. They are thus constantly subject to a double uncertainty: about their reputation and about their future activity – that is, about their very survival as holders of a competence whose exercise must be remunerated. Finally, if the modes of codification emanating from administrative agencies continue to have some relevance, they are no longer applied in a bureaucratically implacable way, because the workers have learned to use them as resources whose contributions can be modulated, as is apparent in France, for example, in the legal arrangements governing intermittent work.

The world to which this list applies may seem chaotic if we consider it from the standpoint of a social order subjected to the constraint of an industrial organization placed at least implicitly in the position of a norm. Still, there are as many ways to structure social orders as there are ways of creating wealth. Different types of things, if they are to contribute to the creation of wealth, require different types of persons – or, rather, different types of *personnel* – endowed with different qualities and connected to one another by specific modes of coordination. Thus, to take just one example, factory work, no matter what the level of responsibility may be, requires persons who are physically sturdy and psychologically stable if they are to be recognized as reliable, but it is indifferent to what we shall call their "potential for presence." By contrast, this latter characteristic, which is based both on the ability to make oneself interesting (through one's history, personal allure, and so on) and on the ability to manifest one's attention to others, plays a central role in an enrichment economy. The movements associated with the weakening of industrial requirements and the emphasis on requirements that derive from an enrichment economy can be quite obvious when they are marked by the decline of a profession or of a social status. But they may also imperceptibly affect persons whose trade seems enduring even though the ways of being and lifestyles of those who exercise it have been profoundly modified. We see this, for example, in the case of *farmers.* Transformed into *agricultural workers* by administrative measures retranslated into commercial constraints in the age of intensive agriculture in the 1960s and 1970s, former farmers have been encouraged more and more often by the same administrative agencies, since the 1990s, to concern themselves with maintaining the landscape – that is, to become *custodians of the natural environment,* and at the same time to arrange their living spaces so as to place them at the service of green tourism, as we saw happening in the Aubrac region. These workers may not have changed where they live or even, very much, how they live, but they have taken on new roles in the service of the *land,* inasmuch as this land is valorized by the enrichment economy.

In such an economy, specific investments are necessary to valorize objects from the past, but they are less costly per unit, and significantly less concentrated, than investments in production. They rely on small units, organized in networks, and on a human fabric composed of a myriad of potential *discoverers* and *creators,* whose competencies are multiple and whose performances are by no means always predictable. These investments nevertheless constitute only a small part of worldwide investing, which is delegated to collective agencies of higher rank, national governments in particular, but also regional entities, most notably in the form of educational investments. As for the preferred mode of coordination, it does not take the form of an organization so much as that of a network or even an environment or a milieu comprising a multitude of very diverse beings – things and persons – whose interactions are often attributed to chance and whose interplay operates a selection process presented as "natural."

Still, in these universes, there are specific ways in which persons can make themselves stand out, forms of valuation that have something in common with the forms underlying the valuations of the things whose valorization and circulation is ensured by these same persons. This is easiest to see in the case of those who, in the enrichment world, are called *creators.* The figure of the creator occupies the center of this world; the label can be applied very widely, from plastic artists to cooks, from designers to hairdressers, from photographers specializing in advertising or fashion to designers of clothing, jewelry, or perfumes. Contrary to what is suggested by the term used to designate them, creators in this context do not have the task of bringing forth previously unknown objects. This happens rarely; moreover, such objects are unlikely to be welcomed. These creators have a culture – a tradition – behind them and are thus oriented toward the past. But they support or "interpret" that tradition by introducing slight differences, and they often reactivate past forms that are more or less outdated so as to produce effects of surprise even as they stimulate recognition. The play of difference and repetition on which the collection form depends is thus at the heart of their activity. And this way of valorizing things finds an echo in the way these creators ensure their own valorization and engage in self-promotion.

If creators are to succeed (or at least avoid being eliminated), they have to make names for themselves, so to speak: they have to justify their requirements for monetary gain by attaching value to *their own names*, which function as brands and can be registered legally as such. To valorize a name, it helps to connect it in a lasting way with the memory of two types of performative description, each of which stands out against a background of continuity. One type seeks to highlight the manifestation of the *differences* that presumably inflect the course of the tradition in which they are inscribed. The other type seeks to turn a personal *story* into a narrative composed in a traditional format so as to anchor the selected differences in the continuity of a biography, that of a creator identified by a proper name and by the *projects* in which he or she has participated. Without this articulation, on the one hand with tradition, which brings out novelty with respect to a past that is always capable of being presented anew, and on the other hand with the story of a person to whom the articulation is attributed, the differentiation would appear to be random and would blend in with the flow of life's events or, one might say, with the *world*. It would be, if not imperceptible, at least devoid of memorial power and, consequently, of monetary value.

This is to say that creators need to *make their own case*; more specifically, they need biographers. Contemporary creators play growing roles in the staging of their own lives, about which they can release information in the form of interviews that can be appropriated by interpreters, for example, or, more modestly, they can recapitulate their activities, their qualities, and their "original" personal traits in curricula, in files, or in book form and can arrange to have this material widely circulated. Finally, creators have to be able not only to inscribe differences within things but also to generate discourse on these differences, making ample use of social networks. This latter ability presupposes that the traditional background against which the things in question stand out is familiar to them; they must be able to produce narratives of their own lives that allow them to base their claims to *patents* on these differences. In fact, intellectual property rights can apply only to works, whether these are objects or texts; they cannot apply to what are called "ideas." Yet the differences that a creator introduces often take the form of ideas, associated, as the jargon has it, with "hits": if a creator's ideas succeed in catching on and circulating, they are all the more easily adaptable by competitors with respect to whom the creator then has to maintain visible differences.[16] In the sort of display to which the creator's persona gives rise, the differences associated with the creator's name have to be presented and ordered in such a way as to conform to the classic model of biographies of noteworthy people from the past. On the one hand, each of the new differences displayed must mark a gap with respect to those that came before, so as to reactivate the effect of surprise and spark interpretation. On the other hand, each difference must present some similarity with the differences already associated with the name of the creator in question – that is, it must be a kind of repetition – so as to confer a unity of style on the creator, thus augmenting the memorial power of his or her name. But for these differences both to be attached durably to a name and to be judged relevant, the mediation of a *selector* plays a determining role. This latter is in effect in the position of *gatekeeper*. A selector controls access to funding or to a resource on which the creator's reputation depends; this role is often played by editors or curators. Yet the most powerful gatekeepers of all are often other creators – that is, competitors.

The constraint of self-exploitation

The typical creator whose portrait we have just drawn in schematic form is immersed in an environment that is at once a *common world* and a space of competition. In fact, the principal resources from which creators can benefit are spread throughout the space of their activities and their lives in forms that are both material – such as cafés, theaters, galleries, shops, or museums, all of which can be spaces for exhibition and encounters – and immaterial – such as affects, trends, or ideas. But the most profitable resources of all are persons, the ones whom one must get to know because they are well known, and because it is desirable and useful to approach them personally; of these, gatekeepers are in the first rank. This is evident from the interviews carried out by Cyprien Tasset with people who identified with the expression "precarious intellectuals." For these people, even in periods of penury, the expenditures that were hardest to give up were those concerning housing in places where creators are concentrated, restaurants, cafés, and cultural spaces that one has to frequent in order to remain visible and gain access to information about potential projects.[17] But this common world is also a space of selection, thus of competition, to the extent that each creator's self-valorization is oriented by what he or she knows about the others and the way those others valorize themselves, according to the mode of relations that takes hold in the "intellectual fields" explored by Pierre Bourdieu.

In a space of this type, each actor tends toward self-promotion, since each one individually *is* the enterprise on which his or her survival depends. Here we find the realization of the kind of society that Foucault saw taking shape in theories of German "ordoliberalism":

The individual's life must be lodged, not within a framework of a big enterprise like the firm or, if it comes to it, the state, but within the framework of a multiplicity of diverse enterprises connected up to and entangled with each other, enterprises which are in some way ready to hand for the individual, sufficiently limited in their scale for the individual's actions, decisions, and choices to have meaningful and perceptible effects, and numerous enough for him not to be dependent on one alone. And finally, the individual's life itself – with his relationships to his private property, for example, with his family, household, insurance, and retirement – must make him into a sort of permanent and multiple enterprise.[18]

Nevertheless, the type of promotion proper to this world also takes a generational form, since the creators who have succeeded in making names for themselves seek to protect themselves from competition from the new arrivals, even as they put themselves in positions that allow them to make the newcomers dependent on them and to capture their contributions – that is, to benefit from the strength of their claims, even their challenges, and their work. This is why creators, if they are to achieve lasting success, must either attain positions of power in organizations, for example membership in the leadership teams of exhibition or performance spaces, either public (such as museums) or private (such as foundations), or else accumulate wealth that can be transformed into capital – that is, invested in commercial entities oriented toward the enrichment economy, for instance companies focused on fashion, agencies devoted to trend-spotting, or bureaus set up to advise collectors, galleries, or producers in the performing arts or in the audiovisual sphere. However, taking on positions of this sort tends to immobilize creators, thus producing tension with the mobility that is expected of them and that is necessary if they are to defend their positions in the world of creators.

For the most part, the organizations just mentioned, whether public or private, could not prosper, could not even continue to exist, if they did not have access to an abundant and inexpensive workforce consisting of young degree-holders who aspire to achieve the status of creators. For members of this latter group, even temporary and intermittent employment constitutes both a source of income allowing them to subsist and a means of coming into proximity with the agencies on which their selection depends: that is, a means of promoting their own names, an endeavor in which participation in sponsored projects, even in a very minor capacity, can be helpful. One of the advantages of a workforce of this type is that it limits investments in fixed capital: since the members of this workforce are not integrated into a stable staff (the latter being limited to the administrative core in organizations that employ temporary or intermittent workers), they remain outsiders, and most of the costs involved in their work – energy, working space, computers and other tools – are borne by the workers themselves. This mode of organization turns out to be predominant in enrichment economies. Even in the case of "cultural industries," understood in the very limited sense of the Ministry of Culture and Communication (publishing, audiovisual production and distribution; press agencies and advertising firms), individual enterprises are particularly numerous (53 percent of the businesses in this sphere have no salaried employees). As for the larger companies that concentrate on cultural activities (4 percent have more than twenty salaried employees, and these companies bring in 84 percent of the overall profits), they rely heavily on freelancers and subcontractors.[19]

While degree-holding young people in this field could legitimately consider themselves exploited, they have trouble developing collective arrangements designed to limit the level of their exploitation by reinforcing their power to negotiate or apply pressure. There are several reasons for this.[20] The first has to do with the workers' dispersal in space and time. Lacking the physical framework of an established business, they can of course formulate and coordinate critiques, especially via social networks on the Internet, but when they seek to act they are blocked by the need to coordinate bodies. The second reason has to do with the fact that each one sees his or her own condition as temporary and hopes to move beyond it by acquiring the status of a recognized creator; this leads individuals to tend to see others who are oriented toward the same goals not so much as companions in misfortune as competitors. Finally, beyond the easily denounced abstract entities such as "neoliberalism," "neomanagement," or "financial capitalism," these actors do not have a clear sense of what agencies or persons are responsible for their exploitation; consequently, they do not know to whom to address their claims or against whom they might revolt.

In their case, a distinction that has played a historical role because it has served as support for critiques of capitalism has not made much headway: the opposition between *workers*, who possess only their own power to work, and *owners* of the means of production. This opposition was gradually imposed around the middle of the nineteenth century, when big business was winning out over the artisanal model, and when labor unions – workers' organizations of a new type whose structure was inspired by the forms associated with the political arrangements of democracies – began to supplant the older trade organizations.[21] By relying on this opposition, it was possible to flesh out the idea of exploitation understood as an unequal and unjust division of the fruits of productive labor – measured in monetary terms – between the different groups that contributed to production – that is, to the industrial manufacturing of things whose commercialization nourished the profits accumulated by company owners. However, in the case of the cultural organizations that occupy the center of an enrichment economy, it is very hard to make that opposition coherent, because the "exploiters" have characteristics that often do not differ radically from those of the "exploited" – except perhaps in terms of their success and, generally, by their standard of living – and they proclaim the same "values." In addition, while culture workers may well possess a patrimony consisting in exceptional objects or homes, in most cases they are not owners of the organizations under whose auspices they operate, not even directors or managers, since these organizations are not structured hierarchically on the model of mass-production companies. For these various reasons, the "bosses" to whom claims might be addressed are not easy to identify. Ultimately, it is in the rather rare cases in which their situation depends on a status organized by a central government that the exploited actors in an enrichment economy have the best chance of uniting to defend themselves by calling out administrative agencies on their role, especially at the governmental level, as intermittent workers in the performing arts have done.[22] In fact, the existence of a common status tends to furnish a hook for collective action, bringing together persons who in other respects see themselves as different in professional terms and are often objectively in competition. In addition, the existence of clearly identified political or administrative personnel with responsibility for workers holding this status gives these workers an "interlocutor," whereas in many other cases such an interlocutor is lacking.

The specific modes of exploitation proper to this universe turn out to be closely associated with processes of selection whose effects are manifested throughout entire lifetimes. These processes culminate in one of two liminal positions which mark the failure or success of the selection. The first is the position of "*loser.*" Those who have not succeeded in attaching value to their names and whose earnings have remained weak or in decline are compelled, especially if they have no inherited wealth, to leave the expensive centers where new projects are taking shape. They may then be eliminated from the domain of the enrichment economy (for example, by taking positions, when they can, as mid-level managers in public service at the national or regional level), or they may turn back to rural spaces that are not very productive but that are attractive to tourists, places whose decline has been slowed by the arrival of neo-rurals and artists driven out of metropolitan areas; the presence of these displaced creators in such places may help animate local activity and foster green tourism.[23] The second position, by contrast, is that of the *survivor,*[24] someone who has managed to valorize his or her name. Survivors are thus those who have succeeded in attaching to their names the memory of the differences they are credited with initiating, those who have managed to inscribe those differences in a coherent narrative that is conflated with their own life stories. Their success also presupposes that they have been able to withstand competition from newcomers on the scene.

The circumstances behind the crystallization of social classes

In the preceding pages, seeking to identify the changes that an enrichment economy could impose on society, we depicted several characteristic figures – that of the "loser," the "servant," the *rentier*, and the creator. In this respect, we are following the sociologists or social philosophers who seek to sort out the clusters that constitute, as they see it, the basis for emerging groups destined to play a central role in economic and social life in a more or less near future. Over the last twenty years a number of these scholars have forged terms to designate the groups that they see as embodying the change in the economic orientation of Western societies. Richard Barbrook has produced a detailed and ironic inventory of these terms,[25] including for example "knowledge worker," "cognitarian," "swarm capitalist," and "hacker," terms borrowed from information technology but to which Barbrook has given an extension capable of capturing the specificity and novelty of relations of ownership in the "virtual information age."[26]

Richard Florida used a similar approach when he proposed – in a work that, since its publication in 2002, has stirred up considerable interest, first in the United States and then in Europe – the idea that the specificity of contemporary Western societies, considered in terms of their social structure and their spatial distribution, resides in the development of a "creative class" anchored in the heart of major cities, which are thereby nourished by their dynamism.[27] In Florida's view, all those who play a driving role in processes of "innovation" belong to the creative class, whether their specific competencies are scientific or technical (researchers, engineers, doctors, and so on) or stem, rather, from the world of arts and culture, broadly understood, and whether they are salaried employees of large companies focused on industrial production or individual workers operating as freelancers (borrowing a term from César Graña,[28] Florida calls the latter "bohemians"). According to Florida, this "new class" includes roughly 30 percent of the US workforce.

This view is based on several presuppositions that do not square with our approach.[29] First, it does not take into account the specificity of the objects on which the activity of these actors bears, and consequently it does not make it possible to study the way industrial economies differ from what we have called enrichment economies. Second, it presumes that the "creative class" constitutes a homogeneous totality that is simply added to the accumulated divisions already present in industrial societies. Florida's position is also debatable in that, on the one hand, "creators" are distributed among very unequal situations[30] and, on the other hand, they are by no means necessarily "innovators," at least if this descriptor is understood in the sense it has been given by historians and sociologists of science and technology, which associate it with modernism.

Other problems have to do with the very use of the term "class," which, as we know, can take on very different meanings depending on whether it is used in a Marxist perspective, with reference to the "class struggle," or whether it has a chiefly descriptive orientation, as is the case with Anglo-Saxon scales constructed around the notion of hierarchies of "prestige,"[31] or with INSEE's socio-professional categories. In the latter case, a large number of trades have been grouped around focal points or common features, in relation to a system of criteria in which a hierarchical distinction presupposing a lower or higher level of autonomy and responsibility as a function of the length and type of training – the distinction between salaried employees and employers, between manual labor and intellectual work, between workers who execute and workers who direct – plays a predominant role. Nevertheless, the specificity of these socioprofessional categories and the source of their descriptive power lie in the fact that they were based on conventional forms put in place, in France, between 1936 and 1946 – that is, they were based on collective conventions within sectors, and on the Parodi accords,[32] for the business sector, or on the General Statute concerning government work. The statistical forms seeking to represent the world of work and the forms of political representation that had been overlaid on the articulation between union action and central governments were thus well matched, because they relied on the same processes of qualification.[33] Now it is precisely that order of classes, inseparable from the political order of the welfare state and from an industrial order of production, that has been partially dismantled, first by the re-engineering of businesses in the 1990s and the development of subcontracting, then by deindustrialization, and finally by increasing numbers of precarious jobs and the rise in power of the enrichment economy.

In relation to the object of our study, it is thus only in a very vague sense that we can call on the idiom of social class. Partial communities of interests and equally partial affinities of lifestyles no doubt exist within the various clusters we have sought to identify, starting from stereotypical examples of "losers," "servants," *rentiers*, and creators. But since these clusters are not objectified either in law or by administrative and statistical conventions, they retain a virtual character. To see them *realized* – that is, to see them take the form of social classes – one would have to be able to observe them immersed in *events* and, more precisely, in conflicts during which the persons involved would have to be determined in relation to the stakes with which they are confronted.[34] Events of this type in fact constitute historical *tests* that oblige individuals to come together to increase their power within the existing power relations – that is, to fall back on their dominant loyalties.

Troubled critiques

As we see it, the study of the development of the enrichment economy and the analysis of the forms of valuation on which that economy relies make it easier to understand some of the difficulties that have confronted critiques of capitalism in the early twenty-first century, especially in Western European countries. These critiques, intense between the mid-1960s and the mid-1970s, found themselves virtually reduced to silence between 1985 and 1995 owing to two historical movements of very broad scope that, although relatively independent of one another, were nevertheless concurrent. On the one hand, there was the implosion of a certain number of countries said to be governed by "real socialism"; as a result, the communist-inspired parties and unions whose critical role had been central during the postwar decades lost credibility in Western countries, while the remaining socialist countries, with China in the lead, proceeded to undergo a more or less controlled evolution toward capitalism. And, on the other hand, capitalism demonstrated its capacity to overcome the crisis it had undergone in the 1970s by relying most notably, first, on the reorganization of businesses and on the outsourcing of a large portion of industrial production to countries with cheap labor, often to the very countries that had moved from collective ownership to private property, a development that unsettled and splintered the working class; and, second, by relying on deregulation of financial activities, which favored their expansion on a worldwide scale.

After a period of consternation, critiques of capitalism blossomed anew, at the outset of the twenty-first century, chiefly in the form of a critique of neoliberalism. This critique emphasized, first, the effects imputed to the power of the financial markets;[35] second, the difficulties of nation-states confronting debt and the power of international agencies to regulate markets;[36] third, modes of domination through labor, taking advantage of the shock effects of mass unemployment;[37] fourth, the exploitation of so-called natural resources to the detriment of "autochthonous" peoples in particular;[38] and, finally, the generalization of an "individualist" moral-ity oriented toward personal well-being and attention to feelings.[39] The decline of solidarities and even the dissolution of collectivities have been attributed to this fifth factor, because the individualist morality was accused of promoting individual responsibility and generalized competi-tion at all levels, of granting pre-eminence to accounting instruments in the evaluation of things and persons, and of ignoring the leading ideals held in common, whether these ideals were focused on the future or anchored in the past. These prophecies, moreover, were being refuted starting in the 2000s, on the one hand, by the rise in power of nationalism along with mobilizations and conflicts carried out in the name of a religion and, on the other hand, by the prominence of ecological concerns.

While, in this picture, the decline of industrial power has been widely discussed and considered as a process which both the people in charge and their opponents have never ceased to view as reversible, the development of an enrichment economy has not been fully taken into account. It has either been ignored or dismissed disdainfully, as though it touched only futile sidelines of social life and did not constitute a movement of great importance destined to increase in intensity and thus to produce profound economic and social changes that would have political repercussions. And yet the blossoming of the enrichment economy, without ever being recog-nized as such, has sown confusion among critics of capitalism.

This confusion is manifest if we look at the way workers in the enrich-ment universe have been viewed. On the one hand, they have been seen

as personifying the misdeeds of neoliberalism to the extent that they have
been subjected to working and living conditions marked by precarity. On
the other hand, they have been seen, by other authors and sometimes by
the same authors in different contexts, as representing a sort of embodiment of decadent modernity because of everything that, in their ways
of living and being, evokes the reviled free-market liberalism, given the
arrangements imposed by necessity with which they have had to comply
in order to live or survive, the extended, often international spatial context
with respect to which they conceive their activities, and their orientation
in favor of increased social freedom. Characterized as *bobos* (middle
class, fashionable, left-leaning) or "hipsters," they could then represent
the antithesis of the industrial proletariat, which had been granted the
status of "real people" – this perspective could help orient critical stances
toward a demand for reindustrialization in the national context; in certain
versions, this stance was close to nationalism. From the standpoint of
political decision-makers, culture generally continued to be treated as a
princely distraction, far from the "serious" matters of standardized industrial production and finance, all the more so if the two are associated in
war. Moreover, it was this same schema that critics could take up again
when they constituted artistic creativity as the "outside" of capitalism,
from which resistance could be mounted against the unlimited alienation
produced by capital. Such a schema, developed in particular between 1930
and 1950, is in tension today with the impossibility of closing one's eyes to
the role played by artistic and cultural activities, especially in the domains
of luxury and tourism, whose contribution to the prosperity of capitalism
is hardly negligible.

While rightly stressing the role played in the growth of inequalities by the
rise in power of financial capitalism, these critical analyses have neglected
the ties maintained by finance with the development of an enrichment
economy. In reality, this economy reserves ownership and enjoyment of
exceptional goods to the wealthiest, permitting them to live in virtual
isolation chambers apart from the "common people," about whom they
have little reason to be concerned, since the degradation of the living conditions of the vast majority affects the wealthy only in very indirect ways.
In addition, this economy continues to enrich the wealthiest, or at least
allows them to maintain the level of their fortune. It is, on the one hand, by
benefiting from the profits provided by the luxury economy in which they
invest and, on the other, by storing up inherited or acquired wealth – by
placing their funds in real estate or in collectors' items managed as if they
were assets – that the most fortunate preserve a wealth that would always
be at risk of evaporating were it not placed in material goods whose prices
and liquidity are staked on resources that do not depend on the holders'
own activity but that stem from collective work and are thus, on this basis,
common property. For the high metaprices of which these goods can
boast depend to a large extent on the narratives attached to them, narratives whose validity is always established through reference to a regime of

verification that is aligned with culture and history. These stories, whose efficiency derives from their power to invoke the past, are forged by a multitude of actors, headed by historians who have developed the thematics of "sites of memory"; these historians, underwritten by institutions that belong by definition to the collective realm, benefit very little from the profits procured by their commercialization. And yet the past, whose valorization supports the enrichment economy, constitutes a common good par excellence. The past belongs to everyone.

Conclusion: Action and Structures

The enrichment economy and a critique of capitalism

To suggest how a critique of capitalism might make good use of the situation created by the development of an enrichment economy, we propose to emphasize three themes. The first has to do with the relation between capitalism and central governments; the second deals with the forms of exploitation that are being consolidated in the framework of an enrichment economy; and the third bears upon the role of commercialization in the shifting shape of capitalism.

Recent critiques of capitalism have targeted private entities, extremely wealthy individuals, and international firms and markets operating on a global level rather than nation-states, whose importance has been fading – indeed, they have even been represented as the principal victims of capitalism. The development of financialized global capitalism and the indebtedness of nation-states have even led some observers to think that nation-states have become impoverished and impotent. The theme of the "wealth of nations" – which was at the heart of the economy that could still be called political – has been displaced by that of the wealth accumulated by individual owners of capital or by firms treated as if they have become independent of nations, whose productive capacities have allegedly been expatriated by the power of the financial markets. From this perspective, nation-states have become less important as profit centers, while increased importance is attributed to private entities; the latter are now represented as the principal actors in the dynamics of capitalism. Nevertheless, it is still possible to see nation-states as continuing to constitute the frameworks within which wealth is concentrated. Even if we remain on the level of industrial potential, one indication ought to nuance the belief that nation-states have lost control: the highly significant fact that the industries directly tied to state power – in France and in the United States, these include enterprises devoted to aeronautics, weapons production, and the nuclear sector (civil and military) – have not been outsourced and are represented as national "jewels."

The picture we have sought to draw of the enrichment economy and its development in Europe (and particularly in France) sheds light, as we see it, on the role that central governments still play in the formation and accumulation of wealth. In fact, the exploitation of things found in the strata accumulated in the past, to the primary benefit of those who own and commercialize these things, cannot be achieved without assistance from public action in the context of a nation-state. This is all the more true when what is being commercialized carries the brand of a particular nation and is valorized by narratives that are at least loosely attached to that nation's past. Confronted with the declining profits of industrial enterprises, two simultaneous strategies have been put to work. The first consists in delocalizing the manufacture of standard products, something that would not have been possible without the cooperation of nation-states. The second consists in exploiting resources that cannot be delocalized, or those whose prices depend on their ties to specific localities, and valorizing these goods by means of narratives that lean on national fictions. From this perspective, the enrichment economy has been able to align the interests of the owners of capital who are best placed to make these types of goods prosper (and to profit from them themselves) with the interests of central governments, at a time when the latter have had to confront increased international competition while simultaneously facing the need to keep the best educated among their ranks employed and to contain a workforce contending with unemployment.

Where forms of exploitation are concerned, it is important to highlight the issue of how work time is measured. In an economy organized around industrial capitalism, where investments in fixed capital are considerable and not easy to compress, profit depends on the relation between the number of specimens sold and the costs of production; reducing those costs depends primarily on exploitation of the workforce (surplus labor value). In economies of this type, the critique of exploitation may rely on the relation between salary and hours worked. Now, in an enrichment economy, which takes advantage above all of surplus market value, the gap between production costs and the prices of the things sold is very high, so that profits depend especially on the margin that can be taken on each unit sold (in accordance with an estimated acceptable price). Exploitation of the workforce in the enrichment economy has not disappeared, but it can no longer be grasped by taking the relation between the cost of labor and its duration in work hours into account, as can be done in an industrial economy. The form defined for the salaried workforce by collective conventions put in place after lengthy struggles in the decades following the Second World War is no longer the central form in which workers in the enrichment economy operate. This form is increasingly being replaced by a different regime in which working hours, no longer stabilized by negotiated and pre-established work schedules, have come to blend with living hours, because each worker in this economy is forced to become his or her own exploiter, a *self-trader*: in other words, each worker is both merchant and merchandise. Under this regime, the indefinite extension of individual work time is uncoupled from the earnings received by each worker and from the distribution of wealth among all those who participate in its creation. There is no framework for relating the number of hours worked to global enrichment. It follows that the enrichment economy enriches the richest first of all, without giving those whom it does not enrich, or indeed those whom it impoverishes, those who might well consider themselves exploited, any leverage by which they could bring to light and critique the condition in which they find themselves.

This state of affairs can only be perpetuated to the extent that, since the enrichment economy is not recognized as a specific economic sphere functioning according to a different regime from that of industrial economies, there is no accounting system comparable, for example, to the one that was set up with the creation of national accounting in France – no system that would make it possible to tally the wealth created in the various sectors that make up the enrichment economy and then to depict and monitor the way this wealth is distributed among the various actors who helped produce it. Instead, every individual actor is envisaged as a profit center whose success or failure is attributed uniquely to his or her personality and performances, treated as if these were independent of broader processes of accumulation. This situation blurs both what each actor owes to his or her insertion in a given – and more or less advantageous – environment and what his or her activities contribute to the enrichment of that environment. At the present moment, it may seem utopian to defend the validity of collective arrangements for redistributing revenues – for example, to propose that actors or artists working in a locality whose attractiveness is increased by their presence should benefit not only from compensation in payment for specific activities defined contextually but also from redistribution of part of the overall revenues that the enrichment economy brings to the same locality, and in particular the revenues procured by tourism.

Redistribution of a fraction of the overall profits that are taken into account when salary agreements are negotiated has been one of the foundations for postwar economic growth. Still, such redistribution was called into question after the great turnaround in the late 1970s, and it is harder to reconcile with an enrichment economy than it was with the industrial economy. In an industrial economy, workers can be compensated in relation to the hours worked and in relation to the certified competencies they possess (competencies recognized by collective conventions). By contrast, redistribution of the wealth created by an enrichment economy cannot be based on the length of time spent working, since this time is unlimited, as we have seen, and since reputation can appear to be an adequate recompense in itself, so that it would seem inappropriate to ask that it be transformed into money. The properly collective character of the creation of wealth in the framework of an enrichment economy thus presupposes recourse to other types of arrangements. These can be conceived along the lines of the arrangements that, in historically diverse contexts, have been set up to manage common resources while avoiding the introduction of unregulated competition among all those who benefit from their exploitation, competition that would lead not only to the destruction of collectives in which people live or work but also to the destruction of the resources themselves. In fact, what is designated by the term "culture," however that term is defined, constitutes a common resource par excellence whose preservation presupposes that it be deemed a common good.[1] Any other form of management amounts to neglecting the largest portion of the value chain: in practice, this means not remunerating the actors in this sector, thereby further enriching those who are already the wealthiest and increasing inequalities in the process.

Finally, the critique that often has only a nostalgic past as its vantage point – the critique of industrial society and the great workers' struggles – would no doubt benefit if it did a better job at drawing the consequences from the shifts in capitalism. The commercialization of new goods and new domains, as profits diminish in domains commercialized and exploited earlier, drives the very movement of capitalism, whose capacity for shifting its position may well constitute, along with private property, one of its principal features, a feature probably more characteristic than the reference to a body of salaried workers. In critiques where the capacity of capitalism to shift its ground has been taken into account, this capacity has been wrongly interpreted as making it impossible for capitalism to fail, since every critique would be immediately recuperated and recast as a "complicitous illusion."[2] Such an interpretation rests on an outdated vision of capitalism, according to which it has not been transformed since the nineteenth century, and on an almost aesthetic fixation on the figure of the worker. The shifts in capitalism make sense in relation to the quest for profit – that is, in the quest for a differential between price and metaprice – and consequently in relation to forms of valuation. It is within these forms that critical arguments can be used to cause prices, and thus profits, to vary. When a critique of the prices that prevail in a specific domain that gives rise to a specific form of valuation takes hold and succeeds in diminishing the opportunities for profit, capitalism then has to shift in order to try to commercialize domains that had not been sources of profit previously.

At every moment in history, capitalism in fact works – as tectonic plates are said to work – at the borders between what can and what cannot be commodified, borders that are supported by social and moral norms and that are often written into law. This is undoubtedly why the struggle against commodification has always constituted one of the central aspects of critiques of capitalism. This struggle has often been developed with moral – or, more precisely, humanist – inflections, based on the distinction between human persons, who are exempt from the cosmos of merchandise, and things, which are destined to be merchandise, so that certain non-human beings such as domestic animals or works of art have been able to be protected against commodification only by being classified as quasi-persons. In other cases, the separation between civil society – the domain of commerce par excellence – and the nation-state has served to support the establishment of the border separating the commodifiable from the non-commodifiable. But whatever the difference on which this distinction rests may be, commerce in things that are situated right at the border of what is commodifiable has always benefited from a sort of surplus value, as though the fact of being wrested away, as it were, from the non-commercial domain increased the price of a thing. It is this surplus value – we might call it *prohibited surplus value* – that is realized by those who deal in illegal commerce in non-commodifiable things. Those who profit the most from the development of the enrichment economy have an interest in maintaining the separation between ordinary things, trade in which is supposed to obey only the "laws of the economy," and exceptional things, trade in which is possible but which are nevertheless represented as though they have escaped by virtue of their essence, as it were, from the cosmos of commodities, and this treatment confers on them a supplementary value that supports their prices.

To the extent that the dynamic of capitalism rests on shifts of ground that entail an extension of commodification, it does not simply tend to make the world as it is experienced more uniform (something of which capitalism has often been accused) by taking into account first and foremost the expansion of the industrial economy – an expansion that is held responsible for the loss of local particularities in the perspective of a global unification. This dynamic also takes advantage of the exploitation of differences, as long as these differences are distributed asymmetrically. With the development of the enrichment economy, capitalism has taken maximal advantage of the different forms of valuation that we have analyzed. It is most notably in this way that it has succeeded in increasing the commodification of new objects and in drawing maximal profits from them, as much by bringing the prices of certain objects down (in the standard and trend forms) as by increasing prices of other objects when they are put back in circulation (in the collection and asset forms). Still, even though commodification of things has increased, and to that end has had to resort to four different forms of valuation, it does not cover all the things that make up the world – far from it; a large portion of them remains non-commodified.

Alongside the dynamic of capitalism that leads to a limitless capitalization of reality, there is another dynamic that, relying on common practices, draws from the world things whose indeterminate and sometimes indeterminable character hinders commodification, or else it grasps commercial objects but then transforms them according to a logic of "tinkering" that exempts them from commercial circulation. The dissemination of these practices of tinkering, practices stimulated by critiques, has proved to be a stumbling block for capitalism, which has not succeeded in reappropriating the practices according to a logic of commodification. "Tinkering" is used here not only in the sense of a practice in which amateurs substitute for professionals but also in the Lévi-Straussian sense of any practice that takes hold of things or ideas and recombines them without intellectual property constraints, following the ebb and flow of life. A universe in which the actors were led to pay rights-holders every time they touched an object or uttered a word – the object or the word being always attributed to legally protected origins – would be a universe tolerable only for the possessors of those rights, and would therefore be intolerable.

The question of the degree to which the development of the enrichment economy can be maintained, especially in the countries of Western Europe, as though that economy were immunized to the point where no critique could grasp it firmly, is a question that is meaningful only if it is considered in relation to the other changes that are affecting capitalism on a global level. These changes have in common the fact that they rely in large part on new forms of exploitation of the differential between the local and the global – that is, between what is immobile and what is mobile – whether we are dealing with human beings, commodities, information, or capital. The enrichment economy benefits from the displacement of commodities whose valuation depends on narratives that stress their local roots, and especially from the displacement of the most fortunate actors, which has been facilitated by the development of tourism. The industrial economy has continued to flourish by wagering on the displacement of production sites to countries with cheap labor, and this shift itself has been made possible by the opportunities for profit offered, first by the displacements of capital that have accompanied the changes in the legal framework on which financial activities depend, then by the circulation of information, a process that has grown to an unprecedented degree thanks to the Internet, and finally by the development of transportation systems, for commodities as well as for people, and the concomitant reduction in transportation costs. As they have converged, these transformations and the accompanying displacements have resulted in a considerable increase in inequalities within and between nation-states – to such an extent that the increase worries even the primary beneficiaries of the enrichment economy, as is clear from a remark attributed to Johann Rupert, president of the Richemont group, during the eleventh Business of Luxury Summit held in Monaco in 2015: "If 0.1 percent of the wealthiest 0.1 percent make off with everything, even if they are our clients, it's unjust and it's untenable in the long run. They will be hated and scorned …. They won't want to show off their money any longer."[3]

A necessary condition for the existence and development of these displacements is that their security be guaranteed. The future of capitalism thus depends on the level of security, for which competing nation-states have assumed responsibility; these countries, generating a very high level of control everywhere, democracies included, pose particular threats to critical manifestations that aim to bring to light the ever-increasing inequalities produced by capitalism and to reveal their unacceptable character. If it is acknowledged that capitalism rests on the conjunction between forms of property whose legitimacy and defense are guaranteed by the laws and police forces of the nation-states, on the one hand, and on the exploitation of differentials generated by displacements, on the other hand, capitalism enters into crisis mode when the regimes managing the relations between forms of property and forms of mobility are profoundly destabilized. Such crises ought to offer opportunities for relaunching a critique of capitalism that would not aim to prevent displacements through a policy of closing borders – for that would trigger a return to prioritizing local, national, and identitarian concerns; rather, they would aim to reduce the differentials that make it possible to extract profits from the displacements.

On pragmatic structuralism

The development of a critique depends on the competence of actors who are caught between global determinations that are beyond their control and that, in the absence of overarching discourses, inevitably escape them, on the one hand, and the practical demands of their everyday lives, on the other. In an attempt to reconcile these two dimensions of the act of developing a critique, we have sought to bring together two types of approach that have often been treated as incompatible: the systemic approach, which aims to bring processes of broad scope to light, and the pragmatic approach, which aims to shed light on people's actions by analyzing the cognitive structures underlying their exchanges.

The problem with the systemic approach is that, taking the high ground, as it were, it ends up losing sight not only of the actors but also of the arrangements that motivate and give meaning to their actions. However, it does make it possible both to identify the asymmetries and the power relations that drive capital and to describe this seemingly chaotic movement in a way that attributes to it an orientation – above all a spatial orientation – and a historical meaning.

The problem with the pragmatic approach is that, as it looks closely at practices, at the motives that inspire the actors, at their interactions, and at the tests they apply to things, it ends up losing sight of the constraints surrounding their field of action, a field that the actors themselves tend not to grasp clearly: the actors tend to bracket those constraints or misinterpret them by personifying them, because they seem to be out of reach, so that any direct action against them appears impossible.

Nevertheless, the social phenomena that these two approaches allow us to identify are by no means foreign to one another, as we have tried to demonstrate on the basis of an analysis of the structures of merchandise. The geographical and historical shifts of capital, especially in response to variations in profit margins, are indeed what lead to the commodification of things previously viewed as secondary from the standpoint of profit and, thus, to an extension of the cosmos of commodities. But this movement of commodification would remain incomprehensible, or would be cloaked in mystery, without an analysis of the way things that had previously remained apart from capitalism have been inserted into the cosmos of commodities. Such an analysis presupposes that the things in question have been taken in hand by cognitive structures on which the possibility of appreciating them depends, as does the possibility of coordination among actors who all seek advantage or profit but who must nevertheless reach agreement on prices if an exchange is to take place.

These two approaches are not merely complementary; each also sheds new light on the other. The systemic approach makes it possible to envisage the changes that affect the valorization of things and the distribution of these things among the various forms of valuation, no longer by attributing them to changes in tastes that would depend on a host of external "social" variables, but as functions occupying a central position in the shifts of capitalism on a global level. From another standpoint, the way the pragmatic approach brings to light the role of discourse – whether in analytic or narrative form – in the valuation of things makes it possible to shift the axis of power relations and structures of domination on which the systemic approach insists. Thus the pragmatic approach uncovers a power that lies at the heart of power itself: the power to develop a discourse about things and thereby to valorize them in such a way as to demand the highest possible price for them – and also the power to inscribe this discourse and the profits it generates into the fabric of reality. Yet this power is distributed in a particularly asymmetrical fashion. It lies largely in the hands of actors – individual or collective persons – to whose benefit the movements of capital accrue. The discourses of these actors permeate everyday reality; combating them, especially with the powerful critical lever of irony, is thus a first step toward cutting back the power of capital and perhaps limiting its extension. This is a means available to everyone.

The expression *pragmatic structuralism* will strike many readers as a kind of oxymoron. To defend its validity, we need to clarify the relation between structure and experience – that is, between structure and history – since experience always arises from a confrontation between events, however large or small the scale on which these events are identified. The seeming incompatibility between a structural approach and a pragmatic approach, often treated as irreducible, depends largely on the persistence of a theoretical legacy that has led to conceiving of structure as a given, even as a condition of any experience, which amounts to placing it in a transcendental position with respect to experience. This is the case even in versions where, under the influence of the burgeoning social sciences, structure has been anchored in a collective entity – for example, when reference is made to something like traditions or "cultures."

Yet, as we have learned from the radical empiricism that inspires pragmatism, the priority of structure over experience is in no way necessary, or even probable. If it were, experience would never do anything but reactivate an order already inscribed in pre-existing frameworks, so that, finding itself taken up again in what would then have to be called "consciousness," experience would have no effect other than helping to reinforce that order. And this is indeed what happens with all constructions based on a presumption of circular relations between two agencies, called "objective" and "subjective," agencies that, in thematics of this sort, are distinguished only to be better conflated, since their organization results from the application of one and the same program. But it then becomes difficult to understand the shifting relations between these two planes and the fluctuations or changes that affect them; in particular, it is hard to attribute its rightful place to what can be called *critique* in the sense in which this practice, especially in its most unsettling manifestations, is nourished not only by components integrated into reality as reality is socially constructed and, as it were, prestructured but also by ingredients extracted from the world – that is, precisely from all that reality has had to exclude in order to constitute itself as reality. Thus we are obliged to acknowledge, most notably against Durkheim and against all species of transcendentalism, the autonomy of experience, which, being of one body with "the flow of life," is maintained in "the absolute uniformity of existence."[4]

Does this mean that structure has to be relegated to the warehouse for antiquities? To do that would be to forget the relations – which are often conflictual, moreover – between experience and reflection. Experience is by no means always reflective, and, if it were, the cost of action would rise to the point of making it virtually impossible, as we see from the fact, noted by linguists and experienced by people who are learning to express themselves in a foreign language, that it is almost impossible to speak while reflecting on the grammar rules that express the norms for speech in a given language. Conversely, reflection detached from experience spins around, as it were, in a vacuum and delivers nothing more than "ideologies." Marx developed this idea when he posited the fundamental difference between those who produce their own means for subsistence and have the experience of working, on the one hand, and, on the other, those who live off the work of others and believe they have nothing better to do than to "think" their condition, generally universalizing it. Since Marx, this opposition has in large measure inspired theories of practice.

There are nevertheless a great number of situations in which experience, turning back on itself, as it were, initiates a reflective move. This is usually the case when our experience brings us up short and we are in a way "surprised" because we have run up against something that previous experience has not prepared us to deal with, something that strikes us as an enigma. This situation, on which pragmatists – most notably John Dewey – have commented at length, triggers the beginning of an inquiry. In our view, it is at the heart of these states of things that reference to cognitive structures becomes pertinent. For, unlike experience, inquiry cannot do without instruments of investigation; in other words, it has to turn to previously stocked schemas or models, whether these arise from previously lived experiences or from more formal instruction transmitting things known through hearsay and at a distance, or, as is no doubt most often the case, from a combination of the two. Thus it is by combining "lived" experience with these models that an inquiry may take shape. And it is to these schemas and models, which are deposited in different types of memories but which, if they are to be efficacious, always also end up in languages, that reference to internalized structures almost always points. These operators, precisely because they turn out to be molded into the play of language, are necessarily structured.

If this possibility is taken seriously, it becomes clear that there is no point pitting approaches that stress the irreducible aspects of experience against those that make use of structures. Experiences and structures alike are anchored in the "plane of existence" – provided that we conceive of structures not as absolute predecessors of all experience but, rather, as operators capable of being mobilized to interpret experience when the latter runs up against obstacles that prevent it from being absorbed into the flow of life. This does not mean that these operators are always well adapted to the situations in which they are put to work and are thereby enlightening. In a great number of situations, the actors apply to their experiences schemas that are powerless to open up a path for interpretation that would allow those actors to pursue an interaction with the environment; this is particularly the case when reality is confronted with major changes that put experience in direct contact with the world – that is, with what is uncertain or even unknown. There are inquiries that fail; indeed, this is doubtless the most common case. Nevertheless, without recourse to these operators, actors would have no hold at all on reality and, deprived of critical capacities, would be immersed in a flow of experiences that is opaque to itself.

Turning now to systemic structuralism, could one not defend the idea that an overarching narrative, or perhaps, to use a familiar formula, "the big story," is also a sort of composite of experience and reflection in which empirical information, including statistical data, for example, would back up a function of reflection? Considered in this light, what we have called systemic structuralism would be one of the reflective operators that could be mobilized to organize an overarching narrative deployed in both time and space, as is, for example, the story of "globalization." One may of course challenge this proposition by arguing that the overarching narrative is a story without a subject, on the same basis moreover as any narrative that purports to lean on something like "science," since there is no subject capable of memorizing and ordering a personal experience of the totality that constitutes the horizon to which the overarching narrative aspires.

Before rejecting this proposition as absurd, though, it is important to remember that there are actually many species of "subject" that give rise to discourses oriented, to varying degrees, toward the goal of totalization and that present themselves as if they were offering an image of reality seized from an all-encompassing viewpoint that can and even must be reappropriated by ordinary persons – that is, persons endowed with bodies – whom these "subjects" are charged with enlightening. We are referring of course to institutions, beings devoid of bodies that are nevertheless responsible for expressing *the whatness of what is* and to declare this to one and all. These institutional discourses are often criticized as having an abusive character and as intending to do nothing other than stifle the personal experience of actors by imposing on them a "worldview" corresponding to the interests of the powerful, whatever they may be – that is, these discourses are designed to exercise an effect of domination. But this purely critical concept bumps up against the fact that there is probably no society that does without this type of discourse. This observation suggests that such discourses play an important role in the reflective work to which actors submit their own experiences and, by the same token, in the formation of the cosmos within which disparate ingredients tend to crystallize to the point of presenting structures. Clearly, these overarching narratives may be more or less imaginary, and they are acceptable only insofar as their accuracy is attested by procedures of verification. It is always possible, and often appropriate, to cast doubt on them on the basis of personal experience. It is when doubt is generalized by means of interactions that a dynamic of mutation of the overarching narratives is initiated, and it is only when these narratives are associated with "radical democracy," and thereby confronted with a critique, that the overarching narratives, which use methods stemming more or less from systemic structuralism to organize diverse materials, can help enrich the operators that social actors put to work in order to interpret their own experience.

Appendix

An Experiment in Formalizing the Structures of Commodity Exchange

by Guillaume Couffignal

The purpose of this text is to translate structural elements of the forms of commodity valuation we have identified into mathematical language. Our expectation is that the translation will make it possible both to assess the coherence of these elements and to compare the structures of commodity exchange with those of other types of exchange, ranging from kinship structures in anthropology to economic theories. One advantage of mathematical language is its degree of abstraction, which helps to establish connections among structures drawn from very different fields. In addition, the many discussions we had with Guillaume Couffignal in the course of our work served as a useful constraint, leading us to focus on the structural relations among things and on the maintenance of those relations when transformations occur. We see category theory as a potentially useful tool for developing a substantively less rigid form of structuralism that is capable of following the lineaments of action – a form that we call "pragmatic structuralism."

Luc Boltanski and Arnaud Esquerre

The goal in using mathematical language is to clarify the processes of the commercial circulation of things, as Luc Boltanski and Arnaud Esquerre have described and analyzed them. Let us recall that, according to the authors, the forms of valuation they have identified do not exhaust either "every perspective that can be applied to anything at all" or all possible forms of circulation. For social significations lend themselves to an infinite number of formal organizations, no one of which can be definitive. Recourse to the language of category theory seems appropriate, then, for several reasons. First, the language of categories has an abstract, generalizing character that does not close off interpretation prematurely, while an overly rigid formal language, though it might appear more precise, tends to impose limits on meaning. Second, category theory is a natural formal framework for the problems that arise when objects and mathematical theories are compared.

Moreover, category theory itself has been formulated in many different ways, and no particular presentation can be privileged in any absolute sense. The multitude of presentations in fact offers a wide range of viewpoints and practices. Thus various concepts that may be considered central can also be expressed as particular cases of other concepts. While in this text I have chosen to privilege Kan extensions in order to introduce the notion of (co) limit as a particular case, it would have been entirely possible to make the inverse choice by presenting Kan extensions as particular cases of (co) limits. The same point could be made regarding the very important notion of adjunction, about which I shall say very little here for want of space.

However, this observation has implications that go well beyond the simple affirmation that category theory is self-reflexive. By "speaking about itself," category theory enriches itself, in a sense (it would be more accurate to say "in more than one sense") that can be formalized.

Finally, to synthesize the foregoing points (even if this brief text cannot really give their full flavor), category theory is a highly developed and highly ramified theory that is being further ramified every day. It is thus equipped with a considerable arsenal of mathematical tools with applications to physics and biology, information technology and engineering, and many other fields.[1]

Some basic elements of the language of category theory

The two sections that follow apply especially to the forms of commodity valuation; to make these sections comprehensible, I must present some basic elements of the language of category theory. A more thorough treatment of category theory would fill hundreds of pages; thus it is out of the question to offer anything but a rough outline of its formalization here. For a much more complete and detailed discussion, I can recommend Saunders Mac Lane's *Categories for the Working Mathematician*, and the more recent *Categories and Sheaves*, by Masaki Kashiwara and Pierre Schapira.

Definition 1

A **Category** $\mathscr{C}$[2] consists of

- a set $Ob(\mathscr{C})$ whose elements are the **objects** of $\mathscr{C}$,
- for each pair x, y of objects from $\mathscr{C}$ of a set $\mathrm{Hom}_{\mathscr{C}}(x, y)$ (or simply $\mathrm{Hom}(x, y)$) whose elements are called **arrows** (or **morphisms**) with source x and target y and which are denoted by $x \rightarrow y$. This set (like the preceding one) may be empty.
- for each object x in $\mathscr{C}$ a morphism with source and target x, which is denoted by 1_x. This is called the **identity morphism** or identity on x.
- morphisms such that the target of the first matches the source of the second can be composed, and these compositions are associative and

possess identity morphisms as neutral elements. The composition of two morphisms $f : x \mapsto y$ and $g : y \to z$ is denoted by $g \circ f : x \to z$.

For example, let us assume that the following diagram is a category in which all morphisms (and objects) are represented. Thus the objects of this category are the "points" a, b, c, and d, and its morphisms are f, g, h as well as the composition $g \circ f$ and the identity morphisms corresponding to all four points.

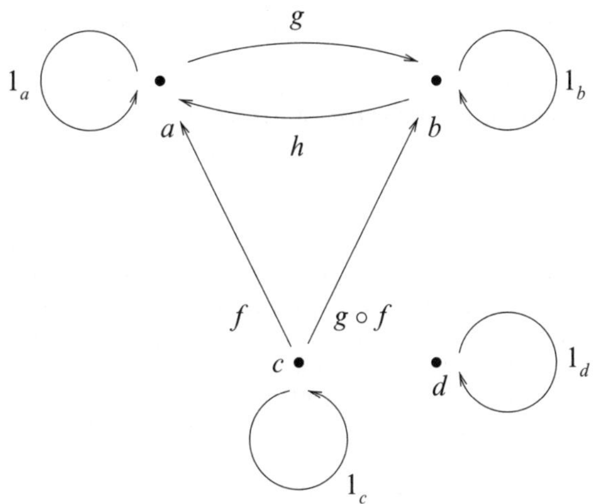

Since we have assumed that this diagram represents a category, it follows by definition 1 that:

- the morphism $g \circ f$ is the composition of the morphism f followed by the morphism g
- The morphisms g and h can be composed, that is, the compositions $h \circ g : a \to a$ and $g \circ h : b \to b$ exist. Since according to the diagram there is only one single morphism with source a and target a (analogous for b), we have necessarily

$$h \circ g = 1_a \text{ and } g \circ h = 1_b.$$

We say that in this situation g (and analogously h) is an **isomorphism**, i.e. a morphism $g : a \to b$ is an isomorphism if there exists a morphism $h : b \to a$, verifying the two previous relations.

- In the same way the morphisms $g \circ f$ and h can be composed, and it follows from the diagram (with the same arguments as before) that

$$h \circ (g \circ f) = f.$$

Since the composition of morphisms is associative, it follows that $h \circ (g \circ f) = (h \circ g) \circ f$. After the previous point we know that $h \circ g = 1_a$, so we rediscover by associativity (and the fact that the identity morphisms are neutral for composition) the previous result:

$$h \circ (g \circ f) = (h \circ g) \circ f = 1_a \circ f = f.$$

A category is thus an oriented graph (whose edges, here called morphisms, are oriented) that is equipped with an associative composition between edges/morphisms as well as with identity morphisms, which play the role of neutral elements for compositions.

Conversely, starting from an oriented graph $\mathcal{G}$ one can produce a **category generated by the oriented graph** $\mathcal{G}$ by formally adjoining the compositions of morphisms and the identity morphisms modulo the relations of associativity and neutrality for the compositions with identity morphisms.

This point will play an important role in the formalization proposed here. We shall assume that commodity structures form categories whose objects are "commodities" and whose morphisms are relations of valuation. For example, a morphism $f : x \rightarrow y$ in this category expresses the fact that f is a point of view that assigns a higher *metaprice* to commodity x than to commodity y. The identity morphism $1_x : x \rightarrow x$ is a way to express the fact that the commodity x has one and the same metaprice, in a "tautological" way (translating the fact that identity morphisms are neutral elements for the composition of morphisms).

Thus, in practice, commodities are most often considered in the form of an oriented graph: x has a higher metaprice than y, which itself has a higher metaprice than z, and so on. This oriented graph can be completed and become a category. For example, the situation just described can be represented graphically as follows:

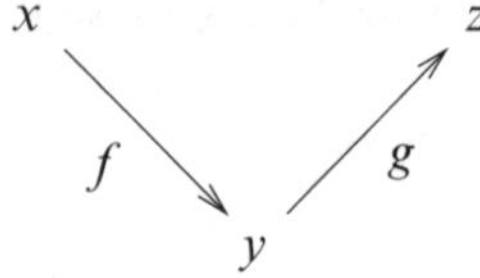

This generates the following category (the identity morphisms are usually not represented but are present nevertheless):

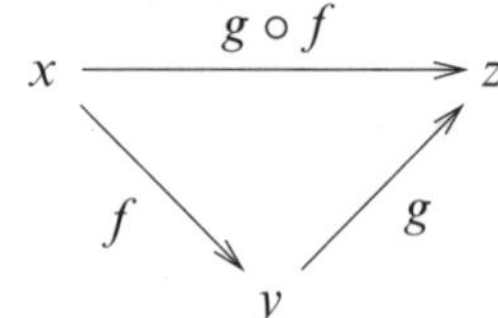

The morphism $g \circ f$ is thus the point of view composed from f and g which expresses the fact that x has a higher metaprice than z.

Categories are omnipresent in mathematics. Here are just a few examples.

Example. A category that appears trivial but plays an important "structural" role is the[3] **terminal** category, which we denote by $*$. It consists of exactly one object and one morphism (the identity morphism).

Example. The category *Ens*, whose objects are sets and whose morphisms are set-theoretical mappings.

Example. Each ordered set can be regarded as a category. Here we denote by $\mathbb{R}_+$ the positive real numbers, which we regard as a category as follows:

- the objects of $\mathbb{R}_+$ are the positive real numbers;
- morphisms between positive real numbers are given by the order relation $\geq$, i.e. for two positive real numbers x and y:

$$x \geq y \text{ means that there is a morphism } x \to y.$$

We usually use the category $\overline{\mathbb{R}}_+$ which denotes positive real numbers to which we "adjoin infinity," that is, we insert a new object, which we denote by ∞ for infinity, thus extending the morphisms of the order relation to infinity.

Without going into detail, we should note that numerous mathematical structures give rise to categories (for example, groups form the category *Grp*, topological spaces the category *Top*, etc.[4]).

It is also possible, starting from any category, to create a new category by formally "reversing" the direction of the morphisms. To illustrate this with an example, we can put the following sentence into the passive mode:

The cat eats the mouse $\rightsquigarrow$ The mouse has been eaten by the cat.

If we display the underlying relations with arrows, we get the following:

The cat $\underset{\text{eats}}{\rightarrow}$ the mouse $\rightsquigarrow$

The mouse $\underset{\text{has been eaten}}{\longrightarrow}$ by the cat.

A similar "form" of operation (setting into passive) also exists in category theory, where it is called the **opposite category** of a category. In the case of a category representing commodities under certain relations of value, we shall interpret the concept of the opposite category as a reversal of the temporal orientation of the *relations of valuation*. This point will be useful for the description of different forms of commodity valuation.

Definition 2

Let $\mathscr{C}$ be a category. The **opposite category** of $\mathscr{C}$, which we denote by $\mathscr{C}^{\mathrm{opp}}$, is the category with the same objects as $\mathscr{C}$, but in which any morphism $x \to y$ is induced by a morphism $y \to x$ in $\mathscr{C}$, so that the composition $f \circ g$ in $\mathscr{C}^{\mathrm{opp}}$ corresponds to the composition $g \circ f$ in $\mathscr{C}$.

As soon as a categorical concept for $\mathscr{C}$ is defined, with the help of this construction, there exists a "dual" or opposite version of the concept that results from applying the foregoing definition to the opposite category $\mathscr{C}^{\mathrm{opp}}$.

We have now introduced an object/notion of category, and in order not to leave the notion "floating on its own in the (mathematical) air," we need the means to "compare" categories with each other. This leads us to the concept of a functor.

Definition 3

Let $\mathscr{A}$ and $\mathscr{B}$ be two categories. A **functor** F from the category $\mathscr{A}$ to the category $\mathscr{B}$, which we denote by $F : \mathscr{A} \to \mathscr{B}$, is given by

– a function that we also denote by F by abuse of notation, from the set of objects from $\mathscr{A}$ to the set of objects from $\mathscr{B}$:

$$F : Ob(\mathscr{A}) \longrightarrow Ob(\mathscr{B})$$
$$x \mapsto F(x)$$

– for each pair of x, y of objects of A a function that we also denote by F by abuse of notation,

$$F : \mathrm{Hom}_{\mathscr{A}}(x, y) \longrightarrow \mathrm{Hom}_{\mathscr{B}}(F(x), F(y))$$
$$f \mapsto F(f)$$

– such that these functions respect the compositions between morphisms and the identity morphisms in $\mathscr{A}$, i.e.

$$F(g \circ f) = F(g) \circ F(f)\ F(1_x) = 1_{F(x)},$$

where $\circ$ also denotes composition in the category $\mathscr{B}$.

A functor $F : \mathscr{A} \to \mathscr{B}$ is the datum of a diagram of objects and morphisms in $\mathscr{B}$, indexed by objects and morphisms in the category $\mathscr{A}$. We shall often use the terms functor and diagram synonymously. A possible view of the functor concept is that it forms a point of view that allows us to "shift," i.e. the structure of the category $\mathcal{A}$ is perceived from the category $\mathcal{B}$. In another logical perspective, a functor $F: \mathcal{A} \to \mathcal{B}$ can be understood as the provision of a model of a theory $\mathcal{A}$ in a theory $\mathcal{B}$. In this view, the theory $\mathcal{B}$ assumes the role of semantics.

Examples

For any category $\mathcal{C}$ there are always at least two functors:

- the identity functor $\mathrm{id}_c: \mathcal{C} \to \mathcal{C}$ to $\mathcal{C}$, which maps every object and morphism to itself;
- the "terminal" functor $T_c: \mathcal{C} \to *$, which maps every object from $\mathcal{C}$ to the only object in $*$ and every morphism in $\mathcal{C}$ to the only morphism in $*$.

Pointing out that these two "trivial" functors exist may sound like an "innocent" remark, but behind this "innocence" lies the fact that the trivial existence of these two functors is of great theoretical importance. In particular, the language provided here is not "empty" and has a certain well-defined content (these functors are obviously defined).

An important property of functors is the fact that they can be composed. If $F: \mathcal{A} \to \mathcal{B}$ and $G: \mathcal{B} \to \mathcal{C}$ are two functors, we define the composition functor $G \circ F: \mathcal{A} \to \mathcal{C}$ as the functor we get by first applying F and then G. This leads us to the following example of a category.

Example. The categories (as objects) and the functors (as morphisms) form a category called C at, the category of categories.[5]

Now that we have introduced the concept of the functor, we must find a means to compare functors.

Definition 4

Let $F: \mathcal{A} \to \mathcal{B}$ and $G: \mathcal{B} \to \mathcal{C}$ be two functors. A **natural transformation** α of the functor F to the functor G, which we denote by $\alpha: F \to G$, is the datum of a family of morphisms in the category $\mathcal{B}$, indexed in the following way by the objects of the category $\mathcal{A}$:

$$\{\alpha_x: F(x) \to G(x)\}_{x \in \mathrm{Ob}(\mathcal{A})},$$

so that for each morphism $f: x \to y$ in $\mathcal{A}$ the following diagram is commutative[6]:

$$
\begin{array}{ccc}
F(x) & \xrightarrow{F(f)} & F(y) \\
\downarrow{\scriptstyle \alpha_x} & & \downarrow{\scriptstyle \alpha_y} \\
G(x) & \xrightarrow[G(f)]{} & G(y)
\end{array}
$$

Natural transformations can also be composed. With the above notation, let $\alpha : F \to G$ and $\beta : G \to H$ be two natural transformations. Then we define the composition $\beta \circ \alpha : F \to H$ by setting for each object x in $\mathcal{A}$:

$$(\beta \circ \alpha)_x = \beta_x \circ \alpha_x : F(x) \to H(x).$$

In this way we get a new kind of category whose objects are the functors.

Example. Let $\mathcal{A}$ and B be two categories. We denote by C at($\mathcal{A}$, $\mathcal{B}$) the category such that:

- the objects are the functors from $\mathcal{A}$ to $\mathcal{B}$,
- the morphisms are the natural transformations between functors from $\mathcal{A}$ to $\mathcal{B}$.
- the identity morphism 1_F is the natural transformation resulting from the identity morphisms $1_{F(a)} F(a) \to F(a)$ for $a \in \mathrm{Ob}(\mathcal{A})$,
- the composition of morphisms is defined as the composition of the associated natural transformations.

Example: Let $\mathcal{A}$ be a category representing a relational commodity structure, and $\overline{\mathbb{R}}_+$ the category of positive real numbers with infinity ∞ adjoined. We denote by the **category of the prices associated to** $\mathcal{A}$ the category of the functors C at $(\mathcal{A}, \overline{\mathbb{R}}_+)$. From a logical point of view, this is the category of models of the structure embodied by $\mathcal{A}$ in the semantics of positive real numbers.

Let $V : \mathcal{A} \to \overline{\mathbb{R}}_+$ be a functor that represents a selling price for a seller of commodities in $\mathcal{A}$. A purchase of the same commodities in the same way also represents a functor $A : \mathcal{A} \to \overline{\mathbb{R}}_+$. We say that there is a **(total) added value** if a natural transformation $\alpha : A \to V$ exists. The natural transformation α measures exactly the seller's monetary profit at purchase. Conversely, if a natural transformation $\beta : V \to A$ exists, it measures the **(total) loss**.

Remark. The above example can be generalized. It assumes numbers (here positive real numbers) as "measures" for prices. But one can now also imagine categories other than $\overline{\mathbb{R}}_+$ (that is, other than numbers), which here implies the intervention of a currency with absolute liquidity, which is used like numbers and can play the role of a *"metric"* (in the sense of Boltanski and Esquerre) for prices and metaprices. After all, we have already seen that it is always possible to define a category C at($\mathcal{A}$, $\mathcal{P}$) of functors for two categories $\mathcal{A}$ and $\mathcal{P}$. Nevertheless, we shall posit that not all categories $\mathcal{P}$ are suitable and that a category must have certain structures like $\overline{\mathbb{R}}_+$ in order to play this role for metaprices. Some of these properties, because they translate linguistic operations, will be examined below.[7]

Definition 5

Let $\mathscr{C}$ be a category. We call an object x from $\mathscr{C}$ **initial object**, if for each object y in $\mathscr{C}$ there exists a uniquely determined morphism of the form

$$x \rightarrow y$$

It results from this definition that an initial object is not necessarily unique, but only unique up to unique isomorphism.

By applying the previous definition to the opposite category $\mathscr{C}^{\mathrm{opp}}$, we define a **terminal object** of a category $\mathscr{C}$. An object x of $\mathscr{C}$ is called terminal if for every object y of $\mathscr{C}$ a uniquely determined morphism of the form

$$y \rightarrow x$$

exists.

Example: In the category $\overline{\mathbb{R}}_+$ the number 0 is the (only) terminal object and ∞ is the only initial object. For the category *Ens* the empty set $\emptyset$ is an initial object and the single-point sets are terminal objects (which are uniquely determined up to unique isomorphism).

We are now approaching the key mathematical tools we shall use in the discussion that follows. The essential concept is that of a Kan extension, which, if it exists, in a given situation (a given diagram) provides a "well defined" functor that satisfies certain given properties in the situation under consideration.

Definition 6

Given a diagram

$$\mathscr{A} \xrightarrow{\;F\;} \mathscr{C}$$
$$\Big\downarrow{\scriptstyle P}$$
$$\mathscr{B}$$

where $\mathscr{A}$, $\mathscr{B}$ and $\mathscr{C}$ are categories and F and P are functors, we say that F has a **left Kan extension along** P if there is a pair $(Lan_P F, \alpha)$ consisting of a functor

$$Lan_P F : \mathscr{B} \rightarrow \mathscr{C}$$

and a natural transformation $\alpha : F \rightarrow Lan_P F \circ P$ which satisfy the following universal property: For each pair (G, β) consisting of a functor $G : \mathscr{B} \rightarrow \mathscr{C}$ and a natural transformation $\beta : F \rightarrow G \circ P$ there is a unique natural transformation $\eta: Lan_p F \to G$, so that for each object a in $\mathscr{A}$ the following diagram is commutative:

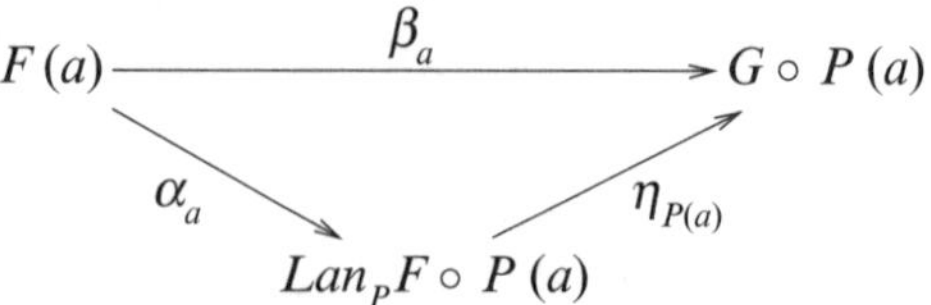

This situation can be presented in a diagram as follows:

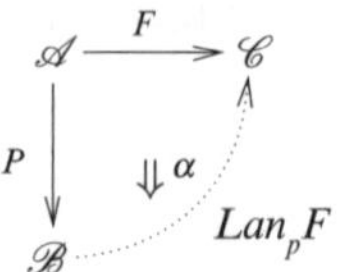

We could reformulate this definition as follows: The set of pairs (G, β), where $G : \mathscr{B} \to \mathscr{C}$ is a functor and $\beta : F \to G \circ P$ is a natural transformation, forms the objects of a category whose morphisms are given by natural transformations between such pairs. That a functor F has a left Kan extension along P means that this category has an initial object, the Kan extension in question.

In a dual way one defines the **right Kan extension** of a functor along another functor. If it exists, we denote the right Kan extension of the functor F along the functor P by $Ran_p F$.

We shall primarily use the following special cases of Kan extensions.

Definition 7

Let $F : \mathscr{A} \to \mathscr{B}$ be a functor. We say that F has **colimits** if there exists a left Kan extension of F along the terminal functor T_o:

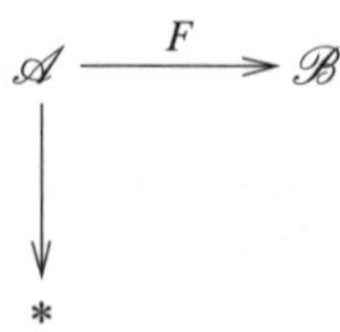

In this case we denote the Kan extension of F along the terminal functor by $colimF$ (instead of $Lan_{T_o} F$).

In a dual way, using the previous definition, we say that F has **limits** if there is a right Kan extension of F along the terminal functor. This is denoted by $limF$.

A functor of the form $* \to \mathscr{B}$ corresponds to the specification of an object of the category $\mathscr{B}$ (which is the image of the unique object in $*$ under the functor to $\mathscr{B}$). So a colimit

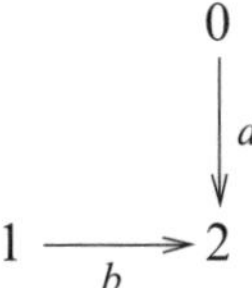

if it exists, corresponds to an object in $\mathscr{B}$, which we also abusively denote by *colimF* and which satisfies the universal property described above.

Example. In the category $\overline{\mathbb{R}}_+$, a functor $F : \mathscr{A} \to \overline{\mathbb{R}}_+$ always admits

- a limit that is given by the supremum $\sup_{a \in \mathscr{A}} F(a)$ of the $F(a)$, and
- a colimit that is given by the infimum $\inf_{a \in \mathscr{A}} F(a)$ of the $F(a)$.

We call a category **complete** if it contains all limits, which means that all functors in that category have limits, and we call it **cocomplete** if it contains all colimits. The previous example shows that the category $\overline{\mathbb{R}}_+$ is complete and cocomplete.

Example. The category *Ens* is also complete and cocomplete. Let us now look at two special cases of limits and colimits, namely the fiber product and the amalgamated sum.

Given the following category, which we shall call *I*

$$
\begin{array}{ccc}
 & & 0 \\
 & & \downarrow a \\
1 & \xrightarrow{\ \ b\ \ } & 2
\end{array}
$$

which consists of three objects 0, 1 and 2 and two morphisms $a : 0 \to 2$ and $b : 1 \to 2$, apart from the identity morphisms (which, as usual, are not represented).

The datum of a functor $F : I \to Ens$ corresponds to the datum of a diagram:

$$
\begin{array}{ccc}
 & & F(0) \\
 & & \downarrow F(a) \\
F(1) & \xrightarrow[F(b)]{} & F(2)
\end{array}
$$

where $F(0)$, $F(1)$ and $F(2)$ are sets and $F(a)$ and $F(b)$ are functions. For greater clarity, we denote these sets and functions as follows:

$$F(0) := A,\ F(1) := B,\ F(2) := \mathscr{C},\ F(a) := f,\ F(b) := g.$$

Since the category of sets is complete, this functor has a limit, which we call the **fiber product** of the above diagram, that is, there exists a set denoted by $limF$ (or $B \times_C A$) and morphisms, which we show dotted below, so that the following diagram commutates:

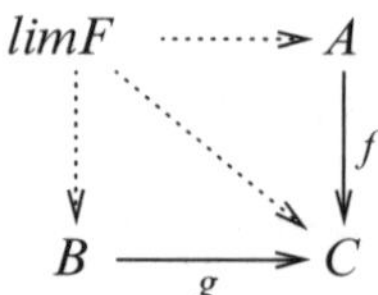

These morphisms satisfy a universal property, which cannot be described in detail here for want of space. The interesting point is that the elements of the set $limF$ can be fully described:

$$limF \simeq \{(x, y) \in B \times A \mid g(x) = f(y)\},$$

i.e. the set that represents the limit is the set of elements from A and B, whose images under the functions f and g respectively agree in C.

Without going into detail, a similar consideration yields the **amalgamated sum** (given by the fiber product in the opposite category), which we represent by the following commutative diagram:

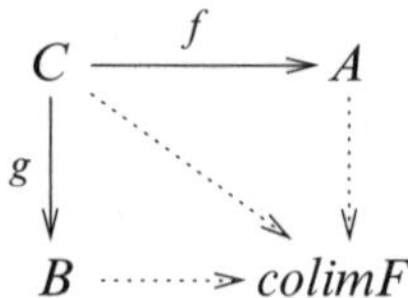

The set $colimF$, which we also call $B \sqcup_C A$, is itself given by

$$colimF \simeq B \sqcup A/\sim,$$

where $B \sqcup A$ denotes the disjoint union of the sets B and A and where we identify in the quotient the points from $B \sqcup A$ related by $\sim$:

$$x \sim y, \text{ if there is a } z \in C \text{ with } g(z) = x \text{ and } f(z) = y,$$

which means, in short, that the colimit is the set of all elements in B and A that are not in the image of the functions g and f, to which the above "quotient" is adjoined.

We can reformulate the previous examples as follows in the form of a "scheme" (using this term here in an illustrative sense rather than as a precise mathematical term), concerning the limits and colimits:

1. a limit "embodies" what appears in a diagram as a common and/or comparable feature and "forgets" the differences in a way determined by the functor (universal property).
2. a colimit "embodies" what appears in the diagram as different and "deletes" what is common and/or comparable in a way determined by the functor (universal property).

We shall now formulate a theorem about a condition of existence of Kan extensions without proving it or providing details. It suffices to state that this theorem allows us to produce, under certain conditions, a functor that fulfills certain properties and that will enable us to compare categories of commodities in a well-defined way (universal property).

Theorem *Consider the following diagram of categories and functors:*

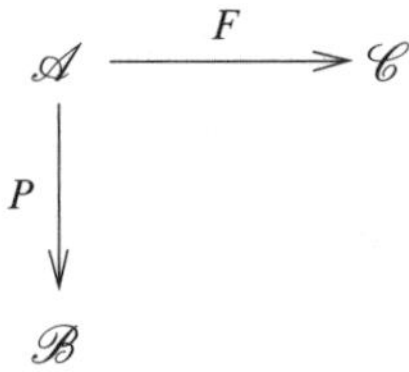

where $\mathcal{A}$ is a (small) category and $\mathcal{C}$ is cocomplete.
Then there exists a left Kan extension:

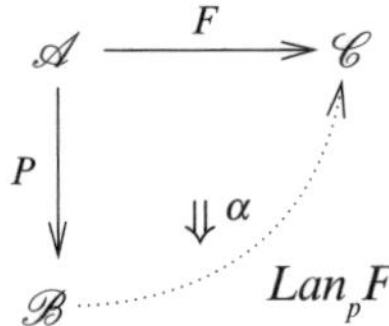

given for every b in $\mathcal{B}$ by the colimit:

$$Lan_P F(b) \simeq colim_{(P(a)\to b)\in(P\downarrow b)} F(a).$$

This notation under the *colim* sign means that we regard the colimit of the (composite) functor:

$$(P \downarrow b) \xrightarrow{U} \mathcal{A} \xrightarrow{F} \mathcal{C}$$
$$g : P(a) \to b \mapsto a \quad\quad \mapsto F(a),$$

where U is a "forgetful functor" ("projection") and $(P \downarrow b)$ denotes the category whose objects are the morphisms in $\mathscr{B}$ of the form $P(a) \to b$ for objects a of A. In this category the morphisms $g \to g'$ are given by commutative diagrams of the form:

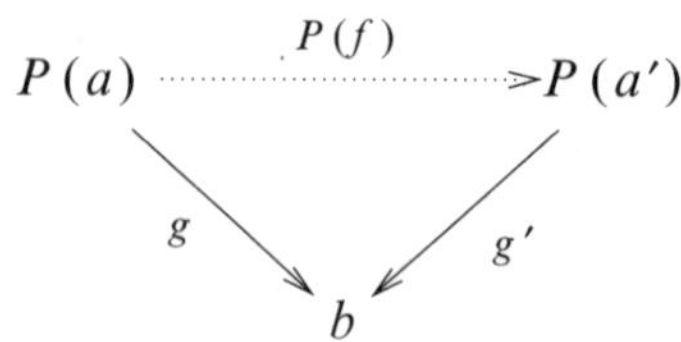

where $f : a \to a'$ is a morphism in the category $\mathscr{A}$.[8]

In a dual way, we have an equivalent result for complete categories. Hence there exists a right Kan extension.

Let us look at an example of the use of Kan extensions in price-setting.

A price is the datum of a functor $F : \mathscr{A} \to \overline{\mathbb{R}}_+$. The category $\overline{\mathbb{R}}_+$ is complete and cocomplete. So by the previous results there exists for each functor $P : \mathscr{A} \to \mathscr{B}$ a left Kan extension

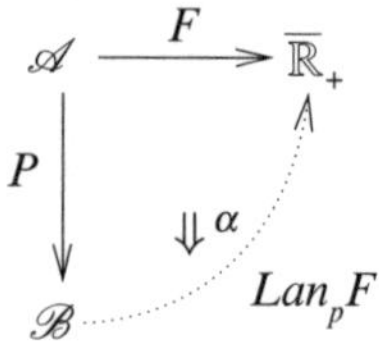

and a right Kan extension

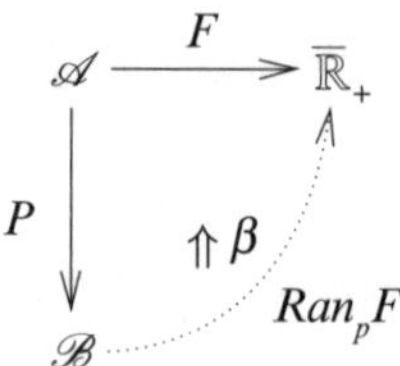

What "sense" can these constructions have? If one understands F as a representative of the metaprice of a seller and the functor P as a shift (actual or narrative) of commodities seen from the viewpoint of $\mathscr{A}$ toward commodities seen from the viewpoint of $\mathscr{B}$ (for example, if P represents the "inclusion" of commodities "structured" according to $\mathscr{A}$ into a more comprehensive structure $\mathscr{B}$, or if P provides the model for a change in the "discourse" about the commodities or an exchange, etc.), the following interpretations result[9]:

– the left Kan extension ($Lan_p F$, α) stands, so to speak, for the maximum profit that is "coherent" with the price F under the shift P, where this new price is given by the functor $Lan_p F$ and the quantification of profit by the natural transformation α (the universal property specifying the "maximum"). The theorem stated above even gives a formula for its calculation.
– in a dual way, the right Kan extension ($Ran_p F$, α) stands, so to speak, for the maximum loss "coherent" with the price F under the shift P.

This brief attempt at a categorical formulation of the investigation of commodity structures has to suffice for now. Category theory and its ramifications have produced an abundance of concepts that could prove useful for an understanding of these structures, and for what Boltanski and Esquerre call "pragmatic structuralism".[10] The limited scope of this text only allows the presentation of some basic elements of the language of such an endeavor. After this general introduction, let us now turn our attention to the formalization of the forms of valuation that the authors of *Enrichment* have identified.

Forms of commodity valuations

In this section we shall look at the initial elements in the formalization of the four "pure" forms of commodity valuation: the standard form, the trend form, the collection form, and the asset form. We use the term "pure" because commodities can of course be considered from different viewpoints. For example, depending on the context of its valuation, the same watch may be considered to fall under the standard form or the collection form. We shall examine these possible types of cases later, especially if they can be understood as "shifts" from one form to another.

Let us now summarize the basic assumptions that have guided our undertaking thus far:

1. A set of commodities under consideration and the relations of "valuation" among these commodities form a category (in the formal sense). For example, the commodities offered in a shop and the valuation relations that exist between them and that justify their price are modeled in a category.
2. The four forms of commodity valuations are modeled in four different types of categories. Each form of valuation is based on its own type of structure, which is formally reflected in the fact that the modeling categories have different structures. Thus, in the above example, if the relations among the commodities offered in a shop are structured by the standard form, the category that models this situation would have a structure specific to the category associated with the standard form.

3. In modeling the different forms, we shall limit ourselves to the concepts of category theory that we have introduced above. Some structural elements of the individual forms, whose modeling would be worthwhile, will therefore not be considered in the following.

4. We have so far limited ourselves to the concepts of limits and colimits. The interest shown in this term is justified by the following scheme: What is structurally determined within a category is given in the form of a limit or colimit of a functor. Conversely, the limit (or colimit) of a functor, if it exists, is a "determination procedure." This concept of determination seems to us to be indispensable for the understanding of commodity structures. For example, assume that a **style** is given if one uses the example of the trend form: A style must be sufficiently determined for it to be a style, i.e. for it to be regarded as such and imitated by the various actors.

5. Furthermore, we have assumed that it is necessary for the price formation and more generally still for shifts between the different forms that things be sufficiently determined in their quality as commodities, as perceived by the various actors involved. A "naked" watch, so to speak, that has neither analytic nor narrative characteristics, has no definable price or metaprice. It is only when a watch is associated with a brand, a style and technical characteristics, and only when the brands, styles and technical characteristics have been sufficiently determined (i.e. recognized as such) by and for the actors, that it is possible to determine its value and associate it with a metaprice.

6. In view of these various observations, our aim in this section is to raise the question of the existence (or non-existence) of limits and colimits for the different types of (formal) categories associated with the four forms of commodity valuation.

7. Finally, this questioning has been guided by the (dual) scheme of limits and colimits, presented earlier, in which a functor is understood as a diagram in a category (the target category):

   a. A limit "embodies" what appears in a diagram as a common and/or comparable element and "forgets" the differences in a way that is determined by the functor (universal property).

   b. A colimit "embodies" what appears different in a diagram and "deletes" what is common and/or comparable in a way determined by the functor (universal property).

The Standard Form

We call *St* a category of commodities considered according to the standard form, i.e. according to a form whose relations of valuation, the morphisms of the category, are given by a structure specific to the standard form.

Consider a diagram in this category, i.e. a functor $F : \mathscr{D} \to St$, where $\mathscr{D}$ is a category.

If we apply the scheme to the limits and colimits of the standard form, it appears that

- the limit of *F*, if it exists, as a common "core" of the objects in the diagram whose differences are excluded, corresponds to the common **properties** of the commodities and the relations considered by the functor *F*. But since a limit, if it exists, is embodied by an object (unique to unique isomorphism) in the category *St*, which we call *limF*, it seems reasonable to assume that the kind of thing represented by *limF* embodies the **prototype** common to the objects and relations of the diagram under consideration.
- According to the previous point, not all limits necessarily exist in a category of the standard type. Not all commodity diagrams have a common prototype. A prototype of prototypes is not imaginable, whereas one could imagine the possibility of imagining a collection of collections.
- The colimit of *F*, if it exists, stands for the "grouping" of the differences among commodities by identifying what they have in common. In the standard form, the differences among commodities are taken into account only if they are comparable and compared, which according to our hypothesis is not compatible with the existence of a colimit. It would be possible for colimits to exist in a category of the standard type, but they would not have a systematic character; rather, they would be contingent for the category under consideration.

Therefore, a commodities category *St* considered according to the standard form is characterized by the existence of some limits embodying the prototypes.

A price associated with such a category is the specification of a functor $St \to \overline{\mathbb{R}}_+$. According to point 5 above, the prototypes are indispensable for the specification of such a functor. The following facts can be derived from this:

1. The prototypes function as upper price and metaprice markers insofar as they do not determine the prices and metaprices of the commodities of which they are the prototypes, but insofar as the price or metaprice of any such commodity cannot be higher than the price or metaprice of the prototype. To put it bluntly, the price or metaprice of such commodities cannot be higher than the price or metaprice of the prototype. In this way, in the case of a seller, the price of a prototype linked to a commodity diagram acts as an upper "limit" in the sense of an upper limit on the profit that can be expected from the sale of a given commodity.
2. Conversely, if the prices or metaprices of the commodities falling under the same prototype (formally represented by a commodity diagram having a limit) are determined, these prices or metaprices constitute the lower limit of the price or metaprice of the prototype.

We shall now use the same approach to analyze the trend form, the collection form, and the asset form. Let us sketch the elements of analysis that allowed us to settle on the proposed solutions.

The Trend Form

We denote by *Td* a category of commodities considered according to the trend form, i.e. according to a form whose relations of valuation, the morphisms of the category, are given by a structure specific to the trend form.

Let us consider a functor $F: \mathcal{D} \rightarrow Td$.

If we apply the scheme as above to the limits and colimits of the trend form, we get:

- The limit of F, if it exists, embodies the common "core" of the objects in the diagram whose differences are excluded. For the "most pertinent dimension of the trend form" is "the fact of anticipating and controlling the life cycle not only of products as material entities but also and especially of the differences supported by those products." While in the standard form there are no colimits, in the trend form the concept of limits is not relevant (while limits may conceivably exist in a category of the trend form type, such limits have no systematic character and are contingent on the specific category considered).
- The colimit of F, on the other hand, can be useful for the trend form. Since it represents the "grouping" of the differences of the commodities by identifying what they have in common, the colimit of F, if it exists, embodies the concept of the **style** under which the commodities are considered. The style is regarded as something that can be recognized by the various actors from a trend perspective, which justifies its modeling as colimit. Since the "style" has no concrete embodiment, it forms an "ideal" and therefore potentially volatile object (after the model of the ideal collections).
- It follows from the previous point that not all colimits necessarily exist in a category of the trend type.

Not every diagram of commodities considered according to the trend form necessarily has a style. Therefore, a category *Td* of commodities considered according to the trend form is characterized by the existence of certain colimits that embody the respective styles.

A price associated with such a category is given by a functor $P: Td \rightarrow \overline{\mathbb{R}}_+$. For the specification of such a functor thus the styles are formative. The following facts about styles can be derived from their property as colimits:

1. The styles function as lower price or metaprice markers to the extent that they determine an amount that is below that of the commodities considered. This reflects the fact that the commodities purchased within the framework of the trend form are acquired primarily on the basis of their style or in their capacity as **signs**. The prices or metaprices of such commodities cannot be lower than the prices and metaprices of the style to which they belong. In this way, the price or metaprice of a

style associated with a commodity diagram acts, in the case of a seller, as a lower "limit" in the sense of a lower limit on the price that can be expected in the sale of a commodity.
2. Conversely, if the price or metaprice of a commodity falling under the same style is determined, that price or metaprice constitutes an upper limit for the price or metaprice associated with the style.

The Collection Form

We denote by *Col* a category of commodities considered according to the collection form, i.e. according to a form whose relations of valuation are given by a structure specific to the collection form.

Let us consider a functor $F: \mathcal{D} \to Col$.

If we apply the scheme to the limits and colimits of the collection form, we find:

- The limit of F embodies a collection (ideal or non-ideal), for which the functor embodies the **governing principle**, to borrow the terms used by Boltanski and Esquerre.
- It follows from the previous point that, unlike the standard form (as far as limits are concerned) and the trend form (as far as colimits are concerned), all limits exist in a category of the collection type. Any diagram of commodities considered according to the collection form always provides a guideline for a collection.
- In a category of commodities considered according to the collection form, colimits do not necessarily exist (i.e., except in a contingent manner). Since commodities viewed through the prism of the collection form are characterized by the importance of more or less divided conventions supporting an (ideal or non-ideal) collection, the concept of colimits does not seem to have a systematic effect.

A category of commodities *Col* considered according to the collection form is characterized by the existence of all limits in this category that embody the collections.

A price associated with such a category is given by a functor $P: Col \to \mathbb{R}_+$. The collections are decisive for the specification of such a functor. The following facts can be derived from the limits:

1. Collections act as upper price or metaprice markers to the extent that they supply an amount which is higher than that of the commodities considered. From this perspective, the price or metaprice of a commodity cannot be higher than the price or metaprice given by the (ideal or non-ideal) collection to which it belongs. In this way, the price or metaprice of a collection associated to a diagram of commodities acts, in the case of a seller, as an upper "limit" in the sense of an upper limit of the profit that can be expected upon the sale of a given commodity.

2. Conversely, when it comes to the determined price or metaprice of commodities belonging to the same collection, these prices or metaprices constitute a lower limit for the price and metaprice of the collection. In everyday language, this expresses the banal observation that a painting cannot cost more than the collection of which it is a part.

The Asset Form

We denote by *Ast* a category of commodities considered according to the asset form, i.e. according to a form whose relations of valuation, the morphisms of the category, are given by a structure specific to the asset form.

Consider a functor $F : \mathscr{D} \to Ast$.

If we apply the scheme for the last time to the limits and colimits of the asset form, the following facts arise:

– Limits do not necessarily exist in a category considered according to the asset form. The reason for this is that the commodities considered through the prism of the asset form are identified by "the differences related to the degree to which objects can easily be converted into money." Since it focuses on their common characteristics, the concept of the limit does not really seem to make sense.
– The colimit of F, on the other hand, embodies the **liquidity** displayed by commodities viewed from the perspective provided by the functor F. Liquidity, as it is widely used in the discourses of social actors when referring to commodities considered according to the asset form, presupposes ideal liquidity along the lines of ideal collections in the collection form. But the difference is that this ideal liquidity is common to all commodities.
– It does not seem exaggerated to assume that all colimits exist in a category of the asset type. The differences between commodities representing a commodity diagram seen in the asset form can always be bracketed, with their liquidity alone being taken into account.

Therefore, a category of commodities *Ast* considered according to the asset form is characterized by the existence of all colimits in that category that embody the various liquidities or liquidity markers.

A price associated with such a category is given by a functor $P : Ast \to \overline{\mathbb{R}}_+$. In this case, the liquidity markers are decisive for the specification of such a functor. The following properties can be derived from the properties of colimits:

1. The liquidity markers function as lower price or metaprice markers to the extent that they provide a lower numerical value than the commodities under consideration. From this perspective, the price or metaprice of a commodity cannot be lower than the price or metaprice given by the liquidity of which it is a part. Thus, in the case of a seller, the price

or metaprice of the liquidity associated with a commodity diagram functions as lower "limit" in the sense of a lower limit on the profit that can be expected from the sale of a commodity.
2. Conversely, when the price or metaprice of a commodity with the same liquidity is referred to, that price or metaprice constitutes an upper limit on the price or metaprice of this liquidity.

The universal properties of limits and colimits, which we have not elaborated in detail, can also be used to model possible strategies for commodity valuation as well as structural "incoherences" in the exchange of commodities.

Some comments on this formalization

We summarize the above formalization in the following table:

Valuation forms	Standard form	Trend form	Collection form	Asset form
Existence of limits "Translations"	in some cases *Prototypes*	$\emptyset$	in all cases *Collections*	$\emptyset$
Existence of colimits "Translations"	$\emptyset$	in some cases *Styles*	$\emptyset$	in all cases *Liquidity markers*

This table invites several comments:

– The categories of the standard form and the trend form are "incomplete" in comparison with the collection form and the asset form insofar as they are not closed under the operations limits and colimits. If one assumes that the social practices inherent in commodities tend to be somewhat closed, the collection form and the asset form appear more stable in this respect. From a "linguistic" point of view, if limits and colimits are regarded as linguistic operations, this means that the structure of the standard form and the trend form is incomplete with respect to these operations. Thus, when one considers that social practices lead to a "transgression" of these operations, the collection form and the asset form constitute, or may constitute, a "refuge" for the expression of these operations.
– In addition, forms of "duality" occur. If we recall that the limits in a category become colimits in the opposite category (and vice versa), and if one interprets this latter term as a "reversal of the temporal orientation of the relations of valuation," the following can be noted: Just like the collection form and the asset form, the standard and trend forms are in a reversed temporal relation to each other. The structure of the standard form is oriented toward **duration**, while the structure of the trend form is oriented toward **brevity**. The collection form gives

preference to narratives turned toward the **past**, the asset form to narratives turned toward the **future**.

Taking into account the above remarks, let us now turn our attention to the shifts between the different forms.

Transitions between the forms

In the previous section, we have associated each of the forms with the existence (or non-existence) of limits and colimits. To the extent that "they are determined," the (co-)limits form markers that play an important role in the attribution of metaprices and prices. Are there shifts (formally speaking: functors) from a category of commodities considered according to the standard form to a category of commodities considered according to the collection form that "respect" the limits? Or shifts from the trend form to the asset form which respect the colimits? etc. If a functor sends the (co-)limits of a category to the (co-)limits of the target category, we say that this functor commutates with (co-)limits.

The formalism we have introduced gives rise to twelve possible cases. The analysis of the different types of functors reveals that some valuation processes are not inherent in the forms, but result from shifts between different forms.

We analyze in list form the "meaning" (or meaninglessness) of each of these cases in the study of the cosmos of commodities:

1. A functor $F : T\,d^{op} \to St$ commuting with limits (if they exist). Such a functor transforms a style (colimit in the trend form) into a "prototype" (limit in the standard form). If one imagines it in the form of a shift, such a functor corresponds to the embodiment of a style in something we shall call the **model**.
2. A functor $F : St^{op} \to Td$ commuting with colimits (if they exist). This case is "dual" to the previous one. It transforms a "prototype" into a style. Such a process leads to the creation of a **brand** (such as Apple and the iPhone, the DS brand for the PSA group, etc.).
3. A functor $F : St \to Col$ commuting with limits. A functor of this type transforms a "prototype" into a (potentially ideal) collection.
4. A functor $F : Col \to St$ commuting with limits. This transforms a collection into a "prototype." Within the framework of the collection form, however, such a shift may be prevented by the "prohibition of reproduction." This kind of prohibition is not based on material impossibility, because there are copies of works that take the place of the originals in museums, which are kept under conditions that are suitable for their best possible preservation. But such a shift would lead to a decrease in the price of a piece and consequently a decrease in the metaprices of all items in the same collection.
5. A functor $F : Col^{op} \to Ast$ commuting with colimits. An example of

such a functor, which transforms a collection into a liquidity marker, is any case in which a collectable object is used as a money substitute (stamps, coins, medals, etc.).

6. A functor $F : Ast^{op} \to Col$ commuting with limits. This functor type, on the other hand, embodies the situations in which stamp collectors or coin collectors find themselves when they ensure that things that were previously investments fall under the collection form.

7. A functor $F : T\,d^{op} \to Col$ commuting with limits. An example of a functor that shifts from a style to a collection is Hermès handbags, etc.

8. A functor $F : Col^{op} \to Td$ commuting with colimits. In this case, collections serve as resources for styles. For example, designers or fashion designers refer to collectables to create objects that are to become a new style.

9. A functor $F : Td \to Ast$ commuting with colimits. This case refers to things that were bought as equipment when they were not fashionable, but would possibly become so and could then be resold at a higher price.

10. A functor $F : Ast \to Td$ commuting with colimits. This functor type shifts a liquidity marker (the colimit in the asset form) to a style. Within this framework belong phenomena such as demonstrative or ostentatious wealth, etc.

11. A functor $F : St^{op} \to Ast$ commuting with colimits. In this case, "prototypes" become liquidity markers. One can think of patents that are not applied for in order to use them directly for production, but because of their future market potential.

12. A functor $F : Ast^{op} \to St$ commuting with limits. This case, in which liquidity markers are shifted to "prototypes," is dual to the previous one.

Possible openings

In the previous section, commodities were considered insofar as they occur in "pure" form (corresponding to the standard, trend, collection and asset forms) and the various displacements between these "pure" forms. In our eyes, however, the social "reality" seems to be characterized for the most part by compositions between these different points of view. And it is also not necessary to assume that such a category $\mathcal{M}$ is generated by only four types of morphisms: standard, trend, collection and asset. It would be interesting to see whether other types of morphisms, i.e. other forms of valuation, can occur. The difficulty lies in knowing how best to investigate these non-homogeneous structures, beyond pursuing the necessary development of the basic categorical theoretical concepts mentioned in the first section. I should like to point out two other approaches that I see as complementary:

1. The first is the approach of the theory of enriched categories as developed in Max Kelly's book. In our view, such a formalism is motivated by the fact that a category of commodities can only "model" a "proper world" reasonably in its specificity if it is "sufficiently" extensive to be able to include in its own world elements that cross its path. Formally speaking, the category $\mathcal{M}$ must have enough operations/structures (limits, colimits, monoidal structures, etc.) and internal possibilities of expression within the framework to which we limit ourselves here, for example (depending on the use/need),[11] as is the case when $\mathcal{M}$ is a cosmos (but other structures are also possible). For example, if $\mathcal{M}$ is a cosmos, we have the concept of an enriched category over $\mathcal{M}$, which is a "type" of category, for which the morphisms between objects no longer form a set, but are given by objects of $\mathcal{M}$, that is, for which the $Hom(x, y)$ are not sets, but objects of $\mathcal{M}$. The category theory we are dealing with in our text already falls under this concept, namely the theory of categories enriched over *Ens* (the category of sets), and the concepts we have introduced can also be defined in the world of categories enriched over a cosmos. The relations between objects in this language are given by the "logic" of $\mathcal{M}$. In the case of categories enriched over $\overline{\mathbb{R}}_+$, relations between two objects can be given by a positive real number (for example $Hom(x, y) = 5$)[12] or by commodities in the enriched over $\mathcal{M}$ case, where $\mathcal{M}$ is a cosmos of commodities. In the latter case, for example, if the objects of an $\mathcal{M}$-category are interpreted as persons, one can imagine an $\mathcal{M}$-category as a structure in which the relations between persons are embodied by commodities from $\mathcal{M}$ and the relations among these commodities (phenomena of **reification of social relations**, etc.). A point of criticism that we can put forward against our formalization of the forms of valuation is that it says nothing or almost nothing about the relations among the commodities: they exist, as if out of the blue, given by "external" considerations and form sets. With the help of the formalization of enriched categories one can again lend more content to the relations/differences between the commodities/persons and above all establish more quantitative theories (the example of the categories enriched over $\overline{\mathbb{R}}_+$, which are generalized metric spaces). Perhaps it is also possible in this context to present more precise formalizations of the forms of valuation?

2. The other possible research approach we would like to mention is given by the concept of localization and derived functors (for the formal aspect, we refer to the book by William G. Dwyer et al. and to the article by Bruno Kahn and Georges Maltsiniotis). Where, briefly put, the previous point refers to the step of creating terms that take into account the differentiations between objects, the second research approach that we propose is, in a sense, a complementary step: the ability to identify what already exists as "similar." Let C be a category. Furthermore, let W be a class of morphisms in the category $\mathscr{C}$. In this case there exists a new category $W^{-1}\mathscr{C}$, which we call the **localization of**

$\mathscr{C}$ to W, which has the same objects as $\mathscr{C}$, but in which we have formally inverted the morphisms in W, that is, we have forced the morphisms in W to be isomorphisms. We recall that two objects in a category are isomorphic if there is an isomorphism "connecting" them, and that isomorphic objects are structurally (i.e. from the point of view of the category considered) identical/identifiable. The difficulty here is to "understand" the category $W^{-1}\mathscr{C}$ (if one formally adds morphisms to a category to make it another category, the new compositions and the associativity of these compositions generally produce a large number of new relationships between the morphisms). Less formally, the morphisms in W provide criteria for identifying the objects they connect and the localization $W^{-1}\mathscr{C}$ is the result of these identifications. In this way, the class of morphisms W provides/describes the objects that are identified, that is, the objects that one wants to see as "equal" (formally isomorphic), and at the same time the way these objects are made "equal" (given by the morphisms in W). There exists a functor called **localization functor**:

$$\gamma : \mathscr{C} \to W^{-1}\mathscr{C}.$$

This sends every morphism from W to an isomorphism in $W^{-1}\mathscr{C}$ and satisfies a universal property that states in a certain sense that this category is "the smallest" category with this property. One can apply the above to a category of commodities $\mathscr{M}$ and, for example, take a class of morphisms for W that represent valuation relations that, for example, fall under the standard form. The category $W^{-1}C$ stands for the structure produced when commodities have been "identified" by these morphisms. Conversely, one can ask oneself whether there is a class of relations of valuation W for a category of commodities $\mathscr{M}$, such that, if one identifies (according to the morphisms) those objects that it contains, one gets a category of the standard type, that is, if $W^{-1}\mathscr{C}$ is a category of the standard type (that is, has certain limits). This formal question can be translated into the following form: If certain analytic features of the relations of valuation between given commodities are expanded, can one see these commodities and their relations as being of the standard form type? We might also turn our attention to the existence and/or the production of functors between categories and to the behavior of these functors under localization:

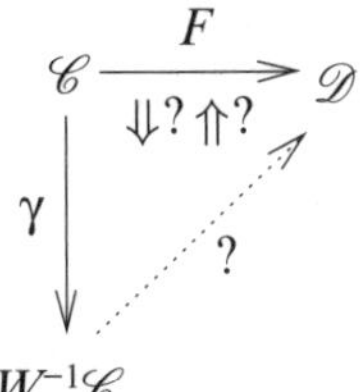

Here we enter the world of **derived functors** (which are special cases of Kan extensions). For example, if $D = \overline{\mathbb{R}}_+$, F represents a price and the existence of derived functors makes it possible to raise the question of the existence of prices, after having "expanded," among certain commodities, the "features" that remain coherent with price F. In my opinion, these considerations would make it possible to produce formal results with regard to a qualitative analysis of the structuring of commodities.

Translated from the French by Annette Werner

Notes

Introduction

1 Walter Benjamin, "Paris, Capital of the Nineteenth Century," trans. Howard Eiland, in *Walter Benjamin: Selected Writings*, ed. Howard Eiland and Michael Jennings, vol. 3 (Cambridge, MA: Harvard University Press, 2002), pp. 32–49.
2 Walter Benjamin, "On the Concept of History," trans. Edmund Jephcott and Howard Eiland, ibid., vol. 4 (Cambridge, MA: Harvard University Press, 2003), p. 391.
3 For details, see chapter 4, note 1.

Chapter 1 The Age of the Enrichment Economy

1 For a synthesis, see Lilas Demmou, "La désindustrialisation en France," working document, Direction Générale du Trésor, nos. 2010–11 (June 2010).
2 Vincent Hecquet, "Emploi et territoires de 1975 à 2009: tertiarisation et rétrécissement de la sphère productive," *Économie et statistique*, nos. 462–3 (2013): 25–68.
3 Martin Fortes, "Spécialisation à l'exportation de la France et de quatre grands pays de l'Union européenne entre 1990 et 2009," *Trésor-Éco*, no. 98 (February 2012).
4 See Alain Touraine, *The Post-Industrial Society: Tomorrow's Social History, Classes, Conflicts and Culture in the Programmed Society* (New York: Random House, [1969] 1971), and Daniel Bell, *The Coming of Post-Industrial Society: A Venture in Social Forecasting* (New York: Basic Books, 1973). For a critique of the relevance of the notion of post-industrial society for characterizing contemporary European societies, see Aurélien Berlan, *La fabrique des derniers hommes: retour sur Tönnies, Simmel et Weber* (Paris: La Découverte, 2012), pp. 317–22.
5 Demmou, "La désindustrialisation en France."
6 See Robert Brenner, *The Boom and the Bubble: The US in the World Economy* (London: Verso, 2003).
7 Hecquet, "Emploi et territoires."
8 Laurent Davezies, *La crise qui vient: la nouvelle fracture territoriale* (Paris: Seuil, 2012).

9 Laurent Davezies, *La République et ses territoires: la circulation invisible des richesses* (Paris: Seuil, 2008), p. 50.

10 Ibid., pp. 58–9.

11 In one-third of French households, the head of the household is retired. For a statistical analysis of the distribution of retirees, see Jean-François Léger, "La répartition géographique des retraités: les six France," *Population & Avenir*, no. 716 (January–February 2014): 4–7. In France, the greatest proportion of retired workers or salaried employees with low incomes is found in the former industrial regions in the northeast. As for retired white-collar workers, found in particularly high numbers in the large urban centers, they are also increasingly numerous in the less urbanized territories in the coastal and southern regions owing to "very selective migratory and economic population flows (retirees with high incomes)"; see also Jean-Marc Zaninetti, "Les retraités en France: des migrations pas comme les autres," *Population & Avenir*, no. 703 (May–June 2011): 4–20.

12 Gwendoline Volat, "L'habitat rural entre 1999 et 2009: des évolutions contrastées," *Le Point sur*, Commissariat général au développement durable, no. 179 (December 2013).

13 Davezies, *La République et ses territoires*, p. 68.

14 This horizon of integral capitalism in which everyone is expected to become a merchant contrasts with that of merchants doing business abroad; see in the eighteenth century, as described by Francesca Trivellato in *The Familiarity of Strangers: The Sephardic Diaspora, Livorno, and Cross-Cultural Trade in the Early Modern Period* (New Haven, CT: Yale University Press, 2009). Trivellato depicts merchants as a distinct category (focusing here on Sephardic Jews from Livorno in Tuscany) and connects them with their merchandise (especially coral and diamonds). See also Fernand Braudel, *Afterthoughts on Material Civilization and Capitalism* (Baltimore: Johns Hopkins University Press, 1977).

15 For literature in French, see especially Nathalie Heinich, *De la visibilité: excellence et singularité en régime médiatique* (Paris: Gallimard, 2012).

16 See Alain Desrosières and Laurent Thévenot, *Les catégories socio-professionnelles* (Paris: La Découverte, 1988), and, for a recent update, Thomas Amossé, "La nomenclature socio-professionnelle: une histoire revisitée," *Annales: Histoire, Sciences Sociales*, 68/4 (2013): 1039–75. The population that interests us can be sought here by relying on surveys by INSEE (the French National Institute of Statistics and Economic Studies). But, given the structure of the surveys and the nomenclatures they use, it is hard to come up with reliable figures, and the findings can always be challenged.

17 In *L'esthétisation du monde: vivre à l'âge du capitalisme artiste* (Paris: Gallimard, 2013), Gilles Lipovetsky and Jean Serroy propose to approach different things from the perspective of aestheticization as a "systematic incorporation of the creative and imaginary dimension in the sectors of commodity consumption." Considered especially in terms of its current development, the "aestheticization of the world triggered by capitalism was to appear," according to the authors, "starting in the second half of the nineteenth century" (p. 39). The idea of "aesthetic capitalism" is also defended by Gernot Böhme, *Ästhetischer Kapitalismus* (Berlin: Suhrkamp, 2016).

18 The Comité Colbert, created in 1954, brings together representatives from the luxury industry and French cultural institutions. See Christian Blanckaert, *Les*

100 mots du luxe (Paris: Presses Universitaires de France, 2010). (Blanckaert has served as director of Hermès international and as presiding delegate of the Colbert Committee.)

19 Romain Sautard, Valérie Duchateau, and Jeannot Rasolofoarison, "Les biens haut de gamme, un avantage comparatif européen," *Trésor Éco*, no. 118 (September 2013). Of 270 prestigious brands surveyed in the world, 130 are French (Benjamin Leperchey, "Le Comité stratégique de filière (CSF) des industries de la mode et du luxe," *Annales des Mines –Réalités industrielles*, no. 4 (2013): 14–19.

20 According to the Ministry of Economy, the "luxury industries" (including fashion, the culinary arts, and outstanding food products, especially wines and spirits, but excluding tourism) employ 170,000 people in France, for a bottom line of 43 billion euros.

21 Sautard et al., "Les biens haut de gamme."

22 In France, the thirty leading brands in the fashion sector have cumulative sales amounting to 15 billion euros, of which 85 percent come from exports; see Leperchey, "Le Comité stratégique."

23 Kenzo and Givenchy moved part of their operations to Poland, Vuitton to Romania; Hermès relied on Nigerian or Madagascan subcontractors. Italian brands did similar things: Prada moved part of its leather goods production to Turkey; Dolce & Gabbana outsourced some of its ready-to-wear apparel to Egypt; and so on. When the product is assembled in the brand's home country, the components subcontracted to a country with low wages are those requiring the most hours of work – for example, in the case of a handbag, the handle. See Maxime Koromyslov, "Le 'Made in France' en question: pratiques et opinions des professionnels français du luxe," *Revue française de gestion*, nos. 218–19 (2011): 107–22.

24 There is no universal legal framework requiring that a product's country of origin be identified. Unlike the American context, for example, the European context is permissive. "The choice in branding at the point of importation and commercialization on national territory is left to the discretion of the manufacturer and thus remains optional" (ibid., p. 111).

25 Ibid., p. 120.

26 See chapter 8, pp. 206–7.

27 Roxana Azimi, "L'élite prend l'art," *M le magazine du Monde* (April 5, 2014).

28 Vincent Marcilhac, *Le luxe alimentaire: une singularité française* (Rennes: Presses Universitaires de Rennes, 2012), p. 27.

29 See Alessandro Stanziani, *Histoire de la qualité alimentaire, XIXe–XXe siècle* (Paris: Seuil, 2005).

30 On the importance of authenticity in gastronomy, see Josée Johnston and Shyon Baumann, "Democracy versus Distinction: A Study of Omnivorousness in Gourmet Food Writing," *American Journal of Sociology*, 113/1 (2007): 165–204.

31 Marie-France Garcia-Parpet, *Le marché de l'excellence: les grands crus à l'épreuve de la mondialisation* (Paris: Seuil, 2009).

32 Marcilhac, *Le luxe alimentaire*, p. 34; and on the growing ascendancy of the big multinational groups over the prestigious vineyards, see Garcia-Parpet, *Marché de l'excellence*, pp. 140–5.

33 Michaela DeSoucey, "Food Traditions and Authenticity Politics in the European Union," *American Sociological Review*, 75/3 (2010): 432–55.

34 Garcia-Parpet, *Marché de l'excellence*, pp. 172–3.
35 Thus, for instance, the association "Bienvenue à la ferme," supported by the Chamber of Agriculture of the Loiret (a region with a significant architectural heritage), describes itself as the "first French network for direct sales and for welcoming [visitors] to farms"; in its annual brochure, local winemakers and producers offer recipes to a cosmopolitan audience, but they nevertheless specify the use of traditional local products: "sauerkraut with fish from the Loire in a baking dish, sauce with butter from Nantes," is presented by two Loire fishermen, a "lamb tagine" is described by locals who raise sheep, and a "stew with ancient vegetables" is proposed by fruit and vegetable growers.
36 Françoise Bonnal traces the notion of "nation branding" back to the publication of Philip Kotler's book, *Marketing Places: Attracting Investment, Industry and Tourism to Cities, States, and Nations* (New York: Free Press, 1993); the notion was first put to work in marketing tourism. See Françoise Bonnal, "Comprendre et gérer la marque France: mode d'emploi pour les acteurs de la marque France," *Revue française de gestion*, nos. 218–19 (2001): 27–43. Currently, many agencies, mostly based in London, specialize in the construction and diffusion of markers of identity and national narratives designed to highlight nations, regions, and cities, associating them with products in order to promote their commercialization; see Melissa Aronczyk, *Branding the Nation: The Global Business of National Identity* (Oxford: Oxford University Press, 2013).
37 Bonnal, "Comprendre et gérer."
38 On the way traditions are invented, see the classic work by Eric Hobsbawm and Terence Ranger, eds, *The Invention of Tradition* (Cambridge: Cambridge University Press, 1983); see also Anne-Marie Thiesse, *La création des identités nationales* (Paris: Seuil, 1999).
39 Bonnal, "Comprendre et gérer."
40 On the generalization of benchmarking, see especially Isabelle Bruno and Emmanuel Didier, *Benchmarking: l'État sous pression statistique* (Paris: Zone Books, 2013); see also Christian Laval, Francis Vergne, Pierre Clément, and Guy Dreux, *La nouvelle école capitaliste* (Paris: La Découverte, 2011).
41 The processes of heritage creation are currently receiving a great deal of attention, especially from historians and anthropologists but also from sociologists, geographers, and economists; the literature on the subject is increasing day by day. One of the most notable editorial projects in this area is a collection edited by Pierre Nora and published by Gallimard: Pierre Nora, ed., *Rethinking France=Lieux de mémoire*, trans. David Jordan, 4 vols (Chicago: University of Chicago Press, [1984–92] 2001). See also Xavier Greffe, *La valeur économique du patrimoine* (Paris: Anthropos, 1990); Alain Berger, Pascal Chevalier, Geneviève Cortes, and Marc Dedeire, eds, *Patrimoines, héritages et développement rural en Europe* (Paris: L'Harmattan, 2010). We should also mention the analysis by an anthropologist who studies the processes of heritage creation in Palma de Mallorca. The author shows that these are twofold processes. On one side, they put up barriers to the growth of gentrification; on the other, they promote the commodification of the zones surrounding sites of heritage creation. See Jaume Franquesa, "On Keeping and Selling: The Political Economy of Heritage Making in Contemporary Spain," *Current Anthropology*, 54/3 (2013): 346–69.

42 See Sharon Zukin, *The Culture of Cities* (Oxford: Blackwell, 1995), pp. 79–108.
43 See, for example, the brochures "Nantes, le voyage," and "Nantes, les adresses CHIK."
44 See Berger et al., *Patrimoines*, pp. 5–10.
45 Stéphane Gerson, "Le patrimoine local impossible: Nostradamus à Salon-de-Provence (1890–1999)," *Genèses*, no. 92 (2013): 52–75.
46 In recent years most households that have changed residences in France have moved to a rural or peri-urban commune, and they justify that choice by their quest for "life in the country." Between 1999 and 2006, rural communes have experienced a net population growth of 0.8 percent, whereas the population in urban centers has remained stable; see Jean Laganier and Dalila Vienne, "Recensement de la population en 2006: la croissance retrouvée des espaces ruraux et des grandes villes," *Insee première*, no. 1218 (2009).
47 On policies of public heritage creation and their expression over the last forty years, see François Hartog, *Regimes of Historicity: Presentism and Experiences of Time* (New York: Columbia University Press, [2003] 2015), pp. 180–6. Thus, for example, whereas the Athens Charter for the Restoration of Historical Monuments focused on isolated single monuments, the Venice charter, thirty years later, included in the notion of historical monument "not only the single architectural work but also the urban or rural setting in which is found evidence of a particular civilization, a significant development or a historic event" (p. 183).
48 To take just one example, Vincent Biot analyzes the way the plateaus known as the Grands Causses, carved out between the gorges of the Tarn and Jonte rivers, have been highlighted. In the nineteenth century these regions still benefited from flourishing economic activities based on livestock farming, especially tanneries, millinery, and trading in wool and silk; during the first third of the twentieth century, these activities all declined, with the exception of glove-making in Millau. Learned local authors undertook to call attention to the aesthetic value of the landscape, following the nineteenth-century writers Charles Nodier, Louis de Malafosse, and especially, a little later, Édouard-Alfred Martel; these authors achieved what Vincent Biot calls the "territorial construction" of this region. See Vincent Biot, "Valorisation patrimoniale et développement touristique des Grands Causses: l'empreinte d'Édouard-Alfred Martel (1859–1938)," in Jean-Yves Andrieux and Patrick Harismendy, eds, *Initiateurs et entrepreneurs culturels du tourisme (1850–1950)* (Rennes: Presses Universitaires de Rennes, 2011), pp. 35–46.
49 See Jacqueline Candau and Ludovic Ginelli, "L'engagement des agriculteurs dans un service environnemental: l'exemple du paysage," *Revue française de sociologie*, 52/4 (2011): 691–718. Candau and Ginelli carried out their investigation among farmers in the Morvan and the Saint-Nectaire regions.
50 The proportion of lodgings in hotels as compared to those in campgrounds and other recognized "tourist accommodations" (holiday cottages, temporary rentals, vacation villages, and so on) can serve as a rough indicator for a first estimate of the proportion of high-end tourism: it is about 45 percent in France, where so-called open-air hotels play an important role. See "Le tourisme en Europe en 2015," *Insee première*, no. 1610 (2016).
51 Tourism is one of the elements that allow geographers to understand the connection between the phenomena of globalization and the processes of reinforcing collective identities: see Peter Burns, "Brief Encounters: Culture, Tourism,

and the Local–Global Nexus," in Salah Wahab and Chris Cooper, eds, *Tourism in the Age of Globalization* (Abingdon: Routledge, 2001), pp. 290–305.

52 International tourism represents a market of 1,200 billion dollars and contributes 9 percent to the world economy; see Frédéric Pierret, "Le tourisme est-il devenu un enjeu stratégique?" *Annales des Mines – Réalités industrielles*, no. 3 (2015): 9–13.

53 Veille info tourisme, Ministère de l'Artisanat, du Commerce et du Tourisme (www.veilleinfotourisme.fr/).

54 According to the assistant director of tourism in the office of tourism, commerce, arts and crafts, and services, Direction Générale des Entreprises (DGE), Ministère de l'Économie, de l'Industrie et du Numérique (interviewed by the authors, February 18, 2016).

55 Davezies, *La République et ses territoires*, p. 38.

56 DGE, available at www.veilleinfotourisme.fr/.

57 Pierret, "Le tourisme."

58 In the European Union, the leading clientele is from Asia (39 percent of overnight stays), closely followed by the North American contingent (37 percent). The United Kingdom is the primary Asian destination; it attracts tourists especially from English-speaking countries and the Commonwealth; France and Italy come next. France draws more tourists from China and Japan than the other European countries: the rapidly growing Chinese clientele overtook the Japanese in 2012. See "Le tourisme en France," *Insee première*.

59 Saskia Cousin and Bertrand Réau, *Sociologie du tourisme* (Paris: La Découverte, 2009), pp. 59–67.

60 Georges Panayotis, "Le tourisme français: un secteur économique majeur au fort potentiel," *Annales des Mines – Réalités industrielles*, no. 3 (2015): 15–19.

61 On "experience management," see B. Joseph Pine II and James H. Gilmore, *The Experience Economy: Work is Theatre & Every Business a Stage* (Boston: Harvard Business School Press, 1999), esp. pp. 15–17.

62 The proportion of overnight stays by the sea in relation to the overall number of nights can serve as an indicator to distinguish, among the European countries that have the highest percentage of tourists (the proportion of overnight stays in relation to the resident population), those whose potential for tourism rests not only on their "cultural" assets but also on the prominence of their coastal regions and on favorable climates that allow for a longer tourist season. This is the case for Spain, which benefits both from cultural tourism and "sea-and-sun" tourism; the proportion of overnight stays on the coast (80 percent) is more than double the proportion in France (around 35 percent). Spain, where the number of nights increased by 3.3 percent between 2012 and 2015 (compared to 0.4 percent in France), attracts a large number of Northern Europeans, especially to its seaside resorts, and it has benefited from "reports detrimental to countries outside of Europe deemed 'risky.'" More generally, the southern coasts attract most of the foreign tourists coming from Europe: see "Le tourisme en Europe," *Insee première*.

63 Saskia Cousin, "L'Unesco et la doctrine du tourisme culturel: généalogie d'un 'bon' tourisme," *Civilisations*, no. 57 (2008): 41–56.

64 For examples of the use of "the symbolics of travel" – an area in which writers such as Nicolas Bouvier and Bruce Chatwin are the current heroes – as instruments for critiquing the "tourism industry," see among others Rodolphe

Christin, *L'usure du monde: critique de la déraison touristique* (Montreuil: L'Échappée, 2014).

65 Cousin, "L'Unesco," pp. 47–8.

66 The Malaga Chamber of Commerce, *Le tourisme culturel en Méditerranée: quelques opportunités pour l'Espagne, la France, le Maroc, la Tunisie*, in *Invest in Med* (Marseille: Etinet, Euromediterranean Tourist Network, 2011): 11.

67 See www.entrepriseetdecouverte.fr/.

68 Jonathan Friedman has analyzed the role played by tourism in the processes of identity affirmation that accompany globalization. For example, in the case of the Ainu people in northern Japan, the rearrangement of living spaces to make them conform better to the expectations of tourists seeking exoticism and the increased production of "traditional" objects for sale to tourists constitute "conscious strategies of identity reconstruction," strategies that accompany calls for autonomy stressing ethnic specificity: see Jonathan Friedman, *Cultural Identities and Global Process* (London: Sage, 1994), pp. 109–13.

69 See Nelson Graburn, ed., *Ethnic and Tourist Arts* (Oakland: University of California Press, 1979); Paul van der Grijp, *Art and Exoticism: An Anthropology of the Yearning for Authenticity* (London: Transaction, 2009); and on authenticity as an argument for tourism, see Dennison Nash, *Anthropology of Tourism* (Oxford: Pergamon Press, 1996).

70 More generally, for countries that draw a significant portion of their revenues from tourism, the demand for security plays a central role; it lies at the heart of professional preoccupations, as we have seen for example in countries such as Egypt and Tunisia, where heritage sites and museums have been targeted in particular.

71 See Gérôme Truc, *Shellshocked: The Social Response to Terrorist Attacks*, trans. Andrew Brown (Cambridge: Polity, 2017).

72 On the filming of television dramas in castles, see Sabine Chalvon-Demersay, "La saison des châteaux: une ethnographie des tournages en 'décors réels' pour la télévision," *Réseaux*, no. 172 (2012): 175–213.

73 As is very often the case in this type of quantitative study, the figures obtained are approximate and thus debatable, in the sense that they depend on the nomenclatures used and the methods adopted – for example, in this case, the decision to include "indirect activities" in the count.

74 Serge Kancel, Jérôme Itty, Morgane Weill, and Bruno Durieux, *L'apport de la culture à l'économie de la France* (Paris: Inspection générale des finances, 2013).

75 Yves Jauneau and Xavier Niel, "Le poids économique direct de la culture en 2013," *Culture Chiffres*, no. 5 (2014): 1–18.

76 By "audiovisual" we refer here to radio, cinema, television, video, and CDs.

77 Kancel et al., *L'apport de la culture*.

78 A commune is a French administrative unit corresponding to a village, city, or incorporated township.

79 The number of museums and monuments open to the public in France, inventoried in a guide published by the Éditions du Cherche-Midi, increased from 7,000 in the 1992 edition to 10,000 in 2001: see Josquin Barré, "L'impact de la variable prix dans le tourisme culturel," in Jean-Michel Tobelem, ed., *La culture mise à prix* (Paris: L'Harmattan, 2005), pp. 105–26.

80 See Jean-Cédric Delvainquière, François Tugores, Nicolas Laroche, and Benoît Jourdan, "Les dépenses culturelles des collectivités territoriales en 2010: 7,6 milliards d'euros pour la culture," *Culture Chiffres*, no. 3 (2014):1–32.

81 Marie Gouyon and Frédérique Patureau, "Vingt ans d'évolution de l'emploi dans les professions culturelles," *Culture Chiffres*, no. 6 (2014): 1–24.

82 Chantal Lacroix, "Les dépenses de consommation des ménages en biens et services culturels et télécommunications," *Culture Chiffres*, no. 2 (2009): 1–7.

83 Olivier Donnat, *Les pratiques culturelles des Français: enquête 1997* (Paris: La Documentation française, 1998), pp. 221, 279, 291.

84 Peter Laslett, *Finnish Life and Illicit Love in Earlier Generations* (Cambridge: Cambridge University Press, 1977), p. 43.

85 Pierre Ansart, *Marx et l'anarchisme* (Paris: Presses Universitaires de France, 1969).

86 See for example Harry Bellet, *Le marché de l'art s'écroule demain à 18 h 30* (Paris: Nil, 2001); Daniel Granet and Catherine Lamour, *Grands et petits secrets du monde de l'art* (Paris: Fayard, 2010); and Don Thompson, *The $12 Million Stuffed Shark: The Curious Economics of Contemporary Art* (New York: Palgrave Macmillan, 2008).

87 See especially Isabelle Graw, *High Price: Art between the Market and Celebrity Culture* (Berlin: Sternberg, 2009); Sarah Thornton, *Seven Days in the Art World* (New York: W. W. Norton, 2008); Pierre-Michel Menger, *The Economics of Creativity: Art and Achievement under Uncertainty*, trans. Stephen Rendell et al. (Cambridge, MA: Harvard University Press, [2009] 2014); Nathalie Heinich, *Le paradigme de l'art contemporain: structures d'une révolution artistique* (Paris: Gallimard, 2014).

88 See Daniel Aaron Silver and Terry Nichols Clark, *Scenescapes: How Qualities Shape Social Life* (Chicago: University of Chicago Press, 2016).

89 See Olaf Velthuis, *Talking Prices: Symbolic Meanings of Prices on the Market for Contemporary Art* (Princeton, NJ: Princeton University Press, 2005).

90 See Alain Quemin, *Les stars de l'art contemporain: notoriété et consécration artistique dans les arts visuels* (Paris: CNRS, 2013); on rankings of personalities, see especially pp. 205–76.

91 Art collectors themselves are ranked, particularly in terms of their notoriety and their visibility, on the site *Larry's List* (www.larryslist.com).

92 According to the highly successful model presented by Robert H. Frank and Philip J. Cook, *The Winner-Take-All Society: Why the Few at the Top Get So Much More than the Rest of Us* (New York: Free Press, 1995).

93 Jean-Jacques Arrighi and Marjorie Martin, "Grand Arles: des difficultés à surmonter, des atouts à exploiter," *Insee études*, no. 31 (2013).

94 See Jean-Maurice Rouquette, ed., *Arles: histoire, territoires et cultures* (Paris: Imprimerie nationale, 2008).

95 The statistics in this section come from Rouquette, *Arles*, and Arrighi and Martin, "Grand Arles."

96 According to the magazine *Bilan* (November 30, 2012).

97 See the reports of the Boston Consulting Group (www.bcg.com) and Gabriel Zucman, *The Hidden Wealth of Nations: The Scourge of Tax Havens*, trans. Teresa Lavender Fagan (Chicago: University of Chicago Press, [2013] 2015), pp. 29–30.

98 On the problems that this two-track consumption poses to the mass distribution sector, see Philippe Moati, *L'avenir de la grande distribution* (Paris: Odile Jacob, 2001) and *La nouvelle révolution commerciale* (Paris: Odile Jacob, 2011).

Chapter 2 Toward Enrichment

1 Michael Thompson, *Rubbish Theory: The Creation and Destruction of Value* (Oxford: Oxford University Press, 1979).

2 See Michel Melot, *Mirabilia: essai sur l'inventaire général du patrimoine culturel* (Paris: Gallimard, 2012), and, for an ethnography of the selection processes, Nathalie Heinich, *La fabrique du patrimoine* (Paris: Éditions de la MSH, 2009).

3 Thorstein Veblen, *The Theory of the Leisure Class* (New York: Penguin Books, [1899] 1979).

4 See Marie-France Garcia-Parpet, *Le marché de l'excellence: les grands crus à l'épreuve de la mondialisation* (Paris: Seuil, 2009).

5 Jean-Pierre Cometti ignores this problem when he addresses the question: see Jean-Pierre Cometti, *Conserver/restaurer: l'oeuvre d'art à l'époque de sa préservation technique* (Paris: Gallimard, 2016).

6 This theme has been developed in American sociology; see especially Paul DiMaggio, "Classification in Art," *American Sociological Review*, 52/4 (1987): 440–55; Sharon Zukin, *The Culture of Cities* (Oxford: Blackwell, 1995), pp. 79–108; on the notion of "symbolic goods," see Michèle Lamont and Marcel Fournier, *Cultivating Differences: Symbolic Boundaries and the Making of Inequality* (Chicago: University of Chicago Press, 1992).

7 Pierre Bourdieu, "Le marché des biens symboliques," *L'Année sociologique* 22 (1971): 49–126.

8 Jean Baudrillard, *The System of Objects*, trans. James Benedict (London: Verso, [1968] 1996).

9 Here we follow Cornelius Castoriadis in *The Imaginary Institution of Society*, trans. Kathleen Blamey (Cambridge, MA: MIT Press, [1975] 1987): "Everything that is presented to us in the social–historical world is inextricably tied to the symbolic. ... the innumerable material products without which no society could live even an instant, are not (not always, not directly) symbols. All of these, however, would be impossible outside of a symbolic network" (p. 117). According to Castoriadis, the "symbolic" can neither be treated (as it often is) as a mere neutral cloak nor as stemming from a "logic" properly speaking that would be superimposed on another kind of order known as "rational" (pp. 117–27).

10 Howard S. Becker, *Art Worlds* (Berkeley: University of California Press, 1982), p. 34.

11 A nineteenth-century elevated railroad track converted in the early twenty-first century to a space for strolling enhanced by contemporary art works, the High Line is in a former industrial district that has become a center for art galleries and luxury shops. See David Halle and Elisabeth Tiso, *New York's New Edge: Contemporary Art, the High Line, and Urban Megaprojects on the Far West Side* (Chicago: University of Chicago Press, 2014).

12 See Edward Anthony Wrigley, *Continuity, Chance & Change: The Character of the Industrial Revolution in England* (Cambridge: Cambridge University Press, 1990), and *Energy and the English Industrial Revolution* (Cambridge: Cambridge University Press, 2010).

13 See Dominique Poulot, *Une histoire des musées en France* (Paris: La Découverte, 2008).

14 On the constitution of the French national patrimony, see Alexandra Kowalski, "The Nation, Rescaled: Theorizing the Decentralization of

Memory in Contemporary France," *Comparative Studies in Society and History*, 54/2 (2012): 308–31; and "State Power as Field Work: Culture and Practice in the French Survey of Historic Landmarks," in Richard Sennett and Craig Calhoun, eds, *Practicing Culture* (London: Routledge, 2007), pp. 82–104.

15 Bénédicte Savoy, *Patrimoine annexé: les biens culturels saisis par la France en Allemagne autour de 1800*, 2 vols (Paris: Éditions de la MSH, 2003).

16 Guido Guerzoni, *Apollo and Vulcan: The Art Markets in Italy, 1400–1700*, trans. Amanda George (East Lansing: Michigan State University Press, [2006] 2011).

17 Cissie Fairchilds, "The Production and Marketing of Populuxe Goods in Eighteenth-Century Paris," in John Brewer and Roy Porter, eds, *Consumption and the World of Goods* (New York: Routledge, 1993), pp. 228–48.

18 Louis Bergeron, *Les industries du luxe en France* (Paris: Odile Jacob, 1998).

19 See Eric Zuelow, ed., *Touring Beyond the Nation: A Transnational Approach to European Tourism History* (Burlington, VT: Ashgate, 2011).

20 Alain Croix, ed., *Initiateurs et entrepreneurs culturels du tourisme (1850–1950)*, Actes du colloque de Saint-Brieuc, June 2–4, 2010 (Rennes: Presses Universitaires de Rennes, 2011).

21 See Pierre Bourdieu and Luc Boltanski, *La production de l'idéologie dominante* (Paris: Demopolis, [1976] 2008).

22 A good indicator is the work *Le partage des bénéfices*, published under the collective name of Darras, which brings together the contributions to a colloquium organized by Pierre Bourdieu in 1965 by sociologists and anthropologists (P. Bourdieu, J.-C. Chamboredon, C. Durand, R. Sainsaulieu, J. Lautman, J. Cuisenier), economists (J.-P. Pagé, C. Gruson, M. Praderie), and statisticians from INSEE (A. Darbel, C. Seibel, J.-P. Ruault). Prefaced by Claude Gruson, a Keynesian economist influenced by social Christianity, then director of INSEE, the work dealt with the fact that "expansion" had not managed to reduce inequality envisaged on several levels: employment, agriculture, schooling, and so on. The papers tended to stress the need for "social mobility." See Darras, *Le partage des bénéfices, expansion et inégalités en France* (Paris: Minuit, 1966).

23 After the first report of the Club of Rome, in 1972, titled "The Limits to Growth." See Peter Wagner, *Modernity: Understanding the Present* (Cambridge: Polity, 2012), pp. 49–52.

24 See for example *La Gueule ouverte*, a successful periodical similar to *Charlie Hebdo*, published by Pierre Fournier with contributions by Cavanna, Wolinski, Reiser, and Cabu; and also Alain Hervé's *Le Sauvage*, similar to *Le Nouvel Observateur*, where André Gorz was a journalist.

25 The number of students grew sixfold between the early 1960s and the first decade of the twenty-first century, from 215,000 to 1.3 million. In 1982, among French people between the ages of twenty-five and fifty-four who were working or actively seeking employment, 2.1 million – that is, 13 percent of this age group – had degrees attesting to post-secondary education. In 2010, the number with similar degrees reached 8 million, or four times as many, and they represented more than a third (36 percent) of people in the workforce between the ages of twenty-five and fifty-four. See Jean-François Léger, "Plus de diplômés, plus d'inégalités territoriales?" *Population & Avenir*, no. 718 (2014): 4.

26 For a detailed description of the reorganization of companies and changes in working conditions, see Luc Boltanski and Ève Chiapello, *The New Spirit of Capitalism*, trans. Gregory Elliott (London: Verso, [1999] 2005).

27 This devaluation of diplomas, which began in the 1980s, became particularly significant starting in the 1990s, and it has only been accentuated since then. In 1982, as we have seen, 2.1 million members of the workforce had higher degrees, while there were 1.6 million workers at the managerial level (cadres); thus there were thirteen members of the workforce with higher degrees for every ten cadres. In 2010, 8 million members of the workforce held higher degrees, while there were 3.6 million cadres, or twenty-two members of the workforce with higher degrees for every ten cadres. In 1990, 45 percent of people with higher degrees were cadres. Twenty years later, the proportion had fallen to 37 percent. At the same time, the territorial distribution of opportunities to get a position as a cadre became more and more unequal: cadres with higher degrees were concentrated in the Paris region and to a lesser extent in the major regional metropolitan centers such as Lyon, Marseille, and Toulouse. See Léger, "Plus de diplômés," pp. 4–7.

28 Here we can speak of the "finite world," as Zygmunt Bauman does in *Globalization: The Human Consequences* (New York: Columbia University Press, 1998) and in *Wasted Lives: Modernity and its Outcasts* (Cambridge: Polity, 2004).

29 This conception of culture in terms of "art for art's sake," exempt from financial considerations, penetrates even into galleries of contemporary art (despite their orientation toward commerce), which proliferated in the postwar years and sought to break with the compromises of the art market during the occupation (after the Jewish-owned galleries had already been eliminated) by turning toward artists whose work embodied both the rejection of "capitalism" and aesthetic research in its most elitist dimensions. The same phenomenon is found in the domain of publishing. See Julie Verlaine, *Les galeries d'art contemporain à Paris: une histoire culturelle du marché de l'art, 1944–1970* (Paris: Publications de la Sorbonne, 2012), pp. 23–45.

30 Maryvonne de Saint-Pulgent, *Jack Lang: batailles pour la culture* (Paris: La Documentation française, 2013), p. 56.

31 On the shift from ethnographic museums to ecomuseums, see Martine Segalen, *La vie d'un musée, 1937–2005* (Paris: Stock, 2005).

32 See Nathalie Heinich and Roberta Shapiro, eds, *De l'artification: enquêtes sur le passage à l'art* (Paris: Éditions de l'EHESS, 2012).

33 The delegation for the plastic arts, established in 1982, created twenty-two positions of regional counselor for the plastic arts under the Direction régionale des affaires culturelles (Regional Office for Cultural Affairs) and the same number of Fonds régionaux d'art contemporain (FRAC, Regional Foundations for Contemporary Art).

34 The critique of the new cultural policies that had the most significant media impact was probably that of Marc Fumaroli, in *L'État culturel: une religion moderne* (Paris: De Fallois, 1991).

35 See Laurent Jeanpierre and Séverine Sofio, "Chronique d'une mort annoncée: les conservateurs de musée face aux commissaires d'expositions dans l'art contemporain français," in Frédéric Poulard and Jean-Michel Tobolem, eds, *Les conservateurs de musée: atouts et faiblesses d'une profession* (Paris: La Documentation française, 2015), pp. 111–39.

36 As François Dosse points out, "Guattari va jouer auprès de Jack Lang le rôle d'une boîte à idées"; see François Dosse, *Gilles Deleuze et Félix Guattari: biographie croisée* (Paris: La Découverte, 2007), p. 450.

37 Félix Guattari and Suely Rolnik, *Micropolitiques* (Paris: Les Empêcheurs de penser en rond/Seuil, 2007), p. 33.

38 Philippe Urfalino, "De l'anti-impérialisme américain à la dissolution de la politique culturelle," *Revue française de science politique*, 45/5 (1993): 823–49.

39 See Thomas Angeletti, "Le laboratoire de la nécessité: économistes, institutions et qualifications de l'économie," Doctoral thesis in sociology, Paris, EHESS, 2013.

40 On the foundation of the economics of conventions, see *L'économie des conventions*, special issue, *Revue économique*, 40/2 (1989). See also Laurent Thévenot, "Les investissements de forme," in *Conventions économiques: cahiers du centre d'études de l'emploi* (Paris: Presses Universitaires de France, 1985), pp. 21–72, and "Essai sur les objets usuels: propriétés, fonctions, usages," in Bernard Conein, Nicolas Dodier, and Laurent Thévenot, eds, *Les objets dans l'action* (Paris: Éditions de l'EHESS, 1993), pp. 85–111. See also Philippe Batifoulier, ed., *Théorie des conventions* (Paris: Economica, 2001), André Orléan, *Analyse économique des conventions* (Paris: Presses Universitaires de France, 2004), and Robert Salais, "Conventions de travail, mondes de production et institutions," *L'Homme et la Société*, nos. 170–1 (2008–9): 151–74.

41 For a synthesis, see Arnaldo Bagnasco and Charles Sabel, *PME et développement économique en Europe* (Paris: La Découverte, 1994). On the development of the "Third Italy" in opposition to the industrial triangle Milan–Turin–Genoa, see also Arnaldo Bagnasco and Carlo Trigilia, *La construction sociale du marché: le défi de la troisième Italie* (Cachan: Les Éditions de l'ENS de Cachan, [1988] 1993). (The "third Italy" designates a region in central and northeastern Italy where clusters of small family-run businesses developed with municipal support in the 1970s and 1980s.)

42 Michael Piore and Charles Sabel, "Préface," *Les chemins de la prospérité: de la production de masse à la spécialisation souple*, trans. Luc Boussard (Paris: Hachette, 1989), p. 10 [preface to the French translation of *The Second Industrial Divide: Possibilities for Prosperity* (New York: Basic Books, 1984)].

43 Piore and Sabel, *The Second Industrial Divide*, p. 214; more generally, see pp. 213–16.

44 See Andrea Colli and Elisabetta Merlo, "Family Business and Luxury Business in Italy (1950–2000)," *Entreprises et histoire*, no. 46 (2007): 113–24.

45 Robert Salais and Michael Storper, *Les mondes de production: enquête sur l'identité économique en France* (Paris: Éditions de la MSH, 1993). A revised English version appeared four years later entitled *Worlds of Production: The Action Frameworks of the Economy* (Cambridge, MA: Harvard University Press, [1993] 1997).

46 Salais and Storper, *Mondes de production*, p. 39.

47 Ibid., p. 117.

48 Pierre Moulinier, "Naissance et développement du partenariat contractuel dans le domaine culturel," in Philippe Poirrier and René Rizzardo, eds, *Une ambition partagée? La coopération entre le ministère de la culture et les collectivités territoriales (1959–2009)* (Paris: Travaux et documents du ministère de la culture, no. 26 (2009), p. 60.

49 Ibid., p. 61.

50 In 2001, in France, one association out of five had a cultural purpose. See Valérie Deroin, "Emploi, bénévolat et financement des associations culturelles," *Culture Chiffres*, no. 1 (2014): 1–12.
51 Ibid.
52 Excerpts from the documentation presented on the site of the Ministry of Foreign Affairs.
53 See Thomas Piketty, *Capital in the Twenty-First Century*, trans. Arthur Goldhammer (Cambridge, MA: Belknap Press of Harvard University Press, [2013] 2014).
54 See www.forum-avignon.org.
55 Monique de Saint Martin, *L'espace de la noblesse* (Paris: Métailié, 1993). See also Michel Pinçon and Monique Pinçon-Charlot, *Châteaux et châtelains: les siècles passent, le symbole demeure* (Paris: Anne Carrière, 2005).
56 Vincent Eblé, *Rapport d'information sur les dépenses fiscales relatives à la préservation du patrimoine historique bâti*, French Senate, recorded October 7, 2015; see www.senat.fr/rap/r15-018/r15-018_mono.html.
57 Ibid., p. 36.
58 As attested by the case of Alain du Plessis de Pouzilhac, cited in Saint Martin, *L'espace de la noblesse*, p. 97.
59 Ibid., p. 99.
60 Ibid., p. 100. In Dominique Schnapper's first book, devoted to the lifestyle of the elites of Bologna, the author makes similar remarks: "In the salons of the old aristocracy, the paintings remain hung in several rows, in the old style, rather than highlighted for display, because their presence is not due to the personal taste of a collector or of an amateur wanting to show off his wealth. The poor state of preservation of works that have been passed down through inheritance over many generations and their awkward presentation signifies the hereditary character of the objects owned"; see Dominique Schnapper, *L'Italie rouge et noire: les modèles de la vie quotidienne à Bologne* (Paris: Gallimard, 1971), pp. 103–4.
61 Saint Martin, *L'espace de la noblesse*, pp. 105–7.
62 Ibid., p. 111.
63 See the site of the French Ministry of Culture, under the heading "European Heritage Days": http://traduction.culture.gouv.fr/url/Result.aspx?to=en&url=https%3A%2F%2Fjourneesdupatrimoine.culture.gouv.fr%2F.
64 Saint Martin, *L'espace de la noblesse*, p. 110.
65 See Marie-Odile Mergnac, *La généalogie: une passion française* (Paris: Autrement, 2003), and Jean-Louis Beaucarnot, *La généalogie* (Paris: Presses Universitaires de France, 1997).
66 See Robert Brenner, *The Economic Capital of Global Turbulence: The Advanced Capitalist Economies from Long Boom to Long Downturn* (London: Verso, 2006).
67 Giovanni Arrighi, *Adam Smith in Beijing: Lineages of the Twenty-First Century* (London: Verso, 2007), pp. 105–12.
68 We are borrowing the notion of "central capitalism" from Jonathan Nitzan and Shimshon Bichler, who have developed an analysis of the dynamic of capitalism in terms of competition for differential accumulation – that is, in terms of relative power. In this logic, the dynamic of capitalism is linked to shifts that, on the one hand, extend commodification and, on the other, come back to "sabotage" the industrial capacities of the competitors; see

Jonathan Nitzan and Shimshon Bichler, *Capital as Power: A Study of Order and Creorder* (New York: Routledge, 2009). Nitzan and Bichler (pp. 219–27) align themselves with the analyses of Thorstein Veblen, who was the first to develop the notion of industrial "sabotage." He stressed the tension between industrial interests, governed by the requirement to produce things, and those of "business," governed by the prices of things: "In the business world the price of things is a more substantial fact than the things themselves" (Thorstein Veblen, *Absentee Ownership and Business Enterprises in Recent Times: The Case of America* (Boston: Beacon Press, [1923] 1967), p. 89; cited in Nitzan and Bichler, p. 221). For Veblen, prices are a matter of property and power, and they play a central role in the dynamics of capitalism (Nitzan and Bichler, pp. 217–27).

69 For a precise and perceptive analysis of these processes, see Wolfgang Streeck, *Buying Time: The Delayed Crisis of Democratic Capitalism*, trans. Patrick Camiller (London: Verso, [2013] 2014), esp. chapter 1, "From Legitimation Crisis to Fiscal Crisis," pp. 1–46.

70 Giovanni Arrighi, whose approach is inspired by the work of Fernand Braudel, decomposes the evolution of capitalism into a series of cycles of accumulation, each of which occupies a specific period (roughly a century) and is centered around a geographic profit center (Genoa, the Netherlands, England, the United States). One of his arguments is that, in each of these cycles, a financial phase follows a manufacturing and commercial phase and that the financial phase precedes and announces the decline of this cycle to the benefit of a new cycle centered on a different geographic pole; see Giovanni Arrighi, *The Long Twentieth Century: Money, Power and the Origins of Our Times* (new edn, London: Verso, 2010). This is why, if Arrighi agrees with David Harvey (*The New Imperialism* [Oxford: Oxford University Press, 2003]) in recognizing the importance of the financial turn operated by capitalism since the 1980s, he takes a different path by interpreting this turn as a sign of crisis and decline. One of his arguments consists in comparing the phase of financialization and optimism of the Reagan–Thatcher period and the financialization that followed the depression of 1873–96, followed by a phase of improvement (what he calls the Edwardian "belle époque") foreshadowing, as he sees it, the crisis of 1929, which marked the end of the cycle of accumulation centered on England, to the benefit of the United States.

71 For a synthesis, see Thomas W. Volscho and Nathan J. Kelly, "The Rise of the Super-Rich: Power Resources, Taxes, Financial Markets, and the Dynamics of the Top 1 Percent, 1949 to 2008," *American Sociological Review*, 77/5 (2012): 679–99.

72 It is hard to find precise information on the way the wealthy use and preserve their money, and on the share of their fortunes that is stored in objects of value rather than in stocks or bonds, as these types of goods are generally conflated under the heading of "household patrimony." In addition, the real price negotiated for exceptional goods is often highly undervalued for tax purposes.

73 The French title of this section is borrowed from a celebrated book by the poet Francis Ponge, *Le parti pris des choses* (1942). The English translation is adapted from a recent English-language version of Ponge's book *Partisan of Things*, translated by Joshua Corey and Jean-Luc Garneau (Chicago: Kenning, 2016).

74 Bruno Cousin and Sébastien Chauvin, "L'entre-soi élitaire à Saint-Barthélémy," *Ethnologie française*, 42/2 (2012): 335–45.

75 We are thinking here of Michel Pinçon and Monique Pinçon-Charlot's very informative work, especially *Les ghettos du gotha: au coeur de la grande bourgeoisie* (Paris: Seuil, 2010) and *Sociologie de la bourgeoisie* (Paris: La Découverte, 2005).

76 Pierre Bourdieu, *Distinction: A Social Critique of the Judgement of Taste*, trans. Richard Nice (London: Routledge & Kegan Paul, [1979] 1986).

77 See Franco Moretti, *The Bourgeois: Between History and Literature* (London: Verso, 2013).

78 The distinction between patrimony and capital is supported in the analyses of Joseph Schumpeter, even though that theorist envisaged it mainly with respect to industrial production. For Schumpeter, the goods one owns, including monetary goods, constitute capital properly speaking only on condition that they are put to work – that is, put into circulation. "Capital is nothing but the lever by which the entrepreneur subjects to his control the concrete goods which he needs, nothing but a means of diverting the factors of production to new uses, of dictating a new direction to production"; Joseph Schumpeter, *The Theory of Economic Development: An Inquiry into Profits, Capital, Credit, Interest, and the Business Cycle*, trans. Redvers Opie (New York: Oxford University Press, [1911, 1926] 1961), p. 116.

79 The number of business schools in France grew from 76 in 1980 to around 250 in 2017.

80 On the notion of hipster, see Mark Greif, "What Was the Hipster?," in *Against Everything* (New York: Pantheon Books, 2016), pp. 209–19.

81 Arjun Appadurai, ed., *The Social Life of Things: Commodities in Cultural Perspective* (Cambridge: Cambridge University Press, 1986). This work marked a refoundation of anthropological work on commodities, reconnecting with an approach developed by Jean Baudrillard. The latter's two seminal works – *The System of Objects* and *The Consumer Society: Myths and Structures* (rev. edn, London: Sage, [1970] 2017) – set forth the premises, in sociology, of a new attention to objects. The interest in things placed on the same level as humans has been developed in particular by Bruno Latour in numerous works; see most notably his *Aramis, or, The Love of Technology*, trans. Catherine Porter (Cambridge, MA: Harvard University Press, [1992] 1996).

82 On the use made here of the notion of test, see Luc Boltanski and Laurent Thévenot, *On Justification: Economies of Worth*, trans. Catherine Porter (Princeton, NJ: Princeton University Press, [1991] 2006).

Chapter 3 Commerce in Things

1 See Jens Beckert and Jörg Rössel, "The Price of Art: Uncertainty and Reputation in the Art Field," *European Societies*, 15/2 (2013): 178–95.

2 See Fabien Accominotti, *Market Chains* (Princeton, NJ: Princeton University Press, forthcoming).

3 See Lucien Karpik, *Valuing the Unique: The Economics of Singularities*, trans. Nora Scott (Princeton, NJ: Princeton University Press, [2007] 2010), chapter 17, "Prices," pp. 209–25.

4 Michel Callon and Fabian Muniesa, "Les marchés économiques comme dispositifs collectifs de calcul" (2003), in Michel Callon, Madeleine Akrich, Sophie Dubuisson-Quellier, et al., *Sociologie des agencements marchands* (Paris: Presses des Mines-Transvalor, 2013), pp. 195–233.

5 See Michel Callon, "Innovation et emprise croissante des forces marchandes," *Le libellio d'AEGIS*, 11/4 (2015): 43–61, and Michel Callon, ed., *The Laws of the Markets* (Oxford: Blackwell, 1998).

6 What Karl Polanyi calls the "catallactic triad: trade, money, and markets," in Karl Polanyi and Harry W. Pearson, *The Livelihood of Man* (New York: Academic Press, [1977] 2011), pp. 75–142. For historical analyses of situations of "commerce without markets," see also three essays by Karl Polanyi: "Traders and Trade," in Jeremy A. Sabloff and C. C. Lamberg-Karlovsky, eds, *Ancient Civilization and Trade* (Albuquerque: University of New Mexico Press, 1975), pp. 133–54; "Ports of Trade in Early Societies," *Journal of Economic History*, 23/1 (1963): 30–45; and "Marketless Trading in Hammurabi's Time," in Karl Polanyi, Conrad M. Arensberg, and Harry W. Pearson, eds, *Trade and Market in the Early Empires: Economies in History and Theory* (Glencoe, IL: Free Press, 1957), pp. 12–26.

7 As Jeanne Lazarus has undertaken to do for banking competencies: see in particular Jeanne Lazarus, "Tenir ses comptes et bien se tenir: l'apprentissage de l'autonomie par la banque," *Politix*, no. 108 (2014): 75–97.

8 Marcel Mauss, *The Gift: The Form and Reason for Exchange in Archaic Societies*, trans. W. D. Halls (New York: W. W. Norton, [1923–4] 2000).

9 Pierre Bourdieu, "Case Study 1: The Twofold Truth of the Gift," *Pascalian Meditations*, trans. Richard Nice (Stanford, CA: Stanford University Press, 2000), pp. 191–202.

10 See especially Alain Testart, *Critique du don: étude sur la circulation non marchande* (Paris: Syllepse, 2006).

11 Philippe Descola, *Beyond Nature and Culture*, trans. Janet Lloyd (Chicago: University of Chicago Press, 2013), pp. 311–21.

12 Georg Simmel, *The Philosophy of Money*, 3rd edn, expanded, trans. Tom Bottomore and David Frisby (London: Routledge, [1900] 2004).

13 Viviana A. Zelizer, "Gifted Money," *The Social Meaning of Money* (New York: Basic Books, 1994), pp. 71–118.

14 Pierre Bourdieu, *The Social Structures of the Economy*, trans. Chris Turner (Cambridge: Polity, [2000] 2005).

15 Clifford Geertz, "Suk: The Bazaar Economy in Sefrou," in Clifford Geertz, Hildred Geertz, and Lawrence Rosen, *Meaning and Order in Moroccan Society* (Cambridge: Cambridge University Press, 1979), pp. 123–313.

16 The opposite is not true: marketing specialists unhesitatingly absorb the work of scholars.

17 We shall not deal with illegal commerce, which raises problems that fall outside the scope of our current project.

18 Viviana A. Zelizer, "What Does Money Mean?," *The Social Meaning of Money* (New York: Basic Books, 1994), pp. 199–216.

19 Here, the term "world" encompasses "everything that happens," and "reality" refers to what is "stabilized by pre-established formats," sustained by institutions, which often have a juridical or para-juridical character. These formats compose a semantics charged with expressing "the whatness of what is"; they establish qualifications, define entities and tests, and determine the relations

that entities and tests must maintain in order to have an acceptable character. See Luc Boltanski, *On Critique: A Sociology of Emancipation*, trans. Gregory Elliott (Cambridge: Polity, [2009] 2011), p. 59.

20 These are typical of the gestures made by experts examining objects intended for sale at auction; see Christian Bessy and Francis Chateauraynaud, *Experts et faussaires* (Paris: Métailié, 1995).

21 Fernand Braudel, *Civilization and Capitalism, 15th–18th Century*, vol. 2: *The Wheels of Commerce*, trans. Siân Reynolds (New York: Harper & Row, [1979] 1982).

22 For an example of the ethnography of a marketplace in French society in the late twentieth century, see Michèle de la Pradelle, *Les vendredis de Carpentras* (Paris: Fayard, 1996).

23 The need for trust between merchants engaged in external commerce and the risks that can lead to the failure of a business when that trust is betrayed are made clear by Francesca Trivellato, *The Familiarity of Strangers: The Sephardic Diaspora, Livorno, and Cross-Cultural Trade in the Early Modern Period* (New Haven, CT: Yale University Press, 2009).

24 While *semantics* is generally defined as the science or study of meanings in language forms, *a semantics* can be understood as a set of specific meanings ascribed to a given set of words or expressions, as opposed to a *pragmatics*, which refers to the way words and expressions are understood in the context of enunciation.

25 On the role of institutions in the establishment of commercial transactions made formally autonomous as compared to personal relations, see Florence Weber, "Transactions marchandes, échanges rituels, relations personnelles: une ethnographie économique après le Grand Partage," *Genèse*, no. 40 (2000): 85–107.

26 Claude Lévi-Strauss, *The Savage Mind*, trans. Doreen Weightman and John Weightman (Chicago: University of Chicago Press, [1962] 1966), pp. 8–9; more generally, see pp. 1–13.

27 It has been shown that the classifications used by INSEE in the realm of food were based on a taxonomy of agricultural products of industrial origin, a taxonomy that did not correspond, on a number of points, to the categories implicitly used by the members of the various social classes. See Luc Boltanski, "Taxinomies populaires, taxinomies savantes: les objets de consommation et leur classement," *Revue française de sociologie*, 11/1 (1970): 34–44.

28 Benoit B. Mandelbrot, *Fractals: Form, Chance, and Dimension* (San Francisco: W. H. Freeman, [1975] 1977).

29 For a critique of the polysemic character of the notion of utility in neoclassical economics, see Jan de Vries, *The Industrious Revolution: Consumer Behavior and the Household Economy, 1650 to the Present* (Cambridge: Cambridge University Press, 2008), pp. 21–5.

30 Ferdinand de Saussure, *Course in General Linguistics*, trans. Wade Baskin, ed. Perry Meisel and Haun Saussy (New York: Columbia University Press, [1916] 2011).

31 Patrice Maniglier, *La vie énigmatique des signes: Saussure et la naissance du structuralisme* (Paris: Léo Scheer, 2006), p. 286.

32 Raymond de Roover, *La pensée économique des scolastiques: doctrines et méthodes* (Paris: Vrin, 1971).

33 See Pierre Bourdieu, *Distinction: A Social Critique of the Judgement of Taste* (London: Routledge & Kegan Paul, [1979] 1986), p. 247.

34 See Caroline Urbain and Marine Le Gall-Ely, *Prix et stratégie marketing* (Paris: Dunod, 2009). According to these authors, "the price differentials observed for a given offer are 50 percent for automobiles and 500 percent for pharmaceutical products, depending on the geographic zone; 300 percent for rail transportation depending on the class of service, rate categories, and usage restrictions; 1000 percent for air transportation depending on the same criteria; at least 300 percent for hotel stays and tourist visits depending on the season and the location; 300–500 percent for industrial products depending on quantities and contractual conditions; 50–500 percent for telecommunications depending on the time of day and the operator; 500 percent for consumer goods depending on the distribution channel" (p. 1). See also Hermann Simon, Florent Jacquet, and Franck Brault, *La stratégie prix* (Paris: Dunod, 2011).

35 See Jean Finez, "La construction des prix à la SNCF, une socio-histoire de la tarification: de la péréquation au yield management (1938–2012)," *Revue française de sociologie*, 55/1 (2014): 5–39.

36 Marion Fourcade, "Cents and Sensibility: Economic Valuation and the Nature of 'Nature,'" *American Journal of Sociology*, 116/6 (2011): 1721–77.

37 See Anthony Kuhn and Yves Moulin, "Proximité des acteurs et transformation des conventions: le cas du marché philatélique numérique," *Revue française de gestion*, no. 213 (2011): 43–56.

38 Albert O. Hirschman, *Exit, Voice, and Loyalty: Responses to Decline in Firms, Organizations, and States* (Cambridge, MA: Harvard University Press, 1970).

39 The critique of the hypothesis of product homogeneity, which is one of the postulates on which the neoclassical theory relies, is the starting point for Edward Chamberlin's analyses, which are aimed at reducing the opposition between competition theory and monopoly theory by showing that most exchanges present various combinations of "forces," some of which go in the direction of competition and others in the direction of monopoly. This led Chamberlin, in the seminal book he published in 1933, to explore a new approach to market exchanges, which he labeled "monopolistic competition"; see Edward Hastings Chamberlin, *The Theory of Monopolistic Competition* (Cambridge, MA: Harvard University Press, [1933] 1962). As Chamberlin writes in his introduction: "With differentiation appears monopoly, and as it proceeds further the element of monopoly becomes greater. Where there is any degree of differentiation whatever, each seller has an absolute monopoly of his own product, but is subject to the competition of more or less imperfect substitutes. Since each is a monopolist and yet has competitors, we may speak of them as 'competing monopolists'" (pp. 8–9). Chamberlin includes among monopolistic effects the localization of points of sale: "Here the broad sense in which the word 'product' is used must constantly be held in mind. Its 'variation' may refer to an alteration in the quality of the product itself – technical changes, a new design, or better materials; it may mean a new package or container; it may mean more prompt or courteous service, a different way of doing business, or perhaps a different location" (p. 71). In stressing the qualification of goods, Chamberlin was a precursor of the economic trends that were to develop, especially in France, in the 1980s, and especially in the economics of conventions; see Michel Callon, Cécile Méadel, and Vololona Rabeharisoa, "L'économie des qualités," in Callon et al., *Sociologie des agencements marchands* (Paris: Presses des Mines, 2013), pp. 143–70.

40 Socio-economic research on value and valuation is currently flourishing, especially in the United States. For a synthetic presentation, see Michèle Lamont, "A Comparative Sociology of Valuation and Evaluation," *Annual Review of Sociology*, 38 (2012): 201–21.

41 Among the many uses of the term "value," ours differs here from the conception proposed by Bruno Latour when he defends the idea that anthropologists of the Moderns "can no longer so easily ignore the real existence of the values to which we hold. They can no longer practice the mental restriction that has served 'intercultural dialogue' for so long – especially now that we are well aware that we are not just in a 'culture' but also in a 'nature.' To speak well of something to someone is first of all to respect the *precise ontological tenor* of the value that matters to him and for which he lives"; see Bruno Latour, *An Inquiry into Modes of Existence: An Anthropology of the Moderns*, trans. Catherine Porter (Cambridge, MA: Harvard University Press, [2012] 2013), p. 144.

42 Émile Durkheim, "Value Judgments and Judgments of Reality" (1911), in *Sociology and Philosophy*, trans. D. F. Pocock (Glencoe, IL: Free Press, [1924] 1953), pp. 80–97; the citations are from pp. 86, 87, and 95.

43 John Dewey, *Theory of Valuation* (Chicago: University of Chicago Press, 1939).

44 David Stark, "What's Valuable," in Jens Beckert and Patrik Aspers, *The Worth of Goods: Valuation and Pricing in the Economy* (Oxford: Oxford University Press, 2011), p. 321.

45 Ibid., p. 6. Stark's use of the term differs from the way in which the notion of worth (*grandeur*) is used in *On Justification*, a work that deals with moral judgments concerning justice and not with the prices paid in exchange for things; see Luc Boltanski and Laurent Thévenot, *On Justification*, trans. Catherine Porter (Princeton, NJ: Princeton University Press, [1991] 2006).

46 Olivier Favereau, "La pièce manquante de la sociologie du choix rationnel," *Revue française de sociologie*, 44/2 (2003): 291.

47 As Niklas Luhmann points out, "uncertainty is and remains a condition of structure," and "expectations are the autopoietic requirement for the reproduction of actions, and to this extent they are structures." See *Social Systems*, trans. John Bednarz, Jr., with Dirk Baecker (Stanford, CA: Stanford University Press, [1984] 1995), p. 288.

48 Olivier Favereau, Olivier Biencourt, and François Eymard-Duvernay, "Where Do Markets Come From? From (Quality) Conventions," in Olivier Favereau and Emmanuel Lazega, eds, *Conventions and Structures in Economic Organizations: Markets, Networks and Hierarchies* (Cheltenham: Edward Elgar, 2003), pp. 213–52.

49 Alfred Schutz, *Collected Papers III: Studies in Phenomenological Philosophy* (The Hague: Martinus Nijhoff, [1932] 1975).

50 Geertz, "Suk."

51 Ibid., p. 198.

52 As Geertz remarks ibid., p. 125.

53 Ibid., pp. 213–17.

54 Bernard Lahire, *Ceci n'est pas qu'un tableau: essai sur l'art, la domination, la magie et le sacré* (Paris: La Découverte, 2015), p. 33.

55 Michel Foucault, *The Birth of Biopolitics: Lectures at the Collège de France, 1978–1979*, trans. Graham Burchell (New York: Picador, [2004] 2010), p. 32.

56 Ibid., p. 59.

57 Ibid., p. 68.
58 See Luc Boltanski, *Mysteries and Conspiracies: Detective Stories, Spy Novels, and the Making of Modern Societies*, trans. Catherine Porter (Cambridge: Polity, [2012] 2014).
59 Gabriel Kessler and Sylvia Sigal, "Comportements et représentations face à la dislocation des régulations sociales: l'hyperinflation en Argentine," *Cultures et Conflits*, special issue: *Survivre: réflexion sur l'action en situation de chaos*, nos. 24–5 (1997): 39; see also Federico Neiburg, "Inflation: Economists and Economic Cultures in Brazil and Argentina," *Comparative Studies in Society and History*, 48/3 (2006): 604–33.

Chapter 4 Forms of Valuation

1 See Claude Lévi-Strauss, *The Savage Mind*, trans. Doreen Weightman and John Weightman (Chicago: University of Chicago Press, [1962] 1966). In a transformation group, in Lévi-Strauss's sense, according to a first definition (which we shall adopt), the permutations are "in mutual solidarity and can be represented in a chart in which each binary feature receives an opposing value," as Patrice Maniglier points out in *Le vocabulaire de Lévi-Strauss* (Paris: Ellipse, 2002), p. 55. According to a second definition, "a transformation group is defined in mathematics by the following properties: 1. The combination of two transformations corresponds to a transformation of the group; 2. these transformations may be associated; 3. there is an identical transformation (which changes nothing); 4. the transformations are non-reversible" (ibid., p. 56).
2 Lucien Karpik, *Valuing the Unique: The Economics of Singularities*, trans. Nora Scott (Princeton, NJ: Princeton University Press, [2007] 2010).
3 See pp. 137, 190, 226, 251, and 299.
4 Axel Honneth, *Reification: A New Look at an Old Idea*, ed. Martin Jay (Oxford: Oxford University Press, [2005] 2007).
5 For theories concerning the agency of things, see Alfred Gell, *Art and Agency: An Anthropological Theory* (Oxford: Oxford University Press, 1998), and Philippe Descola, ed., *La fabrique des images: visions du monde et formes de la représentation* (Paris: Somogy/Musée du Quai Branly, 2010).
6 For an in-depth analysis of this contradiction, see Luc Boltanski, *The Foetal Condition: A Sociology of Engendering and Abortion*, trans. Catherine Porter (Cambridge: Polity, [2010] 2013).
7 In the case of human beings, it is for the most part kinship – which is structured like a grammar, as Claude Lévi-Strauss has shown – that takes charge of what can be called the grammar of engendering and transmission, one function of which is to attenuate or dissimulate the contradiction between constraints of determination (attributing beings to classes in which they are substitutable) and constraints of singularization (in relation to which they are non-substitutable), a contradiction that can never be completely eliminated.
8 This is also why the development of a salaried workforce has been based on a distinction – one whose grounds are always difficult to establish – between a worker's sale of his or her very person and the sale of his or her power to work. See Mikhail Xifaras, *La propriété: étude de philosophie du droit* (Paris: Presses Universitaires de France, 2004).

9 Viviana A. Zelizer, *The Purchase of Intimacy* (Oxford: Oxford University Press, 2005).

10 See Gilles Deleuze, *Difference and Repetition*, trans. Paul Patton (New York: Columbia University Press, [1968] 1994).

11 Pierre Bourdieu, *The Social Structures of the Economy*, trans. Chris Turner (Cambridge: Polity, [2000] 2005).

12 Marc Augé, *Domaines et châteaux* (Paris: Seuil, 1989).

13 Sharon Zukin, *Naked City: The Death and Life of Authentic Urban Places* (Oxford: Oxford University Press, 2010).

14 Lévi-Strauss, *The Savage Mind*; see also Maniglier, *Le vocabulaire de Lévi-Strauss*, pp. 55–6.

15 Lévi-Strauss, *The Savage Mind*, p. 32.

16 Ibid., p. 31.

17 Ibid., p. 34.

18 Eleanor Rosch, "Classification of Real-World Objects: Origins and Representations in Cognition," in P. N. Johnson-Laird and P. C. Wason, eds, *Thinking: Readings in Cognitive Science* (Cambridge: Cambridge University Press, 1977), pp. 212–22.

19 Lévi-Strauss, *The Savage Mind*, p. 17.

20 Ibid., pp. 20–1.

21 On the processes of this type, which play on the relation between "schemas of visual categorization" and "systems of common comprehension," opening up the possibility of a "multiple description," see Bernard Conein, *Les sens sociaux: trois essais de sociologie cognitive* (Paris: Economica, 2005), pp. 51–67.

22 This can nurture the illusion according to which a collector's item has the properties of a person. See Brigitte Derlon and Monique Jeudy-Ballini, *La passion de l'art primitif: enquête sur les collectionneurs* (Paris: Gallimard, 2008).

23 Pascal Boyer, *Religion Explained: The Evolutionary Origins of Religious Thought* (New York: Basic Books, [2001] 2007).

24 "Fictional landscapes," to use Thomas Pavel's term from *Fictional Worlds* (Cambridge, MA: Harvard University Press, 1986), are based on two quite different "discursive and textual conventions"; narratives of valuation often fall back on the convention of "realism," which "strove most conscientiously toward minute referential accuracy" (p. 114). But a competing narrative of valuation may also be based on extensive ontologies such as that of Alexius Meinong, for instance: starting from the observation that "every actual object consists of a list of properties," Meinong proposes a more general version of the notion of object, by stipulating that "to every list of properties there corresponds an object, be it existent or not" (p. 28). This ontology favors the comparison of a particular object presented as actually existing, constituted by the thing to which value is attributed, with other objects for which the question of whether or not they really exist can be suspended, or even with objects whose fictional character is acknowledged.

25 Paul Ricoeur, *Time and Narrative*, trans. Kathleen McLaughlin and David Pellauer (Chicago: University of Chicago Press, 1984–8), vol. 3, pp. 244–9.

26 See Luc Boltanski, *On Critique: A Sociology of Emancipation*, trans. Gregory Elliott (Cambridge: Polity, [2009] 2011).

27 John Searle, *The Construction of Social Reality* (New York: Free Press, 1995).

28 Let us note, in this connection, the growth of the number of museums in the world, including in the so-called emerging countries. At least 652 new museums were created worldwide between 1995 and 2013, including 139 in the United States, 68 in Japan, 67 in Germany, 50 in Spain, 43 in France, and 35 in China. The 23 architects whose designs were most often selected are responsible for 176 museums. See Guido Guerzoni, ed., *Museums on the Map, 1995–2012* (Turin: Fondazione de Venezia/Umberto Allemandi, 2014).

29 Chantal Mouffe, *Agonistics: Thinking the World Politically* (London: Verso, 2013), p. 101.

30 Niklas Luhmann, *Social Systems*, trans. John Bednarz, Jr., with Dirk Baecker (Stanford, CA: Stanford University Press, [1984] 1995), p. 343.

31 Edward Hastings Chamberlin, *The Theory of Monopolistic Competition* (Cambridge, MA: Harvard University Press, [1933] 1962).

32 Gildas Salmon, *Les structures de l'esprit: Lévi-Strauss et les mythes* (Paris: Presses Universitaires de France, 2013), p. 241.

33 Michel de Certeau, *The Practice of Everyday Life*, trans. Steven Rendall (Berkeley: University of California Press, [1980] 1984).

34 Thus one can apply to the forms of valuation what Jean-Pierre Cometti says about language games in Wittgenstein: they establish themselves "between language and actions in contexts of contexts and interlocution concretized by practical activities pursued in common." See Jean-Pierre Cometti, *La démocratie radicale: lire John Dewey* (Paris: Gallimard, 2016), p. 105.

35 On the normative dimension of the situated uses of language on which the pragmatic approach focuses, see Robert Brandom, *Making it Explicit: Reasoning, Representing, and Discursive Commitment* (Cambridge, MA: Harvard University Press, 1994), pp. 3–66.

Chapter 5 The Standard Form

1 See Wendy Espeland and Mitchell Stevens, "Commensuration as a Social Process," *Annual Review of Sociology*, 24 (1988): 313–43.

2 George Akerlof, "The Market for 'Lemons': Quality, Uncertainty, and the Market Mechanism," *Quarterly Journal of Economics*, 84 (1970): 488–500.

3 On the tensions that may be revealed when a standardized and "normalized" object is used once it has left the factory – that is, once it is confronted with "different modes of grasping" associated with "different regimes of engagement" – see Laurent Thévenot, "Essai sur les objets usuels: propriétés, fonctions, usages," in Bernard Conein, Nicolas Dodier, and Laurent Thévenot, eds, *Les objets dans l'action* (Paris: Éditions de l'EHESS, 1993), pp. 85–111, and "Un gouvernement par les normes: pratiques et politiques des formats d'information," in Bernard Conein and Laurent Thévenot, eds, *Cognition et information en société* (Paris: Éditions de l'EHESS, 1997), pp. 206–41.

4 This schema, like the subsequent ones, is not based on quantitative data but is designed to illustrate the models that underlie our analyses.

5 Among the most ambitious recent works, see Patrick Verley, *L'échelle du monde: essai sur l'industrialisation de l'Occident* (Paris: Gallimard, 1997), and Paul Bairoch, *Victoires et déboires: histoire économique et sociale du monde du XVIe siècle à nos jours*, 3 vols (Paris: Gallimard, 1997).

6 Verley, *L'échelle du monde*, p. 153.

7 See Jan de Vries, *The Industrious Revolution: Consumer Behavior and the Household Economy, 1650 to the Present* (Cambridge: Cambridge University Press, 2008).

8 On the use of commerce by women to acquire some space for autonomy in the nineteenth century, see Laurence Fontaine, *Le marché: histoire et usages d'une conquête sociale* (Paris: Gallimard, 2014), pp. 196–8.

9 See David S. Landes, *The Unbound Prometheus: Technological Change and Industrial Development in Western Europe from 1750 to the Present* (2nd edn, Cambridge: Cambridge University Press, 2003), pp. 288ff. The network allowing electricity to be transmitted over long distances was built in France between 1890 and 1910; see Alexandre Fernandez and Jean-Charles Asselain, *Industrialisation et sociétés en Europe occidentale, 1880–1960* (Paris: Messene, 1997), vol. 2, p. 18.

10 See David Hounshell, *From the American System to Mass Production, 1800–1932* (Baltimore: Johns Hopkins University Press, 1984).

11 See Laurence Fontaine, *History of Pedlars in Europe*, trans. Vicki Whittaker (Durham, NC: Duke University Press, [1993] 1996). Pedlars sold mainly new objects, such as watches, grooming and clothing accessories, sewing notions, cutlery, hardware, and, more generally, objects that were "out of the ordinary" destined for a rural, lower-class population and that might be imitations or even counterfeit copies of more "luxurious" or exotic items sold in city shops.

12 Verley, *L'échelle du monde*, p. 276.

13 See Laurence Fontaine, "The Exchange of Second-Hand Goods between Survival Strategies and 'Business' in Eighteenth-Century Paris," in Laurence Fontaine, ed., *Alternative Exchanges: Second-Hand Circulations from the Sixteenth Century to the Present* (Oxford: Berghahn Books, 2008), pp. 97–114.

14 See Daniel Roche, *The Culture of Clothing: Dress and Fashion in the Ancien Regime*, trans. Jean Birrell (Cambridge: Cambridge University Press, 1994), p. 347.

15 Ibid., pp. 344–63.

16 Erwin Panofsky, *Tomb Sculpture: Four Lectures on its Changing Aspects from Ancient Egypt to Bernini*, ed. H. W. Janson (New York: H. N. Abrams, 1964), p. 38.

17 Ibid.

18 David Freedberg, *The Power of Images: Studies in the History and Theory of Response* (Chicago: University of Chicago Press, 1989), p. 181.

19 To facilitate meditation, one had to face an image representing a narrative from the Gospel and contemplate it, as Saint Francis Borgia explained in the fifteenth century, "because the function of the image is, as it were, to give taste and flavour to the food one has to eat, in such a way that one is not satisfied until one has eaten it"; cited ibid.

20 Ibid., p. 177.

21 The arrival of industrially produced consumer products on a massive scale that marked the period between the wars occurred chiefly in the United States at the beginning of the twentieth century. Paul Bairoch mentions fans, washing machines, gramophones, radios, motorcycles, and, of course, automobiles (Bairoch, *Victoires et déboires*, vol. 2, p. 41). A description of many standard objects, each with its history and date of appearance, is provided in Jack Challoner, ed., *Les 1 001 inventions qui ont changé le monde* (Paris: Flammarion, 2008).

22 Aristotle, *Metaphysics*, trans. C. D. C. Reeve (Indianapolis: Hackett, 2016), Z7-8, pp. 112–15.
23 Ibid., Z4, p. 107.
24 For a contemporary reinterpretation of these conceptions, see Richard Sennett, *The Craftsman* (New Haven, CT: Yale University Press, 2008).
25 See Émile Durkheim, *The Evolution of Educational Thought: Lectures on the Formation and Development of Secondary Education in France*, trans. Peter Collins (London: Routledge & Kegan Paul, [1938] 1977), esp. the chapter on Rabelais, pp. 177–88.
26 Karl Marx, *Capital: A Critique of Political Economy*, 4th edn, ed. Frederic Engels, trans. Ben Fowkes (London: Penguin Classics, [1890] 1990), vol. 1, Part 1, chapter 15, "Machinery and Large-Scale Industry," pp. 492–639.
27 The Taylor method made possible the fulfillment of a wish that had haunted manufacturing since the first third of the nineteenth century. Thus one finds in Andrew Ure's *Philosophy of Manufactures; or, An Exposition of the Scientific, Moral, and Commercial Economy of the Factory System of Great Britain* (3rd edn, New York: B. Franklin, [1835] 1969) (on which Marx often sharpened his critical verve) the following remark (pp. 20–1):

> By the infirmity of human nature it happens, that the more skilful the workman, the more self-willed and intractable he is apt to become, and, of course, the less fit a component of a mechanical system, in which, by occasional irregularities, he may do great damage to the whole. The grand object therefore of the modern manufacturer is, through the union of capital and science, to reduce the task of his work-people to the exercise of vigilance and their dexterity – faculties, when concentrated to one process, speedily brought to perfection in the young.

28 Hounshell, *From the American System*, pp. 315–23.
29 Walter Benjamin, "The Work of Art in the Age of its Technological Reproducibility," trans. Edmund Jephcott and Harry Zohn, in *Walter Benjamin: Selected Writings*, ed. Howard Eiland and Michael Jennings, vol. 3 (Cambridge, MA: Harvard University Press, 2002), pp. 101–33.
30 It is conceivable that the stupor generated by the development of the standardization of things, which led to fear of a similar standardization of human beings, played a role in the wave of philosophical and literary interrogations that arose in the United States starting in the 1930s. This tendency invaded the American intellectual world, sweeping away John Dewey's progressive optimism. See Mark Greif, *The Age of the Crisis of Man* (Princeton, NJ: Princeton University Press, 2015).
31 Cited in François Eymard-Duvernay, "Le travail dans l'entreprise: pour une démocratisation des pouvoirs de valorisation," working document, Collège des Bernardins, Department of Economics, April 2011, p. 26. We shall follow Eymard-Duvernay here when he remarks that this position contradicts the standard neoclassical theory that sees the consumer as the only actor capable of exercising a power of valorization.
32 Karl Marx, *Contribution to the Critique of Political Economy*, trans. N. I. Stone from the 2nd German edn (Chicago: Charles H. Kerr, [1897] 1904), pp. 276–83.
33 The efforts to make more fine-tuned adjustments to client demand, which resulted, starting in the 1980s, on the one hand, from the saturation of the markets involving the most common goods and, on the other, from the critique

of massifications, gave rise to the production of more differentiated goods in a context of very lively competition. Let us note, however, that this diversification of what was offered, which was often represented as arising from an insistence on greater authenticity, did not have the effect of profoundly modifying the principal properties of the standard form. The observation reinforces the idea that this form should be characterized through the play of the relation between prototypes and specimens rather than through the uniformity of things offered for sale, which the new production arrangements made it possible to surmount.

34 Peter Drucker, *Concept of the Corporation* (New York: John Day, 1972), pp. 219–20.

35 For a synthetic presentation of Thorstein Veblen's critical ideal, see Raymond Aron, "Avez-vous lu Veblen?" in Aron, *Les sociétés modernes*, ed. Serge Paugam (Paris: Presses Universitaires de France, 2006), pp. 239–66.

36 See Georgi Derluguian's excellent analysis of the problems encountered by the production of goods for mass consumption in the Soviet Union: "What Communism Was," in Immanuel Wallerstein, ed., *Does Capitalism Have a Future?* (New York: Oxford University Press, 2013), pp. 99–129.

37 See Hounshell, *From the American System*, pp. 263–301.

38 See Michel Piore and Charles Sabel, *The Second Industrial Divide: Possibilities for Prosperity* (New York: Basic Books, 1984), and Arnaldo Bagnasco and Charles Sabel, *Small and Medium-Size Enterprises* (London: Pinter, 1995).

39 Among many examples, see Raymond Aron, *18 Lectures on Industrial Society*, trans. M. K. Bottomore (London: Weidenfeld & Nicolson, [1962] 1967). In this book, which was based on the first course Aron gave at the Sorbonne (in 1955–6), the author proposed most notably to reinterpret the notion of historical progress that was associated with the development of industrial society, and to give it a political sense by turning to Montesquieu ("reconcile hierarchy with equality," p. 65); he also proposed to refute the Marxist critique of industrial society inasmuch as it is a capitalist society. It is relevant to our project to note that Aron excluded "religion and art" from the field that can give rise to "progress" inasmuch as he viewed those domains as foreign to both "economics and politics" (p. 62), which, at the time he was writing (the so-called Thirty Glorious Years), still seemed to be a matter of common sense.

40 See Peter Wagner, *A Sociology of Modernity: Liberty and Discipline* (London: Routledge, 1994). See also Wagner, *Modernity: Understanding the Present* (Cambridge: Polity, 2012), especially pp. 4–10.

41 We are borrowing this definition of alienation from the book devoted to the work of François Lyotard by Claire Pagès, *Lyotard et l'aliénation* (Paris: Presses Universitaires de France, 2011), p. 13.

42 Christian Borch, *The Politics of Crowds: An Alternative History of Society* (Cambridge: Cambridge University Press, 2012).

43 Gustave Le Bon, *The Crowd* (New Brunswick, NJ: Transaction, [1895] 1995); Gabriel Tarde, *The Laws of Imitation* (New York: Henry Holt, [1890] 1903).

44 See Sergeï Chakhotin, *The Rape of the Masses: The Psychology of Totalitarian Propaganda*, trans. E. W. Dickes (New York: Alliance Book Corporation, [1939] 1940). On the history and contemporary uses of the theme of mental manipulation, see Arnaud Esquerre, *La manipulation mentale: sociologie des sectes en France* (Paris: Fayard, 2009).

45 See Guy Debord, *The Society of the Spectacle* (New York: Zone Books, [1967] 1994).

46 Anselm Jappe, *Guy Debord*, trans. Donald Nicholson-Smith (Berkeley: University of California Press, 1999), p. 8; for Jappe's analysis of the relation between the notion of the spectacle and that of the "simulacrum," see pp. 132–5.

Chapter 6 Standardization and Differentiation

1 Roger Chartier, *La main de l'auteur et l'esprit de l'imprimeur* (Paris: Gallimard, 2015), p. 25.
2 Among the earliest and most important works on the topic, see Julius von Schlosser, *Les cabinets d'art de merveilles de la Renaissance tardive: une contribution à l'histoire du collectionnisme* (Paris: Macula, [1908] 2012).
3 See Anne Goldgar, *Tulipmania: Money, Honor, and Knowledge in the Dutch Golden Age* (Chicago: University of Chicago Press, 2007).
4 "Treasure should be distinguished from other forms of stored wealth. ... Treasure, in the proper sense of the term, is formed of prestige goods, including 'valuables' and ceremonial objects whose mere possession endow[s] the holder with social weight, power, and influence." Treasure is not "used as a medium of exchange," even though "treasure, like other sources of power, may be of great economic importance": Karl Polanyi and Harry W. Pearson, *The Livelihood of Man* (New York: Academic Press, [1977] 2011), p. 109.
5 In the text he devoted to the notion of work value in Marx, Cornelius Castoriadis analyzed the tension in Marx between a positivist position that would make work the source of all exchange value and a historicist position according to which capitalism would make work value "appear" as a mode of homogenization of things that are heterogeneous in themselves and that would thereby constitute commodities as such. "Marx knows very well, and is the first to say, that the apparent homogenization of products and labor emerges only with capitalism. It is capitalism which brings it into being." See Castoriadis, "Value, Equality, Justice, Politics: From Marx to Aristotle and from Aristotle to Ourselves," in *Crossroads in the Labyrinth*, trans. Kate Soper and Martin H. Ryle (Cambridge, MA: MIT Press, [1978] 1984), p. 276.
6 See Franck Cochoy, *Une histoire du marketing: discipliner l'économie de marché* (Paris: La Découverte, 1999).
7 Patrick Verley, *L'échelle du monde: Essai sur l'industrialisation de l'Occident* (Paris: Gallimard, 1997), p. 182.
8 See Alain Beltran, Sophie Chauveau, and Gabriel Galvez-Behar, *Des brevets et des marques: une histoire de la propriété intellectuelle* (Paris: Fayard, 2001), pp. 184–8, and Joel Stillerman, *The Sociology of Consumption: A Global Approach* (Cambridge: Polity, 2015), pp. 27–30.
9 See Marie-Emmanuelle Chessel, *Consommateurs engagés à la Belle Époque: la Ligue sociale d'acheteurs* (Paris: Presses de Science Po, 2012).
10 Ralph Nader, *Unsafe at Any Speed: The Designed-in Dangers of the American Automobile* (New York: Grossman, [1965] 1972).
11 Walter Benjamin, "Paris, Capital of the Nineteenth Century," trans. Howard Eiland, in *Walter Benjamin: Selected Writings*, ed. Howard Eiland and Michael Jennings, vol. 3 (Cambridge, MA: Harvard University Press, 2002), pp. 32–49. "World exhibitions are places of pilgrimage to the commodity fetish, 'Europe is off to view the merchandise,' says [Hippolyte] Taine in 1855. ... World exhibitions glorify the exchange value of the commodity. They

create a framework in which its use value recedes into the background" (p. 37). And see Benjamin, *Écrits français* (Paris: Gallimard, 1991), p. 296: "World fairs were a school in which the masses forcibly kept away from consumption became penetrated with the exchange value of commodities to the point of identifying with it: 'It is forbidden to touch the objects on display.'" (This sentence, omitted from the published English translation, immediately follows the passage cited above.)

12 Jean-Yves Grenier, *L'économie d'Ancien Régime: un monde de l'échange et de l'incertitude* (Paris: Albin Michel, 1996); Alain Guerreau, "Avant le marché, les marchés: en Europe, XIIIe siècle–XVIIIe siècle," *Annales: Histoire, Sciences Sociales*, 56/6 (2001): 1129–75.

13 Guerreau, "Avant le marché," p. 1139.

14 Ibid., p. 1134. Guerreau continues: "[This] corresponds astonishingly to the duality between the money used for accounting purposes, which entailed purely numerical values, and real, concrete currencies bearing no indications of value." The author distinguished three types of cash in hand, depending on how it was used: for savings, transactions, or speculation.

15 Ibid., p. 1139.

16 Ibid., p. 1138.

17 Laurence Fontaine emphasizes, similarly, that under the Old Regime second-hand objects could be used to pay debts; these goods thus constituted "an alternative form of currency." See Fontaine, "The Exchange of Second-Hand Goods between Survival Strategies and 'Business' in Eighteenth-Century Paris," in Fontaine, ed., *Alternative Exchanges: Second-Hand Circulations from the Sixteenth Century to the Present* (Oxford: Berghahn Books, 2008), pp. 97–114.

18 For a debunking, in the same spirit, of the idea of an "art market," in the case of Italy between the fifteenth and the eighteenth centuries, see Guido Guerzoni, *Apollo and Vulcan: The Art Markets in Italy, 1400–1700*, trans. Amanda George (East Lansing: Michigan State University Press, [2006] 2011), esp. pp. xx–xxiv.

19 Guerreau, "Avant le marché," p. 1164.

20 Ibid., p. 1137.

21 Ibid., p. 1165.

22 Grenier, *L'économie d'Ancien Régime*, p. 87.

23 On the role attributed to space by eighteenth-century economists (Cantillon, Turgot, Necker) and on the spatial stakes of the institutional debate over fairs and markets, see Dominique Margairaz, "La formation du réseau des foires et des marchés: stratégies, pratiques et idéologies," *Annales: Économies, Sociétés, Civilisations*, 41/6 (1986): 1215–42.

24 Grenier, *L'économie d'Ancien Régime*, p. 85 (more generally, see pp. 84–7).

25 See Paul-André Rosental, *Les sentiers invisibles: espace, famille et migration dans la France du XIXe siècle* (Paris: Éditions de l'EHESS, 1999), and Daniel Roche, *Humeurs vagabondes: de la circulation des hommes et de l'utilité des voyages* (Paris: Fayard, 2003).

26 Guerreau, "Avant le marché," p. 1158.

27 Ibid., p. 1140.

28 Bernard Mandeville, *The Fable of the Bees*, 2 vols (New York: Georg Olms, [1714, 1729] 1981, 2017).

29 See Albert Hirschman, *The Passions and the Interests: Political Arguments for Capitalism Before its Triumph* (Princeton, NJ: Princeton University Press, 1977).

30 See Christian Laval, *L'homme économique: essai sur les racines du néolibéra-lisme* (Paris: Gallimard, 2007).

31 For a historical analysis of this theme and a reformulation, see Axel Honneth, *Reification: A New Look at an Old Idea*, ed. Martin Jay (Oxford: Oxford University Press, [2005] 2007).

32 For a recent analysis of this role of the market, see Laurence Fontaine, *Le marché: histoire et usages d'une conquête sociale* (Paris: Gallimard, 2014).

33 César Graña, *Bohemian versus Bourgeois: French Society and the French Man of Letters in the Nineteenth Century* (New York: Basic Books, 1964).

34 In 1930, in response to a survey conducted by *L'Esprit français* on the "current role of capital vis-à-vis intellectual producers," André Breton constructed his text around the opposition between the producer of commodities, even intellectual commodities, and the intellectual who, "through his products, mainly tries to satisfy the needs of his own mind." He then cites Marx: "'A thing can be useful,' says Marx, 'and the product of human labor, without being a commodity. Whoever directly satisfies his wants with the product of his own labor, creates, indeed, use-values, but not commodities. In order to produce the latter, he must not only produce use-values, but use-values for others, social use-values.'" Breton went on to argue that it is "impossible to appraise" the value of intellectual work "by the common measure of work-hours." See André Breton, "On the Relations between Intellectual Labor and Capital," in *Break of Day (Point du Jour)*, trans. Mark Polizzotti and Mary Ann Caws (Lincoln: University of Nebraska Press, [1970] 1999), pp. 64–6.

35 Georges Bataille, *The Accursed Share: An Essay on General Economy*, trans. Robert Hurley, 3 vols (New York: Zone Books, [1949] 1991). The original French text, *La part maudite*, is preceded by "La notion de dépense," written in 1933 (Paris: Minuit, 1949), vol. 1, pp. 29–54; it is available in English as "The Notion of Expenditure," in *Visions of Excess: Selected Writings 1927–1939*, ed. Allan Stoekl, trans. Allan Stoekl with Carol R. Lovitt and Donald M. Leslie, Jr. (Minneapolis: University of Minnesota Press, 1985), pp. 116–29.

36 See Jeremy Rifkin, *The Age of Access: The New Culture of Hypercapitalism* (New York: J. P. Tarcher/Putnam, 2000); see also, after Rifkin, Olivier Bomsel, *L'économie immatérielle: industries et marché d'expériences* (Paris: Gallimard, 2010).

37 See André Gorz, *The Immaterial: Knowledge, Value and Capital*, trans. Chris Turner (London: Seagull Books, 2010), and Yann Moulier-Boutang, *Cognitive Capitalism*, trans. Ed Emery (Cambridge: Polity, 2011).

38 Robert Darnton, *The Case for Books: Past, Present, and Future* (New York: PublicAffairs, 2009), p. 31.

39 Claude Lévi-Strauss, *The Naked Man*, vol. 4 of *Introduction to a Science of Mythology*, trans. Doreen Weightman (New York: Harper & Row, [1971] 1981), p. 627.

Chapter 7 The Collection Form

1 Especially in the wake of Krzysztof Pomian's seminal work: see in particular Krzysztof Pomian, *Collectors and Curiosities: Paris and Venice, 1500–1800*, trans. Elizabeth Wiles-Portier (Cambridge: Polity, [1987] 1990). And, on the curio cabinets, see Julius von Schlosser, *Les cabinets d'art et de merveilles de*

la Renaissance tardive: une contribution à l'histoire du collectionnisme (Paris: Macula, [1908] 2012). For the "curious" in the seventeenth century, see Antoine Schnapper, *Curieux du Grand Siècle: collections et collectionneurs dans la France du XVIIe siècle* (Paris: Flammarion, 1994).

2 Michel Foucault, *The Order of Things: An Archaeology of the Human Sciences* (New York: Pantheon Books, [1966] 1971).

3 For the passage from curio cabinets to collections in the natural sciences, see Antoine Schnapper, *Le géant, la licorne et la tulipe: les cabinets de curiosités en France au XVIIe siècle* (Paris: Flammarion, 1988). See also Noël Coye, "La collection introuvable de l'abbé Breuil," in Odile Vincent, ed., *Collectionner? Territoires, objets, destins* (Paris: Créaphis, 2011), pp. 52–70.

4 See Benoît de L'Estoile, "L'anthropologie après les musées?" *Ethnologie française*, 38/4 (2008): 665–70.

5 See Dominique Pety, *Poétique de la collection au XIXe siècle: du document de l'historien au bibelot de l'esthète* (Paris: Presses Universitaires de Paris Ouest, 2010).

6 Honoré de Balzac, *Cousin Pons*, trans. Ellen Marriage, part 2 of *Poor Relations* (Philadelphia: Avil, [1847] 1901).

7 Anatole France, *The Crime of Sylvestre Bonnard*, trans. Lafcadio Hearn (New York: Dodd-Mead, [1881] 1922).

8 Balzac, *Cousin Pons*, p. 9.

9 Bénédicte Savoy, *Patrimoine annexé: les biens culturels saisis par la France en Allemagne autour de 1800*, 2 vols (Paris: Éditions de la MSH, 2003).

10 See Francis Haskell, *Rediscoveries in Art: Some Aspects of Taste, Fashion, and Collecting in England and France* (Ithaca, NY: Cornell University Press, 1976).

11 Michel Merlot, *Mirabilia: essai sur l'inventaire général du patrimoine culturel* (Paris: Gallimard, 2012), p. 24.

12 See Hervé Sciardet, *Les marchands de l'aube: ethnographie et théorie du commerce aux Puces de Saint-Ouen* (Paris: Economica, 2003).

13 See France, *The Crime of Sylvestre Bonnard*. The plot is complex; it may be based on a symbolic structure including a sexual dimension.

14 Ibid., pp. 57, 72, 58–9.

15 Steven Gelber, "Free Market Metaphor: The Historical Dynamics of Stamp Collecting," *Comparative Studies in Society and History*, 34/4 (1992): 742–69.

16 See especially Susan Pearce, *Collecting in Contemporary Practices* (London: Sage, 1998).

17 Krzysztof Pomian, *Des saintes reliques à l'art moderne: Venise–Chicago, XIIIe siècle* (Paris: Gallimard, 2003).

18 This point of view is defended most notably by Bernard Lahire, in *Ceci n'est pas qu'un tableau: essai sur l'art, la domination, la magie et le sacré* (Paris: La Découverte, 2015). For Lahire, "the comparison between holy relics and works of the great masters imposes itself almost naturally on the scholar" (p. 278). According to this author, "in the first place, just as relics were associated with singular persons who stood out from among ordinary mortals (Jesus, the saints), works of art are those of more or less well known singular artists. The magic of the relic, like that of the work of art, is based on this intimate bond between a being deemed exceptional – saint or artist – and singular objects" (ibid.). "After the market in relics, the market in art was built up. ... While both relics and works of art are sold and bought, commerce in relics has remained predominantly illicit, whereas the art market has developed legally,

getting all the actors in the art world to connect economic values and aesthetic values" (ibid., pp. 278–9).

19 Yves Gagneux, *Reliques et reliquaires à Paris (XIXe–XXe siècle)* (Paris: Cerf, 2007), p. 287.

20 See Arnaud Esquerre, *Les os, les cendres, et l'État* (Paris: Fayard, 2011).

21 See Judith Ickowicz, *Le droit après la dématérialisation de l'oeuvre d'art* (Dijon: Les Presses du réel, 2013).

22 For example, the accumulation of pebbles produced by Luigi Lineri and exhibited in 2012 in Paris at the Halle Saint-Pierre, Musée de l'art brut.

23 Joseph Ferdinand Cheval was a rural postman in the late nineteenth century who collected stones and other materials as he was making his rounds: over a period of thirty-three years, he built his "ideal palace" in Hauterives in southern France. The structure, considered a prime example of naïve architecture, is populated with exotic stone animals and imaginary creatures and complemented by a mausoleum Cheval completed before his death in 1924.

24 See the early works of Annette Messager, who defined herself as a "collector," or those of Henri Cueco, which he brought together in *Le collectionneur de collections* (Paris: Seuil, 1995).

25 See the catalog Musée des arts décoratifs, *Ils collectionnent* (Paris: Adrien Maeght, 1974).

26 Like the stoneware once produced industrially whose trajectory has been reconstituted in minute detail by Thierry Bonnot in *La vie des objets* (Paris: Éditions de la MSH, 2002).

27 This valorization through reference to the past differs from the "memorial value" (*Erinnerungswert*) proposed by Aloïs Riegl in that it is a justification of prices, not a value incorporated in things. See Aloïs Riegl, *The Modern Cult of Monuments: Its Character and its Origin*, trans. Kurt Walter Forster (Cambridge, MA: MIT Press, [1903] 1982).

28 What we are calling "lack" here is close to what Serge Reubi calls "lacunae." See Serge Reubi, "La lacune, miroir des pratiques de collections," *Traverse*, no. 3 (2012): 81–90.

29 As Guido Guerzoni remarks in *Apollo and Vulcan: The Art Markets in Italy, 1400–1700*, trans. Amanda George (East Lansing: Michigan State University Press, [2006] 2011), p. 130: "Originality was not always welcome, and often the purchasers were fixated on certain works (Titian painted no less than eleven versions of the *Ecce homo*), unconcerned that others owned similar or identical works; they were not always attracted by the subtle fascination of the unique and original piece but gave to reproductions a value whose importance vanishes in the age of technical reproducibility."

30 Gérard Labrot, "Éloge de la copie: le marché napolitain (1614–1764)," *Annales: Histoire, Sciences Sociales*, 59/1 (2004): 7–35.

31 Charlotte Guichard, "La signature dans le tableau aux XVIIe et XVIIIe siècles: identité, réputation et marché de l'art," *Sociétés & représentation*, no. 25 (2008): 52.

32 This valorization of authenticity is perhaps never more evident than when "authenticity" is highlighted in the context of commercial enterprises where it is especially difficult to support. This is the case, for example, when workshops that produce "chromos" (chromolithographs) "by the dozens," according to Raymonde Moulin (citing a study by Francine Couture bearing on this kind of enterprise in Montreal), strive to "construct a fictional artistic identity" so

as to "individualize the authors or pseudo-authors" of the pictures they are offering for sale: see Raymonde Moulin, *L'artiste, l'institution, et le marché* (Paris: Flammarion, 1992), pp. 34–44. The case of ArtCo, studied by Julie Verlaine, offers another example. This company, founded in 1949, had sought to commercialize reproductions of works of modern art made through a new procedure, the "Aeply process," which combined different techniques with the goal of producing perfect copies, in the sense that nothing would allow them to be distinguished from the originals. These copies, which were supposed to be produced in "limited numbers," were presented as being "neither originals nor reproductions." To characterize them, the company invented the term "multiple originals": see Julie Verlaine, "Une histoire de la société ArtCo: le commerce des reproductions d'art après la Seconde Guerre mondiale," *Vingtième Siècle: Revue d'histoire*, no. 108 (2010): 141–51.

33 This is the case, for example, with "art deco," which began to be labeled as such in the 1960s through the intermediary of exhibit commissioners and critics who set up a series of exhibits in various museums in Europe and the United States. The process of creating a specifically "art deco" style, one of whose characteristics was its plasticity and its hybridization according to sites and countries, has been analyzed in detail by Élodie Lacroix di Méo: see "Les enjeux identitaires de la patrimonialisation de l'art déco," in Jean-Claude Nemery, Michel Rautenberg, and Fabrice Thuriot, eds, *Stratégies identitaires de conservation et de valorisation du patrimoine* (Paris: L'Harmattan, 2008), pp. 52–62.

34 In the ethnographic work Olav Velthuis has devoted to art galleries in Amsterdam and New York, he describes the arrangements that make it possible to isolate "the sacred world of art" from "the profane world of commerce." He analyzes, in the way Erving Goffman distinguishes the "stage" from the "wings," the opposition between the space of presentation (the "front space") and the space of negotiation (the "back space"), or the primary market, in which gallery owners maintain prices that are supposed to be associated with the artistic value of the work, and the secondary market, which is purely speculative. See Olav Velthuis, *Talking Prices: Symbolic Meanings of Prices on the Market for Contemporary Art* (Princeton, NJ: Princeton University Press, 2005), pp. 42–52.

35 See Nathalie Heinich, *Le paradigme de l'art contemporain: structures d'une révolution artistique* (Paris: Gallimard, 2014), esp. pp. 223–30. In recent works, especially works by journalists specializing in contemporary art and adopting a stance at once fascinated and critical, one can find numerous anecdotes about the way the major collectors "manipulate" the rankings of artists. There is a story, for example, about François Pinault systematically purchasing works by Reberolle in order to store them away; another about Charles Saatchi negotiating all the works of Sandro Chia with the intention of bringing down their prices, or, conversely, using various maneuvers to try to bring up the prices of works by Damien Hirst; see in particular Harry Bellet, *Le marché de l'art s'écroule demain à 18 h 30* (Paris: Nil, 2001), and Don Thompson, *The $12 Million Stuffed Shark: The Curious Economics of Contemporary Art* (New York: Palgrave Macmillan, 2008).

36 See Isabelle Graw, *High Price: Art between the Market and Celebrity Culture* (Berlin: Sternberg, 2009), and also Isabelle Graw and Daniel Birnbaum, eds, *Canvases and Careers Today: Criticism and its Markets* (New York: Sternberg,

2008). The latter work seeks to analyze the way the increasing role played both by collectors and by the organizational arrangements on which major sales of art works depend modified the economic environment in which, from the Impressionist era until roughly the 1970s, the value attributed to works was shaped. The formation of that environment was masterfully described in a book that has become a classic: Harrison C. White, *Canvases and Careers: Institutional Change in the French Painting World* (Chicago: University of Chicago Press, [1965] 1993).

37 As recent studies have shown, the increased importance of awards is by no means limited to the art world. It can also be observed not only in the large companies where the management techniques that use benchmarking originated but also, more and more often, in the public domain, and most notably in that of the management and orientation of university research. On this point, see Alain Desrosières, *L'argument statistique*, Vol. 2: *Gouverner par les nombres* (Paris: Mines ParisTech, 2008), esp. pp. 27–32; Emmanuel Didier, *Prouver et gouverner: une analyse politique des statistiques publiques* (Paris: La Découverte, 2014); Isabelle Bruno and Emmanuel Didier, *Benchmarking: l'État sous pression statistique* (Paris: Zone Books, 2013); and, on the new ways of managing research, see Isabelle Bruno, *À vos marques, prêts … cherchez! La stratégie européenne de Lisbonne, vers un marché de la recherche* (Paris: Croquant, 2008).

38 Michael Thompson, *Rubbish Theory: The Creation and Destruction of Value* (Oxford: Oxford University Press, 1979), pp. 13–33.

39 In the case of stamp collectors, there are numerous examples in an article by Anthony Kuhn and Yves Moulin on the formation of conventional differences: "Le rôle des conventions de qualité dans la construction d'un marché: l'évolution du marché philatélique français (1860–1995)," *Entreprises et histoire*, no. 53 (2008): 54–67.

40 See Elizabeth Edwards, Chris Gosden, and Ruth B. Phillips, eds, *Sensible Objects: Colonialism, Museums and Material Culture* (New York: Berg, 2006).

41 See John MacGregor, *The Discovery of the Art of the Insane* (Princeton, NJ: Princeton University Press, 1989).

42 Thompson, *Rubbish Theory*, pp. 13–33.

43 For an investigation that consisted in following operations of selection on the ground, see Nathalie Heinich, *La fabrique du patrimoine* (Paris: Éditions de la MSH, 2009).

44 Pierre Cabanne, *Les grands collectionneurs*, vol. 2 (Paris: Éditions de l'Amateur, 2004), pp. 297–8 [Vol. 1 is available in English translation: *The Great Collectors* (New York: Farrar, Strauss, 1963)].

45 Claude Lévi-Strauss, *The Savage Mind*, trans. Doreen Weightman and John Weightman (Chicago: University of Chicago Press, [1962] 1966), pp. 191–6.

46 Mieke Bal, "Telling Objects: A Narrative Perspective on Collecting," in John Elsner and Roger Cardinal, eds, *The Cultures of Collecting* (London: Reaktion Books, 1994), pp. 97–115.

47 A celebrated example is that of the polemics surrounding "La bella Principessa," an image on vellum that was allegedly cut out of a fifteenth-century book about the House of Sforza and preserved in Warsaw. The dispute has to do with whether or not the image is by Leonardo da Vinci's own hand. Assessed by Christie's at between \$12,000 and \$15,000, the same image, if it were judged by experts as actually being by da Vinci, would probably be worth around

$150,000,000. See Martin Kemp, *La bella Principessa: The Story of a New Masterpiece by Leonardo da Vinci* (London: Hodder & Stoughton, 2010); Kemp is one of the experts trying to authenticate the drawing.

48 It can be precisely in order to abolish their memorial power that objects once thought to be immortal can be deliberately destroyed or reduced to the state of trash, as in cases of iconoclasm; see Olivier Christin, *Une révolution symbolique: l'iconoclasme Huguenot et la reconstruction catholique* (Paris: Minuit, 1991).

49 At least if we agree to give any credence to the claims of an advertising campaign seeking to create a demand for this model, whose original specimens were produced by the Lip watchmaking firm around the 1940s.

50 The artist Christian Boltanski has played with these differences in memorial value in museum exhibits where he showed all the things – photos, lamps, ribbons, and the like – that belonged to a recently deceased unknown person. In this gesture of public memorialization, which would have been easily identifiable and in a sense banal had it aimed to celebrate the memory of an illustrious individual, we can recognize an equivalent of what used to be called a "vanity." For all mortals have the same value; see, for example, the catalog *List of Exhibits Belonging to a Woman of Baden-Baden, Followed by an Explanatory Note* (Oxford: Museum of Modern Art, 1973).

51 Many contemporary artists have placed the question of authenticity at the heart of their own work in order to challenge it; Daniel Spoerri is a good example, with his "snare-pictures," created by others but signed and thus "guaranteed" by the author.

Chapter 8 Collection and Enrichment

1 David Ricardo, *On the Principles of Political Economy, and Taxation* (Baltimore: Johns Hopkins Press, [1819] 1928).

2 In the figure of Balzac's Cousin Pons, an old bachelor ignored or rejected by women who has reoriented his impulses toward gastronomy and art, we can perhaps see the origin of this stereotype, which came to be widely deployed later on, especially if we turn to psychoanalysis for support. Psychoanalytic literature on collections and collectors is quite abundant, stimulated by the fact that Freud himself was a collector. See especially Michelle Moreau Ricaud, *Freud collectionneur* (Paris: Campagne Première, 2011); Gérard Wajcman, *Collection, suivi de L'avarice* (Caen: Jous, 1999); and Werner Muensterberger, *Le collectionneur: anatomie d'une passion* (Paris: Payot, 1994). Jean Baudrillard takes up the thematics that associates collecting and sexuality in the chapter of *The System of Objects* that deals with collecting (London: Verso, [1968] 1996), pp. 87–9.

3 See Luc Boltanski, "Pouvoir et impuissance: projet intellectuel et sexualité dans le Journal d'Amiel," *Actes de la recherche en sciences sociales*, 1/5–6 (1975): 80–108.

4 Steven Gelber, *Hobbies, Leisure and the Culture of Work in America* (New York: Columbia University Press, 1999), pp. 114–24.

5 On the notion of *otium* as an activity cultivated in Roman antiquity, see Paul van der Grijp, *Passion and Profit* (London: Transaction, 2006), p. 11.

6 Russell Belk, *Collecting in a Consumer Society* (London: Routledge, 1995).

7	See Jeanne Lazarus, "Le crédit à la consommation dans la bancarisation," *Entreprises et histoire*, no. 59 (2010): 28–40.

8	Georges Bataille, *The Accursed Share: An Essay on General Economy*, trans. Robert Hurley (New York: Zone Books, 1991), p. 37:

> This surplus eventually contributes to making growth more difficult, for growth no longer suffices to use it up. At a certain point the advantage of extension is neutralized by the contrary advantage, that of luxury .... Henceforth what matters *primarily* is no longer to develop the productive forces but to spend their products sumptuously.
>
> At this point, immense squanderings are about to take place: After a century of populating and of industrial peace, the temporary limit of development being encountered, the two world wars organized the greatest orgies of wealth – and of human beings – that history has recorded. Yet these orgies coincide with an appreciable rise in the general standard of living: The majority of the population benefits from more and more unproductive services; work is reduced and wages are increased overall.

9	This rarely discussed issue has been reconsidered recently in the language of contemporary sociology by Andrew Abbott in "The Problem of Excess," *Sociological Theory*, 32/1 (2014): 1–26.

10	Malcolm Bull, *The Mirror of the Gods: How Renaissance Artists Rediscovered the Pagan Gods* (Oxford: Oxford University Press, 2005).

11	Max Weber, *The Protestant Ethic and the Spirit of Capitalism*, trans. Talcott Parsons (Los Angeles: Roxbury, [1829] 1998).

12	On the production of things destined for the poor as the new horizon of capitalism, see Coimbatore Krishnao Prahalad, *The Fortune at the Bottom of the Pyramid: Eradicating Poverty through Profits* (Upper Saddle River, NJ: Pearson Education, 2009). And, for an in-depth commentary, see Laurence Fontaine, *Le marché: histoire et usages d'une conquête sociale* (Paris: Gallimard, 2014).

13	Jean-Paul Sartre, *Critique of Dialectical Reason*, vol. 1: *Theory of Practical Ensembles*, trans. Alan Sheridan-Smith (London: NLB, [1960] 1976), pp. 122ff.

14	See Aurélie Corne and Laurent Botti, "*Benchmarking*, attraction et valeur touristique du territoire: une analyse par le secteur hôtelier français," *Management & avenir*, no. 84 (2016): 179–96.

15	This exhibit, titled "Coup de sac!," was held at MUDAC, Lausanne, from June 19 to October 6, 2013.

16	Werner Sombart was one of the first economic historians to stress the importance of the luxury economy in the formation of capitalism, especially in Italy: see Werner Sombart, *The Future of Capitalism* (Berlin-Charlottenburg: Buchholz & Weisswange, 1932), and, for an interesting commentary on Sombart's positions and the often moralizing critics who opposed him, see Guido Guerzoni, *Apollo and Vulcan: The Art Markets in Italy, 1400–1700*, trans. Amanda George (East Lansing: Michigan State University Press, [2006] 2011), pp. 11–19.

17	On the moral debates that accompanied the development of luxury in the eighteenth century, see Audrey Provost, *Le luxe, les Lumières et la Révolution* (Seyssel: Champ Vallon, 2014).

18	A document published monthly by the Comité Colbert, an association of company leaders founded in 1954 to promote the French luxury industry.

19 *Lettre du Comité Colbert*, no. 33, March–April 1984.
20 Ibid.
21 See Judith Ickowicz, *Le droit après la dématérialisation de l'oeuvre d'art* (Dijon: Les Presses du réel, 2013).
22 See Anne Jourdain's work on artisanal art: "Réconcilier l'art et l'artisanat: une étude de l'artisanat d'art," *Sociologie de l'art*, 21 (2012): 21–42, and "La construction sociale de la singularité: une stratégie entrepreneuriale des artisans d'art," *Revue française de socio-économie*, 6 (2010): 13–30.
23 For a perspective on the luxury industry that is both internal and critical, see Marie-Claude Sicard, *Luxe, mensonge et marketing* (Paris: Pearson, 2010).
24 On the analysis of these techniques and on their use in marketing and in politics, see Christian Salmon, *Storytelling: la machine à fabriquer des histoires et à formatter les esprits* (Paris: La Découverte, 2007).
25 Thorstein Veblen, *The Theory of the Leisure Class* (New York: Penguin Books, [1899] 1979).
26 Our analysis is based primarily on the annual financial reports for fiscal year 2013 (published in 2014) of the two companies: LVMH, Consolidated Financial Statements, December 31, translation of the French financial documents, fiscal year ended December 31, 2013 (hereafter LVMH 2013), www.lvmh.fr/wp-content/uploads/2014/10/lvmh_2013_financial_documents_va.pdf, and Kering, *Investor Presentation* 2013 (hereafter Kering 2013), www.kering.com/en/finance/publications/. The 2018 figures come from the annual financial reports published by each company in 2019: LVMH, Consolidated Financial Statements, December 31, 2018, https://r.lvmh-static.com/uploads/2019/02/comptes-consolides_lvmh_va.pdf and the 2018 financial document, www.kering.com/en/finance/publications/.
27 Alessandro Schiliro, *Luxury Apparel Brands: World Market Analysis, 2013–2018 Trends*, Xerfi Global, December 2013, p. 34.
28 Kering 2013, p. 16.
29 Ibid.; Kering gives its source as Capgemini/RBC 2013 World Wealth Report.
30 LVMH, Consolidated Financial Statements 2018, and Kering, 2018 financial document.
31 Kering 2013, p. 206.
32 LVMH 2013, p. 31.
33 On the methods used for the financial evaluation of brands, see Adel Beldi, Édouard Chastenet, Jean-Claude Dupuis, and Mohamed Talfi, "Pertinence des méthodes d'évaluation financière des marques: une étude empirique internationale," *Revue française de gestion*, no. 207 (2010): 153–68.
34 Kering 2013, p. 10.
35 Ibid., p. 9.
36 Ibid.
37 Ibid., p. 22.
38 Ibid., p. 38.
39 Ibid., p. 34.
40 Louis Vuitton exhibit, "Volez, Voguez, Voyagez," Grand Palais, Paris, December 4, 2015–February 21, 2016.
41 Ibid.
42 In 2014, Nathalie Moureau, Dominique Sagot-Duvauroux, and Marion Vidal carried out a survey among contemporary art collectors that received 322 responses. (It is difficult, as the authors acknowledge, to evaluate the extent

to which their sample is "representative" of collectors in general, since there is no agreed-on population of collectors with administratively defined contours.) On the basis of this survey, they constructed a "typology" of collectors, identifying "quasi-professional collectors," with collections that include more than 200 pieces whose maximum annual purchase price can exceed 200,000 euros, "invested collectors," with collections that include from 100 to 200 works whose acquisition prices vary from 10,000 to 50,000 euros, "steady" collectors, and "independent collectors." These collectors, especially those in the first two categories, frequent the art world assiduously, have connections with galleries, or visit workshops (in the case of 88 percent of the collectors in these categories) in order to spot "promising" artists who are not yet highly rated but who have a chance, they think, to rise in the more or less near future; according to the authors, "the majority of collectors – including the wealthiest," declare that they are "incapable of following the steep climb of the prices associated with the current workings of the art market." See Nathalie Moureau, Dominique Sagot-Duvauroux, and Marion Vidal, "Collectionneurs d'art contemporain: des acteurs méconnus de la vie artistique," *Cultures études*, 1/1 (2015): 1–20.

43 See Pierre Cabanne, *Les grands collectionneurs*, vol. 2 (Paris: Éditions de l'Amateur, 2004), pp. 365–79.

44 See Nathalie Heinich and Roberta Shapiro, eds, *De l'artification: enquêtes sur le passage à l'art* (Paris: Éditions de l'EHESS, 2012).

45 The concept of immortality is invoked here in the sense Hannah Arendt gave it in *The Human Condition* (Chicago: University of Chicago Press, 1958), pp. 167–74.

46 There are numerous examples in the work of Francis Haskell, who shows the importance of the role played by collectors in the formation of judgments of taste. See Francis Haskell, *L'amateur d'art*, trans. Pierre-Emmanuel Dauzat (Paris: Librairie Générale Française, 1997) [a collection of essays published in English between 1981 and 1994]; *Rediscoveries in Art: Some Aspects of Taste, Fashion and Collecting in England and France* (Ithaca, NY: Cornell University Press, 1976); and *The Ephemeral Museum: Old Master Paintings and the Rise of the Art Exhibition* (New Haven, CT: Yale University Press, 2000).

47 On the notion of "regime of singularity," see Nathalie Heinich, *L'élite artiste: excellence et singularité en régime démocratique* (Paris: Gallimard, 2005).

48 Pierre Bourdieu, *The Rules of Art: Genesis and Structure of the Literary Field*, trans. Susan Emanuel (Stanford, CA: Stanford University Press, 1996).

49 Raymonde Moulin, *L'artiste, l'institution et le marché* (Paris: Flammarion, 1992).

50 In the case of old works that are already widely recognized, works that Moulin calls "established paintings," one way of dealing with the growing scarcity of works on offer, which may extend all the way to their exhaustion, consists in "rediscovering" – that is, "recuperating" – the work of previously neglected artists: see Raymonde Moulin, *The French Art Market: A Sociological View*, abridged trans. Arthur Goldhammer (New Brunswick, NJ: Rutgers University Press, 1987), pp. 144–51; for a more extensive discussion, see Raymonde Moulin, *Le marché de la peinture en France* (Paris: Minuit, 1967), pp. 417–32.

51 This process was attested, for example, by the exhibit "Modernités plurielles, 1905–1970," presented at the Pompidou Center in Paris in 2013–14 under the direction of Catherine Grenier. This vast exhibit aimed to sketch out a new

version of art history by placing alongside famous paintings, veritable icons of modern art, works by peripheral artists that had been kept in the collections of the National Museum of Modern Art, in certain cases without ever having been shown to the public. A number of those canvases had been created by artists who had more recently become sought after by emerging collectors in their countries of origin.

52 As the survey by Moureau, Sagot-Duvauroux, and Vidal has shown, this is how the collectors most committed to their activity seek ties with institutions, for example by collaborating on projected exhibits and working with exhibit organizers (35 percent collaborate in this way), by participating in the publication of catalogs of artists present in their collections (33 percent), by joining a society of friends of a given museum (60 percent), by lending works to museums (27 percent), or by serving on museum boards or purchasing committees (14 percent). The fact that "their artistic choices are confirmed by a museum" confers on them an "authority" that spills over onto the estimation of the metaprices of all the works they possess. As the authors of the survey also note, "the simple fact of belonging to a purchasing committee of an institution affords a power to influence" (Moureau et al., "Collectionneurs d'art contemporain").

53 See Michel Houellebecq, *The Map and the Territory*, trans. Gavin Bowd (New York: Alfred A. Knopf, [2010] 2012).

54 Interview with Benjamin Leperchey, December 2015. The idea was expressed in similar terms by the same highly placed official in an article: "Luxury is an ambassador for France abroad: if the major French houses profit from the aura of France to 'nourish' their brands, the reverse is undeniably true." The Comité stratégique de filière (CSF) of the fashion and luxury industries thus includes, in addition to representatives of professional federations, representatives of those who "give the orders" – that is, the major luxury houses such as Balenciaga, Dior, Hermès or Vuitton – and representatives of government agencies such as the Public Investment Bank (BPI) or the Ministry of Culture and Communication. See Benjamin Leperchey, "Le Comité stratégique de filière (CSF) des industries de la mode et du luxe," *Annales des Mines – Réalités industrielles*, no. 4 (2013): 14–19.

55 David Harvey, "The Art of Rent: Globalization and the Commodification of Culture," in *Spaces of Capital: Towards a Critical Geography* (New York: Routledge, 2001), pp. 404, 396.

56 Ibid., p. 408.

Chapter 9 The Trend Form

1 For example, for France, see Daniel Roche, *The Culture of Clothing: Dress and Fashion in the Ancien Régime*, trans. Jean Birrell (Cambridge: Cambridge University Press, 1994).

2 Pierre Bourdieu with Yvette Delsaut, "Le couturier et sa griffe: contribution à une théorie de la magie," *Actes de la recherche en sciences sociales*, 1/1 (1975): 7–36. A synthesis of the research Bourdieu devoted to the role of objects in the process of domination can be found in *Distinction: A Social Critique of the Judgement of Taste*, trans. Richard Nice (London: Routledge & Kegan Paul, [1979] 1986).

3 See Patrice Maniglier, ed., *Le moment philosophique des années 1960 en France* (Paris: Presses Universitaires de France, 2011); see especially David Raboin, "Structuralisme et comparatisme en sciences humaines et en mathématiques; un malentendu?," ibid., pp. 37–58.

4 On this topic we are thinking especially of Roland Barthes, *Mythologies*, trans. Annette Lavers (New York: Noonday Press, [1957] 1972); *The Fashion System*, trans. Matthew Ward and Richard Howard (New York: Hill & Wang, [1967] 1983); and "Semantics of the Object" (1966), in *The Semiotic Challenge*, trans. Richard Howard (New York: Hill & Wang, [1985] 1988), pp. 179–90.

5 Jean Baudrillard, *The System of Objects*, trans. James Benedict (London: Verso, [1968] 1996), and *The Consumer Society: Myths and Structures* (rev. edn, London: Sage, [1970] 2017).

6 Patrick Aspers reaches the same conclusions in *Orderly Fashion: A Sociology of Markets* (Princeton, NJ: Princeton University Press, 2010), pp. 49–54.

7 Ferdinand de Saussure, *Course in General Linguistics*, trans. Wade Baskin, ed. Perry Meisel and Haun Saussy (New York: Columbia University Press, [1916] 2011).

8 Peter Drucker, *Concept of the Corporation* (New York: John Day, 1972).

9 See Maxine Berg, "New Commodities, Luxuries and Their Consumers in Eighteenth-Century England," in Maxine Berg and Helen Clifford, eds, *Consumers and Luxury: Consumer Culture in England, 1650–1850* (Manchester: Manchester University Press, 1999), pp. 63–87.

10 Creamware, which became fashionable around 1760, is a good example. This was "fine earthenware, glazed and translucid," on which its inventor, Josiah Wedgwood, "placed reproductions of designs ordered from independent artists inspired by oriental decors." See Jean-Claude Daumas and Marc de Ferrière Le Vayer, "Les métamorphoses du luxe vues d'Europe," *Entreprises et histoire*, no. 46 (2007): 6–16.

11 Cissie Fairchilds, "The Production and Marketing of Populuxe Goods in Eighteenth-Century Paris," in John Brewer and Roy Porter, eds, *Consumption and the World of Goods* (New York: Routledge, 1993), pp. 228–48.

12 Edgar Morin, *The Stars*, trans. Richard Howard (Minneapolis: University of Minnesota Press, [1957] 2005).

13 Bourdieu with Delsaut, "Le couturier et sa griffe," p. 18.

14 See Sylvain Parasie, "Une critique désarmée: le tournant publicitaire dans la France des années 1980," *Réseaux*, no. 150 (2008): 219–45.

15 See James Gilmore and Joseph Pine II, *Authenticity: What Consumers Really Want* (Boston: Harvard Business School Press, 2007), esp. pp. 12–13 and 77–8.

16 See Guillaume Erner, *Sociologie des tendances* (Paris: Presses Universitaires de France, 2008), pp. 109–12.

17 See Diego Rinallo and Francesca Golfetto, "Representing Markets: The Shaping of Fashion Trends by French and Italian Fabric Companies," *Industrial Marketing Management*, 35/7 (2006): 856–69.

18 See Alain Chatriot, "La construction récente des groupes de luxe français: mythes, discours et pratiques," *Entreprises et histoire*, no. 46 (2007): 143–56.

19 In the approach developed by Pierre Bourdieu, the taste for imitation characterizes the middle classes, whose members want to distinguish themselves from the lower classes and move closer to the upper classes but lack the financial means necessary for acquiring truly distinctive objects (Bourdieu, *Distinction*, esp. pp. 251–2).

20 See Léa Bulci, "Les bureaux du style, ces gens qui 'font' la tendance," *mad-moiZelle*, August 3, 2012, www.madmoizelle.com/bureaux-style-117208.

21 Erner, *Sociologie des tendances*, p. 111.

22 For an analysis of the chain of value that, in the case of fashion, goes from "trendsetters" to "designers," manufacturing workshops, global distribution enterprises, and retailers who sell the products, see Aspers, *Orderly Fashion*.

23 "At Dammartin I arrive in the evening. I put up at the *Image Saint-Jean*. I am assigned a room, pretty clean, hung with old tapestry, with a glass against the wall. This room is a last return to the taste for bric-à-brac, which I have forsworn long since" (Gérard de Nerval, *Sylvie: Recollections of Valois* (New York: Home Book Company, [1853] 1981), p. 133). The period of his life to which Nerval is referring, in which bric-à-brac played a big role, is presented at the beginning of *Petits châteaux de bohème*, in which Nerval described the life he led on the rue du Doyenné (Gérard de Nerval, *Poésies et souvenirs* (Paris: Gallimard, 1980), pp. 84–7).

24 André Orléan, *The Empire of Value: A New Foundation for Economics*, trans. M. B. DeBevoise (Cambridge, MA: MIT Press, [2011] 2014), pp. 50–61.

25 See Henri Peretz, "Soldes 'haut de gamme' à Paris," *Ethnologie française*, 35/1 (2005): 47–54.

26 See Corinne Degoutte, "Stratégies de marques dans la mode: convergence ou divergence des modèles de gestion nationaux dans l'industrie du luxe (1860–2003)," *Entreprises et histoire*, no. 46 (2007): 125–42.

27 See Frédéric Godart, *Sociologie de la mode* (Paris: La Découverte, 2010), p. 51.

28 See Maurizio Lazzarato, Yann Moulier-Boutang, Antonio Negri, and Giancaro Santilli, *Des entreprises pas comme les autres: Benetton, le Sentier à Paris* (Aix-en-Provence: Publisud, 1993).

29 On April 24, 2013, Rana Plaza collapsed, killing 1,135 people and injuring around a thousand more. The building, situated in a suburb of Dhaka that harbored many workshops in the garment industry, had shown signs of cracking, but no repairs had been made. These workshops, subcontractors for international brands, were not highly mechanized; they concentrated large numbers of hand-workers, mostly women, who were subjected to working conditions that harked back to those of the early nineteenth century.

30 For a denunciation of these practices, see Naomi Klein, *No Logo: No Space, No Choice, No Job: Taking Aim at the Brand Bullies* (Toronto: A. A. Knopf Canada, 2000). Klein's book reached a broad audience and its message was supported by a number of NGOs, but to little concrete effect. Still, during the last decade or so, the vigilance of the NGOs has led the leading firms in the garment industry to stress, in their annual reports, the "ethical" dimension of their activities and to affirm their observance of norms involving health and working conditions in the countries where their products are produced (see Aspers, *Orderly Fashion*, pp. 160–2).

31 See Ashley Mears, *Pricing Beauty: The Making of a Fashion Model* (Berkeley: University of California Press, 2011).

32 See Bruno Cousin, "Segrégation résidentielle et quartiers refondés: usages de la comparaison entre Paris et Milan," *Sociologie du travail*, 55/2 (2013): 214–36.

33 See John B. Thompson, *Merchants of Culture: The Publishing Business in the Twenty-First Century* (Cambridge: Polity, 2010), pp. 74–5.

34 See Chatriot, "La construction récente des groupes de luxe français."

35 See Andrea Colli and Elisabetta Merlo, "Family Business and Luxury Business in Italy (1950–2000)," *Entreprises et histoire*, no. 46 (2007): 113–24.
36 See the list of marketing manuals in chapter 8, p. 199.

Chapter 10 The Asset Form

1 See Camille Herlin-Giret, "Les mondes de la richesse: travailler et faire travailler le capital," doctoral thesis, Université Paris-Dauphine, July 2016.
2 Karl Marx, *Capital*, 4th edn, ed. Frederic Engels, trans. Ben Fowkes (London: Penguin Classics, [1890] 1990), vol. 1, part 2, chapter 4, p. 247.
3 See Nathalie Moureau, *Analyse économique de la valeur des biens d'art: la peinture contemporaine* (Paris: Economica, 2000), pp. 197–200.
4 See William J. Baumol, "Unnatural Value: or Art Investment as Floating Crap Game," *American Economic Review*, 76/2 (1986): 10–14.
5 See Nicolette Marinelli and Giulio Palomba, "A Model for Pricing Italian Contemporary Art Paintings at Auction," *Quarterly Review of Economics and Finance*, 51 (2011): 212–24.
6 See Elroy Dimson, Peter L. Rousseau, and Christophe Spaenjers, "The Price of Wine," *Journal of Financial Economics*, 118 (2015): 431–49.
7 See Dominic Taylor and Les Coleman, "Price Determinants of Aboriginal Art, and its Role as an Alternative Asset Class," *Journal of Banking & Finance*, 35 (2011): 1519–29.
8 See Orley Ashenfelter and Kathryn Graddy, "Auctions and the Price of Art," *Journal of Economic Literature*, 41/3 (2003): 763–86.
9 See Christophe Spaenjers, William N. Goetzmann, and Elena Mamonova, "The Economics of Aesthetics and Record Prices for Art since 1701," *Explorations in Economic History*, 57 (2015): 79–94.
10 Lionel Bochurberg and Sylvie Lefort, "Les ventes aux enchères sur l'internet," *Legicom*, nos. 21–2 (2000): 136.
11 See the list of marketing manuals in chapter 8, p. 199.
12 Raymonde Moulin, *The French Art Market: A Sociological View*, abridged trans. Arthur Goldhammer (New Brunswick, NJ: Rutgers University Press, 1967), p. 84.
13 These criticisms have been advanced by Noah Horowitz, in *Art of the Deal: Contemporary Art in a Global Financial Market* (Princeton, NJ: Princeton University Press, 2011), pp. 143–87.
14 As Taylor and Coleman suggest in "Price Determinants of Aboriginal Art."
15 For exchanges to be carried out easily and often, the determination of goods has to be based on stable markers and has to be readily accessible, so as to limit anxiety on the part of actors as to the existence of asymmetries in the information available; see Bruce Carruthers and Arthur Stinchcombe, "The Social Structure of Liquidity: Flexibility, Markets, and States," *Theory and Society*, 29 (1999): 353–82.
16 See Taylor and Coleman, "Price Determinants of Aboriginal Art."
17 See Anthony Kuhn and Yves Moulin, "Le rôle des conventions de qualité dans la construction d'un marché: l'évolution du marché philatélique français (1860–1995)," *Entreprises et histoire*, no. 53 (2008): 54–67.
18 Jonathan Grant, "The Socialist Construction of Philately in the Early Soviet Era," *Comparative Studies in Society and History*, 37 (1995): 476–93.

19 Hubert Duez, *Secrets d'un brocanteur* (Paris: Seuil, 1999), p. 65. For an especially illuminating analysis of the formation of prices in flea markets, see Hervé Sciardet, *Les marchands de l'aube: ethnographie et théorie du commerce aux Puces de Saint-Ouen* (Paris: Economica, 2003).

20 See Clifford Geertz, "Suk: The Bazaar Economy in Sefrou," in Clifford Geertz, Hildred Geertz, and Lawrence Rosen, *Meaning and Order in Moroccan Society* (Cambridge: Cambridge University Press, 1979), pp. 123–313. Hernando de Soto shows, similarly, that the myriad micro-enterprises in the suburbs of Lima are distinguishable from capital, in the proper sense of the term, only to the extent that, since their property is not based on institutional and legal arrangements, the revenues that can be drawn from it are entirely dependent on local connections and personal relationships, familial in particular. See Hernando de Soto, *The Mystery of Capital: Why Capitalism Triumphs in the West and Fails Everywhere Else* (New York: Basic Books, 2000).

21 To get a sense of the advice given by financial specialists to buyers of art aiming to minimize the tax implications of this type of investment, see for example Ralph Lerner, "Art and Taxation in the United States," in Clare McAndrew, *Fine Art and High Finance: Expert Advice on the Economics of Ownership* (New York: Bloomberg Press, 2010), pp. 211–48. For the French case, see Herlin-Giret, "Les mondes de la richesse."

22 On the importance that this mode of evaluation has taken on, and on its extension from the evaluation of businesses to that of public investments or even to the calculation of the costs that may be involved in preserving the well-being of future generations, see Jonathan Nitzan and Shimshon Bichler, *Capital as Power: A Study of Order and Creorder* (New York: Routledge, 2009), especially pp. 147–66. And for a sociological analysis of the processes of capitalization, see Fabien Muniesa, "A Flank Movement in the Understanding of Valuation," in Lisa Adkins and Celia Lury, eds, *Measure and Value* (Chichester: Wiley-Blackwell, 2012), pp. 24–38, and Horacio Ortiz, "Value and Power: Some Questions for a Global Political Anthropology of Global Finance," in Raul Acosta, Sadaf Rizvi, and Ana Santos, eds, *Making Sense of the Global: Anthropological Perspectives on Interconnections and Processes* (Cambridge: Cambridge University Press, 2010), pp. 63–81.

23 See André Orléan, *The Empire of Value: A New Foundation for Economics*, trans. M. B. DeBevoise (Cambridge, MA: MIT Press, [2011] 2014), and, for an empirical application, *De l'euphorie à la panique: penser la crise financière* (Paris: Rue d'Ulm, 2009).

24 See Charles Kindleberger and Robert Z. Aliber, *Manias, Panics and Crashes* (New York: Macmillan, 2011).

25 See Takato Hiraki, Akitoshi Ito, Darius A. Spieth, and Naoya Takezawa, "How Did Japanese Investments Influence International Art Prices?," *The Journal of Financial and Quantitative Analysis*, 44/6 (2000): 1489–514.

26 See Jeanne Lazarus, *L'épreuve de l'argent: banques, banquiers, clients* (Paris: Calmann-Lévy, 2012), pp. 222–5.

27 See Taylor and Coleman, "Price Determinants of Aboriginal Art."

28 If about half (twenty-six) of the fifty Flemish artists viewed as "canonical" at the end of the twentieth century have been famous for 350 years, we must not forget that those in the other half are no longer celebrated as major artists. See Victor Ginsburgh, François Mairesse, and Sheila Weyers, "De la narration à

la consécration: l'exemple de la peinture flamande de Van Eyck à Rubens," *Histoire & mesure*, 23/2 (2008): 145–76.
29 See Spaenjers et al., "The Economics of Aesthetics."
30 See Moulin, *The French Art Market*, pp. 143–6.
31 See Julie Verlaine, *Les galeries d'art contemporain à Paris: une histoire culturelle du marché de l'art, 1944–1970* (Paris: Publications de la Sorbonne, 2012), p. 22.
32 See the ArtPrice annual report, *The Art Market in 2014*, https://imgpublic.artprice.com/pdf/rama2014_en.pdf.
33 On auctions as arrangements for reducing the uncertainty about value, especially in the case of collector's items, see Charles Smith, *Auctions: The Social Construction of Value* (New York: Free Press, 1989).
34 For example, by invoking the notion of *expenditure*, in Georges Bataille, *The Accursed Share: An Essay on General Economy*, trans. Robert Hurley (New York: Zone Books, [1949] 1991).
35 In *Seven Days in the Art World* (New York: W. W. Norton, 2008), a work based on a large number of field studies and written for a broad public by the sociologist Sarah Thornton, one can find a description, very rich on the ethnographic level and very perspicacious, of the major auctions of contemporary art in New York (pp. 1–39). The author stresses the difference between innovative collectors eager to extend and modify the contours of their collections, which pass through the primary market by and large, and collectors who are oriented more toward the accumulation of assets, who turn to the secondary market and to auctions so as to know "with certainty that they've paid the market price" (p. 12). Thornton also describes with pertinence the signs that attest to the existence of personal relations among the members of the latter group, for whom major sales also constitute social rituals and occasions to reinforce their bonds.

Chapter 11 Profit in a Commercial Society

1 See Joseph Schumpeter, *The Theory of Economic Development: An Inquiry into Profits, Capital, Credit, Interest, and the Business Cycle*, trans. Redvers Opie (New York: Oxford University Press, [1911, 1926] 1961).
2 Max Weber, *The Protestant Ethic and the Spirit of Capitalism*, trans. Talcott Parsons (Los Angeles: Roxbury, [1829] 1998).
3 The question of exchange is at the heart of Claude Lévi-Strauss's *The Elementary Structures of Kinship*, trans. John Richard Von Sturmer, James Harle Bell, and Rodney Needham (Boston: Beacon Press, [1949] 1969). The kinship systems studied in this work have in common the fact that they allow the circulation of women among lineages or segments of society over several generations, in a way that precludes the accumulation of women, who constitute, in these societies, a form of wealth of the highest importance, at certain points in the network. In fact, such accumulations would lead to the division of society into separate and potentially antagonistic groups. Without being directly assimilable to an exchange of gifts, the exchange of women is thus placed under the sign of reciprocity. This model can be understood as a sort of metaphor for a non-capitalist mercantile society – that is, a society whose structures are based on exchange as an alternative to violence but that is equipped

with arrangements making it possible to dissociate exchange from the quest for a decisive and lasting advantage, equivalent to what capitalist societies term profit. If we pursue this metaphor, we see, on the one hand, that it is not exchange or even commerce that poses a problem in capitalist societies but the fact that commerce, motivated in these societies by the possibility of profit, leads to the accumulation of goods in profit centers and to the formation of inequalities whose effects are cumulative. And, on the other hand, we see that the formation of these inequalities is virtually inevitable if it is not countered by structural arrangements designed to cause goods to circulate in such a way that they will be redistributed. In fact, the existence of multiple differentials that are unequally distributed, even contextual, which the actors are likely to grasp in the course of their commercial relations in order to get a strategic advantage over their partner(s), has every chance of giving rise to inequalities that will accumulate if the exchange is not regulated by a "third party" (which may not be a person or even an institution but may be assimilated into common practice) that will recall the requirement of reciprocity.

4 We are following the analyses of Richard Swedberg, in *Schumpeter: A Biography* (Princeton, NJ: Princeton University Press, 1991).

5 Edward Hastings Chamberlin, *The Theory of Monopolistic Competition* (Cambridge, MA: Harvard University Press, [1933] 1962).

6 We are following the interpretation of Frank H. Knight, *Risk, Uncertainty and Profit* (Boston: Houghton Mifflin, 1921), as proposed by Nathalie Moureau and Dorothée Rivaud-Danset, in *L'incertitude dans les théories économiques* (Paris: La Découverte, 2004), pp. 6–9.

7 Here we are following the interpretation of Thorstein Veblen, *The Theory of Business Enterprise* (New York: C. Scribner's Sons, [1904] 1932), as proposed by Jonathan Nitzan and Shimshon Bichler, in *Capital as Power: A Study of Order and Creorder* (New York: Routledge, 2009), pp. 219–23.

8 Karl Marx, *Wages, Price, and Profit* (Peking: Foreign Languages Press, [1865] 1965).

9 Fernand Braudel, *The Wheels of Commerce*, vol. 2 of *Civilization and Capitalism, 15th–18th Century*, trans. Siân Reynolds (New York: Harper & Row, [1979] 1982).

10 Marx, *Wages, Price, and Profit*, p. 27.

11 Ibid., pp. 33–4.

12 Ibid., p. 39.

13 See chapter 10, pp. 240–1.

14 For an in-depth analysis of the notion of value in Marx, see Anselm Jappe, *Les aventures de la marchandise: pour une nouvelle critique de la valeur* (Paris: Denoël, 2003).

15 For example, see John Elster, *Making Sense of Marx* (Cambridge: Cambridge University Press, 1985), pp. 171–85.

16 Marx, *Wages, Price, and Profit*, p. 38.

17 See Cornelius Castoriadis, *Capitalisme moderne et révolution* (Paris: UGC, 1979), esp. the chapter dealing with the critique of "reducing the rate of profit," pp. 205–22.

18 Let us recall the debates – sometimes rather convoluted, it must be said – that marked the late Marxism of the 1960s and 1970s, bearing on the question whether so-called non-productive wage-earners could be assimilated to "proletarians," a category in which "laborers" occupied the center. These debates

unfolded in particular between Serge Mallet's *The New Working Class*, trans. Andrée Shepherd and Bob Shepherd (Nottingham: Bertrand Russell Peace Foundation for Spokesman Books, [1963] 1975), and, a few years later, Nikos Poulantzas's *Political Power and Social Classes*, trans. Timothy O'Hagan (London: NLB/Sheed & Ward, [1968] 1973), followed by his *Classes in Contemporary Capitalism*, trans. David Fernbach (London: NLB, [1974] 1975).

19 Braudel, *The Wheels of Commerce*, p. 168: "When goods travelled, they naturally increased in price the farther they went. This was what I shall call the 'trading profit.' Can this be described as a universal rule? With near certainty."

20 Ibid., p. 231.

21 Ibid., p. 230.

22 Ibid., p. 406.

23 Ibid., p. 405.

24 Ibid., pp. 400–1.

25 A number of works inspired by Braudel have deepened our knowledge of the practical modalities on which profits drawn from displacements of merchandise are based. These works have stressed the formation of extensive intercultural networks that allow the circulation of raw materials and objects among widely separated groups that depend on different "local traditions": thus these studies emphasize the "cultural," "ethnic," and "linguistic" dimensions of exchanges whose success does not by any means depend solely on "the rationality of the agents" proclaimed by "neoclassical analysis." That success depends above all on the capacity to exploit a plurality of *differentials*, which presupposes, on the one hand, at the local level, the establishment of relations of "cooperation" and "trust," based on arrangements such as "reputation," "reciprocity," knowledge of local customs, and generosity, and, on the other hand, good knowledge of global power relations, in particular among political entities. It is this ability to shift from the local to the global level that allows operators to play on the prices of commodities – even though these may be translated into different metrics at the various stages of their trajectory – and makes it possible to anticipate prices from the perspective of profit. This means, too, as the authors of these works stress, that the forces that contribute to market success and on which the formation of capitalism is based move away from the currently dominant economic conceptions when they supply themselves with a homogeneous and transparent transaction space. See Anthony Molho and Diogo Ramada Curto, "Les réseaux marchands à l'époque moderne," *Annales: Histoire, Sciences Sociales*, 58/3 (2003): 569–79. (This article is the preface to an issue of *Annales* devoted to market networks, following a seminar held at the European University Institute in Florence in 2001–2.)

26 Guido Guerzoni, *Apollo and Vulcan: The Art Markets in Italy, 1400–1700*, trans. Amanda George (East Lansing: Michigan State University Press, [2006] 2011), pp. 1–19.

27 We are borrowing this use of *value*, along with part of the reasoning developed here (in particular the use of "point of view"), from Patrice Maniglier, "De Mauss à Claude Lévi-Strauss: cinquante ans après: pour une ontologie Maori," *Archives de Philosophie*, no. 69 (2006): 37–56. See also Ferdinand de Saussure, *Course in General Linguistics*, trans. Wade Baskin, ed. Perry Meisel and Haun Saussy (New York: Columbia University Press, [1916] 2011).

28 As Francesca Trivellato emphasizes, letters between merchants had four functions that printed documents could not perform: "They certified contracts

and property rights in court; they allowed a merchant to ask and respond to specific questions and concerns that he might have about market conditions; they informed traders about the aptitude and reliability of associates, commissioners, and suppliers; and, when necessary, they also assured secrecy." See Francesca Trivellato, *The Familiarity of Strangers: The Sephardic Diaspora, Livorno, and Cross-cultural Trade in the Early Modern Period* (New Haven, CT: Yale University Press, 2009), p. 172.

29 See Olivier Pétré-Grenouilleau, *Les traites négrières: essai d'histoire globale* (Paris: Gallimard, 2004).

30 Gabriel Mendoza Zarate, "La fabrique de la critique: les travailleurs 'sous-traités' de l'industrie électronique au Mexique," doctoral thesis, EHESS, Paris, 2014.

31 See Frédéric Godart, *Sociologie de la mode* (Paris: La Découverte, 2010), pp. 31–7.

32 Hubert Duez, *Secrets d'un brocanteur* (Paris: Seuil, 1999), p. 9:

> I am a seller of old furnishings and objects. During twenty-five years of practice, I have acquired knowledge, know-how, and skill in knowing what to buy. … This is doubtless what they call experience. … As with all my colleagues, my training took place on the job. To learn, we have purchased, by mistake, fakes or things that were "not very good." We have all sold "very good" pieces that we mistakenly thought were only "decent." … That is why we never reveal anything, either about our sources or about our knowledge.

33 Ibid., pp. 23–4.

34 Ibid., p. 22.

35 Ibid., pp. 52–3.

36 Ibid., p. 97. One more example: "I recently saw a flask from Nevers with its leather strap slid through delicate twisted loops. However, in the eighteenth century, loops were simple, narrow protuberances. Only those from Urbino, in the sixteenth century, were elaborately wrought" (ibid.).

37 Ibid., p. 17.

38 Ibid., p. 20.

39 Ibid., p. 23.

40 Ibid., p. 29.

41 See Emmanuel Didier, "Mesurer la délinquance en France depuis 1970: entre expertise et publicité," *Ethnologie française*, 45/1 (2015): 109–21.

42 Benoît Heilbrunn and Bertrand Barré, *Le Packaging* (Paris: Presses Universitaires de France, 2002), pp. 111–14. The authors take as their example Guerlain's Shalimar perfume.

43 Guerzoni, *Apollo and Vulcan*, pp. 30–1.

Chapter 12 The Enrichment Economy in Practice

1 Our work is based largely on a study carried out during two month-long stints in Laguiole (August 2013 and August 2014) and a stay in Thiers during the week of the Salon de la coutellerie (May 2014), visits financed by the Laboratory of Comparative Ethnology and Sociology (LESC, at the University of Paris Ouest-Nanterre La Défense), for which we wish to express our thanks; we also spent time consulting the MUCEM archives in Marseille

(spring 2014), and we analyzed the journal *Excalibur*, devoted to cutlery, along with documents relating to the law on consumption (impact report, summary of debates, and so on). Quotations from individual informants not otherwise attributed are from personal interviews we conducted during our study.

2 Rivière's study, which took 1962 as its primary focus, was published in seven volumes over several years starting in 1970. See Georges-Henri Rivière, ed., *L'Aubrac: étude ethnologique, linguistique, agronomique et économique d'un établissement humain (Recherche coopérative sur programme)*, vol. 1 (Paris: Éditions du CNRS, 1970).

3 See ibid., vol. 3 (1972), pp. 26–52.

4 See Nina Gorgus, *Le magicien des vitrines: le muséologue Georges-Henri Rivière* (Paris: Éditions de la MSH, [1999] 2003), pp. 203–10.

5 Jean Cuisinier, Aubrac 29, Collection RCP Aubrac, MUCEM archives, Marseille, 1964.

6 Jean-Luc Chodkiewicz, *L'Aubrac à Paris: une enquête d'ethnologie urbaine* (Paris: Éditions du CTHS, 2014), p. 101 [a study carried out in 1965–6].

7 Albert Calmels, *Guide touristique de l'Aubrac: Saint-Chély-d'Aubrac et Laguiole* (Paris: Éditions de la solidarité aveyronnaise, 1981).

8 Reported in a 2012 study published by the Aveyron Departmental Tourism commission.

9 Field notes, Laguiole, August 2013.

10 The price for one night at the time of writing is between 20 and 30 euros.

11 A one-night stay here costs between 70 and 90 euros.

12 Rivière, *L'Aubrac*, vol. 3, p. 51.

13 See www.projet-pnr-aubrac.fr.

14 Archives, RCP Aubrac, typescript titled "Économie et société."

15 Archives, RCP Aubrac, document titled "Réunion de travail: Artisanat," Paris, June 14, 1965; Georges-Henri Rivière was present at the meeting.

16 This festival, also known as Corpus Christi, is traditionally celebrated sixty days after Easter. The celebration in Aubrac is illustrated photographically in the framework of the RCP in Jean-Dominique Lajoux, *Aubrac: des racines et des hommes* (Paris: Delachaux et Niestlé, 2014), pp. 206–9.

17 Conversation with a cutler, August 2013.

18 Field notes, Laguiole, August 2013.

19 Jean-Jacques Pietraru, "Éditorial," *Excalibur*, no. 60 (2013): 3.

20 Field notes, Laguiole, August 2013.

21 Judith Ickowicz, *Le droit après la dématérialisation de l'oeuvre d'art* (Dijon: Les Presses du réel, 2013).

22 Gérard Pacella, "La collection des couteaux, armes blanches et outils tranchants," *Excalibur*, no. 20 (2001): 42.

23 Ibid., p. 47 (more generally, see pp. 40–7).

24 *Excalibur*, no. 68 (2013): 46.

25 Ibid., pp. 66–71.

26 Aveyron Departmental Tourism Commission.

27 Camille Pagé, *La coutellerie depuis l'origine jusqu'à nos jours*, vol. 2: *La coutellerie moderne* (Châtellerault: H. Rivière, 1896), p. 273.

28 Ibid., p. 302.

29 Archives, RCP Aubrac.

30 Interview, field notes, August 2014.

31 Field notes, August 2014.

32 Ibid.

33 Ibid.

34 Ruling, Council of State, January 31, 1973.

35 See Stéphane Ferret, *Le Bateau de Thésée: le problème de l'identité à travers le temps* (Paris: Minuit, 1996).

36 Pagé, *La coutellerie depuis l'origine jusqu'à nos jours*, vol. 2, p. 405.

37 Ibid., p. 437.

38 Ibid., p. 438.

39 Field notes, Laguiole, August 2014.

40 Ibid.

41 Ibid.

42 John L. Comaroff and Jean Comaroff, *Ethnicity, Inc.* (Chicago: University of Chicago Press, 2009).

43 Interview with the entrepreneur, fall 2014.

44 Field notes, Laguiole, August 2013.

45 Ibid.

46 Law no. 2014-344, March 17, 2014.

47 Discussion during the first reading of a proposed law in the Commission on Economic Affairs, National Assembly, Thursday, June 11, 2013; see www.assemblee-nationale.fr/14/cr-eco/12-13/c1213087.asp.

48 Discussion during the first reading in a public session in the Senate, September 2013.

49 Field notes, Laguiole, August 2013.

50 Discussion during the first reading in the Commission on Economic Affairs, National Assembly, Thursday, June 11, 2013.

51 Razzy Hammadi, rapporteur charged with preparing the report on the proposed law, www.assemblee-nationale.fr/14/cr-eco/12-13/c1213087.asp.

52 Discussion during the first reading in a public session in the Senate, September 2013.

Chapter 13 The Shape of the Enrichment Society

1 See Joseph Schumpeter, *The Theory of Economic Development: An Inquiry into Profits, Capital, Credit, Interest, and the Business Cycle*, trans. Redvers Opie (New York: Oxford University Press, [1911, 1926] 1961).

2 See Simona Cerutti's analyses concerning the problems that arose in Turin in the eighteenth century over the transmission of goods belonging to deceased foreigners whose family ties were unknown: Simona Cerutti, "A qui appartiennent les biens qui n'appartiennent à personne? Citoyenneté et droit d'aubaine à l'époque moderne," *Annales: Histoire, Sciences Sociales*, 62/2 (2007): 355–83, and *Étrangers: étude d'une condition d'incertitude dans une société d'Ancien Régime* (Paris: Bayard, 2012).

3 Among many others, see Sharon Zukin, one of the first sociologists to study the processes of urban gentrification, in *Loft Living: Culture and Capital in Urban Change* (New Brunswick, NJ: Rutgers University Press, 1982), and *Naked City: The Death and Life of Authentic Urban Places* (Oxford: Oxford University Press, 2010).

4 Michel Rautenberg, "Une politique culturelle des produits locaux dans la region Rhône-Alpes," *Revue de géographie alpine*, 86/4 (1998): 81–7

5 Michel Rautenberg, personal communication. For a comparative study, see Rautenberg, "Industrial Heritage, Regeneration of Cities and Public Policies in the 1990s: Elements of a French/British Comparison," *International Journal of Heritage Studies*, 18 (2012): 1–12, https://halshs.archives-ouvertes.fr/halshs-00721541/document.

6 Stéphane Gerson, "Le patrimoine local impossible: Nostradamus à Salon-de-Provence (1980–1999)," *Genèses*, no. 92 (2013): 52–75.

7 Charles Tilly, *The Contentious French* (Cambridge, MA: Belknap Press of Harvard University Press, 1986).

8 See Nancy Fraser and Axel Honneth, *Redistribution or Recognition? A Political-Philosophical Exchange* (London: Verso, 2015).

9 See Roberta Shapiro, "Du smurf au ballet: l'invention de la danse hip-hop," in Nathalie Heinich and Roberta Shapiro, eds, *De l'artification: enquêtes sur le passage à l'art* (Paris: Éditions de l'EHESS, 2012), pp. 171–92.

10 For a detailed analysis of the "workers' repertory of actions" during the 1960s and 1970s, see Xavier Vigna, *L'insubordination ouvrière dans les années 68: essai d'histoire politique des usines* (Rennes: Presses Universitaires de Rennes, 2007).

11 On the problems posed by collective mobilizations in the realm of culture, see Irène Pereira, *Les travailleurs de la culture en lutte: le syndicalisme d'action directe face aux transformations du capitalisme et de l'État dans le secteur de la culture* (Paris: D'ores et déjà, 2010).

12 See Zeev Sternhell, *La droite révolutionnaire, 1885–1914: les origines françaises du fascisme* (Paris: Seuil, 1978).

13 See Sabine Chalvon-Demersay, *Le triangle du 14e: de nouveaux habitants dans un vieux quartier de Paris* (Paris: Éditions de la MSH, 1984).

14 See Luc Boltanski, *Les cadres: la formation d'un groupe social* (Paris: Minuit, 1982).

15 For France, see Raymond Aron, *Dix-huit leçons sur la société industrielle* (Paris: Gallimard, 1962).

16 See Thomas Piketty, *Capital in the Twenty-First Century*, trans. Arthur Goldhammer (Cambridge, MA: Belknap Press of Harvard University Press, [2013] 2014).

17 Cédric Houdré and Juliette Ponceau, eds, *Les revenus et le patrimoine des ménages* (Paris: INSEE, 2014).

18 The cost of a residence represented four years' income for the households buying between 2002 and 2006, as opposed to only three years between 1997 and 2001. The market price for residences in old buildings more than doubled between 2000 and 2007. After leveling off in 2008–9, prices rose again, especially in the Paris region (+25.6 percent).

19 For an approach to these phenomena from the perspective of social anthropology, see the analyses that Marc Augé has devoted to the multiplication in weekly publications, starting in the 1980s, of sales listings for "quality" homes or "exceptional" properties. An example from 1986–7: "Near the Gorges du Verdon. Templar command post, 1 km away from a delightful village close to the Gorges du Verdon; its authenticity and the quality of its restoration make it a rare find. More than 300 m² living space on 1 hectare of land. It is a house with stories to tell … It has kept its two Templar chapels. Swimming pool with pool house. Price: 4,750,000 francs." Marc Augé, *Domaines et châteaux* (Paris: Seuil, 1989).

20 Piketty, *Capital in the Twenty-First Century*, pp. 117–18.
21 Ibid., p. 166.
22 Ibid., p. 173.
23 Ibid., pp. 179–80.
24 Ibid., p. 261.
25 Ibid., p. 351.
26 Ibid., p. 379.
27 Ibid., p. 418.
28 As attested by the 2014 edition of the regular publication INSEE devoted to household incomes and holdings: Houdré and Ponceau, *Les revenus et le patrimoine des ménages*.
29 Ibid.
30 Those with "very high incomes" declare more than 93,000 euros by consumption unit; these are 1 percent of the most affluent (610,000 persons). As for the tax on wealth, whose threshold was raised in 2011 from 79,000 euros to 1.3 million euros, it concerns 290,000 households (as opposed to 590,000 earlier).
31 According to INSEE, the "very high incomes" are found among "those persons situated in the top 1 percent of the distribution of income declared by consumption unit."
32 Cédric Houdré, Nathalie Missègue, and Juliette Ponceau, "Inégalités de niveau de vie et pauvreté en 2011," in *Les revenus et le patrimoine des ménages*, pp. 9–16.
33 Ibid.
34 See Bertrand Garbinti and Pierre Lamarche, "Qui épargne? Qui désépargne?" in *Les revenus et le patrimoine des ménages*, pp. 25–38.

Chapter 14 Creators in the Enrichment Society

1 See Robert Castel, *Les métamorphoses de la question sociale* (Paris: Fayard, 1994).
2 Cyprien Tasset, "Les intellectuels précaires: genèses et réalités d'une figure critique," doctoral thesis, EHESS, Paris, 2015, esp. pp. 116–20.
3 Tasset chose to work on the 2007 "generation" survey because it entailed a more detailed presentation of the results than later surveys did.
4 According to the classifications established by INSEE, the intermediate professions include elementary school teachers and related professions, mid-level health-care workers and social workers, clergy and other religious workers, mid-level administrators in the public sector and in business, technicians, supervisors and foremen, and so on.
5 Marie Gouyon, "Revenus d'activité et niveaux de vie des professionnels de la culture," *Culture Chiffres*, no. 1 (2015): 1–28.
6 To the "professionals," in the restrictive sense of the Ministry of Culture and Communication, one would need to add, among culture workers, the category of "intermediaries" (as it is analyzed in particular in a collective work by Laurent Jeanpierre and Olivier Roueff, eds, *La culture et ses intermédiaires: dans les arts, le numérique et les industries créatives* (Paris: Éditions des archives contemporaines, 2014), but the category would have to be oriented toward the enrichment economy.

7 Gouyon, "Revenus d'activité," p. 1.

8 Ibid., p. 2.

9 Among the cultural professions, freelance work and temporary contracts account for 62 percent of workers' annual income on average, as opposed to 24 percent for the working population as a whole. The proportion of freelance workers is highest among visual and plastic artists (around 50 percent), and the proportion of temporary contracts is highest in the performing arts (72 percent). These figures are from the 2008–12 jobs survey, presented in DEPS, *Chiffres clefs 2014* (Paris: Ministère de la Culture et de la Communication, 2014), pp. 26–7 (cited in Tasset, "Les intellectuels précaires," pp. 106–7).

10 Tasset, "Les intellectuels précaires."

11 Gouyon, "Revenus d'activité," p. 11.

12 This theme, which has given rise to a considerable number of glosses on the part of economists and sociologists specializing in the arts and in culture, has been stimulated by media disclosures of the high income levels attained by stars in sports, the film industry, and the arts, and also by the success of the widely read work by Robert H. Frank and Philip J. Cook, *The Winner-Take-All Society: Why the Few at the Top Get So Much More Than the Rest of Us* (New York: Free Press, 1995).

13 Randall Collins, *The Credential Society: An Historical Sociology of Education and Stratification* (New York: Academic Press, 1979).

14 For an overview of the way these arrangements were set up, see Abram de Swaan, *In Care of the State: Health Care, Education and Welfare in Europe and the USA in the Modern Era* (Cambridge: Polity, 1988).

15 See Maurizio Lazzarato, *Marcel Duchamp and the Refusal of Work*, trans. Joshua David Jordan (Los Angeles: Semiotext(e), 2014).

16 See Pierre Bourdieu, *Manet: A Symbolic Revolution*, trans. Peter Collier (Cambridge: Polity, [2013] 2017).

17 Tasset, "Les intellectuels précaires."

18 Michel Foucault, *The Birth of Biopolitics: Lectures at the Collège de France, 1978–1979*, trans. Graham Burchell (New York: Picador, [2004] 2010), p. 241.

19 See Valérie Deroin, "Statistiques d'entreprises des industries culturelles," *Culture Chiffres*, no. 4 (2008): 1–8.

20 See Irène Pereira, *Les travailleurs de la culture en lutte: le syndicalisme d'action directe face aux transformations du capitalisme et l'État dans le secteur de la culture* (Paris: D'ores et déjà, 2010).

21 See William Sewell, *Work and Revolution in France: The Language of Labor from the Old Regime to 1948* (Cambridge: Cambridge University Press, 1980).

22 Social conflicts involving intermittent workers in the performing arts have attracted a good deal of attention from sociologists, who have often viewed these workers as "innovators." See especially Pierre-Michel Menger, *Les intermittents du spectacle: sociologie du travail flexible* (Paris: Éditions de l'EHESS, 2011); Grégoire Mathieu, *Les intermittents du spectacle: enjeux d'un siècle de luttes* (Paris: La Dispute, 2013); Antonella Corsani and Maurizio Lazzarato, *Intermittents et précaires* (Paris: Éditions Amsterdam, 2008).

23 On cases of what is now called rural gentrification or *greenification*, processes through which new social environments are constituted (processes that are often united by ecological, political, and/or creative preoccupations and that are concerned with lifestyles along with agricultural as well as intellectual or artistic

activities), see the testimony gathered by the Mauvaise Troupe collective, *Constellations: trajectoires révolutionnaires du jeune XXIe siècle* (Paris: L'Eclat, 2014), and, more particularly on the Limousin region, "Vivre en collectif sur le plateau de Millevaches," pp. 338–50. For an economic and statistical account of the effects of the implantation of newcomers in the Limousin mountains, see Frédéric Richard, Julien Dellier, and Greta Tommasi, "Migration, Environment and Rural Gentrification in the Limousin Mountains," *Journal of Alpine Research*, 102/3 (2014), https://journals.openedition.org/rga/2561; and Frédéric Richard, Marius Chevalier, Julien Dellier, and Vincent Lagarde, "Circuits courts agroalimentaires de proximité en Limousin: performance économique et processus de gentrification rurale," *Norois*, no. 230 (2014): 21–39.

24 For a phenomenological analysis of the "survivor," see Elias Canetti, *Crowds and Power*, trans. Carol Stewart (New York: Viking, [1960] 1962), epilogue, pp. 465–70.

25 Richard Barbrook, *The Class of the New* (London: Mute, 2007).

26 On hackers, see Nicolas Auray's work, especially "Le prophétisme hacker et son contenu politique," *Alice*, no. 1 (1998): 65–79, and Nicolas Auray and Danielle Kaminsky, "The Professionalisation Paths of Hackers in IT Security: The Sociology of a Divided Identity," *Annals of Telecommunications*, 62/11–12 (2007): 1313–26.

27 Richard Florida, *Cities and the Creative Class* (New York: Routledge, 2005), and *The Rise of the Creative Class* (New York: Basic Books, 2002).

28 César Graña, *Bohemian versus Bourgeois: French Society and the French Man of Letters in the Nineteenth Century* (New York: Basic Books, 1964).

29 For a pertinent critique of the theory of the creative class, see especially Stefan Krätke, *The Creative Capital of Cities: Interactive Knowledge, Creation and the Urbanization Economies of Innovation* (Chichester: Wiley-Blackwell, 2011).

30 See Cyprien Tasset, "Les 'intellos précaires' et la classe créative: le recours à la quantification dans deux projets concurrents de regroupement social," in Isabelle Bruno, Emmanuel Didier, and Julien Prévieux, *Stat-Activisme: comment lutter avec des nombres* (Paris: La Découverte, 2004), pp. 117–32.

31 See Dominique Merllié, *Les enquêtes de mobilité sociale* (Paris: Presses Universitaires de France, 1994).

32 Alexandre Parodi, the French minister of labor, issued decrees in 1945 establishing a classification grid for workers' salaries, which were set by the central government at the time. Workers were ranked as manual laborers (unskilled), specialized workers (those who had undergone a brief apprenticeship), and qualified workers (those who had earned a certificate of professional aptitude). This ranking system came to be known as the Parodi accords.

33 See Alain Desrosières, *The Politics of Large Numbers: A History of Statistical Reasoning*, trans. Camille Naish (Cambridge, MA: Harvard University Press, [1993] 1998).

34 This is precisely the approach Marx adopted in the two studies in which he pushed his analyses of social classes the farthest: *The Class Struggles in France (1848–1850)* (New York: International, [1850] 1934), and *The Eighteenth Brumaire of Louis Bonaparte*, trans. D. D. L. (New York: Mondial, [1852] 2005).

35 For example, see Nancy Fraser, "A New Form of Capitalism? Response to Boltanski and Esquerre," *New Left Review*, 106 (2017), https://newleftreview. org/issues/II106/articles/nancy-fraser-a-new-form-of-capitalism.

36 For example, see Wolfgang Streeck, *Buying Time: The Delayed Crisis of Capitalism*, trans. Patrick Camiller (London: Verso, [2013] 2014).
37 For example, see David Harvey, *The New Imperialism* (Oxford: Oxford University Press, 2003).
38 For example, Sian Sullivan, "Banking Nature? The Spectacular Financialisation of Environmental Conservation," *Antipode*, 45/1 (2013): 198–217.
39 See for example Eva Illouz, *Cold Intimacies: The Making of Emotional Capitalism* (Cambridge: Polity, 2007).

Conclusion

1 On the question of what is "common," see Michael Hardt and Antonio Negri, *Commonwealth* (Cambridge, MA: Belknap Press of Harvard University Press, 2009).
2 See Jacques Rancière, *Le spectateur émancipé* (Paris: La Fabrique, 2008), pp. 40–4.
3 Comment cited by Kate Abnett, "Les inégalités économiques fragilisent le luxe," *Le Monde*, August 1, 2016.
4 Cf. Émile Durkheim, *Pragmatism and Sociology*, trans. J. C. Whitehouse (Cambridge: Cambridge University Press, [1955] 1963), p. 35.

Appendix

1 On this topic, the curious reader may wish to consult the articles by the physicist and mathematician John Baez on his website: math.ucr.edu/home/baez/ as well as on his blog: johncarlosbaez.wordpress.com/.
2 Translator's note: Here the text deviates from the usual definition in category theory. In the standard definition of a category, the objects form a class, not necessarily a set. The special case considered here, in which the objects form a set, is usually referred to as a **small category**.
3 The use of the definite article "the" is intended. The terminal category is unique in a categorical sense, i.e. unique up to a uniquely determined isomorphism (of categories).
4 Translator's note: This is only correct if one uses the usual category concept instead of the concept of small category designated in definition 1.
5 We exclude in this text cardinality problems and refer to the book of Saunders MacLane as well as to the books of Masaki Kashiwara and Pierre Schapira.
6 The commutativity of this diagram means the following equality of compositions of morphisms: $\alpha_y \circ F(f) = G(f) \circ \alpha_x$.
7 At this stage of our thinking, good candidates are those categories which Jean Bénabou calls cosmos, that is, complete and cocomplete closed symmetric monoidal categories, of which two examples are $\overline{\mathbb{R}}_+$ and *Ens*. A cosmos allows the development of a "good" theory of enriched categories (see for example the classic work of Max Kelly in the references). Even if one can define a concept of weaker enriched categories, the framework of a cosmos seems to provide a more expressive language to transfer a fine-grained critical analysis into the sphere of commodities.
8 The category $(P \downarrow b)$ is an example of a so-called comma category.

9 For these interpretations to be more "justified," we would have to examine special features of the functor P (such as being fully faithful); however, we lack the space to do that here.

10 In particular, we have not addressed the very rich concepts of equivalence of categories and adjunction that can be easily introduced with the help of the material provided, nor the construction techniques for categories such as comma categories. The notion of comma category makes it possible to produce a category, i.e. in our case relations of valuation, based on functors. For example, for two given (price) functors $F : \mathscr{A} \to \overline{\mathbb{R}}_+$ and $G : \mathscr{B} \to \overline{\mathbb{R}}_+$, the comma category $(F \downarrow G)$ embodies the generation of relations of valuation (and the coherence between these relations) derived from the prices F and G.

11 Here I am thinking in particular of the concept of internal homomorphisms, i.e. the concept of the existence of an object of the category that (internally) represents "morphisms." For example, in the category of sets the morphisms are functions and the "set" of functions from the set X to the set Y is also a set, which we denote by Y^X.

12 The categories enriched over $\overline{\mathbb{R}}_+$ represent a generalization of metric spaces (see the groundbreaking article by F. William Lawvere). This case allows us to consider commodities as directly differentiated by a numeric value, a positive real number, which embodies the relative metaprice/price between commodities. In contrast to the framework of metric spaces, this framework allows a formulation of the fact that different commodities may have the same metaprice/price (i.e. relative metaprice/price zero). In a metric space in fact, two points with distance zero are equal. In this enriched framework this simply means that they are isomorphic (in terms of enriched categories over $\overline{\mathbb{R}}_+$), but not necessarily the same as the structure of a metric space would require.

References

Abbott, Andrew, "The Problem of Excess," *Sociological Theory*, 32/1 (2014): 1–26.

Abnett, Kate, "Les inégalités économiques fragilisent le luxe," *Le Monde*, August 1, 2016.

Accominotti, Fabien, *Market Chains*. Princeton, NJ: Princeton University Press, forthcoming.

Akerlof, George, "The Market for 'Lemons': Quality, Uncertainty, and the Market Mechanism," *Quarterly Journal of Economics*, 84 (1970): 488–500.

Amossé, Thomas, "La nomenclature socio-professionnelle: une histoire revisitée," *Annales: Histoire, Sciences Sociales*, 68/4 (2013): 1039–75.

Ansart, Pierre, *Marx et l'anarchisme*. Paris: Presses Universitaires de France, 1969.

Appadurai, Arjun, ed., *The Social Life of Things: Commodities in Cultural Perspective*. Cambridge: Cambridge University Press, 1986.

Arendt, Hannah, *The Human Condition*. Chicago: University of Chicago Press, 1958.

Aristotle, *Metaphysics*, trans. C. D. C. Reeve. Indianapolis: Hackett, 2016.

Aron, Raymond, "Avez-vous lu Veblen?," in Aron, *Les sociétés modernes*, ed. Serge Paugam. Paris: Presses Universitaires de France, 2006, pp. 239–66.

——— *Dix-huit leçons sur la société industrielle*. Paris: Gallimard, 1962.

——— *18 Lectures on Industrial Society*, trans. M. K. Bottomore. London: Weidenfeld & Nicolson, [1962] 1967.

Aronczyk, Melissa, *Branding the Nation: The Global Business of National Identity*. Oxford: Oxford University Press, 2013.

Arrighi, Giovanni, *Adam Smith in Beijing: Lineages of the Twenty-First Century*. London: Verso, 2007.

——— *The Long Twentieth Century: Money, Power and the Origins of Our Times*. New edn, London: Verso, 2010.

Arrighi, Jean-Jacques, and Marjorie Martin, "Grand Arles: des difficultés à surmonter, des atouts à exploiter," *Insee études*, no. 31 (2013).

ArtPrice, *The Art Market in 2014*, https://imgpublic.artprice.com/pdf/rama2014_en.pdf.

Ashenfelter, Orley, and Kathryn Graddy, "Auctions and the Price of Art," *Journal of Economic Literature*, 41/3 (2003): 763–86.

Aspers, Patrick, *Orderly Fashion: A Sociology of Markets*. Princeton, NJ: Princeton University Press, 2010.

Augé, Marc, *Domaines et châteaux*. Paris: Seuil, 1989.

Auray, Nicolas, "Le prophétisme hacker et son contenu politique," *Alice*, no. 1 (1998): 65–79.

Auray, Nicolas, and Danielle Kaminsky, "The Professionalisation Paths of Hackers in IT Security: The Sociology of a Divided Identity," *Annals of Telecommunications*, 62/11–12 (2007): 1313–26.

Azimi, Roxana, "L'élite prend l'art," *M le magazine du Monde*, April 5, 2014.

Bagnasco, Arnaldo, and Charles Sabel, *PME et développement économique en Europe*. Paris: La Découverte, 1994.

_____ *Small and Medium-Size Enterprises*. London: Pinter, 1995.

Bagnasco, Arnaldo, and Carlo Trigilia, *La construction sociale du marché: le défi de la troisième Italie*. Cachan: Les Éditions de l'ENS de Cachan, [1988] 1993.

Bairoch, Paul, *Victoires et déboires: histoire économique et sociale du monde du XVIe siècle à nos jours*, 3 vols. Paris: Gallimard, 1997.

Bal, Mieke, "Telling Objects: A Narrative Perspective on Collecting," in John Elsner and Roger Cardinal, eds, *The Cultures of Collecting*. London: Reaktion Books, 1994, pp. 97–115.

Balzac, Honoré de, *Cousin Pons*, trans. Ellen Marriage. Part 2 of *Poor Relations*. Philadelphia: Avil, [1847] 1901.

Barbrook, Richard, *The Class of the New*. London: Mute, 2007.

Barré, Josquin, "L'impact de la variable prix dans le tourisme culturel," in Jean-Michel Tobelem, ed., *La culture mise à prix*. Paris: L'Harmattan, 2005, pp. 105–26.

Barthes, Roland, *The Fashion System*, trans. Matthew Ward and Richard Howard. New York: Hill & Wang, [1967] 1983.

_____ *Mythologies*, trans. Annette Lavers. New York: Noonday Press, [1957] 1972.

_____ "Semantics of the Object" (1966), in *The Semiotic Challenge*, trans. Richard Howard (New York: Hill & Wang, [1985] 1988), pp. 179–90.

Bataille, Georges, *The Accursed Share: An Essay on General Economy*, trans. Robert Hurley. New York: Zone Books, [1949] 1991.

_____ "La notion de dépense," in *La part maudite*. Paris: Minuit, 1949, pp. 29–54.

_____ "The Notion of Expenditure," in *Visions of Excess: Selected Writings 1927–1939*, ed. Allan Stoekl, trans. Allan Stoekl with Carol R. Lovitt and Donald M. Leslie, Jr. Minneapolis: University of Minnesota Press, 1985, pp. 116–29.

Batifoulier, Philippe, ed., *Théorie des conventions*. Paris: Economica, 2001.

Baudrillard, Jean, *The Consumer Society: Myths and Structures*. Rev. edn, London: Sage, [1970] 2017.

_____ *The System of Objects*, trans. James Benedict. London: Verso, [1968] 1996.

Bauman, Zygmunt, *Globalization: The Human Consequences*. New York: Columbia University Press, 1998.

_____ *Wasted Lives: Modernity and its Outcasts*. Cambridge: Polity, 2004.

Baumol, William, "Unnatural Value: or Art Investment as Floating Crap Game," *American Economic Review*, 76/2 (1986): 10–14.

Beaucarnot, Jean-Louis, *La généalogie*. Paris: Presses Universitaires de France, 1997.

Becker, Howard S., *Art Worlds*. Berkeley: University of California Press, 1982.

Beckert, Jens, and Jörg Rössel, "The Price of Art: Uncertainty and Reputation in the Art Field," *European Societies*, 15/2 (2013): 178–95.

Beldi, Adel, Edouard Chastenet, Jean-Claude Dupuis, and Mohamed Talfi, "Pertinence des méthodes d'évaluation financière des marques: une étude empirique internationale," *Revue française de gestion*, no. 207 (2010): 153–68.

Belk, Russell, *Collecting in a Consumer Society*. London: Routledge, 1995.

Bell, Daniel, *The Coming of Post-Industrial Society: A Venture in Social Forecasting*. New York: Basic Books, 1973.

Bellet, Harry, *Le marché de l'art s'écroule demain à 18 h 30*. Paris: Nil, 2001.

Beltran, Alain, Sophie Chauveau, and Gabriel Galvez-Behar, *Des brevets et des marques: une histoire de la propriété intellectuelle*. Paris: Fayard, 2001.

Benjamin, Walter, *Écrits français*. Paris: Gallimard, 1991.

_____ "On the Concept of History," trans. Edmund Jephcott and Howard Eiland, in *Walter Benjamin: Selected Writings*, ed. Howard Eiland and Michael Jennings, vol. 4. Cambridge, MA: Harvard University Press, 2003.

_____ "Paris, Capital of the Nineteenth Century," trans. Howard Eiland, in *Walter Benjamin: Selected Writings*, ed. Howard Eiland and Michael Jennings, vol. 3. Cambridge, MA: Harvard University Press, 2002.

_____ "The Work of Art in the Age of its Technological Reproducibility," trans. Edmund Jephcott and Harry Zohn, in *Walter Benjamin: Selected Writings*, ed. Howard Eiland and Michael Jennings, vol. 3. Cambridge, MA: Harvard University Press, 2002, pp. 101–33.

Berg, Maxine, "New Commodities, Luxuries and Their Consumers in Eighteenth-Century England," in Maxine Berg and Helen Clifford, eds, *Consumers and Luxury: Consumer Culture in England, 1650–1850*. Manchester: Manchester University Press, 1999, pp. 63–87.

Berger, Alain, Pascal Chevalier, Geneviève Cortes, and Marc Dedeire, eds, *Patrimoines, héritages et développement rural en Europe*. Paris: L'Harmattan, 2010.

Bergeron, Louis, *Les industries du luxe en France*. Paris: Odile Jacob, 1998.

Berlan, Aurélien, *La fabrique des derniers hommes: retour sur Tönnies, Simmel et Weber*. Paris: La Découverte, 2012.

Bessy, Christian, and Francis Chateauraynaud, *Experts et faussaires*. Paris: Métailié, 1995.

Biot, Vincent, "Valorisation patrimoniale et développement touristique des Grands Causses: l'empreinte d'Édouard-Alfred Martel (1859–1938)," in Jean-Yves Andrieux and Patrick Harismendy, eds, *Initiateurs et entrepreneurs culturels du tourisme (1850–1950)*. Rennes: Presses Universitaires de Rennes, 2011.

Blanckaert, Christian, *Les 100 mots du luxe*. Paris: Presses Universitaires de France, 2010.

Bochurberg, Lionel, and Sylvie Lefort, "Les ventes aux enchères sur l'internet," *Legicom*, nos. 21–2 (2000): 131–47.

Böhme, Gernot, *Ästhetischer Kapitalismus*. Berlin: Suhrkamp, 2016.

Boltanski, Christian, *List of Exhibits Belonging to a Woman of Baden-Baden, Followed by an Explanatory Note*. Oxford: Museum of Modern Art, 1973.

Boltanski, Luc, *Les cadres: la formation d'un groupe social*. Paris: Minuit, 1982.

_____ *The Foetal Condition: A Sociology of Engendering and Abortion*, trans. Catherine Porter. Cambridge: Polity, [2010] 2013.

_____ *Mysteries and Conspiracies: Detective Stories, Spy Novels, and the Making of Modern Societies*, trans. Catherine Porter. Cambridge: Polity, [2012] 2014.

_____ *On Critique: A Sociology of Emancipation*, trans. Gregory Elliott. Cambridge: Polity, [2009] 2011.

_____ "Pouvoir et impuissance: projet intellectuel et sexualité dans le Journal d'Amiel," *Actes de la recherche en sciences sociales*, 1/5–6 (1975): 80–108.

_____ "Taxinomies populaires, taxonomies savantes: les objets de consommation et leur classement," *Revue française de sociologie*, 11/1 (1970): 34–44.

Boltanski, Luc, and Ève Chiapello, *The New Spirit of Capitalism*, trans. Gregory Elliott. London: Verso, [1999] 2005.

Boltanski, Luc, and Laurent Thévenot, *On Justification*, trans. Catherine Porter. Princeton, NJ: Princeton University Press, [1991] 2006.

Bomsel, Olivier, *L'économie immatérielle: industries et marché d'expériences*. Paris: Gallimard, 2010.

Bonnal, Françoise, "Comprendre et gérer la marque France: mode d'emploi pour les acteurs de la marque France," *Revue française de gestion*, nos. 218–19 (2001): 27–43.

Bonnot, Thierry, *La vie des objets*. Paris: Éditions de la MSH, 2002.

Borch, Christian, *The Politics of Crowds: An Alternative History of Society*. Cambridge: Cambridge University Press, 2012.

Bourdieu, Pierre, "Case Study 1: The Twofold Truth of the Gift," *Pascalian Meditations*, trans. Richard Nice. Stanford, CA: Stanford University Press, 2000, pp. 191–202.

_____ *Distinction: A Social Critique of the Judgement of Taste*, trans. Richard Nice. London: Routledge & Kegan Paul, [1979] 1986.

_____ *Manet: A Symbolic Revolution*, trans. Peter Collier. Cambridge: Polity, [2013] 2017.

_____ "Le marché des biens symboliques," *L'Année sociologique*, 22 (1971): 49–126.

_____ *The Rules of Art: Genesis and Structure of the Literary Field*, trans. Susan Emanuel. Stanford, CA: Stanford University Press, 1996.

_____ *The Social Structures of the Economy*, trans. Chris Turner. Cambridge: Polity, [2000] 2005.

Bourdieu, Pierre, and Luc Boltanski, *La production de l'idéologie dominante*. Paris: Demopolis, [1976] 2008.

Bourdieu, Pierre, with Yvette Delsaut, "Le couturier et sa griffe: contribution à une théorie de la magie," *Actes de la recherche en sciences sociales*, 1/1 (1975): 7–36.

Boyer, Pascal, *Religion Explained: The Evolutionary Origins of Religious Thought*. New York: Basic Books, [2001] 2007.

Brandom, Robert, *Making it Explicit: Reasoning, Representing, and Discursive Commitment*. Cambridge, MA: Harvard University Press, 1994.

Braudel, Fernand, *Afterthoughts on Material Civilization and Capitalism*. Baltimore: Johns Hopkins University Press, 1977.

_____ *The Wheels of Commerce*, Vol. 2 of *Civilization and Capitalism, 15th–18th Century*, trans. Siân Reynolds. New York: Harper & Row, [1979] 1982.

Brenner, Robert, *The Boom and the Bubble: The US in the World Economy*. London: Verso, 2003.

_____ *The Economic Capital of Global Turbulence: The Advanced Capitalist Economies from Long Boom to Long Downturn*. London: Verso, 2006.

Breton, André, "On the Relations between Intellectual Labor and Capital," in *Break of Day (Point du Jour)*, trans. Mark Polizzotti and Mary Ann Caws. Lincoln: University of Nebraska Press, [1970] 1999, pp. 64–6.

Bruno, Isabelle, *À vos marques, prêts … cherchez! La stratégie européenne de Lisbonne, vers un marché*. Paris: Croquant, 2008.

426   *References*

Bruno, Isabelle, and Emmanuel Didier, *Benchmarking: l'État sous pression statistique*. Paris: Zone Books, 2013.

Bulci, Léa, "Les bureaux du style, ces gens qui 'font' la tendance," *madmoiZelle*, August 3, 2012, www.madmoizelle.com/bureaux-style-117208.

Bull, Malcolm, *The Mirror of the Gods: How Renaissance Artists Rediscovered the Pagan Gods*. Oxford: Oxford University Press, 2005.

Burns, Peter, "Brief Encounters: Culture, Tourism, and the Local–Global Nexus," in Salah Wahab and Chris Cooper, eds, *Tourism in the Age of Globalization*. Abingdon: Routledge, 2001, pp. 290–305.

Cabanne, Pierre, *Les grands collectionneurs*, 2 vols. Paris: Éditions de l'Amateur, 2004.

_____ *The Great Collectors*. New York: Farrar, Strauss, 1963 [trans. of *Les grands collectionneurs*, Vol. 1].

Callon, Michel, "Innovation et emprise croissante des forces marchandes," *Le libellio d'AEGIS*, 11/4 (2015): 43–61.

Callon, Michel, ed., *The Laws of the Markets*. Oxford: Blackwell, 1998.

Callon, Michel, and Fabian Muniesa, "Les marchés économiques comme dispositifs collectifs de calcul" (2003), in Michel Callon, Madeleine Akrich, Sophie Dubuisson-Quellier, et al., *Sociologie des agencements marchands*. Paris: Presses des Mines, 2013, pp. 195–233.

Callon, Michel, Cécile Méadel, and Vololona Rabeharisoa, "L'économie des qualités," in Michel Callon, Madeleine Akrich, Sophie Dubuisson-Quellier, et al., *Sociologie des agencements marchands*. Paris: Presses des Mines, 2013, pp. 143–79.

Calmels, Albert, *Guide touristique de l'Aubrac: Saint-Chély-d'Aubrac et Laguiole*. Paris: Éditions de la solidarité aveyronnaise, 1981.

Candau, Jacqueline, and Ludovic Ginelli, "L'engagement des agriculteurs dans un service environnemental: l'exemple du paysage," *Revue française de sociologie*, 52/4 (2011): 691–718.

Canetti, Elias, *Crowds and Power*, trans. Carol Stewart. New York: Viking, 1962.

Carruthers, Bruce, and Arthur Stinchcombe, "The Social Structure of Liquidity: Flexibility, Markets, and States," *Theory and Society*, 29 (1999): 353–82.

Castel, Robert, *Les métamorphoses de la question sociale*. Paris: Fayard, 1994.

Castoriadis, Cornelius, *Capitalisme moderne et révolution*. Paris: UGC, 1979.

_____ *The Imaginary Institution of Society*, trans. Kathleen Blamey. Cambridge, MA: MIT Press, [1975] 1987.

_____ "Value, Equality, Justice, Politics: From Marx to Aristotle and from Aristotle to Ourselves," in *Crossroads in the Labyrinth*, trans. Kate Soper and Martin H. Ryle. Cambridge, MA: MIT Press, [1978] 1984, pp. 260–339.

Certeau, Michel de, *The Practice of Everyday Life*, trans. Steven Rendall. Berkeley: University of California Press, [1980] 1984.

Cerutti, Simona, "A qui appartiennent les biens qui n'appartiennent à personne? Citoyenneté et droit d'aubaine à l'époque moderne," *Annales: Histoire, Sciences Sociales*, 62/2 (2007): 355–83.

_____ *Étrangers: étude d'une condition d'incertitude dans une société d'Ancien Régime*. Paris: Bayard, 2012.

Chakhotin, Sergeï, *The Rape of the Masses: The Psychology of Totalitarian Propaganda*, trans. E. W. Dickes. New York: Alliance Book Corporation, [1939] 1940.

Challoner, Jack, ed., *Les 1 001 inventions qui ont changé le monde*. Paris: Flammarion, 2008.

Chalvon-Demersay, Sabine, "La saison des châteaux: une ethnographie des tournages en 'décors réels' pour la télévision," *Réseaux*, no. 172 (2012): 175–213.

_____ *Le triangle du 14e: de nouveaux habitants dans un vieux quartier de Paris.* Paris: Éditions de la MSH, 1984.

Chamberlin, Edward Hastings, *The Theory of Monopolistic Competition.* Cambridge, MA: Harvard University Press, [1933] 1962.

Chartier, Roger, *La main de l'auteur et l'esprit de l'imprimeur.* Paris: Gallimard, 2015.

Chatriot, Alain, "La construction récente des groupes de luxe français: mythes, discours et pratiques," *Entreprises et histoire*, no. 46 (2007): 143–56.

Chessel, Marie-Emmanuelle, *Consommateurs engagés à la Belle Époque: la Ligue sociale d'acheteurs.* Paris: Presses de Science Po, 2012.

Chodkiewicz, Jean-Luc, *L'Aubrac à Paris: une enquête d'ethnologie urbaine.* Paris: Éditions du CTHS, 2014.

Christin, Olivier, *Une révolution symbolique: l'iconoclasme Huguenot et la reconstruction catholique.* Paris: Minuit, 1991.

Christin, Rodolphe, *L'usure du monde: critique de la déraison touristique.* Montreuil: L'Échappée, 2014.

Cochoy, Franck, *Une histoire du marketing: discipliner l'économie de marché.* Paris: La Découverte, 1999.

Colli, Andrea, and Elisabetta Merlo, "Family Business and Luxury Business in Italy (1950–2000)," *Entreprises et histoire*, no. 46 (2007): 113–24.

Collins, Randall, *The Credential Society: An Historical Sociology of Education and Stratification.* New York: Academic Press, 1979.

Comaroff, John, and Jean Comaroff, *Ethnicity, Inc.* Chicago: University of Chicago Press, 2009.

Cometti, Jean-Pierre, *Conserver/restaurer: l'oeuvre d'art à l'époque de sa préservation technique.* Paris: Gallimard, 2016.

_____ *La démocratie radicale: lire John Dewey.* Paris: Gallimard, 2016.

Conein, Bernard, *Les sens sociaux: trois essais de sociologie cognitive.* Paris: Economica, 2005.

Corne, Aurélie, and Laurent Botti, "*Benchmarking*, attraction et valeur touristique du territoire: une analyse par le secteur hôtelier français," *Management & avenir*, no. 84 (2016): 179–96.

Corsani, Antonella, and Maurizio Lazzarato, *Intermittents et précaires.* Paris: Éditions Amsterdam, 2008.

Cousin, Bruno, "Segrégation résidentielle et quartiers refondés: usages de la comparaison entre Paris et Milan," *Sociologie du travail*, 55/2 (2013): 214–36.

Cousin, Bruno, and Sébastien Chauvin, "L'entre-soi élitaire à Saint-Barthélémy," *Ethnologie française*, 42/2 (2012): 335–45.

Cousin, Saskia, "L'Unesco et la doctrine du tourisme culturel: généalogie d'un 'bon' tourisme," *Civilisations*, no. 57 (2008): 41–56.

Cousin, Saskia, and Bertrand Réau, *Sociologie du tourisme.* Paris: La Découverte, 2009.

Coye, Noël, "La collection introuvable de l'abbé Breuil," in Odile Vincent, ed., *Collectionner? Territoires, objets, destins.* Paris: Créaphis, 2011, pp. 52–70.

Croix, Alain, ed., *Initiateurs et entrepreneurs culturels du tourisme (1850–1950)*, Actes du colloque de Saint-Brieuc, June 2–4, 2010. Rennes: Presses Universitaires de Rennes, 2011.

Cueco, Henri, *Le collectionneur de collections.* Paris: Seuil, 1995.

Darnton, Robert, *The Case for Books: Past, Present, and Future*. New York: PublicAffairs, 2009.

Darras [Groupe d'Arras], *Le partage des bénéfices, expansion et inégalités en France*. Paris: Minuit, 1966.

Daumas, Jean-Claude, and Marc de Ferrière Le Vayer, "Les métamorphoses du luxe vues d'Europe," *Entreprises et histoire*, no. 46 (2007): 6–16.

Davezies, Laurent, *La crise qui vient: la nouvelle fracture territoriale*. Paris: Seuil, 2012.

_____ *La République et ses territoires: la circulation invisible des richesses*. Paris: Seuil, 2008.

Debord, Guy, *The Society of the Spectacle*. New York: Zone Books, [1967] 1994.

Degoutte, Corinne, "Stratégies de marques dans la mode: convergence ou divergence des modèles de gestion nationaux dans l'industrie du luxe (1860–2003)," *Entreprises et histoire*, no. 46 (2007): 125–42.

Deleuze, Gilles, *Difference and Repetition*, trans. Paul Patton. New York: Columbia University Press, [1968] 1994.

Delvainquière, Jean-Cédric, François Tugores, Nicolas Laroche, and Benoît Jourdan, "Les dépenses culturelles des collectivités territoriales en 2010: 7,6 milliards d'euros pour la culture," *Culture Chiffres*, no. 3 (2014): 1–32.

Demmou, Lilas, "La désindustrialisation en France," working document, Direction Générale du Trésor, nos. 2010–11 (June 2010).

DEPS [Département des études de la prospective et des statistiques], *Chiffres clefs 2014*. Paris: Ministère de la Culture et de la Communication, 2014.

Derlon, Brigitte, and Monique Jeudy-Ballini, *La passion de l'art primitif: enquête sur les collectionneurs*. Paris: Gallimard, 2008.

Derluguian, Georgi, "What Communism Was," in Immanuel Wallerstein, ed., *Does Capitalism Have a Future?* New York: Oxford University Press, 2013, pp. 99–129.

Deroin, Valérie, "Emploi, bénévolat et financement des associations culturelles," *Culture Chiffres*, no. 1 (2014): 1–12.

_____ "Statistiques d'entreprises des industries culturelles," *Culture Chiffres*, no. 4 (2018): 1–8.

Descola, Philippe, *Beyond Nature and Culture*, trans. Janet Lloyd. Chicago: University of Chicago Press, 2013.

Descola, Philippe, ed., *La fabrique des images: visions du monde et formes de la représentation*. Paris: Somogy/Musée du Quai Branly, 2010.

DeSoucey, Michaela, "Food Traditions and Authenticity Politics in the European Union," *American Sociological Review*, 75/3 (2010): 432–55.

Desrosières, Alain, *L'argument statistique*, Vol. 2: *Gouverner par les nombres*. Paris: Mines ParisTech, 2008.

_____ *The Politics of Large Numbers: A History of Statistical Reasoning*, trans. Camille Naish. Cambridge, MA: Harvard University Press, [1993] 1998.

Desrosières, Alain, and Laurent Thévenot, *Les catégories socio-professionnelles*. Paris: La Découverte, 1988.

Dewey, John, *Theory of Valuation*. Chicago: University of Chicago Press, 1939.

Didier, Emmanuel, "Mesurer la délinquance en France depuis 1970: entre expertise et publicité," *Ethnologie française*, 45/1 (2015): 109–21.

_____ *Prouver et gouverner: une analyse politique des statistiques publiques*. Paris: La Découverte, 2014.

DiMaggio, Paul, "Classification in Art," *American Sociological Review*, 52/4 (1987): 440–55.

Dimson, Elroy, Peter L. Rousseau, and Christophe Spaenjers, "The Price of Wine," *Journal of Financial Economics*, 118 (2015): 431–49.

Donnat, Olivier, *Les pratiques culturelles des Français: enquête 1997.* Paris: La Documentation française, 1998.

Dosse, François, *Gilles Deleuze et Félix Guattari: biographie croisée.* Paris: La Découverte, 2007.

Drucker, Peter, *Concept of the Corporation.* New York: John Day, 1972.

Duez, Hubert, *Secrets d'un brocanteur.* Paris: Seuil, 1999.

Durkheim, Émile, *The Evolution of Educational Thought: Lectures on the Formation and Development of Secondary Education in France*, trans. Peter Collins. London: Routledge & Kegan Paul, [1938] 1977.

_____ *Pragmatism and Sociology*, trans. J. C. Whitehouse. Cambridge: Cambridge University Press, [1955] 1963.

_____ "Value Judgments and Judgments of Reality" (1911), in *Sociology and Philosophy*, trans. D. F. Pocock. Glencoe, IL: Free Press, [1924] 1953, pp. 80–97.

Dwyer, William G., Philip S. Hirschhorn, Daniel M. Kan, and Jeffrey H. Smith, *Homotopy Limit Functors on Model Categories and Homotopical Categories.* Providence, RI: American Mathematical Society, 2004.

Eblé, Vincent, *Rapport d'information sur les dépenses fiscales relatives à la préservation du patrimoine historique bâti*, French Senate, recorded October 7, 2015, www.senat.fr/rap/r15-018/r15-018_mono.html.

Edwards, Elizabeth, Chris Gosden, and Ruth B. Phillips, eds, *Sensible Objects: Colonialism, Museums and Material Culture.* New York: Berg, 2006.

Elster, John, *Making Sense of Marx.* Cambridge: Cambridge University Press, 1985.

Erner, Guillaume, *Sociologie des tendances.* Paris: Presses Universitaires de France, 2008.

Espeland, Wendy, and Mitchell Stevens, "Commensuration as a Social Process," *Annual Review of Sociology*, 24 (1988): 313–43.

Esquerre, Arnaud, *La manipulation mentale: sociologie des sectes en France.* Paris: Fayard, 2009.

_____ *Les os, les cendres, et l'État.* Paris: Fayard, 2011.

Eymard-Duvernay, François, "Le travail dans l'entreprise: pour une démocratisation des pouvoirs de valorisation," Working document, Collège des Bernardins, Department of Economics, April 2011.

Fairchilds, Cissie, "The Production and Marketing of Populuxe Goods in Eighteenth-Century Paris," in John Brewer and Roy Porter, eds, *Consumption and the World of Goods.* New York: Routledge, 1993, pp. 228–48.

Favereau, Olivier, "La pièce manquante de la sociologie du choix rationnel," *Revue française de sociologie*, 44/2 (2003): 275–95.

Favereau, Olivier, Olivier Biencourt, and François Eymard-Duvernay, "Where Do Markets Come From? From (Quality) Conventions," in Olivier Favereau and Emmanuel Lazega, eds, *Conventions and Structures in Economic Organizations: Markets, Networks and Hierarchies.* Cheltenham: Edward Elgar, 2003, pp. 213–52.

Fernandez, Alexandre, and Jean-Charles Asselain, *Industrialisation et sociétés en Europe occidentale, 1880–1960*, 2 vols. Paris: Messene, 1997.

Ferret, Stéphane, *Le Bateau de Thésée: le problème de l'identité à travers le temps.* Paris: Minuit, 1996.

Finez, Jean, "La construction des prix à la SNCF, une socio-histoire de la tarification: de la péréquation au yield management (1938–2012)," *Revue française de sociologie*, 55/1 (2014): 5–39.

Florida, Richard, *Cities and the Creative Class*. New York: Routledge, 2005.

_____ *The Rise of the Creative Class*. New York: Basic Books, 2002.

Fontaine, Laurence, "The Exchange of Second-Hand Goods between Survival Strategies and 'Business' in Eighteenth-Century Paris," in Fontaine, ed., *Alternative Exchanges: Second-Hand Circulations from the Sixteenth Century to the Present*. Oxford: Berghahn Books, 2008, pp. 97–114.

_____ *History of Pedlars in Europe*, trans. Vicki Whittaker. Durham, NC: Duke University Press, [1993] 1996.

_____ *Le marché: histoire et usages d'une conquête sociale*. Paris: Gallimard, 2014.

Fortes, Martin, "Spécialisation à l'exportation de la France et de quatre grands pays de l'Union européenne entre 1990 et 2009," *Trésor-Éco*, no. 98 (2012).

Foucault, Michel, *The Birth of Biopolitics: Lectures at the Collège de France, 1978–1979*, trans. Graham Burchell. New York: Picador, [2004] 2010.

_____ *The Order of Things: An Archaeology of the Human Sciences*. New York: Pantheon Books, [1966] 1971.

Fourcade, Marion, "Cents and Sensibility: Economic Valuation and the Nature of 'Nature,'" *American Journal of Sociology*, 116/6 (2011): 1721–77.

France, Anatole, *The Crime of Sylvestre Bonnard*, trans. Lafcadio Hearn. New York: Dodd-Mead, [1881] 1922.

Frank, Robert H., and Philip J. Cook, *The Winner-Take-All Society: Why the Few at the Top Get So Much More than the Rest of Us*. New York: Free Press, 1995.

Franquesa, Jaume, "On Keeping and Selling: The Political Economy of Heritage Making in Contemporary Spain," *Current Anthropology*, 54/3 (2013): 346–69.

Fraser, Nancy, "A New Form of Capitalism? Response to Boltanski and Esquerre, *New Left Review*, 106 (2017), https://newleftreview.org/issues/II106/articles/nancy-fraser-a-new-form-of-capitalism.

Fraser, Nancy, and Axel Honneth, *Redistribution or Recognition? A Political-Philosophical Exchange*. London: Verso, 2015.

Freedberg, David, *The Power of Images: Studies in the History and Theory of Response*. Chicago: University of Chicago Press, 1989.

Friedman, Jonathan, *Cultural Identities and Global Process*. London: Sage, 1994.

Fumaroli, Marc, *L'État culturel: une religion moderne*. Paris: De Fallois, 1991.

Gagneux, Yves, *Reliques et reliquaires à Paris (XIXe–XXe siècle)*. Paris: Cerf, 2007.

Garbinti, Bertrand, and Pierre Lamarche, "Qui épargne? Qui désépargne?," in Cédric Houdré and Juliette Ponceau, eds, *Les revenus et le patrimoine des ménages*. Paris: INSEE, 2014, pp. 25–38.

Garcia-Papet, Marie-France, *Le marché de l'excellence: les grands crus à l'épreuve de la mondialisation*. Paris: Seuil, 2009.

Geertz, Clifford, "Suk: The Bazaar Economy in Sefrou," in Clifford Geertz, Hildred Geertz, and Lawrence Rosen, *Meaning and Order in Moroccan Society*. Cambridge: Cambridge University Press, 1979, pp. 123–313.

Gelber, Steven, "Free Market Metaphor: The Historical Dynamics of Stamp Collecting," *Comparative Studies in Society and History*, 34/4 (1992): 742–69.

_____ *Hobbies, Leisure and the Culture of Work in America*. New York: Columbia University Press, 1999.

Gell, Alfred, *Art and Agency: An Anthropological Theory*. Oxford: Oxford University Press, 1998.

Gerson, Stéphane, "Le patrimoine local impossible: Nostradamus à Salon-de-Provence (1890–1999)," *Genèses*, no. 92 (2013): 52–75.

Gilmore, James, and Joseph Pine II, *Authenticity: What Consumers Really Want*. Boston: Harvard Business School Press, 2007.

Ginsburgh, Victor, François Mairesse, and Sheila Weyers, "De la narration à la consécration: l'exemple de la peinture flamande de Van Eyck à Rubens," *Histoire & mesure*, 23/2 (2008): 145–76.

Godart, Frédéric, *Sociologie de la mode*. Paris: La Découverte, 2010.

Goldgar, Anne, *Tulipmania: Money, Honor, and Knowledge in the Dutch Golden Age*. Chicago: University of Chicago Press, 2007.

Gorgus, Nina, *Le magicien des vitrines: le muséologue Georges-Henri Rivière*. Paris: Éditions de la MSH, [1999] 2003.

Gorz, André, *The Immaterial: Knowledge, Value and Capital*, trans. Chris Turner. London: Seagull Books, 2010.

Gouyon, Marie, "Revenus d'activité et niveaux de vie des professionnels de la culture," *Culture Chiffres*, no. 1 (2015): 1–28.

Gouyon, Marie, and Frédérique Patureau, "Vingt ans d'évolution de l'emploi dans les professions culturelles," *Culture Chiffres*, no. 6 (2014): 1–24.

Graburn, Nelson, ed., *Ethnic and Tourist Arts*. Oakland: University of California Press, 1979.

Graña, César, *Bohemian versus Bourgeois: French Society and the French Man of Letters in the Nineteenth Century*. New York: Basic Books, 1964.

Granet, Daniel, and Catherine Lamour, *Grands et petits secrets du monde de l'art*. Paris: Fayard, 2010.

Grant, Jonathan, "The Socialist Construction of Philately in the Early Soviet Era," *Comparative Studies in Society and History*, 37 (1995): 476–93.

Graw, Isabelle, *High Price: Art between the Market and Celebrity Culture*. Berlin: Sternberg, 2009.

Graw, Isabelle, and Daniel Birnbaum, eds, *Canvases and Careers Today: Criticism and its Markets*. New York: Sternberg, 2008.

Greffe, Xavier, *La valeur économique du patrimoine*. Paris: Anthropos, 1990.

Greif, Mark, *The Age of the Crisis of Man*. Princeton, NJ: Princeton University Press, 2015.

——— "What Was the Hipster?," in Greif, *Against Everything: Essays*. New York: Pantheon Books, 2016, pp. 209–19.

Grenier, Jean-Yves, *L'économie d'Ancien Régime: un monde de l'échange et de l'incertitude*. Paris: Albin Michel, 1996.

Guattari, Félix, and Suely Rolnik, *Micropolitiques*. Paris: Les Empêcheurs de penser en rond/Seuil, 2007.

Guerreau, Alain, "Avant le marché, les marchés: en Europe, XIIIe siècle–XVIIIe siècle," *Annales: Histoire, Sciences Sociales*, no. 6 (2001): 1129–75.

Guerzoni, Guido, *Apollo and Vulcan: The Art Markets in Italy, 1400–1700*, trans. Amanda George. East Lansing: Michigan State University Press, [2006] 2011.

Guerzoni, Guido, ed., *Museums on the Map, 1995–2012*. Turin: Fondazione de Venezia/ Umberto Allemandi, 2014.

Guichard, Charlotte, "La signature dans le tableau aux XVIIe et XVIIIe siècles: identité, réputation et marché de l'art," *Sociétés & représentation*, no. 25 (2008): 47–77.

Halle, David, and Elisabeth Tiso, *New York's New Edge: Contemporary Art, the High Line, and Urban Megaprojects on the Far West Side*. Chicago: University of Chicago Press, 2014.

Hardt, Michael, and Antonio Negri, *Commonwealth*. Cambridge, MA: Belknap Press of Harvard University Press, 2009.

Hartog, François, *Regimes of Historicity: Presentism and Experiences of Time*. New York: Columbia University Press, [2003] 2015.

Harvey, David, "The Art of Rent: Globalization and the Commodification of Culture," in Harvey, *Spaces of Capital: Towards a Critical Geography*. New York: Routledge, 2001, pp. 394–411.

_____ *The New Imperialism*. Oxford: Oxford University Press, 2003.

Haskell, Francis, *L'amateur d'art*, trans. Pierre-Emmanuel Dauzat. Paris: Librairie Générale Française, 1997.

_____ *The Ephemeral Museum: Old Master Paintings and the Rise of the Art Exhibition*. New Haven, CT: Yale University Press, 2000.

_____ *Rediscoveries in Art: Some Aspects of Taste, Fashion, and Collecting in England and France*. Ithaca, NY: Cornell University Press, 1976.

Hecquet, Vincent, "Emploi et territoires de 1975 à 2009: tertiarisation et rétrécissement de la sphère productive," *Économie et statistique*, nos. 462–3 (2013): 25–68.

Heilbrunn, Benoît, and Bertrand Barré, *Le Packaging*. Paris: Presses Universitaires de France, 2002.

Heinich, Nathalie, *De la visibilité: excellence et singularité en régime médiatique*. Paris: Gallimard, 2012.

_____ *L'élite artiste: excellence et singularité en régime démocratique*. Paris: Gallimard, 2005.

_____ *La fabrique du patrimoine*. Paris: Éditions de la MSH, 2009.

_____ *Le paradigme de l'art contemporain: structures d'une révolution artistique*. Paris: Gallimard, 2014.

Heinich, Nathalie, and Roberta Shapiro, eds, *De l'artification: enquêtes sur le passage à l'art*. Paris: Éditions de L'EHESS, 2012.

Herlin-Giret, Camille, "Les mondes de la richesse: travailler et faire travailler le capital," doctoral thesis, Université Paris-Dauphine, July 2016.

Hiraki, Takato, Akitoshi Ito, Darius A. Spieth, and Naoya Takezawa, "How Did Japanese Investments Influence International Art Prices?" *Journal of Financial and Quantitative Analysis*, 44/6 (2000): 1489–514.

Hirschman, Albert O., *Exit, Voice, and Loyalty: Responses to Decline in Firms, Organizations, and States*. Cambridge, MA: Harvard University Press, 1970.

_____ *The Passions and the Interests: Political Arguments for Capitalism Before its Triumph*. Princeton, NJ: Princeton University Press, 1977.

Hobsbawm, Eric, and Terence Ranger, eds, *The Invention of Tradition*. Cambridge: Cambridge University Press, 1983.

Honneth, Axel, *Reification: A New Look at an Old Idea*, ed. Martin Jay. Oxford: Oxford University Press, [2005] 2007.

Horowitz, Noah, *Art of the Deal: Contemporary Art in a Global Financial Market*. Princeton, NJ: Princeton University Press, 2011.

Houdré, Cédric, and Juliette Ponceau, eds, *Les revenus et le patrimoine des ménages*. Paris: INSEE, 2014.

Houdré, Cédric, Nathalie Missègue, and Juliette Ponceau, "Inégalités de niveau de vie et pauvreté en 2011," in *Les revenus et le patrimoine des ménages*. Paris: INSEE, 2014, pp. 9–16.

Houellebecq, Michel, *The Map and the Territory*, trans. Gavin Bowd. New York: Alfred A. Knopf, [2010] 2012.

Hounshell, David, *From the American System to Mass Production, 1800–1932*. Baltimore: Johns Hopkins University Press, 1984.

Ickowicz, Judith, *Le droit après la dématérialisation de l'oeuvre d'art*. Dijon: Les Presses du réel, 2013.

Illouz, Eva, *Cold Intimacies: The Making of Emotional Capitalism*. Cambridge: Polity: 2007.

Jappe, Anselm, *Les aventures de la marchandise: pour une nouvelle critique de la valeur*. Paris: Denoël, 2003.

_____ *Guy Debord*, trans. Donald Nicholson-Smith. Berkeley: University of California Press, 1999.

Jauneau, Yves, and Xavier Niel, "Le poids économique direct de la culture en 2013," *Culture Chiffres*, no. 5 (2014): 1–18.

Jeanpierre, Laurent, and Olivier Roueff, eds, *La culture et ses intermédiaires: dans les arts, le numérique et les industries créatives*. Paris: Éditions des archives contemporaines, 2014.

Jeanpierre, Laurent, and Séverine Sofio, "Chronique d'une mort annoncée: les conservateurs de musée face aux commissaires d'expositions dans l'art contemporain français," in Frédéric Poulard and Jean-Michel Tobolem, eds, *Les conservateurs de musée: atouts et faiblesses d'une profession*. Paris: La Documentation française, 2015, pp. 111–39.

Johnston, Josée, and Shyon Baumann, "Democracy versus Distinction: A Study of Omnivorousness in Gourmet Food Writing," *American Journal of Sociology*, 113/1 (2007): 165–204.

Jourdain, Anne, "La construction sociale de la singularité: une stratégie entrepreneuriale des artisans d'art," *Revue française de socio-économie*, 6 (2010): 13–30.

_____ "Réconcilier l'art et l'artisanat: une étude de l'artisanat d'art," *Sociologie de l'art*, 21 (2012): 21–42.

Kahn, Bruno, and Georges Maltsiniotis, "Structures de dérivabilité", *Advances in Mathematics*, 218, no. 4 (2008): 1286–1318.

Kancel, Serge, Jérôme Itty, Morgane Weill, and Bruno Durieux, *L'apport de la culture à l'économie de la France*. Paris: Inspection générale des Finances, 2013.

Karpik, Lucien, *Valuing the Unique: The Economics of Singularities*, trans. Nora Scott. Princeton, NJ: Princeton University Press, [2007] 2010.

Kashiwara, Masaki, and Pierre Schapira, *Categories and Sheaves*. Vol. 332. Berlin Springer 2005.

Kelly, Max, *Basic Concepts of Enriched Category Theory*. Vol. 64, CUP Archive, 1982.

Kemp, Martin, *La bella Principessa: The Story of a New Masterpiece by Leonardo da Vinci*. London: Hodder & Stoughton, 2010.

Kessler, Gabriel, and Sylvia Sigal, "Comportements et représentations face à la dislocation des régulations sociales: l'hyperinflation en Argentine," *Cultures et Conflits*, special issue: *Survivre: Réflexion sur l'action en situation de chaos*, nos. 24–5 (1997): 37–77.

Kindleberger, Charles, and Robert Z. Aliber, *Manias, Panics and Crashes*. New York: Macmillan, 2011.

Klein, Naomi, *No Logo: No Space, No Choice, No Jobs: Taking Aim at the Brand Bullies*. Toronto: A. A. Knopf Canada, 2000.

Knight, Frank H., *Risk, Uncertainty and Profit*. Boston: Houghton Mifflin, 1921.

Koromyslov, Maxime, "Le 'Made in France' en question: pratiques et opinions des professionnels français du luxe," *Revue française de gestion*, nos. 218–19 (2011): 107–22.

Kotler, Philip, *Marketing Places: Attracting Investment, Industry and Tourism to Cities, States, and Nations*. New York: Free Press, 1993.

Kowalski, Alexandra, "The Nation, Rescaled: Theorizing the Decentralization of Memory in Contemporary France," *Comparative Studies in Society and History*, 54/2 (2012): 308–31.

_____ "State Power as Field Work: Culture and Practice in the French Survey of Historic Landmarks," in Richard Sennett and Craig Calhoun, eds, *Practicing Culture*. London: Routledge, 2007, pp. 82–104.

Krätke, Stefan, *The Creative Capital of Cities: Interactive Knowledge, Creation and the Urbanization Economies of Innovation*. Chichester: Wiley-Blackwell, 2011.

Kuhn, Anthony, and Yves Moulin, "Proximité des acteurs et transformation des conventions: le cas du marché philatélique numérique," *Revue française de gestion*, no. 213 (2011): 43–56.

_____ "Le rôle des conventions de qualité dans la construction d'un marché: l'évolution du marché philatélique français (1860–1995)," *Entreprises et histoire*, no. 53 (2008): 54–67.

Labrot, Gérard, "Éloge de la copie: le marché napolitain (1614–1764)," *Annales: Histoire, Sciences Sociales*, 59/1 (2004): 7–35.

Lacroix, Chantal, "Les dépenses de consommation des ménages en biens et services culturels et télécommunications," *Culture Chiffres*, no. 2 (2009): 1–7.

Lacroix di Méo, Élodie, "Les enjeux identitaires de la patrimonialisation de l'art déco," in Jean-Claude Nemery, Michel Rautenberg, and Fabrice Thuriot, eds, *Stratégies identitaires de conservation et de valorisation du patrimoine*. Paris: L'Harmattan, 2008, pp. 52–62.

Laganier, Jean, and Dalila Vienne, "Recensement de la population en 2006: la croissance retrouvée des espaces ruraux et des grandes villes," *Insee première*, no. 2018 (2009).

Lahire, Bernard, *Ceci n'est pas qu'un tableau: essai sur l'art, la domination, la magie et le sacré*. Paris: La Découverte, 2015.

Lajoux, Jean-Dominique, *Aubrac: des racines et des hommes*. Paris: Delachaux et Niestlé, 2014.

Lamont, Michèle, "A Comparative Sociology of Valuation and Evaluation," *Annual Review of Sociology*, 38 (2012): 201–21.

Lamont, Michèle, and Marcel Fournier, *Cultivating Differences: Symbolic Boundaries and the Making of Inequality*. Chicago: University of Chicago Press, 1992.

Landes, David S., *The Unbound Prometheus: Technological Change and Industrial Development in Western Europe from 1750 to the Present*. 2nd edn, Cambridge: Cambridge University Press, 2003.

Laslett, Peter, *Finnish Life and Illicit Love in Earlier Generations*. Cambridge: Cambridge University Press, 1977.

Latour, Bruno, *Aramis, or, The Love of Technology*, trans. Catherine Porter. Cambridge, MA: Harvard University Press, [1992] 1996.

_____ *An Inquiry into Modes of Existence: An Anthropology of the Moderns*, trans. Catherine Porter. Cambridge, MA: Harvard University Press, [2012] 2013.

Laval, Christian, *L'homme économique: essai sur les racines du néolibéralisme*. Paris: Gallimard, 2007.

Laval, Christian, Francis Vergne, Pierre Clément, and Guy Dreux, *La nouvelle école capitaliste*. Paris: La Découverte, 2011.

Lawvere, F. William. "Metric Spaces, Generalized Logic, and Closed Categories," *Rendiconti del seminario matematico e fisico di Milano*, 43, no. 1 (1973): 135–66.

Lazarus, Jeanne, "Le crédit à la consommation dans la bancarisation," *Entreprises et histoire*, no. 59 (2010): 28–40.

_____ *L'épreuve de l'argent: banques, banquiers, clients*. Paris: Calmann-Lévy, 2012.

_____ "Tenir ses comptes et bien se tenir: l'apprentissage de l'autonomie par la banque," *Politix*, no. 108 (2014): 75–97.

Lazzarato, Maurizio, *Marcel Duchamp and the Refusal of Work*, trans. Joshua David Jordan. Los Angeles: Semiotext(e), 2014.

Lazzarato, Maurizio, Yann Moulier-Boutang, Antonio Negri, and Giancaro Santilli, *Des entreprises pas comme les autres: Benetton, le Sentier à Paris*. Aix-en-Provence: Publisud, 1993.

Le Bon, Gustave, *The Crowd*. New Brunswick, NJ: Transaction, [1895] 1995.

Léger, Jean-François, "Plus de diplômés, plus d'inégalités territoriales?," *Population & avenir*, no. 718 (2014): 4–7.

_____ "La répartition géographique des retraités: les six France," *Population & avenir*, no. 716 (2014): 4–7.

Leperchey, Benjamin, "Le comité stratégique de filière (CSF) des industries de la mode et du luxe," *Annales des Mines – Réalités industrielles*, no. 4 (2013): 14–19.

Lerner, Ralph, "Art and Taxation in the United States," in Clare McAndrew, *Fine Art and High Finance: Expert Advice on the Economics of Ownership*. New York: Bloomberg Press, 2010, pp. 211–48.

L'Estoile, Benoît de, "L'anthropologie après les musées?" *Ethnologie française*, 38/4 (2008): 665–70.

Lettre du Comité Colbert, no. 33, March–April 1984.

Lévi-Strauss, Claude, *The Elementary Structures of Kinship*, trans. John Richard Von Sturmer, James Harle Bell, and Rodney Needham. Boston: Beacon Press, [1949] 1969.

_____ *The Naked Man*, Vol. 4 of *Introduction to a Science of Mythology*, trans. Doreen Weightman. New York: Harper & Row, [1971] 1981.

_____ *The Savage Mind*, trans. Doreen Weightman and John Weightman. Chicago: University of Chicago Press, [1962] 1966.

Lipovetsky, Gilles, and Jean Serroy, *L'esthétisation du monde: vivre à l'âge du capitalisme artiste*. Paris: Gallimard, 2013.

Luhmann, Niklas, *Social Systems*, trans. John Bednarz, Jr., with Dirk Baecker. Stanford, CA: Stanford University Press, [1984] 1995.

Mac Lane, Saunders, *Categories for Working Mathematicians*. 2nd edn. Berlin: Springer 1998.

MacGregor, John, *The Discovery of the Art of the Insane*. Princeton, NJ: Princeton University Press, 1989.

Malaga Chamber of Commerce, *Le tourisme culturel en Méditerranée: quelques opportunités pour l'Espagne, la France, le Maroc, la Tunisie*, in *Invest in Med*. Marseille: Etinet, Euromediterranean Tourist Network, 2011.

Mallet, Serge, *The New Working Class*, trans. Andrée Shepherd and Bob Shepherd. Nottingham: Bertrand Russell Peace Foundation for Spokesman Books, [1963] 1975.

Mandelbrot, Benoit B., *Fractals: Form, Chance, and Dimension*. San Francisco: W. H. Freeman, 1977.

Mandeville, Bernard, *The Fable of the Bees or, Private Vices, Publick Benefits*, 2 vols. New York: Georg Olms, [1714, 1729] 1981, 2017.

Maniglier, Patrice, "De Mauss à Claude Lévi-Strauss: cinquante ans après: pour une ontologie Maori," *Archives de Philosophie*, no. 69 (2006): 37–56.

______ *La vie énigmatique des signes: Saussure et la naissance du structuralisme*. Paris: Léo Scheer, 2006.

______ *Le vocabulaire de Lévi-Strauss*. Paris: Ellipse, 2002.

Maniglier, Patrice, ed., *Le moment philosophique des années 1960 en France*. Paris: Presses Universitaires de France, 2011.

Marcilhac, Vincent, *Le luxe alimentaire: une singularité française*. Rennes: Presses Universitaires de Rennes, 2012.

Margairaz, Dominique, "La formation du réseau des foires et des marchés: stratégies, pratiques et idéologies," *Annales: Économies, Sociétés, Civilisations*, 41/6 (1986): 1215–42.

Marinelli, Nicolette, and Giulio Palomba, "A Model for Pricing Italian Contemporary Art Paintings at Auction," *Quarterly Review of Economics and Finance*, 51 (2011): 212–24.

Marx, Karl, *Capital: A Critique of Political Economy*, 4th edn, ed. Frederic Engels, trans. Ben Fowkes. London: Penguin Classics, [1890] 1990.

______ *The Class Struggles in France (1848–1850)*. New York: International, [1850] 1934.

______ *Contribution to the Critique of Political Economy*, trans. N. I. Stone from the 2nd German edn. Chicago: Charles H. Kerr, [1897] 1904.

______ *The Eighteenth Brumaire of Louis Bonaparte*, trans. D. D. L. New York: Mondial, [1852] 2005.

______ *Wages, Price, and Profit*. Peking: Foreign Languages Press, [1865] 1965.

Mathieu, Grégoire, *Les intermittents du spectacle: enjeux d'un siècle de luttes*. Paris: La Dispute, 2013.

Mauss, Marcel, *The Gift: The Form and Reason for Exchange in Archaic Societies*, trans. W. D. Halls. New York: W. W. Norton, [1923–4] 2000.

Mauvaise Troupe collective, *Constellations: trajectoires révolutionnaires du jeune XXIe siècle*. Paris: L'Eclat, 2014.

Mears, Ashley, *Pricing Beauty: The Making of a Fashion Model*. Berkeley: University of California Press, 2011.

Melot, Michel, *Mirabilia: essai sur l'inventaire général du patrimoine culturel*. Paris: Gallimard, 2012.

Menger, Pierre-Michel, *The Economics of Creativity: Art and Achievement under Uncertainty*, trans. Stephen Rendell et al. Cambridge, MA: Harvard University Press, [2009] 2014.

______ *Les intermittents du spectacle: sociologie du travail flexible*. Paris: Éditions de l'EHESS, 2011.

Mergnac, Marie-Odile, *La généalogie: une passion française*. Paris: Autrement, 2003.

Merllié, Dominique, *Les enquêtes de mobilité sociale*. Paris: Presses Universitaires de France, 1994.

Merlot, Michel, *Mirabilia: essai sur l'inventaire général du patrimoine culturel*. Paris: Gallimard, 2012.

Moati, Philippe, *L'avenir de la grande distribution*. Paris: Odile Jacob, 2001.

______ *La nouvelle révolution commerciale*. Paris: Odile Jacob, 2011.

Molho, Anthony, and Diogo Ramada Curto, "Les réseaux marchands à l'époque moderne," *Annales: Histoire, Sciences Sociales*, 58/3 (2003): 569–79.

Moretti, Franco, *The Bourgeois: Between History and Literature*. London: Verso, 2013.

Morin, Edgar, *The Stars*, trans. Richard Howard. Minneapolis: University of Minnesota Press, [1957] 2005.

Mouffe, Chantal, *Agonistics: Thinking the World Politically*. London: Verso, 2013.

Moulier-Boutang, Yann, *Cognitive Capitalism*, trans. Ed Emery. Cambridge: Polity, 2011.

Moulin, Raymonde, *L'artiste, l'institution, et le marché*. Paris: Flammarion, 1992.

_____ *The French Art Market: A Sociological View*, trans. Arthur Goldhammer. Abridged edn, New Brunswick, NJ: Rutgers University Press, [1967] 1987.

_____ *Le marché de la peinture en France*. Paris: Minuit, 1967.

Moulinier, Pierre, "Naissance et développement du partenariat contractuel dans le domaine culturel," in Philippe Poirrier and René Rizzardo, eds, *Une ambition partagée? La coopération entre le ministère de la culture et les collectivités territoriales (1959–2009)*. Paris: Travaux et documents du Ministère de la Culture, no. 26 (2009), pp. 47–92.

Moureau, Nathalie, *Analyse économique de la valeur des biens d'art: la peinture contemporaine*. Paris: Economica, 2000.

Moureau, Nathalie, and Dorothée Rivaud-Danset, *L'incertitude dans les théories économiques*. Paris: La Découverte, 2004.

Moureau, Nathalie, Dominique Sagot-Duvauroux, and Marion Vidal, "Collectionneurs d'art contemporain: des acteurs méconnus de la vie artistique," *Cultures études*, 1/1 (2015): 1–20.

Muensterberger, Werner, *Le collectionneur: anatomie d'une passion*. Paris: Payot, 1994.

Muniesa, Fabien, "A Flank Movement in the Understanding of Valuation," in Lisa Adkins and Celia Lury, eds, *Measure and Value*. Chichester: Wiley-Blackwell, 2012, pp. 24–38.

Musée des arts décoratifs, *Ils collectionnent*. Paris: Adrien Maeght, 1974.

Nader, Ralph, *Unsafe at Any Speed: The Designed-in Dangers of the American Automobile*. New York: Grossman, [1965] 1972.

Nash, Dennison, *Anthropology of Tourism*. Oxford: Pergamon Press, 1996.

Neiburg, Federico, "Inflation: Economists and Economic Cultures in Brazil and Argentina," *Comparative Studies in Society and History*, 48/3 (2006): 604–33.

Nerval, Gérard de, *Poésies et souvenirs*. Paris: Gallimard, 1980.

_____ *Sylvie: Recollections of Valois*. New York: Home Book Company, [1853] 1981.

Nitzan, Jonathan, and Shimshon Bichler, *Capital as Power: A Study of Order and Creorder*. New York: Routledge, 2009.

Nora, Pierre, ed., *Rethinking France=Lieux de mémoire*, trans. David Jordan et al., 4 vols. Chicago: University of Chicago Press, [1984–92] 2001.

Orléan, André, *Analyse économique des conventions*. Paris: Presses Universitaires de France, 2004.

_____ *De l'euphorie à la panique: penser la crise financière*. Paris: Rue d'Ulm, 2009.

_____ *The Empire of Value: A New Foundation for Economics*, trans. M. B. DeBevoise. Cambridge, MA: MIT Press, [2011] 2014.

Ortiz, Horacio, "Value and Power: Some Questions for a Global Political Anthropology of Global Finance," in Raul Acosta, Sadaf Rizvi, and Ana Santos, eds, *Making Sense of the Global: Anthropological Perspectives on Interconnections and Processes*. Cambridge: Cambridge University Press, 2010, pp. 63–81.

Pacella, Gérard, "La collection des couteaux, armes blanches et outils tranchants," *Excalibur*, no. 20 (2001).

Pagé, Camille, *La coutellerie depuis l'origine jusqu'à nos jours*, 6 vols. Châtellerault: H. Rivière, 1896–1904.

Pagès, Claire, *Lyotard et l'aliénation*. Paris: Presses Universitaires de France, 2011.

Panayotis, Georges, "Le tourisme français: un secteur économique majeur au fort potentiel," *Annales des Mines – Réalités industrielles*, no. 3 (2015): 15–19.

Panofsky, Erwin, *Tomb Sculpture: Four Lectures on its Changing Aspects from Ancient Egypt to Bernini*, ed. H. W. Janson. New York: H. N. Abrams, 1964.

Parasie, Sylvain, "Une critique désarmée: le tournant publicitaire dans la France des années 1980," *Réseaux*, no. 150 (2008): 219–45.

Pavel, Thomas, *Fictional Worlds*. Cambridge, MA: Harvard University Press, 1986.

Pearce, Susan, *Collecting in Contemporary Practices*. London: Sage, 1998.

Pereira, Irène, *Les travailleurs de la culture en lutte: le syndicalisme d'action directe face aux transformations du capitalisme et de l'Etat dans le secteur de la culture*. Paris: D'ores et déjà, 2010.

Peretz, Henri, "Soldes 'haut de gamme' à Paris," *Ethnologie française*, 35/1 (2005): 47–54.

Pétré-Grenouilleau, Olivier, *Les traites négrières: essai d'histoire globale*. Paris: Gallimard, 2004.

Pety, Dominique, *Poétique de la collection au XIXe siècle: du document de l'historien au bibelot de l'esthète*. Paris: Presses Universitaires de Paris Ouest, 2010.

Pierret, Frédéric, "Le tourisme est-il devenu un enjeu stratégique?," *Annales des Mines –Réalités industrielles*, no. 3 (2015): 9–13.

Pietraru, Jean-Jacques, "Éditorial," *Excalibur*, no. 60 (2013): 3.

Piketty, Thomas, *Capital in the Twenty-First Century*, trans. Arthur Goldhammer. Cambridge, MA: Belknap Press of Harvard University Press, [2013] 2014.

Pinçon, Michel, and Monique Pinçon-Charlot, *Châteaux et châtelains: les siècles passent, le symbole demeure*. Paris: Anne Carrière, 2005.

______ *Les ghettos du gotha: au coeur de la grande bourgeoisie*. Paris: Seuil, 2010.

______ *Sociologie de la bourgeoisie*. Paris: La Découverte, 2005.

Pine, B. Joseph, II, and James H. Gilmore, *The Experience Economy: Work Is Theatre & Every Business a Stage*. Boston: Harvard Business School Press, 1999.

Piore, Michael, and Charles Sabel, "Préface," *Les chemins de la prospérité: de la production de masse à la spécialisation souple*, trans. Luc Boussard. Paris: Hachette, [1984] 1989, pp. 10–17.

______ *The Second Industrial Divide: Possibilities for Prosperity*. New York: Basic Books, 1984.

Polanyi, Karl, "Marketless Trading in Hammurabi's Time," in Karl Polanyi, Conrad M. Arensberg, and Harry W. Pearson, eds, *Trade and Market in the Early Empires: Economies in History and Theory*. Glencoe, IL: Free Press, 1957, pp. 12–26.

______ "Ports of Trade in Early Societies," *Journal of Economic History*, 23/1 (1963): 30–45.

______ "Traders and Trade," in Jeremy A. Sabloff and C. C. Lamberg-Karlovsky, eds, *Ancient Civilization and Trade*. Albuquerque: University of New Mexico Press, 1975, pp. 133–54.

Polanyi, Karl, and Harry W. Pearson, *The Livelihood of Man*. New York: Academic Press, 2011.

Pomian, Krzysztof, *Collectors and Curiosities: Paris and Venice, 1500–1800*, trans. Elizabeth Wiles-Portier. Cambridge: Polity, [1987] 1990.

_____ *Des saintes reliques à l'art moderne: Venise–Chicago, XIIIe siècle*. Paris: Gallimard, 2003.

Ponge, Francis, *Partisan of Things*, trans. Joshua Corey and Jean-Luc Garneau. Chicago: Kenning, [1942] 2016.

Poulantzas, Nikos, *Classes in Contemporary Capitalism*, trans. David Fernbach. London: NLB, [1974] 1975.

_____ *Political Power and Social Classes*, trans. Timothy O'Hagan. London: NLB/ Sheed & Ward, [1968] 1973.

Poulot, Dominique, *Une histoire des musées en France*. Paris: La Découverte, 2008.

Pradelle, Michèle de, *Les vendredis de Carpentras*. Paris: Fayard, 1996.

Prahalad, Coimbatore Krishnao, *The Fortune at the Bottom of the Pyramid: Eradicating Poverty through Profits*. Upper Saddle River, NJ: Pearson Education, 2009.

Provost, Audrey, *Le luxe, les Lumières et la Révolution*. Seyssel: Champ Vallon, 2014.

Quemin, Alain, *Les stars de l'art contemporain: notoriété et consécration artistique dans les arts visuels*. Paris: CNRS, 2013.

Raboin, David, "Structuralisme et comparatisme en sciences humaines et en mathématiques: un malentendu?," in Patrice Maniglier, ed., *Le moment philosophique des années 1960 en France*. Paris: Presses Universitaires de France, 2011, pp. 37–58.

Rancière, Jacques, *Le spectateur émancipé*. Paris: La Fabrique, 2008.

Rautenberg, Michel, "Industrial Heritage, Regeneration of Cities and Public Policies in the 1990s: Elements of a French/British Comparison," *International Journal of Heritage Studies*, 18 (2012): 1–12, https://halshs.archives-ouvertes.fr/ halshs-00721541/document.

_____ "Une politique culturelle des produits locaux dans la région Rhöne-Alpes," *Revue de géographie alpine*, 86/4 (1998): 81–7.

Reubi, Serge, "La lacune, miroir des pratiques de collections," *Traverse*, no. 3 (2012): 81–90.

Ricardo, David, *On the Principles of Political Economy, and Taxation*. Baltimore: Johns Hopkins Press, [1819] 1928.

Ricaud, Michelle Moreau, *Freud collectionneur*. Paris: Campagne Première, 2011.

Richard, Frédéric, Marius Chevalier, Julien Dellier, and Vincent Lagarde, "Circuits courts agroalimentaires de proximité en Limousin: performance économique et processus de gentrification rurale," *Norois*, no. 230 (2014): 21–39.

Richard, Frédéric, Julien Dellier, and Greta Tommasi, "Migration, Environment and Rural Gentrification in the Limousin Mountains," *Journal of Alpine Research*, 102/3 (2014), https://journals.openedition.org/rga/2561.

Ricoeur, Paul, *Time and Narrative*, 3 vols, trans. Kathleen McLaughlin and David Pellauer. Chicago: University of Chicago Press, 1984–8.

Riegl, Aloïs, *The Modern Cult of Monuments: Its Character and its Origin*, trans. Kurt Walter Forster. Cambridge, MA: MIT Press, [1903] 1982.

Rifkin, Jeremy, *The Age of Access: The New Culture of Hypercapitalism*. New York: J. P. Tarcher/Putnam, 2000.

Rinallo, Diego, and Francesca Golfetto, "Representing Markets: The Shaping of Fashion Trends by French and Italian Fabric Companies," *Industrial Marketing Management*, 35/7 (2006): 856–69.

Rivière, Georges-Henri, ed., *L'Aubrac: étude ethnologique, linguistique, agronomique et économique d'un établissement humain (recherche coopérative sur programme)*, 7 vols. Paris: Éditions du CNRS, 1970.

Roche, Daniel, *The Culture of Clothing: Dress and Fashion in the Ancien Régime*, trans. Jean Birrell. Cambridge: Cambridge University Press, 1994.

_____ *Humeurs vagabondes: de la circulation des hommes et de l'utilité des voyages.* Paris: Fayard, 2003.

Roover, Raymond de, *La pensée économique des scolastiques: doctrines et méthodes.* Paris: Vrin, 1971.

Rosch, Eleanor, "Classification of Real-World Objects: Origins and Representations in Cognition," in P. N. Johnson-Laird and P. C. Wason, eds, *Thinking: Readings in Cognitive Science.* Cambridge: Cambridge University Press, 1977, pp. 212–22.

Rosental, Paul André, *Les sentiers invisibles: espace, famille et migration dans la France du XIXe siècle.* Paris: Éditions de l'EHESS, 1999.

Rouquette, Jean-Maurice, ed., *Arles, Histoire, territoires et cultures.* Paris: Imprimerie nationale, 2008.

Saint Martin, Monique de, *L'espace de la noblesse.* Paris: Métailié, 1993.

Saint-Pulgent, Maryvonne de, *Jack Lang: batailles pour la culture.* Paris: La Documentation française, 2013.

Salais, Robert, "Conventions de travail, mondes de production et institutions," *L'Homme et la Société*, nos. 170–1 (2008–9): 151–74.

Salais, Robert, and Michael Storper, *Les mondes de production: enquête sur l'identité économique en France.* Paris: Éditions de la MSH, 1993.

_____ *Worlds of Production: The Action Frameworks of the Economy.* Cambridge, MA: Harvard University Press, [1993] 1997.

Salmon, Christian, *Storytelling: la machine à fabriquer des histoires et à formatter les esprits.* Paris: La Découverte, 2007.

Salmon, Gildas, *Les structures de l'esprit: Lévi-Strauss et les mythes.* Paris: Presses Universitaires de France, 2013.

Sartre, Jean-Paul, *Critique of Dialectical Reason*, Vol. 1: *Theory of Practical Ensembles*, trans. Alan Sheridan-Smith. London: NLB, [1960] 1976.

Saussure, Ferdinand de, *Course in General Linguistics*, trans. Wade Baskin, ed. Perry Meisel and Haun Saussy. New York: Columbia University Press, [1916] 2011.

Sautard, Romain, Valérie Duchateau, and Jeannot Rasolofoarison, "Les biens haut de gamme, un avantage comparatif européen," *Trésor Éco*, no. 118 (2013).

Savoy, Bénédicte, *Patrimoine annexé: les biens culturels saisis par la France en Allemagne autour de 1800*, 2 vols. Paris: Éditions de la MSH, 2003.

Schiliro, Alessandro, *Luxury Apparel Brands: World Market Analysis, 2013–2018 Trends.* Xerfi Global, December 2013.

Schlosser, Julius von, *Les cabinets d'art et de merveilles de la Renaissance tardive: une contribution à l'histoire du collectionnisme.* Paris: Macula, [1908] 2012.

Schnapper, Antoine, *Curieux du Grand Siècle: collections et collectionneurs dans la France du XVIIe siècle.* Paris: Flammarion, 1994.

_____ *Le géant, la licorne et la tulipe: les cabinets de curiosités en France au XVIIe siècle.* Paris: Flammarion, 1988.

Schnapper, Dominique, *L'Italie rouge et noire: les modèles de la vie quotidienne à Bologne*. Paris: Gallimard, 1971.

Schumpeter, Joseph, *The Theory of Economic Development: An Inquiry into Profits, Capital, Credit, Interest, and the Business Cycle*, trans. Redvers Opie. New York: Oxford University Press, [1911, 1926] 1961.

Schutz, Alfred, *Collected Papers III: Studies in Phenomenological Philosophy*. The Hague: Martinus Nijhoff, [1932] 1975.

Sciardet, Hervé, *Les marchands de l'aube: ethnographie et théorie du commerce aux Puces de Saint-Ouen*. Paris: Economica, 2003.

Searle, John, *The Construction of Social Reality*. New York: Free Press, 1995.

Segalen, Marine, *La vie d'un musée, 1937–2005*. Paris: Stock, 2005.

Sennett, Richard, *The Craftsman*. New Haven, CT: Yale University Press, 2008.

Sewell, William, *Work and Revolution in France: The Language of Labor from the Old Regime to 1948*. Cambridge: Cambridge University Press, 1980.

Shapiro, Roberta, "Du smurf au ballet: l'invention de la danse hip-hop," in Nathalie Heinich and Roberta Shapiro, eds, *De l'artification: enquêtes sur le passage à l'art*. Paris: Éditions de L'EHESS, 2012, pp. 171–92.

Sicard, Marie-Claude, *Luxe, mensonge et marketing*. Paris: Pearson, 2010.

Silver, Daniel Aaron, and Terry Nichols Clark, *Scenescapes: How Qualities Shape Social Life*. Chicago: University of Chicago Press, 2016.

Simmel, Georg, *The Philosophy of Money*, 3rd edn, expanded, trans. Tom Bottomore and David Frisby. London: Routledge, [1900] 2004.

Simon, Hermann, Florent Jacquet, and Franck Brault, *La stratégie prix*. Paris: Dunod, 2011.

Smith, Charles, *Auctions: The Social Construction of Value*. New York: Free Press, 1989.

Sombart, Werner, *The Future of Capitalism*. Berlin-Charlottenburg: Buchholz &Weisswange, 1932.

Soto, Hernando de, *The Mystery of Capital: Why Capitalism Triumphs in the West and Fails Everywhere Else*. New York: Basic Books, 2000.

Spaenjers, Christophe, William N. Goetzmann, and Elena Mamonova, "The Economics of Aesthetics and Record Prices for Art since 1701," *Explorations in Economic History*, 57 (2015): 79–94.

Stanziani, Alessandro, *Histoire de la qualité alimentaire, XIXe–XXe siècle*. Paris: Seuil, 2005.

Stark, David, "What's Valuable," in Jens Beckert and Patrik Aspers, *The Worth of Goods: Valuation and Pricing in the Economy*. Oxford: Oxford University Press, 2011, pp. 319–38.

Sternhell, Zeev, *La droite révolutionnaire, 1885–1914: les origines françaises du fascisme*. Paris: Seuil, 1978.

Stillerman, Joel, *The Sociology of Consumption: A Global Approach*. Cambridge: Polity, 2015.

Streeck, Wolfgang, *Buying Time: The Delayed Crisis of Democratic Capitalism*, trans. Patrick Camiller. London: Verso, [2013] 2014.

Sullivan, Sian, "Banking Nature? The Spectacular Financialisation of Environmental Conservation," *Antipode*, 45/1 (2013): 198–217.

Swaan, Abram de, *In Care of the State: Health Care, Education and Welfare in Europe and the USA in the Modern Era*. Cambridge: Polity, 1988.

Swedberg, Richard, *Schumpeter: A Biography*. Princeton, NJ: Princeton University Press, 1991.

Tarde, Gabriel, *The Laws of Imitation*. New York: Henry Holt, [1890] 1903.

Tasset, Cyprien, "Les intellectuels précaires: genèses et réalités d'une figure critique," doctoral thesis, EHESS, Paris, 2015.

_______ "Les 'intellos précaires' et la classe créative: le recours à la quantification dans deux projets concurrents de regroupement social," in Isabelle Bruno, Emmanuel Didier, and Julien Prévieux, *Stat-Activisme: comment lutter avec des nombres*. Paris: La Découverte, 2004, pp. 117–32.

Taylor, Dominic, and Les Coleman, "Price Determinants of Aboriginal Art, and its Role as an Alternative Asset Class," *Journal of Banking & Finance*, 35 (2011): 1519–29.

Testart, Alain, *Critique du don: étude sur la circulation non marchande*. Paris: Syllepse, 2006.

Thévenot, Laurent, "Essai sur les objets usuels: propriétés, fonctions, usages," in Bernard Conein, Nicolas Dodier, and Laurent Thévenot, eds, *Les objets dans l'action*. Paris: Éditions de l'EHESS, 1993, pp. 85–111.

_______ "Un gouvernement par les normes: pratiques et politiques des formats d'information," in Bernard Conein and Laurent Thévenot, eds, *Cognition et information en société*. Paris: Éditions de l'EHESS, 1997, pp. 206–41.

_______ "Les investissements de forme," in *Conventions économiques: cahiers du Centre d'études de l'emploi*. Paris: Presses Universitaires de France, 1985, pp. 21–72.

Thiesse, Anne-Marie, *La création des identités nationales*. Paris: Seuil, 1999.

Thompson, Don, *The $12 Million Stuffed Shark: The Curious Economics of Contemporary Art*. New York: Palgrave Macmillan, 2008.

Thompson, John B., *Merchants of Culture: The Publishing Business in the Twenty-First Century*. Cambridge: Polity, 2010.

Thompson, Michael, *Rubbish Theory: The Creation and Destruction of Value*. Oxford: Oxford University Press, 1979.

Thornton, Sarah, *Seven Days in the Art World*. New York: W. W. Norton, 2008.

Tilly, Charles, *The Contentious French*. Cambridge, MA: Belknap Press of Harvard University Press, 1986.

Touraine, Alain, *The Post-Industrial Society: Tomorrow's Social History, Classes, Conflicts and Culture in the Programmed Society*. New York: Random House, [1969] 1971.

Trivellato, Francesca, *The Familiarity of Strangers: The Sephardic Diaspora, Livorno, and Cross-Cultural Trade in the Early Modern Period*. New Haven, CT: Yale University Press, 2009.

Truc, Gérôme, *Shellshocked: The Social Response to Terrorist Attacks*, trans. Andrew Brown. Cambridge: Polity, 2017.

Urbain, Caroline, and Marine Le Gall-Ely, *Prix et stratégie marketing*. Paris: Dunod, 2009.

Ure, Andrew, *Philosophy of Manufactures; or, An Exposition of the Scientific, Moral, and Commercial Economy of the Factory System of Great Britain*. 3rd edn, New York: B. Franklin, [1835] 1969.

Urfalino, Philippe, "De l'anti-impérialisme américain à la dissolution de la politique culturelle," *Revue française de science politique*, 45/5 (1993): 823–49.

van der Grijp, Paul, *Art and Exoticism: An Anthropology of the Yearning for Authenticity*. London: Transaction, 2009.

_______ *Passion and Profit*. London: Transaction, 2006.

Veblen, Thorstein, *Absentee Ownership and Business Enterprises in Recent Times: The Case of America*. Boston: Beacon Press, 1967.

_____ *The Theory of Business Enterprise*. New York: C. Scribner's Sons, [1904] 1932.

_____ *The Theory of the Leisure Class*. New York: Penguin Books, [1899] 1979.

Velthuis, Olaf, *Talking Prices: Symbolic Meanings of Prices on the Market for Contemporary Art*. Princeton, NJ: Princeton University Press, 2005.

Verlaine, Julie, *Les galeries d'art contemporain à Paris: une histoire culturelle du marché de l'art, 1944–1970*. Paris: Publications de la Sorbonne, 2012.

_____ "Une histoire de la société ArtCo: le commerce des reproductions d'art après la Seconde Guerre mondiale," *Vingtième Siècle: revue d'histoire*, no. 108 (2010): 141–51.

Verley, Patrick, *L'échelle du monde: essai sur l'industrialisation de l'Occident*. Paris: Gallimard, 1997.

Vigna, Xavier, *L'insubordination ouvrière dans les années 68: essai d'histoire politique des usines*. Rennes: Presses Universitaires de Rennes, 2007.

Volat, Gwendoline, "L'habitat rural entre 1999 et 2009: des évolutions contrastées," *Le Point sur*. Commissariat général au développement durable, no. 179 (December 2013).

Volscho, Thomas W., and Nathan J. Kelly, "The Rise of the Super-Rich: Power Resources, Taxes, Financial Markets, and the Dynamics of the Top 1 Percent, 1949 to 2008," *American Sociological Review*, 77/5 (2012): 679–99.

Vries, Jan de, *The Industrious Revolution: Consumer Behavior and the Household Economy, 1650 to the Present*. Cambridge: Cambridge University Press, 2008.

Wagner, Peter, *Modernity: Understanding the Present*. Cambridge: Polity, 2012.

_____ *A Sociology of Modernity: Liberty and Discipline*. London: Routledge, 1994.

Wajcman, Gérard, *Collection, suivi de L'avarice*. Caen: Jous, 1999.

Weber, Florence, "Transactions marchandes, échanges rituels, relations personnelles: une ethnographie économique après le Grand Partage," *Genèse*, no. 40 (2000): 85–107.

Weber, Max, *The Protestant Ethic and the Spirit of Capitalism*, trans. Talcott Parsons. Los Angeles: Roxbury, [1829] 1998.

White, Harrison C., *Canvases and Careers: Institutional Change in the French Painting World*. Chicago: University of Chicago Press, [1965] 1993.

Wrigley, Edward Anthony, *Continuity, Chance & Change: The Character of the Industrial Revolution in England*. Cambridge: Cambridge University Press, 1990.

_____ *Energy and the English Industrial Revolution*. Cambridge: Cambridge University Press, 2010.

Xifaras, Mikhail, *La propriété: étude de philosophie du droit*. Paris: Presses Universitaires de France, 2004.

Zaninetti, Jean-Marc, "Les retraités en France: des migrations pas comme les autres," *Population & avenir*, no. 703 (2011): 4–20.

Zarate, Gabriel Mendoza, "La fabrique de la critique: les travailleurs 'sous-traités' de l'industrie électronique au Mexique," doctoral thesis, EHESS, Paris, 2014.

Zelizer, Viviana A., "Gifted Money," in Zelizer, *The Social Meaning of Money*. New York: Basic Books, 1994, pp. 71–118.

_____ *The Purchase of Intimacy*. Oxford: Oxford University Press, 2005.

_____ "What Does Money Mean?," in Zelizer, *The Social Meaning of Money*. New York: Basic Books, 1994, pp. 199–216.

Zucman, Gabriel, *The Hidden Wealth of Nations: The Scourge of Tax Havens*, trans. Teresa Lavender Fagan. Chicago: University of Chicago Press, [2013] 2015.

Zuelow, Eric, ed., *Touring Beyond the Nation: A Transnational Approach to European Tourism History*. Burlington, VT: Ashgate, 2011.
Zukin, Sharon, *The Culture of Cities*. Oxford: Blackwell, 1995.
_____ *Loft Living: Culture and Capital in Urban Change*. New Brunswick, NJ: Rutgers University Press, 1982.
_____ *Naked City: The Death and Life of Authentic Urban Places*. Oxford: Oxford University Press, 2010.